$2895

Introduction to Managerial Economics

THOMAS J. HAILSTONES
JOHN C. ROTHWELL
Xavier University

Prentice-Hall, Inc., Englewood Cliffs, New Jersey 07632

Library of Congress Cataloging in Publication Data

Hailstones, Thomas J
   Introduction to managerial economics.

   Includes bibliographical references and index.
   1. Managerial economics. I. Rothwell, John,
1929-   joint author. II. Title.
HD30.22.H34 1979   330'.02'4658   78-20948
ISBN 0-13-486290-2

Editorial/production supervision and interior design by Natalie Krivanek.
Cover design by Rudolph Svezia.
Manufacturing buyer: John Hall.

Printed in the United States of America

10 9 8 7 6 5 4

Prentice-Hall International, Inc., *London*
Prentice-Hall of Australia Pty. Limited, *Sydney*
Prentice-Hall of Canada, Ltd., *Toronto*
Prentice-Hall of India Private Limited, *New Delhi*
Prentice-Hall of Japan, Inc., *Tokyo*
Prentice-Hall of Southeast Asia Pte. Ltd., *Singapore*
Whitehall Books Limited, *Wellington, New Zealand*

Contents

9. Pricing: Monopolistic Competition and Oligopoly   277

10. Pricing in Practice   313

11. Antitrust Regulation   351

12. Capital Expenditure Analysis   383

13. Cost of Capital   415

Preface

Often there is a wide gap between economic theory and the application of economic analysis, particularly at the microeconomic level. The theory of the firm is one thing, the application of economic analysis to the problems of the firm is another. It was for this reason that the National Association of Business Economists was formed fifteen years ago by a group of business economists who realized that most of the research analyses, publication and discussion of traditional economics offered little help in solving the day-to-day economic problems of the firm. On the other hand, the body of knowledge known as managerial economics, especially as developed in the past two decades, serves as a very useful tool of business management.

This text in managerial economics endeavors to bridge the gap between economic theory and the application of economic analysis. It reviews traditional analysis and shows the application of this analysis to the understanding and solution of economic problems of the firm and industry. Frequently a student will learn microeconomic principles or theory and then ask: "What can I do with it?" This text shows what can be done with it and how it can be applied. As a result, microeconomics comes alive. It takes on new zest and meaning. This is accomplished in a manner that the student with a modest knowledge of economic principles and a modicum of mathematics can grasp the fundamentals of managerial economics. In fact, the review material is of sufficient thoroughness that a good student can assimilate sufficient economic concepts to handle fundamental managerial economics without a prerequisite course in principles of economics.

Although there are many complex, sophisticated and highly quantitative aspects of managerial economics, this text is designed as a beginning. It stresses fundamentals and basic applications. It melds theory and practice. It deals with practical problems and cases. In addition to its pragmatic value, knowledge obtained through this text can be used as a stepping stone to the study of higher levels of managerial economics.

The authors wish to thank their many colleagues and students for offering constructive comments on the original manuscript. In particular a note of appreciation is due Dr. K. K. Seo and Mrs. Louise Lo, both of the University of Hawaii, for their helpful suggestions on specific parts of the book. A special *mahalo* is extended to Masayo Matsukawa and Gail Masaki, as well as to Mrs. Marjorie Schmidt, for their stenographic assistance with the manuscript.

T.J.H.
J.C.R.

Managerial Economics and the Role of the Business Economist

Traditional economics is often divided into two segments: macroeconomics and microeconomics. Macroeconomics deals with aggregates of the economy, such as total production, total employment and unemployment, total income, total money supply, and the general price level. Microeconomics, on the other hand, treats issues and problems of the individual consumer, the business firm and the industry, including demand and supply, profit maximization, and competition. Further, there are many special areas of economics, such as agricultural economics, multinational economics, urban and regional economics, comparative economic systems, mathematical economics, econometrics, and managerial economics.

TRADITIONAL ECONOMICS
VS. MANAGERIAL ECONOMICS

For years much of economics was confined to the ivory tower of the theorist on the university campus. Since World War II, however, there has been an increased effort to apply traditional economics, particularly microtheory, to the economic problems of business firms, nonprofit organizations, and government agencies. Thus evolved the concept of managerial economics.

Managerial economics, sometimes referred to as business economics, is a relatively new area of economic analysis and has become more widespread in the past few decades. *Managerial economics* is the application of economic theory and analysis to practices of business firms and other institutions, such as health care facilitites and government agencies. Managerial economics deals with managerial decisions in comparing and selecting among economic alternatives.

Managerial economics uses more than microeconomic theory. It requires, also, the application and integration of practices, principles, and techniques from the areas of accounting, finance, marketing, production, personnel, and other functions or disciplines associated with economics. Since sales and profits of the firm and industry are affected by the national economic climate, managerial economics must relate the concept of macroeconomics to the problems of the business firm. Since the current success, prosperity, or problems of the firm are often linked to what is happening to the status of such measures as the GNP, the general level of employment, and the

2

Consumer Price Index, there is a need to relate the economics of the firm with the national economy. Likewise future sales and profits of the firm must be projected within the constraints of the growth and development of the national economy. Similarly, the operations of nonprofit organizations and government agencies are affected by the economic climate of a region or general business conditions of the nation.

PROFIT MAXIMIZATION THEORY

Microtheory is based in large part on the assumption that the individual, the firm, and the industry, will seek to maximize profit, both in the short and the long run. In using this as a guiding principle, however, managerial economics recognizes that short-run profit may be sacrificed in the interest of long-run profit. The business economist must recognize, too, that other factors beside profit maximization may have to be taken into consideration by an officer or manager of a firm when rendering a final decision on an economic problem. The firm in many instances may be interested in a reasonable profit rather than in maximizing profit to the nth degree. The actions of the firm on economic matters may to some extent be influenced by related legal, moral, public, and community obligations. Minority problems and environmental issues may also have a bearing on managerial decisions. Most firms and industries desire to avoid illegal or unethical practices, even if it means less profit. A monopolist or oligopolist may charge less than "what the traffic will bear" for the sake of maintaining better consumer relations and improving its public image. Firms will often contribute large sums of money to civic and charitable organizations, which certainly reduces the amount of profit that can be paid out in dividends or retained for future development of the company. Often firms are more generous than necessary with worker wage and fringe benefits. More and more firms today are concerned about the deterioration of the natural environment and may be accepting less than maximum profit as a result of expenditures for anti- and depollution devices.

This does not imply that all firms are altruistic. Certainly a number of the twelve million business enterprises in the American economy exploit every opportunity, by fair means or foul, to maximize profit. Hence our society enacts laws regarding the economic conduct of individuals and business firms. Consequently, a firm may be forced to take, or avoid taking, certain measures that will affect profit maximization.

Today's antitrust laws, designed to protect, preserve, and promote competition, for example, prevent many firms from taking actions that may enhance their profits, particularly at the expense of other firms or at a cost to the general public. Labor laws that give workers the right to organize and bargain collectively can restrict profit maximization measures. Minimum wage laws also limit the profit maximization axiom, especially for the marginal firm. More recently, firms have had to contend with the Fair Employment Practices Act, a number of federal and state antipollution acts, the federal Occupational Safety and Health Act, and various consumer protection laws. Accordingly a firm must be careful whom it hires or fires in terms of racial discrimination; it should attain and maintain a proper ratio of minority employees. It may have to install costly antipollution devices or sometimes close down certain of its operations. It must have the proper equipment and take necessary measures for the safety of its employees. Living within the law imposes a cost. This cost may or may not be passed on to the consumer. In many cases these laws lessen the firm's ability to maximize profits. Since the requirements of these laws cannot be ignored without running the risk of severe penalty, they have to be taken into consideration when making final decisions on the economics of the firm.

With the large number of reservations, restrictions, and requirements on business firms today, one may truly question whether our economic system still can be labeled a free enterprise system. This issue will not be debated here. Much of the constraint on businesses has been imposed for the purpose of preventing exploitation or promoting the common good; thus it can justifiably be said that the freedom of our economic system is not complete but qualified. The firm has a right to do business and compete, but it does not have the right to infringe upon the rights and freedom of its competitors, to exploit consumers, or to endanger the safety of its workers.

Within this context of voluntary or involuntary constraints, a firm will seek to optimize its profit. That is, it will seek profits, not necessarily maximum, compatible with the firm's general objectives and overall goals, both economic and noneconomic. Consequently, when the economist uses profit maximization as a guide in his economic analysis, he must remember that final decisions on economic issues will be tempered by other considerations.

In spite of the widespread acceptance of some sense of public and civic responsibility among many business firms and their officials, one world-renowned economist stoutly maintains that the sole responsibility of the business firm is to make a profit for its stockholders. Others suggest, however, that the profit motive ought to be deemphasized. They recommend, for example, that the managers of a business enterprise should be judged not only on their ability to make profits, but also on the extent to which the firm fulfills some social commitment as well. In order to appraise social commitment, a different type of board of directors is recommended, one made up of stockholders, consumers, businessmen, and government officials. Nevertheless, profit is still the prime determinant of managerial efficiency; and the concepts of managerial economics apply in analyzing problems and issues for managerial decisions.

ECONOMICS AND NONPROFIT INSTITUTIONS

Many concepts of managerial economics apply to nonbusiness or nonprofit institutions as well. The activities of government agencies, courts, hospitals, churches, and universities, for example, are limited by budget constraints. The implementation of cost reduction measures, the selection of more productive alternatives, the enhancement of revenues, and the adoption of other measures can help to maximize the service and the social contribution of these institutions. Governments should try to obtain the maximum benefit for taxpayers from spending their tax dollars; government agencies can measure their efficiency through cost-benefit analysis. Hospitals should seek to handle more patients and give better care at lower cost by applying economic techniques. Even our universities can gain much by practicing what they preach about managerial economics.

GROWING USE OF THE ECONOMIST

The application of economics has become more widespread over the past few decades, and the role of the economist has taken on new meaning. He has come out of his ivory tower and been asked to apply some of his knowledge and theories to practical problems and issues. The growing importance of the economist since the end of World War II has been rather dramatic. On the macroeconomics scale, of course, this movement was furthered by the passage of the Employment Act of 1946. At the federal level, this act obligates the administration in office to take measures at its disposal to bring about conditions that promote "maximum employment, production, and purchasing power." It further requires the President to submit to Congress an economic report each year. In this report the President usually reviews the national economic conditions of the past year, presents the outlook for the forthcoming year, and sets down those measures he would like to see adopted to bring about the conditions of maximum employment, production, and purchasing power. To aid the President, the act established a Council of Economic Advisers. It is the job of the Council to analyze the status of the economy and make recommendations to achieve the objectives of full employment, stable prices, and a healthy rate of growth for the nation's economy. The actions of the President and his Council of Economic Advisers in dealing with national problems of unemployment, inflation, recession, energy, wage and price controls, and many other issues make national news. Congressional hearings, newspaper accounts, and magazine articles have popularized the role of the economist in determining matters of national economic policy.[1]

At the microeconomics level, the use of managerial economics and the role of the economists have grown just as much, but in a less dramatic fashion. The actions of business economists generally do not merit the national attention and publicity given to those of economists dealing with national economic issues and policies. It is not hot news wire copy or a flash TV news report item, for example, when a major company hires a new business economist.

THE MARKET FOR BUSINESS ECONOMISTS

Before World War II, relatively few economists were hired outside of the universities and a few government agencies. Business enterprises, banks, institutions, and most government agencies had little use for economists. In fact, as late as 1947, one young college graduate, upon receipt of his degree in Economics and Business Administration, was going to be moved by a large automobile manufacturer off the assembly line into an office position. Since he had majored in economics and minored in accounting, the employment manager offered him a position in the accounting department. When the young man indicated that he preferred not to work in the accounting department, the employment manager queried, "Well, what can be done with economics?" He had no idea how economics could be used by the company and there was no such job listing. The young man himself was befuddled because at that stage he, too, did not fully appreciate how economics could be applied in a business environment. Nevertheless, four years and a couple of graduate degrees later, the young man was offered a position as an economist in the

---

[1] In addition to the President's Council of Economic Advisers, fifteen states now have councils of economic advisers, or similar types of organizations, to inform governors and/or the legislatures about important state and regional economic matters.

newly formed financial analysis division of the company. Today that company has an economics department with a sizable staff.

Today the job market for economists is large. Many government agencies, particularly the departments of Agriculture, Labor, Commerce, the Treasury, State, Defense, HEW, and HUD hire economists by the hundreds. The bureaus of the Budget and the Census, the Department of Justice, and the Postal Service require the services of economists. Many states have industrial or economic development departments that employ economists to do research, analysis, and drafting of development plans. Local chambers of commerce in large cities often employ economists to do various studies regarding urban economics.

Large commercial banks, the Federal Reserve banks, and the Federal Home Loan banks provide employment opportunities for economists. At these banks, economists provide services ranging from elementary research to forecasting and assisting in determining policies for the institution. Each of the twelve Federal Reserve banks, for example, has an economic research staff that, among other things, provides studies and analysis for publication in the banks' monthly and special periodicals. A number of the major commercial banks also publish monthly economic letters or bulletins, containing economic studies and analyses.

Major firms in such industries as steel, auto, chemicals, lumber, petroleum, airline transportation, insurance, public utilities, merchandising, publishing, and plastics usually keep business economists on their staffs. Trade associations, likewise, may have an economist, or a staff of economists, to do industry economic studies. Major labor unions employ economists, particularly for analyzing the profit position of the firm and the cost of union demands for use by union negotiators.

Some firms that may not need a full-time business economist often hire an economic consultant—an individual or a firm—when special problems arise. Lawyers, too, increasingly are employing economists as expert witnesses in litigation on antitrust matters, public utility rate hearings, and suits for loss of family income due to a wrongful death (one that is due to the fault or neglect of another), usually by accident, of a family member. Thus, the consultant field offers business economists another source of employment.

Size of the Profession

Currently there are over 15,000 economists in the United States. Of course, not all of these are business economists. Many, 11,263, are university professors or government employees. About five thousand economists are employed by business firms or trade associations. The

American Economic Association (AEA) has a membership of seven thousand. The more recently organized National Association of Business Economists (NABE) has two thousand dues-paying members. Naturally, there is some duplication of membership between the AEA and the NABE, since some economists belong to both organizations. The NABE, however, is made up primarily of business economists employed by various companies. The NABE was formed in 1959 by a small group of business economists who felt that much of the theoretical and traditional economics discussed at AEA meetings and most of the articles in the AEA's prestigious *American Economic Review* had very little immediate practical meaning to business economists dealing with the daily problems of business firms. The annual and special meetings of the NABE deal primarily with those matters relevant to the operation of business firms and various institutions. The NABE publication, *Business Economics*, contains many articles on economic analysis and techniques for solving business problems.

The growing need for, and importance of, the economist today is shown in a recent issue of *Chemical Age*: Economists are listed as the highest paid scientists, ahead of physicists, chemists, biologists, mathematicians, and others. Table 1-1 shows that the economist is well paid in relation to other federal scientific personnel. An NABE survey of its members shows an annual salary range from $10,000 to *more than* $50,000 for its members, with $27,000 the average annual salary.

Entry into the Profession

How does one become an economist? *When* does one become an economist? The answer is not as simple as it is for some professions. A lawyer, for example, can show membership in his profession by passing the state bar examination; an accountant can become a CPA through examination; even an engineer can become a PE (professional engineer). In economics, as in many other academic specialties, there is no qualifying examination that shows a person to be an economist. Usually a bachelor's degree in economics, or some related field in which the person has learned the fundamentals of economics, is a prerequisite. Some individuals get into the profession by a kind of osmosis, filtering into economics from a related field, such as engineering, finance, or marketing. A master's degree in economics is helpful for a beginner wishing to enter the profession. It can open many doors. Those with doctoral degrees in economics have the road into the profession paved for them in most cases. But

TABLE 1-1. Mean Annual Salaries of Professional Scientific, and Technical Personnel in the Federal Government, by Occupational Field, by Sex: 1974 (In thousands of dollars. As of October)

Occupational Field	1974		
	Total	Male	Female
Scientific personnel	21.2	21.5	18.1
Physical sciences	23.2	23.6	18.4
General physical	26.9	27.1	20.1
Chemistry	21.4	22.0	17.9
Physics	24.0	24.1	20.3
Life sciences	18.7	18.8	16.3
General biological	20.1	20.8	16.1
Agricultural sciences	17.6	17.6	16.6
Animal sciences	22.2	22.4	18.6
Microbiology	19.8	21.2	16.7
Plant sciences	19.4	19.6	15.9
Mathematics and statistics	22.2	23.0	18.6
Mathematics	20.8	21.4	18.3
Statistics	21.6	22.4	18.7
Social sciences	22.4	23.2	18.9
General	21.4	22.5	19.1
Economics	22.7	23.3	18.8
Geography and cartography	18.7	18.8	16.7
Psychology	23.0	23.6	19.6
Health personnel	17.8	23.5	14.6
Health officers	28.5	28.3	30.1
Nursing personnel	14.0	13.9	14.0
Engineering personnel	23.2	23.2	18.5

Source: *Statistical Abstract of the United States*, 1976.

even here a younger member of the profession probably will start at the bottom of the ladder, doing research, engaging in fundamental analysis, and solving minor problems. Often he or she will serve as a junior assistant to a senior economist. Time and experience, coupled with wisdom, will lead the junior economist to a higher level doing analysis of greater sophistication.

A number of persons enter the economics profession through teaching. They may spend all or most of their lives as college teachers rising to the rank of associate professor or professor. While following a teaching career, an economist may decide to do some consulting on a part-time project basis with the government or with private enterprise. Often a university professor will shift to full-time government service either temporarily or permanently. A number of business economists have come from the university ranks. Often they are professors of noted teaching, research, and writing ability who become business economists at a higher level within the firm or institution into which they transfer.

A novice economist may begin by taking the civil-service examination in that field in order to work for one of the government agencies. Lower-level entry jobs usually require a written exam. For higher-level positions an unassembled exam is used (judgment of qualifications for a position is made on the basis of education, experience, and related factors). Job opportunities are also listed at the employment markets established in connection with the annual national meeting of the AEA and at annual regional meetings such as those of the Midwest Economic Association and the Southern Economic Association. In addition to university openings, job opportunities with government agencies, banks, and business firms are listed at these employment centers. A special employment service has been established by the AEA. For business economists, another important source of employment information is NABE job listings in its publication *Business Economics.*

THE ROLE OF THE BUSINESS ECONOMIST

The position of economist with a firm or institution is usually a staff function rather than a line function; that is, the economist is not generally in the line of command, or authority, like a foreman, manager, superintendent, general manager, or a vice president. He may serve in an advisory capacity to someone in a line position, such as a vice president or president. The economist may do research, engage in analysis, or conduct studies for any number of departments, such as marketing or finance, or for particular officials in the company. If there is a large economics department to service the firm or institution, however, the economist may hold a line position within the department, such as chief economist, senior economist, junior economist, or the like. Many times the economist, because of his overall knowledge of the company and the national economy may be asked to serve on important company committees. Occasionally economists who have managerial talent as well as economic wisdom may be raised to the executive level, such as a vice president of the firm.

Sometimes one hears the question "What specifically can the economist do for the firm?" On occasion, persons from related positions or neophyte economists appointed to a newly created position of economist within the firm themselves ask what they are supposed to do in the new position. And here lies the problem. The economist has no set list of duties. There is a wide variety of functions that the economist can perform. An economist with one company may do a type of work completely different from that done by an economist with another company. Within a firm, moreover, the economist may perform many tasks, working on different types of studies and analyses. Within each company or institution, especially where the position is new or taken over by a newly appointed person, the job of the economist will develop over time. Much will depend on the company's needs and the economist's expertise. Other persons or departments within the company may already be performing what may be considered the usual functions of an economist. Perhaps this will require a coordinated effort or a realignment of functions. In one company the economist may spend considerable time on demand analysis, pricing, and economic forecasting. In another, the economist may spend the major portion of his time doing cost and profit analysis. In still another, the economist's chief function may be dealing with labor issues, such as wages, costs, and fringe benefits. In still others he may be heavily involved with investment analysis or acquisition and merger studies.

If the economist works for a bank or investment house, his functions will concentrate on finance. If he works for a government agency, his work will fit the needs of the agency. Thus, he may be involved with agricultural pricing, the effect of minimum wage laws, the cost of welfare programs, the benefits of new highways, the setting of postal rates, the cost of pollution, the economic impact of tariff laws, or a hundred other subjects.

Obviously the scope of economics and the function of the economist vary widely. Even business economists working in private industry engage in a wide spectrum of duties. The accompanying list shows a few of the various types of studies and analysis in which the business economist may be involved:

1. Profit Analysis
2. Cost Determination
3. Production Possibilities Charts
4. Pricing
5. Demand Analysis
6. Market Penetration Studies
7. Economic Forecasting
8. Sales Forecasting
9. Marginal Analysis
10. Break-Even Analysis
11. Competitive Market Studies
12. Antitrust Issues

13. Plant-Location Studies
14. Mergers and Acquisitions
15. Labor-Cost Studies
16. Inventory Problems
17. Investment Analysis
18. Capital Budgeting
19. Cost of Capital
20. Government Regulations

The economist will not usually make the actual business decisions on economic matters relating to the firm. The business economist will be asked to present data, analyze issues and problems, suggest alternative solutions, and recommend plans of action. Some person or group in a line position, however, will generally be responsible for making the final decision. The economist, nevertheless, can have an important influence on that business decision. The final decision on a business problem may determine whether a project succeeds or fails, make a difference in thousands or millions of dollars in revenue or profit, or impact the economic life of the firm itself. Consequently, whether he plays a direct or indirect part, in the business decision, the economist must exercise prudent judgment supported by ample data and thorough analysis in making his recommendations.

Process of Analysis

In pursuing economic studies, engaging in economic analysis, and solving business problems, the business economist, like any good analyst, should use a scientific approach to his work. The following process of analysis is one often used, and it can serve as a guide, especially to beginners in this field.

1. Define the Issues or Problems.   In looking at an economic situation remember that more than one issue or problem may be involved. But the economist should be able to define the major problem or central issue and keep it separated from the minor issues or problems. Is it primarily a matter, for example, of reducing cost or increasing revenue?

2. Obtain the Facts.   The business economist should seek out and gather all the facts and data related to the issue or problem. Once he has assembled the facts, he must work out and sift the relevant data from the irrelevant data. Often, presenting too many facts may cloud the real issue.

3. Analyze the Data and Formulate Alternatives.   The relevant facts and data must be studied regarding their bearing on the problem, alternative solutions to the problem must be formalized; then the alternatives must be analyzed and weighed in terms of their cost and economic impact on the problem. Here some imagination should be used in formalizing alternatives. Good analyses of two or three alternatives may be misleading if a fourth and better alternative exists and remains undetected or not analyzed.

4. Recommend a Solution. After analyzing and weighing the alternatives, the business economist must recommend a solution to the issue or problem. Sometimes it is advisable to give alternative recommendations based on different contingencies and indicate some order of preference or probability. The economist's analyses should be thorough enough to give him confidence in the wisdom of his recommendation.

It is suggested that you follow this process or one similar to it while seeking solutions and answers to the problems and cases presented in the following chapters of the textbook.

WHAT ABOUT THE NONECONOMIST?

Managerial economics is important even for the person who does not intend to become an economist. First, if he is working for a firm or institution that does not have an economist, the individual in a decision-making capacity must often do his own economic analysis as he tries to solve business or institutional problems. A knowledge of managerial economics can be helpful to him in such instances. Second, if the firm or institution does have an economist, or uses the services of one, the manager who has some knowledge of managerial economics can better understand, question, and even at times challenge the analysis and recommendations of the economist.

SUMMARY

The study of economics is divided into two broad categories: macroeconomics, dealing with aggregates, and microeconomics, dealing with problems of individuals, business firms, and industries. Managerial economics, or business economics, evolved from efforts to apply microeconomic theory to the problems of the business firm.

Although profit maximization is a guiding principle in macroeconomic analysis, it is modified for a number of reasons in the study of managerial economics. The concepts of managerial economics can also be applied to nonprofit organizations and government agencies.

The employment of economists in government, banks, and business firms has grown substantially since the end of World War II, currently there is a substantial market for the services of business economists. Economists are generally well paid and perform a variety of duties for their employers. Today there are over 15,000 practicing economists in the United States.

In dealing with economic problems or issues, it is important to follow a somewhat scientific procedure. One recommended procedure is to (1) define the problem or issues, (2) gather and sort the facts, (3) analyze the data and formulate alternatives, (4) recommend a solution. With this in mind we can turn to the next chapter on profit analysis.

QUESTIONS FOR ANALYSIS AND DISCUSSION

1. Distinguish between macroeconomics and microeconomics. Explain how the business economist may be involved in both areas of study.
2. What is the profit maximization theory? Do you think that a firm should attempt to maximize profit? Why or why not?
3. What are some of the voluntary or involuntary constraints on profit maximization?
4. Do you think that the efficiency of business executives should be judged on the basis of profit maximization? Why or why not?
5. Explain how managerial economics may apply to nonprofit institutions.
6. How has the Employment Act of 1946 promoted a widespread understanding and popularity of economics?
7. How has the use of the business economist been growing in the past few decades? Do you know any economists?
8. What are some sources of employment for business economists?
9. In what types of work are economists engaged?
10. Give a process the business economist can follow in seeking answers to and making decisions on business problems.

SELECTED READINGS

Arthur, Henry B. "Help from the Company Economist." *Harvard Business Review*, September–October 1961.

Boulding, Kenneth E. *Economics As a Science*. New York: McGraw-Hill Book Company, Inc., 1970.

Brook, Kathleen, and F. Ray Marshall. "The Labor Market for Economists." *The American Economics Review*, May 1974.

Brown, Alan A., Egon Neuberger and Malcolm Palmatier. *Perspectives In Economics — Economists Look at Their Fields of Study*. New York: McGraw-Hill Book Company, Inc., 1971.

Business Economics Careers. Cleveland: National Association of Business Economists, 1975.

Daniel, Eleanor S. "The Economist In Life Insurance." *Business Economics*, September 1970.

"Economists for All Seasons." *The New York Times*, September 18, 1973.

"Ethical Problems of Business Economists." *Business Economics*, Fall, 1967.

Heldring, Frederick. "A Businessman's Evaluation of the Work of the Business Economist." *Business Economics*, January 1974.

Hough, Robbin R. *What Economists Do.* New York: Harper & Row Publishers, 1972.

Jones, Sydney L. "Are Economists Answering the Right Questions?" *Business Economics*, January 1975.

Lowes, B. and J.R. Sparkes. "Business Economics and Management Policy Planning." *Business Economics*, March 1976.

Maher, John E. *What Is Economics.* New York: John Wiley & Sons, Inc. 1969.

McLaughlin, Robert R. "The Corporate Economist in the Microtheory." *Business Economics*, May 1973.

Moor, Roy E. "The State of Business Economics." *Business Economics*, January 1974.

Parsons, S.A. *How to Find Out About Economics.* Elmsford, N.Y.: Pergman Press, Inc., 1973.

"Private Prophet: Corporate Economists Give In-house Advice." *The Wall Street Journal*, March 26, 1974.

2

Business and Economic Profit

We all know that consumption is the ultimate end of economic activity. Furthermore, in a broad social context, it is the function of business firms to provide goods and services for members of the society to consume. In a narrower content, however, it is the objective of the firms to make a profit. Some theorists contend that the proper role of the business firm is to provide goods and services and that the motivation to do so is the opportunity to make profit. Others contend that the primary function of the firm is to make a profit and that the means of doing this is providing goods and services for members of the community. In a way "providing goods and services" and "making a profit" are dual objectives of the firm. To be successful a firm must work toward both objectives and cannot neglect either. If a firm is so altruistic in providing goods and services that it neglects its profit position, it may not be around very long to provide the goods and services. On the other hand, if it becomes so greedy for profit that it neglects the quality of the goods and services it produces, it will not make a profit for long.

Profit is the lifeblood of the business firm. Just as the laborer is entitled to a wage in exchange for his labor, the landlord to rent for the use of his land, and the capitalist to interest for the use of his funds, the entrepreneur or business firm is entitled to reap a profit for providing goods and services.

FUNCTION OF PROFIT

Capitalism is a system in which capital or producers' goods are used for the production of additional goods and services. This capital may be in the form of machinery, buildings, and equipment, or it may be represented by money that can be used to purchase capital goods. Under the free-enterprise, capitalist system, such capital goods are owned and used primarily by the individuals and firms in the economy rather than by government bodies. Moreover, profit is the incentive for obtaining and using capital goods to produce additional goods and services.

In a truly free-enterprise capitalist system, individuals must be free — with certain limitations — to obtain, own, use, or sell land, machinery, tools, buildings, material, and other capital goods. Furthermore, under the concept of private property, individuals are entitled to the fruits of production resulting from the use of land, labor, and capital, whether used separately or combined. Thus, when the farmer grows corn on his own land with the aid of his own labor and his capital, the gain becomes his property and he can dispose of it as he desires. The company that manufactures hats is entitled to ownership of the hats produced. After paying for the factors of production that it uses in producing the hats, the hat manufacturer is entitled to what remains of the sales income.

Although consumption is the ultimate end of economic activity, for most business firms the immediate end is profit. In an endeavor to make a profit, businesses cater to consumer demand. Through the prices they are willing to pay, consumers give businesses enough revenue, more or less, to reimburse the companies for the costs of the factors of production used in producing the goods and services. The stronger the demand, the greater the profit potential and the greater the incentive to produce. Thus, profits play a crucial role in the operation of business firms and of a free-enterprise economy.

ECONOMIC PROFIT

Profit is a residual of income over and above all economic costs (both explicit and implicit) that results from the operation of a business.

Profits are dynamic in that they are constantly changing in amount. New business firms are established in hope of making a profit, others fail because of the lack of profit. During the ten-year period 1965–75, several million new firms were established in the United States. But during the same period, millions of other firms went out of business. We had a net increase of approximately 800,000 firms in the decade. Furthermore, several hundred thousand going concerns were sold or reorganized. Starting a business involves a risk, but the opportunity for profit induces hundreds of thousands of individuals annually to try to become successful entrepreneurs. More important than the success or failure of an individual business enterprise, however, is the freedom our economic system gives to an individual to go into business for himself.

Profit and Competition

Pure economic profit is a return to the entrepreneur solely from the operation of the business. It excludes any incidental income, such as that resulting from the sale of assets or the return for the use of one's own factors of production utilized in the input mix. If the profit is inadequate or if the firm suffers a loss, it may go out of business or into bankruptcy. The amount of profit that is neither excessive nor minimal but is the amount necessary to induce the entrepreneur to stay in business is called *nominal profit*. Generally, the economist considers nominal profit to be an economic cost of doing business. It is the return necessary to induce the entrepreneur to initiate and continue his efforts in operating the business. It is an implicit cost for the services of the entrepreneur. Any amount of profit over and above nominal profit can be called *pure profit*. Under highly competitive conditions, profit is a temporary phenomenon. Any time a pure profit exists, competitive forces, such as greater supply and lower prices, come into play to eliminate any such pure profit. This is so because of the nature of perfect competition as we shall see subsequently.

At the other extreme, if a pure profit situation exists in a monopoly, the monopolist may be able by various means to block effectively the entry of new firms into the industry. Consequently, profit becomes more than a temporary phenomenon. In addition, since by definition his output makes up the total supply of goods in a market, the monopolist can alter the supply and therefore market price by changing output. In this way a price can be set that will yield the greatest profit. Under various forms of monopoly, or limited competition, profits may be larger than they would be under highly competitive conditions.

The cost and revenue situation for an individual firm and its profit position will depend to a large extent on the type of competition that prevails in its industry. Therefore, we shall return to the subject of pricing and profits under various types of competition in subsequent chapters.

The Entrepreneur

The existence of natural resources, labor, and capital does not necessarily result in the production of goods and services. Before production can take place, these factors must be brought together. Someone must organize, control, and direct the use of manpower and resources to mold or blend them into finished goods or services. Until this is accomplished, the factors of production are only potentially important.

Who organizes and directs the factors of production depends upon the nature of the economic society. In America and similar free enterprise, capitalist economies, private entrepreneurs occupy strategic positions as the primary organizers and directors of business and industry. In some countries the state may be the entrepreneur.

An individual entrepreneur may establish and operate a corner drug store, a restaurant, fruit market, or other small business enterprise. A small group of individuals may pool resources and abilities to form a law partnership, a CPA firm, or an automobile dealership. In larger firms, such as General Motors, United States Steel, or General Electric, the stockholders are the entrepreneurs. In the case of most large firms, however, a small group of enterprising individuals originally served as entrepreneurs to organize the firm. In the process they induced other investors to become partial owners, or entrepreneurs, through the purchase of stock. Consequently, the average stockholder today may not be an entrepreneur in the same sense as is the owner of a small business enterprise. The latter plays a more active role in operating the business than does the average stockholder of a large corporation.

The enterpreneur is a risk-taker. Since nearly all production is for future use, risk is inevitable. From the time production is begun on a farm or in a factory, there are many possibilities of financial loss. Physical disaster in the way of fire, flood, storms, and other hazards affecting the product or merchandise may occur. Goods may be stolen. Mismanagement may result in cost overruns. Consumers' tastes may change. Demand and prices may decline. Even the most efficient management cannot eliminate the possibilities of loss from some or all of these hazards.

Management is considered to be a prerogative of the entrepreneur. It is, however, a form of labor, and any compensation that the owner-manager of a business may get for his or her management services is a form of wages. In the case of corporations, the stockholders are the entrepreneurs, in the sense that they take the risks. The officers, although their salaries may amount to hundreds of thousands of dollars annually, are hired employees. They do, of course, manage the finances and direct the operations of the corporation. These are delegated prerogatives of the entrepreneurial owners.

Entrepreneurship is an important factor in directing the structure of production in the economy. Manpower, resources, and capital must be combined in optimum proportions to generate the production of goods and services to satisfy consumer wants and at the same time yield a profit. The actual or anticipated demand of consumers for goods and services is translated into a demand for natural resources, for the services of workers, and for investment funds. Workers are dependent upon entrepreneurs for advances in the form of wages, which the employer hopes to recover when the goods are sold. These entrepreneurial functions may be performed directly by the entrepreneur or owner, as they frequently are in smaller firms, or they may be delegated to managers, as they are in larger corporations. Nevertheless, it is the function of entrepreneurship, one way or another, to "put it all together," if the enterprise is going to be successful.

PROFIT AND INCOME DISTRIBUTION

In a free-enterprise, or market, economy, prices and income are determined largely by the supply and demand for the factors of production. However, the government occasionally steps in to modify the market function, as in the case of veterans' benefits, social security, minimum-wage laws, and farm subsidies.

The study of income distribution is divided into two parts: (1) personal distribution and (2) functional distribution. The study of the many conditions, such as wealth, education, social status, and the like, that determine the actual division of income among individuals, deals with the personal distribution of income. Such a study is important, for it helps to throw light on the economic and social conditions that determine the division of income among the millions of income recipients. Ample statistics are readily available to show income differences by occupations, age, color, sex, and geographic location. We shall not deal with personal income distribution here, but rather concentrate on functional distribution of income.

Functional distribution of income is largely concerned with the conditions that determine the shares received by each of the factors of production — labor, land, capital, and entrepreneurship — for their respective contributions to the productive process. The question of functional distribution is a question of the shares going to wages, rent, interest, and profit. In short, income is a function of the productive contribution of each of the various factors of production.

The problem of income distribution becomes more perplexing as our economy becomes more complex. In the early days of the self-sufficing economy, individuals and families frequently produced directly the goods and services required for their own needs. If there were any surplus, families would exchange goods with each other. In this early system an individual generally used his own labor or that of his family, his own land, his own tools; he directed the production of the goods and services he needed. Assuming the institution of private property to exist, it was obvious that he was entitled to sole ownership of the fruits of his production.

In a modern industrial economy, however, the problem of income distribution is more involved. One who desires to produce must still use the basic factors of production. But in bringing these factors together, the entrepreneur may use the labor of one or several other persons, the land of another, and the capital of a third. By combining the factors, a good or a service is produced that has a certain value. Then the big question arises: What should be the share of, or payment to, each of the factors for its particular contribution to the total product? In a barter economy, remuneration could be made in kind: that is, each factor could be compensated with a certain share of the particular good produced. In our modern economy, remuneration to the factors of production — labor, land, capital, and entrepreneurship — is made by paying out money as wages, rent, interest, and profits, respectively.

We see a manifestation of this problem today, when, for example, a labor union strikes for higher wages. The striking employees are interested in maintaining, or enlarging, their portion of the economic pie. At other times, landlords try to increase their share by raising rents. As the money supply tightens, the capitalist often raises his interest rates, and the entrepreneur will frequently raise prices in order to increase his profit. This problem of distribution has plagued economists for two centuries, and we still have no solution for it.

The theory of distribution is not generally presented as a single or as a completely integrated theory. It is usually presented as a group of theories concerning each factor of production. A theory about one factor cannot be studied, however, without regard to the whole. If a particular theory allocates more income to one factor of production, such as labor or land, it may mean that the other factors receive less. Nevertheless, each factor might increase its total remuneration without detriment to the others if the total output were increased. Any increase in productivity through better use of any, or all, factors of production can be beneficial to all. Since we cannot explore all distribution theories here without unduly lengthening this book we will review only the theories of profit. This, after all, is the major concern of the entrepreneur and the business manager.

THEORIES OF PROFIT

Profit is a return to the entrepreneur, and it may arise from various sources or causes. There are, consequently, several theories of profit: the risk-bearing theory, the innovation theory, the monopoly theory, the managerial-efficiency theory, and the windfall theory.

It is often conceded that economic profit is a return to the entrepreneur in exchange for the risk undertaken by him in the operation of a business enterprise. Because the other factors of production have contractual agreements for payment for their services — wages, rent, and interest — economic profit is a residue that may exist after these other factors have been compensated. Since at times there may be no profit at all or even a loss, the entrepreneur assumes a certain amount of risk. Consequently, according to risk-bearing theory, if all goes well, he is entitled to any and all return over all costs. Moreover, since the other factors take little or no risk, they are entitled to only the agreed-upon remuneration.

Due to the risk involved, the profit potential of the product must be high enough to induce the entrepreneur to undertake the organization, development, and operation of the business. Usually the more risky the business, the greater must be the promise of profit. Furthermore, the presence of risk discourages a number of would-be producers, at least at the beginning. This can result in higher profits for those venturesome entrepreneurs who assume the risk and become successful.

The risk-bearing theory explains who should receive the economic profit and why. Unfortunately, it does not explain the source of, or the reason for, profit. In many cases profits are not commensurate with the risk involved. In fact, a venture may be so risky that it is doomed to failure and no profits will be realized. In other cases, such as with the existence of patent rights, the control of the source of raw materials, or the grant of a public-utility franchise, profits may be assured with a minimum of risk.

The risk-bearing theory considers only the risks inherent in operating the business. Such risks include consumer acceptance or rejection of a product, a change in prices, or the entry into the market of competitors with a new and better product. Loss from such business risks may be guarded against to some extent by wise and prudent management. The loss from external risks, such as fire, theft, or liability suits, can be reduced or eliminated by insurance coverage.

A substantial risk was undertaken by Henry Ford in using his own and borrowed funds when he established the world's largest single factory for producing automobiles. Walt Disney and his investors poured millions of dollars into the development of Disneyland before they realized a penny of revenue from its operations. Numerous small-business men risk their capital, time, and effort in business enterprises each year in an endeavor to make a profit. Some succeed and are rewarded with a profit; many others are not so fortunate and become bankrupt.

Innovation

For decades economists held innovation to be the prevalent source of profit. According to this theory, profit occurs because of innovation. The entrepreneur who develops a new product, a new process, or a more efficient method of producing a product may earn an economic profit. Actually, the innovation theory is tied in very closely with our explanation of profit under conditions of perfect competition. Assuming a no-profit situation, what can the producer do to achieve a profit? Since the cost of productive agents and the market price of the finished goods are determined by the forces in the market, the only way he can increase his profit is to reduce cost with new and better machinery or more efficient production techniques, or to introduce a new and better product that will not be bound by the market price for the existing product. In short, he may produce some innovation that will increase his economic profit by either decreasing his cost or increasing his revenue.

Let us assume that an entrepreneur finds a new production technique that reduces his cost. Although he may pay the same price as other producers for productive agents, assume that his techniques of using such agents will reduce his cost per unit of output. In such case the innovator will make a profit. As the innovation lowers his costs of production, economic profit will appear. These profits, according to the innovation theory, will exist until squeezed out by the forces of competition. Among other things, as new firms appear and the market supply is increased, prices will fall, decreasing revenue and profits. The firm or firms will again be in an equilibrium, or no-profit, position until another innovation or series of innovations occurs and the entire process is repeated.

Innovations are continually taking place, and innovation profits are very much in evidence. On a large scale such developments in the United States economy as electric power, the rise of the corporate form of business, the automobile, the airplane, developments in the appliance field, radio, television, and computers, all have brought about innovation profits. The forces of competition, however, have brought about higher production, relatively lower prices and dwindling profits for most of these goods in the past decades. Smaller innovations have been numerous in recent years. The ball-point pen is a classic example of innovation profit. When first put on the market after World War II, ball points sold at a price of $12.50 and profits were phenomenal. But within a few years, dozens of new firms had entered the market, and prices fell to 69 cents and lower, eliminating most of the innovation profit by the early 1950s.[1] A similar innovation pattern developed more recently with the hand-held calculator. It was introduced in the early 1970s at prices in excess of $300. Within a few years, numerous companies were selling various models for as little as $9.95 and they had gained widespread use even by school children. Other substantial innovations in recent years have been television for home entertainment, introduction of the basic oxygen furnace and the development of a continuous casting process in making steel, the development of the motorized home in the housing industry, the use of jet engines in the aircraft industry, the development of high-speed computers, and the popularity of CB radios in motor vehicles.

All profit cannot be attributed to innovation, however, since frequently profit exists without innovations, and profit often continues to exist long after the innovation has run its course.

Monopoly Profit

Profit may arise or be maintained because of the existence of a monopoly or a market with relatively few producers. Sometimes a firm will secure sufficient control over a market so that competition is discouraged and profit maintained. *Monopoly profit* results from the ability of the producer to influence price in such a manner that profits can continue to be made over an extended period of time.[2]

A monopolist may be successful in controlling prices and/or limiting the entry of other firms into the industry through the use of patent rights, by the exclusive ownership of the source of raw materials, or through efficient management. It may be, too, that the size

---

[1] Subsequent innovations, both technical and marketing, in the production and distribution of ball-point pens by such companies as Paper Mate and Bic International, however, brought them substantial profits in the 1960s and 1970s.

[2] Profit that arises from such a situation is sometimes referred to as *economic rent*, since it is income from the use of factors of production that have an inelastic supply. This may be further explained by stating that if competition existed, others would duplicate the product, the supply of goods on the market would increase, prices would fall, and profit would soon disappear. If the monopolist, however, can prevent anyone from producing the same commodity, his income exists because there is limited supply of such commodities, and such income, therefore, can be termed economic rent. The monopolist is actually receiving more for his product than he would if there were an ample supply of the product. In many cases that start out with innovation profits, the income ceases to be innovation profit and becomes economic rent if a monopolistic situation prevails.

of the market is small compared with the optimum scale of operations of the monopolist, so that it is unprofitable for other firms to enter the industry. Public utility companies that operate under franchises are special examples of producers that receive profits because they enjoy a degree of legal monopoly.

In some industries where there are relatively few firms and in which collusive practices are used to limit the total output, monopoly profits may exist. In still other cases the capital expenditures necessary to enter a particular business may be large enough to deter many would-be producers from entering the market.

In the United States economy, and in some others, monopoly or monopolistic profits are widespread. Usually it is the occurrence, or prospects, of substantial innovation profit that leads to development of various measures to prevent or limit competition, which in turn results in monopoly profit.

Managerial Efficiency

One can argue that profit arises as a result of managerial efficiency. It can be shown, in many instances, that management can through more efficient operations reduce the cost of doing business, anticipate and offset changes that will adversely affect the company's income, adopt new marketing techniques, improve product quality, and expand the product line in order to increase profit. There is no doubt that business acumen regarding product development, pricing structure, and marketing models can enhance profits.

But again, not all profit can be attributed to managerial efficiency. In some cases, good profits exist in spite of poor management. In other cases a capable manager may be in position where a profit cannot be made whatever the efficiency of his management. This often happens in the sports world. A coach may have an undefeated football team for several years. As a result of his fine reputation as a coach, he may be hired by a different school whose football fortunes have not been all that the alumni desire. After transfer to the new school the former coach-of-the-year may end up with a disastrous season, and his team may continue at the bottom of the conference until he is finally fired. In such a case, the efficiency of the coach may not have changed, but rather the material with which he had to work.[3]

---

[3] Dick Williams, while manager of the Oakland Athletics, for example, won three American League pennants and three World Series in a span of three years. On his next job, as manager of the San Diego Padres, he was fired in the middle of his first year because of the poor league standing of his team. In another cele-

Similarly, a top-level business executive may be transferred from one department to another or change companies. Although he may exercise better judgment and display more efficiency in the new position than his predecessor did, his superior ability may not be apparent in the income statement. A business recession, a sudden change in consumer taste, restrictive legislation affecting the manufacture of his product, or other unforeseen adverse external factors may depress profits and cloud his true managerial skills.

Sometimes a change in management can turn a losing situation into a profitable operation. Such was the historic change in the late 1940s when Henry Ford II, with the able assistance of Ernest Breech, took over the management of the Ford Motor Company. The company had been losing millions of dollars annually and was in a relatively poor financial position compared with its former days of glory when it was the leading producer and money-maker in the industry. The policies, organization, techniques, and practices adopted by the new management returned the company to a leading position in the industry, and it has been making a healthy profit for the past three decades. Similar and more recent turnabouts have occurred in various firms in other industries.

If we grant that profit may arise because of managerial efficiency, as it frequently does, then we may ask about the disposition of such profit. In the early history of industrial development, when the owner often operated his own business, performing the functions of both entrepreneur and manager, this was less of a problem. In current corporate practice, however, it is customary to hire managers to operate the business. Under such circumstances, should the owner receive all the profit for his risk-bearing function, or should management receive the profit because of its efficiency? One possible solution to this problem is the adoption of the bonus system. In this way, the owners, who are legally and economically entitled to the profit, share it with management. This permits management to share the profit if and when that reaches a certain predetermined level. Such a policy recognizes that profit may arise because of, and certainly is affected by, managerial efficiency.

Recently, for example, one of the highest-paid executives in the nation, a board chairman, received a salary of $408,000 plus $381,000 in bonuses and other compensations for a total income of $789,000 for the year. Another board chairman was the third-

---

brated case, Bunkie Knudsen, considered a managerial whiz when he was vice-president of General Motors Corporation, lasted less than two years after being hired as president of the Ford Motor Company.

highest-paid executive in the country. Fifteen top executives each received total compensation of $500,000 or more. Publication of corporate executives' salaries showed that 300 earned over $200,000 annually, Most of the incomes were a combination of salaries and bonuses. At the other end of the management ladder, however, many junior executives or middle-level managers receive only a few hundred or a few thousand dollars annually in bonuses. Bonuses fluctuate with profits. In the auto industry, for example, several top executives who received bonuses of $500,000 or more in 1974 received no bonuses in 1975 because of poor car sales.

A number of firms have profit-sharing plans from which all employees, including the nonmanagers, receive a share in the profits. Many advantages and disadvantages can be listed and analyzed for such profit-sharing systems. Some claim that profit sharing is contrary to the free enterprise system because the entrepreneurs or shareholders take the risk and should receive all the profit. Others claim that since labor takes no risk and does not suffer from the losses of the business, it is not entitled to any of the profit. Hundreds of companies, however, especially those in the Council of Profit Sharing Industries, maintain that profit sharing enhances productivity and is a means of recognizing the workers' contribution to greater productivity and profits.

Windfall Profit

Regardless of the structure of competition in the economy, profit often arises by mere chance. With the outbreak of World War II and the cessation of automobile production, for example, junk-car dealers with dormant stocks found a lucrative market for spare parts and could sell their scrap to the steel mills at a good price. In another case, many fur dealers in the mid-1950s were burdened with large inventories of inexpensive furs. The emergence of the Davy Crockett fad, with the demand for coonskin caps and other fur-trimmed items, provided a profitable outlet for the sale of their excess products. In the mid-1960s many people who had been collecting silver dollars and silver certificates enjoyed a windfall gain when the market price of silver rose substantially. In the early 1970s, owners of gold profited substantially when, as a result of market forces and the United States's devaluation of the dollar, the price of gold rose from $35 per ounce to nearly $200 per ounce. In other cases, oil, gold, coal, and minerals are sometimes discovered on farm land.

Unexpected changes in the market prices of commodities often result in windfall profits or losses. Land values change with shifts in population or changes in business and industrial centers. These and other such situations bring about profits that are not due to risk bearing, innovation, or monopoly. Such profits do not arise from the normal operations of the business, but result from factors generally outside of and beyond the control of the business.

Recapitulation

Profit may arise from a multiplicity of causes. One can find numerous examples to show the occurrence of profit from each of the causes just cited. Others can be found to show that a combination of causes, such as innovation and managerial efficiency, may be responsible for generating large profits. Cases exist, also, in which the lack of efficient management led to substantial losses for firms with valuable innovations. It is the hope of profit that usually induces individuals and companies to seek innovations, undertake risks, develop managerial efficiency, and endeavor to gain monopolistic powers. Speculation, likewise, is often undertaken in the hope that unexpected change will bring about windfall profits.

Profit is a dynamic, unstable, and uncertain form of income. It is a temporary phenomenon especially under vigorous competitive conditions. Even though monopolistic practices may be used to protect and maintain profit, the appearance of substitutes and imitations constitutes an ever-present threat to the profit of the firm.

ECONOMIC PROFIT VS. ACCOUNTING PROFIT

The concept of economic profit is often misunderstood, and it is frequently confused with the terms *business* or *accounting profit.* The net income or loss shown on the accountant's income statement is usually the difference between the total income of the business and its total expenses in a given period. The accountant generally lists only the *explicit* costs of operating the business. These costs consist of actual payments of cash or of bookkeeping entries for the expense accounts, such as wages, material, and depreciation. In order to find the true economic profit, however, the economist will also consider any *implicit* cost involved. These costs consist of allowances for the owner's own factors of production, such as labor, land, or capital, that are used in operating the business. This is necessary in order to reduce any income to a true economic profit.

As an example, let us assume that there are two book stores with identical shop facilities located in a busy downtown section. Assume further that Mrs. Reader, the entrepreneur of the Colonial Book Shoppe, pays rent for her store, borrows $5,000 to stock her inventory, and hires a manager to operate the store. We will also assume that the entrepreneur of the 20th Century Book Store, Ms. Bookman, uses her own savings to buy her store and to finance her inventory and manages the store herself. If the two stores had identical sales for a given period, their respective income statements might appear as follows:

Colonial Book Shoppe Income Statement (Mrs. Reader)			20th Century Book Store Income Statement (Ms. Bookman)		
Net Sales		$150,000	Net Sales		$150,000
Cost of goods sold		120,000	Cost of goods sold		120,000
Gross profit on sales		$ 30,000	Gross profit on sales		$ 30,000
Operating expenses:			Operating expenses:		
Rent	$4,500		Wages	$6,000	
Wages	6,000		Insurance	450	
Salary	7,500		Depreciation		
Insurance	450		taxes, etc.	900	
Interest	300		Other	750	
Other	750	19,500			8,100
Net income		$10,500	Net income		$ 21,900

Initially, it appears that the 20th Century Book Store is making more than double the profit of the Colonial Book Shoppe. A closer inspection of the figures, however, shows that the economic profit of the two firms may be identical. Note that Mrs. Reader paid an annual rent of $4,500, a manager's salary of $7,500, and interest of $300 on a $5,000 loan. These payments, along with the others, are explicit costs; the accounting profit of $10,500 corresponds closely to the true economic profit from operating the business. There still has to be an opportunity cost allowance, however, for the entrepreneurial services of Mrs. Reader. If this were assumed to be $3,000, then the true economic profit from the business would be $7,500.

In the case of the 20th Century Book Store, however, the business profit of $21,900 is nowhere near the true economic profit. Certain implicit costs must be considered.

Since Ms. Bookman, the entrepreneur, is working also as manager in her own store, this use of her services is a cost of doing business. The imputed value of her service as a manager can be determined by calculating what she could earn employed in a similar job by someone else. This is known as *opportunity cost*. Specifically, opportunity cost can be measured by determining what amount of income a factor of production could earn if used in a similar or the next best capacity elsewhere. Assuming the salary Mrs. Reader is paying to her manager is typical for that type of work, it is readily determinable that Ms. Bookman probably could have earned at least $7,500 per year managing another book store.

In addition, Ms. Bookman is using $5,000 of her own funds to finance her inventory. This means that her money tied up in inventory could have been earning interest if invested elsewhere. If the current yield or interest rate on investments is 6 percent for example, it is costing her $300 ($5,000 × .06 = $300) in opportunity interest to use her own money in the business. An opportunity rent also should be determined. This can be done by calculating the net rent that could be earned by renting the building to someone else. In this case assume that Ms. Bookman could rent her store for $4,500, the same rent Mrs. Reader is paying. Since the depreciation, taxes, and maintenance costs of the building amount to $900 per year, the implicit net rental income from the store would be thirty-six hundred dollars. Thus, implicit net rental income plus the depreciation charge, taxes, and maintenance cost is equal to the gross rental income of $4,500, which is equivalent to the rent paid by Mrs. Reader.

Now, if we were to add the total imputed costs, $11,400 ($7,500 + $300 + $3,600) to the operating expenses of the 20th Century Book Store, the total operating expenses would increase from $8,100 to $19,500. Consequently, it then would show the same economic profit as the Colonial Book Shoppe, $10,500. Assuming that $3,000 of this is nominal profit, or the imputed cost for the entrepreneurial services of Ms. Bookman, it leaves a true economic profit of $7,500, identical to that received by Mrs. Reader.

Does this mean that the 20th Century Book Store did not earn $21,900? Not at all. It is merely saying that of the $21,900 total earnings, only $7,500 can be attributed to economic profit. The remainder is earned from the use of other factors of production. Another way to look at the situation is to say that the Colonial Book Shoppe had a business income of $10,500, of which $7,500 was economic profit and $3,000 was for entrepreneurial services. On the other hand, the 20th Century Book Store, or Ms. Bookman in particular, had a business income of $21,900, but it should be allocated as follows: $7,500 as salary income, $3,600 as net rental income, $300 an interest income, $3,000 as nominal profit and $7,500 as economic profit.

Ascertaining the true economic profit and distinguishing between various forms of income is an important function of economic analysis. Many entrepreneurs, especially those operating small businesses, are misled because they do not understand the true nature of economic profits. Suppose, for example, that the gross profit on sales of the 20th Century Book Store fell to $15,000. Deducting the operating expenses as shown in the statement above, $8,100, would leave a business profit of $6,900. Ms. Bookman might think that her business is doing well since it shows a $6,900 business profit. But actually, the business is operating at an economic loss. If she subtracts her imputed costs, should would have the following breakdown of her sixty-nine-hundred-dollar business income: salary, $7,500; rental income, thirty-six hundred dollars; interest income, $300; entrepreneurial cost, $3,000; and an economic loss, $7,500. Actually her business would not be making a profit at all but suffering $7,500 loss. If the situation continued, she would do better economically to sell or rent her store, reinvest her money in government bonds or elsewhere, and go to work for someone else.

PROFIT AS A MEASURE OF EFFICIENCY

Profit is frequently used as a measure of efficiency of business operations. Suppose that in the previous example, two firms had the same inputs, material, financial and labor resources—but one firm was able to show a greater profit. This could be a manifestation of greater entrepreneurial efficiency. Perhaps the more profitable firm may have a lower cost due to a better utilization of its inputs, or it may be capable of producing a superior product. Since profit is dependent on sales and price, as well as costs, which in turn are determined in large part by consumer demand, it can be said that in a free market the firm with the greater profit is making more efficient use of resources in satisfying consumer demand.

The entrepreneur, or owner, likewise uses profits as a measure to determine the efficiency of his investment. There must be some way to determine whether the time, effort and resources involved in the production process are being used efficiently or whether they could be put to better use in some other alternative. One method of making this determination is by measuring the rate of return. In this regard some firms measure profit as a percentage of the sales dollar. Others measure profit as a rate of return on assets. From the viewpoint of economic analysis, however, the best measure is profit as a rate of return on investment.

Although profit per dollar of sales is a measure commonly used by businesses, it can be misleading. Sales volumes vary among firms and between industries. What may be a good return in one industry may be a poor return in another. A firm in one industry, for example, may have a 12 percent profit per dollar of sales, but have relatively few sales. Consequently, its total profit might be very low. A firm in another industry might have a 4 percent profit per dollar of sales, but have a large sales volume. Consequently, its profit could be very large in spite of its low profit per sales dollar. In either case the profit, either as a percentage of sales or as a total figure, does not give a good direct indication of managerial efficiency.

The second method, rate of return on assets, is somewhat better as an economic measure. It measures profit as a percentage return on the use of assets by the business. But here again some problems arise. If Entrepreneur A has $500,000 invested in machinery, equipment, and other assets and the business shows a net profit, over all costs both explicit and implicit, of $50,000 it could be said that profit as a rate of return on assets is 10 percent ($50,000 ÷ $500,000 = .10). Suppose Entrepreneur B has an identical situation, but he borrows $250,000 for the purchase of additional machinery and as a result he can show a net profit of $75,000 per annum. It might be said that the rate of return on assets is still 10 percent ($75,000 ÷ $750,000 = .10). Since the entrepreneur has only $500,000 invested in the business, however, is the rate of return not better stated as 15 percent ($75,000 ÷ $500,000 = .15)?

This is what leads to the third measure — profit as a rate of return on investment. In this respect, the resources used in the business are computed as total monetary investment. Reducing profit to a rate of return on investment gives a truer measure as to how the investment is being used. Furthermore, it is a more equitable means of comparing the economic efficiency of one firm with that of another or one industry versus another. In addition, profit as a rate of return on investment can be used to determine whether the investment might be put to a better productive alternative, or to determine whether it is best to disinvest and hold assets in a more liquid form, such as stocks, bonds or cash savings.

But even in calculating the rate of return on investment, problems arise. A firm may be making a good rate of return on investment, but perhaps its rate could be improved by making more profitable use of its borrowed funds. After all, one can have a good return on investment and not maximize the return on assets. Sometimes difficulty arises, too, in determining the value of the investment. Should it be measured by original cost or by reproduction cost? Here again a good return on original investment may not be a good return when one considers the reproduction cost of the investment. This is very much akin to the problem of the small investor who buys a stock for $50 that is paying a $3 annual dividend. No doubt his investment does yield 6 percent. But suppose his stock rises in value to $75 and the dividend is still $3 per annum. What now is his yield? Considering his original investment it is still 6 percent. But, considering that he now has an investment worth $75, his current yield is only 4 percent. Consequently, if the company does not increase the dividend, he might consider liquidating the stock and investing in something with a more lucrative current return.

Public utilities frequently encounter the problem of original versus reproduction cost in evaluating investment. The company may desire to use reproduction costs, especially during periods of inflation, as a basis of calculating its rate of return on investment, but the public service commission may use original cost or some other variation in its appraisal.

For industry in general one of the most widely used measures is the rate of profit on stockholders' equity as computed by the Federal Trade Commission. In this measure stockholders' equity includes paid-in capital plus retained earnings.[4] Tables 2-1 and 2-2 show some examples of profit per dollar of sales and profit on stockholders' equity as published in the FTC quarterly report on earnings.

Although there seems to be a correlation between profits per dollar of sales and rate of profit on stockholders' equity, the correlation does not exist in all individual cases. Note that food and kindred products — which had a relatively low profit per dollar of sales, 3.7 percent, after taxes for the second quarter of 1976 — had a fairly good, 16.3 percent, rate of profit after taxes on stockholders' equity. On the other hand, iron and steel, which had a higher profit per dollar of sales, 4.8 percent, had a modest 11.3 percent rate of return on stockholders' equity.

This in large part may be explained by the degree of capital intensity of an industry. In a highly capital-intensive industry like steel, a high profit per dollar of sales may yield a relatively low rate of return on stockholders' equity. This is so because it takes a large amount of capital expenditure to generate a dollar of sales, and a given profit divided by a large capital expenditure will yield a low rate of return on stockholders' equity. On the other hand, in a low capital-intensive industry, such as the food industry, a relatively low profit per dollar of sales may yield a high rate of return on stockholders' equity.

[4] *Stockholders' equity* consists of capital stock (net of treasury stock), capital surplus, minority interest, earned surplus and earned reserves, and reserves not reflected elsewhere (the bulk of the last item is surplus reserves because not all companies include such reserves with earned surplus as called for on the report form).

TABLE 2-1. Profits per Dollar of Sales, by Industry

Industry	Profit before income taxes (cents) 2Q 1976	Profit after taxes (cents) 2Q 1976
All Manufacturing Corporations	9.5	5.9
Nondurable Manufacturing Corporations	9.5	5.9
Food and Kindred Products	6.2	3.7
Tobacco Manufactures	16.1	9.0
Textile Mill Products	5.4	2.9
Paper and Allied Products	10.6	6.7
Printing and Publishing	10.1	5.6
Chemicals and Allied Products	13.0	8.1
Industrial chemicals and synthetics[1]	12.7	7.6
Drugs[1]	19.4	12.7
Petroleum and Coal Products	12.9	9.0
Rubber and Miscellaneous Plastics Products	7.6	4.5
Other Nondurable Manufacturing Corporations	5.4	2.9
Durable Manufacturing Corporations	9.6	5.8
Stone, Clay and Glass Products	9.9	6.2
Primary Metal Industries	7.2	4.8
Iron and Steel[1]	7.3	4.8
Nonferrous Metals[1]	7.2	4.7
Fabricated Metal Products	9.2	5.3
Machinery, except Electrical	12.2	7.5
Electrical and Electronic Equipment	8.1	4.6
Transportation Equipment	9.7	5.8
Motor vehicles and equipment[1]	11.3	6.9
Aircraft, guided missiles and parts[1]	6.1	3.6
Instruments and Related Products	14.4	8.6
Other Durable Manufacturing Corporations	7.9	5.0
All Mining Corporations	15.2	10.3
All Retail Trade Corporations	NA	NA*
All Wholesale Trade Corporations	4.3	2.9

[1] Included in major industry above.
*NA Not available.
Source: *Quarterly Financial Report for Manufacturing Corporations.* Federal Trade Commission, September 1976.

TABLE 2-2 Annual Rates of Profit on Stockholders' Equity, by Industry (Percent)

Industry	Before income taxes[2] 2Q 1976	After taxes 2Q 1976
All Manufacturing Corporations	25.5	15.7
Nondurable Manufacturing Corporations	24.7	15.5
Food and Kindred Products	27.4	16.3
Tobacco Manufactures	28.5	16.0
Textile Mill Products	18.7	10.1
Paper and Allied Products	25.8	16.3
Printing and Publishing	29.4	16.3
Chemicals and Allied Products	27.8	17.2
Industrial chemicals and synthetics[1]	27.2	16.3
Drugs[1]	27.9	18.2
Petroleum and Coal Products	21.0	14.8
Rubber and Miscellaneous Plastics Products	22.6	13.4
Other Nondurable Manufacturing Corporations	25.2	13.6
Durable Manufacturing Corporations	26.4	16.0
Stone, Clay and Glass Products	24.8	15.5
Primary Metal Industries	16.2	10.7
Iron and steel[1]	17.1	11.3
Nonferrous metals[1]	14.7	9.5
Fabricated Metal Products	30.6	17.7
Machinery, except Electrical	26.5	16.2
Electrical and Electronic Equipment	23.8	13.5
Transportation Equipment	34.4	20.7
Motor vehicles and equipment[1]	38.0	23.1
Aircraft, guided missiles and parts[1]	24.1	14.0
Instruments and Related Products	27.2	16.3
Other Durable Manufacturing Corporations	27.5	17.5
All Mining Corporations	24.2	16.4
All Retail Trade Corporations	NA	NA*
All Wholesale Trade Corporations	35.4	24.0

[1] Included in major industry above.
[2] Based on profit figure which includes net income (loss) of foreign branches and equity in earnings (losses) of nonconsolidated subsidiaries, net of foreign taxes.
*NA Not available.
Source: *Quarterly Financial Report for Manufacturing Corporations.* Federal Trade Commission, September 1976.

PRICE-LEVEL ACCOUNTING

Even using profit as a rate of return on investment (ROI) as a measure of efficiency can be misleading, as can other measures of profit. This is particularly so during an inflationary period such as we have experienced since 1966. A firm may show an improved profit picture in conventional terms. But this may be due primarily to higher prices. In fact, a firm could show a very good profit while the volume of its sales was declining. Very often when revenue and profit are measured in dollar volume, an increase in either may disguise a declining sales volume.

From another point of view, if profits rise either because of an increase in sales price or in sales volume, a firm's financial situation may not be enhanced in real terms. This will happen if the general price level increases in greater proportion than dollar profits. In short, even though the firm has more total profit, the purchasing power of that profit may be less than a previous year's profit because of rising prices.

Another difficulty with ROI is that profit may be rising as measured against the original or historic cost of assets and investment. But if one considers the current value of the assets, as measured by their replacement cost, the ROI will be lower during an inflationary period. An ROI of 7 percent using original cost may convert to an ROI of only 5 percent using current or replacement cost.

To eliminate false impressions about profits, price-level, or current-value, accounting (sometimes called *inflation accounting*) techniques can be used. By adjusting nonmonetary assets and nonmonetary liabilities for inflation (deflation), current-dollar profit can be converted into real or constant-dollar profit. Several statistical methods are available to make this conversion, and a number of different price indexes, such as the consumer price index and the Gross National Product implicit price deflators, can be used.

When this is done, of course, it will give the firm a different view of what is happening to its real profit and its rate of return on investment. Moreover, where a manager's efficiency is judged by his profit contribution, using price level accounting techniques may give a different set of guidelines and a different measure of this efficiency.

PROFIT MAXIMIZATION

In economic analysis it is assumed that a business firm, whether a monopolist or one engaged in pure competition, seeks to maximize profit. To act otherwise is economically irrational. Although profit maximization is a healthy guiding principle, many firms do not push profits to the nth degree.

First, short-run profit maximization may endanger long-run profit maximization. In such case the firm may sacrifice some short-run profit in the interest of maximizing profits over a longer period of time. Second, issues other than economic issues have an influence on a company's actions. Customer relations and the desire for a good public image may have an effect on the pricing and profit structure of the company. The company, too, must operate within the confines of the antitrust laws. Involvement of minority groups and pressures to preserve the natural environment effect costs and profits. This is not to say that the business firm is altruistic, at least not completely, but that it will seek to maximize profit only within reasonable limits considering the legal, social, political, and economic constraints under which it operates.

THE ENTREPRENEURS' SHARE
OF THE NATIONAL INCOME

As stated previously, profit is the most dynamic and uncertain segment of our total income. It is a residual and a noncontractual form of income. Consequently there may be nothing left out of revenue after paying other factor costs of doing business. Profit invariably changes from quarter to quarter and from year to year. The entrepreneurs' share of the national income varies from year to year and will fluctuate widely between periods of prosperity and depression. Moreover, the entrepreneurs' share of the national income has been declining over the past three decades, as shown in Table 2-3. On the other hand, compensation to employees, consisting primarily of wages and salaries, has increased from 66.3 percent to 76.2 percent of the national income during the same period.

Close scrutiny of related data indicates that proprietors' income tends to be a bit more stable than corporate profits. This occurs because proprietors' income goes in part to farmers, other self-employed persons, and many small service enterprises whose income sometimes is more related to a return of services rendered than to profit.

SUMMARY

Profit is a return to the entrepreneur arising from the operation of a business enterprise. *Profit* can be defined in simple terms as the excess of revenue over costs. Measures of cost, however, can vary

TABLE 2-3 Profits before Taxes as a Percentage of National Income
(1946-77)

Year	National Income (billions)	Proprietors' Income (billions)	Corporate Profits (billions)	Total Entre-preneurial Income (billions)	Total as a Percentage of National Income
1946	$ 178.3	$36.6	$ 16.6	$ 53.2	29.8
1950	236.2	38.4	33.7	72.1	30.5
1955	328.0	42.5	44.6	87.1	26.5
1960	412.0	47.0	46.6	93.6	22.7
1965	566.0	56.7	77.1	133.8	23.6
1970	798.4	65.1	67.9	133.0	16.6
1975	1217.0	86.0	99.3	185.3	15.2
1977	1520.5	98.2	139.8	238.0	15.7

Source: *Economic Report of the President*, 1976.

widely. Profit, being a residual, differs from other forms of income, such as wages, rent, and interest, which are contractual in nature.

The *entrepreneur* is a risk-taker who organizes and directs the factors of production in order to produce a good or a service. His reward for success is profit. Risk-bearing, innovation, fortuitous circumstances, managerial efficiency, or monopoly may be causes of, or factors contributing to, profit.

Economic profit may differ from accounting profit. In calculating profit, the latter considers primarily explicit cost. Economic profit considers also the implicit or imputed cost of using one's own factors of production. Implicit cost can be measured by observing the return to a factor of production in its alternative use. This is referred to as *opportunity cost*.

Profit is often used as a measure of managerial efficiency. In this respect one might look at profit per dollar of sales, profit as a rate of return on assets, or profit as a rate of return on stockholders' equity. More and more business firms are considering the use of price level accounting, which adjusts profit for the effect of inflation on the cost of non-cash assets.

Although profit maximization is assumed to be the prime objective for a firm in theoretical economic analysis, in actual experience this objective may be modified to some extent for a multitude of reasons.

QUESTIONS FOR ANALYSIS AND DISCUSSION

1. Distinguish between nominal profit and pure profit.
2. Explain the role of the entrepreneur in starting a business.
3. Distinguish between personal income distribution and functional distribution.

4. Innovation profit is ephemeral in nature. Explain.
5. Which of the several theories of profit do you think is the most appropriate?
6. What is the difference between accounting profit and economic profit?
7. How is opportunity cost used in determining economic profit?
8. Profit is a measure of efficiency. What are some of the criteria against which profit can be measured?
9. Is profit per dollar of sales or profit as a rate of return on investment the better measure of economic efficiency?
10. In recent years it has been suggested that the efficiency of business firms be measured by their total social contribution rather than by profit. Do you agree with this suggestion? Why or why not?

PROBLEMS AND CASES

1. John Stallworth, proprietor of the Kentucky Gourmet Restaurant, is currently making an economic profit of $15,000 per annum on the $200,000 he borrowed to establish his restaurant. This is a cause of dissatisfaction to him, since he feels that after three years of operation he ought to be making more profit. After studying his costs of operation, he decides to reduce his insurance protection, fire and liability, to a minimum. This will reduce his insurance premiums from $3,000 to $1,000 per year. He figures that by assuming more risk he can raise his profit to a more respectable level of $17,000 per year.

   (a) Is this truly an increase in economic profit?
   (b) If you were to purchase this business from Mr. Stallworth, would you be willing to pay a purchase price based on a profit of $17,000 per annum?

2. Slugger Williams, a major-league baseball player, gave up baseball at the prime of his career because of his dislike for training and travel. Averages indicate that he still would have been able to play eight to ten more years in the majors. Upon retiring he became the owner-proprietor of a sporting goods store. During the first few years of operation, the store yielded him a profit of $15,000 in addition to the $12,000 he earned as manager. Williams was happy about the success of his new business venture. One of his former college classmates, currently a junior economist at a local bank, informed Williams that he was not actually making a profit, but suffering an economic loss. The economist pointed out that since Williams could be earning at least $50,000 playing baseball, instead of running the store, he has to subtract $50,000 in opportunity cost from his revenue. Consequently, his friend tells him that instead of making a profit of $15,000, the sporting goods store is actually losing $35,000 annually.

   (a) Do you agree or disagree that the business is suffering a loss? Why or why not?
   (b) How should opportunity cost for the use of one's own effort in managing the business be calculated?

3. During the middle of a recession, Jim Mechanic, MBA, accepted a position of general manager of a small tool shop that was on the verge of bankruptcy. As a result of his efforts to reduce cost, improve marketing techniques, and as a

result of the improvement of general business conditions in the economy, the financial picture of the firm was turned around. The firm was able to pay off some of its debts, avoid bankruptcy, and show an improved profit position. Mechanic asked for a 50 percent increase in salary, contending that the improvement in the company's financial position was due to his managerial efficiency. The owners were reluctant to grant the request, contending that profit was a reward for risk-taking. They stated that the current profits were merely offsetting some of the previous losses they suffered.

(a) As an outside member of the board of directors, how would you decide?

(b) What other factors beside managerial efficiency and assumption of risk would you consider in making your decision?

4. In 1960, Jim Smith, president and principal stockholder of the Slick Oil Refinery Company, decided to invest some of his company's surplus funds in land. At that time he was able to purchase several sizable tracts of land in the Orlando, Florida, area for a total of two hundred and fifty thousand dollars. With the advent and development of Disney World in the late 1960s and early 1970s, the value of his landholdings in the area tripled in value and was still rising. By 1975, he had sold all his landholdings in the area for one million dollars. A friend commented on Smith's luck and the windfall profit of seven hundred and fifty thousand dollars. Upon hearing the remark, Smith became somewhat indignant and informed his friend that the profit was not due to luck or a windfall, but resulted from managerial efficiency.

(a) In such a discussion would you side with Mr. Smith or his friend regarding the nature of the economic gain?

(b) Regardless of what you consider the cause of the profit, does $750,000 represent a true economic profit figure?

5. Howard Schultz bought 100 shares of stock at $50 per share. At the time of purchase the stock paid an annual dividend of $2 per share. Four years later, the market value of his stock rose to $75 and the dividend had been raised gradually to $4 per share. Schultz was pleased with his success in the stock market and figured that he was receiving a yield of 8 percent ($4 ÷ $50 = .08) on his investment, since he had bought the stock for $50 per share. A friend of his, who was a broker, tried to convince Schultz that he should sell his stock and invest in some other stock or in government notes yielding 8 percent or more, because his stock was yielding only 5.3 percent on its current value of $75 per share $4 ÷ $75 = 5.3).

(a) What is the current yield or return on Mr. Schultz's investment?

(b) Do you see any problem akin to this in calculating profit as rate of return of stockholders' equity?

6. The accompanying tables show income and expenses of the Ford Motor Company for the years 1975–76. After analyzing them, calculate the following for 1976:

(a) Profit per dollar of sales

(b) Rate of return on assets

(c) Stockholders' equity

(d) Rate of return on stockholders' equity

Ford Motor Company and Consolidated Subsidiaries
Consolidated Statement of Income
For the Years Ended December 31, 1976 and 1975 (in millions)

	1976	1975
Sales	$28,839.6	$24,009.1
Costs and Expenses		
Costs, excluding items listed below	24,494.7	21,090.2
Depreciation	589.7	583.8
Amortization of special tools	431.0	435.3
Selling and administrative	1,166.5	1,036.7
Employee retirement plans	505.5	426.7
Provision for supplemental compensation	65.3	0
Total costs and expenses	27,252.7	23,572.7
Operating Income	1,586.9	436.4
Interest income (expense), net	16.0	(145.2)
Equity in net income of unconsolidated subsidiaries and affiliates	136.3	107.0
Income before Income Taxes	1,739.2	398.2
Provision for income taxes	730.6	151.9
Income before Minority Interests	1,008.6	246.3
Minority interests in net income of consolidated subsidiaries	25.5	18.8
Income before Cumulative Effect of an Accounting Change	983.1	227.5
Cumulative effect of change (as of January 1, 1975) to flow-through method of accounting for investment tax credit	—	95.2
Net Income	$ 983.1	$ 322.7
Income a Share before Cumulative Effect of an Accounting Change	$10.45	$2.44
Cumulative effect a share of change (as of January 1, 1975) to flow-through method of accounting for investment tax credit	—	1.02
Net Income a Share	$10.45	$3.46
Net Income a Share Assuming Full Dilution	$ 9.68	$3.31
Cash Dividends a Share	$ 2.80	$2.60

Reprinted from the Ford Motor Company Annual Report, pp. 29-31. Stockholder Relations, Ford Motor Company, Dearborn, Michigan.

Ford Motor Company and Consolidated Subsidiaries
Consolidated Balance Sheet
December 31, 1976 and 1975 (in millions)

Assets	1976	1975
Current Assets		
Cash	$ 754.1	$ 271.4
Marketable securities, at cost, which approximates market	910.0	624.8
Receivables	1,702.5	1,387.7
Inventories	4,356.0	3,806.8
Income taxes allocable to the following years	98.1	221.0
Other current assets	421.8	343.4
Total current assets	8,242.5	6,655.1
Investments and Other Assets		
Equities in net assets of unconsolidated subsidiaries and affiliates	1,385.9	1,252.3
Other investments, at cost, and other assets	280.7	257.7
Total investments and other assets	1,666.6	1,510.0
Property		
Land, plant and equipment, at cost (Note 9)	10,247.9	9,908.3
Less accumulated depreciation	5,689.8	5,281.4
Net land, plant and equipment	4,558.1	4,626.9
Unamortized special tools	1,021.7	949.0
Net property	5,579.8	5,575.9
Excess of Cost of Investments in Consolidated Subsidiaries Over Equities in Net Assets	279.2	279.2
Total Assets	$15,768.1	$14,020.2

Liabilities and Stockholders' Equity	1976	1975
Current Liabilities		
Accounts payable and accrued liabilities	$ 4,953.2	$ 4,025.8
Income taxes	423.8	151.2
Short-term debt of consolidated subsidiaries	531.5	711.5
Long-term debt payable within one year	88.3	101.0
Total current liabilities	5,996.8	4,989.5
Long-term Debt	1,411.4	1,533.9
Other Liabilities and Deferred Credits		
Accrued liabilities, noncurrent	492.3	464.5
Deferred supplemental compensation awards	25.9	32.1
Unawarded supplemental compensation	66.4	1.0
Deferred income taxes	492.2	453.4
Deferred investment tax credits	15.9	23.4
Total other liabilities and deferred credits	1,092.7	974.4

Ford Motor Company and Consolidated Subsidiaries
Consolidated Balance Sheet
December 31, 1976 and 1975 (in millions)
(continued)

Liabilities and Stockholders' Equity	1976	1975
Minority Interests in Net Assets of Consolidated Subsidiaries	160.2	145.9
Stockholders' Equity		
Capital stock, par value $2.50 a share, 1976 — 94.5 million shares and 1975 — 94.3 million shares	236.4	235.7
Capital in excess of par value of stock	399.2	389.1
Earnings retained for use in the business	6,471.4	5,751.7
Total stockholders' equity	7,107.0	6,376.5
Total Liabilities and Stockholders' Equity	$15,768.1	$14,020.2

7. The accompanying exhibit (on pages 45-46) shows the rate of return on stockholder's equity for all manufacturing corporations by industry group for the years 1950-75.

(a) Plot on graph paper the rate of return for the category "all manufacturers corporations" for each of the years shown.

(b) Recessions affected the United States economy in 1954, 1958, and 1960-61. There also were recessions in 1967, 1970, and 1974-75. What happened to the rate of return in each of these years? (Check appropriate sources for the 1976 and 1977 rate of return figures.)

(c) Which category of industry, durable goods or nondurable goods, tends to have the higher rate of return on stockholders' equity? Which of the two categories tend to have the more stable rate of return?

(d) Select a manufacturing (or nonmanufacturing) company in which you are interested. Calculate its rate of return on stockholders' equity. Compare that figure with the rate of return for the appropriate industry group as shown in the exhibit.

Jet-Spray Car Wash

In January 1965, Richard Carter, an excavation worker in his thirties, decided to go into the car-wash business. He owned property near a busy intersection on a major thoroughfare in the city. The property was within a few hundred feet of a several-hundred-room travel and convention motel, the largest in the city or regional area. It was also near several smaller motels and in a fair-sized business district in the middle of a large residential area. This location was also near a major interstate highway from

Relation of Profits after Taxes to Stockholders' Equity and to Sales, All Manufacturing Corporations, by Industry Group, 1950–75

Durable Goods Industries

Ratio of Profits after Federal Income Taxes (annual rate) to Stockholders' Equity—Percent

Year or Quarter	All Manufacturing Corporations	Total Durable	Motor Vehicles and Equipment	Aircraft and Parts	Electrical Machinery, Equipment, and Supplies	Machinery (except electrical)	Fabricated Metal Products	Primary Iron and Steel Industries	Primary Nonferrous Metal Industries	Stone, Clay, and Glass Products	Furniture and Fixtures	Lumber and Wood Products (except furniture)	Instruments and Related Products	Miscellaneous Manufacturing (including Ordnance)
1950	15.4	16.9	25.3		20.9	14.1	16.0	14.3	15.1	17.7	15.2	17.5	16.7	12.3
1951	12.1	13.0	14.3		14.0	13.0	13.4	12.3	13.8	14.2	11.3	11.9	13.2	9.7
1952	10.5	11.1	13.9		13.7	11.3	10.1	8.5	11.6	11.7	8.6	8.5	11.6	7.0
1953	10.5	11.1	13.9		13.1	9.8	9.8	10.7	11.1	11.8	8.2	7.1	11.4	8.2
1954	9.9	10.3	14.1		12.4	8.6	7.6	8.1	10.4	12.5	6.0	6.3	12.3	7.5
1955	12.6	13.8	21.7		12.3	10.3	10.0	13.5	15.5	15.6	9.2	11.1	12.5	8.5
1956	12.3	12.8	13.1		11.4	12.6	10.7	12.7	16.4	14.9	11.6	8.7	12.4	11.6
1957	10.9	11.3	14.2	17.7	12.5	10.7	9.3	11.4	9.3	12.4	8.5	4.7	12.0	7.7
1958	8.6	8.0	8.2	13.2	10.2	6.9	7.3	7.2	6.0	10.2	6.3	5.7	10.6	8.2
1959	10.4	10.4	14.5	8.1	12.5	9.7	8.0	8.0	7.9	12.7	8.9	9.4	13.1	9.3
1960	9.2	8.5	13.5	7.3	9.5	7.5	5.6	7.2	7.1	9.9	6.5	3.6	11.6	9.2
1961	8.9	8.1	11.4	9.8	8.9	7.8	5.9	6.1	7.1	8.9	4.9	4.1	10.6	9.9
1962	9.8	9.6	16.3	12.7	10.0	9.1	7.9	5.4	7.5	8.9	7.9	5.6	12.0	9.4
1963	10.3	10.1	16.7	11.3	10.1	9.6	8.3	7.0	7.6	8.7	8.3	8.2	12.1	8.8
1964	11.6	11.7	16.9	12.2	11.2	12.5	10.1	8.8	9.8	9.6	10.1	9.9	14.4	9.5
1965	13.0	13.8	19.5	15.2	13.5	14.1	13.2	9.8	11.9	10.3	13.4	10.1	17.5	10.7
1966	13.4	14.2	15.9	14.4	14.8	15.0	14.7	10.2	14.8	9.9	14.2	10.0	20.9	15.4
1967	11.7	11.7	11.7	12.9	12.8	12.9	12.7	7.7	10.9	8.2	12.1	8.6	18.0	13.1
1968	12.1	12.2	15.1	14.2	12.2	12.3	11.7	7.6	10.8	9.2	12.2	14.6	16.6	12.4
1969	11.5	11.4	12.6	10.6	11.1	12.2	11.3	7.6	12.2	9.2	12.6	13.0	15.6	11.6
1970	9.3	8.3	6.1	6.8	9.1	9.8	8.5	4.3	10.6	6.9	7.9	5.6	14.3	10.0
1971	9.7	9.0	13.1	5.8	9.5	8.7	8.3	4.5	5.1	9.2	9.5	11.4	13.6	9.0
1972	10.6	10.8	14.7	7.7	10.8	10.6	10.7	6.0	5.9	10.1	13.4	16.3	14.9	10.8
1973	12.8	13.1	15.1	10.3	13.0	13.4	13.8	9.5	10.8	11.2	13.2	22.4	15.9	11.5
1974	14.9	12.6	6.9	10.6	11.1	13.2	17.1	10.8	15.8	10.6	NA	NA	10.1	11.7
1975	11.6	10.2	6.2	11.0	9.0	13.6	13.1	10.7	5.2	6.8	NA	NA	13.7	8.5

(continued)

		Nondurable Goods Industries									
Year of Quarter	Total Non-dur-able	Food and Kin-dred Prod-ucts	To-bacco Man-ufac-tures	Tex-tile Mill Prod-ucts	Ap-parel and Related Prod-ucts	Paper and Allied Prod-ucts	Print-ing and Pub-lish-ing[1]	Chem-icals and Allied Prod-ucts	Petro-leum Refin-ing	Rub-ber and Mis-cella-neous Plastic Prod-ucts	Leather and Leather Prod-ucts
				Ratio of Profits after Federal Income Taxes (annual rate) to Stockholders' Equity—Percent							
1950	14.1	12.3	11.5	12.7	10.1	16.2	11.5	17.8		16.9	10.9
1951	11.2	8.1	9.5	8.2	2.9	13.9	10.3	12.2	15.2	14.8	2.1
1952	9.7	7.6	8.4	4.2	4.4	10.5	9.1	10.9	13.3	11.1	5.8
1953	9.9	8.1	9.4	4.6	5.1	10.1	9.4	10.7	13.4	11.3	6.0
1954	9.6	8.1	10.2	1.8	4.5	9.9	9.2	11.6	12.7	10.6	5.9
1955	11.4	8.9	11.4	5.7	6.1	11.5	10.2	14.7	13.4	13.2	8.5
1956	11.8	9.3	11.7	5.8	8.1	11.6	13.0	14.2	13.9	12.2	7.2
1957	10.6	8.7	12.5	4.2	6.3	8.9	11.7	13.3	12.5	11.1	7.0
1958	9.2	8.7	13.5	3.5	4.9	8.1	9.0	11.4	10.0	9.1	5.7
1959	10.4	9.3	13.4	7.5	8.6	9.5	11.4	13.7	9.8	11.0	8.5
1960	9.8	8.7	13.4	5.8	7.7	8.5	10.6	12.2	10.1	9.1	6.3
1961	9.6	8.9	13.6	5.0	7.2	7.9	8.5	11.8	10.3	9.3	4.4
1962	9.9	8.8	13.1	6.2	9.3	8.1	10.3	12.4	10.1	9.6	6.9
1963	10.4	9.0	13.4	6.1	7.7	8.1	9.2	12.9	11.3	9.2	6.9
1964	11.5	10.0	13.4	8.5	11.7	9.3	12.6	14.4	11.4	10.6	10.5
1965	12.2	10.7	13.5	10.9	12.7	9.4	14.2	15.2	11.8	11.7	11.6
1966	12.7	11.2	14.1	10.1	13.3	10.6	15.6	15.1	12.4	12.2	12.9
1967	11.8	10.8	14.4	7.6	12.0	9.1	13.0	13.1	12.5	10.3	11.9
1968	11.9	10.8	14.4	8.8	13.0	9.7	12.5	13.3	12.3	12.3	13.0
1969	11.5	10.9	14.5	7.9	11.9	10.1	12.6	12.8	11.7	10.3	9.3
1970	10.3	10.8	15.7	5.1	9.3	7.0	11.2	11.4	11.0	7.1	9.4
1971	10.3	11.0	15.8	6.7	11.2	4.8	10.7	11.8	10.3	9.6	8.2
1972	10.5	11.1	15.4	7.5	12.0	9.0	12.1	12.9	8.7	10.3	9.1
1973	12.6	12.8	14.8	9.0	10.5	12.9	12.8	14.8	11.6	12.0	9.4
1974	17.2	14.0	15.6	8.2	NA	17.8	13.2	18.2	21.0	14.4	NA
1975	12.9	14.4	15.9	4.4	NA	12.6	12.9	15.2	12.5	8.0	NA

Source: *Statistical Abstract of the United States*, 1973, 1975, and 1976, p. 523.

which people exited to stay at some of the motels in town. Carter's property, which he inherited, had a 75-foot frontage and was 500 feet long. He sold a portion that was toward the rear to an adjacent auto dealer for $25,000.

Carter had only limited business experience, and after a visit to California, where he went through a two-week car-wash program sponsored by the equipment supplier, he had a car wash built on half of his property. The building and equipment cost him about $65,000, of which $40,000 was for equipment. To finance this, he borrowed $55,000 from the Thrifty Savings and Loan Company. One year after the Jet-Spray Car Wash began operations, he borrowed another $20,000 to erect a building for rental purposes adjacent to the car wash. During the first year, he rented this building to a dry cleaner for $475 a month. In the second year it was leased to a carpet company for $550 per month with an option to renew the lease for five more years. The carpet company, which had plants and offices in other large, nearby towns, used the building for offices, sales promotion, and pick-up. It put in new equipment and installed a battery of small telephone offices for its sales promotion. Carter had a twenty-five-year mortgage from the Savings and Loan Company at 8¼ percent interest. His monthly payments on the mortage amounted to $700. According to his best estimates, the land on which the car wash and the rental property were located was worth $100,000. The buildings were worth $85,000, making the total value of his business $185,000.

In the first few years of business, the car wash, Carter felt, operated profitably. (His income statement is shown in this report.) It had a full crew of eight persons in the summer and twelve in the winter. On slow days in winter, however, it operated with a minimum crew of eight persons. The Jet-Spray Car Wash had three or four regular and reliable workers. Most others regarded the job as temporary. Often, Carter would not know how many men he would need on a particular day, because of the variability of the weather. Some days he turned down men who wanted to work. Other days he had to get on the phone in an effort to hire more workers for the day. The average pay was about the minumum wage. The car wash also had a tip box for workers placed at the end of the line where customers picked up their cleaned automobiles. During the first three years of operation, about 52,000 cars per year went through the car wash, with the winter months heavier than the summer months.

Carter did very little advertising. For a while he did advertise in one or two local papers and also placed signs in store windows, barber shops, motels, and a few other convenient locations. The usual charge for a car wash was $1.75, but the person who had the car washed received a ticket that entitled him to return within the next ten days and have his car washed for $1.00. The next time in, however, the person had to pay $1.75, but was eligible to receive another $1.00 car wash in the next ten days. This practice, however, was dropped in late 1967. In its place, Carter substituted punch cards that granted a free car wash to a customer who had paid for ten car washes. Wednesday was "ladies' day," when women could have their cars washed for $1.25.

Although Jet-Spray Car Wash had these practices, Carter stopped advertising these or any other information about the car wash in late 1965. Carter was thinking about raising his car-wash price to a flat $2.00. He felt that this was the price trend in the car-wash business, and that he could not service all the cars that came on rush days anyway. He had no idea, however, about how many, if any, customers he might lose because of the higher price. Carter thought also about installing gas pumps as a promotion measure, but decided against it because of the money and trouble involved. There was no fully automatic or complete car wash within four miles of Jet-Spray Car Wash. There was, however, a twenty-five-cent do-it-yourself car-wash operation within four or five blocks.

For two years, Carter employed a woman to operate the cash register for $70 per week. He generally managed and supervised the car wash. In his absence one of his nephews, who was attending a local college, supervised the car-wash operation. In the first few years of operation, Carter had a few opportunities both to sell and to lease his car wash but he declined all offers. In the fall of 1972, he was approached again about leasing the car wash. At that time he thought of installing new equipment, such as wrap-around brushes, hood brushes, window brushes, a hot soaper, and a pressure washer. This equipment would have cost him $20,000. He could purchase it for one-third down and five years to pay the remainder at an 8 percent carrying charge. At the time, however, Carter was a little short of working capital. He had previously borrowed $4,000, which he repaid, from a friend to obtain some auxiliary equipment in 1970. He subsequently borrowed $10,000 from the same friend for replacement of some of his equipment and for working capital. He still owed about $6,000 on this loan. Carter could not increase his mortgage loan from the bank because it had originally lent him money, not only on the land and buildings, but also on the equipment. He had a home valued at $45,000 which still had a $38,000 mortgage. He had life insurance of about $8,000 carried on a plan through one of his former employers on which he could not borrow anything. His friend was unable to extend a further loan. Carter was reluctant to approach a commercial bank because he knew he had no unattached assets to offer as collateral for a loan of $20,000. He also felt that it might press him a bit to take on regular monthly payments on another loan. He was interested in replacing his current equipment, which was becoming a little obsolete, with some new equipment. With new equipment, he could give a better and faster car wash and handle more cars on rush days. On these days the cars were often backed along his U-shaped driveway to the major thoroughfare, a distance of several hundred feet. Carter thought that with new equipment he could increase his sales to 67,000 cars annually primarily by capitalizing on rush-day business. The new equipment also would allow him to reduce his work force by about four men during the peak season. This, of course, would reduce his labor cost.

About this time, Carter was again approached to lease his operation. The potential leasee formerly had been manager of the Sunshine Car Wash in another section of town. He offered Carter $1,000 a month for five years, with the option of renewing the lease for five more. He was willing to pay the first year's rent in advance. The potential leasee wanted to put in more equipment and have permission to make changes in the building. He wanted, for example, freedom to install gas pumps to sell gas in connection with the car wash. He wanted the equipment that he put in to belong to him after two years. He wanted complete freedom to run the operation. He wanted to make sure all bills were paid before the lease contract was signed. He was willing to pay in advance the last half of the fifth year plus half of the first year, $12,000.

About the same time, Carter was approached by the car dealer to whom he had previously sold a portion of his property about the possibility of selling his whole operation. The car dealer was interested in the land for future development and in the car wash as an interim investment. The car dealer stated, however, that he would be interested whether Carter leased the property or not. He talked about a purchase price in the vicinity of $160,000. Carter had previously asked $200,000 for the property and the business and would have been willing to settle for $180,000. He was not certain whether he should take $160,000. Carter owned, from his excavating days, his own tractor and related digging equipment and generally had made about $250 per week doing business as an independent operator. Carter now had to decide whether to try to borrow funds from some source and continue to operate the car wash himself, to lease it to the prospective leasee, or to sell it outright to the car dealer.

(a) What was the economic profit of Jet-Spray Car Wash?
(b) Should Mr. Carter borrow funds and continue to operate Jet Spray, lease the business, or sell it outright?

Jet-Spray Car Wash
Operating Statement, 1972

Receipts		$75,782.71
Operating Expenses		
Wages	$27,987.27	
Operating Supplies	4,106.92	
Light, Heat, Power	4,613.87	
Taxes	3,811.03	
Office Supplies and Expenses	1,191.76	
Advertising	1,282.38	
Claims Paid	901.57	
Maintenance	773.04	
Uniforms	543.59	
Miscellaneous Expenses	305.04	
Insurance	292.27	
Legal and Professional	716.60	
Auto Expenses	500.00	
Telephone	195.27	
	$47,220.61	
Depreciation	5,959.02	$53,179.63
Operating Income		$22,603.08
Interest Expense		4,426.31
Net Income		$18,176.77

P&G's Aren't Chips Off the Old Spud,
But They Are Selling

Its Pringle's Potato Chips Have No Lumps
or Bumps But Spark a Controversy

People in the potato-chip business aren't very chipper these days. Potato-chip manufacturers, or chippers, are apt to look back with a bit of nostalgia to the summer of 1968 — the glorious, golden days of the chipping business — when an appreciative public would graciously forgive a burnt-looking chip or two while snatching the cellophane-wrapped goodies from the grocery shelves.

Then, later that same year, Procter & Gamble Co. came along and changed potato-chip history. After 10 years of research and development, the Cincinnati soapmaker produced what no one thought possible — the "perfect" potato chip.

Called Pringle's Newfangled Potato Chips, P&G's product doesn't have any lumps, bumps or black edges. Stamped from dehydrated potato mash, each Pringle's chip is molded to exactly the same size, flash-fried in 15 seconds to precisely the same curl, and salted. The chips then are stacked neatly into a cardboard container that resembles a tennis-ball can. In this moistureproof, recappable can, P&G says, unopened Pringle's stay crisp for a year while other potato chips turn soggy after six weeks on the shelf.

In the fall of 1968, Pringle's were test-marketed in Evansville, Ind., and they promptly sliced off an estimated 20% of the local potato-chip market. Although P&G doesn't like to brag about it — in fact the company declines even to talk about it — Pringle's are currently gobbling into potato-chip sales in 40% of the country.

A "SERIOUS CHALLENGE." All this hasn't gone unnoticed by chippers. "The arrival of Pringle's on the scene in a big way would seem to present the potato-chip industry with the most serious challenge in its history," warned the monthly trade magazine, Potato Chipper. The magazine went on to predict ominously: "Whatever happens, it's doubtful the potato-chip industry will ever be the same."

That prediction turned out to be all too true. As Pringle's nibbled into the potato-chip market from one side, ingredient and manufacturing costs cut into the $1.25 billion industry from the other. In the past five years, raw-potato prices leaped 50%, labor costs jumped 31% and packaging-material prices rose 20%. And these costs are still climbing.

Under such pressure, a few small chippers crumbled last year and closed up shop. With annual potato-chip consumption hovering at its 1969 level of an average of five pounds a person, even those still in business aren't sure how long they'll survive. "Potato chippers can't weather too many 1973s," says Francis Dodd, president of the Potato Chip Institute, the chippers' trade group that, among other things, provides chip fanciers with recipes for such delicacies as "Lamb Chip Chops" and "Baked Chipped Snapper."

A BOW TO GEORGE CRUM. But most manufacturers aren't ready to cash in their chips and fade away just yet. In a spirit that would make

George Crum proud, chippers are fighting for the purity of their product. (For those not versed in potato-chip lore, George Crum was an Indian chef at Moon Lake House Hotel in Saratoga Springs, N.Y. In 1853, angered by a customer's request for thinner-than-usual French fries, Mr. Crum testily whittled his potatoes into paper-thin slices, cooked them in boiling fat for about three minutes and salted them. The result of his pique was the first potato chips, or, as they were then known Saratoga Chips.)

Chippers insist that real potato chips are exactly as Chef Crum made them. Pringle's and other products like General Mills Inc.'s boxed Chipos, which although made from dehydrated potatoes aren't of uniform size, are "synthetics" masquerading as real potato chips, they say.

To emphasize their point, chippers filed suit against Pringle's and Chipos, seeking to force them to label their products "snacks" rather than potato chips. The chippers lost, promptly took their case to the Food and Drug Administration and lost again. Undeterred, they're still fighting, hoping that the FDA will reconsider.

"Do you think a consumer would be deceived if a manufacturer came out with a product made out of ground beef with additives shaped as a sirloin and called it a sirloin steak made from ground beef?" argues Lawrence Burch, the Potato Chip Institute's executive director, who admits that chippers "get emotional" on the subject of Pringle's.

At the 1973 potato-chip annual convention, passions ran deep enough for members to change their designation of October from the traditional National Potato Chip Month to National "Real" Potato Chip Month. And to fight off the Pringle's threat, members were assessed extra dues under a "stay-in-business" campaign. "A lot of them thought the giant was here and it's going to slay us," remembers Joseph Whelan, vice president of advertising for Jays Foods, Chicago's largest chipper.

In such a frame of mind, most chippers have about as much enthusiasm for Pringle's as lovers of haute cuisine have for hash houses. "They taste like cardboard," grumbles one Pringle's competitor who like most other chippers, started his business with little more than a potato slicer and a vat of oil.

What chippers find particularly hard to swallow is that consumers willingly pay more for Pringle's. Nine ounces of Pringle's sells for about 88 cents while 10 ounces of other chips sells for about 69 cents. Chippers concede, however, that P&G's eye-catching, red, recappable can appeals to people who munch only a few chips at a sitting.

Pringle's have other appealing features as well. Unlike regular potato chips, which require more delicate handling than eggs, Pringle's crush-proof can and year-long shelf life allow P&G to send them through normal warehouse distribution channels with minimal breakage and shipping costs. On the other hand, chippers must maintain a costly sales force and truck fleet to hand-deliver a fresh product to grocery stores.

Yet even the "perfect" potato chip has its flaws. Industry observers who have studied P&G's patents say the Pringle's process is tremendously complicated and expensive. "It's a real Rube Goldberg," says Ora Smith, the Potato Chip Institute's research director, who adds that, like other chippers, P&G is staggering under rising raw-material and packaging costs. "They make one chip at a time."

Even chip by chip, Pringle's potential market is no small potatoes. Industry experts estimate that when Pringle's reaches nationwide distribution, sales could easily top $120 million. Although P&G won't disclose its marketing plans, last October it said it would build a second Pringle's plant in Greenville, N.C.

(a) In what ways are Pringle's Potato Chips an innovation?

(b) To what extent does the innovation permit its producer to break away from the normal market price?

(c) Is there any evidence that imitators are coming into the market?

(d) Is the innovation forcing any established potato chip producers out of business?

(e) Why are smaller producers more likely to be forced out of business by the innovation than are large producers?

(f) What will happen to innovation profit if the innovation becomes widespread?

The Alpha Company

The balance sheets of the Alpha Company for January 1971 and January 1975 are shown in Exhibit A. The company was organized late in 1970 and began operation on January 1, 1971, with a capital stock of $250,000. Most of the money from the sale of the stock was invested in buildings, machinery, and equipment. Shortly afterward, the company borrowed money to purchase additional machinery and equipment. For the year 1975, the company showed a profit of $30,000.

EXHIBIT A. The Alpha Company Balance Sheet

Assets	1971	1975
Cash	$ 25,000	$ 25,000
Buildings & Mach.	200,000	230,000
Equipment	25,000	25,000
Notes Receivable	—	10,000
	$250,000	$290,000

1971 1975 Liabilities and Net Worth		
Notes Payable	—	$ 25,000
Capital Stock	$250,000	250,000
Retained Earnings	—	15,000
	250,000	290,000

EXHIBIT B. Various Price Indexes (1967 = 100)
(1971-1975)

	Consumer Price Index (CPI)	Wholesale Price Index (WPI)	GNP Implicit Price Deflators (IPD)		
			All Items	Domestic Investment	Structures
1971	121	114	96	96	94
1975	161	175	126	137	141

During the period 1971 and 1975 various indexes of prices are shown in Exhibit B.

(a) Using conventional accounting methods (historical costs) what is the rate of return on stockholders' investment for 1975?

(b) Assume that all buildings, machinery, and equipment were purchased on or shortly after January 1971. Using the CPI and price-level accounting techniques adjust the 1975 balance sheet to reflect current (1975) values.

(c) On the basis of the current-value adjustments, what is the rate of return on stockholder' equity for the year 1975?

(d) What would be the rate of return on stockholders' equity on the basis of current values if the GNP Implicit Price Deflators for Structures were used to make the balance sheet adjustments?

(e) Which of you think is the better measure, the CPI or the IPD, in this case for making current value adjustments? Why?

(f) Would there be any difference in the current values if the buildings, machinery, and equipment were purchased periodically over the five-year period. Why, or why not?

(g) Suppose the 1975 profit of $30,000 were deflated to 1971 constant dollars, and the deflated profit measured against the stockholders' equity in terms of historical cost. What would be the rate of return on stockholders' equity?

SELECTED READINGS

Childs, John F. *Earning per Share and Management Decisions*. Englewood Cliffs, N.J.: Prentice-Hall, Inc., 1971.

Current-Value Accounting: Economic Reality in Financial Reporting. New York: Touche Ross & Company, 1976.

Dudick, Thomas F. *Profile for Profitability*. New York: John Wiley & Sons, Inc., 1972.

Hawkins, David F. *Corporate Financial Reporting*, Homewood, Ill.: Richard A. Irwin, Inc., 1971. Chap. 15, "Price-Level Accounting."

Knight, Frank, *Risk, Uncertainty & Profit.* Chicago: University of Chicago Press, 1971.

Liles, Patrick R. "Who Are The Entrepreneurs?" *MSU Business Topics.* Lansing, Michigan, Winter 1974.

Passer, Harold C. "The Long Term Outlook for Corporate Profits as a Share of National Income." *Business Economics,* January 1974.

Quarterly Financial Report for Manufacturing Corporations. Washington, D.C.: U.S. Government Printing Office (Current Issue).

Weiss, H.L. "The Profit Ethic." Schenectady, N.Y.: General Electric Co., May 1974.

3

Price Determination: Demand and Supply Analysis

If the business firm is to be successful and generate profit, it must have ample sales to provide revenue sufficient to more than cover the cost of production. Sales revenue depends directly on price and quantity sold. In short, sales depend on demand. Consequently, in order to make prudent managerial economic decisions about prices and sales, one needs a thorough understanding and analysis of the theory and application of demand.

Furthermore, supply likewise affects price, whether a firm is buying or selling commodities or services. The total market supply, including that of a firm, influences the price it can get for the product it is selling. On the other hand, in buying materials or labor, the total supply available along with the demand will determine the price a firm must pay for its inputs. Consequently, in this chapter we shall be analyzing both demand and supply.

ROLE OF DEMAND

The forces of demand and supply are relied upon in a free-market system to determine prices. Consumers manifest their demand in the prices they are willing to pay for various products. Business firms seeking profit cater to consumer demand by offering goods and services at various prices. Thus, for an individual commodity, a market is established in which its price is determined by the supply of the producers and demand of the buyers.

If either demand or supply changes it will cause adjustments in the amount of goods and services sold, or price, or both. If sports enthusiasts, for example, accelerate their purchases of tennis racquets, sport shops will order inventory replacements and additional racquets from manufacturers, who in turn will produce more tennis racquets. Depending on the availability and cost of resources, these additional tennis racquets may be supplied at the same or at a different price. In this way, consumer demand is made known to the producers through the market structure. At other times, producers will try to anticipate the demands of consumers and provide goods beforehand to meet anticipated demand. The system does not work perfectly. At times there are lags and leads in the market: gluts and shortages occur, and prices fluctuate. Nevertheless, considering the wide variety in quality, shape, size, and color of the billions of items produced and sold each year, the system somehow seems to do an excellent job of satisfying consumer demand.

The demand for goods and services of all kinds can be traced to the demand for goods and services that directly satisfy consumer wants. The demand for tennis racquets, for example, gives rise to a demand for wood, gut, steel, and leather; that, in turn, gives rise to a demand for iron and steel with which to make tools and machines for fabricating and processing wood, gut, steel, and leather. The demand for a good or service that grows out of the desire to satisfy the demand for some other good or service is referred to as a *derived demand*.

DEMAND

In analyzing the impact of demand on the prices, we must distinguish between personal or individual demand and market demand. *Market demand* is merely the aggregate of personal demand.

Personal Demand and Utility

Demand implies something more than a need or want. In addition to a need or want, an individual must have purchasing power if he is to satisfy his want. One may have a strong desire, for example, for a new model Lincoln Continental, but unless he has the ability to buy it, his desire will have no influence on the market. Personal demand therefore implies a desire plus some purchasing power. It signifies the quantity of a good that an individual stands ready to buy at each of several prices at a particular time or under given conditions.

The *utility* (usefulness) of a good to an individual at a particular time depends upon the number of units that he has recently consumed or that he may own. If the number of units consumed or owned is large, the marginal utility of an additional unit is apt to be lower than it otherwise would be. Hence, the price of a commodity will affect the quantity that an individual will buy at a given time. A homemaker, for example, may buy one dozen eggs at the grocery at a given price, buy fewer if the price is higher, but buy two dozen eggs if the price is low enough. Merchants are aware of the relationship between prices and the quantities bought. This is one reason they conduct sales at reduced prices and give quantity discounts.

Market Demand

Market demand consists of the total quantity of a good that would be bought in the aggregate by individuals and firms at each of several prices at a given time. *Demand* is formally defined as a schedule of the total quantities of a good or service that will be purchased at various prices at a given time. A precise schedule of this kind for a specific commodity or services is difficult to construct because it requires us to know just how many units would actually be purchased at various prices. Although we may not have a specific measure, it is generally conceded that at a given time consumers will buy more units of a good at lower prices than they will at higher prices. The reason is multifold. First, consumers willing to purchase a commodity at a high price may buy more of the product at a lower price. Second, some lower-income consumers may not be able to afford the product at a higher price but will buy it at a lower price. Third, some consumers who can afford to buy the product at a high price, but may not because they do not think that it is worth the price, will buy the product at a lower price. A lower price for a good or service, therefore, nearly always results in the sale of a larger amount of a product. A higher price, other things remaining the same, usually tends to limit the amount that will be purchased. Thus, we can conclude that the quantity of a good or service that will be purchased tends to vary inversely with the price.

The statement "tends to vary inversely" does not imply that the variation in the amount sold is always proportionate to the change in price. A reduction of 25 percent in the price of a good, for example, probably would not result in a 25 percent rise in the number of units sold; nor would an increase of 50 percent in the price likely result in a corresponding decrease in the amount that would be purchased. In some cases, the change in the quantity sold might be more than proportional to the change in price; in others, it might be less.

A Demand Schedule

Since the quantity of most goods purchased tends to vary inversely with price, we can use a hypothetical schedule of prices and quantities to illustrate this relationship. Let us assume that on Wednesday, at 9:00 A.M., retailers, bakers, food processors, and other buyers at the Kansas City market would purchase at various prices the amounts of grade-A eggs shown in column D (demand), Table 3–1. Observe that the larger amounts of eggs would be bought at lower prices.

The relationship between price and the quantity that would be purchased is represented graphically in Figure 3–1. The vertical line, OY, indicates at regular intervals the price; the horizontal line, OX, shows the quantity in dozens. Thus, to locate the point for the demand at twenty-five cents, for example, a horizontal line is drawn to the right from that price. A vertical line also is drawn upward from 2500 on to the quantity line to a point that intersects the price line

TABLE 3-1. Demand Schedule for Eggs

Price per Dozen	Dozens of Eggs That Will Be Bought		
	D	D_1	D_2
$.50	650	1,100	200
.45	1,000	1,480	550
.40	1,400	1,820	920
.35	1,800	2,200	1,300
.30	2,150	2,550	1,650
.25	2,500	2,900	2,000
.20	2,800	3,250	2,350
.15	3,200	3,600	2,710
.10	3,550	3,980	3,100
.05	3,900	4,200	3,450

(y). This shows that twenty-five hundred dozen eggs will be purchased at twenty-five cents per dozen. The same thing can be done for other prices and quantities.

When all the points have been plotted in this way, they suggest a line that slopes downward to the right. If the price and the quantity changes were infinitely small, and if they varied according to the proportions indicated in the schedule, the result in the graph would really be such a line. For our purposes, therefore, we may construct a line to indicate demand. The demand line then is a graphic way of

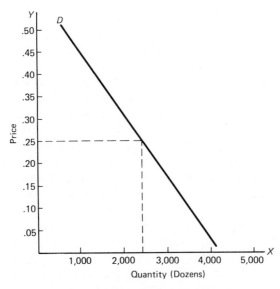

Figure 3-1. Demand Line for Eggs

showing how the quantity of eggs that would be bought varies inversely with price. A demand schedule may be represented by a straight line or by a curve. The line may have a shallow or a steep slope, it may be continuous or discontinuous, smooth or jagged, depending on the nature of the demand for the particular product and the ability to obtain sufficient information to plot the demand schedule. In actuality, there are all kinds and shapes of demand lines.

Although the typical demand line moves downward to the right, it is not uncommon to find a product for which the demand will move downward to the right over a given range of prices, but then eventually curve backward to the left. This would indicate that in certain price ranges, less of the product would be purchased even at lower prices. Prestige items are sometimes in this category. Diamonds, for example, are a status symbol to many people. If the price were lower, more people would buy diamonds. But if the price were so low that almost anyone could afford to buy diamonds, they might lose their prestige and perhaps fewer people would want to buy them.

Changes in Demand

Remember that we defined demand as a *schedule of amounts* that would be purchased at various prices under a given set of conditions. That implies, of course, no change in population, income, tastes, uses for the product, substitutes, or other conditions. Notice on the demand line in Figure 3-1 that at a price of twenty-five cents, twenty-five hundred dozen eggs would be sold. If the price were twenty cents, instead of twenty-five cents, more eggs would be sold. Does this mean that there is an increase in demand? No, not at all. Even though we altered the price from twenty-five cents to twenty cents and sold more, this is not a change in demand. Nothing has happened to the demand schedule. It merely indicates that at a lower price more goods are sold. This is known as a movement along the demand line, sometimes referred to as a *change in the quantity demanded*. It should not be confused with a change in demand. To have a change in demand, as opposed to a change in the quantity demanded, a greater or lesser amount of the product would have to be bought at given prices. An increase in demand, for example, is shown in Table 3-1.

Column D_1 is a schedule representing an increase in the amount that will be purchased at each of the prices as compared with column D. When a demand line for D_1 is plotted, it will be drawn to the right of the line for D, as shown in Figure 3-2. It will reveal that at a price of twenty-five cents, for example, twenty-nine hundred dozen eggs

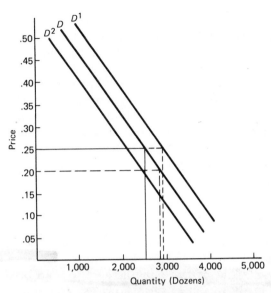

Figure 3-2. Changes in the Demand for Eggs

will be purchased. A decrease in demand, on the other hand, means that a smaller quantity will be purchased at the various prices. In Table 3-1, column D_2 shows a decrease in demand, compared with column D. The demand line D_2 lies to the left of line D as shown in Figure 3-2.

A change in demand (increase or decrease) may be caused by many different factors. A change in population, for example, may cause an increase in demand over a period of time. This can be seen in the demand for autos today compared with that of a few decades ago. There are now more people driving more cars. A change in income can also change demand. Again with higher incomes today, more people can afford to buy cars. Moreover, higher family income has increased the number of two- and three-car families. Another important factor affecting demand is changing consumers' taste. The change in men's tastes, for example, brought about an increase in demand for leisure suits in place of formal suits. The change in taste from skirts and dresses to pants suits has a substantial impact on the demand for various kinds of women's clothing. Advertising can also affect the demand for products or services. Consumers may buy more or less of a product depending on the effectiveness of advertising. Witness the emphasis on advertising by soap producers, automobile manufacturers, and breweries that results in higher sales at existing prices. The demand for a given product can be altered, too, by the change in price or a competing or complementary product. A decrease in price by Competitor A can cause a decrease in sales for Competitor B. On the other hand, a decrease in the price of stereo sets resulting in greater sales could cause an increase in the sale of records as more people owned stereos. The development of new uses for a product, such as plastic for sewer pipe, the development of substitutes, such as the twenty-four-hour automatic bank teller, and many other factors can bring about changes in demand. We will see more about these changes in the process of measuring the elasticity of demand in the next chapter.

SUPPLY

As with the concept of demand, there are also two aspects of supply: personal supply and market supply. Personal or *individual supply* is a schedule of the quantities of a good or service that an individual is ready to sell at various prices. To determine the supply any person might offer to sell, one would need to know exactly how much he would sell at various prices. For example, if food were very scarce and one possessed a limited amount, he might be induced to sell some at a certain price. If the price offered were higher, he might sell a larger quantity, and at a still higher price, he might be willing to sell even more. But if his life depended on his retaining a minimum amount of food for his own nutrition, he would not part with all the remainder at any price.

Market Supply

The *market supply* is composed of the total quantities of a good that all sellers stand ready to offer for sale. *Supply* is defined as a schedule of the total quantities of a good or service that will be offered for sale at various prices at a given time. Remember: We are considering here the behavior of a great many individuals or firms. The market supply refers to total quantities of a homogeneous product or service. Supply, like demand, is always specific. It means one thing, for example, to talk about the total supply of refrigerators in the market. It means another thing to measure the individual supply of Frigidaire, Coldspot, General Electric, Westinghouse, and various other makes and models of refrigerators. Obviously the supply of and the demand for home model refrigerators constitute a different market from the demand for compact dormitory refrigerators.

A Supply Schedule

For analysis, it is convenient to construct a market supply schedule just as we did with demand. Therefore, let us set up a hypothetical market supply schedule for grade-A eggs on the Kansas City market at 9:00 A.M. on Wednesday, as shown in columns 1 and 2 of Table 3-2.

The same procedure used in drawing the demand line for eggs can be used to plot the supply line (shown by S in Figure 3-3). Supply indicates the number of units of a good or service that will be offered for sale at different prices at a given time. Again this assumes that there is no change in other conditions, such as the costs of materials and labor, worker productivity, alternative use of inputs, and other factors affecting the quantity offered for sale. The supply line rises from left to right, indicating that larger amounts of eggs will be offered for sale at higher prices. Because a larger amount can be sold at a higher price, supply has not, therefore, increased. There is merely a movement along the supply line, or an increase in the quantity offered for sale. This is sometimes referred to as an increase in the *quantity supplied*. More will be offered for sale at higher prices for two obvious reasons: First, those willing to produce and sell at one price will be encouraged to produce and offer more at higher prices. Second, many high-cost producers who are unwilling to produce and sell at lower prices because it would be unprofitable may find it profitable to enter the market at higher prices.

In order to have an increase in supply as opposed to an increase in the quantity supplied, a greater quantity would have to be offered at given prices. An increase in supply, for example, is shown in Table

TABLE 3-2. Supply Schedules for Eggs
(Dozens of eggs that will be offered for sale)

Price	S	S_1	S_2
$.50	4,800	5,300	4,300
.45	4,350	4,850	3,850
.40	3,900	4,400	3,400
.35	3,450	3,950	2,950
.30	3,000	3,500	2,500
.25	2,500	3,100	2,100
.20	2,100	2,600	1,600
.15	1,650	2,100	1,100
.10	1,200	1,700	700
.05	850	1,300	300

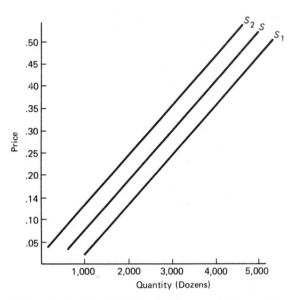

Figure 3-3. Supply Line for Eggs and Changes in
the Supply Curve

3-2. The third column, S_1 indicates that at fifty cents more eggs will
be offered for sale than was indicated in the first schedule, S. For
each price a greater quantity will be offered for sale. A decrease in
supply means that a smaller quantity will be offered for sale at various prices. When we plot the supply line for S_1, it will lie to the right
of that for S; and the line for S_2, showing a decrease in supply, will
lie to the left of S, as shown in Figure 3-3.

Changes in Supply

Market supply is the counterpart of market demand. In the case
of reproducible goods, the quantity demanded usually tends to
vary inversely with price. The quantity supplied on the other hand,
tends to vary directly with price; that is, a higher price usually — but
not always — results in a greater amount offered for sale. But remember, just as with demand, when price changes, and a greater or
lesser amount is offered for sale, that is not a change in supply. It
is merely a movement along the supply line or a change in the
quantity supplied.

When supply changes, a different quantity will be offered for sale
at each price. An *increase in supply* means that a larger amount will
be offered; and a decrease in supply, that a smaller quantity will be

offered at each of the various prices. This is shown in Table 3-2 and Figure 3-3. A change in supply, (increase or decrease) may be caused by many different factors, such as a change in the cost or availability of raw materials or labor, the availability of substitute raw materials, a change in worker productivity, a change in production techniques, a change in alternative uses of raw materials and labor, the use of more efficient machinery, and other changes that can affect the quantity of goods offered for sale at various prices.

PRICE DETERMINATION BY DEMAND AND SUPPLY

To see how demand and supply determine price in a free market, let us look again at the demand for and the supply of eggs on the Kansas City market at 9:00 A.M. on Wednesday as reproduced in Table 3-3.

At what price will eggs sell? The market price will be established by the interaction of demand and supply. It will be set at the point where "demand and supply are equal." To put it another way, the price will be determined where the quantity purchased equals the quantity offered for sale. Since the market will be cleared of all eggs at that price, it is known as the *equilibrium price*.

To demonstrate relationship of prices to demand and supply, we can reconstruct the demand and supply lines for the schedules in Table 3-3, in the manner shown in Figure 3-4. With reference to price and quantity, the lines intersect at a point that indicates a price of twenty-five cents and a quantity of twenty-five hundred dozens. What is the significance of this? It simply means that at a price of

TABLE 3-3. Demand and Supply Schedules for Eggs
(Dozens that will be bought and sold)

Price per Dozen	Demand	Supply
$.50	650	4800
.45	1000	4350
.40	1400	3900
.35	1800	3450
.30	2150	3000
.25	2500	2500
.20	2800	2100
.15	3200	1650
.10	3550	1200
.05	3900	850

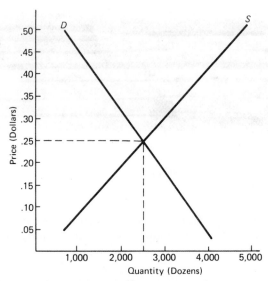

Figure 3-4. Demand and Supply Set the Market Price

twenty-five cents, twenty-five hundred dozen eggs will be bought, by the various purchasers, and an equal amount will be offered for sale by the producers. Any large-scale user of eggs willing to pay this price can purchase all the eggs he wants. Any supplier can sell at the same price. No buyer need pay more than twenty-five cents because he can buy all he wants at that price. A buyer unwilling to pay that much, however, will not be able to buy any eggs.

On the supply side, all producers willing to sell their eggs at twenty-five cents or less can sell all their product at the market price. But those who are not willing to sell at that price will have to keep their eggs because buyers can obtain all they want at the twenty-five-cent price. Therefore, the market price of twenty-five cents is the equilibrium price. It will not change until there is a change in the relationship between demand and supply.

With these market conditions of demand and supply, if the price were anything other than twenty-five cents, the quantities consumers would be willing to buy and the amount of eggs offered for sale by producers would be out of balance. In such a situation, market forces would serve to adjust the price to twenty-five cents, or the equilibrium level. At a price of thirty cents, for example, the quantity of eggs offered for sale would exceed by 850 dozens the quantity demanded. Consequently, not all the eggs would be sold. Notice however, that some producers are willing to sell their eggs at twenty-eight cents, twenty-six cents, and lower prices. They will offer to sell their eggs at the lower prices rather than hold onto them. Notice, too, that certain buyers would not pay thirty cents for eggs, but will pay twenty-seven cents, twenty-five cents, or less. Therefore, as market conditions force the price of eggs downward, the amount offered for sale decreases and the quantity demanded increases until the demand and supply come into balance at the equilibrium price of twenty-five cents.

If a price of twenty cents exists in such a market, the opposite action takes place. At that low price, the quantity demanded exceeds the quantity supplied by seven hundred dozens and some consumers would have to go without eggs. Notice, however, that according to Figure 3-4, some buyers are willing to pay more than twenty cents for a dozen eggs. Rather than go without, they offer higher prices of twenty-two cents, twenty-four cents, and upward. As the price is bid upward, a dual corrective action takes place in the market. The higher prices will deter some buyers from making purchases and induce sellers to offer more for sale. The corresponding increase in the amount offered for sale and the decrease in the amount purchased finally bring supply and demand into balance at the equilibrium price of twenty-five cents. In a freely competitive market, no other price can prevail. At other prices, either a surplus or a shortage will exist in the short run, as shown in Figure 3-5, until corrective forces adjust the price to the equilibrium level.

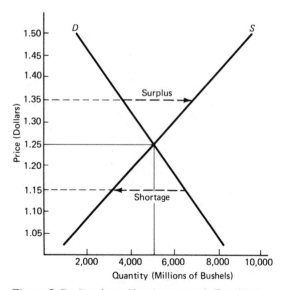

Figure 3-5. Surplus, Shortages, and Equilibrium in the Demand and Supply of Corn

If someone desired to set the price at other than the market price established by the free forces of supply and demand, the market would have to be rigged or the forces of supply and demand changed. This happens, for example, when the government sets a parity price for an agricultural commodity that is higher than the market price. If the government does not find a way to limit output or increase demand, a surplus will appear. The opposite happens when the government establishes a ceiling price on a commodity lower than the market price during a wartime period. In this case the government must find a way, such as rationing, to limit demand or take measures to increase the amount produced. Otherwise shortages will result and black markets will develop. Business firms, too, charged with price fixing are often found guilty of collusion with other firms in efforts to interfere with the forces of the free market, especially with the restriction of supply.

To support agricultural prices, for example, if the free market price of corn were $1.25 per bushel and Congress set a parity price for farmers at $1.35 per bushel, large gluts would develop on the market. As seen in Figure 3-5, at a price of $1.35 the amount supplied would be 6.6 million bushels but the quantity demanded would be less than four million bushels. One way the government can maintain such a price is by offering to buy surplus corn from farmers at $1.35 per bushel. This in effect would increase the total demand for corn, as shown in Figure 3-6. It would leave the government, however, with

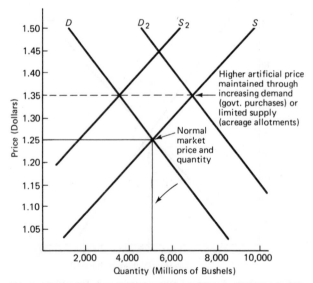

Figure 3-6. Market Price and Quantity vs. Higher Artificial Price Set by the Government

an excessive stock of corn. In order to avoid this as much as possible, an endeavor can be made to limit the supply. Consequently, the guarantee of a parity price to the farmer is generally accompanied by a restriction on production designed to limit the supply of a commodity. For example, if the acreage restriction on the production of corn was sufficient to limit the supply, as shown by line S^2, the higher price could be sustained on the market without the occurrence of surplus or the need for large government purchases, as shown in Figure 3-6.

On the other hand, suppose the equilibrium price had been $1.25 per bushel, but as a result of a strong wartime demand, the price level rose to $1.30 per bushel. If the government decided to establish a ceiling price of $1.25, shortages would occur in the market as shown in Figure 3-7. The normal market force would tend to move the price level up to $1.30, the free market price. Some attempt may be made to ease price pressures by limiting demand through some type of nonprice, rationing program. In the absence of an increase in supply or decrease in demand, however, the only way that the government can enforce the $1.25 ceiling price is through strict regulation and penalties for violators. Nevertheless, the existence of shortages and the readiness of some buyers to pay a higher price lead to black-market operations.

The number of possible relationships between demand and supply

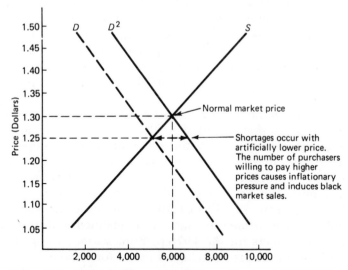

Figure 3-7. Market Price and Quantity vs. Lower Artificial Price Set by Government Price Controls

is practically infinite. For instance, demand may increase while supply decreases, or vice versa. Or both demand and supply may increase, but demand may increase more than supply. Demand may increase while supply remains constant, or vice versa.

We can rely on a few simple principles in any changing relationship between demand and supply. An increase in demand relative to supply will result in a higher price; a decrease in demand will result in a lower price. On the other hand, an increase in supply will reduce the price, and a decrease in supply will raise the price, other factors remaining unchanged.

Tracing the effect of multiple changes in demand and supply becomes more complex. When both demand and supply change in the same direction, each tends to offset the effect of the other on price but to augment the effect of the other on the amount sold. When they change in the opposite direction (for example, when demand increases and supply decreases), they tend to augment the effect of each other in regard to price but to offset the effect of each other on the amount sold.

When demand or supply changes, in either the same or the opposite direction as the other, but the degree of change in one is greater than in the other, this, too, complicates the result. The slopes of the demand and supply lines are important because they, too, have an effect on how much price and quantity sold will be affected with given changes in supply and demand. Hence, we focus on elasticity of demand in the next chapter.

These principles show why world oil prices quadrupled in the early 1970s when the Organization of Petroleum Exporting Countries (OPEC) imposed a petroleum export embargo. To reach and maintain the higher price desired by the producers it was necessary to reduce the supply. Thus, the embargo. The skyrocketed price had an almost catastrophic effect on industrial nations that were large importers of oil.

The foregoing principles can also be used to explain the surge in world food prices that occurred in the early 1970s, as a result of worldwide crop shortages. On the other hand, the bumper United States food crop in 1977 caused prices of farm products to drop and farm income to decline. The price of wheat, for example, fell from $2.88 per bushel in September 1976 to $2.17 in September 1977. Corn decreased from $2.60 to $1.59 per bushel in the same period. As a result, the Department of Agriculture planned to restrict acreage allotments to farmers for the 1978 planting season; it hoped to limit supply in its effort to maintain higher prices for farmers.

SOME SUGGESTED METHODS
OF ESTIMATING DEMAND

As we said earlier in this chapter, it is rather difficult to develop a good measure of demand or to construct a reasonably accurate demand schedule. A number of them have been calculated with varying degrees of accuracy. The techniques used to construct such demand lines include controlled market experiments, consumer questionnaires, cost-saving estimates, and correlation analysis.

Controlled Market Experiments

This frequently used technique prices a commodity in various but similar markets and notes the quantity sold. There are several good test markets throughout the United States, they have common population characteristics, the same income patterns, and similar degrees of economic competition. By offering its product at different prices in each of several markets, a firm may obtain some indication of the demand for its product and be able to construct an approximate demand line. After using a universal price of seventy-nine cents, for example, it may select five markets in which to experiment. In one, it may shift the price to eighty-one cents; in another, eighty-three cents; in a third, seventy-seven cents; in a fourth, seventy-five cents; and in another, leave the price at seventy-nine cents. From such data, the firm may be able to construct an approximate demand line. These data could then be used to set a new universal price for the product.

The same market may be used by altering the price over a period of several weeks and observing changes in sales volume. A classic experiment in the 1960s in Grand Rapids, Michigan, tried to measure the demand for three types of Valencia oranges. Several similar stores were selected in the test area. During a month, orange prices were altered in four-cent intervals above and below a base price. After the experiment the analysts were able to construct demand schedules for each of the three types of oranges.[1]

A similar method may be used for the introduction of new products into the market. The product can be test-marketed at different

---

[1] Marshall R. Goodwin, W. Fred Chapman, and William T. Hanley, *Competition between Florida and California Valencia Oranges in the Fruit Market*. University of Florida, Institute of Food and Agriculture Services, Bulletin 704, December 1965, Gainesville, Florida.

prices in various but similar markets in order to obtain some idea of demand before establishing a common price for the product.

Another way to conduct the controlled experiment is through the use of mail-order catalogues or mail promotion. The product might be offered to similar groups, or categories, of customers at different prices. Thus sales volume at the various prices could be used to construct a potential demand schedule.

Consumer Questionnaires

Some notion of the demand for a product can be obtained by using consumer questionnaires. Consumers are asked, in personal interviews, or more often, by mail: "What do you think a product is worth? How much would you be willing to pay for it? How many would you buy at ten dollars, nine dollars, eight dollars, seven dollars, etc.?" Although some notion of demand may be obtained in this manner, the measure will by no means be precise. There may be considerable differences between what customers say they will do and what they would do if making an actual purchase. It might, however, give some idea of the upper and lower limits of price. Whatever method is used, responses can be tabulated, computerized, and a demand schedule drafted therefrom.

Cost-saving Estimates

Sometimes a technique is used, particularly in capital goods industries, that relates cost-savings from the use of new machines or equipment, to possible prices firms may be willing to pay for a product. In the machine-tool industry, for example, an analyst using the services of an engineer and/or financial expert may be able to show that, under given conditions, installing a new machine may result in certain cost-savings. From this, he could conclude that a firm purchasing such a machine would be willing to pay some amount within a given price range for it.

Under another set of conditions (smaller firm, older machinery to be replaced, less output, lower wage scale, etc.) another company may have a different cost-saving from the installation of the same machine. Consequently, it may find it profitable to purchase the machine, but only at a lower price range. By categorizing and analyzing the cost-savings of a number of firms, the analyst may be able to convert such data into some type of demand schedule showing the relationship of price to quantity sold. From the demand schedule, the firm may then be able to determine the best possible price for its product.

A fourth method often used for estimating the relationship between price and the quantity sold is by correlation analysis of past data. One can collect data on price changes that have occurred over the years, whether the changes were initiated by the particular firm doing the analysis, by its competitors, by retailers through sales promotions, or as a result of changes in excise taxes on the product. The data can be put in tabular form showing prices in descending order and the amount of sales by period (day, week, month, etc.) corresponding to each price. Through the use of a scattergram, line of regression, and correlation analysis, some relationship between price and the amount sold may be indicated. A major problem with using historical data in this manner is holding constant all other variable factors, except price. Changes will occur, such as those in income, advertising, new products, substitutes, and changes in the price of competitors' products. These may seriously distort any attempt to construct a true demand line. Consequently, one must use some of the statistical techniques available to ferret out the effects of the other variables on the quantity sold if a true measure of demand is desired.

An insight into the problem of measuring demand in this fashion can be gleaned by examining the table (page 74) showing the price of newsprint and the quantity consumed by publishers.

If one uses the data in the table, a demand line might be constructed by plotting the quantity consumed at each price. This would be misleading, however, since the price changes occurred over a period of years. During that time, the demand for newsprint could have been changed for a number of reasons, such as population growth, changing income levels, an increase or decrease in advertising expenditures, the appearance of substitutes, and changes in the prices of competing products. Consequently, one must try to eliminate the effects of these other factors on the demand for newsprint.

Some effort in this direction can be made adjusting the quantity sold by the change in population. This can be done by dividing the consumption figures by the population growth. Thus, dividing colume 3, consumption, by column 5, the population index (1967 = 100) will yield population-adjusted consumption as shown in column 8. These figures in column 8, however, must be further adjusted for changes in income. This can be accomplished by dividing column 8 by the index of real per capita disposable income shown in column 7. This refines the consumption data for changes in population and income as shown in column 9. This is not a precise demand line, however, because it assumes that the consumption of newsprint

Sale of Newsprint, 1967-1975

(1) Year	(2) Price per Ton	(3) Consumption	(4) Population[a]	(5) Population Index	(6) Real per Capita Disposable Income[b]	(7) Per Capita Income Index	(8) Consumption Adjusted for Population Change[c]	(9) Consumption Adjusted for Population and Income Changes[a]
1967	$140	$6,907	198.7	100	$3,371	100.0	6,907	6,907
1968	141	7,025	200.7	101	3,464	102.8	6,955	6,834
1969	146	7,344	202.7	102	3,515	104.3	7,200	7,041
1970	151	7,130	204.9	103	3,619	107.4	6,923	6,639
1971	157	7,057	207.0	104	3,714	110.2	6,785	6,404
1972	163	7,569	208.8	105	3,837	113.8	7,209	6,651
1973	170	7,658	210.4	106	4,062	120.5	7,224	6,355
1974	210	7,022	211.9	106.6	3,968	117.7	6,587	5,966
1975	256	6,364	213.5	107.5	4,007	118.9	5,920	5,352

[a]Millions.
[b]1967 constant dollars.
[c]Thousands of tons.

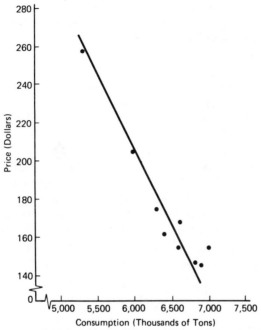

Figure 3-8. Demand for Newsprint

changes directly proportionately to changes in population and income. This it may or may not do. Even if it did, the demand line would still have to be modified because other factors mentioned must be taken into consideration. If all competing product prices change at the same rate as the consumer price index or the GNP implicit price deflators, the prices of newsprint could be further adjusted by dividing them by the appropriate price index. In the absence of specific data on this and other factors, however, some approximation or semblance of a demand line can be constructed.

Plotting the data on prices in column 2 versus the consumption figures in column 9 gives the scattergram[2] shown in Figure 3-8. The data in the scattergram tend to show some relationship between price and amount consumed, with less consumption at higher prices and greater consumption at lower prices. A line representing this relationship between price and consumption can be drawn through the scattergram. This line, usually called a *line of regression*, approximates the demand for newsprint. If this line were drawn perfectly, the sum of the deviations, pluses and minuses, of the actual data, Y,

[2] A Scattergram is a chart showing a series of observations between two variances. In this case it is between price and consumption of newsprint.

from the line of regression, Yc, would equal zero or be minimal.[3] It is said that the line approximates the demand for newsprint because the data have not been adjusted for all the factors affecting consumption. An adjustment was made for population and income changes. The prices of newsprint, however, could be adjusted further for changes in all other products by dividing them by the Consumer Price Index or by adjusting for changing prices of competitors. Advertising outlays, likewise, could be taken into account. After making such adjustments, however, the demand line would still slope downward to the right in typical demand line fashion.

Several endeavors have been made to measure demand for various products, such as wheat, beef, houses, food, frozen fruit pies, sugar, steel, and other commodities. Numerous other studies have been made by individuals and by industries or trade groups. The results have become proprietary information and are not generally available to the public. (The next chapter gives additional information on demand-line studies and the measurement of elasticity of demand.)

SUMMARY

The profit of a firm is dependent on revenue and cost. Revenue in turn depends on the price and quantity of goods sold; the forces of demand and supply in large part determine price.

Demand is a schedule of quantities that will be purchased at various prices at a given time. Generally more of a good will be purchased at lower prices. A typical demand line slopes downward to the right, indicating greater sales at lower prices. As price changes, the quantity purchased will change. This is not a change in demand, however, since the demand line has not changed. It is merely a movement on the demand line, otherwise known as *a change in the quantity demanded*. In order to have a change in demand, more or less of the good must be purchased at given prices. In short, the demand line has to shift in one direction or another. A change in demand may result from such factors as a population change, a change in income, new uses for the product, the appearance of substitutes, or changes in taste.

Supply is a schedule of quantities that will be offered for sale at various prices at a given time. Usually more will be offered for sale at higher prices. A typical supply line slopes upward to the right indicating larger amounts offered at higher prices. Supply may

---

[3] The line of regression, or demand line, can be calculated more precisely by using the method of least squares found in business-statistics textbooks. The formula for least squares is $Yc = a + b\,(x)$. This formula is used in Chapter 6 to calculate the trend line for forecasting GNP and sales.

change—increasing or decreasing—for a number of reasons, including increased productivity and reduction in the cost of materials.

Price in the market will be established where supply and demand are in balance. When demand increases, the price will rise and the amount sold will increase, and vice versa. When supply increases, the price will fall and the amount sold will rise. Multiple variations of changes in demand and supply will affect price in many ways. In order to obtain or maintain a price other than that determined by demand and supply, the market must somehow be rigged or controlled.

Several methods are available for estimating demand. These include controlled experiments, consumer questionnaires, cost-savings estimates, and correlation analysis. Much care must be exercised in constructing a demand line by any of these methods, and such demand lines must be used or applied with reservation.

QUESTIONS FOR ANALYSIS AND DISCUSSION

1. What are the three basic elements contained in the definition of demand?
2. Most demand lines slope downward to the right. Why?
3. Differentiate between a change in demand and a movement on a demand line.
4. Name several factors that can cause a change in demand.
5. A supply line generally slopes upward to the right. Why?
6. Explain why under competitive market conditions price cannot be higher or lower than that established by the free forces of demand and supply.
7. If both demand and supply increase, but demand increases more than supply, what will happen to price?
8. Name several factors that can cause an increase in supply.
9. If the government desires to maintain a parity price that is higher than the market price as determined by supply and demand, how can it do so in the absence of outright price regulation?
10. Explain how price controls can lead to black-market operations.

PROBLEMS AND CASES

Changes in Demand and Supply and the Effect on Price and the Quantity Purchased

Situation I: Simple change

Change in Supply or Demand	Price	Amount Purchased
Increase demand	Increase	Increase
Decrease demand	Decrease	Decrease
Increase supply	Decrease	Increase
Decrease supply	Increase	Decrease

Situation II: Compound change — both in the same direction

When both demand and supply are changing in the same direction, the tendency will be for each to offset the effect of the other on price and to intensify the effect on quantity purchased.

When both demand and supply are changing in the same direction but one changes more than the other, the line that changes more will exert the greater influence, but its effect on price will be less, and its effect on quantity purchased will be greater than it would be if the other line had remained unchanged.

Situation III: Compound change — both in opposite directions

When both demand and supply are changing in opposite directions, the tendency will be for each to intensify the effect of the other on price and to counteract the effect of the other quantity purchased.

When both demand and supply are changing in the opposite directions, but one changes more than the other, the line that changes more will exert the greater influence, but its effect on price will be greater and its effect on quantity purchased will be less than it would be if the other line had remained unchanged.

1. In order to facilitate your handling of demand and supply situations, do the following:

    (i) Draw graphs showing the effect of changes (a), (c), (e), (g), (h), (k), (l), and (m) below.

    (ii) State what effect (increase or decrease) these changes have on price and quantity purchased.
Give effects of compound changes in conformity with Situations II and III.

    (iii) For each change for which you made a graph, there is a converse change for which you made no graph. The one graph, however, will reveal the the effects of either change. For each graph that you have drawn, give the number of the related converse situation, which is also shown by that graph.

    (a) Demand increases, no change in supply.

    (b) Demand decreases, no change in supply.

    (c) Supply increases, no change in demand.

    (d) Supply decreases, no change in demand.

    (e) Demand and supply increase equally.

    (f) Demand and supply decrease equally.

    (g) Demand and supply increase, but demand increases more than supply.

    (h) Demand and supply increase, but supply increases more than demand.

    (i) Demand and supply decrease, but demand decreases more than supply.

    (j) Demand and supply decrease but supply decreases more than demand.

    (k) Demand decreases, but supply increases equally.

    (l) Demand increases, but supply decreases more.

    (m) Demand increases, but supply decreases less.

    (n) Demand increases, but supply decreases equally.

    (o) Demand decreases, but supply increases more.

    (p) Demand decreases, but supply increases less.

2. In order to know its market better, the Xepex Corporation hires an economic and marketing consulting firm to analyze the market for Commodity X.

From the survey, they estimate the demand (D) and supply (S) for Commodity X as shown in the table below. They also make other estimates for possible increases and decreases in demand and supply. As a member of the market and economic research team, you are asked to plot these data and answer the following questions for the company.

Estimated Demand and Supply Schedules for Commodity X

	Demand		Price per Unit		Supply	
D^2	D^1	D		S	S^1	S^2
0	1,000	500	$7.70	8,500	9,000	8,000
500	1,500	1,000	6.75	8,000	8,500	7,500
1,000	2,000	1,500	6.00	7,500	8,000	7,000
1,500	2,500	2,000	5.40	7,000	7,500	6,500
2,000	3,000	2,500	4.80	6,500	7,000	6,000
2,500	3,500	3,000	4.20	6,000	6,500	5,500
3,000	4,000	3,500	3.75	5,500	6,000	5,000
3,500	4,500	4,000	3.35	5,000	5,500	4,500
4,000	5,000	4,500	2.90	4,500	5,000	4,000
4,500	5,500	5,000	2.60	4,000	4,500	3,500
5,000	6,000	5,500	2.30	3,500	4,000	3,000
5,500	6,500	6,000	2.00	3,000	3,500	2,500
6,000	7,000	6,500	1.70	2,500	3,000	2,000
6,500	7,500	7,000	1.45	2,000	2,500	1,500
7,000	8,000	7,500	1.25	1,500	2,000	1,000
7,500	8,500	8,000	1.05	1,000	2,500	500

(a) What should be the market price according to the original findings about demand (D) and supply (S)?

(b) What will be the price using D^1 and S^1?

(c) What will be the price if D^2 and S^2 occur?

(d) Suppose demand increases to D^1 but supply decreases to S^2. What will happen to the market price?

(e) If competition increases supply to S^1 but demand decreases to D^2, what will happen to price?

3. In 1972, approximately eleven million autos were sold in the United States; in 1973 the figure rose to twelve million. Fuel shortages in late 1973 and early 1974, and anticipated gasoline rationing sometime in 1974, strengthened the trend toward economy- and compact-car sales. As a result of the shift of demand toward compact cars, some auto plants laid off workers, while those producing compacts were operating at greater than normal capacity. In fact, facilities at some plants were converted from producing standard and luxury-sized cars to producing compact cars at the cost of millions of dollars.

(a) Can the demand and supply of automobiles be properly expressed as twelve million units?

(b) Under the circumstances cited, what should have been happening to the price of compact cars vis-à-vis large luxury models?

4. While home for the Christmas holidays in 1973, two college students were discussing price controls, fuel scarcities, energy shortages, and meat shortages. Joe Sharp, an MBA student, contended that the Economic Stabilization Act, which was due to expire in April 1974, should be permitted to expire rather than be renewed, saying, "If controls were removed and prices permitted to rise, it would bring about an increase in the supply and eliminate the shortages." Joe's long-time friend Pete Smart, an MA economics student, contended that higher prices would not increase the supply of the scarce commodities. After debating for nearly an hour they come to you to settle their argument.

(a) How would you respond?
(b) Might they both be right but just hung up on terminology?
(c) What other factor besides price would you relate to the discussion of supply?

5. Belle Ring and Goldie Fobb operate the Academic Jewelry Supply Company. Their main line of products consists primarily of class rings, watch fobs, pendants, and other items of jewelry sold to colleges and high schools. For many years the cost of a major input, gold, was stable at thirty-five dollars per ounce. The industrial price was the same as the monetary price. This, of course, made the task of forecasting costs and price fairly certain.

In the late 1960s and early 1970s, the free-market price of gold began to rise and then fluctuate considerably. The demand for gold for both industrial uses and monetary purposes increased substantially. Uncertainty in world monetary circles led to gold speculation and devaluation and revaluation of various currencies. In the late 1960s, the world monetary authorities decided to permit a two-tier price for gold. They would maintain the monetary price at a given level, but permit the price of gold in the free markets of the world to fluctuate. The United States devalued the dollar in 1971 by raising the monetary price of gold to $38.00 per ounce and again in 1972 to $42.22 per ounce.

Since you are a member of the Junior Board of Directors and have some knowledge of economics, Ring asked you to prepare a report explaining what is happening to the demand and supply of gold and why the price has risen so high and fluctuates so widely. In gathering data to shed some light on the matter, you find the information presented in exhibits 1, 2, and 3.

In preparing your report, it is suggested that you answer the following questions:

(a) On the basis of United States industrial demand (consumption) and supply, what would have happened to the cost of gold in the 1960s if the price had not been established at $35.00 per ounce by monetary authorities? Why?
(b) Was the pegged price of thirty-five dollars per ounce acting as a price support or a price ceiling in the 1960s?
(c) Is there any relationship between currency devaluation and the price of of gold in the free market? If so, what?

Exhibit 1. Gold Production

(In millions of dollars; $35 per fine ounce through 1971; $38 through Sept. 1973; $42.22 (thereafter)

Period	World Production	Africa			North and South America					Asia			Other	
		South Africa	Ghana	Zaire	United States	Canada	Mexico	Nicaragua	Colombia	India	Japan	Philippines	Australia	All Other
1967	1,410.0	1,068.7	26.7	5.4	53.4	103.7	5.8	5.2	9.0	3.4	23.7	17.2	28.4	59.4
1968	1,420.0	1,088.0	25.4	5.9	53.9	94.1	6.2	4.9	8.4	4.0	21.5	18.5	27.6	61.6
1969	1,420.0	1,090.7	24.8	6.0	60.1	89.1	6.3	3.7	7.7	3.4	23.7	20.0	24.5	60.0
1970	1,450.0	1,128.0	24.6	6.2	63.5	84.3	6.9	4.0	7.1	3.7	24.8	21.1	21.7	54.1
1971		1,098.7	24.4	6.0	52.3	79.1	5.3	3.7	6.6	4.1	27.0	22.2	23.5	
1972		1,109.8	27.5	5.3	54.3	77.2	5.6	3.0	7.1	4.0	32.2	23.0	28.7	
1973		1,073.6				75.2								

Source: *Federal Reserve Bulletin*, April 1974.

81

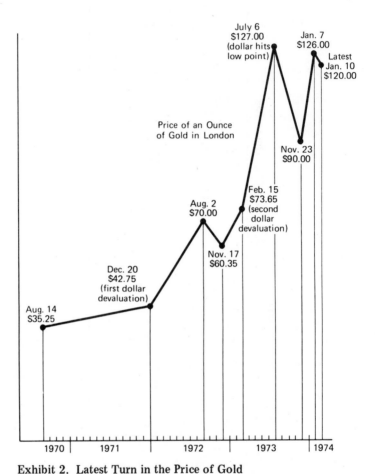

Exhibit 2. Latest Turn in the Price of Gold
Source: Reprinted from U.S. News & World Report, Jan. 21, 1974, p. 22. Copyright 1974 U.S. News & World Report, Inc.

(d) Explain in terms of demand and supply, devaluation, and other factors why the price of gold has risen.
(e) What is the probable cause of the fluctuations in the price of gold?
(f) Has the quantity supplied increased in response to the increase in the price of gold?
(g) Would you advise Academic Jewelry Supply Company to maintain its gold-supply inventory at a high or a low level?
(h) Since the company takes orders and quotes prices as much as a year in advance, how would you advise it to protect its profit margins from being eroded by uncertaintites in the price of gold?
(i) What has happened to the price of gold between January 1974 and the present?

Exhibit 3 Gold Production, Consumption, Price, and World Production
(1950-75)

Year	Mine Production (1,000 fine ounces)	Value (millions)	Industrial Consumption (millions)	Price per Ounce	World Production (1,000 fine ounces)
1950	2,324	$ 84	$ 98	$ 35.00	32,700
1955	1,880	66	46	35.00	36,300
1960	1,667	58	105	35.00	38,200
1965	1,765	60	185	35.00	46,200
1967	1,733	72	295	41.51	46,600
1968	1,478	58	259	37,26	46,200
1970	1,743	63	217	36.41	47,500
1971	1,495	62	286	41.26	46,500
1972	1,450	85	427	58.60	44,700
1973	1,176	115	658	97.81	43,100
1974	1,112	181	743	159.74	39,600
1975	1,042	168	645	161.49	38,700

Source: *Statistical Abstract of the United States*, 1976, p. 721.

Economic Growth and the Beef Industry*

Beef Consumption. The consumption of beef at any given time is determined largely by available supplies. Over a period of time, however, supply can be changed. Thus, beef consumption in the longer run is influenced by both demand and supply factors.

Beef certainly is among the elite of farm commodities. With the increased incomes and employment generated by economic growth, consumers have demonstrated their taste for beef by increasing per captia consumption sharply. When supplies have not been adequate to maintain or increase per capita consumption, the price of beef has been bid up sharply. Annual cash receipts from the sale of beef cattle have risen 44 per cent over the past decade to the present total of $11 billion — a fourth of total cash receipts from farm marketings.

Per capita consumption of beef increased sharply from 1950 to 1969, while that of the other red meats declined during the same period. (See Exhibit 1.) Per capita consumption of poultry also rose during this period. However, much of the increased consumption of poultry can be attributed

*Acknowledgement is due Emanuel O. Melichar of the Board of Governors of the Federal Reserve System for careful review and many excellent suggestions on methodology.

Source: Raymond J. Doll and Blaine W. Bickel; Federal Reserve Bank of Kansas City, *Monthly Review*, February 1970.

EXHIBIT 1 Per Capita Meat Consumption
(in pounds)

Year	Beef	Veal	Pork	Lamb & Mutton	Total Red Meats	Poultry Meat	Total Red and Poultry Meats
1950	63.4	8.0	69.2	4.0	144.6	24.7	169.3
1951	56.1	6.6	71.9	3.4	138.0	26.1	164.1
1952	62.2	7.2	72.4	4.2	146.0	26.8	172.8
1953	77.6	9.5	63.5	4.7	155.3	26.7	182.0
1954	80.1	10.0	60.0	4.6	154.7	28.1	182.8
1955	82.0	9.4	66.8	4.6	162.8	26.3	189.1
1956	85.4	9.5	67.3	4.5	166.7	29.6	196.3
1957	84.6	8.8	61.1	4.2	158.7	31.4	190.1
1958	80.5	6.7	60.2	4.2	151.6	34.0	185.6
1959	81.4	5.7	67.6	4.8	159.5	35.2	194.7
1960	85.0	6.1	64.9	4.8	160.8	34.1	194.9
1961	87.7	5.6	62.0	5.1	160.4	37.4	197.8
1962	88.8	5.5	63.5	5.2	163.0	36.9	199.9
1963	94.3	4.9	65.3	4.8	169.3	37.5	206.8
1964	99.8	5.2	65.3	4.2	174.5	38.3	212.8
1965	99.3	5.2	58.5	3.7	166.7	40.8	207.5
1966	104.0	4.5	58.0	4.0	170.5	43.8	214.3
1967	105.9	3.8	63.9	3.9	177.5	45.7	223.2
1968	109.4	3.6	66.0	3.7	182.7	45.1	227.8
1969	110.7	3.3	64.7	3.4	182.1	47.1	229.2

Source: U.S. Department of Agriculture.

to reduced prices made possible by technological breakthroughs in production efficiency, while it appears that greater consumption of beef resulted largely from increasing demand — as time passed, the Nation consumed more beef at a given price or the same amount at a higher price.

Cattle Prices. At any given time, the relationship between the price and quantity of a good consumed tends to be inverse. That is, as the price falls, the quantity consumed will increase and vice versa. Some interesting observations can be made from studying the annual quantity-price relationship, as measured by per capita consumption of beef and veal and prices received by farmers for cattle.[1] Exhibit 2 indicates that, during the past 40 years, there have been a number of periods during which the anticipated inverse quantity-price relationship has prevailed; but, in certain years, abrupt shifts have occurred — all upward. Prior to 1947, quantity-price relationships were quite unstable — for explainable reasons — but there was a per-

[1] Demand for beef cattle is derived largely from demand for beef and veal. Therefore, prices received by farmers for cattle are closely related to beef prices and are influenced by the same supply and demand factors. This close association permits our analysis to use the price received by farmers for cattle, while measuring quantity by per capita consumption of beef and veal.

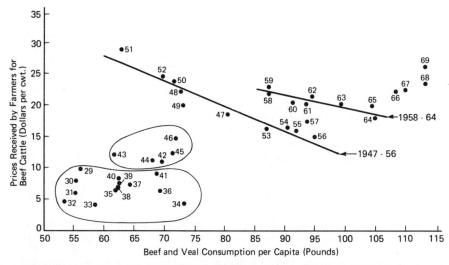

Exhibit 2. Annual Beef Cattle Prices and per Capita Consumption of Beef and Veal (1929-69)

sistent tendency for demand to move upward. More importantly, since 1946, the quantity-price relationship has tended to remain stable for a number of years and then to shift abruptly upward and not return to its preceding level. This suggests that several irreversible increases in demand for beef have occurred in abrupt stages — perhaps as a result of economic growth, changing taste for beef and veal, inflation, a combination of these events, or other factors. An upward shift in demand occurs when the same quantity is consumed at a higher price, or more is consumed at a constant price — thereby forming a new quantity-price relationship. The relationships shown in Exhibit 2 suggest that several upward shifts have occurred in recent decades. Before documenting these events with the results of a statistical study of the demand for beef in recent years, it is interesting to review supplies and prices from 1929 to date.

During the 1929-41 period, there was no apparent relationship between beef and veal consumption and the prices farmers received for their cattle. This was the period of the Depression, during which unemployment increased rapidly early in the period and then remained high. Associated with this development, incomes declined sharply, and economic conditions generally were chaotic. During the 1929-32 part of this period, when the Depression was developing and intensifying, the per capita consumption-cattle price relationship suggests a rather persistent decline in demand for cattle. During the 1933-41 part of the period, Exhibit 2 suggests some improvement, although the relationships from year to year are quite poor in that they do not follow an orthodox pattern. In 1941, a substantially larger quantity of beef was consumed at a slightly higher price than in 1940. This probably can be attributed to the beginning of the development of the wartime economy. Because of the conditions just described, the 1929-41 period has been circled to designate it as abnormal.

Just prior to and during World War II, the economy changed from depressed conditions in which many resources were underemployed to one in which strains on resource use became severe and economic growth was so rapid that inflationary conditions prevailed. During this period, the quantity-price relationship between per capita supplies of beef and veal, and prices received by farmers for cattle showed strong upward pressure. However, because of price and wage controls and meat rationing, market forces were not permitted to operate in a normal manner. These controls were rigidly imposed from 1942 to mid-1946. Consequently, this period also is designated as abnormal in Exhibit 2.

When these restrictions were removed in mid-1946, market forces immediately adjusted for the changes held in abeyance during the War period. In 1947, more beef was consumed at a higher price than in any previous year. For the next 10 years, there was an orthodox quantity-price relationship at a level substantially higher than had prevailed prior to that time. A straight line on the chart represents the relationship during this period.

From 1956 to 1958, the level of the quantity-price relationship rose abruptly. This increase probably was associated with the relatively large cyclical increase in beef supplies caused by the drought liquidation that occurred during the 1953-56 period and which consumers were only willing to consume at lower prices. Then, as the drought ended and supplies were reduced sharply from 1956 to 1958, consumers indicated their unwillingness to return to the quantity-price relationship of the 1947-56 period. They had become accustomed to a higher level of beef consumption and their incomes enabled them to bid higher for the more limited supplies.

Thus, conditions prevailing from 1956 to 1958 set the stage for the 1958-64 period — during which the quantity-price relationships again exhibited an orthodox inverse relationship, but at a higher level. During this period, consumption changed inversely to 4.8 pounds for every one dollar change in price, which is a higher ratio (more elastic) than the 4.5-to-1 ratio of the prior period. As the quantity-price line becomes more elastic, a small drop in price results in a larger-than-proportional increase in the quantity consumed. With this type of demand for cattle, gross income from cattle sales rises with increased marketings because the increase in volume of cattle sold more than offsets the effect of any decline in cattle prices. Consequently, to the extent that technological improvements enable producers to decrease costs of beef production, there is a strong incentive to expand output. This is particularly true for those producers and stages of production where economies of size are important.

The last five years shown on Exhibit 2 again form an unusual pattern in that both the quantity and price have risen abruptly from year to year. A somewhat similar pattern existed from 1942 to 1947; some parallels can be drawn between the two periods. The present period is currently the most war-oriented period since World War II; a high level of strain on resources has been experienced with the concurrent rising incomes and prices and relatively rapid rise in the rate of inflation. Under these conditions, consumers historically have increased their consumption of beef — despite increasing prices — and they apparently are continuing this pattern. The major difference between the current period and that of 1942 to 1947 is that the shift in the first period was very abrupt from mid-1946 — when price controls and rationing were removed — to 1947. Market forces cur-

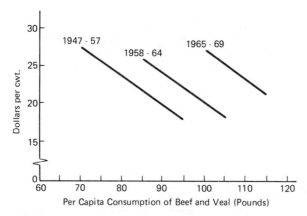

Exhibit 3. Computed Demand Curves for Beef Cattle
Deflated by Wholesale Price Index (1947-69)

rently are not being inhibited by price and wage controls as they were in
the earlier period.

The quantity-price relationships for the 1965-69 period strongly suggest
another upward shift in demand for beef. If the shift proves irreversible,
as has been characteristic of the quantity-price relationship for the past 40
years, a new curve will develop somewhere around the 1969 level — or
perhaps even higher, although the elasticity for the new curve — when it
evolves — may be different than for the preceding periods. Based on the
historical record, it seems reasonable to assume that the elasticity will
remain high; that is, quantity consumed will change relatively rapidly and
widely in an inverse manner with a change in cattle prices.

Because of the importance of demand changes for the cattle outlook, an
effort was made to compute a curve, or curves, that reflect such changes
since 1947. Although the computations are somewhat technical, the methodology and results can be described rather simply.

By the use of different multiple regression techniques — including single
and simultaneous equations estimates — numerous attempts were made
to determine the impact of various factors on the price of beef cattle.
Through this experimentation, a model was developed which employed
the most simplified technique consistent with good results.[2]

Factors of greatest importance in determining real cattle prices (actual
prices deflated by the wholesale price index) during the 1947-69 period
were supplies of beef and veal as measured by per capita consumption, per
capita consumption of pork, and total employment. Exhibit 3 shows the

[2] Separate supply and demand equations were estimated to test various
explanatory factors. Variables with the greatest impact on supply and/or
demand were then applied in a simultaneous equations solution. Use of
this method, which is substantially more complicated than estimation of a
single equation that includes both supply and demand factors, did not
yield better results, so the single equation approach is reported in this
article. Equations also were computed in which percentage changes from
year to year were used instead of absolute numbers. When percentage
changes were used an $R2 = .65$, which is significant, was obtained.

statistically computed relationships between per capita consumption of beef and veal and the price of cattle for the three periods 1947-57, 1958-64, and 1965-69 after adjusting for variability in per capita supplies of pork and total employment.[3] The graph illustrates the shifts in demand for beef cattle between 1947 and 1969. Consumers bought more beef at the same price, or the same amount at a higher price, in the 1958-64 period than in 1947-57, and a similar increase occurred during 1965-69. Both shifts occurred in addition to any impact of supplies of pork and total employment. The equation also suggests that the response of beef consumption to a change in the price of cattle is much more inelastic than suggested by the simple quantity-price relationships shown in Exhibit 2. The quantity-price relationship shown by the equation has been adjusted for changes in pork supply, total employment, and the wholesale price index, in the estimating process.[4]

For forecasting purposes, the model used in Exhibit 3 offers advantages over extrapolation of the simple relationships in Exhibit 2, since the specific impact of the more important variables influencing cattle prices has been evaluated more rigorously.[5]

The 1970 Forecast. The model just described incorporates the belief that demand for beef has been increasing as population and per captia consumption have grown, and that demand currently is substantially higher than in other recent years. It also quantifies the impact of per capita beef consumption (supply), per capita consumption of pork, and employment on cattle prices at this higher level of demand. Estimated future values for these variables can be substituted into the equation and the deflated price of cattle computed. This price can then be converted to a current price by multiplying by the expected wholesale price index.

For example, if it is assumed that per capita beef and veal consumption in 1970 will be 115 pounds, per capita pork consumption 63 pounds, total employment 85.2 million, and the wholesale price index at 116.2, the price received by farmers for beef cattle would be $26.42 per hundredweight (shown by the dot in the shaded area of Exhibit 4), as compared with roughly a $26 average for 1969. Under these conditions, the outlook is for improved cattle prices in 1970. As more reliable estimates of per

[3] A single equation was estimated by multiple regression, with dummy variables used to differentiate each of the three periods in which different levels of demand (not explained by changes in employment or the supply of pork) were thought to prevail.

[4] It also should be pointed out that the slopes of these lines measure the average price elasticity for the entire 1947-69 period.

[5] When the equation was estimated using current instead of deflated cattle prices, a rather interesting result was obtained. The quantity-price relationships for the 1947-57, 1958-64, and 1965-69 periods shifted just as they did when real prices were used. However, when current prices were used, the curves for the 1958-64 period fell below that of the 1947-57 period, but that for the 1964-69 period was substantially above the curves for either of the preceding periods. Since price stability was maintained much better during the 1958-64 period than during either the preceding or subsequent periods, this result suggests that price inflation during the post-World War II period may have had a relatively favorable impact on cattle prices.

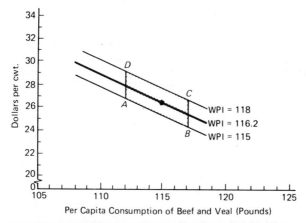

Exhibit 4. Computed 1970 Cattle Prices in Current Dollars under Different Assumptions as to Supplies of Beef and Veal and Pork, Employment, and Wholesale Price Index

capita supplies of beef and pork, employment, and the wholesale price index become available, conclusions can be altered.

For example, if per capita consumption of beef and veal should be only 112 pounds, per capita pork consumption 61 pounds, employment 84.4 million, and the wholesale price index 115.0, computed cattle prices would be $26.71 (point A) instead of $26.42. If all of the estimates in the preceding sentence were accurate, except that per capita consumption of beef and veal were 117 pounds instead of 112 pounds, the computed cattle price would be $24.47 (point B). On the other hand, if per capita consumption of beef and veal were 117 pounds, that of pork 65 pounds, employment 86 million, and the wholesale price index 118.0, the computed price would be $26.72 (point C). If the data in the preceding sentence were identical, except that per capita consumption of beef and veal were 112 pounds, the computed price would be $29.02 (point D). These points were computed so the shaded parallelogram — within which cattle prices would be expected to fall in 1970 if some combination of estimates within the ranges stated above should prevail — could be drawn.

The following exhibits, 5-8, relating to meat consumption, livestock production, wholesale prices, and population, are based on data from the Statistical Abstract of the United States.

(a) What happened to the price of beef in 1970? Was it higher or lower than anticipated by the article? If different, what factors do you think accounted for the difference?

(b) What happened to the price of farm products compared with "all commodities" in the Wholesale Price Index between 1969 and 1970?

(c) What factors accounted for the dramatic increase in beef prices between 1970 and 1973?

(d) In relation to Exhibit 6, plot the per capita consumption of beef and veal (combined) vis à vis prices received by the farmer for beef cattle, 1970–1975. Does it appear that there has been a further upward shift in the demand for beef and veal? If so, what factors account for the increase in demand?

EXHIBIT 5. Per Capita Consumption of Meat
(in pounds)

	1969	1970	1971	1972	1973	1974	1975
Beef	110.8	113.7	113.0	114.8	109.6	116.8	119.6
Veal	3.3	2.9	2.7	2.2	1.8	2.3	4.1
Lamb and mutton	3.4	3.3	3.1	3.4	2.7	2.3	2.0
Pork	65.0	66.4	73.0	67.7	61.6	66.6	54.8

EXHIBIT 6. Livestock Production and Prices Received by Farmers
(1969–1972)

	Calves			Hogs		Sheep		
	All Cattle Production[1]	Price[2] Beef	Price Calves	Production	Price	Production	Price Sheep	Price Lam
1969	37,147	26.20	31.60	26,600	22.20	1,065	8.10	27.
1970	39,304	27.10	34.50	21,900	22.70	1,098	7.51	26.
1971	39,376	29.00	36.40	23,026	17.50	1,062	6.59	25.
1972	41,381	33.50	44.60	21,585	25.10	994	7.29	29.
1973	41,100	42.80	56.60	19,987	38.40	891	12.90	35.
1974	42,650	35.60	35.20	20,101	34.20	805	11.30	37.
1975	40,680	32.30	27.20	16,824	46.10	772	11.20	42.

[1] Production (millions of pounds).
[2] Prices per 100 pounds.

EXHIBIT 7. Wholesale Price Index

	1957–59 = 100		1967 = 100	
	All Commodities	Farm Products	All Commodities	Farm Products
1966	105.9	105.6	99.8	105.9
1967	106.1	99.7	100.0	100.0
1968	108.7	102.2	102.5	102.5
1969	113.0	108.5	106.5	109.1
1970	117.1	110.7	110.4	111.0
1971	120.9	112.6	113.9	113.8
1972	127.3	124.6	119.1	122.4
1973	143.9	170.0	134.7	159.1
1974	171.0	189.6	160.1	177.4
1975	186.9	196.7	174.9	184.2

EXHIBIT 8. Population, Labor Force, Employment, and per Capita Income (1967–1975)

Year	Population (millions)	Total Labor Force (Millions)[a]	Civilian Labor Force Employment (millions)[b]	Per Capita Disposal Income (current dollars)	Constant (1967) Dollars
1967	198.7	80.8	74.4	$2,740	$3,371
1968	200.7	82.3	75.9	2,930	3,464
1969	202.7	84.3	77.9	3,111	3,515
1970	204.9	85.9	78.6	3,348	3,619
1971	207.0	86.9	79.1	3,588	3,714
1972	208.8	89.0	81.7	3,837	3,837
1973	210.4	91.0	83.4	4,285	4,062
1974	211.9	93.2	85.9	4,646	3,973
1975	213.5	94.8	84.8	5,077	4,014

[a]Includes numbers of the Armed Forces.
[b]Excludes numbers of the Armed Forces.

Sudden Surplus After Scarcity in 1973, World Meat Supplies Become Very Plentiful

Prices Fall, Global Trade Is Disrupted as Output Soars, Consumption Lags

Even More Meat Is Expected

Last summer, when many supermarket meat counters were bare and prices were soaring out of sight, a lot of people worried that the days of ample supplies of meat were over.

Well, less than 10 months later, those days are back again.

As of May 1, the latest date for which figures are available, the U.S. had

Source: Reprinted by permission of *The Wall Street Journal*, © Dow Jones & Company, Inc. (June 7, 1974). All rights reserved.

1.029 billion pounds of beef, pork and veal (mostly beef) in freezer storage, up 46% from a year earlier and the largest stock in 22 years. Poultry stocks also are piling up; at 382 million pounds on May 1, the supply of chickens and turkeys was up 88%. Government statisticians say the June 1 figures, not released yet, are even higher.

Not surprisingly, prices have fallen sharply. Choice beef now wholesales in Chicago for about 65 cents a pound, down from a record 91 cents on Feb. 6. Wholesale pork and poultry have dropped, too.

Many people complain that supermarkets haven't passed along the full amount of the wholesale-price declines to retail customers. More and more meat bargains are showing up at retail, however, and are sure to become increasingly common, meat and poultry handlers predict. One Chicago chain recently offered lean ground beef for 59 cents a pound if the customer bought at least $3 of groceries. This was down from $1.09 earlier this year and the lowest advertised ground-beef price in four years. Several East Coast and Midwest supermarket chains recently sold large turkeys at 29 cents a pound, down from $1 and higher last Thanksgiving and Christmas. Elsewhere, turkey specials at 39 cents a pound were widespread last week.

World-wide Expansion. The U.S. isn't alone; meat supplies are expanding in many other countries around the world. Last week, Japan prohibited beef imports for the rest of the year to protect domestic beef producers because prices in Japan are 30% below a year ago. The European Common Market is thinking about cutting back on chicken production and is faced with disposing of nearly 90,000 tons of beef that accumulated through a price-support program. "We have a beef mountain," lamented a Common Market agriculture minister after a recent London meeting at which meat imports were banned and export subsidies were instituted.

(Unfortunately, the mountains of meat can't be easily diverted to feed starving people in Africa, India and elsewhere. "All that stuff is in freezers, which makes it very awkward to handle and distribute to areas with little or no refrigeration," a U.S. government official says.)

One reason for the meat pileup is that many people have slowed down the steadily increasing consumption that was the trend in recent years. At first they were reacting to record meat prices. Now, rapid inflation in most of the meat-eating countries of the world has caused people to cut back on expenses of all sorts — including food, despite lower meat prices.

At the same time, meat production is increasing. The U.S., Canada, Japan and the Common Market countries are expected to boost their aggregate red-meat production by nearly 4% this year — beef by 4% and pork by 2%, according to Philip L. Mackie and Suzanne Early, economists at the U.S. Agriculure Department's Foreign Agricultural Service. These areas, which account for two-thirds of the world's beef production, are expected to boost poultry output, too; their total production of meat may hit a record 92.5 billion pounds this year.

World-wide meat production rose steadily for 11 years and then dropped in both 1972 and 1973 as farmers held back breeding stock to expand their herds. Now that prices are falling, marginal breeding stock is being marketed along with the regular flow of supplies, which are themselves heavier because the cattle put on extra weight as feeders held them overly long in a vain hope that prices would soon climb again.

More Beef in 1975. The meal-production buildup of the past two years could accelerate dramatically next year, especially for beef. Mr. Mackie and Mrs. Early, the Foreign Agricultural Service economists, say that "if slaughter rates return to the level of the 1960s and if carcass weights increase on trend, world-wide beef and veal output could swell by an additional 20% to 25% in 1975."

Another Agriculture Department economist adds: "In 1975, output will be so large that the world beef trade will fall sharply and the weight of low beef prices should continue to exert downward price pressure on veal, pork, poultry, fish and even dairy products."

That's gloomy news for the countries that export meat, which already are feeling the pinch of lagging demand and spurting production. Argentina, which is among the world's largest beef exporters, had a 52.5% drop in its beef shipments in the first four months of 1974. In a recent report to the European Common Market, Argentine Ambassador Ildefonso Recalde estimated that if the trend continued, Argentina would earn $200 million less from beef this year than in 1973. Argentina joined with neighboring beef exporters Paraguay, Colombia and Uruguay to map a commercial strategy to increase beef sales to European nations.

"It's a dreary picture," says Peter Bartlett, executive officer of the Australian Meat Exporters Federal Council, a trade group. He forecasts a decline in Australia's exports of all types of meat in the year ending this month to about 700,000 long tons (2,240 pounds each). "We had been expecting about 850,000 tons," he adds ruefully. Beef makes up the bulk of Australia's meat exports, which in the year ended June 20, 1973, hit a record 823,000 long tons.

One problem the Australians face is the increased value of the Australian dollar. Since the end of 1972, it has risen 26% against the U.S. dollar to a current exchange rate of one to 1.50. That means U.S. customers would have to pay more and more just to keep the returns to Australian meat producers even; but, of course, prices in the U.S. have fallen. Imported beef now brings 67 cents a pound in New York, down from a record $1.30 late last summer.

Nonetheless, Australian cattlemen are undaunted. Normally, the grass would have run out by this time and cattlemen would be driving herds to the slaughterhouses. But Australia has had an incredible run of good weather this year with just enough rain to keep the pastures green. Instead of selling off their animals, ranchers are continuing to fatten them. Because 1973 was very profitable, they aren't facing the need to sell now to obtain operating funds.

This full-steam-ahead attitude bothers the U.S. cattle industry, which worries that with import bans in Europe and Japan, Australians will ship increasing amounts of meat to an already-depressed U.S. market. Cattlemen are pressing the government to reimpose meat-import controls, which were lifted in June 1972 because of shortages. Agriculture Secretary Earl L. Butz says the administration is thinking about it, but in the spirit of free trade would rather try to talk Japan and Europe into reopening their markets.

Meanwhile, the Agriculture Department's index of prices received by U.S. farmers for meat animals fell 8% to 159% of the 1967 average during the month ended May 15; prices of hogs, cattle and calves all declined. In the same month, the index of prices paid by farmers for feed dropped only

3% to 173% of the 1967 average, a level still 12% above a year ago. Many cattlemen complain they are losing $100 to $200 a head, though some experts contend these are "paper losses" to a large extent.

Feedlot Fallout. As a result, some livestock-feeding operations are going out of business, or at least are cutting back sharply on the number of animals they are fattening for market.

This shows up particularly clearly in the cattle-feeding industry, where feedlots with capacities of 8,000 to 16,000 cattle were hit especially hard by plummeting prices. Many of these lots were capitalized by urban investors, and they supplied about one-eighth of the grain-feed beef that recently filled supermarket shelves. The burned investors withdrew what was left of their money last year, and the absence of feedlots this size could leave a noticeable gap between the relative handful of giant feedlots and the far more numerous farm-and-ranch operations, livestock economists say.

But some cattlemen, generally those whose capital and facilities are wholly committed to beef production, seem to be taking the opportunity to rebuild. "If the price of grain comes down like it appears it's going to, family-sized, fully automated operations stand to make money," says Marvin McLain, administrator of the Agriculture Department's Packer and Stockyards Administration. He contends that these smaller operations were at a disadvantage during the beef buildup in the early 1970s because they were outbid for feeder stock by well-heeled, nonfarm investors. Now that the industry has been left largely to the best-run of both the larger and family-sized lots, "it may be that the 500-head lots turn out to be the most durable ones we have," says Philip Raup, a University of Minnesota economist studying corporate farming.

Feedlot Cooperatives Are Seen. One way the smaller lots might evolve is by joining forces. S.A. Ewing, head of the animal-science department at Iowa State University, thinks the shake-out may inspire the growth of a third kind of feedlot — a modestly scaled, cooperative enterprise involving a half-dozen or so farmer-feeders who pool their resources to build confinement sheds in which to fatten their cattle. The farmers share the costs while benefitting from the efficiencies of larger scale than they could afford on their own and by having their cattle close to their corn. But managerial and capital requirements for such a venture are high, and waste-disposal problems are more acute. One such venture has operated in northwest Iowa for a year, and more Midwestern producers are showing interest, Prof. Ewing says.

Despite the shake-out, there is little evidence that the U.S. beef herd is contracting. It is true that placement of cattle in feedlots is down 10% or so from last year, but the total number of cattle and calves on U.S. farms continues to rise. There were a record 127.5 million cattle in the U.S. on Jan. 1, 1974, and "a further rise to more than 130 million is expected by Jan. 1, 1975," says George H. Hoffman, an Agriculture Department economist specializing in the domestic livestock industry.

Agriculture Department sources also say pork supplies will grow this year. The number of hogs on U.S. farms on Dec. 1, 1973, was 61 million, up from 59.2 million a year earlier. An interim report issued for 14 major pork-producing states as of March 1 indicated that the rise in hog numbers is continuing.

The department forecasts that turkey production this year will rise 8% to a record 2.1 billion pounds and that chicken output will return to the 1972 record level of 9.12 billion pounds after a 2% decline last year.

(a) What happened to meat prices in 1973 as a result of shortages?

(b) What was the percentage increase in the U.S. meat supplies (beef, pork, and veal) in 1974 as compared with that in 1973?

(c) What was the percentage decrease in the wholesale price of beef in Chicago between January 1974 and June 1974?

(d) During this time, what was happening to the consumption of beef?

(e) Does the demand for beef appear to be elastic or inelastic with regard to price?

(f) What measures were some foreign nations taking to limit supplies of beef in their respective countries?

(g) As meat production was increasing, what was happening to the consumption of beef?

(h) What caused the worldwide shortage of meat in 1972 and 1973?

(i) What is expected to happen to beef production and prices in the next few years?

(j) As Argentina produces more beef, what do they anticipate happening to income from beef sales?

(k) As meat prices fall what is happening to the number and level of operations of cattle feedlots?

(l) In what ways does the cattle industry manifest conditions approaching pure competition?

Demand Analysis: Elasticities of Demand

Even when a demand schedule can be constructed, the producer, retailer, or other seller often faces a problem of selecting the best price at which to market the product or service. True, a greater amount of sales can be made at lower prices. But a good manager will want to know whether increased revenue from additional sales offsets the reduction in revenue from the lower price. A change in price does not always result in a proportional change in sales. Thus, price selection presents a real problem to producers and sellers. Fortunately, the economist has a tool to measure the change in relationship between price and the amount sold. *Price elasticity of demand*, as it is known, is a measure of consumer responsiveness to a change in price. Whether a seller will benefit by an increase or a decrease in price depends on the degree of price elasticity. Later, we shall see that there are types of elasticity other than price elasticity.

MEASURING PRICE ELASTICITY OF DEMAND

Price elasticity may be measured or defined in two ways. *Point elasticity* is a measure of elasticity at a given price. *Arc elasticity* measures the average elasticity over some given range of prices. Point elasticity can be measured through the use of partial derivatives. Since most decisions regarding elasticity of demand relate to changes in price, however, we will concern ourselves with arc elasticity. We can illustrate price elasticity of demand by constructing three demand lines and measuring their elasticities. Notice that according to demand schedule D_1, in Figure 4-1, 3200 units are sold at the price of $20, but at a price of $16, 4000 units will be sold. We can now measure price elasticity in either of two ways: by using the formula method, or by using the total revenue method.

Formula Method

The formula for elasticity measures the relative change in amount sold compared with the relative change in price. In its simplest form it may be stated thus:

$$\text{Price elasticity} = \frac{\text{Percent change in quantity}}{\text{Percent change in price}}$$

This formula can also be written as $E_p = \Delta q / \Delta p$, where the symbol

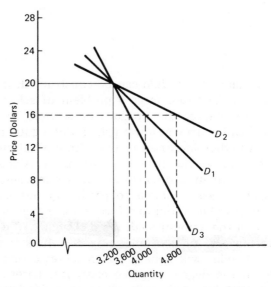

Figure 4-1. Demand Lines Showing Different Elasticities

delta (Δ) is used to represent small percentage increments or decrements of change.

Some minor problems arise in applying the formula. The percentage changes, for example, can be computed by using the original price and quantity as bases. If this is done, however, the result will be a different measure of elasticity, depending on whether the price is moved up or pushed down. If the price is decreased from $20 to $16, notice that the four-dollar price change is a 20 percent change compared with the original price base of $20. The change in quantity sold, from sixteen hundred to two thousand units, is 25 percent. If the 20 percent change in price is divided into the 25 percent change in quantity, the measure of elasticity is 1.25 (.25 ÷ .20 = 1.25). On the other hand, if the price were raised from $16 to $20 and the amount sold decreased from 4000 units to thirty-two hundred units, the percentage change in price according to the formula would be 25 percent (4 ÷ 16 = .25) and the relative change in amount would be 20 percent (800 ÷ 4000 = .20). In this case, elasticity of demand would measure .8(.20 ÷ .25 = .8).[1] Thus, it appears that there could be a different measure of elasticity between two points, depending on the direction of the price change.

[1] Since price and quantity on a typical demand line move in opposite directions, price elasticity will always be a negative figure. It is customary, however, to drop the minus sign when measuring elasticity.

Any such confusion can be avoided by selecting a constant base for measuring percentage changes in price and quantity. This can be done by using average bases for price and quantity. In doing so, the percentage change will be identical whether moving the price up or down. In our example above, the absolute price change of $4 would be divided by $18 (the average between $20 and $16) and equal to 22 percent. The relative change in sales also would be 22 percent (800 ÷ 3600 = .22). Consequently, whether the price were raised or lowered, the measure of price elasticity of demand would be the same, 1.0 (.22 ÷ .22 = 1.0).[2] This measure of elasticity, 1.0, means that a given change in price will bring about a proportional change in the quantity sold. A 1 percent decrease in price results in a 1 percent increase in the quantity sold and vice versa. A 5 percent increase in price will result in a 5 percent decrease in quantity, and so forth.

A coefficient of elasticity of 1.0 is known as *unitary elasticity*[3] and is the point of demarcation between an elastic and inelastic demand. Any measure greater than 1.0 is known as an *elastic demand*, and any measure less than 1.0 is referred to as an *inelastic demand*.

Let us now measure the price elasticity for the demand schedule D_2 in Figure 4-1. It can be seen that when price is changed from $20 to $16, a 22 percent change ($4 ÷ $18 = .22), the quantity demanded increases from thirty-two hundred to forty-eight hundred units, an increase of 40 percent (1600 ÷ 4000 = .40). On this schedule, the measure of elasticity is 1.8 (.40 ÷ .22 =1.8). This means that a 2 percent change in price, for example, will result in a 3.6 percent change in the quantity demand. In this case, consumer demand is elastic and the amount sold will change in greater proportion than the change in price.

Demand schedule D_3, on the other hand, shows less consumer responsiveness to a price change. Notice that a 22 percent decrease in price from $20 to $16 results in an 11 percent increase in quantity sold. This yields a measure of elasticity of demand of .5, which indicates that the demand is price inelastic. Therefore, a given change in price will bring about a less than proportional change in the quantity demanded. A 1 percent decrease in price, for example, will result in a

[2] The formula for this is generally written:

$$\frac{\dfrac{Q_2 - Q_1}{(Q_1 + Q_2)/2}}{\dfrac{P_1 - P_2}{(P_1 + P_2)/2}} = \text{price elasticity} \quad \therefore \quad \frac{\dfrac{4000 - 3200}{(3200 + 4000)/2}}{\dfrac{20 - 16}{(20 + 16)/2}} = \frac{\dfrac{800}{3600}}{\dfrac{4}{18}} = \frac{.22}{.22} = 1.0$$

[3] Sometimes this is referred to as *unit elasticity*.

.5 percent increase in the quantity sold. A 4 percent price rise will result in a 2 percent decline in sales.[4]

The measure of price elasticity can be extremely important to a manufacturer or seller. It indicates what is going to happen to the amount of total revenue as prices and sales change. It is important, also, to the consumers. Total revenue received by sellers, after all, represents the total expenditures of buyers for the product. More spent by consumers on one commodity, of course, means that there will be less to spend on other goods and services.

The total revenue method of measuring price elasticity shows more directly what happens to total revenue with price changes. Moreover, it shows clearly the significance of a coefficient of elasticity. This can be demonstrated by taking the three measures of elasticity and arranging them in tabular form as shown in Table 4-1 below.

Column 2 in the table represents the measures of price elasticity calculated for the data from Figure 4-1 by the formula method. The top line value in column 3 represents the total revenue, $64,000, in each case from the sale of products when the price is $20. Notice that, when the price is lowered to $16 on demand schedule D_1, the total revenue remains the same. Since the coefficient of elasticity is 1.0, the change in quantity demanded is proportional to the change in price. At the lower price, the decrease in revenue resulting from the decrease in price is offset by the increase in revenue from the increase in sales. Consequently, total revenue, $64,000, remains the same. In this case the seller may be indifferent about his price. Whether he is or not will depend on his costs of production.

On demand schedule D_2, where price elasticity is 1.8, notice that total revenue increases as the price decreases. In this case, the de-

---

[4] Another method sometimes used to calculate the percentage change and hold the base constant is to use the lower (or upper) extremity of the change as a base whether the move is upward or downward. In the case above, if $16 and 3200 units were used as the bases in computing the percentage changes, the measure of elasticity, whether lowering or raising prices, would be 1.0. Lowering the price from $20 to $16, for example, will result in a 25 percent change when the lower extremity is used as a base of the change ($4 ÷ $16 = .25). If the amount sold at the lower price, $16, is 4000 units compared with the 3200 units that would be sold at the higher price, $20, this also represents a 25 percent change (800 ÷ 3200 = .25). This yields a measure of elasticity of 1.0 (.25 ÷ .25 = 1.0). Since the same price and quantity bases and the same absolute changes are involved when the price is raised from $16 to $20, the measure of elasticity is the same in either direction. Since the formula is designed to measure the effects of only small increments or decrements in price, any mathematical error will be minimal.

TABLE 4-1. The Three Measures of Elasticity

	Formula Method	Total Revenue Method	
Demand Schedule	$Ep = \dfrac{\Delta q}{\Delta P}$	$20 x 3200 = $64,000	Type of Elasticity
D_1	$\dfrac{.22}{.22} = 1.0$	$16 x 4000 = 64,000	Unitary
D_2	$\dfrac{.40}{.22} = 1.8$	$16 x 4800 = 76,800	Elastic
D_3	$\dfrac{.11}{.22} = .5$	$16 x 3600 = 57,600	Inelastic

crease in revenue resulting from the lower price is more than offset by the increase is revenue from the additional sales. The net result is that total revenue increases from $64,000 to $76,800. In such a situation the manufacturer or producer may find it beneficial to increase output and lower price in order to improve sales. An elastic demand, however, can be a disadvantage if one desires to raise the price. If the producer with demand schedule D_2 were to raise his price from $16 to $20, for example, notice that total revenue would drop from $76,800 to $64,000.

Demand schedule D_3, has an inelastic demand of .5 as measured by the formula method. In column 3 you can observe that if price is lowered from $20 to $16, total revenue will fall from $64,000 to $57,600 because the change in quantity sold is less than proportional to the change in price. In this case the increase in revenue from the additional sales is insufficient to make up for the decrease in revenue resulting from the decrease in price. The net result is that total revenue decreases as price decreases. In such a case the producer would not find it beneficial to decrease his price. On the other hand, notice that when demand is price inelastic, a rise in the price will not cause a corresponding decline in sales. Since consumer responsiveness is less than proportional to the change in price, the increase in revenue from a higher price will more than offset the decrease in revenue from the decrease in sales. Under such circumstances, the seller may benefit from raising his price. It is very interesting to note, as we shall see later, that many government antitrust suits against price fixing occur in industries with relatively few firms and a highly inelastic demand.

This can be related to the formula method by pointing out that if the coefficient of elasticity is 1.0, total revenue will remain constant when price is changed. If elasticity is greater than 1.0, total revenue will move in the opposite direction as a price change; if elasticity is less than 1.0, total revenue will move in the same direction as a price change.

RANGE OF PRICE ELASTICITY

Price elasticity of demand may range from perfect elasticity at one extreme to perfect inelasticity at the other. A product or service for which there is a perfectly elastic demand would be one for which an infinite quantity would be purchased at a given price. In short, a producer could sell his entire supply at a given market price. Agriculture offers one of the best examples of a perfectly elastic demand. Once the price of wheat or other grain is established by supply and demand or by government parity, the farmer can sell all his available supply at that price. A perfectly elastic demand is represented graphically as a straight horizontal line, D_1, as shown in Figure 4-2.

A perfectly inelastic demand would exist if the same quantity of a product would be bought regardless of the price. It would mean that change in price would result in no change in the quantity demanded. Such a demand is represented by a straight vertical line, D_2, as shown in Figure 4-2. Except in a limited price range, very few, if any, goods or services have a perfectly inelastic demand. Approaching it, however, is the demand for automobile license plates. Whether the price is thirty dollars, twenty dollars, ten dollars, or five dollars, no economically rational motorist will purchase more than one set of license plates for his car. If the price is raised, he will still have to buy that one set. Thus demand may be perfectly inelastic within a certain price range. There is, however, a price at which it may not be worthwhile to purchase license plates for some old jalopies, or at which

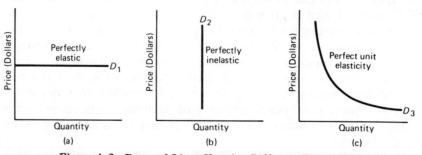

Figure 4-2. Demand Lines Showing Different Elasticities

owning a second or third car may become too expensive. In such a situation, a raise in the price would result in a decrease in the quantity demanded.

There is some tendency among market analysts to say that the more horizontal a demand line, the more it tends to be elastic. This, however, is not always true. Except for a perfectly elastic or inelastic demand, any straight-line demand schedule, will have certain parts of the line that are elastic, other segments that are inelastic, and at some point it will measure unitary elasticity. Related to this is the not infrequent notion that a 45° line represents unitary elasticity. This also is untrue on a conventional type of demand chart. Both of these misconceptions can be clarified by reference to the Figure 4-3. Notice on this demand line that a change in price from eighteen dollars to sixteen dollars, a price change of 11.8 percent, brings about a change in quantity demanded from twenty to forty units, an increase of 66.7 percent (using the midpoint as the base of the percentage change). At the lower end of the vertical axis a price change from four dollars to two dollars, which represents a 66.7 percent change in price, results in an increase in quantity demanded from 160 to 180 units, or a quantity change of 11.7 percent. At one end of the scale price elasticity of demand is 5.7 (66.7 ÷ 11.7). At the other end of the demand schedule price elasticity is only .017(.117 ÷ .667 = .017). Observe further that the point at which price changes from eleven

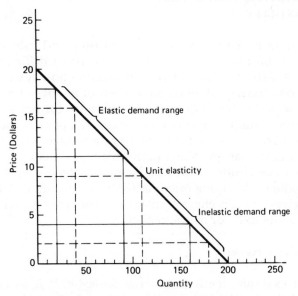

Figure 4-3. Demand Line Showing Varying Measures of Price Elasticity

dollars to nine dollars and the quantity demanded moves from ninety units to 110 units, unitary elasticity exists. (.20 ÷ .20 = 1.0). Any change in price through the range of twenty dollars to eleven dollars is elastic; any change in price between nine dollars and one dollar is inelastic. On this demand line, the point of maximum revenue for the seller would be in the vicinity of ten dollars, since a price change in either direction, up or down, would result in a decrease in revenue. Remember that on a straight-line demand schedule it is possible for a good or service to be elastic at some price ranges and inelastic at others, since it is percentage changes that are being measured. For a demand schedule to possess unitary elasticity throughout, it would have to be represented by a hyperbola as shown in Figure 4-2. On such a line changes in price and quantity are proportional throughout.

The measure of elasticity can be applied to supply also. Because of the slope of the supply line, it should be remembered that quantity changes move in the same direction as price changes. If a given percentage change in the price of a good, however, results in a greater percentage change in the quantity supplied, the supply is elastic. If a price change results in a lesser percentage change in the quantity offered, the supply is inelastic. If a price change results in a proportionate change in the quantity offered for sale, unitary elasticity exists.

CHARACTERISTICS THAT AFFECT PRICE ELASTICITY

Constructing an empirical demand schedule and calculating price elasticity are burdensome tasks. First, it is often difficult to gather sufficient statistical information to determine how much of a good or service consumers will purchase at each of a series of prices. But it can be done and is being done more and more for firms by business economists and market analysts. Secondly, if a price is changed in an effort to observe the change in quantity demanded, the analyst must ferret out other changes taking place, such as a change in income or advertising expenditures, that also have an influence on the demand for the product. Measuring price elasticity is, indeed, a difficult task.

Nevertheless, certain characteristics of products or services tend to give them an inelastic or elastic tendency.

Necessities vs. Luxuries

Milk, for example, tends to be price inelastic. It is an essential ingredient of the family diet, and it has relatively few substitutes. Consequently, if the price rose by 20 percent, milk sales probably would not fall by that amount, since parents would be reluctant to deprive their children of milk. Conversely, a pleasure boat is not a necessity, and a 20 percent increase in its price may quickly deter many potential customers from making a purchase.

Size of Expenditure

Items that constitute a small percentage of total budget expenditures tend to have an inelastic demand. Salt or a book of matches is a minimal-cost item in the family budget. Therefore, their prices may be increased by 40, 75, or 100 percent without substantially affecting the quantities demanded. But buying big ticket items is another matter. If you were prepared to buy a bass boat for six thousand dollars and you were suddenly informed that the price was seven thousand dollars, you might very well decide against the purchase. A large percentage change on a small expenditure does not affect one's total budget nearly as much as the same, or even a more modest, percentage change on a large-budget item. Consequently, small-expenditure items tend to have less elasticity than large-expenditure items.

Product Durability

Consumer reaction to price change is affected also by the durability of a good. If worn-out durable goods can be patched up or repaired, the owner may prefer to continue using an existing asset, such as an overcoat, television set, or punch press, instead of purchasing a high-priced replacement. Such a choice, however, is not available with the utilization of perishable goods. If the wick or mantle of a camping lamp burns out, the only reasonable alternative is to purchase a new wick. The same is true with such items as raw materials for industrial production, gasoline for cars, and food for the table. It is apparent that perishable or nondurable goods tend to have less elasticity than durable goods.

Complementary vs. Substitute Goods

A similar analysis can be made for complementary goods in comparison with substitute goods. A person does not cease driving a five-thousand-dollar car simply because the replacement cost of tires, (complementary goods) which he may need, rises by 10–20 percent. He may, however, substitute retreads for new tires. If airline cargo charges increase, however, a manufacturer may ship by rail, by truck, by water, or other means of transportation. If the admission price of a pro-football game were raised, a young couple may decide to go to a movie instead or watch television. Substitute goods or services tend to have greater price elasticity of demand than do complementary goods and services, because the user can turn to alternatives if prices rise.

Multiple Uses

Price elasticity of demand is also affected by the number of actual and potential uses that exist for a service or product. In this way it is related to the substitution effect. If a product has only one or relatively few uses, lowering the price may induce a limited increase in sales. If the product has multiple uses, however, and its price is lowered, it will have many more sources for increased sales from actual and potential users. Consider, for example, the effect of reducing the price of atomic energy to the effect of reducing the price of electricity. The latter has a much wider variety of uses.

Some goods and services happen to have characteristics of both elasticity and inelasticity, and it is difficult to ascertain in which direction the elasticity leans. A color television, for example, is a moderate expenditure, it is durable, and there are substitute sources of entertainment; all this tends to make the demand for color television elastic. But many Americans consider television a basic necessity. Moreover, one can buy television sets with installment credit. Thus the demand for television becomes less price elastic. Similar mixed characteristics exist in the demand for automobiles which have a price elasticity somewhere between .5 and 1.5.

The elastic characteristics of some goods and services may offset or modify their inelastic characteristics, and vice versa. Table 4-2 indicates, nevertheless, the effect that each characteristic tends to have on the measure of elasticity:

TABLE 4-2

Characteristics that Tend toward Elasticity	Characteristics that Tend toward Inelasticity
Luxuries	Necessities
Large expenditures	Small expenditures
Durable goods	Perishable goods
Substitute goods	Complementary goods
Multiple uses	Limited uses

CROSS ELASTICITY OF DEMAND

The quantity demanded of a particular good or service is affected not only by changes in its price but also by the changes in the price of other goods and services. Assume, for example, that two commodities are close substitutes and that the price of Commodity B is decreased while the price of Commodity A remains the same. Consumers will begin shifting from buying Commodity A to buying Commodity B. This substitution effect will cause a decrease in the demand for Commodity A and an increase in the quantity demand for product B. From a practical point of view, a rise in the price of steak may reduce the consumption of steaks and increase the demand for hamburger and chicken. A rise in the price of butter may result in greater consumption of margarine. Certainly a decrease in the price of a Kawasaki motorcycle would lead to higher sales at the expense of Harley-Davidson and Suzuki bikes, provided that their prices did not fall. Higher bond prices can lead to an increase in the sale of stocks. This relationship, a change in the demand for one commodity or service as a result of a change in the price of another, is known as *cross elasticity of demand*. It is an important concept in a competitive industry where the price actions of one competitor can have a strong effect on the demand, or market share, of other products. Consequently, cross elasticity is sometimes referred to as *market share* elasticity. The formula for cross elasticity can be written as follows:

$$\text{Cross elasticity, } E_x = \frac{\text{Percent change in the quantity of } A}{\text{Percent change in the price of } B}$$

or

$$E_x = \frac{\Delta q(A)}{\Delta p(B)}$$

Cross elasticity exists not only between substitutes but also between complementary products. In contrast to substitutes that show a positive cross elasticity, complementary goods show a negative cross elasticity. With substitute goods, as the price of one good increases, demand for the substitute rises. With complementary goods, when the price of a basic commodity goes up, the demand for the complementary good falls along with the sales for the basic commodity. The sales of records and tapes, for example, may very well decline if the price of stereo sets rises and fewer stereo sets are bought. Since many firms are concerned not only with total sales but also with market penetration, the cross elasticity formula may be stated in terms of market share. In this case, the formula would be written

$$\text{Market share elasticity}, E_{ms} = \frac{\text{Percent change in the market share of } A}{\text{Percent change in the price of } B}$$

If a firm knows from experience what effect a change in the price of its competitor's product will have on its own sales, the information may be analyzed graphically as shown in Figure 4-4. Such information is useful in studying the impact of monopolistic and oligopolistic pricing. In the chart the intersect, P_1S_1, represents the existing price and the market share of Firm A. The price at P_1 may be equal to the competitor's price, or take into account any customary differential, such as that existing between major brands and independent brands of gasoline. S_1, at the intersect, represents Firm A's market share under existing pricing conditions. If Firm A lowers its price by moving down the vertical scale it will gain an increasing share of the market. Thus, if it lowers price 2 percent, its share of the market would increase by 6 percent. On the other hand, if Firm A raises its price 2 percent its share of the market will be reduced by 6 percent. Similarly, if Firm B changed its price the same effect would occur. A price rise by Firm B would, in effect, be a relative decrease in the price of Firm A's product. Consequently, if Firm B raises price 2 percent it will be equivalent to a 2 percent decrease in the price of Firm A's product, and Firm A's market share will rise 6 percent. On the

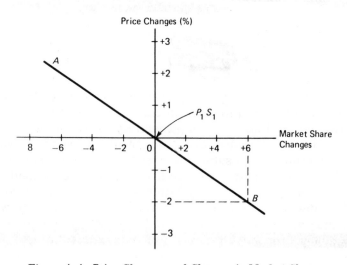

Figure 4-4. Price Changes and Changes in Market Share

other hand, if Firm B lowers its price 2 percent and Firm A does not, it will be similar to a 2 percent rise in price for Firm A, and its market share will decline by 6 percent.

INCOME ELASTICITY OF DEMAND

The level of consumer income is a major factor affecting the demand for most goods and services. As the incomes of individuals, families, and business firms change, the demand for particular commodities and the demand for goods and services in general change. In most situations, an increase in consumer income tends to bring about an increase in the demand for particular goods. As income rises, especially during prosperity, consumers buy more at given prices, causing the demand line to shift to the right. With a decline in employment and income, on the other hand, the demand for many products and services declines and the demand line shifts downward to the left.

This relationship between changing income and changes in demand is known as *income elasticity of demand*. If the demand for a product increases in greater proportion than the increase in income, income elasticity will be greater than 1.0, and the product is said to be *income elastic*. If the increase in sales is less than the increase in income, however, income elasticity will be less than 1.0 or income inelastic. If the change in income and demand is proportional, the product possess unitary income elasticity. The formula for measuring income elasticity of demand is shown below:

$$\text{Income elasticity, } E_i = \frac{\text{Percent change in quantity}}{\text{Percent change in disposable income}}$$

or,

$$E_i = \frac{\Delta q}{\Delta DI}$$

Income elasticity, or *income sensitivity*, as it is often called, varies for different commodities and services. It is usually low for basic necessities, since these items are bought even when incomes are minimal. There may be little need, therefore, to buy more of them as incomes increase. Many conveniences, luxuries, and services, however, tend to have a high income elasticity. Consumers can afford more of these items only as income increases. In planning for growth, it is important for managers in various firms and industries to know something about the income elasticity of their products. They should know whether the demand for their products increases at the same, a

TABLE 4-3. Personal Consumption Expenditure Items Classified According to Sensitivity to Changes in Disposable Personal Income[1]

$$S = \frac{\Delta\%Q}{\Delta\%DI}$$

Above-average Sensitivity

Durable goods

Item	S
Boats and pleasure aircraft	3.1
Radios, phonographs, parts, and records	2.5
Pianos and other musical instruments	2.3
New cars and net purchases of used cars	2.0
Luggage	1.9
Jewelry and watches	1.8
Cooking and portable heating equipment	1.7
Tools	1.7
Furniture	1.6
Writing equipment	1.6
Miscellaneous electrical appliances except radios	1.6
Floor coverings	1.4
Wheel goods, durable toys, and sport equipment	1.4
Durable house furnishings, n.e.c.	1.4
Products of custom establishments, n.e.c.	1.3
Monuments and tombstones	1.3
Tires and tubes	1.3
Books and maps	1.2
Automobile parts and accessories	1.2
Refrigerators, and washing and sewing machines	1.0

Nondurable goods

Item	S
Purchased meals and beverages — dining and buffet cars	1.6
Flowers, seeds, and potted plants	1.6
Stationery and writing supplies	1.4
Semidurable house furnishings	1.1
Clothing and accessories except footwear	1.1
Purchased meals and beverages — hotels	1.0

Average Sensitivity

Durable goods

Item	S
Ophthalmic products and orthopedic appliances	0.8

Nondurable goods

Item	S
Food purchased for off-premises consumption	[2] 1.0
Purchased meals and beverages — tips	[2] 1.0
Purchased meals and beverages — retail, service, and amusement establishments	[2] 1.0
Nondurable toys and sport supplies	[2] 1.0
Cleaning and polishing preparations	.9
Food produced and consumed on farms	.8
Toilet articles and preparations	.8
Food furnished government and commercial employees; and withdrawn by nonfarm proprietors	.8

Services

Item	S
Care of electrical equipment (except radios) and of stoves	[2] 1.0
Personal business services, n.e.c.	[2] 1.0
Accident and health insurance — net payments	1.0
Dancing, riding, shooting, skating, and swimming places	[2] 1.0
Chiropractors — services	.9
Amusement devices and parks	.9
Boat and bicycle rental, storage, and repair	.9
Baths and masseurs	.9
Admissions — professional baseball	.9
Miscellaneous curative and healing professions — services	.9

Below Average Sensitivity

Durable goods

Item	S
China, glassware, tableware, and utensils	[3] 0.7

Nondurable goods

Item	S
Miscellaneous household paper products	[3] .7
Drug preparations and sundries	.6
Purchased fuel (except gas) and ice	.6
Tobacco products and smoking supplies	.5
Gasoline and oil	.5
Magazines, newspapers, and sheet music	.5
Purchased meals and beverages — schools and fraternities	.5

Services

Item	S
Intercity bus — fares	[3] .7
Chiropodists and podiatrists — services	[3] .7
Admissions — professional hockey	.6
Funeral and burial services	.6
Interest on personal debt	.6
Foundation expenditures for education and research	.6
Foundation expenditures for religious and welfare activities	.6
Automobile insurance — net payments	.6
Upholstery and furniture repair	.6
Services furnished without payment by financial intermediaries except insurance companies	.6
Net purchases from second-hand furniture dealers	.6
Housing — clubs, schools, and institutions	.5
Owner-occupied nonfarm dwellings — space rental value	[4] .5
Moving expenses and warehousing	[4] .5
Trust services of banks	.5

Services[1]

Item	S
Ticket brokers' mark-up on admissions	2.1
Admissions — legitimate theaters and opera	[4]1.9
Fur storage and repair	1.6
Watch, clock, and jewelry repairs	1.5
Steam railway (excluding commutation) fares	1.4
Photo developing and printing	1.3
Sleeping and parlor car — fares and tips	1.3
Baggage transfer, carriage, storage, and excess charges	1.3
Private flying operations	1.3
Domestic service	1.3
Taxicab — fares and tips	1.2
Dressmakers and seamstresses (not in shop) — charges	1.2
Net payments — mutual accidents and sick benefit associations	1.2
Practical nurses and midwives — services	1.2
Rug, drapery, and mattress cleaning and repair	1.2
Miscellaneous personal services	1.2
Cleaning, dyeing, pressing, alteration, storage, and repair of garments, n.e.c. (in shops)	1.0
Billiard parlors and bowling alleys	1.2
Express charges	1.1
Photographic studios	1.1
Housing — transient hotels and tourist cabins	1.1
Radio repair	1.0
Automobile repair, greasing, washing, parking, storage, and rental	1.0
Osteopathic physicians — services	.9
Commercial, business, and trade schools — fees	.9
Dentists — services	.9
Telegraph, cable, and wireless	.9
Laundering in establishments	.9
Fire and theft insurance on personal property — net payments	.8
Veterinary service and purchase of pets	.8
Classified advertisements	.8
Correspondence schools — fees	.8
Commercial amusements, n.e.c.	.8
Athletic and social clubs — dues and fees	.8
Beauty parlor services	.8
Costume and dress suit rental	.8
Entertainments of nonprofit organizations, except athletics	.8
Golf instruction, club rental, and caddy fees	.8
Other instruction (except athletics) — fees	.8
Physicians — services	.8
Shoe cleaning and repair	.7
Admissions — motion-picture theaters	.7
Social welfare and foreign relief agencies	.7
Barber shop services	.7
Admissions — other amateur spectator sports	.7
Private duty trained nurses — services	.7
Street and electric railway and local bus — fares	.9
Tenant-occupied nonfarm dwellings — space rent	[4].5
Cemeteries and crematories	.5
Steam railway — commutation fares	.5
Rental value of farm houses	[4].4
Telephone	[4].4
Religious bodies	[4].3
Legal services	.3
Privately controlled hospitals and sanitarium services	.3
Postage	[4].3
Museums and libraries	.3
Miscellaneous household operation services	.3
Water	[4].2
Expense of handling life insurance — life insurance companies	.2
Gas	[4].2
Electricity	[4].2

[1] The classification is based on the relationship of personal consumption expenditures for each item with disposable personal income and a time factor for the period 1929–40. The figures in the S column indicate the percent change which is associated with a 1 percent change in disposable income; for example, an increase of 1 percent in disposable personal income is associated with an increase of 1.8 percent in the expenditures on jewelry and watches, all other factors being equal.
[2] Value between 0.95 and 1.00.
[3] Value between 0.65 and .70.
[4] Coefficient of partial determination less than 0.7.
Source: adapted from U.S. Department of Commerce, Office of Business Economics. *Survey of Current Business*, January 1950.

slower, or a faster rate than does the general level of income in the economy. Table 4-3 gives some typical measures of income sensitivity for various goods and services as calculated by the Department of Commerce's Office of Business Economics. Observe the types of goods and services that tend to have high income sensitivity and those that have low income sensitivity.

PROMOTIONAL ELASTICITY

It is also possible to measure promotional elasticity, or the relationship between changes in advertising expenditure and the resultant change in the quantity of a good or service sold. In this case the formula can be stated:

$$Ea = \frac{\text{Percent change in quantity}}{\text{Percent change in promotional expenditure}}$$

A measure such as promotional elasticity may be less meaningful than some other measures of elasticity, especially price elasticity. In price elasticity, for example, an inelastic demand means that total revenue will decrease if price is lowered, and total revenue will also decline if the demand is elastic and the price is raised. With promotional elasticity, however, any measure of elasticity or inelasticity will produce an increase in total revenue. A measure of 1.0 or above means that total revenue will rise in greater proportion than would an increase in promotional expenditure. A measure of 0.5 indicates that total revenue would rise less than proportionally to a rise in promotional expenditure. But even with this, total revenue in dollars may increase more than promotional expenditure and result in an increase in gross revenue. Assume sales are one million units, the price level is one dollar, and advertising expenditure is one hundred thousand dollars per year. If advertising expenditure is increased by 50 percent to $150,000 and as a result sales increase by 25 percent to 1,250,000 units (or $1,250,000), there is still a positive gain to the firm. Its gross revenue would be increased by $200,000 ($250,000 – $50,000) although promotional inelasticity of demand exists.

INDUSTRY ELASTICITY VS. FIRM ELASTICITY

Thus far we have been talking about the general demand for particular products and suggesting that a measure of elasticity may be calculated. But the degree of elasticity for a product may differ, depending on whether it is measured from the viewpoint of an individual firm, or seller, or from the viewpoint of a total industry. An industry may be faced with a highly price-inelastic demand for its product, yet demand to the individual firms in that industry may be very price elastic. Much depends on the number of firms competing in the market and the reaction of other firms to changes in price by one or a few firms.

A good case in point is that of agricultural products. By and large, the demand for wheat is price inelastic, and the price is set by the interaction of total supply and demand as affected by government parity. Since there are nearly a million wheat farmers in the United States, no one of these producers individually can influence the price of wheat. They must sell at the market price as determined by overall supply and demand. On the other hand, each will be able to sell his total individual supply at the market price. Consequently, each of them faces a perfectly elastic demand for his product, even though the general demand for wheat is inelastic.

In the case of a pure monopolist, where there is only one producer, the elasticity of demand for the product of the firm is identical to the elasticity of demand for the product in the market in general. This is so because the firm's market and the industry market are identical. If more firms were to share in that market, however, the demand lines of the individual firms would tend to be more elastic than that of the market in general as long as they were producing identical products. This is so because of the probable substitution effect, or cross elasticity of demand, as one firm changes price. Reaction of firms in an industry to a change in price by one of them also affects the degree of elasticity. Firm A, for example, may lower its price and count on some substitution effect to bring about an increase in its sales. But if firms B, C, and D also lower their prices, the increase in sales to firm A from the lower price may be far less than anticipated. In fact, as a result of price retaliation, it is possible to change a firm's potentially elastic demand into an inelastic demand.

QUANTITY SOLD AS A FUNCTION OF PRICE

We usually think of quantity sold as a function of, or dependent upon, price, and express this relationship as $q = f(p)$. It should be clear now, however, that many other factors besides price affect sales. Quantity sold is influenced by the level of disposable income, the price of other goods, (both complementary and substitute goods), advertising or promotion outlays, and by other considerations, such as quality and service. Thus, just as it is proper to write $q = f(p)$, all factors affecting quantity sold can be combined into one equation and expressed as follows: $q = f(p, DI, p_x, a, \ldots)$, etc. In the equation, p is the price of the product itself, DI is the level of disposable income, p_x is the price of other commodities, and a is the advertising outlay.

In the fast-foods industry, for example, McDonald's, which has sold over 25 billion hamburgers, maintains that its success as a leader in the industry is due just as much to the quality of its product, the cleanliness of its shops, and its service as it is to price. It is evident, too, that McDonald's sales are affected substantially by advertising.

DEMAND AND PRODUCT DIFFERENTIATION

Sometimes firms are faced with difficult demand situations. A firm with an inelastic demand may desire to increase its output to obtain a lower cost per unit of output, but knows that its total revenue will decline. Perhaps total revenue may decline more than cost. Even a firm with an elastic demand may be concerned that by increasing its output and lowering its price, it will be selling its product to some customers at a price below that which the customers are willing to pay for the product. In short, there will exist consumer surplus for some buyers. It is apparent that some customers are willing to pay more than others for a product. What can the firm do to take advantage of this fact and improve its profit picture under the above conditions?

First of all the firm must remember that its demand line is a series of alternative relationships between prices and sales. It may be able to sell 1000 units at $100, 2500 units at $90, 4250 units at $80, and so on down the demand schedule. In this case its choice is to sell 1000 units at $100 or 2500 units at $90. It is not 1000 units at $100 plus 2500 additional units at $90 and so forth. The firm under some circumstance, such as a close-out sale, the sale of a nonrepeatable purchase item, etc., may endeavor to sell at the highest possible price until all who are willing to pay that price have made their purchases and then lower its price in order to sell as much as it can at that price. In this way it certainly would be maximizing its revenue. If the firm did this as a matter of practice, or did it perennially on items of repeatable purchase, however, customers would soon get wise to the process and hold back on buying until the price came down.

Another way in which the firm can maximize its revenue is through product differentiation. Suppose a firm were faced with the demand line for its carpet sweepers as shown in Figure 4–5(A). It has a choice of selling a limited number of sweepers at a high price, more at a middle price and most at a lower price. In order to sell a larger amount,

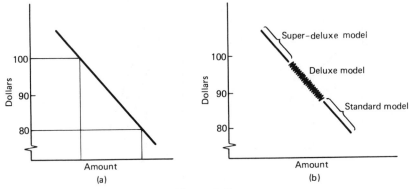

Figure 4-5.

it must lower its price. But in lowering its price to obtain greater sales, it will be selling sweepers to many customers who might be willing to pay more. How then can the firm get some customers to pay the higher price while still selling to others at a lower price? This can be done through product differentiation. The firm may develop three very similar but slightly differentiated models of its products. Almost all parts and units of the sweeper may be the same in order to hold down the cost of production, but frills will be added to the two "better" models. It can then sell the standard model to those who will pay only the lower price, a deluxe model to those willing to pay a slightly higher price and a super-deluxe model to those willing to pay the highest price. In this way, the firm can obtain higher prices from those willing to pay them. In short, the firm will segment its demand line into three parts, or into three separate demand lines, as shown in Figure 4-5(B). In this way it obtains maximum advantage of the demand for its product. A firm with an inelastic demand for its product actually can sell more and increase its total revenue with this method. The firm with the elastic demand, of course, would obtain a greater than the usual increase in revenue through increased sales. This, of course, is done with sweepers, automobiles, encyclopedias, electric razors, bicycles, hotel rooms, tires, tourist trips, television sets, and hundreds of other products and services. In fact, many sellers advertise the lower price but push the higher-priced model or service when consumers come to buy.

SOME PROBLEMS OF MEASURING ELASTICITIES

As we mentioned earlier, constructing a demand line is not easy. In collecting price and quantity data, it may not be possible to hold constant all other factors that affect quantity sold when price is

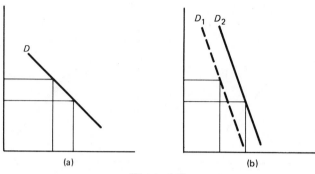

(a)   (b)

Figure 4-6.

changed. This is especially true if the data are collected over a period of time. A market analyst or economist, for example, may plot price and quantity data that he has collected over a few months or years as shown in Figure 4-6(A). Analyzing the data, he may conclude that the demand for the product is price elastic and therefore the price should be reduced to increase revenue. It may be, however, that after the price change there was also an increase in disposable income. In such a case, in measuring the increased quantity sold, as price was lowered, he is including also some additional sales that result from higher income. He does not have a true measure of price elasticity because all factors, exclusive of prices, have not remained the same: income has increased, and demand has shifted to the right. Instead of measuring quantity sold on a given demand line as shown in Figure 4-6(A), he is comparing price and quantity sold on one demand line, D_1, with the price and quantity sold on a second demand line, D_2, as shown in Figure 4-6(B). This may lead him to conclude that demand for the product is price elastic, whereas in reality the demand could be price inelastic. The bulk of the increase in sales could be coming from income elasticity rather than from price elasticity. In such a case he would do better to recommend that the price of the product be maintained or increased, rather than decreased, in order to maximize revenues.

Price and cross elasticity are affected not only by a change in price, but by the response or reaction of competitors to a price change. If Firm A reduced its price, for example, Firm B may decide to match the price reduction, ignore it, or take some other action, such as offering a purchase bonus to the buyers. What Firm B and other competitors do will certainly affect the sales of Firm A (through price elasticity and cross elasticity for its product).

On a typical demand line, a greater quantity of the product or service will be sold at a lower price. The increase in quantity sold

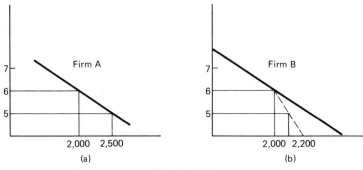

Figure 4-7.

will come from the factors cited on page 58, plus some substitution effect, as sales are diverted from other firms. Consequently, assuming no positive response to a price reduction by its competitors, Firm A may look upon its demand line as shown in Figure 4-7(a).

In Figure 4-7(a), if Firm A lowers its price from $6 to $5 its anticipated sales will increase from 2000 to 2500 units. Since price elasticity is

$$1.22 \left(\frac{\text{rel. } \Delta \ q}{\text{rel. } \Delta \ p} = \frac{.22}{.18} = 1.22\right)$$

its total revenue will increase from $12,000 to $12,500. If competitors respond by meeting the price reduction, however, the demand line would shift as shown in Figure 4-7(b). At a price of $5, Firm A's total sales would be only 2,200 units and its total revenue would decline to $11,000. The price elasticity, if measured in this case would be

$$.55 \left(\frac{\text{rel. } \Delta \ q}{\text{rel. } \Delta \ p} = \frac{.10}{.18} = .55\right)$$

On the other hand, if Firm A calculated that it had an inelastic demand and it raised its price in order to obtain more revenue, its success would again depend in large part on the response of its competitors. If competitors raised their prices also, Firm A would lose no sales through cross elasticity or substitution effect. But if competitors decide not to raise their prices, Firm A may lose more sales than anticipated because there would be a substitution effect as Firm A's customer moved to relative lower-priced competitors' products. Consequently, in constructing a measure of price elasticity or cross elasticity, due consideration must be given to the probable reaction of competitors.

In measuring price elasticity of demand, therefore, it is important to hold all other factors constant in order to observe the effect of price changes on quantity sold. This may not be possible, since the firm may have no control over these other variables. Consequently, in order to get a true measure of price elasticity, it is also necessary while trying to measure it, to find ways to ferret out the effect of other changes that may be taking place, such as income changes, changes in the prices of substitute products, changes in the quality of products, or changes in promotional expenditures. Similar precautions must be taken when measuring income, market share, promotional, and other types of elasticities.

SOME SUGGESTED METHODS OF MEASURING
PRICE ELASTICITY OF DEMAND

The several methods for constructing demand schedules suggested in the previous chapter can be employed for measuring elasticity of demand. After all, it is necessary to obtain some type of demand schedule if one is going to measure price, income, cross, and promotional eleasticities. Once a true demand schedule, or one as nearly true as possible, is plotted, price elasticity and other types of elasticity, for example, can be measured by using the formulas explained earlier in this chapter.

Controlled experiments in a test market, for example, may yield adequate data about sales at different prices to permit the calculation of price elasticity. Consumer questionnaires also may give sufficient information. Likewise, a demand line obtained through regression analysis can be used to measure price elasticity. In the previous chapter, for instance, we constructed a demand line for the consumption of newsprint. Measuring the price elasticity on that line by using the price of $146 per ton at which consumption is 704 million tons and the price of $151 at which 663 million tons of newsprint were consumed yields a 1.76 measure of price elasticity of demand.[5] Mea-

---

[5] Using the formula, given on page 99, for determining the price elasticity of demand yields the following:

$$\frac{\dfrac{Q_2 - Q_1}{Q_1 + Q_2/2}}{\dfrac{P_1 - P_2}{P_1 + P_2/2}} = \frac{\dfrac{704 - 663}{704 + 663/2}}{\dfrac{151 - 146}{146 + 151/2}} = \frac{\dfrac{41}{684}}{\dfrac{5}{148.5}} = \frac{.060}{.034} = 1.76$$

suring the elasticity by using the prices of $163, with consumption of 665 million tons, and $170, at which consumption is 635 million tons, yields a measure of price elasticity of demand of 1.08. Using the prices of $170 and $210 with their respective amounts of consumption indicates price elasticity of .3, showing that there are various degrees of elasticity along the given demand schedule.

In the 1962 orange price experiment, cited in Chapter 3, the analysts were able to construct a demand schedule and measure price elasticity of demand. By using a sufficient number of stores in the test market and offering customers three different types of oranges, they were also able to obtain some measures of price cross elasticity of demand. Sometime during the test period, each of three types of oranges were offered for sale at nine different prices. Price changes ranged thirty-two cents by four-cent intervals. By altering the price of one type of orange, they could determine the change in the amount sold and thus measure price elasticity. By changing the price of one type of orange and holding the prices of the others constant, they were able to observe the effect on the sale of the other oranges and thus obtain data to measure cross elasticity of demand. Since the test period was thirty-one days, it was short enough to avoid complexities caused by changing incomes and changing tastes.

In 1964, the Office of Business Economics of the Department of Commerce conducted a household survey and obtained sufficient information to derive income elasticity of demand for automobiles. In addition to income, five other variables affecting demand, such as age and geographic location, were factored into the study. The measures of income elasticity ranged from .25 to 1.0, according to the different variables.

Early studies by Roos and Von Szelski indicate price elasticity of demand for automobiles to be little more than 1.0. This helps to explain the reluctance of auto firms to rely on price reduction to increase sales.[6]

The 1950 study of demand by the Office of Business Economics showed the income elasticity of demand of automobiles to be 2.0 and the price elasticity to be 1.3. A later study of Gregory Chow,[7] for the 1960s, however, showed both price and income elasticities to be less. The lessening of elasticities was attributed to a number of factors, such as easier credit and the deterioration of substitute means of transportation. The latter meant, that the automobile was becoming a necessity.

[6]C.F. Roos and V. Von Szelski, *The Dynamics of Automobile Demands* (New York: General Motors Corporation, 1939).

[7]Gregory Chow, "Statistical Demand Functions and Their Use for Forecasting," in Arnold C. Harberger, ed., *The Demand for Durable Goods* (Chicago: University of Chicago Press, 1960).

Studies by Burk[8] in the 1960s showed income elasticity of demand for food to be quite low at .24, and elasticity was less among higher-income groups than among lower income groups. This is quite natural, since food is a fundamental necessity and higher- and middle-income groups have an ample supply of food. Consequently, as their incomes rose, these groups spent very little more for food.

The widely publicized Houthakker-Taylor elasticity studies of the 1960s cover more than eighty commodities and reveal a variety of elasticity measures, including some commodities on which income elasticity shifted from positive to negative as incomes rose.[9] A study of the price–quantity relationship of tobacco in several different countries revealed low income and price elasticities in the demand for cigarettes.[10] Moreover, high taxes and price increases did little to curtail the consumption of cigarettes. Other studies have indicated low price and income elasticities for public utility services, as might be expected in the use of a basic utility. On the other hand, studies show that income elasticity of demand for furniture and clothing is greater than unity.

RESERVATIONS IN THE USE OF DEMAND LINES

Although the methods and measures just cited, plus some others, have been used often, they may not result in the construction of a perfect demand line or curve for a good or service. They can, if developed with as much accuracy as possible, however, give some indication of a demand schedule. Furthermore, more than one method may be utilized as a means of comparing and verifying results. Certainly, developing some plausible and reasonably accurate demand schedule is better than having none at all and merely guessing at the relationship between price and quantity sold.

Even when a reasonably accurate measure of demand in constructed, however, it has limitations when used for determining the price and output of the firm. Probably the most serious weakness, or omission, of demand analysis is that it tells nothing about the cost of production. The best price, or the maximum revenue position, on the demand line may require an output greater than optimal as far as costs are concerned. Consequently, that price, although yielding

---

[8] Marguerite C. Burk, "Ramifications of the Relationship between Income and Food," *Journal of Farm Economics*, February 1962.

[9] H.S. Houthakker and L.D. Taylor, *Consumer Demand in the United States, 1929–1970* (Cambridge, Mass: Harvard University Press, 1966).

[10] A.P. Koutsoyannis, "Demand Functions for Tobacco," *The Manchester School of Economics and Social Studies*, January 1963.

maximum revenue, may not result in maximum profit. Therefore, analysis of demand has to be related to cost analysis in order to make sound judgments about pricing. We will learn subsequently that the firm must seek optimum price and cost if it desires to maximize profit.

Before going into cost analysis, however, let us explore one other aspect of demand. That is the forecasting of demand for the product or service of a firm, since demand will bear heavily on the economic and managerial planning of the firm both in the short and the long run.

SUMMARY

There are several types of demand elasticities. Price elasticity, for example, is a measure of consumer responsiveness to a change in price. It can be measured by the formula method or the total revenue method. A coefficient of elasticity of 1.0 is considered unity elasticity. This indicates that a given price change will elicit a proportional change in the quantity sold. A coefficient of more than 1.0 indicates an elastic demand; a measure of less than 1.0 indicates an inelastic demand. A knowledge of elasticity is important in formulating the pricing policies of a firm.

Products that are necessities, those involving small expenditures, perishable goods, and complementary goods tend toward inelasticity. On the other hand, luxuries, high-priced goods, durable goods, and substitute goods tend toward elasticity.

Cross elasticity is a measure of consumer responsiveness of the quantity purchased of one product to the change in the price of another product. This, along with price elasticity, is important to the pricing policies of a firm. Also important is income elasticity of demand, since it indicates to some extent the future spending directions of consumers. Demand and sales can also be affected by promotional (advertising) outlays, and attempts have been made to measure promotional elasticity of demand.

The elasticity of demand for the product of a particular firm may differ from the elasticity of demand for the product of the industry or the market. Generally, the price elasticity of demand for the firm will tend to be more elastic than that for the entire industry. This is so because of the competitive element within the industry and the occurrence of cross elasticity.

A number of problems arise when endeavoring to measure elasticity of demand. A major concern when attempting to measure price elasticity, for example, is that of eliminating the influence on demand of such factors as population change, changes in income, and changes in the prices of competing products. Again, one must be careful when attempting to measure elasticities of demand and cautious in using them.

QUESTIONS FOR ANALYSIS AND DISCUSSION

1. Give the formulas for the following:
   a. price elasticity of demand
   b. income elasticity of demand
   c. cross elasticity of demand
   d. promotional elasticity of demand
2. What are the guidelines for determining whether a product has an elastic, inelastic, or unit elasticity of demand by using the total revenue method?
3. Distinguish between perfect elasticity, perfect inelasticity, and unit elasticity of demand. Indicate what demand line represents each of these types of demand.
4. What is the relationship between price elasticity of demand and marginal revenue?
5. What characteristics of a good tend to make it inelastic?
6. Indicate whether the demand for the following tends to be price elastic or price inelastic: (a) shoelaces, (b) portable home air-conditioning units, (c) college textbooks, (d) professional entertainment, (e) new homes.
7. What is market share elasticity? Why is it important to a firm?
8. How is it possible for the demand for the product of an industry to be inelastic, but the demand for the product of an individual firm in that industry to be price elastic?
9. How can a firm with an inelastic demand sell more of its product at a lower price without decreasing its total revenue?
10. Explain briefly some of the methods that can be used to gather data necessary to construct a demand schedule.
11. What cautions must be exercised in any attempt to measure price elasticity of demand from empirical data on sales and prices?

PROBLEMS AND CASES

1. Changes in Demand and Supply and the Effect on Price and the Quantity Purchased as Influenced by Elasticity.

   In the previous chapter, as an assignment, you drew some graphs showing the effect of changes in supply and demand on the price and quantity of a good purchased. The effect of such changes, however, will be influenced by the slope or elasticity of the demand and supply lines. Below are some axioms that can be followed in approximating the influence of elasticities on price and the amount purchased with changes in demand and supply:

   Change in demand: With a given change in demand, the more elastic the supply, the less will be the proportionate change in price, and greater will be the proportionate change in quantity purchased.

The less elastic the supply, the greater will be the change in price, and the less the change on amount purchased.

Change in supply: With a given change in supply, the more elastic the demand, the less will be the proportionate change in price, and the greater the proportionate change in quantity purchased.

The less elastic the demand, the greater the change in price, and the less the change in quantity purchased.

In order to facilitate your handling of demand and supply situations involving degrees of elasticity, do the following:

(a) Draw graphs showing the effect of changes (1) and (3) below.

(b) State what effect these changes have on price and quantity purchased.

(c) For each change for which you drew a graph there is a converse change for which you drew no graph. The one graph, however, will reveal the effects of either change. For each graph that you have drawn, give the number of the related converse situation (also revealed by the graph).

> (1) Demand increases, no change in supply
>> (i) supply elastic
>> (ii) supply inelastic
>
> (2) Demand decreases, no change in supply
>> (i) supply elastic
>> (ii) supply inelastic
>
> (3) Supply increases, no change in demand
>> (i) demand elastic
>> (ii) demand inelastic
>
> (4) Supply decreases, no change in demand
>> (i) demand elastic
>> (ii) demand inelastic

2. Mr. E.Z. Knott operates the Rainbow Tie Company. He collects data that indicate he can increase his sales from the current level of 315,000 ties per month to 405,000 per month by reducing the price at which he sells to retailers from $16.50 to $13.50 per dozen. If his cost per tie does not increase, would you advise Mr. Knott to reduce his price?

3. Jack Salmon and Bill Trout own a small manufacturing company that produces fishing equipment. Their shop produces and sells 140,000 trolling motors in competition with other producers at a price of $33.95 per motor. It is generally known in the industry that sales are related to income and that the income elasticity of demand is in the vicinity of 1.34 for trolling motors. Salmon contends that by improving their Zephyr trolling motor and selling at a lower price they can outsell most of their competitors. Trout has some doubts about lowering price, but finally agrees to go along with the idea. Thereupon they cease production of the Zephyr motor temporarily in order to experiment with an improved model.

One year later they begin producing and selling Zephyr II, the improved model, at a price of $27.95. In the intervening year, real personal disposable income of the nation increased by 5 percent. During the first year, sales of Zephyr II reached 180,000 per year.

(a) Was Mr. Salmon right in his suggestion to lower price?

(b) What is the true measure of price elasticity of demand?

4. Dick Wash is a brand manager of a bar soap in the soap division of a large manufacturer of toiletries. The company sells, among other brands, Bubble brand soap in competition with other soaps. The going price for most of these soaps is twenty-three cents per bar. The sales of Bubble amount to one million bars per month. Wash feels that because of its superior qualities, Bubble soap can be sold at a higher price of 27 cents without losing sales, provided that it is properly promoted.

   With the aid of his assistants, Wash designs an advertising and promotion campaign to extoll the superiority of Bubble soap to be put into effect when the price is increased. Subsequently, he requests both a budget increase of $300,000 per year for advertising and promotion and authority to raise the price of Bubble soap from twenty-three to twenty-seven cents per bar.

   You are the division manager and the request comes across your desk. You observe that the request would increase advertising expense by thirty percent. From your recent experience with other bar soaps, you know that promotional elasticity of demand is in the vicinity of 1.4.

   (a) What would the measure of price elasticity of demand be if prices are raised, the $300,000 is spent for advertising and promotion, and sales remained at 1 million bars per month?

   (b) What would be the increase in total revenue resulting from conditions in the above question?

   (c) What would be the increase in total revenue if the advertising budget increase were approved and utilized, but the price increase were not approved?

   (d) Would you approve either or both of the requests regarding the price change and the advertising and promotional budget?

5. A market test conducted for the Spinner Novelty Company indicated the following monthly sales for its newly designed yo-yo, which it recently put into production on a limited scale. At a price of 89 cents, 23,000 units were sold; at 84 cents, 27,000 units; and at 79 cents, 32,000 units. Before engaging in mass production of the yo-yo, the manager and owner meet to select the market price to use in its forthcoming promotional campaign.

   (a) Draw a graph showing the demand line for the new yo-yo.

   (b) Measure the price elasticity of demand.

   (c) At what price would you recommend Spinner Supply Company market its new yo-yo?

6. Mr. D.C. Volt is the owner and president of a small manufacturing company that makes electronic controls to open and close garage doors. By pressing a mobile control unit located in an automobile, or elsewhere, one can open and close a garage door automically. Volt is discussing with his production supervisor, Mr. Overhead, the feasibility of reducing the price of his control unit in order to increase sales. You, as a part-time economic consultant, are asked by Volt to advise him on the matter.

   He assures you that a price cut would be wise management and marketing strategy because the demand for his product is price elastic. You ask him how he knows that. He points out that in 1971 he sold 100,000 units at a price of $105 per unit. In 1972 the price was lowered to $95 per unit and sales rose to one hundred and twenty-two thousand units.

You ask for a few days to think the matter over before giving him an answer. Meantime, in gathering data for your analysis of the situation, you find that between 1971 and 1972, the dates used by Volt, personal income for the economy rose about 7 percent, that the income elasticity of demand for products of this nature is estimated at about 1.25, that competitors increased their prices by an average of ten percent because of inflation, that Volt, against the wishes of Overhead, reduced the quality of his product by using less expensive and less reliable components, that new housing starts rose 15 percent in 1972 and that automobile registrations were up by 10 percent in 1972 over 1971.

(a) Using Mr. Volt's price and sales figures, what would be the price elasticity of demand if all other factors had remained unchanged?

(b) Prepare a graphic presentation to show how each of the other factors you uncovered would affect the measure of price elasticity implied by Mr. Volt and calculated by you in the above question.

(c) Without trying to quantify the effects, indicate whether each of these "other factors" exaggerates or modifies the measure of price elasticity in question (a).

(d) What advice would you give to Mr. Volt in regard to his proposal to cut price to increase sales?

UAW* Correspondence with "Big 3" Auto Firms.
The following is the text of a letter to the "Big 3" auto firms on one-hundred-dollar price-cut plan.

Mr. Lester L. Colbert, President   August 16, 1957
Chrysler Corporation
Detroit Mich.

Dear Mr. Colbert:

Like millions of Americans, we in the UAW view with deep concern the growing problem of inflation. We believe that inflation, if permitted to go unchecked, can assume proportions that will threaten the stability of the American economy, weaken our ability to lead the fight of the free world against the forces of Communist tyranny, and cause widespread hardship and human suffering through reduction of the living standards of millions of American families.

Much is being said about the growing problem of inflation, but unfortunately little is being done. We can all agree that in our free society, free labor and free management, in addition to having privileges, share joint responsibilities. One of these joint responsibilities is to find a way to raise

*United Automobile Workers of America
Source: UAW, Solidarity House, Detroit, Michigan, Oct. 1, 1957.

collective bargaining above the level of a struggle between competing economic pressure groups. We in the UAW believe that collective bargaining, to be sound and socially responsible, must serve the public need. In practical terms, this means that free labor must shape its economic demands and free management must determine its pricing policies so that they will not only protect and advance the interest of workers and stockholders but will also protect and advance the interest of all American consumers. This joint responsibility to the whole of our society and to the well being of the whole nation transcends in importance the more narrow responsibilities that labor and management have to their respective groups. In a real sense, neither free labor nor free management can in the long pull advance their particular interests in an economic or social vacuum. They can, in effect, only advance their particular interests as those interests are compatible with the interests of the whole community.

Based upon the unanimous action of the UAW International Executive Board, I am writing to suggest a positive and practical proposal for making an effective beginning in stopping and reversing the inflationary trend. This is a tangible and effective way for both management and labor to carry out their joint responsibility to all of the American people.

The UAW recognizes that management has an obligation to its stockholders to obtain for them a reasonable return on their investment. You surely recognize, in turn, that the Union has an obligation to its members and to their families to help them to obtain for themselves a fair share in the fruits of their labor.

Neither stockholders nor workers, however, have a right to insist on levels of income obtained through inflationary prices that deny to other citizens their full and proper equity in the national product.

In today's inflationary context, this means, in our judgment, that you must accept your responsibility to resist pressure to increase car prices and we must accept our corresponding responsibility to do what we can to facilitate your resistance to such pressure.

But we do not believe that our joint responsibility ends with mere resistance to further price increases in the auto industry. The inflationary crisis presents a challenge to leadership. Our industry is in a uniquely favorable position to provide such leadership in reversing the inflationary trend.

We, therefore, propose that, instead of giving another whirl to the inflationary spiral, the auto industry bring the full weight of its great influence to bear on the side of lower prices. We of the UAW are prepared to make our full contribution toward facilitating such action by your corporation and the other leading companies in the industry.

But we cannot make that contribution without the cooperation of corporations such as yours. The UAW has no power to set prices in the automotive industry. Price decisions are in the exclusive hands of management and are jealously guarded as "management prorogatives." Under these circumstances, there are obvious limits to what we can do as a union to combat inflation.

Recognizing the increasing seriousness of the current inflationary situation, we are prepared to go even further now if we can obtain your corporation's cooperation with respect to prices.

As you know, we are now in process of preparing for 1958 negotiations with your corporation and other leading auto producers. This coming January, 3,000 delegates, representing our local unions throughout the United States and Canada, will meet in special convention to formulate the demands we will present when negotiations begin. Those of us who share in the leadership of the UAW will have the responsibility of drafting recommendations to that special convention.

We would, in any event, avoid making recommendations that would necessitate price increases. We offer now to draft recommendations that will facilitate price decreases if you will agree to put a substantial price reduction into effect when you introduce your new 1958 models.

Specifically we propose:

1. That your corporation and other leading auto producers reduce prices on 1958 models to levels averaging at least $100 below the prices for comparable 1957 models.

2. That, if you do put such price reductions into effect, we for our part will give full consideration to the effect of such reductions on your corporation's financial position in the drafting of our 1958 demands and in our negotiations.

Your are doubtless aware that the second part of this proposal is self-enforcing. It is an old maxim in collective bargaining that "you cannot wring water from a stone." If price reductions should have any adverse effect upon the industry's financial position, we would have no alternative but to take that fact into account in our negotiations.

Nevertheless, we are prepared to give further assurance that our bargaining will be conducted within the framework of the economic conditions resulting from a price reduction of $100 per car.

If, in the course of negotiations, a question should arise as to whether the granting of our demands would necessitate a restoration of part or all of the $100 per car price reduction, we would be willing to submit that question to impartial review and to be guided in further negotiations by the results of such review.

In our opinion, however, it is most unlikely that any necessity would arise for invoking the public review procedure. The very availability of such a procedure for an objective determination of the facts would serve, in itself, to give factual considerations great weight in our face-to-face negotiations and to avoid needless argument and controversy concerning the facts. Besides, we are confident that a $100 per car price reduction put into effect by your corporation would create a wholly new atmosphere for negotiations in which joint concern for the public interest would be paramount and would foster a cooperative effort to reach a fair and honorable settlement based upon the facts.

Even more important, however, is the effect such dramatic price action would have on the general economic climate. Corporations in other industries now tempted to raise prices would be under strong public pressure to exercise restraint. We are confident that many would follow leadership furnished by the automotive industry in lowering prices. Free management and free labor would have provided a graphic demonstration of their ability to act jointly and unselfishly in the public interest.

The leading automobile corporations are in a singularly advantageous position to assume leadership in reversing the inflationary trend. Despite a decline in their passenger car production of 19 per cent from the 1955 peak, rates of return on investment of the three corporations controlling over 97 per cent of U.S. car production are far above the average for manufacturing corporations generally. Present profit margins therefore provide ample room for substantial price reductions. Such price reductions, in all probability, would mean greatly increased unit sales. Because of the great importance of overhead costs in car production, a significant increase in unit sales would offset substantially or even wholly the effect of reduced prices on profits. It goes without saying that increased unit sales would also make an important contribution to the general welfare by reducing unemployment and underemployment not only of auto workers but also among workers of the many supplying industries that are now operating considerably below capacity.

There is every reason to believe that prices have a significant effect on car sales, and that reduced prices would markedly increase unit sales. No one is in a better position to speak on this subject than the dealers who are in daily contact with the consumer and see at first hand his reaction to the price tags on cars. Great weight must, therefore, be given to the remarks recently made by one of the dealers' leading spokesmen, Mr. Carl E. Fribley, past president of the National Automobile Dealers' Association, who said:

> "As long ago as September 8, 1956, when I spoke to dealers of Maine, I suggested that increased manufacturing costs of 1957 automobiles should be absorbed by the manufacturers. It was my belief that dealers would be unable and the public unwilling to absorb much higher prices even on the greatly improved 1957 models.
>
> "I further pointed out that while it was the prerogative of manufacturers to price cars at wholesale, dealers throughout America had a tremendous interest and stake in the final pricing. My concluding remarks in Maine stressed the fact that pricing of '57 models could mean the difference between a 6½ to seven-million car year, or a 5½ to six-million car year.
>
> "Today, almost eight months later, I can see nothing that would change these remarks."

Mr. Fribley's estimate of a loss of sales amounting to one million cars because of last year's price increase may be either too high or too low. The accuracy of his figure could be determined only if put to a test by an actual price reduction. But, without question, a substantial decrease in prices would bring a substantial increase in sales.

(It should be noted that a $100 price cut at the wholesale level would actually mean an approximate $140 cut to the consumer at the retail level.)

This means that there would be little risk involved in reducing car prices. Assuming Mr. Fribley's figure is correct, a $100 per car price reduction offset by gains from your corporation's share of a one-million car increase in the industry's sales would leave profits that would still be at enviable levels from the standpoint of most industrialists.

During the first six months of this year, your corporation produced 721,082 cars (21.3 percent of the industry's total) and made profits of $190.7 million before taxes and $89.7 million after taxes, equal to an annual rate of 27.8 percent on investment. Had each of these cars sold for $100 less, profits before taxes would have been $118.6 million. After taxes they would have been $55.8 million, equal to an annual rate of return of 17.3 percent on investment as compared with an average of 12.1 percent for all manufacturing corporations during the latest 12-month period for which data are available.

Based on a $100 per car price reduction, your rate of profit on sales before taxes would have been 6 percent. If we assume now that the same rate of profit on sales were obtained on sale of an additional 106,000 cars (your company's proportionate share for six months of an increase of one million per year for the industry as a whole), the additional profits available based on an estimate average wholesale price of $1,700 per car would amount to $10.7 million, making the total profits for the six-month period $129.3 million before taxes. This would mean an annual rate of return on investment of 40.0 percent before taxes and 19.2 percent after taxes as compared with the average of 12.1 percent for all manufacturing.

The foregoing estimated rates of return, it should be noted, are extremely conservative because they make no allowance whatsoever for the greatly increased profit margins which would result from decreased overhead cost per unit as production increased.

GM LETTER

(The letter to GM was identical to the letter to Chrysler, except for substitution of the following for the corresponding paragraphs above in the Chrysler letter:)

During the first six months of this year, your corporation produced 1,543,323 cars (45.7 percent of the industry's total) and made profits of $997 million before taxes and $481 million after taxes, equal to an annual rate of 21.0 percent on investment. Had each of these cars sold for $100 less, profits before taxes would have been $843 million. After taxes they would have been $406 million, equal to an annual rate of return of 17.7 percent on investment as compared with an average of 12.1 percent for all manufacturing corporations during the latest 12-month period for which data are available.

Based on a $100 per car price reduction, your rate of profit on sales before taxes would have been 14.6 per cent. If we assume now that the same rate of profit on sales were obtained on sale of an additional 228,000 cars (your company's proportionate share for six months of an increase of one million per year for the industry as a whole), the additional profits available based on an estimated average price of $1,700 per car would amount to $56.9 million, making the total profits for the six-month period $899.9-million before taxes. This would mean an annual rate of return on investment of 39.3 percent before taxes and 18.9 percent after taxes as compared with the average of 12.1 percent for all manufacturing.

FORD LETTER

(The letter to Ford was identical to the letter to Chrysler, except for substitution of the following for the corresponding paragraphs above in the Chrysler letter:)

During the first six months of this year, your corporation produced 1,015,311 cars (30.1 percent of the industry's total) and made profits of $365.4 million before taxes and $171.0 million after taxes, equal to an annual rate of 17.2 percent on investment. Had each of these cars sold for $100 less, profits before taxes would have been $263.9 million. After taxes they would have been $126.7 million, equal to an annual rate of return of 12.8 percent on investment as compared with an average of 12.1 percent for all manufacturing corporations during the latest 12-month period for which data are available.

Based on a $100 per car price reduction, your rate of profit on sales before taxes would have been 9.1 percent. If we assume now that the same rate of profit on sales were obtained on sale of an additional 150,000 cars (your company's proportionate share for six months of an increase of one million per year for the industry as a whole), the additional profits available based on an estimated average wholesale price of $1,700 per car would amount to $23 million, making the total profits for the six-month period $286.9 million before taxes. This would mean an annual rate of return on investment of 28.9 percent before taxes and 13.9 percent after taxes as compared with the average of 12.1 percent for all manufacturing.

The paramount issue for present purposes, however, is not the degree to which your corporation's profits would be affected if car prices were reduced.

Neither is the paramount issue the degree to which our members could look forward to progress toward their legitimate aspirations in next year's negotiations if you reduce car prices.

Transcending both by far are the interests of the American people as a whole in a stable price level. For that reason, we are confident our members will be willing to take the consequences in collective bargaining if the price reductions we propose should make it impossible to meet all of their just demands and still maintain a reasonable rate of profit.

In other words, we are not asking you to take any risk that we are not prepared to share.

We urge you with all the emphasis at our command to join with us in this undertaking. Clearly the current inflationary trend cannot be permitted to continue indefinitely. Unless free labor and free management voluntarily take effective steps to halt it, and soon, the inflationary spiral will be stopped either by the onset of recession or by the intervention of government acting on behalf of a justifiably aroused people.

The time has come — in fact it is long overdue — for a dramatic and electrifying step to prove to all concerned that democracy is capable of mobilizing on a voluntary basis the resources of wisdom and responsibility in management and labor needed to solve its economic problems.

Free labor and free management in the automobile industry have the opportunity to a greater degree than in most other industries to provide such a demonstration of the potentialities of voluntary action by free men. If we make full use of that opportunity, the constructive effects of our action will be felt throughout the entire economy. Men and women everywhere will at last begin to have hope of ending the inflation that threatens their living standards and their security.

With this opportunity goes a heavy responsibility. We must not fail to take full advantage of the possibilities within our power to make a major contribution toward arresting and reversing the inflationary trend. We are prepared to do our part. We sincerely hope you will do your part in a joint effort that is in our common interest because it is in the interest of the nation as a whole.

Should you wish any clarification or elaboration of this proposal, we shall be glad to meet with you to discuss in in full detail.

We urge your prompt and sympathetic consideration.

Sincerely yours,

WALTER P. REUTHER, President
International Union. UAW

(a) The average price of a passenger automobile in 1957 was approximately two-thousand five-hundred dollars. What then was the coefficient of price elasticity of demand implied in Mr. Fribley's figures?

(b) Search for one or more other measurements of price elasticity for automobiles. How does Mr. Fribley's implied measurement compare with the other figure(s)?

(c) What other factors besides price affect the demand for automobiles?

(d) How does the rate of return on investment for the auto industry quoted by the UAW compare with the rate of return shown in Table 4-3 on page 110?

(e) Do you see any weakness(es) in the UAW's computation of the return on investment?

SELECTED READINGS

Clower, Robert W., and John F. Due. *Microeconomics.* Homewood, Ill.: Richard D. Irwin, Inc., 1972.

Cole, Charles L. *Microeconomics: A Contemporary Approach.* New York: Harcourt Brace Jovanovich, Inc., 1973.

Dooley, Peter C. *Elementary Price Theory,* 2nd ed. New York: Appleton-Century-Crofts, 1973.

Hirshleifer, Jack. *Price Theory and Applications.* Englewood Cliffs, N.J.: Prentice-Hall, Inc. 1976.

Lancaster, Kelvin. *Introduction to Modern Microeconomics.* Chicago: Rand McNally & Company, 1974.

Leftwich, Richard H. *The Price System and Resource Allocation.* New York: Holt, Rinehart & Winston, Inc., 1973.

Mansfield Edwin, *Microeconomics,* 2nd ed. New York: W.W. Norton & Company, Inc., 1975.

Maxwell, W. David. *Price Theory and Application in Business Administration.* Pacific Palisades, Calif.: Goodyear Publishing Company, Inc., 1970.

Stigler, George J., and James K. Kindahl. *The Behavior of Industrial Prices.* New York: National Bureau of Economic Research, Inc., 1970.

Thompson, Arthur A., Jr. *Economics of the Firm: Theory and Practice.* Englewood Cliffs, N.J.: Prentice-Hall, Inc. 1973.

Trescott, Paul B. *The Logic of the Price System.* New York: McGraw-Hill Book Company, Inc. 1970.

Watson, Donald S. *Price Theory and Its Uses.* Boston: Houghton Mifflin Company, 1973.

5

Business Fluctuations and Economic Indicators

Business fluctuations affect the production, sales, profits, and employment of industries and firms and the welfare of individuals. Fluctuation of consumer income will affect the sales and profit of some firms more than others. A recession or prosperity can affect various firms in different ways. Since business cycles affect entire industries, individual firms, and personal welfare, a business person should know something about business cycles in order to render wise managerial decisions. One can make even better managerial decisions if one can correctly anticipate the upswings and downswings of business fluctuations. The most prudent decisions can be made if the manager or executive knows, in addition, the effect that national monetary and fiscal measures used to stabilize the economy will have on the firm.

A *business cycle* is often defined as a cumulative upswing of production, employment, income, prices, and other business activity that is followed by a cumulative downswing. Business cycles are sometime described as fluctuations around a norm, the norm being the average economic growth line of the economy.

CHANGES IN BUSINESS ACTIVITY

In the analysis of economic activity, four types of business changes or fluctuations can be distinguished:

Trend

The *trend* is the general directional movement upward, downward, or sidewise in economic activity over an extended period of time. Trends may also be calculated for various sectors of the economy. A trend upward, downward, or sidewise can be calculated also for any industry or an individual.

Seasonal Fluctuations

Seasonal fluctuations are periodically recurring variations in business activity during a given period, usually one year. The cause of a seasonal fluctuation may be natural or conventional. We produce more farm commodities, for example, in summer than in winter. Thus, changes in agricultural production and employment are brought about by a natural cause: the weather. Similar variations in production occur in the construction industry, in coal mining, and in the manufacture of bathing suits, galoshes, and snow tires. Our custom of presenting gifts at Christmas leads to an increase in department-store sales in November and December. This fluctuation is caused by an artificial, or conventional, force.

Managers need to know how much seasonal fluctuations affect sales and production of the firm. Otherwise, they may be misled by such changes. By constructing and using a seasonal index, sales and production figures, for example, can be adjusted to expunge the seasonal factor and make the data for different months and different years more comparable.

Random Fluctuations

Random or *irregular fluctuations* are changes in business activity resulting from some unexpected or unusual event. Such factors as pestilence, a serious flood, or inclement weather can seriously affect the economy of certain regions of the nation. Wars, currency devaluation, a rapid increase in population, material or energy shortages, changes in the tax laws, the imposition of price controls, or the passage of certain types of legislation can affect the economy as a whole. For example, the cyclones in India in 1971 caused a serious decline in the level of business activity in that nation. Production of war materials stimulated the American economy during the war in Vietnam. Floods in the eastern United States in the spring of 1972 seriously impaired the production of some firms in that area; devaluation of the dollar in 1972 and 1973 affected firms in different ways, and the petroleum shortages of 1974 had a pronounced effect on the United States economy and its various industries.

Cyclical Fluctuations

Cyclical fluctuations are recurring fluctuations in the level of business activity that would come about even though there were no seasonal, irregular, or other forces. Cycles are caused by forces inherent in the economy itself. The economy operates in a pattern that tends to accelerate at times, but in so doing, builds up the forces that eventually bring about a deceleration or decline in business activity.

TYPES OF BUSINESS CYCLES

The American economy has experienced numerous business cycles in the past two hundred years. Some of these cycles have been severe, others mild. Some cycles have been long, others short. Some firms are affected more than others by the length and depth of a business cycle. Business fluctuations are usually categorized as major cycles, minor cycles, and long-wave cycles.

Major Cycles

Major cycles are those that show a wide oscillation of business activity. They are especially characterized by serious depressions. According to Wesley G. Mitchell, serious economic depressions occurred in the United States in 1812, 1818, 1825, 1837, 1847, 1857, 1873, 1884, 1890, 1893, 1903, 1907, 1910, 1913, and 1920.[1] Another noted business cycle analyst, Alvin Hansen, who supports this conviction, points out that there were seven major cycles between 1870 and 1937.[2] Since World War II, however, the occurrence of major cycles has been neither as frequent nor as severe. Certainly they have not disappeared. The 1974–75 depression, for example, was the longest and most severe since the Great Depression of the 1930s.

Minor Cycles

Minor cycles are business cycles of relatively mild intensity in which the fluctuations are noticeable but not severe. They are characterized primarily by a minor downward movement. We have had numerous minor cycles in the past. Since World War II minor cycles have occurred in 1949, 1953–54, 1957–58, 1960–61, and 1970 plus mini-recession in 1967.[3] There is evidence that a minor cycle occurs on the average of every four or five years. Some of the post-World War II minor cycles might have developed into more severe, if not major, depressions were it not for the use of expansionary economic measures by the government.[4]

Long-wave Cycles

Studies by American and European economists reveal the presence of *long-wave cycles* (or *fluctuations*) in economic activities. These cycles last fifty to sixty years. The upswing period of the long-range

[1] Wesley C. Mitchell, *Business Cycles and Unemployment* (New York: McGraw-Hill Book Company, Inc., 1928).

[2] Alvin Hansen, *Business Cycles and National Income* (New York: W.W. Norton & Company, Inc., 1951), p. 24.

[3] Some analysts, including the authors, would classify 1974-75 as a major cycle.

[4] See Philip A. Klein, *Business Cycles in the Postwar World* (Washington, D.C.: American Enterprise Institute for Public Policy Research, 1976) for further discussion of recent business cycles.

cycle, for example, may very well contain several minor and even major cycles. Thus, it is possible to experience a short-run decline in economic activity during a long-run expansion period, just as it is possible to have short-run expansion during a long-run contraction period.

MEASURING BUSINESS FLUCTUATIONS

It is sometimes difficult to distinguish the effect of cyclical fluctuations from the impact of other types of economic change, such as the trend, the seasonal, and the random. Changes in the level of business activity, or of production, employment, income, and prices, may be brought about by any one or any combination of forces. In looking at the total economy, the GNP, for example, is the product of the trend, seasonal, cyclical, and random factors. In order to determine to what extent a change in business activity is the result of a cyclical fluctuation, we must isolate the cyclical force. This is generally done through a process of elimination.

The original data are made up of the trend, multiplied by the seasonal variation, multiplied by the cyclical fluctuation, multiplied by random forces. In formula this appears as $Y = TSCR$, in which Y equals the original data, T is the value of the trend, S is the value of the seasonal variation, C is the value of cyclical fluctuation, and R is the value of the random forces. We then calculate the trend and the seasonal values and divide these values into the original data. The residual represents CR. Since there is no completely satisfactory statistical method of measuring the random force, the cyclical element will usually include some influence of the random forces. Let us, following this process through, using a hypothetical chart showing the level of business activity over a period of time.

Adjustment for Seasonal Fluctuation

In Figure 5–1, the original data, or Y values, shown by the sawtooth line, represents $TSCR$ at any point. Let us select point A on the line and assume that we are at that particular level of business activity because of the four forces at work. In order to determine the cyclical effect, let us first deseasonalize the data. This is done by dividing $TSCR$ by S, a seasonal index, and our data then become

$$\frac{TSCR}{S} = TCR$$

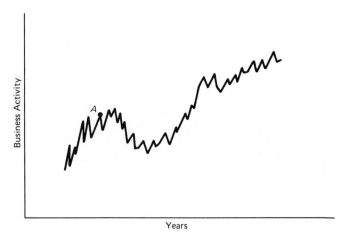

Figure 5-1. Business Activity — Original Data

A seasonal index can be constructed, as you learned in your course in business or economic statistics, by computing the value of the original data for each month. The value for each month is then divided by the average monthly value for the year. The result expresses the value of each month as a percentage of the average monthly value. If these specific monthly values are computed for a number of years, the average or typical percentage values for each month can be obtained. These values then make up the seasonal index.[5]

A *seasonal index* is a series of relative comparisons of typical data for each month compared with the average monthly data, that is, the total annual data divided by 12 months. Therefore, if the seasonal index for February were 80, it would mean that data for that month were typically 20 percent below the monthly average. If the index for November were 150, it would mean that activity in that month was usually 50 percent greater than the monthly average. Thus, if sales for a specific commodity were $700 million in February, they could be adjusted for seasonal variation by dividing $700 by .80, which would mean that, were it not for the seasonal lag, sales would probably be $875 million. Similarly, sales of $1.313 billion in November, if adjusted by the seasonal index of 150, would also equal $875 million. Such a situation could indicate that no net changes had taken place except those resulting from seasonal forces. If, however, sales in November actually were $1.600 billion, and the seasonally adjusted sales were $1.066 billion, one would conclude

[5] This, and other methods for computing a seasonal index, can be found in textbooks on business or economic statistics.

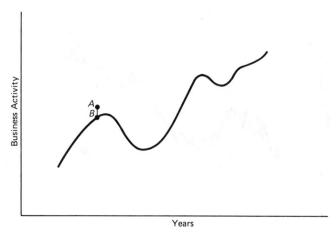

Figure 5-2. Business Activity — Deseasonalized

that a net increase of 22 percent over and above the seasonal fluctuation had taken place. The 22 percent increase could be the result of the cyclical factor or the random factor, or both. After adjusting our original sawtooth line in Figure 5-1 for seasonal variation, it would appear as shown in Figure 5-2.

In this figure, the difference between point A on the original line and point B on the deseasonalized line represents the difference in activity due to seasonal fluctuation.

Any manager who does not know whether his firm's sales are affected by seasonal variation, and the extent to which they may be affected, is missing a good tool of business analysis. Without this knowledge, a manager may easily have misconceptions about sales, prices, and profits of the firm.

Adjustment for the Trend

The elimination of the trend from the original data is our next step. By eliminating T from our TCR factors, we arrive at

$$\frac{TCR}{T} = CR$$

To do this, a trend line must be computed. This can be accomplished by any one of several methods that attempt to average out the fluctuations, that is, by averaging the highs against the lows. To compute a trend line, one may use a moving average, a measure of

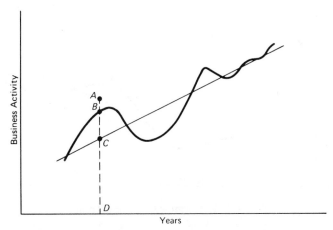

Figure 5-3. Business Activity — Trend

"least squares," or the unsophisticated "eyeball" method.[6] If the trend line is accurate, the deviation of the actual data from the trend line will be at a minimum. In short, if we have a perfect trend line, the average deviation from this line will equal zero. The trend line will also represent the average growth or decline in business activity. Therefore, it often becomes the norm for economic or business activity. A trend line for our data would appear as shown in Figure 5-3.

Residual Equals Business Cycle

In this figure, the ordinate of the trend is at point C. The total value of the trend at this point is represented by the difference between C and D. At B we were ahead of the average level of business activity for that period. The difference between A and B, you will recall, represents the seasonal variation.

The difference between point C on the trend line and point B on the curved line represents the cyclical fluctuation. It should now be apparent why business cycles are often described as fluctuations above and below a norm, the norm being the trend line of business activity. The cycle is measured in deviations from this trend line. These deviations may be measured in absolute or in relative terms.

---

[6] Probably the most used is the "least squares" formula, which can be found in any basic textbook in business statistics. It reads:

$$YC = a + b\,(x)$$

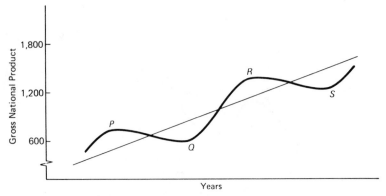

Figure 5-4. Business Cycle and Trend

For example, at point P in Figure 5-4, it can be seen that the economy is operating at $780 billion, or $180 billion above the trend line; at point S it is below the trend.

For comparison, it is sometimes better to measure the relative deviations. This can be done by dividing the trend line value into the deseasonalized data for a corresponding period. For example, let us measure four positions on the chart. Assume that at point P the economy was at a level 30 percent (180 ÷ 600) greater than the trend; at point Q it was 20 percent (180 ÷ 900) below normal; at point R it was 20 percent (240 ÷ 1200) above normal; and at point S it was 10 percent (150 ÷ 1500) below the trend line.

Frequently, business cycles are depicted as fluctuations around a norm, with the trend line used as the norm. The norm is represented as a straight horizontal line, and the value of the cycle is given in percentage figures above or below the norm as shown in Figure 5-5.

This type of chart makes it easy to determine at a glance the percentage of business activity above or below the trend. It can be very misleading, however, to someone who does not understand the makeup of the chart. For example, some readers looking at such a chart are likely to get the impression that business activity was higher at point P than it was at point S. The truth of the matter is that business activity was at a higher absolute level at point S. Relative to the norm, however, point S was at a lower level. It is important to remember that the norm represents different absolute amounts at various periods. The value of the norm at point P is $600 billion, its value at point S is $1,500 billion.

Figure 5-6 shows a practical application of the foregoing approach to measuring business activity. The first part depicts the actual GNP

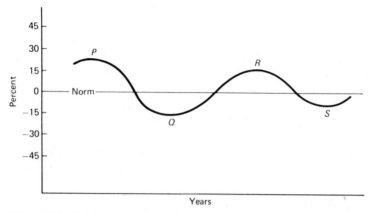

Figure 5-5. Business Cycles as Measured in Percentage Deviation from the Trend

with a trend line constructed through it. The lower part of the chart shows the trend line as the norm, with percentage deviations above and below the trend.

The trend line may also be represented as an index number trend. In such case the trend line represents average percentage growth or business or economic activity.

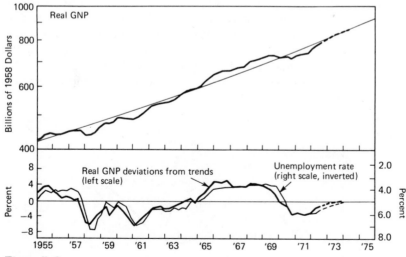

Figure 5-6.

Source: *The Morgan Guaranty Survey*, December 1, 1972.

CHARACTERISTICS OF THE BUSINESS CYCLE

Early observations led to the theory that the economy periodically suffered from "crises." It was suggested that business activity proceeded at some normal pace for a considerable period of time and then experienced a sharp decline from which a recovery to normal was made, only to be followed by another crisis later. Further study and analysis soon proved that a crisis was not an isolated phenomenon but an integral part of a dynamic cyclical movement. Eventually it was realized that the economy experienced periods of expansion as well as contraction.

Phases of the Cycle

Today the business cycle is considered to have four distinct phases: prosperity, recession, depression, and recovery. *Prosperity* exists whenever there is an overall high level of economic or business activity, although it is not necessary that full employment exist. A *recession* occurs whenever there is a noticeable widespread decline in the level of business activity. *Depression* is a period in which the overall level of economic activity has dropped to its lowest ebb during one cycle. *Recovery* occurs when the level of business activity begins to rise. The duration or intensity of any of the four phases has little to do with their definitions; that is, a business cycle consists of a series of changes that includes all four phases, whether the degree of change is as great as we experienced in the 1930s, or as slight as we experienced in 1970. The four phases of the business cycle are shown in Figure 5-7. It has become customary, however, for many lay persons and even business analysts to refer to a mild depression, such as the economy experienced in 1960 and 1970, as an economic or business *recession*.

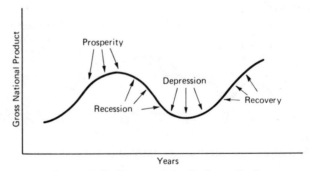

Figure 5-7. Phases of the Business Cycle

Duration and Intensity of Cycles

There is no definite duration or degree of oscillation for the cycle since the variations in the length and intensity of cycles from the average are very pronounced. There have been many cycles of greater, and many of less, duration than the four-to-five-year average. The degree of intensity also varies. Since the end of World War II, for example, we have had six recessions or depressions: those of 1949, 1954, 1958, 1960, 1970, and 1974–75.

Recently, however, it has become customary to avoid the term *depression* and refer to a mild depression as a *recession*. This practice is supported by the National Bureau of Economic Research (NBER), a prime compiler and analyzer of business cycle data. In response to the question of whether a recession did occur in early 1967, the NBER defined a *recession* as a period in which the real GNP declines in two consecutive quarters. Thus 1967 was not officially a recession, since the GNP declined in only one quarter. Some analysts, however, refer to 1967 as a "mini-recession." In the spring of 1971, however, the NBER labeled 1970 as a recession year.

The NBER definition clarifies the designation as a recession. It also allows one to refer to any drop in economic activity of two or more consecutive quarters as a recession. The NBER definition, however, still leaves us without a specific definition of a depression. Consequently, there has been much discussion and controversy whether the five-consecutive-quarter GNP decline of 1974–75, the longest and deepest since the 1930s, was a recession or a depression. In the absence of a quantitative definition of a depression, some business cycle analysts suggest that a depression occurs when double-digit unemployment exists. If we accept this definition, then 1974–75 came close to being a depression period. It is, however, still inconclusive. Although national unemployment reached 9.2 percent at one point in the 1974–75 period, it averaged 8.5 percent in 1975. During that same period, however, unemployment in many cities and in some states exceeded 10 percent. Does this mean the national economy experienced a recession, but that a depression existed in many sectors within the economy?

Some attempts have been made to ascertain the average length of each phase of the cycle, but any such measures are very subjective. There is no clear line of demarcation, for example, between a recession and a depression. Precisely when does the economy finish a recession and enter a depression? At what point does a recovery begin? When does the recovery develop into prosperity? Various analysts answer these questions differently. Nevertheless, available studies do indicate that recovery and recessionary periods are relatively short, and that periods of prosperity last longer than depressions.

One suggestion that, if adopted widely, would give more uniformity to the measure of business cycles comes from the NBER. It suggests that the period from the trend line up the peak of the cycle be labeled prosperity; the period from the peak back to the trend line, recession; from the trend line down to the trough of the cycle, depression; and the period from the bottom of the trough back up to the trend line, recovery (Figure 5–8).

One problem with this suggestion, as with most measures of business fluctuations, is that an analyst can seldom pinpoint the peak or trough of a business cycle until it has been passed. This is owing to the lag in data for the indicators. It is usually several weeks, and sometimes months, before data for a particular date become available. For example, NBER did not officially label 1970 as a depression (recession) year until April 1971, when it had all the necessary quantitative data to reinforce its prognosis.

The amplitude of business fluctuations is less difficult to measure. But even here, various studies indicate different degrees of variation in economic activity. Then, too, it depends on what the analyst is measuring. Capital goods production, for example, fluctuates more intensely than that of consumer goods, and the sale of durable consumer goods has a greater degree of oscillation than that of nondurable consumer goods. Variations are usually measured from the norm or trend line, and various analysts calculate the trend differently. Consequently, the measures of amplitude of any fluctuation will differ. Nevertheless, some notion of the amplitude of business

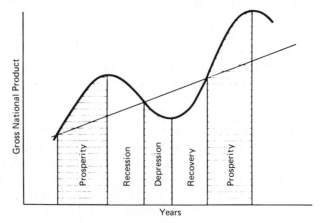

Figure 5–8.

TABLE 5-1. Amplitude of Fluctuations
(1923-1975)

Peaks		Troughs	
Years	Deviation from Normal	Years	Deviation from Normal
1923	+ 16	1924	− 3
1926	+ 13	1927	+ 1
1929	+ 20	1932	− 51
1937	+ 5	1938	− 38
1943	+ 50	1946	− 15
1948	+ 5	1949	− 10
1953	+ 18	1954	− 3
1957	+ 9	1958	− 10
1960	+ 7	1961	− 5
1968	+ 28	1970	+ 18
1973	+ 37	1975	+ 15

Source: *American Business Activity Since 1790* (Cleveland, Ohio: The Cleveland Trust Co., April 1976).

cycles can be obtained from Table 5-1, which shows a range from a +50 to a −51.

Actual vs. Potential GNP

Another way of observing the importance of business cycles is by measuring the differences between actual and potential GNP, as shown in Figure 5-9. The size of the production gap can, in turn, be related to the amount of unemployment in the economy. Moreover, at any time it can be determined how much total production must be increased to reach potential GNP and eliminate excess unemployment. From other, more historical data, shown in Table 5-2, it can be observed also that we do not necessarily reach full employment with each prosperity period. Sometimes, we crest the cycle without attaining our full potential of production and employment. In Table 5-2, benchmark employment is that employment consistent with the concept of full employment.

INDEXES OF ECONOMIC AND BUSINESS ACTIVITY

Since there are many facets to economic and business activity, there are likewise many records. Some of these statistical records are meaningful because they give a clear reflection of the general level of

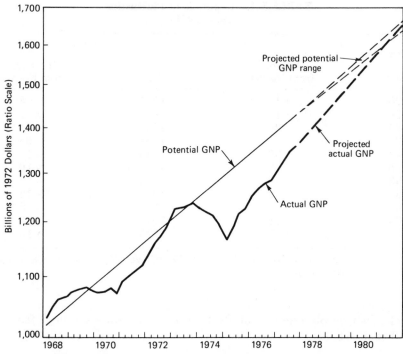

Figure 5-9. Actual and Potential Gross National Product
Source: Economic Report of the President, 1978.

economic activity. Others may accurately reveal changes occurring in a specific aspect of economic activity or in a particular industry but give little indication of what is happening to the general level of production, employment, and income. Some analysts meld several types of business activity into one general indicator in an effort to measure changes in the economy as a whole. For purposes of analyzing business cycles, statistical indexes are usually divided into three broad categories: representative indicators, composite indicators, and general business indicators.

Representative Indicators

Representative indicators are indexes that measure particular aspects of business activity but, at the same time, tend to reflect what is happening to the economy in general. They usually measure a basic type of business activity that is an essential part of the economy. Consequently there is a close correlation between fluctuations in the particular activity and changes in the total economy. The list of these

TABLE 5-2. Potential Gross National Product and Benchmark
Unemployment Rate, 1952-77
[Billions of 1972 dollars, except as noted]

Year	Potential GNP	Actual GNP	GNP gap (potential less actual)	Benchmark Unemployment Rate (percent)
1952	584.9	598.5	- 13.6	4.0
1953	608.2	621.8	- 13.6	4.0
1954	629.7	613.7	16.0	4.0
1955	651.4	654.8	- 3.4	4.0
1956	673.9	668.8	5.1	4.0
1957	697.2	680.9	16.3	4.0
1958	721.3	679.5	41.8	4.0
1959	746.2	720.4	25.8	4.1
1960	771.9	736.8	35.1	4.1
1961	798.6	755.3	43.3	4.1
1962	826.4	799.1	27.3	4.1
1963	857.1	830.7	26.4	4.2
1964	890.3	874.4	15.9	4.3
1965	925.0	925.9	- .9	4.4
1966	960.8	981.0	- 20.2	4.5
1967	996.3	1,007.7	- 11.4	[1] 4.4
1968	1,031.7	1,051.8	- 20.1	4.4
1969	1,068.3	1,078.8	- 10.5	4.4
1970	1,106.2	1,075.3	30.9	4.5
1971	1,145.5	1,107.5	38.0	4.6
1972	1,186.1	1,171.1	15.0	4.7
1973	1,228.2	1,235.0	- 6.8	4.8
1974	1,271.7	1,217.8	53.9	4.8
1975	1,316.9	1,202.1	114.8	4.8
1976	1,363.6	1,274.7	88.9	4.9
1977	1,412.0	[2] 1,337.6	[2] 74.4	4.9

[1] Shift in benchmark unemployment rate from 1966 to 1967 because of 1967 change in sampling procedure in the Current Population Survey.
[2] Preliminary.
Source: Economic Report of the President, 1978.

representative indexes includes iron and steel production, bank clearings, railway carloading, electrical power output, and others.

Index of Iron and Steel Production. Iron and steel are used widely in our economy. If businesses intend to expand their activities, they must have iron and steel for buildings, machinery, equipment, raw material, and the like. Thus, a rise in the output and sale of iron and steel usually indicates a rise in the general level of business activity. Likewise, a decrease in the output of iron and steel production indicates a slow down of business activity. During the peak prosperity period of the mid-1960s, for example, iron and steel production was close to 90 percent of capacity. In 1970, however, average production dropped below 75 percent of capacity. During this period the GNP dropped noticeably and unemployment reached 6 percent. In the prosperity years of 1973 and early 1974, iron and steel production was at record levels. But, it dropped more than 20 percent in the 1974–75 depression period. Changes in the index of iron and steel production often precede slightly changes in the general level of business activity. By watching steel orders and observing movements in the iron and steel index, an expert analyst may be able to forecast changes in the general level of business activity.

Bank Clearings or Bank Debits.   Between 85 and 90 percent of our business transactions is paid for through the use of checks. Naturally, there is a high correlation between the level of business activity and bank clearings or bank debits. Bank debits are considered the better indicator, however, because they record all checks deposited against individual accounts. Bank clearings record only those checks that are processed through the clearinghouses.

To be useful indicators of business activity, of course, bank clearings and debits must be adjusted for price changes. Furthermore, "bank debits ex New York" are usually a more accurate measure. Since many purely financial transactions take place in the New York money market, banks there often engage in activities that have little effect on the general level of economic activity. Consequently, a better measure of economic activity is attained by using an index that excludes data concerning New York.

Railway Carloadings.   The more we produce, the more we transport. Today, the railroad is still a principal means of transporting commodities. Therefore, there is a good relationship between carloadings and the level of business activity. Other transportation indexes are available, such as trucking, air freight, and waterways. Although railway carloadings has been used for decades as an indicator, this transportation index has some noticeable defects. For one thing, it primarily measures the movement of heavy commodities. Also, the increase in truck and airline transportation is gradually rising, compared with that of rail transportation. Nevertheless, the large declines in carloadings in the 1974–75, 1970, and previous recessions corresponded to the declines in the general level of economic activity.

Electric Power Output.   Electricity is a major source of industrial power. Thus, it is a fairly good indicator of the general level of economic activity. It does however, tend to emphasize industry activity and neglect trade, transportation, finance, agriculture, and other activities in which there is not a close relationship with the use of electric energy. From another point of view, the electrical energy shortages that occurred in several parts of the nation during the 100-plus days of the coal miners' strike in early 1978 had an adverse effect on the general level of business activity.

Other Representative Indicators.   Many other indexes of particular business activities have been used as reflectors of the general level of business activity. These include production of paperboard, integral to packaging, and of bituminous coal, widely used in the generation of industrial power. Although at times, such as the prosperity of 1971–73 and the depression of 1974–75, the relationship between automobile production and the level of business activity was good, it is some times erratic. Still other indexes, including construction, manufacturers' unfilled orders, profits, wholesale prices, agricultural output, business failures, job-vacancy ads, and stock market prices, have been suggested as representative indicators but each has some defect when used by itself. In 1977, for example, the economy expanded vigorously but the Dow Jones stock average declined steadily.

Composite Indicators

Composite indicators are those that measure several aspects of business activity. These indexes also take in a wide sphere of economic activity. As a result, they are fairly reliable business-cycle indicators. Several of these indexes have been used over recent years. Three are outstanding: industrial production, the gross national product, and manufacturing capacity utilization rate.

Federal Reserve Board Index of Industrial Production.   Although there are several indexes of industrial production, Federal Reserve Board's Index of Industrial Production is the most commonly used. It is based on a broad sampling of manufacturing and mining establishments. Although it covers nearly one-fourth of all workers in manufacturing and mining, it does not include those in agriculture and construction. Furthermore, services are excluded entirely. The makeup of this index is rather complex. It is, however, a good indicator of the level of business and reflects clearly changes in the economy's activity. Because industrial goods production fluctuates more intensely than nonmanufactured goods and services, however, the Federal Reserve index tends to exaggerate changes in total business activity. Note in Figure 5–10(a) that the durable segment of the manufacturing index fluctuates more widely than does the nondur-

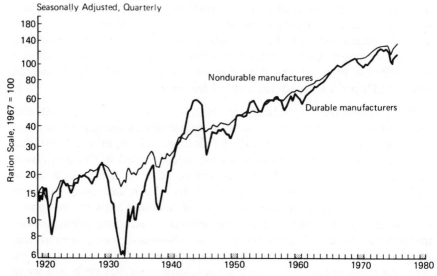

Figure 5-10(a). Federal Reserve Index of Industrial Production for Manufacturing
Source: *Federal Reserve Chart Book*, 1976.

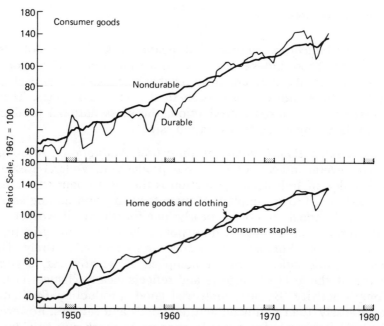

Figure 5-10(b). Federal Reserve Index of Industrial Production (1950-75)
Source: *Federal Reserve Chart Book*, 1977.

able element. The same relationship holds true for durable and nondurable consumer goods production. This is shown in Figure 5-10(b). During the 1970 recession, the Federal Reserve Index fell four percentage points to 106.6 (1967=100). It rose to 125.8 in 1973 but fell in the depression of 1974-75 to as low as 110.1. It was back to 130.1 in June 1976, and rose to 138 by mid-1977, as shown in Table 5-2.

Gross National Production. Since the GNP measures almost all facets of production — manufacturing and nonmanufacturing goods, durable and nondurable goods, and services — it is the best available indicator of the general level of economic activity. It includes economic activities of practically every individual, firm, and industry in the economy as well as that of the various government sectors. It weighs each segment of the economy according to its actual production contribution. Changes in the real, or constant-dollar, GNP indicate fluctuations in business activity more accurately than do changes in the current-dollar GNP.

Related GNP data, such as national income, personal income, or disposable personal income, can also be utilized as economic indicators. Furthermore, it is possible to analyze various segments of the GNP, such as consumption, investment, and government; it also is possible with GNP data to measure fluctuations in different industrial sectors of the economy, such as those in durable goods, agriculture, and services.

In addition, one can use the Federal Reserve flow-of-funds data and the Department of Commerce input-output tables with certain reservations to measure changes in business activity.

Capacity Utilization Rates. A third type of composite index is one that measures manufacturing capacity utilization rates. There are three widely used indexes in this category. One is the Federal Reserve series maintained by the Federal Reserve Board of Governors. This series measuring manufacturing capacity utilization is different from the Federal Reserve Index of Industrial Production, which measures actual production. The others are the Commerce Series published by the Department of Commerce, Bureau of Economic Analysis, and the Wharton Series, published by the Wharton School of Finance at the University of Pennsylvania. Table 5-3 shows the movements in each of these series. The values differ because each uses a somewhat different base to represent 100 percent capacity. It is generally felt that on the Federal Reserve Index, the economy does not reach the bottleneck stage until capacity utilization hits about 87 percent. At about that level, the economy is forced into

TABLE 5-3. Industrial Production and Capacity Utilization 1967–77
(Seasonally adjusted)

| Period | Total Industrial Production | | Manufacturing Capacity Utilization Rate, Percent[1] | | | |
| | Index, 1967 = 100 | Percent Change from Year Earlier | Federal Reserve Series | | Commerce Series[2] | Wharton Series[3] |
			Total Manufacturing	Materials		
1967 proportion	*100.00*					
1971	109.6	1.7	78.0	83.1	80	86.4
1972	119.7	9.2	83.1	88.0	83	91.8
1973	129.8	8.4	87.5	92.4	86	97.1
1974	129.3	-.4	84.2	87.7	83	93.0
1975	117.8	-8.9	73.6	73.6	77	80.4
1976	129.8	10.2	80.2	80.4	81	87.5
1977: Jan	132.3	5.1	80.4	79.4		
Feb	133.2	4.4	80.9	80.2		
Mar	135.3	5.4	82.1	81.6	83	88.4
Apr	136.1	5.8	82.3	82.1		
May	137.0	5.6	82.8	82.7		
June	137.8	6.2	83.0	83.0	84	90.3
July	138.8	6.2	83.1	83.0		
Aug	138.2	5.2	82.9	82.6		
Sept	138.8	6.3	82.9	82.8		90.9

[1] Output as percent of capacity.
[2] Annual data are averages of four monthly indexes.
[3] Quarterly data entered in last month of quarter. Annual data are averages of quarterly data.
Source: Economic Indicators, October 1977.

using outmoded and marginal facilities that add to the cost of the operation. At about that stage, too, businesses must add additional capacity and/or replace depreciated and obsolete capacity. Consequently, investment in the economy may receive a boost with any further increase in capacity. Table 5-3 shows that capacity utilization peaked in 1973 and fell substantially in 1974-75. The changes correspond with the peaks and troughs of business cycles.

General Business Indicators

A *general business indicator* is a series of indexes of several different business activities combined into one general index of business activity. There are several such indexes. A few examples will indicate their use.

Index of American Business Activity. This index is compiled and published by the Cleveland Trust Company and uses several different indexes and measurements to cover the period from 1790 until the present. The data are expressed also as deviations from a norm. In this index, the norm is the long-run trend. Although this index displays a very clear picture of the fluctuations in business activity over the entire history of the United States, its major weakness is its dependence on different sub-indexes to cover various years of such a long period of time. The measurement used for some years is not necessarily comparable with those for other periods. Therefore, the comparison of the intensity, or magnitude, of fluctuations in various periods must be made with some reservations. Nevertheless, it is one of the best indicators of its type available, and one of the few indexes that extends back to the eighteenth century.

"Business Week" Index. This index is compiled and published weekly in graphic and tabular form in *Business Week*. It reflects the combined movements of several individual series, including raw steel production, automobiles, electric power, crude oil, paperboard, machinery, other transportation equipment, construction, and railroad carloadings. The movements of the *Business Week* Index are shown in Figure 5-11. The figure makes the depression in the economy in 1974-75 readily apparent.

Statistical Indicators of Business-cycle Changes. These statistical indicators include twenty-six indexes, each measuring a different aspect of economic activity, selected by the National Bureau of Economic Research because of their close correlation with the general level of business activity. The indicators are separated into three major categories designated as *leading*, *coincident*, and *lagging*.

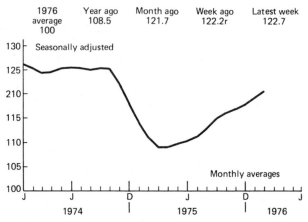

| 1976 average 100 | Year ago 108.5 | Month ago 121.7 | Week ago 122.2r | Latest week 122.7 |

Figure 5-11. *Business Week* Index

Source: Reprinted from the April 19, 1978 issue of *Business Week* by special permission. Copyright © 1978 by McGraw-Hill, Inc., New York, N.Y. 10020. All rights reserved.

The group of leading indicators includes twelve indexes whose turning points, upward and downward, usually precede peaks and troughs in the general level of business activity. The group of coincident indicators consists of eight other indexes whose turning points usually correspond with the peaks and troughs in the general level of business activity. The turning points of the six lagging indicators, of course, occur after the turning points in the general level of business activity.

The current status of these indicators, along with their interpretation and the business outlook is published weekly by Statistical Indicator Associates.

| *Leading Indicators* | *Coincident Indicators* |

Leading Indicators	Coincident Indicators
1. Average Hours Worked	13. Nonagricultural Employment
2. Unemployment Claims	14. Unemployment Rate
3. Net Business Formation	15. GNP (current dollars)
4. Durable Goods Orders	16. GNP (1972 dollars)
5. Plant and Equipment Contracts	17. Industrial Production
6. Housing Permits	18. Personal Income
7. Inventory Changes	19. Manufacturing and Trade Sales
8. Industrial Material Prices	20. Retail Sales
9. Common Stock Prices	
10. Corporate Profits (net)	
11. Price/Labor Cost	
12. Consumer Debt Change	

Data for each of the twenty-six indicators and composite data for each group — leading, coincident, and lagging — are published in tables each week and shown graphically as well. In addition, percentage expanding charts are published every month. These charts are based on simple arithmetic. If nine of the twelve leaders are expanding, the percentage expanding for that group for that month is 75 percent. Figure 5–12a shows that leaders lead and laggers lag. Figure 5–12a clearly shows that leading indicators with definite downward movement preceding both the mini-recession of early 1967 and the recession of 1970. Notice, too, both the downward turning point of the leaders before the 1974–75 depression and the upward turning point preceding the subsequent expansion in the economy occurred prior to the turning points of most coincident and lagging indicators. Figure 5–12b shows the movement of each of the individual leading indicators. Again, note the clear forewarning of a downturn preceding the depression of 1974–75.

"Business Conditions Digest." The Department of Commerce, puts out a monthly publication called *Business Conditons Digest.* This publication contains graphs, charts, and tables for more than one hundred NBER business cycle indicators series. Regularly it plots thirty or more NBER Leading Indicators, several other United States Series with Business Cycle Significance, and a number of International Comparisons of Industrial Production. A complete list of these indicators is shown on pages 161–168. Figure 5–13 shows the movement of six leading indicators from *Business Conditions Digest.* Notice, again, how clearly the indicators reveal the approach of the recessions of 1953–54, 1957–58, 1960–61, 1970, and 1974–75. These series are presented in convenient form for analysis and interpretation by specialists in business-cycle analysis. The Department of Commerce, however, makes no attempt to interpret them or to make business forecasts.

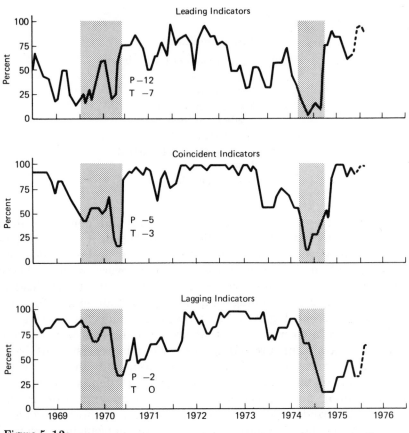

Figure 5-12a.
Source: *Statistical Indicator Reports*, Statistical Indicator Associates, April 21, 1976.

Although many busy executives and managers like to read and use indicators that have interpretations included, it is apparent that the movements of specific indicators will not have the same effect on all firms or industries. Many forecasters and business analysts, consequently, prefer to develop or select a special group of economic and business indicators for their own use and interpretation. In one particular Midwestern group of business economists that meets quarterly to exchange thoughts on the level of business activity and future outlook, there is a representative of a steel producer, an auto manufacturer, a machine tool firm, a commercial bank, the Federal Reserve Bank, an insurance company, a soap and detergent producer, a chemical company, a university, a department store chain, a groc-

Figure 5-12b.
Source *Statistical Indicator Reports*, Statistical Indicator Associates, April 5, 1978.

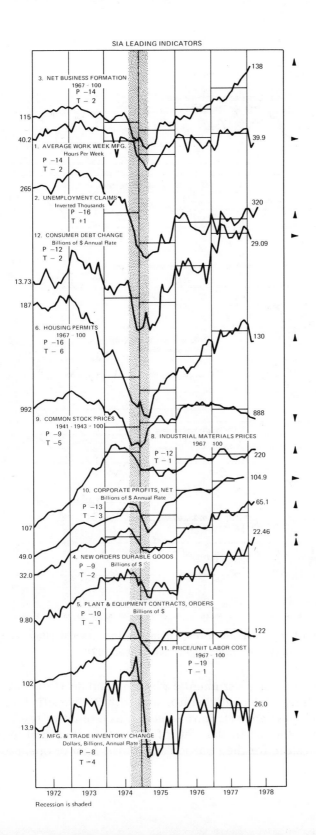

SIA LEADING INDICATORS

3. NET BUSINESS FORMATION
1967 - 100
P −14
T − 2

115

138

40.2

1. AVERAGE WORK WEEK MFG.
Hours Per Week
P −14
T − 2

39.9

265

2. UNEMPLOYMENT CLAIMS
Inverted Thousands
P −16
T +1

320

12. CONSUMER DEBT CHANGE
Billions of $ Annual Rate
P −12
T − 2

29.09

13.73

187

6. HOUSING PERMITS
1967   100
P −16
T − 6

130

992

9. COMMON STOCK PRICES
1941 - 1943 = 100
P −9
T −5

888

8. INDUSTRIAL MATERIALS PRICES
1967   100
P −12
T − 1

220

10. CORPORATE PROFITS, NET
Billions of $ Annual Rate
P −13
T − 3

104.9

65.1

107

22.46

49.0

4. NEW ORDERS DURABLE GOODS
P −9   Billions of $
T −2

32.0

5. PLANT & EQUIPMENT CONTRACTS, ORDERS
Billions of $
P −10
T − 1

9.80

122

11. PRICE/UNIT LABOR COST
1967   100
P −19
T − 1

102

26.0

13.9

7. MFG. & TRADE INVENTORY CHANGE
Dollars, Billions, Annual Rate
P − 8
T −4

1972   1973   1974   1975   1976   1977   1978

Recession is shaded

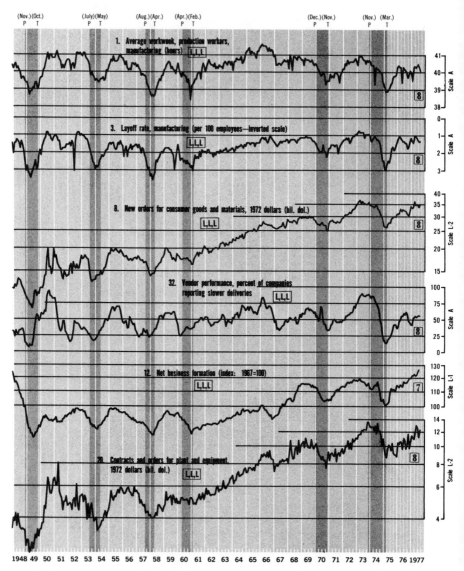

Figure 5-13. Cyclical Indicators, Composite Indexes and Their Components
Source: *Business Conditions Digest,* November 1976.

ery store chain, a governmental planning and development agency, a
public utility, a conglomerate, and other diversified companies.
Several of these analysts have selected, as a result of test and experimentation, the particular set of indicators that best reports the
changes in store for their particular business firm or operation.

SUMMARY

Business activity and profits are affected by changes in economic activity, particularly business cycles. Other changes affecting business profits are trend movements, seasonal fluctuations, and random events. One can use various statistical techniques to adjust raw data on business activity to show the effect of each of these forms of business change. When this is done, it will, for example, show business cycles to be fluctuations above and below the trend line.

A typical business cycle has four phases: prosperity, recession, depression, and recovery. The duration and intensity of business cycles vary, and cyclical fluctuations affect different firms and industries differently. If a manager or executive knows ahead of time when business changes are about to occur, he can make wiser decisions about the operation of the business firm.

There are several indicators of business activity. Among the representative indicators are the indexes of iron and steel production, bank clearings or bank debits, railway carloadings and electrical output. Composite indexes include GNP data, the Federal Reserve Index of Industrial Production and capacity utilization rates. There are also several good general business indicators, such as the Index of American Business Activity and the *Business Week* Index. Lead-lag indicators are a widely used type of index for anticipating changes in business activity. Those published by Statistical Indicator Associates and the Department of Commerce are readily available.

By experimentation and observation a manager may compile his own set of indicators, using those types of other business activities that have the most direct impact on his business.

QUESTIONS FOR ANALYSIS AND DISCUSSION

1. Of what importance is it to a business manager to know the difference be-between a seasonal and cyclical fluctuation?
2. Name some random or irregular forces that have substantially affected the level of business activity on either a regional or a national basis.
3. Do you think it is important to distinguish between a recession and a slow-down in the economy? Why or why not?
4. What advantages do you see in using a chart showing actual versus potential GNP when analyzing the state of the economy?
5. Can you name some other representative indicators besides those mentioned in this chapter?
6. Define a recession.
7. Why should some economic indicators be more susceptible to wider fluctuations than others?

8. What is the current status of the Federal Reserve Board Index of Industrial Production and the industrial capacity utilization rate? Have they been improving in the past six months?

9. What is the advantage to a business manager's following the lead-lag indicators?

10. Knowledge of business indicators is helpful in implementing management measures to offset undesirable fluctuations in business activity. Can you see any way in which knowledge of such indicators may tend to augment business fluctuations?

PROBLEMS AND CASES

1. Check an appropriate source, such as the Department of Commerce *Business Conditions Digest* or the Statistical Indicator Associates *Statistical Indicator Reports* for the current status of the lead-lag indicators. How do they stand in regard to percentage expanding and/or contracting? What is your prediction for the economy for the next six months or year based on the status of the indicators?

2. Is there a production gap, between actual and potential GNP, in the economy at the present time? What is the current level of unemployment? How would you classify the current status of the economy in regard to the phases of the business cycle?

3. Joe Slide and Pete Rule, two young engineers, invent, produce, and market a new hand calculator. Their little shop, with ten employees, is located in an old downtown store that they rent and have converted into a workshop. In addition to performing the usual functions of a small calculator, their Electrometric Calculator can compute measurements in the metric as well as in the regular system and can readily convert from one into the other. Their product, introduced in February, had limited success. Aiming at junior high school, high school, and college markets, they purposely keep the price of the Electrometric at a minimum. After several months of disappointing sales, business picked up dramatically in July, August, and September of 1974, so much so that they had a two-month backlog of orders, although they hired five more employees.

    Being very pleased with their new-found success, Rule enthusiastically suggests to Slide that they borrow $150,000 from the bank to build a new, larger plant in a suburban industrial park and add to their work force. Furthermore, he recommends that the price of the Electromatic be raised and that they borrow another $150,000 to develop a more expensive, deluxe model. Slide is less certain that they should expand capacity, particularly if they must borrow from the bank. Knowing that you are a student of economics and/or business, he asks your advice:

    (a) What would you advise him?

    (b) Point out some of the important factors that should be considered before plant capacity is expanded.

    (c) In what other ways can the partners increase output and sales without having to expand plant capacity?

4. John D. Pull, manager of the window-shade division of a middle-sized manufacturing company, is concerned about the fluctuations in his production

and sales. He complains to you that over the years it has been difficult to keep production, sales, and inventories in balance, because he is unable to tell when sales are going to increase or decrease. Consequently, he frequently finds his department with excessive inventories, but at other times he runs short of inventory. As a result he feels that he is not maximizing his profit. You suggested that he select a series of lead-lag indicators that will reveal to him possible changes that could take place in the sale of window shades. When he states that he does not know anything about such indicators, you volunteer to obtain some information for him.

(a) From the list of indicators contained in the accompanying exhibit pick out what you would consider the four best indicators for Mr. Pull.

(b) Upon hearing what you did for the window-shade department, Mr. Lamp of the office-furniture department asked if you can do the same for him. In his case what indicators would you select?

5. Has the United States economy experienced any recessions since that of 1974-75? If so, was the downswing(s) portended in the economic indicators?

EXHIBIT 1. Cyclical Indicators

Series Title	Timing Classification[3]	Unit of Measure	Average	
			1976	1977
I. CYCLICAL INDICATORS				
A. Composite Indexes				
910. Twelve leading indicators	L,L,L	1967 = 100	124.7	131.1
920. Four coincident indicators	C,C,C	do	122.3	130.1
930. Six lagging indicators	Lg,Lg,Lg	do	120.7	126.7
Leading Indicator Subgroups:				
913. Marginal employment adjustments	L,L,L	do	96.2	96.9
914. Capital investment commitments	L,L,L	do	106.7	111.9
915. Inventory investment and purchasing	L,L,L	do	102.0	102.7
916. Profitability	L,L,L	do	108.1	108.1
917. Money and financial flows	L,L,L	do	107.9	112.3
B. Cyclical Indicators by Economic Process				
B1. Employment and Unemployment				
Marginal Employment Adjustments:				
*1. Average workweek, prod. workers, mfg.	L,L,L	Hours	40.0	40.3
21. Avg. weekly overtime, prod. workers, mfg.[2]	L,C,L	do	3.1	3.4
2. Accession rate, per 100 employees, mfg.[2]	L,L,L	Percent	3.9	4.0
5. Avg. weekly initial claims (inverted[4])	L,C,L	Thousands	384	371
3. Layoff rate, per 100 employ., mfg. (inv.[4])[2]	L,L,L	Percent	1.3	1.2
4. Quit rate, per 100 employees, mfg.[2]	L,Lg,U	do	1.7	1.9
Job Vacancies:				
60. Ratio, help-wanted advertising to persons unemployed[2]	L,Lg,U	Ratio	0.389	0.515
46. Help-wanted advertising	L,Lg,U	1967 = 100	95	118

EXHIBIT 1. continued

Series Title	Timing Classifi-cation[3]	Unit of Measure	Average 1976	Average 1977

I. CYCLICAL INDICATORS — Con.
  B. Cyclical Indicators by Economic Process
    B1. Employment and Unemployment — Con.

Series Title	Timing Classifi-cation[3]	Unit of Measure	1976	1977
Comprehensive Employment:				
48. Employee hours in nonagri. estab-ments	U,C,C	A.r., bil. hrs.	151.50	156.4
42. Persons engaged in nonagri. activities	U,C,C	Thousands	84,188	87,30
41. Employees on nonagri. payrolls	C,C,C	do	79,443	82,14
40. Employees in mfg., mining, construction	L,C,U	do	23,332	24,23
90. Ratio, civilian employment to total population of working age[2]	U,Lg,U	Percent	56.06	57.1
Comprehensive Unemployment:				
37. Total unemployed (inverted[4])	L,Lg,U	Thousands	7,288	6,85
43. Unemployment rate, total (inverted[4])[2]	L,Lg,U	Percent	7.7	7.
45. Avg. weekly insured unemploy. rate (inv.[4])[2]	L,Lg,U	do	4.5	3.
*91. Avg. duration of unemployment (inverted[4])	Lg,Lg,Lg	Weeks	15.8	14.
44. Unemploy. rate, 15 weeks and over (inv.[4])[2]	Lg,Lg,Lg	Percent	2.5	2.
B2. Production and Income				
Comprehensive Output and Income:				
50. GNP in 1972 dollars	C,C,C	A.R., bil. dol.	1274.7	1337.
52. Personal income in 1972 dollars	C,C,C	do	1038.1	1092.
*51. Pers. income less transfer pay., 1972 dollars	C,C,C	do	893.3	945.
53. Wages and salaries in mining, mfg., and construction, 1972 dollars	C,C,C	do	221.8	233.
Industrial Production:				
47. Industrial production, total	C,C,C	1967 = 100	129.8	137.
73. Industrial production, durable mfrs.	C,C,C	do	121.7	129.
74. Industrial production, nondurable mfrs.	C,L,L	do	140.9	148.
49. Value of goods output, 1972 dollars	C,C,C	A.r., bil. dol.	580.1	612.
Capacity Utilization:				
82. Capacity utilization rate, mfg., FRB[2]	L,C,U	Percent	80.2	82.
83. Capacity utilization rate, mfg., BEA2		do	81	NA
84. Capacity utilization rate, materials, FRB[2]	L,C,U	do	80.4	81.9
B3. Consumption, Trade, Orders, and Deliveries				
Orders and Deliveries:				
6. New orders, durable goods	L,L,L	Bil. dol.	50.79	59.0
7. New orders, durable goods, 1972 dollars	L,L,L	do	35.01	38.0
*8. New orders, cons. goods and mtls., 1972 dol.	L,L,L	do	32.35	34.9
25. Chg. in unfilled orders, durable goods[2]	L,L,L	do	0.31	1.4
96. Mfrs.' unfilled orders, durable goods[5]	L,Lg,U	Bil. dol., EOP	167.26	184.5
*82. Vendor performance[2]	L,L,L	Percent	54	5
Consumption and Trade:				
56. Manufacturing and trade sales	C,C,C	Bil. dol.	199.77	NA
*57. Manufacturing and trade sales, 1972 dollars	C,C,C	do	133.47	NA
75. Industrial production, consumer goods	C,L,C	1967 = 100	136.2	143.

EXHIBIT 1. continued

Series Title	Timing Classifi- cation[3]	Unit of Measure	Average	
			1976	1977
I. CYCLICAL INDICATORS—Con.				
B3. Consumption, Trade, Orders, and Deliveries —Con.				
54. Sales of retail stores	C,L,U	Mil. dol.	53,542	58,924
59. Sales of retail stores, 1972 dollars	U,L,U	do	39,813	41,540
55. Personal consumption expend., autos	L,C,C	A.r., bil. dol.	55.0	63.8
58. Index of consumer sentiment ⓐ	L,L,L	I Q 1966 = 100	85.4	86.8
B4. Fixed Capital Investment				
Formation of Business Enterprises:				
*2. Net business formation	L,L,L	1967 = 100	117.6	NA
13. New business incorporations	L,L,L	Number	31,244	NA
Business Investment Commitments:				
10. Contracts and orders, plant and equipment	L,L,L	Bil. dol.	15.56	18.39
20. Contr. and orders, plant and equip., 1972 dol.	L,L,L	do	11.02	12.28
24. New orders, cap. goods indus., nondefense	L,L,L	do	12.84	15.31
27. New orders, capital goods industries, nondefense, 1972 dollars	L,L,L	do	9.15	10.27
9. Construction contracts, commercial and industrial buildings, floor space	L,C,U	Mil. sq. ft.	51.43	62.96
11. New capital appropriations, mfg.	U,Lg,U	Bil. dol.	12.45	NA
97. Backlog of capital appropriations, mfg.[5]	C,Lg,Lg	Bil. dol., EOP	47.53	NA
Business Investment Expenditures:				
61. Business expend., new plant and equipment	C,Lg,Lg	A.r., bil. dol.	120.49	137.02
69. Machinery and equipment sales and business construction expenditures	C,Lg,Lg	do.	175.55	NA
76. Industrial production, business equip.	C,Lg,U	1967 = 100	136.3	149.1
86. Nonresid. fixed investment, total, 1972 dol.	C,Lg,C	A.r., bil. dol.	116.8	127.1
Residential Construction Commitments and Investment:				
28. New private housing units started, total	L,L,L	A.r., thous.	1,538	1,986
29. New building permits, private housing	L,L,L	1967 = 100	112.2	144.4
89. Fixed investment, residential, 1972 dol.	L,L,L	A.r., bil. dol.	47.7	56.9
B5. Inventories and Inventory Investment				
Inventory Investment:				
30. Chg. in business inventories, 1972 dol.[2]	L,L,L	do	8.5	11.6
*36. Change in inventories on hand and on order, 1972 dollars (smoothed[6])[2]	L,L,L	do	8.18	NA
31. Chg. in book value, mfg. and trade invent.[2]	L,L,L	do	24.5	NA
38. Chg. in mtl. stocks on hand and on order[2]	L,L,L	Bil. dol.	0.51	NA
Inventories on Hand and on Order:				
71. Mfg. and trade inventories, total[5]	Lg,Lg,Lg	Bil. dol., EOP	306.32	NA
*70. Mfg. and trade invent., total, 1972 dol.[5]	Lg,Lg,Lg	do	225.90	NA
65. Mfrs.' inventories of finished goods[5]	Lg,Lg,Lg	do	53.75	NA
77. Ratio, inventories to sales, mfg. and trade, constant dollars[2]	Lg,Lg,Lg	Ratio	1.67	NA
78. Materials and supplies, stocks on hand and on order[5]	L,Lg,Lg	Bil. dol., EOP	131.72	NA

EXHIBIT 1. continued

Series Title	Timing Classifi- cation[3]	Unit of Measure	Average 1976	1977
I. CYCLICAL INDICATORS — Con.				
B6. Prices, Costs, and Profits — Con.				
Sensitive Commodity Prices:				
92. Chg. in sensitive prices (smoothed[6])[2]	L,L,L	Percent	1.17	0.69
23. Industrial materials prices ⓦ	U,L,L	1967 = 100	200.7	210.4
Stock Prices:				
19. Stock prices, 500 common stocks ⓦ	L,L,L	1941–43 = 100	102.01	98.20
Profits and Profit Margins:				
16. Corporate profits after taxes	L,L,L	A.r., bil. dol.	92.1	102.9
18. Corp. profits after taxes, 1972 dollars	L,L,L	do	67.5	NA
79. Corp. profits after taxes, with IVA and CCA	L,C,L	do	63.3	NA
80. do in 1972 dol.	L,C,L	do	46.8	NA
15. Profits (after taxes) per dol. of sales, mfg.[2]	L,L,L	Cents.	5.4	NA
17. Ratio, price to unit labor cost, mfg.	L,L,L	1967 = 100	123.1	122.9
Cash Flows:				
34. Net cash flow, corporate	L,L,L	A.r., bil. dol.	153.5	NA
35. Net cash flow, corporate, 1972 dollars	L,L,L	do	109.0	NA
Unit Labor Costs and Labor Share:				
63. Unit labor cost, private business sector	Lg,Lg,Lg	1967 = 100	168.7	179.0
68. Labor cost (cur. dol.) per unit of gross domestic product (1972), nonfin. corp.	Lg,Lg,Lg	Dollars	0.890	0.947
62. Labor cost per unit of output, mfg.	Lg,Lg,Lg	1967 = 100	145.4	154.6
64. Compensation of employees as percent of national income[2]	Lg,Lg,Lg	Percent	76.0	NA
B7. Money and Credit				
Money:				
85. Change in money supply (M1)[2]	L,L,L	Percent	0.48	0.60
102. Change in money supply plus time deposits at commercial banks (M2)[2]	L,C,U	do	0.91	0.72
*104. Chg. in total liquid assets (M7) (smoothed[6])[2]	L,L,L	do	0.84	0.95
*105. Money supply (M1), 1972 dollars	L,L,L	Bil. dol.	223.5	223.9
106. Money supply (M2), 1972 dollars	L,L,L	do	517.1	536.5
Velocity of Money:				
107. Ratio, GNP to money supply (M1)[2]	C,C,C	Ratio	5.610	5.825
108. Ratio, pers. income to money supply (M2)[2]	C,Lg,C	do	1.965	1.975
Credit Flows:				
33. Change in mortgage debt[2]	L,L,L	A.r., bil. dol.	53.47	NA
112. Change in business loans[2]	L,L,L	do	-5.05	8.11
113. Change in consumer installment debt[2]	L,L,L	do	19.98	NA
110. Total private borrowing	L,L,L	do	199.25	NA
Credit Difficulties:				
14. Liabilities of business failures (inv.[4]) ⓦ	L,L,L	Mil. dol.	250.94	NA
39. Delinquency rate, instal. loans (inv.[4])[2] [5]	L,L,L	Percent, EOP	2.40	NA
Bank Reserves:				
93. Free reserves (inverted[4])[2] ⓦ	L,U,U	Mil. dol.	134	-251
94. Borrowing from the Federal Reserve[2] ⓦ	L,Lg,U	do	84	462

EXHIBIT 1. continued

Series Title	Timing Classifi- cation[3]	Unit of Measure	Average 1976	Average 1977
I.CYCLICAL INDICATORS — Con.				
B7. Money and Credit — Con.				
Interest Rates:				
119. Federal funds rate[2] ⓤ	L,Lg,Lg	Percent	5.05	5.54
114. Treasury bill rate[2] ⓤ	C,Lg,Lg	do	5.00	5.26
115. Treasury bond yields[2] ⓤ	C,Lg,Lg	do	6.78	7.06
116. Corporate bond yields[2] ⓤ	Lg,Lg,Lg	do	8.59	8.20
117. Municipal bond yields[2] ⓤ	U,Lg,Lg	do	6.64	5.68
118. Mortgage yields, residential[2] ⓤ	Lg,Lg,Lg	do	8.82	8.68
67 Bank rates on short-term bus. loans[2] ⓤ	Lg,Lg,Lg	do	7.52	NA
*109. Average prime rate charged by banks[2] ⓤ	Lg,Lg,Lg	do	6.84	6.82
Outstanding Debt:				
66. Consumer installment debt[5]	Lg,Lg,Lg	Bil. dol., EOP	179.93	NA
*72. Commercial and industrial loans outstanding, weekly reporting large comm. banks	Lg,Lg,Lg	Bil. dol.	116.42	121.81
*95. Ratio, consumer install. debt to pers. income[2]	Lg,Lg,Lg	Percent	12.33	NA
II. OTHER IMPORTANT ECONOMIC MEASURES				
B. Prices, Wages, and Productivity				
B1. Price Movements				
310. Implicit price deflator, GNP		1972 = 100	133.9	141.3
320. Consumer prices (CPI), all items ⓤ		1967 = 100	170.5	181.5
320c. Change in CPI, all items, S/A[2]		Percent	0.4	0.5
322. CPI, food		1967 = 100	180.8	192.2
330. Wholesale prices (WPI), all commodities ⓤ		do	183.0	194.2
331. WPI, crude materials		do	205.1	214.3
332. WPI, intermediate materials		do	189.3	201.7
333. WPI, producer finished goods		do	173.2	184.5
334. WPI, consumer finished goods		do	169.0	178.9
B2. Wages and Productivity				
340. Average hourly earnings, production workers, private nonfarm economy		do	185.0	198.5
341. Real average hourly earnings, production workers, private nonfarm economy		do	108.5	109.4
345. Average hourly compensation, nonfarm bus.		do	192.6	209.6
346. Real avg. hourly comp., nonfarm business		do	113.0	115.4
370. Output per hour, private business sector		do	116.5	119.3
C. Labor Force, Employment, and Unemployment				
441. Total civilian labor force		Thousands	94,773	97,401
442. Total civilian employment		do	87,485	90,546
37. Number of persons unemployed		do	7,288	6,855
444. Unemployed males, 20 years and over		do	3,041	2,727

EXHIBIT 1. continued

Series Title	Timing Classifi- cation[3]	Unit of Measure	Average 1976	Average 1977
II. OTHER IMPORTANT ECONOMIC MEASURES — Con.				
C. Labor Force, Employment, and Unemployment — Con.				
445. Unemployed females, 20 years and over		do	2,546	2,486
446. Unemployed persons, 16–19 years of age		do	1,701	1,642
Labor Force Participation Rates:				
451. Males, 20 years and over[2]		Percent	79.8	79.7
452. Females, 20 years and over[2]		do	47.0	48.1
453. Both sexes, 16–19 years of age[2]		do	54.6	56.2
D. Government Activities				
D1. Receipts and Expenditures				
501. Federal Government receipts		A.r., bil. dol.	332.3	373.9
502. Federal Government expenditures		do	386.3	423.5
500. Federal Government surplus or deficit[2]		do	-54.0	-49.6
511. State and local government receipts		do	264.7	294.5
512. State and local government expenditures		do	246.2	265.3
510. State and local govt. surplus or deficit[2]		do	18.4	29.2
D2. Defense Indicators				
516. Defense Department obligations, total		Mil. dol.	9,217	NA
525. Military prime contract awards in U.S.		do	4,235	NA
548. New orders, defense products		Bil. dol.	2.46	2.74
564. National defense purchases		A.r., bil. dol.	86.8	94.3
E. U.S. International Transactions				
E1. Merchandise Trade				
602. Exports, total except military aid		Mil. dol.	9,572	NA
604. Exports of agricultural products		do	1,925	NA
606. Exports of nonelectrical machinery		do	1,838	NA
612. General imports, total		do	10,044	NA
614. Imports of petroleum and products		do	2,658	NA
616. Imports of automobiles and parts		do	1,096	NA

Series Title	Unit of Measure	Average 1975	Average 1976	1977
II. OTHER IMPORTANT ECONOMIC MEASURES— Con.				
E2. Goods and Services Movements Except Transfers Under Military Grants				
618. Merchandise exports	Mil. dol.	26,772	28,674	NA
620. Merchandise imports	do	24,511	31,004	NA
622. Merchandise trade balance[2]	do	2,261	-2,330	NA
651. Income on U.S. investments abroad	do	4,332	5,342	NA
652. Income on foreign investment in the U.S.	do	2,844	2,890	NA
668. Exports of goods and services	do	36,900	40,817	NA
669. Imports of goods and services	do	32,860	39,918	NA
667. Balance on goods and services[2]	do	4,041	899	NA

EXHIBIT 1. continued

Series Title	Unit of Measure	1975	Average 1976	1977

I. OTHER IMPORTANT ECONOMIC MEASURES — Con.
  A. National Income and Product
    A1. GNP and Personal Income

Series Title	Unit of Measure	1975	1976	1977
50. GNP in 1972 dollars	A.r., bil. dol.	1202.1	1274.7	1337.6
200. GNP in current dollars	do	1528.8	1706.5	1890.4
213. Final sales, 1972 dollars	do	1212.0	1266.2	1326.1
224. Disposable personal income, current dollars	do	1084.4	1185.8	1308.6
225. Disposable personal income, 1972 dollars	do	857.3	890.3	930.3
217. Per capita GNP in 1972 dollars	A.r., dollars	5,629	5,923	6,168
227. Per capita disposable pers. income, 1972 dol.	do	4,014	4,137	4,290

A2. Personal Consumption Expenditures

Series Title	Unit of Measure	1975	1976	1977
231. Total, 1972 dollars	A.r., bil. dol.	775.1	821.3	860.3
233. Durable goods, 1972 dollars	do	112.7	127.5	138.0
238. Nondurable goods, 1972 dollars	do	307.6	321.6	333.3
239. Services, 1972 dollars	do	354.8	372.2	389.0
230. Total, current dollars	do	980.4	1094.0	1210.1
232. Durable goods, current dollars	do	132.9	158.9	179.4
236. Nondurable goods, current dollars	do	409.3	442.7	480.1
237. Services, current dollars	do	438.2	492.3	550.6

A3. Gross Private Domestic Investment

Series Title	Unit of Measure	1975	1976	1977
241. Total, 1972 dollars	do	141.6	173.0	195.6
243. Total fixed investment, 1972 dollars	do	151.5	164.5	184.0
30. Change in business inventories, 1972 dol.[2]	do	-9.9	8.5	11.6
240. Total, current dollars	do	189.1	243.3	294.3
242. Total fixed investment, current dollars	do	200.6	230.0	276.6
245. Chg. in bus. inventories, current dol.[2]	do	-11.5	13.3	17.8

A.4. Government Purchases of Goods and Services

Series Title	Unit of Measure	1975	1976	1977
261. Total, 1972 dollars	do	263.0	264.4	271.1
263. Federal Government, 1972 dollars	do	96.7	96.5	101.4
267. State and local governments, 1972 dollars	do	166.3	167.9	169.7
260. Total, current dollars	do	338.9	361.4	395.0
262. Federal Government, current dollars	do	123.3	130.1	145.4
266. State and local governments, current dollars	do	215.6	231.2	249.5

A5. Foreign Trade

Series Title	Unit of Measure	1975	1976	1977
256. Exports of goods and services, 1972 dollars	do	89.9	95.8	98.0
257. Imports of goods and services, 1972 dollars	do	67.4	79.8	87.3
255. Net exports of goods and serv., 1972 dol.[2]	do	22.5	16.0	10.7

167

EXHIBIT 1. continued

Series Title	Unit of Measure	1975	Average 1976	1977
II. OTHER IMPORTANT ECONOMIC MEASURES				
A5. Foreign Trade				
252. Exports of goods and services, current dol.	do	147.3	162.9	175.6
253. Imports of goods and services, current dol.	do	126.9	155.1	184.7
250. Net exports of goods and serv., current dol.[2]	do	20.4	7.8	-9.0
A6. National Income and Its Components				
220. National income	do	1217.0	1364.1	1520.3
280. Compensation of employees	do	930.3	1036.3	1155.8
282. Proprietors' income with IVA and CCA	do	86.0	88.0	97.9
286. Corporate profits with IVA and CCA	do	99.3	128.1	140.3
284. Rental income of persons with CCA	do	22.3	23.3	25.3
288. Net interest	do	79.1	88.4	100.9
A7. Saving				
290. Gross saving (private and govt.)	do	195.1	237.0	274.3
295. Business saving	do	179.2	206.6	NA
292. Personal saving	do	80.2	65.9	67.8
298. Government surplus or deficit[2]	do	-64.3	-35.6	-20.4
293. Personal saving rate[2]	Percent	7.4	5.6	5.2

NOTE: Series are seasonally adjusted except for those indicated by ⓤ, which appear to contain no seasonal movement. Series indicated by an asterisk (*) are included in the major composite indexes. Dollar values are in current dollars unless otherwise specified. For complete series titles (including composition of the composite indexes) and sources, see "Titles and Sources of Series" at the back of BCD. NA = not available. a = anticipated. EOP = end of period. A.r. = annual rate. S/A = seasonally adjusted (used for special emphasis). IVA = inventory valuation adjustment. CCA = capital consumption adjustment. NIA = national income accounts.

[1] For a few series, data shown here have been rounded to fewer digits than those shown elsewhere in BCD. Annual figures published by the source agencies are used if available.

[2] Differences rather than percent changes are shown for this series.

[3] The three-part timing code indicates the timing classification of the series at peaks, at troughs, and at all turns: L = leading; C = roughly coincident; Lg = lagging; U = unclassified.

[4] Inverted series. Since this series tends to move counter to movements in general business activity, signs of the changes are reversed.

[5] End-of-period series. The annual figures (and quarterly figures for monthly series) are the last figures for the period.

[6] This series is a weighted 4-term moving average (with weights 1, 2, 2, 1) placed at the terminal month of the span.

Source: *Business Conditions Digest*, January 1978.

168

6

Economic
and Business Forecasting

There are many types and methods of economic or business forecasting. Forecasts can be made for short-run, intermediate, and long-run periods. One of the most common is the annual GNP forecasts, or forecasts of the yearly economic outlook.

In forecasting for a short-run period of one year or less, an analyst may do well using the various economic indicators to ascertain what the next several months hold in store for the economy. The lead-lag indicators, for example, may clearly spell out that the economy is in an expansionary or contractionary stage and that the momentum of various forces within the economy may carry it in that particular direction for a number of months. On the other hand, the indicators may reflect a period of leveling off of an expansion, or a bottoming out of a contraction phase, with the possibility of a turning point occurring in the next few months. The economic indicators in this respect can be very useful and give a fairly accurate picture of the short-run outlook for the economy.

ANNUAL FORECAST

An annual forecast of the GNP and related data, such as national income, personal income, and disposable income, in either current or constant dollars, can be constructed by the analyst or a forecast obtained from other sources. If the analyst himself is to construct it, he can use several techniques. One frequently used method is to forecast the three basic components of the GNP: consumption expenditures, private investment (including net exports), and government purchases of goods and services. Information on each of these can be compiled from various sources. It is possible to find out the attitude of consumers from the Survey of Consumer Finances published by the University of Michigan. Estimates of intended investment of businesses can be obtained through the Securities and Exchange Commission and the Department of Commerce. Another excellent source of investment information is the annual McGraw-Hill *Survey of Business Investment*. Estimates for government expenditures can be obtained by studying various proposed government budgets.

On the other hand, the analyst may rely on forecasts made by others. These may be more sophisticated than one he could construct and using them will save him time, money, and effort. Business periodicals publish a number of respectable GNP forecasts. Other commercial forecasts can be purchased inexpensively. Some of these forecasts, such as the Wharton forecast, are based upon econometric models of the economy. The Wharton forecast and others are often referred to as *machine forecasts* because they are computerized. Computerization, of course, permits the handling of many variables and facilitates adjustments in forecasts resulting from changing variables. It is a current practice for these forecasts to predict the GNP within a certain range. This allows for small changes in contingencies. Several forecasts may be used by the analyst for verification. Economists often take a number of the better-known forecasts and compile a consensus, or standard forecast. Table 6–1 lists a number of forecasting units or economists and indicates their respective GNP forecasts for 1978. Note that the forecasts ranged from a high of $2.108 trillion to a low of $2.055 trillion. The standard forecast for 1978 was considered to be $2.085 trillion — $2.095 trillion with about 4.5 percent real growth and 6.0 percent inflation during the year. More details of these forecasts are shown by Table 6–2, the twenty-sixth annual edition of a GNP forecast by Prudential, a large insurance company.

LONG-RANGE GNP FORECASTING

There are several methods of projecting economic growth or of estimating the future GNP, but remember that they are estimates and not precise measurements. Projected growth can be based on experience, or new data can be constructed regarding the future.

Growth-Rate Formula

The future trend line of the GNP may also be projected by using the following steps: (1) Calculate the average annual increase in the GNP for the past few decades or some similar time period. (2) Make adjustments necessary in this average to account for any factor that will cause the economy to expand at a faster or slower rate in the future. (3) Apply this growth rate cumulatively for the number of years in the period between the present and the year for which one desires to estimate the GNP. This, of course, is merely a variation of the compound interest-rate formula and can be stated as follows: $GNP_1 = GNP_0 \ (1 + r)^n$ where GNP_1 is the future gross national product, GNP_0 is the current GNP, r is the annual rate of economic

TABLE 6-1. Economic Forecasts for 1978

| Economists | 1978 GNP (billions of dollars) | Percentage | | 1978 Average Unemployment |
		Real Growth in GNP	Price Increase	
Townsend-Greenspan*	$2,108	4.8	6.4	6.5
Kent Econ. Development Inst.*	2,105	4.8	6.3	6.5
Univ. of Calif. at L.A.*	2,105	4.9	6.2	6.6
Eggert Economic Enterprises (Robert J. Eggert)	2,104	4.5	6.5	6.7
Harris Trust & Savings (Beryl W. Sprinkel	2,103	4.6	6.5	6.5
U.S. Steel (Elizabeth A. Bossong)	2,099	4.9	5.8	6.4
Provident Nat. Bank (Jack W. Lavery)	2,098	4.4	6.2	6.7
Equitable Life Assurance (Francis H. Schott)	2,098	4.5	6.4	6.6
MAPCAST, General Electric*	2,098	4.0	6.6	6.6
New York Stock Exch. (Wm. C. Freund)	2,097	4.5	6.5	6.5
Nat. Assn. of Mut. Sav. Banks	2,096	4.5	6.0	6.5
Goldman Sachs (Gary M. Wenglowski)	2,096	4.8	6.1	6.5
Data Resources*	2,096	4.5	6.1	6.6
Loeb Rhoades (Ernst Anspach)	2,094	4.4	6.1	6.7
Irving Trust (Gordon B. Pye)	2,094	4.7	6.0	6.6
Research Inst. of America (Haig Babian)	2,090	4.0	6.4	6.8
Bank of N.Y. (Robert Ortner)	2,090	4.5	5.9	6.5
U.S. Trust Co. of N.Y. (Thomas W. Synnott III)	2,090	4.6	5.7	6.6
Schroder Naess & Thomas (Morris Cohen)	2,088	4.5	5.8	6.7
Wharton EFA, Univ. of Pa.*	2,088	4.5	5.7	6.8
Prudential Insurance (J. Robert Ferrari)	2,086	4.0	6.3	6.7
Phila. Nat. Bank (A. Gilbert Heebner)	2,086	4.1	6.1	6.7
The Conference Board (Albert T. Sommers)	2,085	4.3	5.9	6.7
Brown Bros. Harriman (Edward J. Campbell)	2,084	4.2	5.9	6.8
Mc-Graw-Hill (Gordon W. McKinley)	2,084	4.8	5.3	6.5
T. Rowe Price (Ben. E. Laden)	2,083	4.4	5.7	6.5
Security Pacif. Nat. Bank (Edmund A. Mennis)	2,081	4.1	5.8	6.6
Chemical Bank (Richard Scott-Ram)	4,081	4.6	5.4	6.5

TABLE 6-1. continued

| Economists | 1978 GNP (billions of dollars) | Percentage | | 1978 Average Unemployment |
		Real Growth in GNP	Price Increase	
Georgia State University*	2,081	3.4	6.6	6.9
GT&E (Daniel A. Hodes)	2,078	3.8	5.9	6.7
Argus Research (Jeffrey A. Nichols)	2,075	3.4	6.4	7.2
RSQE, Univ. of Michigan*	2,075	3.6	6.0	6.8
White Weld (A. Gary Shilling)	2,068	4.5	4.9	6.8
Peter L. Bernstein, Inc. (Peter L. Bernstein)	2,065	4.0	5.3	7.1
United Calif. Bank (Raymond Jallow)	2,060	2.9	5.9	7.3
Chase Econometric Assoc.*	2,055	2.8	5.9	7.4 .
Average	$2,088	4.3	6.0	6.7

* Econometric Models
Source: *Business Week*, December 26, 1977.

TABLE 6-2. Components of 1978 Forecast

| | Billions of Dollars | | Year-to-Year % Change | |
	1977	1978	1977	1978
Consumers				
Consumer Spending for Goods and Services	1207.5	1320.0	10½	9½
Housing Outlays	90.5	102.0	33	12½
Business				
New Plant and Equipment	185.0	208.5	14½	12½
Inventory Change	18.5	21.0	*	*
Government				
Federal Purchases	146.5	164.0	12½	12
State and Local Purchases	250.0	279.0	8	11½
Net Exports	−10.0	−8.5	*	*
Total GNP	1888.0	2086.0	10½	10¼
Real Growth			4¾	4
Price Inflation			5¾	6¼

*Percentage changes not meaningful
Source: Prudential 1978 Economic Forecast, November 27, 1977.

growth and n is the number of years between the current year and desired future year for which the GNP is estimated.

This method suffers from some weaknesses. First, the rate of economic growth based on past periods may differ depending on the years observed. The average annual rate of real GNP growth in the past five years (1971-76) for example is 2.8 percent compared with 4.5 for the past fifteen-year period, (1961-76). Second, the rate of growth may change for some unforeseeable reason in the future. Third, actual GNP may deviate from projected GNP in any given year because of business fluctuations. Nevertheless, certain estimates of the GNP made on this basis are possible. If a growth rate of 4 percent is used, the estimated GNP for 1985 in constant 1975 dollars is $2.244 trillion.[1] Using the same formula, but applying a maximum growth rate of 5 percent would yield a real GNP for 1985 in the vicinity of $2.5 trillion. Various estimates of the constant-dollar GNP for 1985 based on selected growth rates are shown in Table 6-3. Current-dollar GNP estimates can be made by adding an anticipated inflationary factor. If an annual inflationary factor of 3 percent is added to an assumed 4 percent real growth rate, the current dollar GNP estimate for 1985 will be $2.982 trillion.

Labor-force Model of Projecting the GNP

A model based on the size and productivity of the labor force also can be used to estimate the GNP for future years. Since one can ascertain the probable size of the population for any future date, we can readily calculate the expected labor force. Past trends can be projected in order to estimate the productivity of workers in the future. An adjustment can be made for the number of hours worked per year per member of the labor force to take into account any

---

[1] As stated earlier, the formula $GNP_1 = GNP_0 (1 + r)^n$ is a variation of the compound interest formula $S = P(1 + i)^n$ in which S equals a future sum of money, P equals the beginning principal, i equals the interest rate percentage, and n equals the number of periods (years) the interest rate is applied. If one converts to the GNP formula, GNP_1 is the sum of GNP in the future, GNP_0 is the beginning (1975) GNP, r is the assumed percentage rate of economic growth, and n is the number of years the percentage growth ratio is to be applied.

Thus:
$$GNP_1 = GNP_0 (1 + r)^n$$
$$GNP_{85} = GNP_{75} (1 + .04)^{10}$$
$$GNP_{85} = 1,516 (1.4802)^*$$
$$GNP_{85} = 2,244$$

*The value 1.4802 is found in conventional compound interest tables, $S = (1 + i)^n$

TABLE 6-3. Estimated GNP for 1985 by Growth Rates
(billions of dollars)

GNP 1975 (billions of dollars)	Growth Rate (percent)	Estimated GNP 1985	
		Constant 1975 Dollars	Current Dollars*
	4	$2,244	$2,982
$1,516	4½	2,354	3,124
	5	2,469	3,273

*Assumes a 3 percent annual inflation factor.

possible reduction in the average length of the work week. Multiplying the annual productivity per worker times the number of hours worked times the number of available workers will give the potential GNP in any particular year or period in the future.

An Example. Let us take the economic data for 1975 and project them to 1985. A check of the figures for 1975 reveals that the total population was 213.6 million.[2] Of this total, 94.8 million, or 44.4 percent, were in the total labor force. Of these, 2.2 million were in the armed services and 92.6 million were in the civilian labor force. If we subtract the average unemployment for the year, 7.8 million, from 94.8, it leaves total employment, including the armed forces, of 87.0 million. The average weekly hours of work in nonagricultural employment amounted to 36.1; therefore, each worker put in 1,877 hours for 1975 (36.1 hours times 52 weeks). Multiplying the total employed labor force, 87.0 million, by the average annual hours (1,877) yields a total of 163.3 billion man-hours of work for the year. Since the GNP for 1975 was $1.516 trillion, the productivity was equal to $9.28 per man-hour ($1.516 trillion ÷ 163.3 billion total man-hours worked).[3]

Now the question arises: What will be the approximate size of the GNP in 1985, for example? In making such a prediction, a number of assumptions must be made. Differences in estimates about the future GNP arise primarily because of differences in assumptions made by forecasters. Final results can also differ because forecasters may have different opinions regarding future changes that will take place in the

[2] These figures are contained in *Economic Indicators* prepared by the Council of Economic Advisers and published monthly by the U.S. Government Printing Office.

[3] These calculations can be computed also on the basis of civilian labor force figures, excluding the armed forces. Since the military contributes to the GNP, however, total labor force, including the armed forces, is used here.

various elements that go into the forecasting of the GNP. Final results, however, can usually be reconciled by taking these differences into consideration. Regardless of these differences, a procedure such as that which follows can be used to calculate production and income in the future. For example, one estimate of the total population for 1985 by the Census Bureau is 235.7 million. On the basis of this projection, plus some upward adjustment in the labor force participation rate (percent of total population in the labor force), it is estimated that there will be 107.7 million in the total labor force in 1985. It is further estimated that the number of persons in the armed services will be approximately two million. Considering full employment to be a condition in which 4 percent or less of the civilian labor force is unemployed, full employment, including the armed forces, will in 1985 approximate 103.5 million (107.7 – 2.0 × .96 + 2.0 = 103.5).[4]

The figure necessary for the next step is one about which some differences may arise, that is, the estimate of the average weekly hours of work. A number of economists estimate that the average length of the work week will be less than 40 hours by 1985. Using a 40-hour week for comparison, however, the total man-hours worked in 1985 can be obtained by multiplying 40 hours by 52 weeks. This gives a total of 2,080 man-hours per worker per year. If this figure is then multiplied by the number of employed persons to be in the labor force, 103.5 million, it will yield a total of 215 billion man-hours of work for the year 1985.

The next step involves an estimate of the increase in productivity per man-hour between now and 1985. The annual increase in productivity per man-hour prior to 1948 was 2 percent, but since 1948 it has been about 3 percent. It can safely be said, therefore, that the productivity per man-hour will increase about 2.5 percent annually for the next several years. If this 2.5 percent annual cumulative percentage is applied to the 1975 productivity per man-hour figure, $9.28, it results in a productivity per man-hour of $11.88 for the year 1985.

The final step is to multiply the total man-hours to be worked in 1985, 215 billion hours, by the anticipated productivity per man-hour, $11.88, to obtain an estimate of the probable GNP for the year 1985 in terms of 1975 dollars. Thus, the estimate for the GNP for 1985 is $2.554 trillion, an increase of 68 percent during the 1975–85 period. These steps are enumerated in Table 6–4.

The GNP will be in the neighborhood of $10,836 per capita in

[4] If the more recently suggested 5 percent full employment/unemployment rate is used, final forecast figures for the GNP will be lower.

TABLE 6-4. Projection of GNP for 1985
(in constant 1975 dollars)

	Actual GNP and Related Figures for 1975	Estimated GNP and Related Figures for 1985
Total Population (millions)	213.5	235.7
Total Labor Force (millions)	94.8	107.7
Armed Forces (millions)	2.2	2.0
Civilian Labor Force (millions)	92.6	105.7
Minus Unemployment (millions)	7.8	4.2
Total Employment (millions)	87.0	103.5
Total Average Annual Hours per Worker	1,877	2,080
Equals Total Man-hours (billions)	163.3	215.0
Times Output per Man-hour	$ 9.28	$ 11.88
Equals GNP (billions)	$1,516.	$2,554.

1985 dollars. Since disposable personal income is generally 70 percent of the GNP, the total disposable personal income will be $1,787 trillion. This will mean that per capita disposable personal income will be about $7,582, or an increase of 47 percent over the 1975 disposable personal income figure.

Reservations. Such calculations, it must be remembered, are only rough estimates. They are based on certain assumptions that may or may not bear out. For example, if our calculation of the average weekly hours were 37.5 instead of forty, the estimated GNP would change from $2.554 trillion to $2.397 trillion. Adjustments either upward or downward in the population estimate, in the labor force participation rate, in the number of persons in the armed services, in the average annual hours per worker, in the unemployment rate, or in the output per man-hour, and, of course, the price level, would cause a change in the calculations. In fact, one would do well to make several models, each based on slightly different assumptions, in order to show the various possibilities in the GNP estimates for a given year in the future.

Extrapolating the Trend Line

One fairly simple and often-used method of showing future economic growth and estimating the GNP at a distant date is by extrapolating the trend line of a time series of the GNP. This method has certain weaknesses and must be used with definite reservations. The estimated GNP will be fairly accurate, provided that economic variables, such as the growth rate, population changes, technological development, productivity, hours of work, and the rate of unemployment, remain constant. Of course, actual growth may deviate from the trend line because of cyclical fluctuations. Furthermore, the actual growth rate may be greater or less than the trend line if the economy expands at a slower or faster pace than the extrapolated line. Another difficulty with this method is that it is possible to have different trend lines, depending on the dates used in calculating the trend line.

An example of a trend line extrapolation is shown in Figure 6-1. Note that the GNP for 1980 is expected to be in excess of $1.4 trillion in 1969 dollars. If converted into 1975 dollars, this projection would be about $2.3 trillion. If the trend line is going to be extrapolated as a means of forecasting the long-run GNP, the result will depend in large part on the accuracy of the trend line.

Free-hand Method.   A simple trend line can be drawn by the free-hand method, sometimes referred to as the *eyeball method.* With this method the analyst draws a line through the time series of fluctuations in an attempt to offset the peaks and troughs of the actual data. With the free-hand method, the analyst is only guessing at the trend. If done properly, the deviations of the actual data from the trend line values will equal zero. In short, the plus values above the trend line would equal the minus values below the trend line, and the sum of the deviations would be zero. But such a free-hand trend line is difficult to draw accurately. Moreover, the sighting ability of

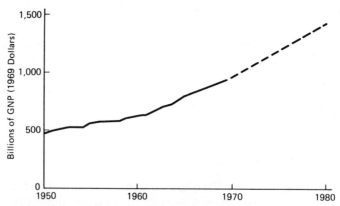

Figure 6-1. Projection of GNP (1969-80)
Source: *U.S. Manpower in the 1970s*, U.S. Department of Labor.

analysts may differ. This could result in differently sloped trend lines, even when the analysts are using identical data. Consequently, extrapolation of the trend line based on this technique can result in different long-run forecasts.

Least-squares Method. A more satisfactory technique of constructing a straight-line trend is by the method of "least squares." Analysts applying this method and using identical data will come up with the same trend line and identical GNP forecasts. Furthermore, it is a more accurate method. With the least-squares method, instead of guessing at the trend line, one computes it mathematically. Once this trend line is constructed, the deviations of the actual data from the trend line values when squared will be minimal. In short, they will be less than they could be from any other straight line that could be drawn through the data. This, incidentally, is where the method gets its name. The deviations squared will be minimum rather than zero, as would be the case if the deviations were not squared, because more emphasis is given to extreme values by the process of squaring.

The formula for calculating a straight-line trend via the method of least squares is

$$Yc = a + bX$$

In this formula, X represents the independent variable (in this case periods of years); Yc, the value of the trend line at a given period; a, the value of the trend line when X is zero; and b, the amount by which the trend line value increases for each increase unit of time (year). Consequently, the value of a shows the height or value of the trend line with reference to the Y axis of a graph when the X axis is equal to zero and b defines the slope of the line. It can be said also that b represents the increase in value along the Y axis of the graph for each unit of value (years) along the X axis of the graph.

Of course, the formula $Yc = a + bX$ gives us two unknowns, a and b. But, the value of these can be solved by using the following normal equations in which time is designated by X and the values in the series by Y.

$$\Sigma Y = Na + b \Sigma X$$
$$\Sigma XY = a \Sigma X \, b \Sigma X^2$$

These formulas can be reduced by shifting the origin of the series of data in a manner that $X =$ zero. In short, instead of starting the time series at the beginning, it can start with a middle value and work the years both plus and minus so that $X = 0$. The formula then becomes:[5]

$$a = \frac{\Sigma Y}{N}$$

$$b = \frac{\Sigma XY}{\Sigma X^2}$$

After the values for a and b are determined, they can then be converted into a trend line by plotting the values for $Yc = a + b$ (1),

[5] In the equation the $Yc = a + b\ (X)$, the coefficients of the two unknowns, a and b, are 1 and X respectively.
1. The two equations needed for using the method of least squares are obtained by the following procedure:
    a. Multiply each observation equation by the coefficient of the first unknown, and the sum of the resulting equations.
    b. Multiply each observation equation by the coefficient of the second unknown, and the sum of the resulting equations.
    Putting the two steps into symbolic language results in the following:

Observation equations multiplied by 1

In general: $1\ (Y = a + bX)$

Specifically: $Y_1 = a + bX_1$

$Y_2 = a + bX_2$

$Y_3 = a = bX_3$

·   ·

·   ·

·   ·

$Y_N = Na + bX_N$

Normal Equation I $\Sigma Y = Na + b\Sigma X$

Observation equations multiplied by X

In general: $X\ (Yc = a + bX)$

Specifically: $X_1 Yc_1 = aX_1 = bX_1^2$

$X_2 Yc_2 = aX_2 + bX_2^2$

$X_3 Yc_3 = aX_3 + bX_3^2$

·   ·

·   ·

·   ·

$X_N Y_N = aX_N + bX_N^2$

Normal Equation II $\Sigma\ XY = a\Sigma X + b\Sigma X^2$

$Yc = a + b$ (2), etc. Let us exemplify the least-squares method using data contained in Table 6-5.

To compute the trend equation, mark off the X values as integers from the middle year 1970 as origin, let Y = GNP, compute XY and X^2, and total these columns. Applying these data to the formula it becomes:

$$a = \frac{\Sigma Y}{N} = \frac{\$11,492 \text{ billion}}{11} = \$1.045 \text{ trillion}$$

$$b = \frac{\Sigma XY}{\Sigma X^2} = \frac{\$9,048 \text{ billion}}{110} = \$82 \text{ billion}$$

and the trend equation is Yc = $1.045 trillion + $82 billion X. This means that the trend line value at the point of origin, or midpoint year, 1970, is $1.045 trillion. The trend line value for any subsequent years equals $1.045 trillion plus $82 billion for each year beyond 1970 and less $82 billion for each year before 1970. Thus the trend line value for 1971 is $1.127 trillion (1.045 + 82), and for 1975 it is $1.455 trillion (1.045 + (82 × 5). These trend line values, Yc, are shown in Table 6-5. These figures are plotted in Figure 6-2.

Once the trend line has been constructed, it can then be extrapolated to future years (as shown in Figure 6-2), to obtain a projec-

---

In fitting a trend line to values that are equidistant along the horizontal, or X, axis of a graph one can save much time and labor by using a short-cut method. This is useful particularly when a time series is involved and the X axis is in terms of time or years. A midpoint of the X axis can be selected so that the sum of the negative X values equals exactly the sum of the positive X values, so that $\Sigma X = 0$.

If $X = 0$ then the normal equations become:

1. $$\Sigma Y = Na + b \Sigma X$$
$$\Sigma Y = Na$$
$$a = \frac{\Sigma Y}{N}$$

2. $$\Sigma XY = a \Sigma X + b \Sigma X^2$$
$$\Sigma XY = b \Sigma X^2$$
$$b = \frac{\Sigma XY}{\Sigma X^2}$$

In the formula above, each equation has only one unknown. This avoids the time and effort involved in solving simultaneous equations.

TABLE 6-5. Arithmetic Straight Line Fitted by Least Squares
to Gross National Product, 1965–1975

| Year | X | GNP (billions) | | | |
		Y	XY	X^2	Yc
1965	-5	688	-3,440	25	635
1966	-4	753	-3,012	16	717
1967	-3	796	-2,388	9	799
1968	-2	867	-1,734	4	881
1969	-1	936	- 936	1	963
1970	0	982	0	0	1,045
1971	+1	1,063	1,063	1	1,127
1972	+2	1,171	2,342	4	1,209
1973	+3	1,307	3,921	9	1,291
1974	+4	1,413	5,652	16	1,373
1975	+5	1,516	7,580	25	1,455
		11,492	9,048	110	

tion of the GNP. Note that, according to the projection, the GNP in
1985 should equal $2.275 trillion (1.045 + (82 × 15) = $2,275). If
one desires, an adjustment may be made in this forecast to take into
consideration price changes, or the effect of inflation on the forecast.

The forecast of $2.275 trillion may seem like a precise figure, and
it is, considering that in the historical GNP data for the period 1965–
75, actual GNP for each year was above or below the trend line value
calculated for that particular year. Since actual GNP values deviate
from the trend line values for the historical data, will they not
invalidate the forecast? No, not at all. The projection merely reveals
the trend value for each of the future years, such as 1980, not the
actual GNP. In all probability, actual GNP in any future years will
deviate from the trend line. But we can now use past data to approximate the probable deviation of actual GNP from the trend line, or
forecasted GNP, for subsequent years. This is done by calculating
the standard error (SE) of the estimate.

We can calculate the standard error for past data by observing the
deviations of the actual values from the trend line values, and put
them into the following formula:

$$SE = \sqrt{\frac{\Sigma(Y - Yc)^2}{N - 2}}$$

In this formula, the square root is taken of the summation of the

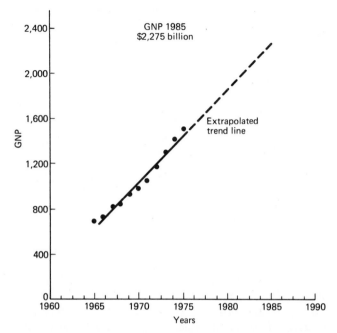

Figure 6-2. Straight Line Fitted by Least Squares to Gross National Product (1965-75), Projected to 1985

deviations squared divided by the number of items in our GNP series.[6] Using Table 6-5 data, we can construct Table 6-6.

The values from this table can then be inserted into the formula and become

$$SE = \sqrt{\frac{\$20,125 \text{ billions}}{9}}$$

$$SE = \sqrt{\$2,236 \text{ billions}}$$

$$SE = \$47 \text{ billions}$$

The standard error of the estimate, $47 billion, represents the

[6] The justification for dividing $(Y - Yc)^2$ by $N - 2$, rather than by N alone, is that deviations from the line of regression are taken from a straight line. This straight line requires two constants, a and b, to locate. As a result two degrees of freedom are lost in estimating the values of these constants by computing them from the sample data.

TABLE 6-6. Information Necessary for Calculating *SE*

Year	Y	(Billions of Dollars)		
		Yc	Y - Yc	$(Y - Yc)^2$
1965	$ 688	$ 635	+53	$ 2,809
1966	753	717	+36	1,296
1967	796	799	-3	9
1968	867	881	-14	196
1969	936	963	-27	729
1970	982	1,045	-63	3,969
1971	1,063	1,127	-64	4,096
1972	1,171	1,209	-38	1,444
1973	1,307	1,291	+16	256
1974	1,413	1,373	+40	1,600
1975	1,516	1,455	+61	3,721
	$11,492			$20,125

average error of estimates that may be expected in predicting the GNP in the trend equation.

Statistical inference indicates that there are certain characteristics of the standard error of the estimate. Among these is the fact that 68 percent of the Y values, will, in a normal distribution, fall within one standard error of the estimate, plus or minus; 95 percent will fall within two standard errors; 99 percent of the Y values will be within three standard errors of the estimate, plus or minus. Applying these characteristics to the GNP forecast will indicate that there is a 68 percent probability that actual GNP in 1985 will be within a range of $2.322 trillion and $2.228 trillion, a 95 percent chance that it will be within a range of $2.369 to $2.181 trillion and a 99 percent probability that it will be within a range of $2.416 trillion and $2.134 trillion.

It is important for an economist or business manager to have some idea of what lies ahead in the long run for the national economy. Certainly, changes in the economy and its rate of growth will affect business operations. None of the preceding methods of forecasting the GNP is perfect, certainly using one of them in an attempt to foresee probabilities is better than burying one's head in the sand and pleading ignorance about the future of the economy.

BUSINESS FORECASTING

Many businessmen are interested in the future growth of the economy. But usually they are more interested in how the change or growth of the economy will affect their sales or profits. Fortunately, the alert business manager can use his knowledge about economic growth, or related data, to predict what probably is going to happen to his future sales.

Some of the methods, or techniques, used in forecasting the GNP can be used to forecast future sales, either from the viewpoint of an industry or from the viewpoint of the firm. The growth rate formula, for example, can be used to project the annual rate of sales growth from a past period into future years. A trend line of sales over past years can be constructed and extrapolated into the future.

Correlation Analysis

Another commonly used method of projecting sales is through correlation analysis. This process relates an unknown and dependent variable, in this case sales, to a known and independent variable, such as the GNP. By calculating from past data, a correlation between the two variables can be determined and a "line of regression" can be constructed. If the future growth of the independent variable, GNP, is known, the line of regression can be extrapolated to determine sales, the unknown variable, in the future.

Before attempting such a correlation the forecaster should make certain of the following: (1) that a true rather than a casual relationship exists between the two variables to be related; (2) that the relationship will continue; and (3) that data about the independent variable are available. Armed with such information, the forecaster can compile a table or plot a scattergram, showing the relationship between the two variables. From these data, a line of regression can be plotted using the formula $Yc = a + bX$. A standard error of the estimate for the historical data can then be calculated. Finally, the line of regression can be extrapolated to a future value, or a value to be attained in a future year. When the independent variable reaches a particular level on the X axis, the value of Y, the dependent variable, can be read on the Y axis of the chart. The standard error or the estimate can then be applied to determine the probable range in the forecast of the dependent variable.

Let us exemplify this by utilizing the GNP forecast shown in Figure 6-2. Table 6-7 shows the relationship between GNP and the sales of the Zero Corporation for the years 1956-70. These are also shown in the scattergram plotted in Figure 6-3. The data can be inserted into the formula $Yc = a + bX$, in which X represents a given value of the independent variable, GNP; a represents the value of the line of regression, Yc, when X is zero; and b equals the amount by which the dependent variable (sales) increases for each unit increase in X. This

TABLE 6-7. Correlation Between Sales of Zero Corporation
and Gross National Product, 1956-70

Year	GNP, (billions)X	Sales, (millions)Y	$(X - \bar{X})$	$(Y - \bar{Y})$	$(X - \bar{X})(Y - \bar{Y})$	$(X - \bar{X})^2$
1956	419	462	-223	-200	44,600	49,729
1957	441	462	-201	-200	40,200	40,401
1958	447	470	-195	-192	37,440	38,025
1959	484	529	-158	-133	21,014	24,964
1960	504	555	-138	-107	14,766	19,044
1961	523	564	-119	-98	11,662	14,161
1962	564	590	-78	-72	5,616	6,084
1963	595	617	-47	-45	2,115	2,209
1964	636	664	-6	2	12	36
1965	688	713	46	51	2,346	2,116
1966	753	766	111	104	11,544	12,321
1967	796	791	154	129	19,866	23,716
1968	867	868	225	206	46,350	50,625
1969	936	922	294	260	76,440	86,436
1970	982	958	342	296	101,232	116,964
Sum	9,635	9,931	0*	0	435,203	486,831
Mean	642	662				

*The summations of the figures in the $(X - \bar{X})$ and $(Y - \bar{Y})$ columns may not
exactly equal zero because of the rounding off of the $\bar{X}$ and $\bar{Y}$ values.

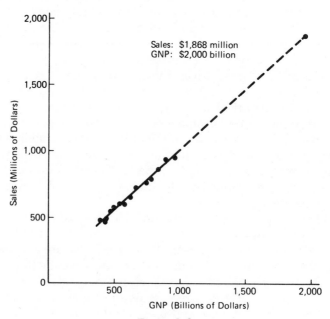

Figure 6-3.

formula, of course, has two unknown variables that can be solved as follows:

$$1. \quad a = \bar{y} - \left(\frac{\Sigma(x - \bar{x})(y - \bar{y})}{\Sigma(x - \bar{x})^2}\right) \cdot \bar{x}$$

In the preceding formula, x represents the independent variable, GNP, and y represents the dependent variable (sales) $\bar{x}$ is the mean of the xs and $\bar{y}$ is the mean of the ys. Thus in substituting from Table 6-7 we have the following:

$$2. \quad a = \$662 - \frac{\$435,203}{\$486,831} \cdot (642)$$

$$= \ 662 - \ 574$$

$$= \ +88$$

In solving for b the formula reads:

$$3. \quad b = \frac{(x - \bar{x})(y - \bar{y})}{(x - \bar{x})^2}$$

Again substituting from Table 6-7, we have:

$$b = \frac{\$435,203}{\$486,831} = .89$$

Thus, $Yc = \$88 + .89X$.

This indicates that at the point of origin, or zero on the X axis of a graph, the value of Yc will be $88 million. For every $1 billion increase in GNP along the X axis, Yc will increase by $890,000. Thus when the GNP was $982 billion in 1970, the Yc line equaled $962 million ($88 + .89 [982] = $962), and when the GNP was $419 in 1956, the Yc value was $461 million ($88 + .89 [419] = $461). These and other Yc values are shown in Table 6-8 and plotted in Figure 6-3.[7]

[7] Another common formula used in solving for a and b is

$$a = \frac{\Sigma x^2 \, \Sigma y - \Sigma x \cdot \Sigma xy}{n \cdot \Sigma x^2 - (\Sigma x)^2}$$

$$b = \frac{n \cdot \Sigma xy - \Sigma x \cdot \Sigma y}{n \cdot \Sigma x^2 - (\Sigma x)^2}$$

TABLE 6-8.

X ($ billions)	Y ($ millions)	Yc ($ millions)	$(y - Y_c)$ ($ millions)	$(Y - Y_c)^2$ ($ millions)
419	462	461	-01	1
441	462	480	-18	324
447	470	486	-16	256
484	529	519	10	100
504	555	537	18	324
523	564	553	11	121
564	590	590	0	0
595	617	618	-1	1
636	664	654	10	100
688	713	700	13	169
753	766	758	8	64
796	791	796	-5	25
867	868	860	8	64
936	922	921	1	1
982	958	962	-6	16
				$1,566

The data from Table 6-8 can be used also to determine the standard error of the estimate. Substituting the data from the table into the formula results in the following

$$SE = \sqrt{\frac{\Sigma (y - yc)^2}{N - 2}}$$

$$= \sqrt{\frac{1,566}{13}}$$

$$= \sqrt{120}$$

$$= \$11.0 \text{ million}$$

Now we have sufficient information to make a reasonable projection of sales for the Zero Corporation. First, we can extrapolate the line of regression (Yc line) as shown in Figure 6-3. It indicates that when the GNP reaches $2.000 trillion, the sales of Zero Corporation will be in the vicinity of $1.868 billion. Secondly, using Figure 6-2, we can expect the GNP to reach the $2 trillion level around the year 1981. Thus it can be anticipated that Zero Corporation sales will reach the $1.868 billion level about that time.

Thirdly, applying the characteristics of the standard error of the estimate to this projection indicates that there will be a 68 percent probability that the sales of Zero Corporation will range between

$1.879 billion and $1.857 billion, a 95 percent chance that the range will be between $1.890 billion and $1.846 billion, and a 99 percent probability that the sales will fall with a range of $1.901 billion and $1.835 billion.

The closer the correlation between the two variables or the less the standard error of the estimate, the smaller the range of probability in the projection and the sharper the forecast.[8] The accuracy of the forecast for a particular variable will depend on the reliability of the forecast of the independent variable. The forecast of sales as related to GNP, for example, is only as good as the GNP forecast. Consequently, it is important to use a reliable forecast for the independent variable.

An unexpected slowdown or acceleration in the rate of economic growth (GNP) in the near future can cause the GNP forecast and the sales forecast to be too high or too low. Consequently, an adjustment should be made in the forecast as near-future economic conditions change. Moreover, changes in the rate of inflation can seriously distort the current dollar forecast of the GNP. If a higher rate of inflation occurs (higher compared with the past years for which the trend line was calculated), the current-dollar GNP forecast will be underestimated. The higher rates of inflation in the 1970s, compared with the 1956–70 period for which the trend line in the above forecast was computed, for example, will result in a higher GNP than forecast. The forecast, however, can be adjusted upward to take into account the higher rates of inflation.

Some business economists maintain a "rolling forecast." They do this by making a 10–15 year forecast every three to five years. Thus, the most recent changes in rates of growth of the GNP, price changes (inflation) and sales, are taken into consideration each time a new forecast is made. Another technique of avoiding the effect of changing price levels is to forecast in terms of constant-dollar values.

This brings to mind another reservation about the use of correlation analysis, that is, the relationship between the dependent and the independent variable. Instead of being content with one measure, it is worthwhile to test a number of independent variables. One may have a better fit than another. The sales of a product or service may be related to GNP, of course. But there may exist a closer relationship between sales and personal income or disposable income. The sale of plumbing fixtures is certainly related to personal income and disposable income, but a better relationship may exist between sales of plumbing fixtures and housing starts.

---

[8] The coefficient of correlation between the GNP and sales of Zero Corporation is .99, which is extremely high since a perfect correlation is 1.0.

It is possible also to compute a multiple correlation in which the dependent variable is related to more than one independent variable. Moreover, it is possible to take into account a change in the relationship between two variables over time by plotting a curvilinear line of regression as opposed to a straight-line regression.

In addition to projecting sales via correlation analysis, other methods have been used to forecast sales of firms and industries.

Projection of Past Pattern

Just as the GNP can be forecast by projecting a trend line, so too can sales of the past be projected into the future. This is done by observing the sales changes over a period of years, constructing a trend line of sales, and then extrapolating the trend line into the future. A standard error of the estimate can be used with this method to provide a little more information about the character of the projection.

Survey of Buyers' Intentions

Another method used, especially for short-run forecasting, is a survey that tries to determine whether potential customers intend to buy a certain product or service in a forthcoming period. An attempt may be made with this method also to ascertain how many units of a product a customer will buy and at what prices. For periodic or perennial sales items, such as autos, suits, and foodstuffs, a survey may be taken of past purchases. On the other hand, for a product or service purchased infrequently, such as the purchase of lake-front property, a survey may be conducted among potential customers. The Survey Research Center at the University of Michigan, for example, conducts annually and quarterly a "Survey of Consumer Finances." In the survey the center tries to estimate the total demand in the economy for housing, automobiles, major applicances, savings, and other goods and services. The results of this survey can sometimes be used as a beginning point for the forecast of sales for a firm or industry.

Survey of Informed Sources

Another less sophisticated method of forecasting is surveying people who are in a position to know what consumers will probably do in the immediate and near future regarding the purchase of goods and services. A firm may get some measure of the forthcoming demand for its product or service by interviewing salesmen, wholesalers, retailers, jobbers, and others who are fairly close to the consumer. Pooling information from such informed sources may give the firm some indication about the sales outlook for its product or service.

FORECASTING SALES FOR NEW PRODUCTS

If a firm is considering marketing a new product and does not have past data on which to rely to project sales, it will have to improvise and use other means in an effort to predict probable sales. In this regard a number of measures have been used with varying degrees of success.

Evolutionary Approach

If the product is an improvement or evolved from an existing product, it can be assumed that the new product may have the same type of experience as that of an existing product. Color television, for example, evolved from black and white, the jet engine from the propeller engine in aircraft and the rotary engine from the internal combustion engine in automobiles. In this manner it is not too difficult to ascertain what the demand for rotary engines will be in the auto industry if it becomes a nearly complete replacement for the internal combustion engine. In fact, the big three firms in the industry have each purchased rights to produce Wankel (rotary) engines.

Substitute Approach

If a new product is a substitute for an existing product, one can estimate what share of the market the new product may get by replacing some of the existing products. A new textbook, for example, may be a substitute for one of the many existing textbooks being used. Knowing the total sales, the producer of the new book may be able to estimate what share of the market it could obtain. From this, he can approximate the probable sales and determine whether the book would be a financial success for the publisher and the author. The great success and growth of the plastics industry in the past few decades is due to the substitability of plastics for other metals and materials.

Sales-Experience Approach

Frequently a new product, such as soap, toothpaste, foodstuffs, and the like, is tested in a sample market in an effort to determine the probable demand for the product. It may be tested at a particular price or at several different prices by using one or more test markets. From the test market results, a projection can be made regarding regional or national sales. The sales experience usually will indicate a go–no go signal for the product. Many successful products have been launched in this manner, such as P & G's Pringle's (potato chips in a can).

Opinon-Sampling Approach

Through use of a questionnaire, given either in person or by mail, one can get some indication of the acceptance of a new product. In this case, a sampling of the potential consumers may be polled directly. Or there may be a poll of sources who have a feel of consumer reaction, such as retailers, wholesalers, jobbers, and manufacturers' representatives. This poll may give some idea of market acceptance and price range.

In using forecasting methods for new products it is wise to employ more than one method. In this manner results may reinforce one another or give opposite results. Sometimes, too, the results may indicate that the product needs improvement or change. Consequently, one can make changes and test-market the product again before spending heavily for large-scale output of the product.

SUMMARY

Forecasting is an important function and a widely used tool of business economists. Forecasts may be made for the total economy or for a particular segment of economic or business activity. Short-run or annual economic forecasts can be constructed by using various economic and business indicators. Forecasts also can be obtained from professional sources.

Long-range forecasting of business and economic activity is more involved and fraught with greater reservations. Long-range forecasts, however, are very useful for long-range company planning. Projections regarding the future of the economy can be based on the growth rate formula $GNP_1 = GNP_0 (1 + r)^n$ or by using the labor force model. Another forecasting technique is to extrapolate a trend line. Such a trend line can be drawn free-hand or computed by the more sophisticated least squares method using the formula $Y_c = a + bX$. This method also provides a standard error of the estimate.

An economic forecast can be used to predict future levels of business activity, particularly sales. This can be done by correlating a dependent variable, such as company sales, with past values of the GNP, or some other independent variable. A line of regression can be plotted showing the relationship of the dependent variable (sales) to the independent variable (GNP). This line of regression can then be extrapolated to show future sales in relation to future growth in the GNP. A standard error of the estimate can be calculated and applied to the forecast.

Forecasts of specific types of business activity can also be made through projection of past patterns, surveys of buyers' intentions, and surveys of informed sources. Techniques for forecasting sales of new products include the evolutionary approach, substitute approach, and the opinion-sampling approach.

Care must be exercised in the construction and use of a forecast based on any of the methods discussed. All forecasts and forecasting methods require certain reservations regarding their development and use.

QUESTIONS FOR ANALYSIS AND DISCUSSION

1. What are some sources of annual GNP forecasts?
2. Explain the three methods of long-range GNP forecasting.
3. Which of the methods in Question 2 provides the most flexibility for inserting judgments regarding inputs into the forecast?
4. What reservations must be kept in mind when using long-range forecasts?
5. What is the "least-squares" method of computing a trend line?
6. What is the "standard error of the estimate," and how is it used in forecasting?
7. How can correlation analysis be used to forecast sales?
8. What is the distinction and importance of a *causal* compared with *casual* relationship between the dependent and the indepedent variable in a correlation analysis?
9. What are some of the other methods, beside correlation analysis, that can be used to project sales of an existing product?
10. What are some of the methods that be utilized to project sales for a new product or service?

PROBLEMS AND CASES

1. Check the GNP and related data, including prices and unemployment, for 1977 and then answer the following:
   (a) How do the actual data compare with the forecast on pages 172-173?
   (b) If sizable differences exist between the actual and forecasted data, try to explain the differences.

(c) What is the GNP forecast for the current or forthcoming year?

2. Table 6-5 of this chapter shows the GNP in current dollars for the years 1965-75; Figure 6-2 extrapolates a GNP trend line to 1985.

   (a) Check the most recent yearly GNP value against the projected value shown in Figure 6-2 and Table 6-6. If the difference is substantial, attempt to explain what may have caused the difference. (The GNP in 1973, for example, was $1.306, but the trend line projected a GNP of approximately $1,291 for 1973.)

   (b) Given below is the GNP in billions for 1966-77. Obtain the GNP for any subsequent years. Then, using the data for the most recent eleven or thirteen years, calculate a GNP trend line, compute the standard error of the estimate, and extropolate a ten-year trend line.

1966 - $ 753	1974 - $1,413
1967 - $ 796	1975 - $1,528
1968 - $ 869	1976 - $1,707
1969 - $ 936	1977 - $1,890
1970 - $ 982	1978 - $——
1971 - $1,063	1979 - $——
1972 - $1,171	1980 - $——
1973 - $1,306	

3. Mr. Pull, the manager of the window shade division, whom you helped previously, calls again to ask you for some information about a five-year sales forecast he is making. When you ask him the basis of the forecast, he indicates that it was constructed primarily from in-house estimates and "gut feel."

   When you ask whether he tried relating his sales to an independent variable, such as personal income or disposable income, his answer is negative. But he is intrigued with the idea. He asks you to show him how to do it so that he may check the results against his forecast. He sends you the sales figures for 1958-72 and his forecast for 1973-77.

   You obtain the disposable personal income for the respective years and list them side by side with the sales figures. From the data you have, do the following:

WINDOW SHADES

Year	Sales	Disposable Personal Income ($ million)
1958	$ 5,600,000	317
1959	5,200,000	336
1960	5,100,000	349
1961	5,250,000	363
1962	5,600,000	384
1963	6,250,000	403
1964	6,550,000	437

WINDOW SHADES (continued)

Year	Sales	Disposable Personal Income ($ million)
1965	6,850,000	472
1966	7,400,000	510
1967	8,050,000	544
1968	9,500,000	588
1969	11,650,000	630
1970	11,800,000	686
1971	13,350,000	743
1972	14,300,000	801
1973	16,200,000*	
1974	17,500,000*	
1975	19,400,000*	
1976	21,400,000*	
1977	23,800,000*	

*Estimates.

(i) Construct a scattergram showing disposable income and sales.

(ii) Calculate and draw a line of regression, using the least-squares method.

(iii) Compute the standard error of the estimate.

(iv) Extrapolate the regression line approximately eight years (to 1980).

(v) Show in dollar figures the sales forecast for 1977 (disposable income for 1977 was $1.309 trillion).

(vi) Indicate the range of the forecast within one standard error of the estimate.

(a) Is your forecast for 1977 higher or lower than that of Mr. Pull?

(b) If it is substantially different, what could account for the difference?

(c) What other independent variables might you recommend for making a projection of window-shade sales?

4. (a) In addition to the previous problem, pick out either a company with which you are associated or some type of economic or business activity in which you are interested. Collect the sales or activity data from a proper source, select an independent variable, and do a forecast using the method suggested in the previous problem.

(b) As another alternative, do a forecast of window-shade sales using housing starts as an independent variable.

Case of the Fuqua Forecast

On December 28, 1972, without prior announcement and with no fanfare, Fuqua Industries, Inc. issued a preliminary 1972 annual report that contained unaudited figures for 1972 and a forecast of its 1973 earnings. The event was unprecedented.

The only comment made by the company on this departure from the norm was a statement by the chairman of the board, J.B. Fuqua, that was included in the report itself:

"This is the first time you have ever received an annual report on the last day of the corporate fiscal year. It is even more unique to include detailed forecasts for the following year's operations.

"It should be clearly understood that the 1972 figures are unaudited and subject to possible adjustment. However, in a well-managed company the independent auditors do not create financial data, they merely verify that company figures are accurate and presented in a manner consistent with prior years.

"It is clear that the Securities and Exchange Commission will shortly require public companies to make forecasts of future opeations. While we are not fully convinced of the merits of making public projections of future earnings, if this is the kind of music we will have to march to, we are willing to lead the band."

This case describes the reasoning and events behind Fuqua's decision to publish the forecasts, examines Fuqua's budgeting system to show how the forecasts were prepared, and presents the arguments for the format that was used.

A trial balloon. Fuqua Industries now owns 19 subsidiary companies, operating in fields ranging from transportation to retail land development. In 1972, total sales rose to $433,960,000, a 17% increase over the 1971 figure, and net operating income was $18,069,000, 29% greater than the 1971 total. Although classified as a conglomerate, in 1972 the company received 58% and 22% of its earnings from its leisure-time and its transportation subsidiaries, respectively.

In 1972, the debate over whether to permit, require, or prohibit the publishing of forecasts raged in various financial and academic journals. The issue was finally examined by the SEC, which ruled that forecasts would be optional for 1973. At the same time, however, events were already taking place within Fuqua that would lead to the publication of its revolutionary preliminary annual report.

A new course. C.L. Patrick, the president and chief operating officer, explained how the situation started:

"Mr. Fuqua had felt for some time that there was no reason why a company with a good internal control and budgeting system could not publish accurate financial statements for the year and have them mailed out by the

Source: John K. Shank and John B. Calfee, Jr., "Case of the Fuqua Forecast," *Harvard Business Review*, November–December, 1973. Copyright © 1973 by the President and Fellows of Harvard College; all rights reserved.

first of the next year, instead of waiting for the auditors to verify what should already be known.

"Early last summer, he asked me if I could give a good solid estimate of the year-end figures. I said that I could, and that the EPS ought to be around $1.80 to $1.85. Later on that summer he asked me if the figures still looked good, and again I said yes."

J.B. Fuqua decided early in the fall to publish the 1972 figures in a preliminary annual report that would appear at the end of the year. Because final figures would not be available in time, the company had to forecast the data for the last two months of the year. Thus there was some concern over the accuracy of the numbers. Theodore H. Davis, the controller, had some reservations:

"While I was satisfied with the forecasted range of earnings, there was still some uncertainty in our year's results. December is *the* month for our ski and snowmobile sales. Because these sales are so dependent on the weather, and because the weather was something we could not forecast, I was somewhat concerned. Also, provided everything worked out, we were supposed to 'close' 100 condominium units in December. If the closings had been delayed, it would really have affected our shelter group forecasts.

"However, most of our subsidiaries had exceeded their 1970 and 1971 forecasts, and after I saw the forecasted figures in October, I was satisfied that they had been conservatively stated."

Davis was not the only one who was concerned—so was Robert L. Whelan, the partner in charge of the Fuqua Industries account for Ernst & Ernst. Even though his own company had no responsibility for the unaudited figures, he was worried that Fuqua might be exposed to undue criticism:

"In the first place, the company was preparing to file a registration statement, and I felt that the SEC might be opposed to this procedure. We called the company's SEC attorneys, and they indicated that publication of the forecast while in registration would not be proper. J.B. Fuqua solved his problem by postponing the registration statement.

"I was even more concerned, however, that there might be adjustments to the preliminary 1972 figures. Although most subsidiaries had recently taken a physical inventory, the results had not yet been extended, summarized, or compared with the book inventories."

Further horizons. The decision to go beyond 1972 data and publish the 1973 forecasts was made in November. Every year at this time, corporate headquarters reviews the various budgets and forecasts for the coming fiscal year sent in by the divisions. The idea to publish forecasts first came from Sam Norwood, the assistant controller. He suggested that if the company were going to publish its 1972 figures, which included two forecasted months, it should publish the 1973 forecasts as well. Norwood explained:

"I was impressed with the very realistic quality of the forecasts being given us by our subsidiaries, and by the supporting evidence for those figures mustered by the division presidents and controllers.

"Also, I am the resident economist on our corporate staff, and to me 1973 looked like a good year to begin publishing forecasts. The economy appeared strong and looked as though it would continue that way well into 1973. I also thought that the SEC might require companies to publish their forecasts pretty soon anyway."

J.B. Fuqua was intrigued with the idea and asked his executives to examine the possibilities to see if there were any really serious obstacles that would prevent them from publishing the forecasts. Davis and Norwood felt that the numbers were good. They felt the internal budgeting and forecasting system had matured to such a point that all the subsidiaries had a very good feel for their industries and for those factors that could affect earnings and sales. Thus, at the time of preparation, the forecasts were realistic estimates of future prospects of their businesses. Davis was reasonably comfortable with the 1973 estimates:

"I did not feel too uncomfortable with forecasting 1973 earnings. We had previously given forecasts of our operations to our board of directors and to our banks. I was not that concerned because we would have a chance to revise them if conditions changed."

A legal issue.   Lawrence P. Klamon, the senior vice president and general counsel, examined the question of legal liability. Although he agreed that a company was certainly increasing its exposure by forecasting, he felt that the liability problem was overrated:

"The 'Monsanto decision' helped to clear the air concerning what a 'reasonable' forecast is.* In essence, the court ruled that, if forecasts are well prepared, extensively reviewed, honest, reasonable, and the best estimate of people most qualified to make them, then there is a 'reasonable basis,' and if the forecasts are revised and this fact is made public, there is no liability under the various securities acts.

"As a practical matter, securities lawyers and financial officers have lived within the liability laws ever since the 1933 and 1934 securities act were passed. Therefore, if a company has a good forecasting system, a proven track record, and proper procedures for documenting and updating the forecasts, there should be no problem."

Other reservations.   Klamon did see four other potential problem areas:

"First, I was a little concerned about our credibility if we should miss our forecasts. Even if the reason for missing them is beyond your control, the fact that you missed will still hurt your image. And there were plenty of environmental factors that were beyond our control.

"Second, I was also concerned that the financial community might place too much confidence in our numbers. This problem was overcome to a certain extent by explicitly stating our assumptions, but, nevertheless, it still existed.

"Third, being the first one to forecast also left us open to the charge that we were not really committed to the concept, but were only forecasting to generate publicity.

"Finally, it may be okay to forecast when business looks good, as it did for the next year; but what about those years when business looks bad?

"One overstated problem is that, in forecasting, a company gives out valuable information to competitors. I don't give much credence to this argument. In our case, about the only things we are giving out are sales increases and profit margins. A competitor might see that we are making 6%, but so what. The forecasts do not tell him how we are making that margin. Anyway, our competitors generally know what we are doing."

*Douglas v. Anderson, '53 FRD 664 (1971).

Fair-weather predictions. Finding general agreement that the numbers looked good and that the legal liability issue, while still a potential problem, was not as significant as many people were saying, J.B. Fuqua decided to go ahead and publish the 1973 forecast:

"I had for some time been questioning the advisability of giving out numbers only to those who asked for them. We have always had a policy here of giving answers to questions asked by analysts and others. We never volunteered the information, but, if they asked, we could give indications of how things looked, even down to product lines and, in some cases, products.

"The Monsanto court case cleared up the liability question, and companies that continue to use this excuse are using a 'chicken' reason. If we are sued, we will have all the necessary records to prove that, when we made the forecasts, the assumptions were well thought out and reasonable. Of course, we will promptly publish any significant changes in our forecasts.

"Anyway, my people told me there was no great problem in going ahead with the forecasts. And when I read that Sandy Burton [John C. Burton, the chief accountant of the SEC] said he thought forecasts were going to be mandatory, I definitely decided that we should include them in our preliminary annual report.

"I think that forecasting will have a beneficial effect on business as a whole. It will force companies to take a good look at their ability to 'count chickens.' Many businesses have absolutely no idea of what they control, and forecasts will force a more detailed analysis."

When asked how the investment community would view the forecasts, J.B. Fuqua replied:

"Despite our efforts to simplify the presentation, I doubt that the average shareholder can really understand much of the statement. So we feel the real thrust of the forecasts is to the security analyst who'll use them — rather than a phone call to us — to check out his figures against ours."

All the senior executives interviewed noted that there were potential problems, but that the benefits generally outweighed them. Norwood stated:

"Sure, I had reservations. The legal liability problem was there. Also, we were locked into this forecast. Obviously, we didn't want to come up short next year.

"Another of the potential problems I saw was that some of the mystery in our stock might disappear. By forecasting our expected results early in the year, everyone would know generally what our expectations were.

"I think that all companies should forecast publicly. After all, since various levels within our business are required to make and meet forecasts, why shouldn't top management do the same thing for its stockholders and accept the same responsibility it places on lower-level management?"

Patrick thought that Fuqua Industries would benefit from being the first to publicly forecast its results because the company would have a one-year head start on everyone else. He did feel, however, that even though the estimates were conservative, and that it was only human nature to make them so, there was always the possibility that they would not be entirely accurate, especially for individual operations. In his own words:

"We always knew the company would face the possibility of erring in the forecast for a particular area, for example, a lack of snow could almost ruin our snowmobile business and so make our forecast way off-target. Of course, the company would reveal promptly and honestly any serious changes in the forecasts if such an unpredictable event occurred. And one advantage of being a diversified company is that other operations can minimize the effect of a normal casualty in one particular year."

On the whole, Patrick believed that Fuqua Industries had a responsibility to forecast:

"We are a public company and we have been giving out much of this information in terms of 'ball park' figures to any analyst who called. It is our hope that, with forecasts, more analysts will be better able to understand us. Those analysts who do follow us have told me that one reason more do not is that they find us too difficult to understand. Breaking down our operations by product lines should help."

The auditor concurs. Whelan of Ernst & Ernst was initially opposed to the idea of Fuqua industries forecasting its 1973 earnings:

"As an auditor, I originally disagreed strongly with the idea. Even though Ernst & Ernst was not involved, I thought they were taking a big risk, because the chances that the forecasts would be accurate were remote. However, Mr. Fuqua convinced me that, as far as the company was concerned, the exposure was no greater than giving out the information piecemeal to analysts who called. I believe that the decision to forecast should be management's. They must feel comfortable with the idea of forecasting.

"'It will be some time before we resolve the question of whether independent accounting firms should perform any function with a company's forecasts. Even without considering whether we have the expertise to evaluate forecasts, the cost to a company such as Fuqua, with its widely diverse operations and geographical locations, could be prohibitive."

Compiling the forecasts. The foundation for Fuqua's published forecasts was its internally generated budgets and forecasts. No major adjustments were made to these internal figures in order to arrive at the public forecasts. Norwood did not feel that compiling the forecasts was very difficult:

"It was no more difficult than assembling the regular budget and forecast material. However, the length of time we had to prepare the statement was shorter than would normally be the case. We only had three weeks to come up with the preliminary annual report, since it had to be at the printers in time to be ready for mailing by the end of December."

The internal system. Fuqua Industries begins it budgetary and forecasting process in October of each year. By this time, all the subsidiaries have sent to corporate headquarters in Atlanta a preliminary budget for the next year.

At a minimum this budget comprises a compilation of key statistics, an income statement, a balance sheet, a funds-flow statement, a list of major expenditures, and a narrative prepared by the president. The budgets are not made up of percentage adjustments tacked onto last year's figures but, rather, are a total evaluation of the company, the industry, and the environmental climate.

The confidence that Fuqua executives have in their ability to forecast is understandable, considering the on-going nature of their budgetary control system. After headquarters reviews the preliminary budgets and, if necessary, makes adjustments, the budgets are returned to the various subsidiaries in late November or early December. Then, after the books are closed on December 31 and the audit is completed, final budgets are due at corporate headquarters. This is normally in February of the budget year.

Throughout the year various updated reports are required. These reports contain actual figures plus revised forecasts for various future periods. They are what the company terms "forecasts." These forecasts create the framework for a periodic formal reappraisal of the business performance outlook in view of recent history, formally unanticipated economic and competitive conditions, and major shifts in management strategies and tactics.

The forecast updates must be in Atlanta by April 20, July 20, and October 20. The reports included are an income statement, balance sheet, funds-flow statement, and a commentary by the subsidiary president. Each forecast shows actual year-to-date figures, a month-by-month forecast for the next three months, and a quarter-by-quarter forecast for the remainder of the year. The commentary contains specific reasons for year-to-date variations from the budget as well as any changes in outlook.

Besides the annual budget and quarterly forecast reports, corporate headquarters also receives monthly a statement of income, a balance sheet, a funds-flow statement, and a commentary report. Thus, through their various reports, the top management of Fuqua Industries is continually receiving indications of actual progress and of any changes in the subsidiaries' assumptions about the future.

Management felt that its system of quarterly updates on the annual forecast would allow it time, if necessary, to promptly revise the public forecasts. Furthermore, from the monthly reports, it would be able to spot trends and have information readily available if a dramatic change was occurring that would require disclosure.

Because there was so little time in which to assemble the preliminary annual report (see Exhibit I and Exhibit II), Norwood temporarily dropped his other duties to head up the effort. Norwood explained that, while there were some things he would do differently in the future, he thought that the format was a fair presentation:

"We decided to place our forecast figures next to our historical figures and on the same page, because we thought that such an arrangement would make comparison between actual figures and forecasts much easier: it also enhanced our credibility. It showed that we were not trying to make comparisons difficult for the reader.

"Also, this type of format was the same as the one we use on our internal budgets and forecast reports. In the future, we probably should do a better job of highlighting the forecast figures, but in December we were operating with a two-color offset press and we had no time to go into more elaborate printing."

When asked why the product lines were broken down as they were, and why interest expense and profits before and after taxes were broken out, Norwood had this comment:

"We thought that it would be to our advantage to break down our product lines. We thought our stock was undervalued, and we believed that if analysts could see where our earnings come from, they would also see that our stock is undervalued.

"Some thought it would be unwise to break out our snowmobile and

EXHIBIT 1. Fuqua Industries' 1972 Preliminary Annual Report,
Statement of Consolidated Income
(In thousands of dollars)

	Actual 1971	Estimated 1972	Forecast 1973
Net Sales and Revenues	$366,557	$430,000	$484,000
Operating Costs and Expenses	331,072	385,600	431,600
Interest Expense	8,006	8,700	10,000
Total Costs and Expenses	339,078	394,300	441,600
Operating Income Before Taxes	27,479	35,700	42,400
Provision for Income Taxes	13,477	17,700	21,000
Net Operating Income	14,002	18,000	21,400
Extraordinary Item	(3,500)*	–	–
Net Income	$ 10,502	$ 18,000	$ 21,400
Earnings Per Common and Common Equivalent Share (8,541,000 shares in 1971, 9,500,000 shares in 1972, and 10,000,000 shares† in 1973)			
Net Operating Income	$ 1.59	$ 1.85	$ 2.09†
Extraordinary Item	(.41)	–	–
Net Income	$ 1.18	$ 1.85	$ 2.09†
Earnings Per Common Share Assuming Full Dilution (9,731,000 shares in 1971, 9,870,000 shares in 1972, and 10,000,000 shares† in 1973)			
Net Operating Income	$ 1.44	$ 1.80	$ 2.09†
Extraordinary Item	(.36)	–	–
Net Income	$ 1.08	$ 1.80	$ 2.09†

*Loss on the sale of a business.
†Earnings-per-share forecast for 1973 does not include shares which may be issued in either stock dividends or in acquisitions.

lawn mower sales. However, the obvious advantages of showing how good our lawn mower company was finally made us conclude that it was a good idea.

"We are a highly leveraged company, so we broke out interest expense. This is a figure many analysts following Fuqua like to see. We separated operating profit before and after taxes because we wanted to show that we do not play games with our tax rate."

When asked why the forecasts were published using a single number instead of a range, Norwood stated:

"We ruled out ranges because of the potential problems they might cause in adding them up from our various product lines. Even if they were small

EXHIBIT 2. Fuqua Industries' 1972 Preliminary Annual Report,
Summary of Operations
(In millions of dollars)

Sales and Revenues	1971	Estimated 1972	Forecast 1973
Leisure Time			
Snowmobiles & Lawn Mowers	$ 45.8	$ 56.0	$ 68.0
Sporting Goods	31.4	37.0	39.0
Marine Products	34.0	41.0	48.0
Entertainment	27.1	38.0	45.0
Photographic Finishing	17.9	21.0	23.0
Total Leisure	156.2	193.0	223.0
Transportation	131.0	140.0	147.0
Shelter*	41.6	61.0	74.0
Agribusiness	33.0	36.0	40.0
Total Continuing Operations†	361.8	430.0	484.0
Add: Discontinued Operations	6.1	—	—
Less: Restatements of Businesses Purchased	1.3	—	—
Total Sales and Revenues	$366.6	$430.0	$484.0

Earnings	1971	1972	% of Total	Compound Annual Growth (rate %)	Forecast 1973
Leisure Time					
Snowmobiles & Lawn Mowers	$ 7.3	$ 9.7	22%	32%	$11.4
Sporting Goods	3.1	4.1	9	30	4.1
Boats & Boat Trailers	.6	3.3	7	27	4.5
Entertainment	4.5	6.4	14	16	6.8
Photographic Finishing	1.7	2.5	6	9	2.9
Total Leisure	17.2	26.0	58	24	29.7
Transportation	9.2	10.0	22	23	10.0
Shelter*	4.7	2.8	5	56	5.5
Agribusiness	5.3	6.7	15	17	6.9
Total Continuing Operations†	36.4	45.5	100%	23%	52.1
Add: Discontinued Operations	(.8)	(.1)			—
Less: Unallocated Corporate Expenses and Corporate Interest	7.9	9.7			9.7
Less: Restatements of Businesses Purchased	.2	—			—

EXHIBIT 2. continued

Earnings	1971	1972	% of Total	Compound Annual Growth (rate %)	Forecast 1973
Income Before Income Taxes	27.5	35.7		19	42.4
Income Taxes	13.5	17.7			21.0
Net Operating Income	$14.0	$18.0		17%	$21.4

*Does not include Brigadier Industries since acquisition had not been completed.
†Includes all continuing companies for all periods regardless of date of acquisition except that Gulf States Theatres is included only for the periods since June 1, 1972. Gulf States Theatres was only a part of a business complex, and accurate data for prior periods on the theatres are not available.

for each product line, totaling them would give a range that would be quite large for the whole company. Furthermore, this range would not jibe with that for Fuqua as a whole, since the latter would be based on a realistic appraisal that neither all the low, nor all the high, ends would occur at the same time."

Forecasts forever? Six months after the fact, Fuqua Industries reported that, while it had received numerous telephone calls from other companies expressing interest in how Fuqua Industries handled its forecasts, there had been little response from the investment community. It had been assumed that analysts would applaud the disclosure of corporate forecasts. And yet, after sending out 12,000 copies of the preliminary annual report to securities analysts along with a card asking for their reactions, J.B. Fuqua reported that only about 50 replies had been received. He went on to state:

"I thought that there would have been more of a reaction to our forecast. I still believe that the idea is good, but I am not about to take up the banner and commence a crusade in favor of companies publishing their forecasts."

Fuqua Industries, Inc. has sent to analysts its revised July 1973 figures, which, like the audited 1972 figures, are not significantly different from the ones originally forecast. Again, the response has been slight. In view of the lack of interest among analysts, the company is still undecided whether to repeat the procedure next year.

(a) Do you approve or disapprove of Fuqua Industries' action in publishing a forecast of next year's earnings? Why or why not?
(b) If earnings are to be forecast, what are the advantages and disadvantages of breaking the forecast down by product lines?

(c) How can an economic forecast for the United States economy help in making a sales forecast for an individual firm?

(d) Sales and earnings forecasts look good during a period of economic prosperity. What effect might they have during a period of recession?

SELECTED READINGS

Burns, Arthur F. *The Business Cycle in a Changing World.* New York: National Bureau of Economic Research, 1969.

Business Conditions Digest. Washington, D.C.: U.S. Department of Commerce (monthly).

Chisholm, Roger K., and Gilbert R. Whitaker, Jr. *Forecasting Methods.* Homewood, Ill.: Richard D. Irwin, Inc., 1971.

Cloos, George W. *The Seventh Business Cycle. Business Conditions.* Federal Reserve Bank of Chicago, March 1975.

Dauten, Carl A., and Lloyd M. Valentine. *Business Cycles and Forecasting.* South-Western Publishing Co., 1974.

Dederick, Robert C. "NABE and the Business Forecasting," *Business Economics,* January 1971.

DePamphilis, Donald M. "Forecasting Expenditures on Consumer Durable Goods." *Business Economics,* May 1974.

Forrester, Jay W. "Business Structures, Economic Cycles and National Policy." *Business Economics,* January 1976.

Lee, Maurice W. *Macroeconomics: Fluctuations, Growth and Stability.* Homewood, Ill.: Richard D. Irwin, Inc., 1971.

Moore, Geoffrey H. "Economic Forecasting—How Good a Track Record?" *The Morgan Guaranty Survey,* January 1975.

——. "New Work On Business Cycles." *53th Annual Report.* National Bureau of Economic Research, September 1973.

Statistical Indicators. North Egremont, Mass.: Statistical Indicator Associates (weekly).

The American Economy, Prospects for Growth to 1988. New York: McGraw-Hill Publications' Economics Department, 1975.

"The Business Cycle Is Alive and Well," *Business Week,* April 19, 1976.

7

Cost of Production

In addition to demand, another area of great concern and sensitivity to the business firm, or any institutional organization for that matter, is its cost. We can say, as we did in Chapter 2, that profit is simply the difference between revenue and cost. But is it that simple? It is relatively easy to ascertain revenue: Multiply the number of units sold by the price per unit. Cost, however, is another matter. There are numerous methods of assigning cost; costs can vary with output; some costs are hidden. Consequently, it requires a little more analysis to determine the true and exact economic cost of production. Under competitive conditions there may be little that a firm can do regarding its cost per unit of input, since cost per unit of input is the price of a factor of production decided in the resource market by aggregate supply and demand. Nevertheless, the firm can alter its cost per unit of output. A decrease in cost per unit of output can be effected by using better production techniques, through more efficient use of labor and by spreading fixed cost over a greater range of output. Since a firm's cost of production largely determines the supply of goods that it will offer on the market and has an important bearing on its profit position, a closer insight into cost concepts will aid us in analyzing managerial decisions on price and output.

THE PRODUCTION FUNCTION

Output costs are affected by certain production relationships between factor inputs and product output. The relationship between factor inputs and product output is often referred to as the *production function* of the firm. Certain conventional characteristics exhibited in the production function help determine why cost varies with output. Among these are the *principle of substitutability*, *returns to scale*, and the *law of diminishing marginal productivity*.

Principle of Substitutability

A production manager combines inputs in such proportions as will yield the best results, in both quantity and quality. Within limits set by the requirements of technology, a manager can vary the input factors to seek that combination that will prove to be the most economical with respect to production cost. Where labor is plentiful and capital scarce, for example, it is usually more economical to use a larger amount of labor and a smaller amount of capital in the input mix. Where land values are high, a garment factory may be built on a smaller area with many floors and a different arrangement of machinery from what would be the case where land is cheap and the factory could be built over a larger area and with fewer floors. Moreover, within the limits set by the technological process, the factors in the input mix may be varied without a reduction in the volume of production. This is commonly known as the *principle of substitutability*. But it is sometimes called the *principle of variable proportions*.

This principle can be demonstrated with the aid of a three-dimensional (horizontal, vertical and depth) production possibilities chart showing the relationship between two different units of input X and Y, and a single unit of output Q. This chart, Figure 7-1, showing the two-input, one-output relationship, is similar to a topographic map with contour lines (isoelevation lines) which connect all points of equal elevation. In this way the topography — hills, valleys, mountains, and gradients of elevation — of an area can be readily observed. In economic analysis, identical quantities of output that can be produced with various combinations of inputs are shown on a production possibilities chart as *isoquants* (from *iso*, meaning equal, and *quant* for quantity). The chart contains isoquant curves showing all the different combinations of input that produce identical quantities of output. Figure 7-1 shows that the greater the total combination of inputs, X and Y, that are used, the higher will be the quantity of output, Q_1, Q_2 and Q_3 (for contour-map readers, the higher up the mountain).

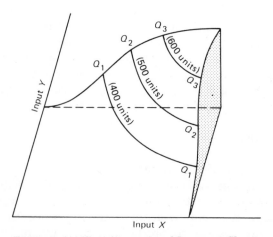

Figure 7-1. Three-dimensional Isoquant Chart

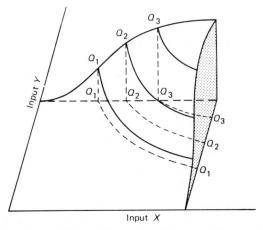

Figure 7-2. Conversion of Three-dimensional Isoquant Curves to a Two-dimensional Chart

For purposes of analysis, we can now transfer these quantities to a two-dimensional chart, remembering, however, that the isoquant lines represent a third dimension: quantity. This can be done as shown in Figure 7-2 where lines Q_1, Q_2, and Q_3 are dropped to the lower surface as Q_1, Q_2 and Q_3. We can then construct a new chart as shown in Figure 7-3 which shows these isoquants on a plane surface. Notice that Q_1, representing 400 units of output, can be produced by various combinations of inputs measured along the vertical and horizontal axis of the chart. Q_1, for example, can be produced

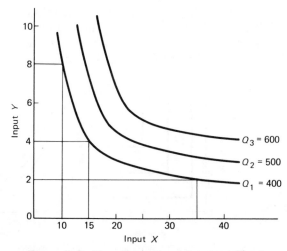

Figure 7-3. Two-dimensional Isoquant Chart

with 8 units of input Y and 10 units of input X. Likewise, Q_1, or 400 units, can be produced with $4Y$ and $15X$, or with $2Y$ and $35X$.

The chart also reveals that, as fewer units of Y are used, it requires an increasing increment of unit X in substitution for a unit of Y. Assume that Y is machinery and X is labor and Q, the product being manufactured, is tennis shoes. Machinery does a considerable amount of the cutting, stitching, and applying of adhesive in the production of tennis shoes, and it can do it more effectively than labor. Consequently, as fewer machines are used, it takes an increasing proportion of laborers to produce the same output.

This relationship between the exchange of X and Y inputs is known as the *marginal rate of substitution of input factors*, or *MRS*. It measures the amount of one unit of input that must be substituted for another, if total production is to remain constant. This can be expressed algebraically:

$$MRS = \frac{\Delta Y}{\Delta X} = \text{the slope of the isoquant}$$

In most instances, the MRS will not be constant. It will diminish, and the slope of the isoquant line change, as the degree of substitution increases. As stated in our previous example, if more and more labor is substituted for machinery in the production of tennis shoes, the increment of labor needed to offset the decrement of a machine will increase as fewer machines are utilized. One can even visualize a situation in which the isoquant may become positively sloped, indicating that there is a limit to the degree that inputs may be substituted for each other without changing the quantity of output. On the other hand, there are rare cases in which inputs may be perfect substitutes for each other and cases in which they do not substitute at all. Figure 7-4 presents three charts showing various degrees of

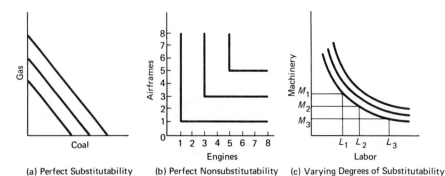

(a) Perfect Substitutability   (b) Perfect Nonsubstitutability   (c) Varying Degrees of Substitutability

Figure 7-4. Three Different Isoquants

substitutability. Figure 7-4 (a) shows input isoquants for the generation of steam in which coal and wood are perfect substitutes for each other, since the steam engine may be fueled completely by coal, entirely by wood, or by various combinations of coal and wood. Figure 7-4 (b) reflects perfect nonsubstitutability between engines and airframes in the production of single-engine aircraft. Each aircraft requires one engine and one airframe, and no number of airframes will compensate for the lack of an engine. Figure 7-4 (c) depicts the usual type of substitutability between labor and machinery found in our example of the production of tennis shoes. It indicates varying degrees of substitution as the input mix changes.

Notice, also, that it takes an increased number of total units of input in any combination to produce Q_2, or 500 units of output, as shown in Figure 7-3. This can be achieved through such combinations of inputs as $8Y$ and $15X$ or $4Y$ and $25X$.

The chart, moreover, can indicate the best combination of inputs to use by relating the cost of inputs to each other. Assume that varying combinations of inputs can be purchased for a given outlay of money. This given outlay is referred to as an *isocost* (equal cost) line. Isocost line C_1 in Figure 7-5 shows that 7.5 units of Y or 32 units of X—$6Y$ and $7X$, $4Y$ and $15X$, or $2Y$ and $22X$—can be purchased for an identical cost. Inspecting this line, one can ascertain that the best combination of inputs for the firm will be $4Y$ and $15X$. Any other combination of inputs will result in less total production, since at no other combination is the isocost line tangent to the isoquant

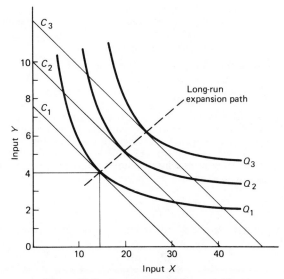

Figure 7-5. Isoquant and Isocost Chart

line.[1] The mixture of inputs at this point also yields the least-cost combination. This is where a firm gets the most output for a given amount of monetary input.

As total expenditures for inputs, and therefore isocost lines, change, different points of tangency on isoquant-isocost maps will appear, such as those shown in Figure 7-5. By connecting these points of tangency, or least-cost combinations, we can chart a least-cost expansion path. Since the least-cost expansion path indicates the inputs required for various levels of output, the least-cost expansion path also can provide the information necessary to plot an output cost line. For any least-cost level of output, indicated on an isoquant, we can determine the quantitites of inputs required to produce that given level of output. Multiplying the input quantities by the prices of the inputs will tell us the total cost of the least-cost combination of output. This can be done for each of the output levels. The outputs and their respective cost can then be plotted on a graph, such as that shown in Figure 7-6.

---

[1] This is so because output along the isoquant line is constant. Therefore, if input Y is reduced, causing the output to decline, input X must be increased sufficiently to increase output enough to offset the decline in output caused by the reduction of input Y. The reduction in output brought about by a small reduction in input Y is equal to the marginal product (MP) of Y, MP_y, multiplied by the change in Y, ΔY. This may be written:

$$(1) \; \Delta Q = MP_y \cdot \Delta Y$$

Likewise, the change in output associated with the increase of input X may be stated as follows:

$$(2) \; \Delta Q = MP_x \cdot \Delta X$$

Therefore, substitution of input X for input Y, ΔQ, in the preceding equations must be the same and can be expressed:

$$(3) \; -MP_y \cdot \Delta Y = MP_x \cdot \Delta X$$

Transposing the variables in Eq. (3) yields the final relationship:

$$(4) \; \frac{\Delta Y}{\Delta X} = -\frac{MP_x}{MP_y} = \text{slope of the isoquant}$$

The slope of the output isoquant, shown in the equation to be equal to $\Delta Y/\Delta X$, is determined by the ratio of the marginal products of the two inputs.

On the graph there is a tangency between the isocost line and the isoquant curve at the point where the inputs are optimally combined. Therefore, the prices of the inputs at the optimal input combination must be equal to the ratio of their marginal products as shown below:

$$(5) \; \frac{P_x}{P_y} = \frac{MP_x}{MP_y}$$

To state it another way, the ratios of marginal product to price must be equal for each input:

$$\frac{MP_x}{P_x} = \frac{MP_y}{P_y}$$

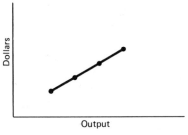

Figure 7-6.

Returns to Scale

The law of substitutability applies when two productive agents in the input mix change, one increasing and the other decreasing. What happens, however, if all productive agents are varied proportionally? Suppose, for example, that all factors in the input mix were doubled. Would output double?

If output changes in proportion to a given change in inputs, of course, constant returns to scale exist: A doubling of all inputs, for example, will double output. On the other hand, when the increase of outputs is in smaller proportion than the increase of inputs, it is an indication of decreasing returns to scale. That is, if the production manager were to double all inputs, output would increase less than 100 percent. Increasing returns to scale, on the other hand, implies that doubling all inputs would more than double output.

Increasing and constant returns to scale may take place, especially in smaller-sized operations, when a manager expands total input without changing the proportions of the mix. Continued expansion of the scale of operation, however, may bring about eventually decreasing returns to scale if the operation becomes rather large and complex. It is often difficult to increase all inputs proportionally. Moreover, resources may not be available, the quantity of inputs may vary, as they do in mining, and the efficiency of workers is not uniform.

Sometimes a business may expand its scale of operation by increasing its input mix without increasing proportionally the element of management. As the scale of operation increases, a heavier burden is placed upon existing management. In addition to decreasing returns to scale, diminishing marginal productivity may be taking place as top management becomes overtaxed.

Returns to scale for a two-input–single-output production function can be demonstrated with an isoquant chart. Figure 7–7 shows a sit-

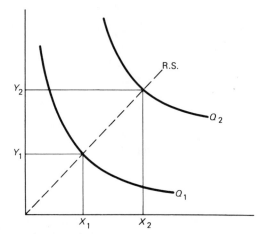

Figure 7-7. Constant Returns to Scale

uation of constant returns to scale (RS). Here it can be seen that by doubling all units of input, the output will double. The points of production can be connected by line RS, which is a straight line. With a little imagination, you can visualize conditions of increasing, decreasing, and varying returns to scale shown in Figure 7-8.

In a way returns to scale has been an important ingredient in the success of many franchise businesses. Instead of adding inputs to an existing operation or location, the franchiser duplicates the inputs, but at a different location. In most cases the franchiser, such as McDonald's, Burger Chef, Kentucky Fried Chicken, Fotomat, Bride & Groom Showcase, and numerous others, have worked out, through experimentation and otherwise, the ideal size of operation for a given economic environment, such as population, income pattern, and flow of traffic. The franchiser knows the best production function, costs, number of employees, financial requirements, parking facilities, and other requirements needed for a successful operation. The franchisee buys the package, and by following the pattern, with slight modifications, he can operate a successful and profitable business. Many of the usual problems and decisions have been worked out in advance for the franchisee.

Law of Diminishing Marginal Productivity

One of the most important economic phenomena affecting cost and output decision-making is the law of diminishing productivity. An essential function of management is to organize materials, capital, and labor so that the best combination of these factors of production

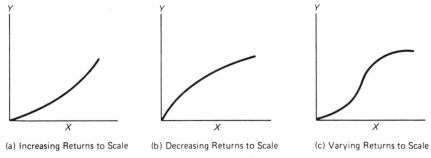

(a) Increasing Returns to Scale   (b) Decreasing Returns to Scale   (c) Varying Returns to Scale

Figure 7-8. Increasing, Decreasing, and Varying Returns to Scale

will be used. There should not be an excess of one factor and a dearth of another. The efficient farmer, for example, realizes that, with a given amount of land, an optimum amount of fertilizer, a certain number of laborers, and a specific number of machines should be used. Likewise, the plant manager knows that the most efficient operation of a given number of machines requires a definite number of employees. If the input factors are not in the optimum proportions, the unit cost will be higher than necessary and/or output less than maximum.

In each production situation, there is an optimum proportion of the factors of production. This optimum or "best" proportion of the factors is determined in part by the law of diminishing marginal productivity.

To illustrate the operation of law of diminishing marginal productivity and show its effects on cost of production, let us assume that an entrepreneur manages his own printing shop with four presses, adequate space, and an ample supply of raw materials. If he hires only one worker who attempts to operate all four presses, the net result will be a limited amount of production, since it will be difficult for one worker to attend to all of the presses, keep the supply of raw material flowing smoothly, bind and package the finished product, and do other jobs directly or indirectly related to the operation of the printing shop. In fact, some of the presses may be idle a good part of the time. If the entrepreneur were to hire a second worker of equal ability, he would find that total output would rise. He would get not only direct benefits from the physical labor of the second worker, but the presses would be operating more of the time. As a result, total output might rise from 20 units to 44 units.

Hiring a third worker might cause total production to rise to 72 units. If a fourth worker were hired, each employee could attend one machine and production might rise still further, to 104 units. In each instance the increase in output per additional worker exceeds that of the previous worker. The change in output per additional worker is known as the *marginal product of labor.*

Marginal Product. The marginal product is defined as the increase in total output resulting from the use of an additional unit of input. In the case cited, input is labor. But how long can marginal product continue to increase? Assuming that all other factors — space, presses, materials — remain fixed, a point eventually will be reached at which the fixed factors become overtaxed or reach their maximum usage, compared with their under-utilization in the early stages of production. Upon hiring a fifth worker, for example, the manager may find that production still rises, since the additional worker may run stock, package materials, and do other jobs that allow the press tenders to devote more time to running the presses. The increase in production, or marginal product, resulting from the employment of the fifth worker, however, may be less than it was with the addition of the fourth worker. Total production may expand by thirty units as a result of hiring the fifth worker, compared with thirty two for the fourth worker, as shown in Table 7-1.

As additional workers are hired and other inputs remain the same, the marginal product will diminish further. A sixth worker may serve as a relief worker, improving the efficiency of all workers by allowing them needed rest periods, and total production may rise to 156 units, an increase of twenty two units. As the employment of additional workers continues, one can imagine a work situation being reached in which the fixed factors are taxed to full capacity and there will be no increase in output. A stage might even be reached, in fact, where workers begin getting in one another's way, resulting in a decline in total production.

Even though increasing marginal productivity is possible, particu-

TABLE 7-1. Input, Output, Marginal Product, and Average Product

Units of Input	Total Output	Marginal Product	Average Product
1	20	—	20
2	44	24	22
3	72	28	24
4	104	32	26
5	134	30	26.8
6	156	22	26
7	168	12	24
8	176	8	22
9	180	4	20
10	180	0	18

larly in the early stages of production, and constant marginal productivity may occur over a certain range of input, diminishing marginal productivity is more common. Consequently, emphasis is placed on the *law of diminishing marginal productivity*, or *diminishing returns*. This law may be stated as follows: As additional units of a factor of production are combined with fixed quantities of other factors, a point will be reached at which the increased output resulting from the use of an additional unit of the variable factor will not be as large as was the increased output due to the addition of the preceding unit. This law applies to the use of any factor in production, and it affects the supply of particular goods and services.

Average Product.   In analyzing the cost of production, average product also is important because it also affects per unit cost. *Average product* is defined as output per unit of input. In Table 7-1, where 3 units of labor input are utilized and the resulting total product is 72 units, for example, the average product is 24 units ($72 \div 3 = 24$). Notice that the average product, like the marginal product, increases, reaches a maximum, and then declines. There is a definite relationship between the average product and the marginal product. Whenever the marginal product is greater than the average product, it pulls up the average product. When the marginal product is less than the average, it reduces the average product. This relationship is shown in Figure 7-9. Note that, even after the marginal product curve reaches its peak and moves downward, the average product curve for a while continues upward until the two are equal. Thereafter, both curves move downward.

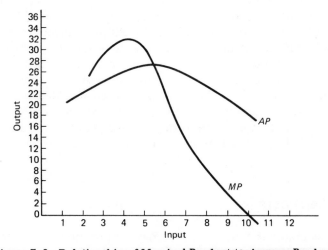

Figure 7-9. Relationship of Marginal Product to Average Product

In order to pull the average product down, the marginal product must be less than the average product, not merely declining. In the table, or on the graph, it can be seen that the marginal product of the fifth laborer declined from 32 to 30 units, but the average product rose from 26 to 26.8 units. This is because the marginal product, 30, although declining, is still larger than the average product, 26. But notice that a point is eventually reached at which the average product, like the marginal product, begins to decline.

The law of diminishing marginal productivity is important for two reasons: First, from the manager's side, it affects production costs, and the task of finding the best combination of productive inputs is one of the most important responsibilities of management. Second, from the viewpoint of the owners of factors of production, under competitive conditions marginal productivity is the most important determinant of the income (price) they will receive in exchange for their labor or other factors of production.

The laws of diminishing productivity and returns to scale and the principle of substitutability are crucial to the operation of a business and influence the demand for the factors of production. The producer will strive to employ factors in that proportion that will mean least cost. Within the limits permitted by technological and quality requirements, the manager will use less expensive factors more freely and higher-priced factors more sparingly.

To what extent will a manager employ or use units of each factor? Certainly, he will want to use them in a manner to achieve the least-cost combination in relation to a desired level of output. Where possible, he will call to his aid the services of engineers, cost accountants, and production experts. If by using capital he can obtain a higher production return for his dollar compared with adding labor, he will continue to add units of capital until the returns from capital, labor, and other input factors yield the same returns. This point of combination of inputs is the *least-cost combination*. It is a point that depends on many variables, and it is constantly subject to change.

Any improvement in technology or any change in the quantity, quality, or price inputs may lead to a new least-cost combination. If the price of one factor rises without a change in others, for example, this factor will be used more sparingly and other factors more liberally.

PRODUCTION COSTS

For most practical purposes, the costs of production are measured in terms of money; the amount of such production costs is made up of payments for labor, capital, materials, and other items directly or indirectly related to the production of a good or service. In addition, as we saw in Chapter 2, an imputed cost allowance is made for the services of the entrepreneur. A certain nominal profit is necessary to induce an entrepreneur to continue producing a particular good or service. This nominal profit is considered by economists as a cost of production. The value of this profit (cost) can be measured by the opportunity cost of the services of the entrepreneur. Any profit over and above this nominal profit is known as *economic profit* or *pure profit*.

External Economies

As an enterprise grows and develops, *external economies* — those realizable outside of individual firms — sometimes arise. These economies result from a greater degree of specialization in procuring, transporting, financing, and distributing materials. In the production and sale of automobiles, for example, external economies have resulted from the separation of assembly from parts manufacturing and the use of separate credit facilities, transportation, and selling franchises. These developments, together with the enormous size of assembly plants, make high level of production and low unit costs possible. In other cases, major department stores, grocery chains, and mail-order houses are able to buy merchandise at lower costs because of their large-scale purchases.

Explicit and Imputed Costs

As we learned in Chapter 2, expenditures for production inputs arising from agreements or contracts are *explicit costs*. These costs are easily recognized because they are stated usually in terms of money; moreover, they are generally paid and recorded.

Costs arising from the use of an entrepreneur's own factors of production, such as the use of one's own land or labor, are *implicit* or *imputed costs*. They generally are not paid out or recorded. In normal accounting procedure, imputed costs are often ignored. The imputed salary costs arising from an entrepreneur's own management services, for example, may not be deducted as a cost in arriving at the taxable income for a proprietorship. In measuring the true economic profit, however, imputed values for the use of one's own land, labor, or capital must be recognized as a part of the real cost of production.

Cost Characteristics

Rarely can the volume of production be increased without changing the cost per unit of output. In some plants and industries — at least for a time — an increase in production results in a decrease in unit cost. In most cases a point eventually is reached beyond which a further increase in production will result in a rise of per unit cost.

Unit cost of production usually varies with the volume of production. When a plant facility is operating at less than full capacity, for example, additional units can be produced, and the increase in production may result in a decrease in the cost per unit produced. The reduction in per unit costs can be attributed to economies within the plant that are made possible by a greater division of labor, a fuller utilization of equipment, better terms in purchasing larger quantities of materials, and other cost savings.

Some industries are said to be *decreasing-cost industries*. Railroad transportation is frequently cited as an example of this kind because of its high fixed cost. On the other hand, agriculture and extractive industries are said to be characterized by increasing costs. Most establishments and industries operate for a while under a condition of decreasing costs, but beyond a certain level of production, they experience increasing per unit cost.

Neither individual firms nor industries are immune to the operation of the law of diminishing marginal productivity. The increased utilization of plant capacity and equipment may make decreasing costs possible for a while. But eventually, increased production pushes the combination of production factors farther and farther away from the ideal proportions, and a tendency toward increasing costs develops. Unit cost will be lowest when a firm is using the optimum combination of inputs. This is known as the *least-cost position*. Production beyond this point results in rising per unit costs. In the long run, a firm or industry may overcome the tendency toward increasing cost by improved technology. If production is pushed beyond a certain point, however, the tendency toward decreasing returns will recur. For example, in the coal-mining industry a producer may utilize modern methods of production and dig coal from large veins near the surface. But if increased demand calls for a larger supply that can be obtained only by recourse to mining of deeper coal, or from smaller veins, the cost per ton will increase.

Categories of Costs

In analyzing the operation of a business firm, an economist will classify costs of production broadly into fixed costs and variable costs. *Fixed costs* are those costs whose total remains constant over a given range of output. Under given condition of capacity, the total fixed cost of a firm does not vary with a change in the volume of production. The aggregate of fixed costs is frequently referred to as *overhead cost*. It includes such items as bond or mortgage interest, certain depreciation on buildings and equipment, property and franchise taxes, and insurance. In addition, a portion of salaries paid for executive and supervisory personnel may properly be regarded as fixed costs, since a minimum managerial staff must be maintained, even when the business is operating at a limited capacity.

Although total fixed costs remain constant over a given range of production, fixed costs per unit of output decrease as output increases. If the total fixed cost in a given firm, for example, is $500,000 and 200,000 units of output are produced, the amount of fixed cost per unit of output is $2.50. But if production is increased to 400,000 units, the fixed cost per unit of output, or the average fixed cost, is $1.25.

Average fixed cost is calculated by dividing total fixed cost by total output. Average fixed cost decreases with increased production as the total fixed cost is spread over a larger and larger number of units, but it never reaches zero. Column 8 of Table 7-2, for example, shows what happens to a $100 total fixed cost when it is converted to average fixed cost.

Total variable costs are those costs of production other than fixed cost, such as the cost of labor, materials, and energy. They vary with changes in output. *Average variable cost* is the variable cost per unit of output. It is found by dividing the total variable cost by total output. Average variable cost decreases as production increases, until the point of diminishing marginal productivity is reached. Thereafter, average variable cost increases as the number of units produced increases.

Table 7-2, for example, shows that the cost of each variable unit of input is forty dollars and that the total variable cost will increase by forty dollars with each additional unit of input. Consequently, total variable cost rises from forty dollars to four hundred dollars as the units of input increases from one to ten. This total variable cost can be converted to an average variable cost by dividing the total variable cost shown in column 6 by the total output shown in column 2. Note that the average variable cost starting out at two dollars per unit of output drops to $1.50 per unit with five units of input or 134 units of output and rises thereafter. It rises to two dollars with 180 units of output. Note, too, that the point of the lowest average variable cost, $1.50, corresponds with the point of diminishing average productivity, or the point of highest average product.

Total cost is the sum of total fixed and total variable costs. *Average total cost* is found by dividing total cost by total output or by adding the average fixed cost and average variable cost at any particular level of output. Total cost increases as output increases, but not proportionately. Average total cost, like average variable cost decreases until

TABLE 7-2.

(1) Input	(2) Total Output	(3) MP	(4) AP	(5) TFC ($)	(6) TVC ($)	(7) TC ($)	(8) AFC ($)	(9) AVC ($)	(10) ATC ($)	(11) MC ($)	(12) AR ($)	(13) TR ($)	(14) MR ($)	(15) Profit ($)
1	20	—	20	100	40	140	5.00	2.00	7.00	—	4	80	4	(-60)
2	44	24	22	100	80	180	2.27	1.82	4.09	1.67	4	176	4	(-4)
3	72	28	24	100	120	220	1.39	1.67	3.05	1.43	4	288	4	68
4	104	32	26	100	160	260	.96	1.54	2.50	1.25	4	416	4	156
5	134	30	26.8	100	200	300	.75	1.50	2.25	1.33	4	536	4	236
6	156	22	26	100	240	340	.64	1.54	2.18	1.82	4	624	4	284
7	168	12	24	100	280	380	.60	1.66	2.26	3.33	4	672	4	292
8	176	8	22	100	320	420	.57	1.82	2.39	5.00	4	704	4	284
9	180	4	20	100	360	460	.56	2.00	2.56	10.00	4	720	4	260
10	180	0	18	100	400	500	.56	2.22	2.78	—	4	720	4	220

a certain level of production is attained. After the point of diminishing average productivity is reached, however, the average total cost increases as production increases. This is shown in column 10 of Table 7-2, indicating that the lowest average total cost is on line 6 at $2.18.

An important concept to the economist is incremental or marginal cost. *Marginal cost* is the increase in the total cost resulting from the production of one more unit of output. Marginal cost is determined in large part by marginal productivity, and the shape of any marginal-cost curve will depend on the nature of the marginal-product curve. Column 3, Table 7-2, is the marginal-product schedule. Column 11 shows the marginal cost for our hypothetical firm. Notice that marginal cost decreases, reaches a minimum, and then rises. Notice, also that, as the marginal product rises, the marginal cost decreases. Then, when the marginal product declines, the marginal cost increases. The point of lowest marginal cost, $1.25, as shown in line 4, corresponds with the point of highest marginal product. This reveals the close, but inverse, relationship between marginal product and marginal cost.

In calculating marginal cost, remember that it refers to the increase in total cost per additional unit of output, not input. The increase in total cost shown in column 7 is the increase in total cost per additional unit of input. This incremental cost per unit of input must be converted to incremental cost per unit of output in order to attain marginal cost. Since the second unit of input, for example, cost $40[2] more but generated an increase of total output of 24 units, the marginal cost, or increased cost per unit of output, will equal $1.67 ($40 ÷ 24 = $1.67) as shown on line 2 of column 11. Similarly, if the successive increments of total cost are divided by the respective marginal products, the marginal cost for each line will be found.

The relationship of these various costs can be seen more vividly when presented in graphic form, as shown in Figure 7-10. On this graph, average fixed cost, AFC, will be represented by a curve continuously decreasing in value as total fixed costs are spread over a larger and larger amount of output. The average variable cost, AVC curve, will decrease, reach a minimum, and then rise because of the law of diminishing marginal productivity. The average total cost, ATC, which is a combination of AFC and AVC, likewise will decline and then rise. Note that when both AFC and AVC are declining,

---

[2] This increase in total cost per additional unit of input is known as the *marginal outlay*. Therefore marginal cost can be found by dividing the marginal outlay by the marginal product, or

$$\frac{MO}{MP} = MC.$$

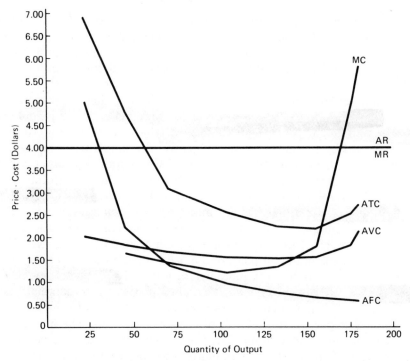

Figure 7-10. Marginal Analysis Chart

ATC will be declining. A point is reached, however, at which AVC starts to rise while AFC is still declining. What happens to the ATC at this point depends on the relative strength of the two curves.

At an early stage, the downward momentum of AFC is usually stronger than the upward force of AVC, so that ATC continues to decline for a while. But eventually the upward force of AVC overcomes the downward momentum of AFC, and ATC rises thereafter. Notice on the graph, also, that the marginal-cost curve, MC, will decrease, reach a minimum, and then rise because of its close relationship with the marginal-product. Whenever marginal cost is less than average variable cost or average total cost, it will effect a reduction in AVC and ATC in much the same manner that the marginal product affects the average product. Whenever MC is greater than AVC or ATC, it will cause them to rise. Moreover, by its very nature MC will or intersect the AVC and the ATC curves at their lowest points.[3]

[3] What is discussed and presented here is a typical hypothetical set of cost functions and cost curves, as shown in Figure 7-10, often found in industry. Since production functions and shapes vary from firm to firm and industry to industry, cost functions and cost curves come in a variety of shapes.

Often business managers will make use of the concept of standard cost, as compared with the use of average total cost. Standard cost per unit of output is determined by adding the material cost, labor cost, and other costs, direct or indirect, associated with predetermined levels of production or capacity. A factor is also added for overhead (fixed cost). The standard cost per unit of output is determined for some level of operating capacity or production level. If a firm customarily produced 200,000 units at normal capacity, standard cost would be determined on the basis of that capacity.

Standard cost gives the firm a good idea of what it costs to produce a unit of output at normal capacity. In this respect it is similar to the average total cost used by the economist. The standard cost can be used to determine selling price and profit per unit. It can also be used in submitting bids on jobs and deciding whether to accept a particular job order.

Standard cost can be misleading, however, if labor cost or material cost changed between the time the standard cost was estimated and the time the actual production took place. In such cases an adjustment for variance has to be made in the accounting records in order to determine the average total cost and calculate the true profit. Actual cost can also deviate from the standard cost if the firm operates at a greater or lesser capacity than normal. In the hypothetical case cited, if labor cost were $8 per unit, material cost $6 per unit, and overhead $4 per unit, the standard cost would be $18 per unit. Overhead per unit is determined by dividing the total overhead to be assigned by the number of units produced. Thus, in the case above, $800,000 ÷ 200,000 = $4 per unit.

If the firm operated at fewer than 200,000 units, however, standard cost would be less than actual or average total cost because total overhead would be underabsorbed. If only 160,000 units were produced, total overhead assigned would be $640,000 (160,000 × $4) instead of $800,000. If the firm operates at 160,000 units, the true overhead burden assigned to each unit of output should be $5 ($800,000 ÷ 160,000) and the average total cost should be $19 per unit, providing there was no variance in labor and material costs.

On the other hand, if the firm operates at 240,000 units of output, the standard cost would be overstated compared with the true cost of production. In such a case, overhead burden would be overabsorbed by $160,000 (240,000 × $4 = $960,000). The actual cost of production is only $17.33 and the true overhead burden per unit is $3.33 ($800,000 ÷ 240,000).

REVENUE AND PROFIT

In an earlier chapter we saw that the demand schedule measures the quantities of a commodity or service that will be purchased at various prices at a given moment of time. It was indicated, also, that under competitive conditions, prices would be determined by the free forces of the market. Conditions are not always competitive, however, and the forces of demand and supply are not always unobstructed. Nevertheless, let us assume for the present that the market price becomes the price at which an individual firm can sell its product. This will allow us to develop some revenue concepts and relate them to the cost concepts in order to analyze the profit position for our hypothetical firm.

Revenues

Average revenue, as defined by the economist, is the price per unit of output sold. It is the market price from the viewpoint of the seller. It may also be computed by dividing total revenue by the number of units sold. *Total revenue* is the amount of revenue received from the sale of a given quantity of goods or services. It can be readily calculated by multiplying the average revenue, or price, by the number of units sold.

An important and more complex concept used by the economist is marginal revenue, which is a counterpart of the marginal-cost concept explained earlier. *Marginal revenue* is defined as the increase in total revenue that results from the sale of one more unit of output. Marginal revenue can be calculated by dividing the increase in total revenue resulting from the use of an additional unit of input[4] by the increase in total product (marginal product). In line 2, Table 7-2, for example, total revenue increased from $80 to $176, or by $96, with the addition of the second unit of input. Since total output increased by 24 units, however, the marginal revenue is $4 ($96 ÷ 24 = $4).[5]

In our example, the values of the marginal revenue and the average revenue are identical. But this will not always be the case. Any time one deals with conditions other than perfect competition, the values of the marginal revenue and the average revenue will differ, as we

---

[4] The increase in total revenue per additional unit of input is commonly called the *marginal revenue product*.

[5] Another way to state this is to say that marginal revenue product divided by marginal product equals marginal revenue, or

$$\frac{MRP}{MP} = MR.$$

shall see later. With a constant price, however, any time the firm sells an additional unit at the market price of four dollars, it adds four dollars to its total revenue, and the marginal revenue must equal the average revenue, or price.

Profit

Total profit in its simplest form is the difference between total revenue and total cost. Whether a firm makes a profit, and how much, depends on the relationship of its revenue to its costs. Even when a firm is suffering a loss, the decision whether to continue to operate or shut down will depend on its cost-revenue relationships. A firm can analyze its profit situation in many ways. It may, for instance, compare its total revenue with its total cost by using a break-even chart, or it may utilize marginal analysis by examining and comparing its marginal revenue and marginal cost.

Total Revenue vs. Total Cost

A firm can determine its most profitable level of output and the levels at which it suffers losses by comparing total revenue with total cost over a given range of output. Moreover, by constructing a break-even chart, it can determine at what point its losses cease and profits begin. This is referred to as the *break-even point*. It may be expressed in terms of the total output, or percentage of capacity utilization. Firms construct and use break-even charts to indicate at what level of production they must operate in order to prevent losses and generate profits. A firm will nautrally endeavor to reach the break-even output or capacity and to go beyond it as far as profitable. It must, however, avoid the temptation to push too far beyond, as it may encounter rapidly rising marginal costs at, or near, full capacity levels. In some situations, total profits may actually decline in spite of higher output. The maximum profit will be garnered at that level of output, or capacity, where there is the largest gap between total revenue and total cost.

As part of a break-even chart, cost can be divided into total fixed cost and total variable cost. If desirable, the variable cost can be further segmented into a variety of cost, such as direct and indirect manufacturing cost, material cost, labor cost, and selling costs.

Having converted the values from Table 7-2 into a break-even chart, we see in Figure 7-11 the total fixed cost of $100 represented by a straight horizontal line. This indicates that the total fixed cost remains constant over the given range of output. Total cost, which continually increases, is represented by a line moving upward to the

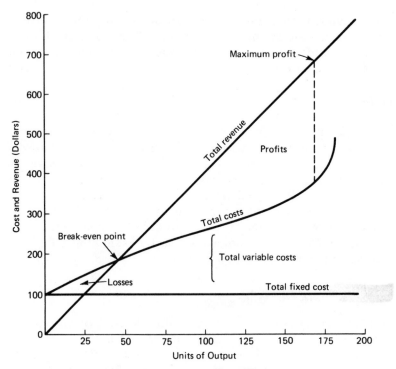

Figure 7-11. Break-Even Chart

right. The total cost taken from Table 7-2 is curvilinear due to the effect of the law of diminishing marginal productivity on the average, marginal, and total cost curves. The difference between total cost and total fixed cost represents the total variable cost. Total revenue is represented by the line moving upward to the right at a constant slope. Since the price at which each unit sells is constant, as sales increase total revenue will increase by uniform amounts. The break-even point is at 46 units of output. Production below that level results in economic losses. Although profits are made at all levels of production beyond the break-even point, maximum profit is made when production is in the vicinity of 168 units. That is where there is the greatest gap between total revenue and total cost.

The same information can be interpolated from the original data (Table 7-2), which indicate that the break-even point will occur somewhere between the second and third units of input, or shortly after the 44th unit of output. Likewise, the maximum profit position will be attained with seven units of input, which corresponds with production in the vicinity of 168 units of output.

Usually firms use a standard cost system for convenience to figure

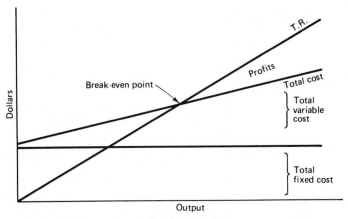

Figure 7-12.

cost per unit of output. Such a system will produce linear, or straight-line, cost curves for break-even charts, such as that shown in Figure 7-12. The break-even chart is a good tool of analysis and serves as a target guide for production goals. Often at year's end, however, the standard cost must be adjusted to allow for variances that caused actual cost to deviate from the standard cost.

Marginal Analysis

In most circumstances, any time a firm can increase its total profit by producing more or fewer units, it will act accordingly. Consequently, the business economist endeavors to analyze a firm's profit situation in terms of changes to total cost and total revenue with additional units of output. This can be done through marginal analysis. Any time the production and sale of an additional, or marginal, unit of output adds more to total revenue than it does to total cost, profits are bound to increase, or losses decrease, whatever the situation may be. The two concepts that indicate how much is added to revenue and to cost with each additional unit of output are marginal revenue and marginal cost. To determine the point of maximum profit, or minimum loss, for a firm, all we need to do is observe their relationship. Consequently, whenever MR is greater than MC (MR > MC), profits will rise, or losses will diminish. On the other hand, if MR is less than MC (MR < MC), profits will decrease, or losses will increase. It will be to the firm's advantage to increase its production so long as its MR > MC. It will be economical to reduce production whenever MR < MC.

In most cases marginal revenue is a constant or decreasing value;

beyond the point of diminishing marginal productivity, marginal cost rises continuously. Therefore, as a firm produces additional units of output, it eventually reaches a point at which MR = MC. This is its maximum profit position, since at any lesser level of production MR > MC and at any greater level of production MR < MC. For our hypothetical firm, for example, we can see that the MR has a constant value of $4, while the MC, after reaching a low of $1.25, continuously increases as production moves toward 180 units. Comparing the MR in column 14 with the MC in column 11, it can be seen that at all levels of production up to and including that associated with the seventh unit of input or 168 units of output, MR exceeds MC. Consequently, the firm will continue to produce up to that point. It will not add the eighth unit of input, however, since the MR is less than the MC for the resulting output. The firm will maximize profits, according to the marginal analysis, at an output level in the vicinity of 168 units. This can be interpolated from Table 7-2 or observed in Figure 7-9. This corresponds with the maximum profit position indicated on the break-even chart illustrated in Figure 7-11.

Minimizing Losses in the Short Run

Thus far we have been dealing with a profitable situation. What happens, however, if a firm is suffering a loss? Suppose, for example, that the average revenue received by the firm were only $2, as determined by demand and supply on the market. Assuming that the costs remained the same, our firm would not be able to make a profit at any level of output. It would, however, minimize its losses with 6 units of input, or 156 units of output. Under such circumstances, should the firm continue to operate or should it shut down? The answer depends on the relationship of revenue to cost, and whether we are concerned with the short-run or the long-run period.

In marginal analysis the *short run* is a period of time in which some factors of production are fixed. The *long run* is a period of time in which all factors of production, including machinery, buildings, and equipment become variable. In the short run, a firm may increase its output, within a given range, by adding workers, buying more raw materials, and/or adding other variable factors without changing its fixed plant, machinery, and equipment. If given sufficient time, however, it could enhance its output greatly by increasing its production capacity by building, buying, or renting additional equipment or a plant. Consequently, in the long run all factors become variable. The actual length of this long-run period varies among industries. Obviously, the long run for the steel industry, which requires construction of huge mills and new furnaces, is much longer than the long-run period of the garment industry, where a firm can purchase additional sewing machines, floor space, and storage capacity within a few weeks.

Even when a firm is minimizing its losses in the short run, its managers still must face the question of whether it is better to continue to operate or to shut down. The answer will depend on the relationship of its fixed to its variable cost and the relationship of the variabile cost to its total revenue. Assume that a firm has a total fixed cost of $120,000, and a total variable cost of $80,000, for a total cost of $200,000. And suppose its total revenue is $100,000. Even though the firm is suffering a loss of $100,000, it is better for it to continue to operate in the short run rather than close down. Notice that by operating, the loss is $100,000, but if the plant were shut down, the loss would be greater. If it were to close down, its total cost would drop by the amount of its variable cost, $80,000; but remember that its revenue would drop to zero. Yet, the firm would still have a fixed cost of $120,000 to pay; hence its loss would be $120,000 instead of $80,000. Although the firm would not be making a profit, it would, by operating, recover all of its variable cost and some of its fixed cost. This is usually referred to as *making a contribution to overhead*. It is a principle that guides managers of firms not only in deciding whether to shut down a plant in the short run, but also in deciding whether to continue certain lines of production that are unprofitable.

To carry our example one step further, notice that if the total revenue for the firm were only $60,000, it would be better to shut down in the short run. In such a case, the variable cost of operating, $80,000, is more than the revenue from operating. By continuing to operate, the total loss incurred would be $140,000 ($120,000 + $80,000 - $60,000 = $140,000). On the other hand, if the firm, in such circumstances, were to shut down, its total loss would be only $120,000, the amount of the total fixed cost.

It benefits a firm to operate at a loss in the short run so long as it can recover its variable cost and make a contribution to overhead. If it cannot recover its variable cost it is more economical to shut down in the short run. One way to determine through marginal analysis whether a firm is recovering its variable cost is by comparing the average revenue with the average variable cost at the point of equilibrium, or the point of minimum losses. If AR is equal to or greater than AVC, it will pay the firm to continue its operation. If AR is less than AVC, it will have less loss by closing down. Before a firm shuts down even in the short run, however, its executives and managers should consider many other offsetting factors, such as the size of the loss, how long they anticipate losses to occur, the effect on customer relations, the dispersal and probably the loss of its experienced work-force as a result of a layoff, and the effect on its unemployment tax rate.

Whether the firm should continue operating at a loss in the long run depends on a multitude of factors. These include cost of new assets, the cost of capital, competition, the general demand for its products, and the general status of the economy. Unless the firm can foresee some improvement in its profit outlook, it would not be wise to pour additional time, effort, and capital into a nonprofitable operation.

PROFIT UNDER COMPETITIVE AND NONCOMPETITIVE CONDITIONS

Pure economic profit is a return to the entrepreneur from the operation of a business. It excludes any payments, explicit or imputed, to nonentrepreneurial factors utilized in the input mix. The amount of profit necessary to induce an entrepreneur to continue in business is called *nominal profit*. It is measured by the opportunity cost of the entrepreneur's services. Nominal profit is considered an economic cost of doing business. Any profit over and above nominal profit is called *pure economic profit*. Under conditions of pure competition, profit, besides being residual and dynamic, is a temporary phenomenon. The forces of pure competition, particularly the entry of new firms, are such that they tend eventually to eliminate pure profit.

Monopoly, or other forms of imperfect competition, may impose barriers to the entry of new firms into the market. Thus, in the absence of competition, profit becomes more than a temporary phenomenon. Moreover, since the output of a monopoly constitutes the total supply on the market, the monopolist can influence the market price by changing his output. Thus, a price can be established within limits that will yield greatest profit for the monopolist. Under a condition of monopoly, or imperfect competition, profit may be larger than it would be under more competitive conditions.

The cost and revenue for an individual firm and what it may be able to do about them depend in part on the type of competition that prevails in its industry.

SUMMARY

Production costs are affected by certain physical relationships between factor inputs and product output, such as the principle of substitutability. Through the use of isoquant and isocost lines, often referred to as *isoquant-isocost maps*, one can determine the least-cost combination for various levels of output. These may be used to chart a long-run expansion path for a firm. The concept of returns to scale also is an important tool of economic analysis.

One of the most frequently applied concepts, however, is the law of diminishing marginal productivity. It states that as units of a given input are added to the input mix, total output will increase in decreasing proportions, if all other inputs remain constant. In effect, the marginal product will increase, reach a maximum, and then decline as a result of the law of decreasing marginal productivity.

Production functions affect certain costs, especially average variable cost, marginal cost, and average total cost. Marginal analysis can be applied to determine the equilibrium output or maximum profit (or minimum loss) position of a firm. This occurs at the point at which marginal revenue equals marginal cost (MR = MC).

Maximum profit can be ascertained also by observing the gap between total revenue and total cost, or by using the widely adopted break-even analysis. Many firms employ break-even charts for setting targets in terms of output or capacity operation.

Costs differ in the short run compared with the long run. At times a firm may continue to operate in the short run even though it is suffering a loss. This will occur whenever a firm by continuing to operate can cover its variable cost and make a contribution to overhead.

QUESTIONS FOR ANALYSIS AND DISCUSSION

1. Describe the principle of substitution.
2. What is an isoquant?
3. Explain the marginal rate of substitution of input factors.
4. What is an isocost line?
5. What is the relationship between an isoquant curve and an isocost line? How can the two be related to determine the optimum input mix?
6. Distinguish between the concepts of diminishing marginal productivity and returns to scale.
7. What evidence do you see of the manifestation of diminishing returns and returns to scale in the growth and development of American industry?
8. Distinguish between explicit and implicit cost.
9. Define each of the following terms used in marginal analysis:

   a. Total fixed cost (TFC)   e. Average variable cost (AVC)
   b. Total variable cost (TVC)   f. Average total cost (ATC)
   c. Total cost (TC)   g. Marginal cost (MC)
   d. Average fixed cost (AFC)   h. Marginal revenue (MR)

10. Why is the point where MR = MC the point of equilibrium output for the firm?

11. Draw and explain a break-even chart.

12. Does the level of output at the break-even point on a break-even chart correspond to the level of output at the point where MR = MC on a marginal analysis chart? Why or why not?

13. Under what conditions might a firm that is suffering an economic loss find it beneficial to continue to operate rather than shut down its operations?

PROBLEMS AND CASES

1. The Sharpe Cutlery Co. had an economist who was endeavoring to figure the best mix of labor and capital for its production runs. Labor cost was $20 per unit; capital was $30 per unit. The economist transferred to a new job before completing his work. You are asked to complete the study for the company. Shown below is the isoquant chart the economist had completed.

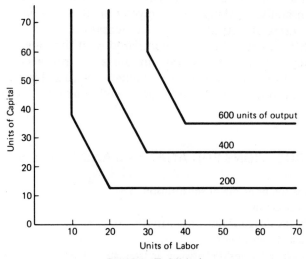

Problem Exhibit 1

(a) Using an isocost line, determine the optimum input mix and the cost of the capital and labor required to produce 400 units of cutlery per day.

(b) How much capital and labor is needed and what is the cost of producing 200 units of output?

2. The manager of a small machine shop asks you to do a production possibility study for him. He informs you that he can use any of three processes in manufacturing his product. Process A requires 2 machine hours and 2 labor hours, process B requires 1 machine hour and 4 labor hours, and process C requires 4 machine hours and 1 labor hour to product a unit of output. The firm can rent all the machine hours it needs at $4 per hour, and

it can obtain any required amount of labor at the prevailing wage of $4 per hour.

(a) Graph a chart showing the production possibilities using as many as 6,000 machine hours and 6,000 labor hours of input.

(b) Draw isoquants for 500, 1,000, and 1,500 units of output.

(c) Assuming that the manager has $16,000 to spend for machine time and labor, draw an isocost line and indicate the best combination of machine time and labor hours to be used in order to maximize his efficiency.

Lightfoot Shoe Company

The Lightfoot Shoe Company, located in New England, produced men's dress shoes. Its shoes were sold mainly to retail shoe stores and department stores in the eastern part of the United States. Buyers retailed the shoes under their respective brand names. Lightfoot had no direct retail outlets of its own.

Most of Lightfoot's production was concentrated in a ten-month period, with the plant operating at about 90 percent capacity during that period and about 15 percent during July and August. During the summer slack period, repairs and renovations were made. Most of the workers took their two-week vacations during the summer and otherwise were furloughed for six weeks without pay.

Lightfoot Company usually sold its shoes at an average price of $18.00 per pair. This price included a 20 percent mark-up on the cost of production, as shown in Exhibit 1.

EXHIBIT 1.

Labor	$ 6.50
Material	4.80
Depreciation	.95
Overhead	1.05
Administrative cost	.50
Selling expense	.30
Repairs and supplies	.90
Total Cost	$15.00
Plus 20 percent markup	3.00
Total	$18.00

In the fall of 1977, Lightfoot received a letter from the vice-president of a large discount chain with several outlets in the Middle West. The vice-president was interested in placing an order for 100,000 pairs of men's dress shoes to be delivered between October 1, 1978, and November 1, 1978, provided that the price would not exceed $14.00 per pair.

The controller of Lightfoot dismissed the potential order as being unprofitable. The president of Lightfoot, however, was not so sure that this could not be done profitably. He hired an economic consultant to analyze the situation and perhaps make some recommendation. The consultant submitted the following breakdown on the cost of producing a pair of shoes.

EXHIBIT 2.

Direct Labor	$ 5.00
Semi-direct Labor	1.00
Material	4.50
Spoilage	.30
Total direct costs	$10.80
Indirect Labor	.50
General overhead burden	.95
Depreciation	1.15
Repairs and Supplies	.70
Administrative and selling expense	.90
Total Cost	$15.00

In addition, the president calculated that if this order of shoes were produced primarily during the slack summer period, direct labor costs would rise by at least 20 percent because some overtime would need to be paid for longer hours and Saturday work. Furthermore, the need for more leather would cause the company to use other than its regular sources of supply. But new suppliers were not willing to extend the usual 2 percent discount Lightfoot had been receiving from its regular suppliers. For his services, the economic consultant received a fee of twenty-five hundred dollars.

(a) Should Lightfoot Shoe Company accept the order for the 100,000 pairs of shoes?

(b) Do you agree with the cost breakdown of the economist?

(c) Does the marginal cost differ from the average variable cost in this case?

(d) What other factors (particularly marketing, production, and financing factors) should be considered before accepting or rejecting this order?

The U.C. Farr Company

U.C. Farr Company was a manufacturer of small binoculars that it sold to wholesalers for $22.50 per pair. These binoculars retailed at about $29 to $30 per pair. The company generally operated its plant at 80 percent of capacity. At that level it produced 50,000 pairs of binoculars monthly. Variable cost changes with output and even the direct per unit cost increases noticeably, giving to spoilage and overtime hours pay for labor, when the firm endeavors to operate beyond 100 percent of its capacity.

Variable and Fixed Cost

Capacity (percent)	60	70	80	90	100	110
Units of Output	37,500	43,750	50,000	56,250	62,500	68.750
Variable Cost	$ 78,000	$ 90,000	$100,000	$115,000	$135,000	180.000
Fixed Overhead	$100,000	$100,000	$100,000	$100,000	$100,000	100.000
Total (V.C. & O.H.)	$178,000	$190,000	$200,000	$215,000	$235,000	280.000
Direct Cost	$450,000	$525,000	$600,000	$675,000	$750,000	825,000
Total Actual Cost	$628,000	$715,000	$800,000	$890,000	$985,000	1,105,000

Since there was some concern about the exact cost of production, Mr. Eyerich, the plant manager calculated the standard cost of a pair of binoculars as follows:

Material cost	$ 5.00
Direct labor cost	$ 7.00
Variable and overhead cost	4.00
Standard cost	$16.00

He obtained the four dollar variable and overhead-cost figure from a flexible budget submitted to him by the company accountant, as shown in the exhibit.

(a) If $16.00 is used as a standard cost, what will be the total overabsorbed or underabsorbed burden at each of the production levels other than normal (80 percent).

(b) Plot the standard-unit cost versus the actual unit cost for each of the six levels of production. At what levels will the actual cost exceed the standard cost, and at which levels will it be below the standard cost?

(c) Plot a marginal-cost curve and an average cost curve for various levels of output from 60 to 100 percent of capacity.

(d) Assume that U.C. Farr receives an order to produce monthly an additional 15,000 pairs of its binoculars for a private-brand label at a price of $15.00 per pair. Should it take the order? Why or why not?

Roundwheel Bicycle Company

C.M. Pedal, the president of a medium-sized bicycle manufacturing firm, has established a profit goal of 6 percent per dollar of sales for his firm. He figures this will yield a comfortable rate of return on stockholders' equity. In addition, he makes use of break-even charts to analyze the profit position of Roundwheel Bicycle Company.

Last year the company had the following sales and cost, while operating at its usual 90 percent of capacity:

	1977	
Sales		$35,000,000
Cost of Goods Sold:		
Material	$15,000,000	
Direct Labor	12,000,000	27,000,000
Gross Profit		$ 8,000,000
Other Expenses		
Factory Overhead	$ 2,500,000	
General Overhead	2,000,000	
Selling Expense	1,400,000	5,900,000
Net Profit		$ 2,100,000

Information has been gathered by Mr. John Dollar, the company's comp-troller, indicating that next year a 10 percent wage package for production workers (direct labor), recently negotiated by the union, will go into effect at the beginning of the next production year. The company usually grants the nonproduction and clerical workers the same percentage pay increase that is given to the production workers. Last year, wage cost for nonproduction or clerical workers comprised 30 percent of factory over-head, 50 percent of administrative overhead, and 40 percent of selling expense. It is expected that material prices will rise by an average of 5 percent for the next year.

In preparation for a forthcoming meeting of the board of directors, Pedal asks you, as price analyst for the company, to prepare the following data:

(a) A break-even chart for the year 1977, indicating the break-even point and showing the profit for the year.

(b) A table showing by how much revenue has to be increased in total and the percentage increase in price in 1978 necessary to maintain a 6 percent profit on sales.

(c) A break-even chart for 1978, showing the break-even output, and pointing how that level of output compares with the break-even out-put for 1977.)

The Rocky Ridge Furniture Company

Mr. Hiram Ash owns and operates the Rocky Ridge Furniture Company, a manufacturing shop in the Appalachian area. It is one of several small producers and it specializes in wooden rocking chairs. The company expe-rienced good sales in the 1960s because the wooden rocking chair was made popular, in part, by its use by President Kennedy. By the mid-1970s, however, sales were disappointing, costs were up, and Ash was losing money on his operation. He kept operating, nevertheless, since a number of his relatives and friends were working in the shop. Although the firm had a one-shift capacity of 10,000 units annually, the plant currently operated at only 60 percent of its capacity because of slow sales. The rockers sold for $18.00, which was the general market price received by most of the producers in the area. Rocky Ridge's cost of production cur-rently was $19.50, as shown in the statement below:

Cost of Rocking Chairs at a Volume of Six Thousand

Labor	$ 5.50
Materials	7.00
Depreciation	4.00
Selling and Administrative Expense	3.00
Total Cost per Unit	$19.50

Ash's son, David, who recently was graduated from college, has been helping out in the plant for the past six months. Observing that the company was losing money, he recommended certain changes in the operation of the business. Among other things, he suggested that the price of rocking chairs be cut by 16 2/3 percent, and that production be trebled by going to two shifts, each operating at 90 percent of capacity. David was confident that at a price of $15 per chair, 18,000 chairs could be sold, particularly if they were marketed through a department store or discount-store chain. He found out that it was possible to obtain a 10 percent discount on wood stock by ordering in larger quantities. In addition, he calculated that productivity per man-hour could be increased by as much as 25 percent by applying labor more efficiently and getting more use out of machinery and equipment. The plant manager agreed that the machinery and equipment were in good condition and could stand more intensive use without hastening their depreciation, so long as the machinery and equipment were given proper maintenance. David also surveyed the local area and estimated that the firm could get an ample supply of workers for a second shift, but calculated that it (the firm) would have to pay a 5 percent wage premium for such labor.

Other members of the family agreed that production might be increased, but they could not understand how it was possible to make a profit by selling rocking chairs for $15.00 when they were unable to make a profit by selling at $18.00. Ash was uncertain what to do, because he knew that even though the company was losing money at the $18.00 price it was at least covering its variable cost and making a contribution to overhead.

(a) Which would you recommend: that the firm continue to produce at the 6000-unit level, or that it implement David's recommendations?

(b) Calculate the unit cost of producing 18,000 rockers per annum.

(c) How will the new unit cost compare with the suggested selling price of $15.00?

(d) Calculate and compare the total profit or loss at the six thousand output level with the proposed 18,000 output level.

SELECTED READINGS

Adams, Walter. *The Structure of American Industry*. New York: Macmillan Publishing Co., Inc., 1971.

Blair, John M. *Economic Concentration: Structure, Behavior, and Public Policy*. New York: Harcourt Brace Jovanovich, Inc., 1972.

Clower, Robert W., and John F. Due. *Microeconomics*. Homewood, Ill.: Richard D. Irwin, Inc., 1972.

Cole, Charles L. *Microeconomics: A Contemporary Approach*. New York: Harcourt Brace Jovanovich, Inc., 1973.

Competition and the Motor Vehicle Industry. A study by General Motors, submitted to the U.S. Senate Subcommittee on Antitrust and Monopoly Hearings, April 10, 1974.

Dooley, Peter C. *Elementary Price Theory*, 2nd ed. New York: Appleton-Century-Crofts, 1973.

Ferguson, C.E., and S. Charles Maurice. *Economic Analysis*. Homewood, Ill.: Richard D. Irwin, Inc., 1974.

Hirshleifer, Jack. *Price Theory and Applications*. Englewood Cliffs, N.J.: Prentice-Hall, Inc., 1976.

Lancaster, Kelvin. *Introduction to Modern Microeconomics*. Chicago: Rand McNally & Company, 1974.

Leftwich, Richard H. *The Price System and Resource Allocation*. New York: Holt, Rinehart & Winston, Inc., 1973.

Mansfield, Edwin. *Microeconomics*, 2nd ed. New York: W.W. Norton & Company, Inc., 1975.

Maxwell, W. David. *Price Theory and Applications in Business Administration*. Pacific Palisades, Calif.: Goodyear Publishing Company, Inc., 1970.

Stigler, George J. and James K. Kindahl. *The Behavior of Industrial Prices*. New York: National Bureau of Economic Research, Inc., 1970.

Stigler, George J. *The Theory of Price*. New York: MacMillan Publishing Co., Inc. 1973.

Thompson, Arthur A., Jr. *Economics of the Firm: Theory and Practice*. Englewood Cliffs, N.J.: Prentice-Hall, Inc. 1973.

Tesler, Lester G. *Competition, Collusion, and Game Theory*. Chicago: Aldine Publishing Company, 1971.

Trescott, Paul B. *The Logic Of The Price System*. New York: McGraw-Hill Book Company, Inc., 1970.

Watson, Donald S. *Price Theory and Its Uses*. Boston: Houghton Mifflin Company, 1973.

8

Pricing:
Pure Competition
vs Monopoly

Cost, prices, output, and profits frequently depend on the structure of competition faced by the firm. Many types of competition exist in the American economy. Since there are millions of firms doing business in hundreds of industries, one can find different types of competition and numerous shades of competition within each type. Competition may range all the way from perfect (pure) competition to pure monopoly. There are fundamental differences between types of competition, but some markets contain elements of more than one type. Furthermore, a firm may find itself in one type of market structure in selling its output, but in a different type of market in buying its inputs. From the standpoint of managerial economics it is important to understand the different forms of competition because they affect a company's pricing and output decisions. In some industries a firm may have no influence whatsoever over the price. In other industries, firms, through their output decision, can have considerable effect on the market price.

PURE COMPETITION

Four basic types of market structures are pure competition, pure monopoly, monopolistic competition, and oligopoly. Among the distinguishing characteristics of markets are the number of firms in an industry, the degree of product differentiation, and the ability of firms in an industry to influence market price. Pure competition is a theoretical and ideal standard against which to measure the economic and social value of other forms of competition. Let us first analyze, therefore, the operation of a firm under purely competitive conditions.

Characteristics of Pure Competition

Pure competition is an ideal set of market conditions that assumes the following characteristics:[1]

1. There are many buyers and sellers of an identical product in a given market. This implies that there are no quality differences, no

---

[1] Although the term *pure competition* is sometimes used interchangeably with the term *perfect competition*, there is a degree of difference in the meanings of the two terms. Perfect competition implies perfect information about markets

brand names, no advertising, nor anything else that would differentiate among the products.

2. All buyers and sellers are well-informed about markets and prices. This assumes that consumers have knowledge of any price differences that may exist. Moreover, it assumes that if one producer can sell at a lower price, competitors will soon learn why and how it can be done.

3. There is freedom to enter into and exit from the market. This means that a firm desiring to produce and/or sell goods in a particular market may do so, without any undue interference. Furthermore, a firm is free to sell its business, to dispose of its assets, or to convert to the production of a different product. Pure competition assumes also that there is perfect mobility on the part of the factors of production. Resources and labor, for example, are free to move into and out of various industries or among firms.

4. Price is determined by the aggregate actions of all buyers and sellers, or by market supply and demand. No individual seller or buyer can influence price. There must be a sufficient number of sellers so that each one's contribution to the total supply is inconsequential. Whether a firm produces more or less, it can have no appreciable effect on the total market supply or price. Hence each seller must accept the market price as determined by aggregate demand and supply.

PROFIT IN THE SHORT RUN

Under these conditions of pure competition each producer faces a perfectly elastic demand line, that is, it can sell its entire supply of a commodity at the market price. Its profit then will depend upon the difference between the average total cost of production and the selling price. It is assumed also that each firm will produce at a level that will maximize its profit.

Individually, a producer or seller can do little or nothing to change the market price. Whether he sells much or little will make no appreciable difference on price. This is not so, however, for the industry as a whole. If many or all producers increase or decrease production, that will change the total market supply and result in a change in price.

---

and prices on the part of all buyers and sellers, perfect mobility of the various factors of production, and perfectly free entry into and exit from a market. In short, perfect competition is a more ideal and a higher degree of competition. In pure competition, for example, information about prices, mobility of factors, or freedom to enter a market may be less than perfect.

A case in point is the growing of wheat in America where there are more than one-half million producers. Whether Farmer Williams increases his production from 1,000 to 10,000, or even 50,000 bushels will have little, if any, effect on the market price of wheat, since there is a total wheat supply of more than 1.3 billion bushels on the United States market each year and 10 billion bushels on the world market. On the other hand, if each wheat farmer in America increased output by an average of 4 percent, it would increase the total United States wheat supply by more than 50 million bushels and would lower the market price in the absence of other changes.

In an industry producing a standardized commodity under a condition of pure competition, how many units of the commodity will each firm supply? The answer for each producer will vary, depending on a number of circumstances. Let us assume a short-run period, just enough time to allow each producer to adjust its output to the most profitable level without enlarging or improving its plant. Under such conditions a producer will attempt to set his output where his marginal cost becomes equal to his marginal revenue.

Adjustment to Price in the Short Run

How much will an individual firm produce? Actually, it is difficult to give a precise figure, for two reasons. First, it is unlikely that management can predict exactly what production cost will be at different levels of output. Second, many firms are likely to be satisfied with a "good" or "reasonable" amount of profit, rather than attempting to squeeze out the last possible dollar of profit from the business.

It is realistic, nevertheless, to assume that, other things being equal, a producer wants to maximize profit. This assumption does not deny that many producers have values and interests other than those that relate to profit. But for the purpose of economic analysis, we will pay attention to only those matters that affect the profit of a business enterprise.

In order to arrive at a logical determination of the firm's output, therefore, we assume that the business manager will undertake to produce the amount that will maximize the firm's profit or minimize its loss. What that output will be depends upon the firm's cost and revenue relationships. Let us assume that for a certain producer, costs and revenues are those shown in Figure 8-1.

According to the marginal analysis chart, the market price (average

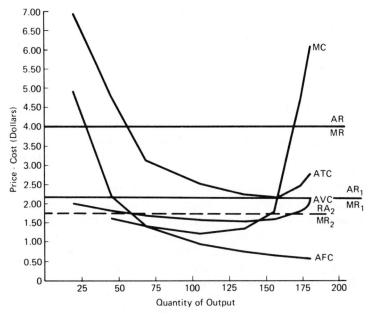

Figure 8-1. Marginal Analysis Chart

revenue) is \$4.00 per unit. At this price the firm can sell all that it might produce. How many units will it produce? It will produce the number that will be the most profitable, about 168.

Figure 8-1 shows that the average total cost (ATC) varies as output changes, whereas average revenue (AR) remains the same. If the firm produces and sells 50 units, it will lose money, since at that point, its ATC will exceed its AR. In fact, it will experience losses up to about 60 units of output, which will be the break-even point. Notice, however, that since the MR is greater than the MC the losses will be diminishing. Beyond 60 units of output the firm will realize profits, and maximize its profit at 168 units, where MR = MC. Beyond that point, profits will decline because after marginal cost and marginal revenue become equal, marginal cost rises above marginal revenue.

Observe that the equilibrium output corresponds with the point of intersection between the marginal revenue line and the marginal cost line at 168 units of output. The difference between average revenue (price) and average total cost at any point represents profit per unit. The profit per unit multiplied by the output measures total profit. The point of intersection of MR and MC is called the *equilibrium point* because once the firm reaches that position, it has no incentive to increase or decrease output. If it is not operating at the equilibrium point, the firm will be moved by the prospect of greater profit to either increase or decrease its production until it attains the equilibrium output. If MR is greater than MC, an expansion of production will increase profit; if MR is less than MC, a contraction of output will increase profit. When MR equals MC, total profit is a maximum.

In addition to average, marginal, and total costs, managers must be concerned with other costs, particularly fixed and variable costs. Understanding these two aspects of costs enables a manager to comprehend why average, total, and marginal costs exhibit the tendencies they do.

Figure 8-1 shows that 180 units can be produced by the business firm without its enlarging its plant. Notice that averaged fixed cost (AFC) varies inversely and proportionately with the number of units produced. AFC continuously decreases as output increases. The average variable cost per unit (AVC), however, decreases until 135 units are produced; then it begins to rise because of the law of diminishing marginal productivity.

The average total cost (ATC) is calculated by dividing the total cost by the number of units at a given level or by adding the AFC and AVC. Marginal cost (MC) shows the increase in total cost that results from the production of an additional unit of output. Marginal cost results only from the use of additional units of variable factors since total fixed cost remains constant and average fixed costs decrease as production increases. Therefore, marginal cost can be ascertained by subtracting the total variable cost at one level of output from the total variable cost (TVC) at the next higher level of output, or by using the figures for total cost in the same way.

The significant relationships between these costs are shown in Figure 8-1. Costs in dollars are measured along the vertical axis; the quantity of production, along the horizontal axis of the chart. Notice that if the price is $4.00 and if fewer than 60 units are produced, the producer will suffer a loss, because only when he produces 60 units or more is average revenue (price) above average total cost (ATC). Observe that after 168 units are produced, marginal cost rises above marginal revenue. Even though some profit or net revenue could be realized by producing and selling 175 units, profit cannot be increased by producing more than 168 units, the number at which marginal revenue and marginal cost are equal.[2]

---

[2] If the firm produces only whole units and the marginal revenue equals the marginal cost at the point of a fractional unit, then it is assumed that the firm will produce that number of whole units closest to the point where MR = MC.

Now let us see what would happen at a different price. Suppose that the price were $2.20 as shown in Figure 8-1. Note that at this price marginal revenue (MR_1) and marginal cost (MC) would intersect at 158 units of output. This means that the most the producer can hope for is to break even. At 158 units of output, average revenue (AR_1) will just equal average total cost (ATC). If additional units are produced, marginal cost (MC) will rise above marginal revenue (MR_1) and average total cost (ATC) will rise above average revenue (AR_1). This means that by producing more, the firm would suffer a loss. If it produces less it will likewise experience losses.

Let us now assume a still lower price (AR_2, MR_2) of $1.75, as shown in Figure 8-1. At this price, we can see that no matter how many units are produced, the firm cannot make a profit because, at any number of units of output, average total cost (ATC) is above average revenue (AR_2). But by producing 154 units, MR_2 will equal MC and losses will be minimized at that point. Although at this point, AR_2 is less than ATC, AR_2 is greater than AVC. This means that the firm will recover the amount of its total variable cost and contribute something toward offsetting the amount of fixed cost. It will not produce more than 154 units, however, because beyond that point MC rises above MR_2.

Under such circumstances it will pay the firm to continue to operate in the short run rather than close. By operating, the net loss will be less than it would be if the firm were to close. As mentioned previously, it will pay the firm to continue to operate in the short run rather than to shut down, so long as it can recover its variable cost. Whether or not it can do so may be ascertained by comparing the AVC with the AR at the equilibrium output.

If the AR is equal to the AVC, the firm will recover its variable cost. If AR > AVC, the firm will also recover a part of its fixed cost; or as stated previously, it will make a contribution to overhead. The size of this contribution can be observed from the graph. Although the fixed cost is not shown on the graph, remember that since ATC is made up of AFC plus AVC, the AFC will be represented by the difference between the ATC and AVC curves.

Visualize, on the other hand, a market in which the product price may be only $1.00. Not only would the firm suffer a loss at any level of output, but even at the equilibrium level, or point of minimum loss, AR would be less than AVC. Consequently, the firm would not recover its variable cost and would find it less costly to shut down rather than operate in the short run.

A change in the market price can affect the profit status of each firm. A change in the per unit cost of inputs, likewise, can affect the profit of each firm by altering its average total cost curve.

COMPETITION, PRICE AND PROFIT IN THE LONG RUN

Economic profits are residual, dynamic, and temporal. Under conditions of pure competition, profit is *residual*, insofar as it is revenue that remains after deducting all costs, both explicit and implicit, including the imputed cost of the entrepreneur's service. Profits are *dynamic* since they are constantly changing. Profits are temporal because under purely competitive conditions, long-run forces tend to reduce or eliminate economic or pure profit. On the other hand, if losses prevail, market forces tend to bring about adjustments that either enhance profit or cause a degeneration of the firm.

Profit Variation among Firms

It should be remembered that all firms under conditions of pure competition pay identical prices for input factors, and all sell their finished products at the same market price determined by demand and supply. Consequently, it is often said that individual firms in pure competition are *price takers* rather than price makers. It is still possible, however, for profits among firms to vary. One of the major reasons for this variance is that some managers are able to use their inputs more efficiently. In the short run, some of them may use better production techniques; they may spread fixed cost over a larger range of output; they may use other measures to lower per unit cost of output. At any given market price, therefore, some firms may be making a profit, others breaking even, and still others suffering a loss. This is demonstrated in Figure 8-2.

In the long run, it is assumed the submarginal firms suffering losses will reorganize their operations in order to make a profit, or else will drop out of business. Remember, pure competition assumes that all sellers are informed about markets, prices, and costs. Therefore, if one firm is, for some reason, able to produce at a lower cost, others will learn how to do it.

The Elimination of Profits

Under conditions of pure competition, market forces tend to eliminate economic profit. This results from the freedom of firms to enter and leave the industry. If profits are being made by firms in the

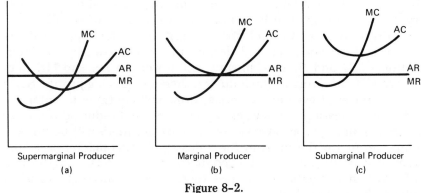

Supermarginal Producer
(a)

Marginal Producer
(b)

Submarginal Producer
(c)

Figure 8-2.

industry, others can learn how to produce and market the product. The lure of profits will induce existing firms to expand output and induce new firms to enter the market. These actions will have a downward effect on the market price.

No individual supplier can affect market price under conditions of pure competition. If a number of existing firms expand output or a number of new firms enter the market, however, the addition to aggregate market supply could very well result in a decrease in market price. As price is lowered, of course, profits will diminish. If profits exist even at the lower price, firms will continue to enter the industry and force prices still lower until a point is reached at which market price equals the average total cost and profit is eliminated. This process is depicted graphically in Figure 8-3.

Assume that market demand (D) and supply (S) in Figure 8-3 (a) establish a market price of $10 per unit. This will become the average revenue (AR) for each of the firms in the industry as shown in Figure

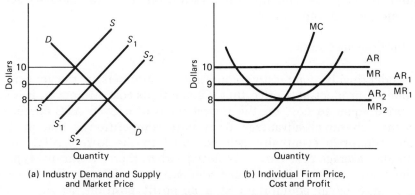

(a) Industry Demand and Supply
and Market Price

(b) Individual Firm Price,
Cost and Profit

Figure 8-3. Long-run Equilibrium Price and Profit

8-3 (b). If this cost and revenue relationship is typical for the industry, individual firms will be making profits. Such profits will induce new firms to enter the industry. As a result, total supply will increase, and market price will decline to $9 as shown by the intersection of S_1 and D. This, in turn, will lower the AR and MR lines for each of the firms in the industry, thereby reducing profits. Since profits still exist even at this price, firms will continue to enter the industry, increasing the market supply to S_2 and reducing the price to $8 per unit. At an average revenue of $8, there will be no economic profit for the firms in the industry. At this market price, the firms will be operating at the point where AR = ATC. Equilibrium will exist in the industry because there is no incentive for firms to enter or leave the industry.

You can picture what would happen if the market price were such that firms in the industry were suffering losses. As some high-cost firms drop out of business, the total supply would decrease, raising the market price and the average revenue of the individual firms. This process would continue until the price were raised sufficiently to eliminate losses for the remaining firms. At that point there would be no further need for firms to leave the industry, and equilibrium would be established. Alternatively, particularly if demand is inadequate, the entire industry might go out of business.

We demonstrated the movement from a short-run profit position to a long-run equilibrium by changes in supply and in the market price. It is also probable that the long-run profit squeeze will be quickened by upward pressures on the costs. As new firms enter the industry, the total demand for raw material, labor, capital, and other inputs may increase. This could raise the market price of inputs and the average total cost curve for individual firms. Consequently, the competitive forces in the market work from two directions — downward pressure on prices and upward pressure on cost — to eliminate economic profit in the long run.

The Long-run Cost Curve

Under highly competitive conditions, consumers in the long run obtain a product at a price that is equal to its cost. Moreover, it is at a price equal to cost on the lowest point of a given ATC curve. A further consumer advantage from pure competition is that in the long run price eventually will be equal to the lowest ATC on a minimal average cost curve. As stated earlier, there are various types, kinds, and sizes of firms under competitive conditions. The typical firm may be in equilibrium at a no-profit position, as shown in Figure 8-3, but other firms may be operating at larger scales and making a profit with the given market price. Pure competition assumes that all firms learn about any cost advantages that may arise for any reason. Consequently, the marginal firms, observing the larger-scale producers enjoying a profit, will be induced to enlarge their scale of operations in order to increase their profits. As firms move toward the larger scale of operations, the total supply in the market will increase, forcing market price downward. If at the larger scale of operation, the industry comes into no-profit equilibrium position, competition may lead some aggressive innovators to produce on a still larger scale in an attempt to reduce cost further in order to generate profits.

If the innovator is successful and does make profit at the larger scale, existing producers may follow suit and new firms may enter the industry at this larger scale of operation. Thus the supply will increase once more, forcing the price down still farther. Eventually an *optimum scale* of operation may be reached. Beyond the optimum scale there will be no further cost advantages arising from size. In fact, average total cost may rise because of inefficiencies, duplications, and diminishing productivity arising from excessive size.

By joining a series with an infinite number of short-run average total cost curves, we can picture a long-run average cost curve as shown in Figure 8-4. One can see that *economies of scale* exist at levels of operation up to the optimum scale since the long-run ATC decreases as the size of operation increases. Beyond the otpimum scale, however, *diseconomies of scale* come into existence, causing the long-run ATC to rise.

Graphic analysis can show how price in the long run equates with the lowest point on the average cost curve at the optimum scale of operation. Figure 8–5 contains a series of short-run cost curves. Assume that the industry is in a no-profit equilibrium position, that the average-sized firm in the industry is operating at Scale *A* and that

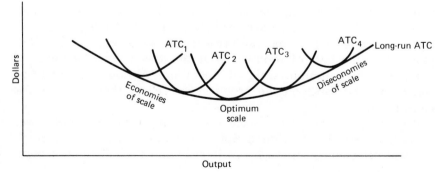

Output

Figure 8-4. Long-run Average Cost Curve

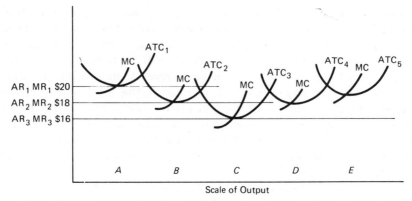

Figure 8-5. Long-run Equilibrium Price at Optimum Scale of Operation

the price level is AR_1. Firms seeking profits will expand to Scale B at which level profits will be made with price AR_1. As existing firms expand production, and new firms enter the industry at this more efficient size of operation, however, the total supply of output on the market will increase and price will fall to AR_2. At this lower price, AR_2, or any price below AR_1, firms operating at Scale A will suffer losses and must move to a larger scale, or find other ways to cut cost in order to avoid going out of business.

When Scale B becomes typical for the industry and economic profits no longer exist, producers in seeking to reduce cost further may move to Scale C. At this scale profits will be made, provided that the market price is AR_2. But again profits will be temporal. Since all producers, under conditions of pure competition, are well-informed, many will expand to the larger size, Scale C, in order to take advantage of cost reductions. But again, as they do, the supply of output will increase and price will fall eventually to AR_3. The process may continue but at some level, such as Scale D, costs will rise instead of decreasing, because of diminishing returns to scale and other complexities of excessive size. The final result under conditions of pure competition is that the price will be reduced to a point that is equal to the cost of production at the lowest point of the ATC curve on the optimum scale of operation. Although competitive forces may be harsh on the producers or sellers, they are ideal for consumers.

The move to even larger-scale operations, and fewer and fewer firms, has prevailed in United States industries, such as auto, steel, tire and petroleum. Although profits have not been eliminated com-

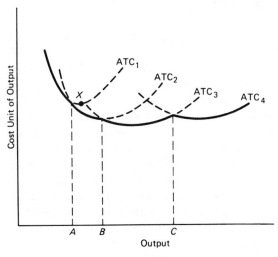

Figure 8-6.

pletely, some firms were forced out of business, and prices have been lower than they would have been with smaller-scale operations.

In the preceding example the short-run average-cost curves are rather uniform as drawn in Figure 8-4. Furthermore, in each of the first three scales of operation, where increasing economies of scale are present, a firm will exceed its least-cost position (lowest point on the ATC curve) on each scale before it becomes feasible to operate at a larger scale. The result is a rather smooth long-run average total cost curve.

In actuality, however, short-run average total cost curves may not be that uniform. Moreover, a firm may be able to move to a larger scale, and even abandon a plant or other facility, before it reaches the least-cost point on an existing scale of operation. This can be demonstrated in Figure 8-6. It can be observed for example that point X is the least-cost combination for ATC_1. Before that point is reached, however, it would be feasible to shift to a larger scale of operation at output level A. At point A or slightly beyond, the ATC_2 is lower than the least-cost position on the ATC_1 scale. Note, too, that the second scale of operation would soon be abandoned in favor of ATC_3, but that the ATC_3 scale would be extended well beyond its least-cost point before converting to a larger scale if that were at all feasible. Observe also that connecting the solid lines of the various short-run ATC curves presents an irregular-shaped long-run average total cost curve.

THE SOCIAL ASPECT OF PURE COMPETITION

Economically, pure competition has many virtues: It tends to maximize the satisfaction of consumers' demands, it allocates resources to their best economic use, and in many cases, it results in minimum prices to consumers. If pure competition prevailed throughout the economy, efficiency would be promoted, and only the most efficient firms and managers would survive. The availability of high profits in any industry would encourage many producers to increase output and induce additional firms to enter the market. Thus, the supplies of goods or services would increase and prices would decline. On the other side of the market, demand for the factors of production would be competitive and their prices also would be established by demand and supply. In the entire process, potential entrepreneurs and managers would be encouraged to develop and produce new types of goods and services to satisfy the needs of consumers.

Pure competition would benefit consumers greatly. In most cases it would result in greater production, the use of more resources and labor, lower prices, and probably less profit than would exist under noncompetitive conditions. But competition does have some drawbacks. At times, it causes unnecessary duplication of plant and equipment. Sometimes it causes waste of valuable resources and manpower, as in the case of American farming. While competition benefits the economy as a whole, it can cause financial hardship for individual producers and displacement of workers as firms are forced out of business by more efficient managers. It is also evident that in some industries, such as public utilities, a large number of firms, each operating at a small scale, could not provide a good or a service as inexpensively as one firm producing at a much larger scale of operation.

From a social point of view, one can say that whereas pure competition maximizes the satisfaction of consumer demands, it does not necessarily maximize the satisfaction of consumer wants or needs because it caters primarily to dollar demand. Moreover, pure competition, or, for that matter, any type of competition, does not consider social or external costs, such as pollution and public services, in its pricing procedure.

Pure competition assumes conditions that are not found readily in the everyday business world. Economists readily admit that perfect, or pure, competition seldom, if ever, exists. The concepts of pure competition and normal competitive price, however, serve as a model for comparing the economic and social consequences of various forms of industrial organization. Pure competition serves as an abstract model against which to compare producer and consumer benefits associated with various forms of imperfect competition. The disadvantages to consumers from monopolistic pricing and other restrictive practices, for example, are difficult to understand unless one realizes what the consumer would gain as a result of greater competition. The reasons for antitrust laws that promote and protect competition can be better understood and more fully appreciated when one understands what is being promoted and protected. A manager can better understand what limits his influence over market price. In this respect the study of pricing and profits under pure competition provides a solid foundation for economic analysis and managerial decisions in the world of reality.

MONOPOLY

At the opposite end of the market spectrum is pure monopoly. *Monopoly* is a market situation in which there is only one producer or seller of a product. Pure monopoly, moreover, assumes that there are no close substitutes for the monopolist's good or service. This assumption, of course, practically eliminates reality from the concept of pure monopoly. It may be true, for example, that Zenith Corporation has a monopoly on the production and sale of Zenith television sets. But so long as consumers can turn to RCA, Admiral, GE, Sony, Hitachi, and numerous other makes of televisions, Zenith does not truly have pure monopoly power. Like pure competition, pure monopoly is more an abstraction than a reality. There are very few markets in which there is a sole supplier.

The Characteristics of Monopoly

The major characteristic of monopoly is the seller's degree of control over price. In most markets, demand and supply establish the market price. In pure competition, we learned, market supply is the aggregate output of many individual producers. With monopoly, however, the market supply and output of the monopolist are identical. Since the monopoly is the only supplier, the total demand on the market becomes a demand line for its product. Consequently, whenever the monopolist increases or decreases output, it will change market supply and affect the market price. Instead of accepting the market price as given and adjusting output to the most profitable position, as the case may be under pure competition, the monopolist can within limits adjust his output in order to attain the most favorable market price. Consequently, the monopolist is often referred to as a *price maker* rather than a price taker. A monopoly does not have complete control over the market price, however, because it cannot force customers to buy at prices they are not willing to pay. Managers must keep this in mind regarding output and pricing decisions.

Because of the complexity of our markets today, it is sometimes difficult to determine what is and what is not a monopoly. A firm may produce a variety of products, of which many sell in competition with identical or similar products. But among its products there may be one item for which there is no competition. Is this firm then a monopoly or is it not? Even a pure monopoly can maintain that it is in competition with other firms. It competes not for the sale of a particular good or service, but for the purchase of the consumer's dollar.

Today, in the American economy pure monopoly in the sale of reproducible goods is practically nonexistent except for government-regulated public utilities. Probably the closest example of a true monopoly was that of the Aluminum Company of America (ALCOA) before World War II. During the first part of this century, it was the only producer of primary aluminum in the United States. But even then it had to compete with the sale of such other materials as steel, copper, wood, and magnesium. The entry of other producers, such as Reynolds Metal Company and Kaiser Aluminum Corporation, during and after World War II destroyed the monopoly position of Alcoa. Other industries that at one time approached monopoly conditions include those that produced shoe machinery, nickel, diamonds, and railroad sleeping cars.

Probably a distinction should be made between the terms *monopoly* and *monopoly power*. The latter term is often used by the courts in antitrust cases when referring to such firms as General Motors Corporation and Bethlehem Steel Company. Although neither is a monopoly, some contend that they can exercise monopoly power because of their influence over market supply and price. Regarding a proposed merger of Bethlehem Steel Corporation and Youngstown Sheet Tube Company the court forbade the merger, declaring that "it would substantially lessen competition and tend to create a monopoly," even though there are dozens of other producers of substantial size in the industry.

The latest development in this regard is the United States Department of Justice plan to prosecute "shared monopoly" cases. These are described as situations in which a few large companies control a monopoly share of a particular industry and work together as if they were a single monopolist. Included in the share-marketing category are the steel, aluminum, and iron-ore industries. In fact, the Antitrust Division has issued "civil investigative demands" (CIDs) to firms in those industries as a prelude to preparing antitrust cases. The CIDs seek to obtain documents, memorandums, and other materials concerning the price actions of the firms involved.

Sources of Monopoly

Monopolies may exist or arise from a number of sources. A primary requisite for establishing and maintaining a monopoly is the erection of legal or economic barriers to the entry of other firms into an industry. The stronger such barriers, the easier to protect a monopoly position. Under competitive conditions the usual response to a profitable industry situation is the movement of additional firms into the market; that will result eventually in the elimination of profits. If, however, a monopoly can effectively keep new firms out of the market, it can continue to reap monopoly profits.

Economies of Scale. In some industries, pure competition or anything close to it is not feasible. Heavy industries, such as steel, auto, and heavy machinery, that require the centralized control of large amounts of capital in order to achieve the economies of large-scale production, veer away from pure competition. If pure competition were to exist, there would have to be so many firms in the industry that none, or very few, could produce enough to take advantage of the low cost associated with economies of scale. Although most large industries are not pure monopolies, they tend to display some monopolistic characteristics. Obviously, we cannot expect to have a sufficient number of steel, auto, or machine tool companies to provide the same degree of competition found in the textile or the grocery industry.

Natural Monopolies. A natural monopoly is said to exist in an industry in which there is an inherent tendency toward economies of scale and decreasing unit costs covering the entire market for the good or service. It is essential, too, that the size of the market must be small compared with the optimum scale of operation. Under such circumstances, the market can be served better by one or a few firms operating at the optimum scale rather than many firms operating at less than optimum scale. Related to this phenomenon of natural monopoly is the probability that waste would arise if, as the result of competition, certain facilities were duplicated. This is especially likely in such high-fixed-cost industries as electric-power production and telephone service, which require heavy investment in plant and equipment.

Some services, like public utilities, by their very nature are better served by monopoly. Confusion, waste, and inconvenience, for example, would result if several utility companies were to compete for the trade of consumers in an urban area. Besides waste through duplication of assets, imagine the unsightliness of three strings of telephone wires and poles, plus those of electric companies, traversing streets and lawns in a new residential subdivision. Just think of the disruption to traffic if three or more gas companies were constantly tearing up streets in order to lay or repair gas lines. What about the safety of passengers and pedestrians if buses from four separate transit companies were to race each other from corner to corner to pick up passengers?

Furthermore, in many public utilities, such as the gas, electric power, and telephone industries, the size of the market in a community may be small compared with the optimum scale of operation. In such cases, the market could not sustain several large-scale companies. The net result of open competition might be that only one, or a few, very efficient and/or economically powerful companies would finally serve the market. This situation could give them unregulated monopoly power, to the disadvantage of the consumer.

In industries clothed with a public interest, where one or two firms can adequately supply all of a service needed for a community, it is desirable to limit within a given territory the number of firms offering these services. Under such circumstances, it becomes imperative for government to exercise its power to regulate services and prices. This is done by granting a monopoly, or franchise, to one or a few firms, subject to control by a public-service commission.

Control of Raw Materials. Ownership or control of essential raw materials can effectively deter competition and so foster monopoly. It is rare that one firm can gain complete control of material resources; in many cases there may be close substitutes for a particular raw material. This method of limiting competition, however, was used for years in the aluminum industry. ALCOA retained a monopoly position for years through its control of nearly all sources of bauxite, the major ingredient of aluminum production. The International Nickel Company of Canada at one time exercised almost a monopoly power through its control of nearly 90 percent of the world's known nickel reserves. In Africa and elsewhere at one time, most of the diamond mines were owned by the DeBeers Company of South Africa, and a large portion of the world's molybdenum supplies were controlled by one company.

Patents. A patent gives the holder the exclusive right to use, to keep, or to sell an invention for seventeen years. It was not the original intent of patent law to give the inventor a permanent monopoly on his invention. Despite some safeguards against an undesirable growth of monopoly arising from patent grants, some large corporations use the control and improvement of patents as an important source of monopolistic power.

Patent control and improvement has played an important role in the development of several well-known modern giant corporations, including National Cash Register, General Electric Company, AT&T, Radio Corporation of America, General Motors, International Business Machines, Westinghouse, and others. Currently, corporations obtain nearly two-thirds of all new patents.

Competitive Tactics. By using aggressive and sometimes unfair methods, a firm may eliminate its rivals or effectively deter the entry of new firms into a market. Temporarily selling below cost to eliminate smaller competitors, vilifying competitors' products, pirating managerial and scientific personnel, coercing competitors, suppliers, or financial sources, and engaging in industrial espionage and sometimes in outright blackmail all have been used to eliminate or prevent competition. Antitrust and federal trade laws have declared these tactics to be illegal yet many aggressive practices still occur in our economy and make it difficult for new firms to enter some industries.

In industries characterized by large-scale operations, the mere existence of some firms that are established and have been doing business for years makes it hard for newcomers to successfully break into the market. A classic case was that of the Kaiser Corporation's problem in entering the auto industry after World War II. Those difficulties forced it to withdraw in a few years. Its entry into the steel industry was equally difficult, although it finally succeeded. More recent is the General Electric Company's rapid exit from the computer manufacturing industry.

PURE MONOPOLY PRICE

The concept of pure monopoly implies a market situation in which there is a single seller of a good for which there is no close substitute. Whether the monopoly exercises its power to obtain the highest possible price for what it sells depends in great measure upon whether it is deterred by threat of potential competition, by desire to maintain the goodwill of consumers and the general public, or by fear of possible government regulation.

Pure monopoly occurs under one of two possible supply situations: The supply may not be reproducible but consist of one unit of a unique good or of a limited number of nonreproducible units of a good for which there is no close substitute, or the supply may be reproducible but controlled by a single seller.

Monopoly Price of a Nonreproducible Supply

If the supply of a good is limited to one unit, the highest price is that which the buyer with the strongest demand is willing to pay. Examples of this situation are to be found in the auctions of unique objects of art—a famous painting, a historical document, or a rare coin or stamp. In such cases, the article can be sold to the highest bidder.

The market situation is considerably different if the seller has several identical or similar nonreproducible units. Since it is unlikely that the subjective bids of the prospective buyers will be identical, the monopolist may sell one unit at a time at the highest current price obtainable. Except in some auction sales, examples of such a selling practice are rare. There are cases, however, in which monopolists seek as high an average price as possible by feeding the supply to the market gradually or by making the limited supply of goods available to various buyers at different prices. A modifcation of these methods is followed in the marketing of diamonds.

Monopoly Price of a Reproducible Supply

The supply of most goods, however, is reproducible. A monopoly usually can produce and maintain the supply at whatever level it chooses. By altering supply, the seller can, within limits, establish the price at that point that will yield the greatest total profit. The location of this point depends upon the nature of the demand for the product and its costs of production. In short, price will be determined by demand and supply, but the monopoly can influence price through its control of supply.

The Monopoly's Demand Line. Under pure competition, demand for the output of a single firm is represented by a straight horizontal line, and the individual producer cannot change the market price either by increasing or decreasing the firm's output. The situation with a monopoly, however, is different. A monopolist is the sole supplier of a good. The demand line for its product slopes downward to the right, because it is identical to the market demand line of all buyers. Hence, the first question to be considered by the monopoly is: How many units of a good can be sold at various prices? The answer will enable the monopolist to determine the number of units to produce and market.

A monopoly market situation is shown in Figure 8-7. Since the monopoly is the only producer, the demand line for the whole industry is also the demand line for the product of the individual monop-

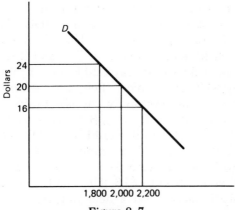

Figure 8-7.

oly. The demand line, *D*, is also the average revenue line for the firm.

In Figure 8-7, the total revenue at 1800 units is $43,200; at 2000 units it is $40,000; at 2200 units it is $35,200. Since demand in this case is priced inelastic, the monopolist can obtain a larger revenue by limiting the supply. If supply increased and sales rose from 1800 to 2200, total revenue would decrease. Of course, if the demand were elastic, the opposite would be true. Consequently, for wise pricing policy the manager must know something about the elasticity of demand for the product.

Monopoly Cost, Revenue, and Profit. A monopoly like most other producers will experience decreasing per unit cost for a while. Eventually, it, too, will reach the production range where MC, AVC, and ATC will rise. How many units the monopoly will produce depends on the relationship of its marginal cost to its marginal revenue.

Remember that the marginal revenue line for the monopolist is not a straight horizontal line as it is under conditions of pure competition. It slopes downward to the right because the market demand line becomes the average revenue (AR) line for the monopolist. This line sloping downward to the right indicates that as the selling price decreases, a larger number of units will be sold.

Since the monopoly is faced with a negatively sloped AR line (demand), its marginal revenue, MR, will be less than the AR line. Moreover, the MR line will decline at a faster rate. In pure competition, by contrast, the seller has a horizontal, or constant, AR line. Every time an additional unit is sold at the market price, that amount is added to the total revenue. Consequently, in pure competition, the AR and the MR lines are equal. With a monopoly, however, the market situation is different. In order for the firm to sell a larger quantity, price must be lowered. The monopoly, for example, may sell 1 unit at $20 or 2 units at $19. Keep in mind that it is not a situation in which it can sell 1 unit at $20 *and* 2 units more at $19 because the buyer who would pay $20 is one of the two buyers who is willing to pay $19. The choice, then, is to sell only 1 unit at $20 or 2 units at $19. If the monopoly chooses to do the latter, its AR will be $19 but its MR will be $18. This is so because the total revenue from the sale of 1 unit would be $20, but the total revenue from the sale of 2 units is $38, an increase of $18. If, instead of selling 2 units at $19 each, it were to sell 3 units at $18, AR would fall to $18 and MR would drop to $16. This can be seen in Table 8-1.

The monopoly is faced with a declining AR as quantity sold increases. Its MR will decline at a steeper rate than does the AR because the monopoly takes a lower price also on the units that it could have sold at a higher price had it chosen to sell fewer units. Thus, if it decides to sell 2 units at $19 rather than 1 unit at $20, its marginal revenue will be $18. Total revenue will increase by $19 from the sale of the second unit, minus the $1 less received from the sale of the original unit it could have sold for $20, had it sold only one unit. Likewise, if the monopolist decides to sell 3 units at $18 instead of 2 units at $19, its total revenue will increase by $18 from the sale of the third unit, as such, minus $1 less on each of the 2 previous units it could have sold for $19 if it had sold only 2 units. In this case, the marginal revenue will be $16.

The relationships of cost and revenue lines for a hypothetical monopoly are shown in Figure 8-8. Notice that the shape of the average total cost (ATC) and the marginal cost (MC) lines, which are both affected by the law of diminishing marginal productivity, are similar to those for a firm in pure competition. On the other hand, note that the AR line of the monopolist slopes downward to the right, identical with the market demand line for the product,

TABLE 8-1. Marginal Revenue—Competition vs. Monopoly

Pure Competition				*Monopoly*			
Quantity Sold	Price	Total Revenue	Marginal Revenue	Quantity Sold	Price	Total Revenue	Marginal Revenue
1	$10	$10	—	1	$20	$20	—
2	$10	$20	$10	2	$19	$38	$18
3	$10	$30	$10	3	$18	$54	$16
4	$10	$40	$10	4	$17	$68	$14
5	$10	$50	$10	5	$16	$80	$12

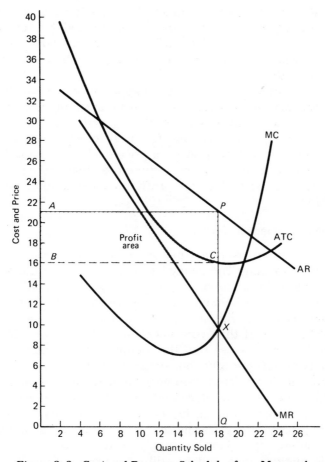

Figure 8-8. Cost and Revenue Schedules for a Monopoly

compared with the horizontal AR line of a firm in pure competition. Note further that the AR and MR lines of the monopoly diverge, while the AR and MR lines of the purely competitive firm are identical.

Under the conditions represented in Figure 8-8, at an output level of 18 units, marginal cost and marginal revenue are equal. This is the equilibrium output and the point of maximum profit for the monopoly. Beyond this point, X, it becomes less profitable to produce additional units. The price at which 18 units would sell is $21. This is shown by the lines PA and PQ, which indicate price and quantity, respectively. The total revenue from the sale of 18 units, then, would be 18 times $21, or $378. In the figure, the total revenue from the sale of 18 units is represented geometrically by the rectangle $OQPA$.

The cost of producting 18 units is 18 times the average total cost of $16., or $288. The total cost is represented by the rectangle *OQCB*, which is less than the total revenue area, *OQPA*, by the size of the profit area, *APCB*. This last area represents the net profit of $90 ($378 - $288).[3]

It is easy to visualize what would happen if additional firms were to enter this market. The resultant increase in supply and decrease in market price would gradually reduce and perhaps eliminate profit. If the monopoly, however, can effectively block the entry of new firms, it can limit supply, prevent a price decline, and continue realizing profits. It is often claimed, therefore, that monopoly results in a higher price and a greater profit than would exist under pure competition.

Limitations on Monopoly Pricing

The public often assumes that monopoly implies an exorbitant price or price gouging. There may be some grounds for the belief that goods produced by a monopoly, or near-monopolist, will be sold at high prices. It would be a mistake, however, to think that monopoly always means an exorbitant price. The monopolist cannot charge more for his product than consumers are willing to pay. If we refer to Figure 8-7, we can see that the monopolist, for example, can sell 2,000 units at $20 per unit, but notice that he cannot sell 2,200 or 2,400 units at that price. Consumers will not buy that many units at that price. The monopolist cannot raise his price to $24 and still hope to sell as many units as he did at the $20 price. A monopolist cannot arbitrarily set a price and sell all he desires to sell at that price. The monopolist can alter his supply in order to obtain the most profitable market price, but he still must price within the scope of consumer demand. Yet the price most profitable to the monopolist might keep a large number of consumers from enjoying the product.

On the other hand, several major economic considerations may deter the monopolist from selling his goods at the highest possible price. These include the following:

Uncertainty. It is improbable that a monopoly would know precisely its demand and cost at different levels of production. This might preclude it from setting a production goal at the level that would prove most profitable.

Discourage Competition. A producer with a monopoly may prefer to keep prices moderate and enjoy a reasonable profit, rather than

---

[3] This area is greater than that of any other rectangle that has the distance from ATC to AR for a chosen number of units as its height and the length equal to the number of units as shown along the *OX* axis.

try to maximize his profit and encourage the entry of competitors, who eventually would force the market price down, thereby reducing profit.

Customer Goodwill. Although it is assumed, in marginal analysis, that a firm will seek to maximize profit, this is not always true in reality. Even monopolists will frequently be satisfied with a reasonable profit. Usually a firm will consider the goodwill of its customers and try not to gouge them with unreasonable prices or poor service. The monopolist, after all, must get its revenue from these customers for many years. Squeezing out the maximum profit in the short run may result in less than maximum or even reasonable profits in the long run.

Preclude Government Regulation. The price of a widely used commodity or service that is generally regarded as a necessity may concern the general public. The monopolist who tries to limit production and charge an unduly high price for such a commodity in order to maximize profit may be inviting government intervention. Traditionally, in the United States, government has been reluctant to compel producers to justify prices or to limit profits. But when a large number of people are convinced that they are being charged an unreasonably high price for a commodity, political pressure may result in public investigation, the enactment of anti-monopoly laws, or the establishment of new (government-fostered) private enterprise.

Although not a monopoly, General Motors (GM) is in a precarious position because of its high profits. Those profits have, over a number of years, aroused the curiosity of the government antitrust division. On the other hand, had GM substantially reduced the price of its cars in order to lower profit, it would certainly have increased its share of the automobile market just when the antitrust division was also asking why GM supplied such a large share of the market. Certain opponents of GM actually suggested that the company be split by spinning off the very profitable Chevrolet Division as a separate corporation.[4] Recently, the drug industry has been subject to damag-

---

[4] General Motors was the first manufacturing company in the United States, if not the world, to realize a profit in excess of $1 billion annually. In some years, its rate of return after taxes has been between 20 and 30 percent. Its rate of return is higher than that of the other major automakers, and the rate of return of the motor vehicle industry is usually higher than the average for durable goods industries. In 1976, for example, GM had a comfortable $2.9 billion profit after taxes. That amounted to a 20 percent rate of return on stockholders' equity of $14.4 billion. The average rate of return for the industry in 1976 was 13.9 percent. The profit of the Ford Motor Company was $983 million on stockholders' equity of $7.1 billion for a rate of return of 13.8 percent. Chrysler had a profit of $423 million, or a 15.1 percent rate of return on stockholders' investment of $2.8 billion.

ing criticism for limited output, high prices, and large profits. In 1973 and 1974, the gasoline shortage and the accompanying high prices and record profits of the oil companies aroused public resentment and brought about a political outcry for restrictions on the oil companies.

SUMMARY

A firm operates within an industry, and each industry is categorized by a certain type of competition. It may be pure competition, pure monopoly, monopolistic competition, oligopoly, or some shade in between. Pure competition is an abstraction often used as a model for comparison with the structure of competition in the real business world. For pure competition to exist, the market must have certain characteristics: numerous buyers and sellers, an identical product for sale, perfect information on the part of buyers and sellers, perfect mobility of the factors of production, free entry into and exit from the market, and price determination by the aggregate forces of demand and supply, rather than by individual firms.

For purposes of economic analysis, costs are categorized as fixed and variable. Important to marginal analysis is the knowledge of average fixed cost (AFC), average variable cost (AVC), average total cost (ATC), and marginal cost (MC). From the revenue side, a measure of average revenue (AR), or price, and marginal revenue (MR) is necessary. A firm in pure competition, as in other forms of competition, will maximize its profit, or minimize its loss, at the output where MR = MC. Profit under pure competition is a temporary phenomenon. A high degree of competition should eventually lower price to the point at which AR = ATC, thus eliminating profit.

In the long run, perfect competition would result in a price for the consumer equal to the lowest point on the ATC curve on the optimum scale of operation. Perfect competition might offer many benefits for consumers, but it also might have some disadvantages for society.

Pure monopoly is at the other end of the competitive spectrum. In pure monopoly there is only one producer or seller and no close substitutes for the product. Since the individual supply of the monopoly is synonymous with the total market supply, the monopoly can exercise some control over price by altering its supply. Like pure competition, however, pure monopoly seldom exists. There are, however, some near-monopolists, and some near and not so near monopolists can exercise what the courts call *monopoly power* regarding price and output.

Sources of monopoly include economies of scale, natural monopolies, control of raw material, patents, and competitive tactics. A monopoly, like a firm in pure competition, will maximize its profit at the point where MR = MC. Because price competition is absent, profits are not necessarily eliminated eventually, as they are in pure competition. Remember that a monopoly can, nevertheless, suffer a loss.

Although a monopolist possesses some control over prices, the degree of control is limited by the structure of consumer demand. Monopoly pricing is also affected by uncertainties in measuring costs, by desire to discourage competition and to preserve consumer goodwill, and at times by concern about potential government regulation.

QUESTIONS FOR ANALYSIS AND DISCUSSION

1. What conditions must be present for pure competition to exist?
2. Why does the individual seller have no effect on the market price under conditions of pure competition?
3. Why is the point at which marginal cost equals marginal revenue the point of equilibrium output for the firm?
4. The average revenue lines and the marginal revenue lines are identical in pure competition. Why?
5. Through graphic analysis, how can you determine: (a) whether a firm is making a profit; (b) if the firm is indeed suffering a loss, whether it should close down or continue to operate in the short run?
6. What market forces cause profits to disappear under conditions of pure competition?
7. Why can a monopolist exert control over price? Is his control absolute?
8. Why do the average revenue lines and the marginal revenue lines diverge under monopolistic conditions whereas they are identical under conditions of pure competition?
9. What are some sources of monopoly?
10. To what extent does pure monopoly exist in the United States economy today?

PROBLEMS AND CASES

1. H.R. Homer, president of the Casey Baseball Bat Company, uses a conventional break-even chart for his profit analysis. He has heard much about marginal analysis, but is not sure of its merits or its application. He asks you to explain and, using data from his firm, compare the two methods of profit analysis for him. He gives you the production and cost schedule shown below, and indicates that his total fixed cost accounts for $25,600 of the total cost. He sells his bats at a market price of $6.40 each.

Production and Total Cost Schedule

Total Output	Total Cost	Total Output	Total Cost	Total Output	Total Cost
1,000	$31,360	6,000	$46,960	11,000	$ 62,560
2,000	35,920	7,000	49,120	12,000	68,320
3,000	39,520	8,000	51,520	13,000	75,520
4,000	42,400	9,000	54,400	14,000	84,400
5,000	44,800	10,000	58,000	15,000	95,200
				16,000	108,160

(a) Construct a marginal analysis table showing the following data: Total Output, TFC, TVC, TC, AFC, AVC, AC, MC, AR, TR, MR, and Profit.

(b) Plot in graphic form a chart, using quantity on the X axis and price-cost on the Y axis, showing the following data: AVC, AC, MC, AR, and MR. From the graph or table answer the following questions:
   (i) What is the equilibrium level of output?
   (ii) At that level, what is the profit or loss per unit of output?
   (iii) What is the total profit or loss?
   (iv) Is the company selling in a purely competitive market?
   (v) Can the AFC be ascertained from the chart? If so, how?
   (vi) If the price were raised to $7.00, what would be the maximum profit level of output?
   (vii) If the price were lowered to $5.50 because of a change in market conditions, would the firm be making a profit or suffering a loss?
   (viii) If it suffered a loss at a price of $5.50, should the firm shut down or continue to operate in the short run? Why or why not?

(c) From the same data, plot a break-even chart, then answer the questions below:
   (i) What is the break-even output?
   (ii) At what level of output are profits maximized?
   (iii) Does the break-even point on the break-even chart correspond in terms of total output with the point at which MR = MC on the marginal analysis chart? Why? Why not?
   (iv) Are the maximum profit levels of output on the break-even chart and the marginal-analysis chart the same?

2. As a government economist, you are asked to help prepare some data for a congressional hearing on the status of competition in a particular industry. From the accompanying information about one of the firms in the industry, you are given the specific task of ascertaining its maximum profit level of output.

(a) From the data, construct a table showing additional data for average cost, marginal cost, total revenue, average revenue, and marginal revenue.

(b) On regular graph paper, draw a marginal-analysis chart showing AC, MC, AR, and MR; then answer the following questions:
   (i) What is the equilibrium output, or the maximum profit position, of the firm?
   (ii) At equilibrium output, what is the price per unit of output?

Total Output	Total Cost	Total Revenue
$ 100	$ 6,000	$ 4,828
200	10,416	9,336
300	13,563	13,374
400	15,684	16,992
500	17,040	20,190
600	18,000	22,968
700	18,816	25,326
800	19,775	27,264
900	21,168	28,782
1,000	23,280	29,880
1,100	26,400	30,558
1,200	30,815	30,816
1,300	36,000	30,654
1,400	40,000	30,072

(iii) At equilibrium output, what is the profit per unit of output and the total profit?

(iv) What line on the chart represents the demand for the products of the firm?

(v) Are the AR and MR identical? Why or why not?

(vi) If asked by the Hearing Committee about the nature of competition in the industry, what would you answer?

(c) It is brought out in the hearings that under perfect (pure) competition, the point at which MR = MC is also the point at which AR = MC. This indicates that a firm continues to produce units of output so long as society is willing to pay a price sufficient to cover the marginal cost of production. You are asked whether this is so in the firm for which you prepared data.

(d) You are asked to explain why the firm may or may not produce to the the point where AR = MC.

(e) You are then asked: If this firm is typical of those in the industry, is the industry acting in the best interest of consumers? Explain why or why not.

The Way Out — Why and How
GE Left Computer Field:
The Road is Marked in IBM
Trial Record

In 1970, General Electric Co. unexpectedly dropped out of the business of making computers and sold the deficit-ridden operation to a competitor, Honeywell Inc.

Source: Scott R. Schmedel, *The Wall Street Journal*, January 12, 1976. Reprinted by permission of *The Wall Street Journal*, © Dow Jones & Company, Inc. 1976. All Rights Reserved.

Until last month, the reasons behind GE's exit hadn't been fully aired in public. But they are currently among the issues in the trial here of the Justice Department's civil antitrust suit against International Business Machines Corp. As a result, highly confidential information about GE's inner workings has come to light. For in seeking to prove IBM's alleged monopoly power over the U.S. computer-systems market, the government has introduced GE documents and testimony.

The documents offer insight into GE's ability to appraise a failure coolly. What's more, they include confidential GE appraisals of competitors.

As to whether IBM had raised insurmountable barriers to GE's success in the industry, deliberately or otherwise, the trial evidence will have to be weighed by the judge. GE documents emphasized IBM's dominance in the industry, but GE's chairman and chief executive, Reginald H. Jones, testified on Dec. 9: "I personally know of no acts or activities of IBM that would have caused our disengagement."

In 1965, IBM considered GE its "strongest competitor," according to a previously secret IBM analysis also disclosed at the trial. But by 1970, GE's products were out of date. Its domestic business-computer manufacturing operations had sustained net losses from 1957 through 1970 totaling $162.7 million. And in 1970 the country was in a recession and GE had just weathered a costly strike. The company was also under financial strain from two other large and unprofitable manufacturing ventures — nuclear power stations and jet aircraft engines — in which it had three- to five-year commitments to customers.

An Article of Faith.   Nuclear power and jet engines were closely related to GE's "core" lines of electrical products and seemed sure to turn profitable. GE management believed, almost as an article of faith, that they couldn't be abandoned. They have since turned profitable.

In contrast, the computer business had never been considered vital to GE, and top management thought it was too late to make a wholehearted commitment to it. It seemed to GE's analysts that if the company was to salvage anything financially from its computer venture, it would have to be the first of "the seven dwarfs," as IBM's main competitors were known, to "disengage."

In October 1969, Fred J. Borch, then GE's chairman, appointed a "ventures task force" of three vice presidents to review computers, nuclear reactors and jet engines. The vice presidents were Mr. Jones — who became GE's chief executive in December 1972 — John B. McKitterick and Robert M. Estes.

The computer group's management had proposed a broad new computer family that would have 20% to 40% better performance than IBM's existing line, at about the same price. This was called the APL plan — for "advanced product line." According to the plan, the new line could generate revenue of $8.2 billion and profit before taxes of $2.34 billion in the 13 years 1969 through 1981. However, the program would amass losses of $538 million through 1973. Profits would appear in 1974, but the cumulative deficit wouldn't be erased until 1977. The cash outflow would total $685 million through 1974.

Mr. Jones has testified at the trial that GE would have had to raise at least $500 million to undertake the plan.

The APL plan was supposed to make GE "a clear No. 2" to IBM, giving it 8% of the market by 1975 and raising that share soon afterward to 10%. That was what GE, which at the time had 4 percent to 5 percent of the market, needed for its computers to be profitable, company officials figured.

Shaky Assumptions. But the plan leaned on some shaky assumptions: that GE could take customers away from IBM, that IBM would tolerate a sizable reduction of its U.S. market share without retaliating, and that GE could achieve key developments by certain deadlines—"invention by schedule," Mr. Jones called it in his testimony. The plan was "fraught with risks," he said, including the likelihood that IBM and others would "leap-frog" APL by bringing out better products.

On Feb. 2, 1970, the task force reported to Mr. Borch and to the three vice chairmen making up GE's "corporate executive office." In the IBM trial record is an 88-page outline of the presentation. Mr. Jones, the outline shows, spoke first:

"Beset with mounting pressure for immediate growth in earnings, carrying an inordinate load of losses from major risk ventures . . . and facing increasing financial demands from its core businesses, General Electric Co. cannot, in our opinion, undertake any half-billion-dollar venture that produces substantial immediate net income losses.

". . . The APL Plan is, in part, based on questionable assumptions . . . it entails very high risks . . . it is doubtful that it could be kept to time and cost schedules . . . We are even more concerned with competitive reaction to such an all-out attack on IBM, one of the world's strongest corporations."

The recommendation, he said, summarizing what was to come, would be: "To disengage ourselves from this business."

Mr. McKitterick then described the industry. The markets were growing fast. The technology and the uses of computers were changing rapidly. He forecast that IBM would continue to dominate, thanks to its "superior sales coverage," low manufacturing costs, and huge base of customers. It had installed 72% of the computers in the world.

IBM had steadily improving profit margins, strength in all technologies, and "overwhelming software," or programming resources. To be sure, it faced antitrust suits, a loss of skilled personnel, increasing specialization by competitors, and some "gradual loss of position, especially in software and peripheral (equipment) technology."

Technology vs. Profits. Still, IBM's competitors, while "impressive" in technical strength, had had meager profits. Specialization in certain products or uses might assure survival, but the position of the "generalists," those competing across the board with IBM, was untenable.

GE was a generalist. It was paying for that with "rapid loss of position" in the U.S. and gradual loss of its stronger position abroad. It hadn't any strong basis for specialization. Its major product lines were "obsolete." They were weak in peripheral, mass-storage, and terminal devices—all key products of the future. GE had "limited technical strength" in most areas. Its customer loyalty was the "lowest of any competitor."

Mr. Jones added these observations:

—IBM had 210 U.S. sales offices with 17,000 salesmen and systems analysts. GE had 38 offices with a staff of 600. To reach its 1975 objective, GE would have to "increase sales force 60-70% per year . . . and . . . develop salesmen who are twice as productive as those of IBM."

—In "hardware" development, "GE has a catch-up job. . . ." To develop APL software "is truly a staggering challenge." GE's manufacturing costs were 47% of its computer revenue, while IBM's were estimated at 20%.

Mr. McKitterick's assessments of the other competitors were, in part:

Control Data Corp.: 4.2% of world installation, growing faster than the market, specialist in larger systems and in vulnerable government programs, technically strong but weak in business applications.

Burroughs Corp.: 2.4% of market, growing substantially faster than the market, specialist in banking and some other uses, technically strong.

NCR Corp.: 2.2% of market; specialist in smaller systems, banking and first-time users; weak in peripherals and software; unprofitable.

Sperry Rand Corp.'s Univac division: 6.8% of market but losing ground, generalist, technically strong except for large-system software but had never fully used its strength; weak marketing organization.

Honeywell: 3.9% of market, growing slower than the market, generalist, technically good but product line incomplete and out of date; had seriously delayed product development in order to be profitable.

RCA Corp.: 2.9% of market and losing market share, generalist but no identifiable market, technically poor except in communications; aging and incomplete product line, no real strength, unprofitable.

Xerox Corp., which has acquired a small computer maker in 1969, wasn't rated.

The Importance of Timing. Mr. Estes, who is GE's general counsel, made the task force's recommendations. A prime element was timing. The industry seemed "on the threshold of a major merger movement." No one dwarf could make a lasting impact. "In the absence of now unanticipated severe constraints on IBM, any competitor over time will exist at the tolerance of this dominant company."

"Should we now temporize," Mr. Estes said, "this merger movement could take place without us — making our already precarious situation disastrous. Conversely . . . if we are timely in our move, we could be a principal beneficiary of such a major merger movement."

What would anyone want with GE's obviously weak operations; "Our potential as a competitor," Mr. Estes noted. "Any dwarf would rest easier" with that potential under his control and would be "deeply concerned" if it went to another. There also was GE's potential as a substantial customer; that was "the hole card."

The next step was to discover who might buy the business. GE wanted to find this out without letting on, inside the company or out, its true intention. Thus, GE would approach competitors to discuss the "structure of the industry" and the hazards posed by "the continuing dominance of IBM." GE would indicate that its options were open: It could buy or sell.

"Luckily, Control Data earlier had proposed some exploratory talks, so GE could respond without appearing to make overtures. Meanwhile, Mr. Estes said, GE's computer management should "exercise maximum ingenuity" to put the APL plan in limbo without creating "a fire-sale atmosphere."

Before putting the whole matter before the board of directors, GE officials approached Control Data, Xerox and Honeywell. By April 24, 1970, management was ready to face the directors. The IBM trial record includes a 55-page outline for a two-hour report the task force made that day. Besides surveying the industry, the report rated how well competitors' operations might match with GE's:

"Operating Match": Honeywell or Burroughs, good; Univac or NCR, fair; Control Data or RCA, poor; Xerox, unrated.

"Financial Capabilities": Xerox, high; Honeywell, RCA, Burroughs, and NCR, medium; Univac, low-plus; Control Data, poor.

$472 Million Invested. GE had invested $472 million in the computer operations it wanted to sell, but the task force said a price of $176 million would cover the depreciated net book value of those assets.

Mr. Jones told the board GE had had two exploratory sessions with Control Data. However, he said, it was clear that that company couldn't finance such an acquisition.

"We have serious reservations about the future of (Control Data)," he continued, and a sale to that company would require GE to hold "a substantial amount of (Control Data's) paper" while Control Data tried to market the poorly matched product lines. No further talks were contemplated.

Prosperous Xerox had seemed a likely condidate but hadn't responded.

GE had then turned to Honeywell and found it ready to talk. Honeywell, stronger in the U.S., and GE, stronger in Europe, would have a combined "installed base" — the number of computers installed and in service — double that of either company. The combination would be "an undisputed Number 2," with assets of $1.24 billion and 12,500 marketing and service employes worldwide. Combined 1970 revenue would be about $932 million. Eliminating duplicate activities and adopting Honeywell's "more liberal" accounting policy could produce a pre-tax profit of $66 million. It was, Mr. Jones told the board, "an optimum fit with a well managed and successful growth company."

He urged that negotiations begin at once, because of "the chances for leaks." Less than a month after the April 24 presentation, GE and Honeywell announced an agreement to put their business-computer assets in a new company that would be controlled and managed by Honeywell. In a transaction effective Oct. 1, 1970, GE turned over its business-computer manufacturing assets to the new company in exchange for $110 million in Honeywell notes, Honeywell stock valued at $124.5 million, and in 18.5% interest in the new company.

GE kept its time-sharing service, which allows simultaneous operation of a computer by many users, and its process-control computers for industry, but sold the process-control line to Honeywell in 1974.

As the first dwarf to withdraw from the manufacture of business computers, GE posted a net gain of $1.7 million in 1970 from the sale to Honeywell. About a year later, RCA abruptly abandoned its computer business at a net loss of $210 million. Sperry Rand bought some of the RCA assets. Last summer, Xerox also dropped out, taking a net write-off of $84.4 million and turning over some of its activities to Honeywell.

The RCA and Xerox case histories are next on the IBM trial agenda.

(a) How would you classify the competitive structure of the computer industry?

   (i) How many firms were in the industry?

   (ii) What was IBM's market share?

(b) What was the profit picture between IBM and the rest of the industry, particularly vis-à-vis General Electric? Why was it so?

(c) What were the nature and status of General Electric Company computer business compared with those of the other "dwarfs" in the industry?

(d) According to the testimony, the industry was ripe for merger of some of the smaller companies. Why did General Electric Company desire to sell rather than merge?

(e) Was there any fear of retaliation by IBM if the "dwarfs" made further inroads into IBM's market share?

(f) How does this case relate to the structure of oligopoly and the move toward larger-scale operation described in the text?

Marketing of Diamonds

In November 1977, DeBeer Consolidated Mines, Ltd. raised its prices on its two thousand different diamonds an average of 17 percent. This followed a 15 percent increase earlier in the year. DeBeers is considered to be a worldwide diamond-marketing monopoly. The price increases were in response to the growing demand for small stones, which are cut and polished primarily in Tel Aviv, Israel. DeBeers's supply of small stones was limited.

Small diamonds were in such demand that Tel Aviv cutters and polishers were offering a 30-40 percent premium over the current market price. To restore some market stability, DeBeers raised its own price for these "melees," rough stones of less than one-quarter carat, by 40 percent.

DeBeers produces 40 percent of the world's diamonds. In addition, it has a strong control over world prices through control of the London-based Central Selling Organization (CSO).

At DeBeers's in London, CSO sells about 80 percent of the world's rough diamonds in its ten showings, or "sights," per year. In addition to its own diamonds, CSO buys almost all of South Africa's diamond production and much of the output of other African nations. CSO also handles diamond sales for Russia in the world market.

DeBeers at the time had a strong cash position, and its $328 million profit in the first half of 1977 was nearly equal to the entire profit of $355 million for the previous year. Toward the end of 1977, DeBeers had $700 million in cash, half held in London and the other half in New York. Its cash was expected to rise to $900 million by the end of 1978.

According to diamond authorities, DeBeers is a benevolent monopoly. With its strong cash position, it can purchase and withhold rough stones from the world market when demand is soft and release them when the market improves. At the end of 1976, for example, DeBeers was holding $260 million worth of rough stones. The CSO sale of rough gems and industrial diamonds was expected to exceed $2 billion in 1977, double the sales for 1975.

(a) How would you classify DeBeers regarding market structure in the diamond industry?

(b) What appears to be the relationship of other firms to DeBeers regarding pricing?

(c) DeBeers claims that it is not a monopoly, but merely engaged in "controlled marketing through a single outlet." Comment.

(d) What differences or similarities do you see between the production and sale of world oil compared with that of diamonds?

9

Pricing: Monopolistic Competition and Oligopoly

Any market structure other than perfect (pure) competition is often called *imperfect competition* in economic analysis. This indicates, of course, that one or a number of the elements of pure competition is missing. At other times, market conditions are visualized as a continuum ranging from pure competition at one extreme to pure monopoly on the other. A firm's place in the spectrum may border on pure competition, be adjacent to monopoly, or be somewhere in between. Although this wide area of competition in which most businesses find themselves is often referred to as imperfect competition, it is actually subdivided into two broader categories. One is *oligopoly*, a market condition with relatively few firms. A specific form of oligopoly is *duopoly*, a market in which two producers account for the total market supply. Another broad category is designated as *monopolistic competition*, a market condition in which a relatively large number of firms produce a similar but differentiated product, with each firm having some degree of control over price.

MONOPOLISTIC COMPETITION

Some notion of the nature of monopolistic competition is revealed by the very name of the concept itself. It implies a mixture of monopoly and competitive characteristics. The monopoly aspect indicates some degree of control over market supply or price. The competitive aspect implies the absence of any influence on price. Melding the two characteristics indicates that there is some control or influence over price, but that the degree of influence is limited.

Monopolistic competition assumes a larger number of firms producing or selling similar products that are close substitutes, as opposed to a homogeneous or identical product associated with conditions of pure competition. In the spectrum of market competition, monopolistic competition fits into a wide range between pure competition and oligopoly. It may border on either one or be somewhere in the middle. The number of firms is less than that found in pure competition. On the other hand, there will be more sellers than are present in oligopoly. Product differentiation is a salient feature of monopolistic competition. It removes the perfect elasticity aspect from the firm's demand line and gives the seller a degree of price elasticity based upon the strength of the product's differentiation.

The case of toothpaste shows the nature of monopolistic competition and its distinction from other forms of competition. Assume a large number of firms selling toothpaste of an identical quality, without brand names, without advertising, and with similar packaging. Assume also that a price of 90 cents per six-ounce tube were established by market supply and demand. Under conditions of pure competition, no seller could get more than the market price for his toothpaste. A buyer would be reluctant to purchase any one seller's toothpaste at a higher price when he could obtain identical toothpaste for 90 cents from several other sellers. If there were only one seller, however, it could change the market price by limiting or expanding its supply.

Product Differentiation

In today's market, a relatively large number of toothpaste producers supply similar but differentiated products. They are different because some toothpaste "prevents cavities," another is powdered, another acts also as a mouthwash, still another "gets teeth whiter," and one is striped. There are many different formulas with numerous ingredients and packaged in a variety of containers. Moreover, there is an even larger number of retail outlets, such as grocery stores, drugstores, department stores, discount stores, "mom and pop" stores, and others. Each may be selling toothpaste under different sales conditions. They may be all selling at, or near, a price determined by the aggregate demand and supply for toothpaste in general. It is the product differentiation, whether real or psychological, that permits an individual firm to have some degree of control over the price at which it sells its particular brand. On the other hand, it is the similarity among the toothpaste brands that restricts or limits the degree of control over price.

Consumers may buy a particular brand of toothpaste because they like the taste, admire the package, or are swayed by a television jingle. Consequently, if the producer of a specific brand, such as Easy White, decided to raise its price a little above the market level, it would not lose all its customers. We can assume that most of the buyers of Easy White would be willing to pay a few cents more than the general market price because of their preference for Easy White. But the firm cannot raise its price too much above the average market price. If its price differential became too great, buyers might feel that Easy White is not all that much different from other brands. When the price reaches a certain level, brand loyalty will diminish and Easy White consumers may shift to other brands of toothpaste. Conversely, if Easy White were to lower its price by a few cents below the average market price, it would probably gain very few customers from the substitution effect. Consumers buy specific brands because they feel there is something different about them. If their preference is strong, they will not leave their favorite brand and shift to Easy White because of a few cents' difference. If Easy White reduces its price substantially, however, some consumers of other brands may feel that the quality or other difference is not great enough to keep them from switching to the lower-priced Easy White toothpaste. In such a case, a price may be reached where the sales of Easy White toothpaste would increase substantially, provided that other toothpaste producers did not react by also lowering their prices.

Product differentiation allows a certain price range within which a seller may raise or lower his price without substantially affecting his sales or those of his competitors. This is the monopolistic aspect of monopolistic competition. On the other hand, if the individual supplier raises its price too high compared with other brands, it will lose customers; if it lowers its price enough, it can draw customers away from other brands. This is the competitive aspect of monopolistic competition.

In monopolistic competition, similar products are usually found at a variety of prices within a general market price range. With a large number of producers or sellers in the market, there may be little concern about competitor reaction to an individual firm's change in price. Instead of aggressive price competition, the firms generally stress product differentiation, use advertising, and emphasize packaging to sell to customers. With a large number of competitors in the market, however, there is less likelihood of firm's engaging in collusive practice to limit output or to fix price.

Monopolistic competition is prevalent in the retail industry. Numerous retail stores in each large city are differentiated as to location, sales personnel, store layout, service, and other aspects of retail selling. Furthermore, they handle various kinds of merchandise produced under monopolistic competitive conditions. In addition to grocery stores and department stores, gasoline service stations, dry cleaners, and barber shops, especially in large urban areas, also tend to approach conditions of monopolistic competition. The manufacture of costume jewelry, metal house furniture, and toys, plus the production of toothpaste, soaps, soft drinks, and beer, all fall within the realm of monopolistic competition.

Short Run: Price, Profit, and Output

The demand line of a firm in monopolistic competition is not a horizontal, perfectly elastic demand line characteristic of pure competition. Nor is the firm's demand line identical to the market demand, as it is in the case of monopoly. Although there are a large number of firms in conditions of monopolistic competition, there may be fewer than there are in pure competition. Moreover, their products are differentiated. As a result, a firm will be able to sell more or less by lowering or raising its price, and its demand line or average revenue will slope downward to the right. Furthermore, because of the substitution effect, the demand for the product of the firm will tend to be more elastic than the demand line for the industry. Of course, the closer monopolistic competition approaches pure competition, the closer to horizontal will be a firm's demand line. The more it moves in toward oligopoly or monopoly, the less elastic the firm's demand line will be, and the closer it will approach the industry demand line.

Since the demand, or average revenue, line slopes downward to the right, the marginal-revenue line will move in the same direction but at a steeper slope. Typical short-run cost and revenue lines for a firm engaged in monopolistic competition are shown in Figure 9-1. Figure 9-1 (a) shows the general price range established in the industry by the intersection of total demand and supply. Figure 9-1 (b) shows a monopolistic competitor making a profit. Observe that the price, although on the high side, is still within the general price range established by this market. Figure 9-1 (b) shows that with this price, the firm will produce 60,000 units and enjoy a profit.

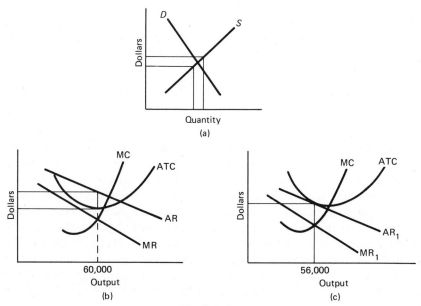

Figure 9-1.

If profits exist in an industry, new firms will be encouraged to enter the industry. As new firms appear with similar but differentiated products, the total supply on the market will increase. This will decrease the market price range and lower the average revenue of each firm in the industry. If there are no strong bars to entry, this process will continue until supply and price are such that profits for the average firm will be eliminated, as shown in Figure 9-1 (c). Notice that at the point of equilibrium, 56,000 units of output, the firm will be making no economic profit. Moreover, in spite of an increase in total market sales, sales of the typical individual firm have dropped.

Conversely, if firms in the industry are suffering losses in the short run, the opposite reaction on market price will occur. As firms drop out of business, the total market supply will decrease, causing the market price to rise. Average revenues will rise until losses are eliminated and equilibrium is established at a no-profit, no-loss position. In the long run under conditions of monopolistic competition, consumers will get a differentiated product at a price equal to the average total cost of production for the industry.

Even though the consumer receives the product at a price that equals its cost of production in the long run, this price is not as low as it would be under conditions of pure competition. Because of its slope, the average revenue line cannot be tangential to the average total cost curve at the lowest point of the ATC curve, as is characteristic of the horizontal average revenue line of pure competition. If one assumes identical costs, equilibrium price under monopolistic competition, therefore, must be higher than the price under pure competition.

OLIGOPOLY

From the point of view of economic analysis probably the most intriguing of market conditions is *oligopoly*, a market condition in which relatively few firms produce identical or similar but differentiated products. Oligopoly may involve a few or more than a dozen firms. The basic characteristics of this form of market structure are the ability of individual firms to influence market price; and concern about retaliation by other firms in setting one's pricing policies. The number of firms supplying a particular good must be small enough for any one of them to influence the market price by altering the amount it offers for sale. Consequently, an increase in supply by any one firm could increase total supply and tend to lower the market price. If one firm reduces its price, it would gain a larger share of the market at the expense of the others. But the other firms might respond by also lowering their prices. This could obliterate the gain of the initial price cutter. Whether the firms and the industry would profit from such price competition would depend on price elasticity of demand for the product of the industry.

Oligopolists generally avoid price competition because of the probable reaction of competitors. Consequently, oligopolists engage in many forms of nonprice competition, in which product differentiation is very prevalent. Besides its presence in the steel, aluminum, and copper industries, oligopoly exists today in the manufacture of automobiles, farm equipment, chemicals, tires, oil, cigarettes, electric motors, tin cans, and tractors. Several oligopolies exist also in nonmanufacturing industries. In some industries, one finds an oligopoly with a *homogeneous* product, such as steel, cement, aluminum, and chemicals. In other industries there exists oligopoly with a *differentiated* product, such as the automobile, aircraft, and cigarette industries.[1]

Some verification of the degree of oligopoly that exists in the American economy can be obtained from a recent report of the Senate Subcommittee on Antitrust and Monopoly. The subcommittee reported that in 1963 there were 24 manufacturing industries in which four firms produced 75-100 percent of the total market supply. In more than 80 additional industries, the four largest firms produced 50-75 percent of the total market supply. There were another 136 industries in which the top four producers accounted for 25-50 percent of the total supply of the industry.

The Kinked Demand Line

Under conditions of oligopoly determination of prices is more complicated than it is under other market structures. An individual firm may or may not be able to predict what amount it can sell at various prices. What happens to sales when an oligopolist establishes or changes price depends in large part on the reaction of competitors. Since an oligopoly involves a market situation in which the number of sellers is few, each firm must consider the response of its rivals. This situation differs from that of monopolistic competition, in which the number of competitors is large enough that an individual

---

[1] Sometimes these are referred to as *pure* oligopoly (identical or homogeneous products) and *differentiated* oligopoly (differentiated or heterogeneous products).

seller can be more independent in regard to the reactions of its competitors. Fear of retaliation by competitors can be a potent factor restricting price competition in an oligopolistic market.

Several reactions by competitors are possible when an oligopolist changes supply and/or price. First, competitors may ignore the price change. In this case the demand and average-revenue line for the individual firm will be known within a reasonable degree of certainty and may appear as DD, shown in Figure 9-2. Secondly, a change in price by an oligopolist may be followed by a similar change by competitors. In this case the demand (average-revenue) line of the oligopolist may appear as D_1D_1 (Figure 9-2). Notice that the demand line D_1D_1 will tend to be less price elastic than demand line DD. This is so because the gain in sales resulting from lower prices will be lessened if competitors also lower their prices. On the other hand, the firm initiating a price increase will not lose as many customers as it otherwise would if competitors, likewise, increase their prices. In short, the substitution effect resulting from the price change will be lessened if other firms respond by matching the price change.

A third, and more interesting, situation may arise. Competitors may follow a price decrease but not follow a price increase. If one firm were to reduce price, its increase in quantity sold might be less than anticipated if rivals also lowered prices. This would tend to eliminate or limit any substitution effect, or gain, in sales at the expense of other firms. The initial price cutter, along with others, would experience some increase in sales, however, as industry sales expanded in response to the lower market price. On the other hand, if a firm raised its price and its competitors did not, the decrease in

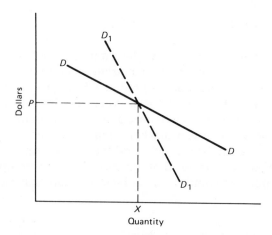

Figure 9-2.

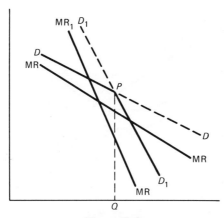

Figure 9-3.

sales of the price changer might be greater than expected as a conse-
quence of its loss of sales to competitors through the substitution
effect. In this case the oligopolist's demand curve would be the same
as that of D for any price above P, but identical with D_1 for any
price below P. Such a demand line would appear as D, P, D_1 (Figure
9-2). This is known as a *kinked demand line*. Such a market situation, of course, can lead to price stability, since the demand line of
the individual firm will tend to be inelastic if price is lowered and
elastic if price is raised. Under these market conditions, price P may
become the maximum revenue point for the firm.

Price stability in oligopoly is also abetted by the discontinuous
nature of the marginal revenue (MR) line that results from a kinked
demand line. At the equilibrium output corresponding with the point
of the kink, there will be a gap in the MR line, as shown in Figure
9-3, which contains the marginal revenue lines accompanying the
demand lines shown in Figure 9-2. Here it can be observed that, for
the upper portion of the oligopolist's demand, line D, the marginal
revenue will follow MR to output at point Q. Beyond that output,
however, the marginal-revenue line for the firm will follow MR_1,
which accompanies the lower part of the oligopolist's demand line,
D_1. Consequently, the firm's marginal revenue, a combination of MR
and MR_1, will be discontinuous (or have a gap) at point Q. Consequently, whenever there is a change in the cost of production,
there may be no incentive to change price or output so long as the
marginal-cost line moves up or down within the gap. This is demonstrated in Figure 9-4, in which the vertical gap in the marginal
revenue can be seen.

Price stabilization may emerge under such a market condition if

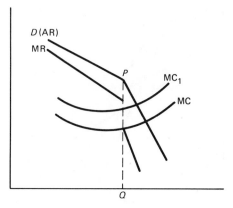

Figure 9-4.

each firm believes that it has little to gain by raising price and that a price war may ensue if it lowers price. This could, of course, lead to collusion, tacit or otherwise, in regard to price determination or market share.

The foregoing analysis does not explain what determines an original price, but merely possible actions and reactions of oligopolistic firms to changes from a given price. Price may have been determined initially by supply and demand, custom, or other factors.

Nonprice Competition

Price rigidity, or the lack of price competition, in oligopoly is offset in part by nonprice competition. Heavy emphasis is placed on product differentiation, for example, and firms resort to widespread advertising to sell their products. Consumers are bombarded with a great variety of styles, models, promotional deals, guarantees, and brand improvements. But seldom do the sellers engage in price competition. This is the pattern of competition in the production and sale of automobiles, television sets, soaps, cigarettes, cosmetics, tires, coffee, and air transportation, in which the emphasis is on nonprice competition. In autos, for example, a car buyer can select from more than 252 domestic models plus numerous foreign models.[2]

The merits and demerits of product differentiation and nonprice competition associated with oligopoly and monopolistic competition are often debated. It can be shown that research for product differentiations sometimes results in improvement in the quality of products,

[2] In 1978, for example, GM offered 138 models; Ford, 64; Chrysler, 39; and American Motors, 11 models.

that brands, models, and styles give the consumer a better and wider choice, that planned obsolescence makes the consumer want to buy newer and better products, and that advertising tells consumers about different products and their uses. It is claimed that advertising also provides or helps pay for numerous intermediary services, such as radio and television entertainment, and newspapers and magazines. Moreover, it provides consumers with numerous small utility products, such as ball point pens, calendars, matches, and other items used as advertising gimmicks. On the other hand, it can also be shown that the product differentiation characteristic of oligopolistic and monopolistic markets results in considerable duplication of facilities, that many product differences are insignificant, that there is a considerable waste of resources and manpower associated with frivolous model and style changes, that planned obsolescence is costly to the economy, and that advertising is often misinformative and results primarily in higher costs for the product.

The tendency toward price stability associated with oligopoly often leads to collusive practices designed to limit output and/or fix prices. This has occurred particularly when there is a highly inelastic demand for the product of the industry and relatively few firms supplying it. A highly inelastic demand, especially with a kinked demand line, makes price competition nonprofitable not only for the firm but also for the industry as a whole. When there are only a few firms, it is easier for them to agree, either tacitly or formally, to limit output or to fix price. Court dockets have recently been filled with antitrust suits against such collusive practices in the electrical, steel, oil, truck, plastic pipe, automobile leasing, and other industries. Let us turn to a few practices leading to price stability.

Pricing by Agreement.   Manufacturers, merchants, farmers, and wage earners sometimes come to an agreement — specific or tacit — that will restrict competition on the basis of price. The inclination of producers or of sellers to protect their own interests is not a recent development. Adam Smith commented on it in his *Wealth of Nations* (1776).[3]

In many European countries, cartels composed of manufacturers or sellers have been taken for granted for a long time. Such practices as production restrictions, division of market territory, control of

---

[3] Adam Smith, *An Investigation into the Wealth of Nations.* Edwin Cannan, ed., Vol. 1, 130, 6th edition. (London: Methuen & Co., Ltd.) 1950. Smith, states: "People of the same trade seldom meet together even for merriment and diversion, but the conversation ends in a conspiracy against the public, or in some contrivance to raise prices. It is impossible to prevent such meetings, by any law which either could be executed, or would be consistent with liberty and justice."

prices, regulation of output, and other measures to protect profits are sanctioned. The result in many cases is the formalization of national or even international oligopolies.

The cartelization of business in the United States has usually been looked upon with suspicion or outright disapproval. Common law and statutes against conspiracies and restraints of trade are invoked to prevent, or to break up, attempts to fix prices or control production. Nevertheless, price agreements — tacit or otherwise — do exist. We shall see more about these practices and the application of antitrust laws to prevent or eliminate them in Chapter 11.

Price Leadership.   In some situations, one firm may be able to set a price that will be adopted by all or most of the industry. This practice of price leadership, when it is found, tends to occur in industries in which one firm has achieved such a dominant position that other firms tend to follow its lead. This can occur also when a few firms dominate the industry. Sometimes, in order to avoid detection, price leadership will be practiced in an oligopoly by using a rotating leader. Of course, this does not mean that price leadership is practiced in all industries in which one or a few companies produce a relatively large share of the total market supply.

Smaller firms may be willing to follow prices established by a leader for several reasons. Some smaller firms may be reluctant to engage in price competition because they realize that the larger firm could enter into a price-cutting war in which the smaller firm would suffer most. With its greater financial resources, and probably a lower ATC curve resulting from a larger scale of operation, the large firm could lower prices to a level that eventually would bankrupt the smaller firm. The smaller firm, too, may willingly accept the price established by the leader, since it is likely to be relatively stable and provide the smaller producer a comfortable profit.

Basing-point Pricing.   It has been the practice in some industries, such as those of steel, automobiles, and cement, to quote "delivered prices" for their products. In this system of pricing, freight charges are computed by the seller from a basing point, designated as the point from which delivery is made no matter where the product may be produced. In the "Pittsburgh plus" system once used in the steel industry, the customer paid a transportation charge equivalent to the cost of shipment between Pittsburgh and the point of destination, even though the steel was produced and shipped from a point other than Pittsburgh. A buyer of steel in Fort Wayne, Indiana, for instance, would be required to pay the factory price at Pittsburgh plus the freight[4] *from Pittsburgh*, although the steel was shipped directly

---

[4] This is also referred to as *phantom freight*.

from a Chicago plant. This, of course, permitted the dominant producers to enter any market and compete successfully with regional producers. Subsequently, some manufacturers established multiple basing points for the quotation of zone prices.

Opponents of the basing-point system argue that it constitutes an exercise of monopoly power and restrains price competition. All firms quote the same delivered prices, and price competition based on transportation cost is prevented. Proponents of the system, however, insist that it is a desirable method of stabilizing prices, and that stable prices are helpful to users of the products. A few decades ago, the United States Supreme Court upheld an order by the Federal Trade Commission against 74 cement manufacturers that ordered them to stop using the basing-point system. The Court stated that the basing-point system was contrary to the spirit of competition and that it constituted an illegal form of price discrimination.[5]

Product Differentiation. Manufacturers of similar commodities that may readily be substituted for one another frequently emphasize the supposed superior characteristics of their products. This practice is known as *product differentiation* and is prevalent in the United States' economy.

The producer of a brand of hair spray, for example, tries to convince consumers that its product is much better than others on the market. Therefore, it may attempt to achieve distinction for its hair spray by giving it an exotic name, by putting it into an eye-appealing container, by adding a certain perfume, by promising more romance, and by making dogmatic, repeated claims that it is superior to other brands of hair spray. The seller can use any or all of the advertising media. The firm's hair spray may be superior to others of a similar nature, but whether it is or not, the firm's objective is to convince consumers that it is. To the extent that it succeeds, the firm lessens competition. Once it has developed a demand for its hair spray, the firm can exercise more control over its price. A major purpose of product differentiation is making the demand line for the product less price elastic and less cross elastic. Then price increases by the seller or price decreases by its competitors will result in a smaller loss of sales through the substitution effect.

The producer of a differentiated product, however, must constantly be concerned about the loss of customers, since buyers' tastes, habits, and preferences are subject to change. A person may use one brand of gasoline for years and then suddenly switch to another brand. A homemaker seeking variety may try another brand of coffee and like it. Not every smoker would "rather fight than

---

[5] *Federal Trade Commission v. Cement Institute*, 333 U.S. 683, 1948.

switch," as the popular advertisement says. Moreover, the possibility of a shift from one brand to another is enhanced if the price of the former is raised. Manufacturers endeavor, therefore, to use advertising to keep their brands in the minds of the public.

Administered Prices.   An *administered price* is a predetermined price that is established by the seller. In establishing the market price for a product, the manufacturer, retail outlet, or other seller takes into consideration the total costs, both fixed and variable. It must estimate its sales over a period of time at prices that would yield an expected profit on the number of units sold. It then sets the price that it feels will yield the maximum or a reasonable amount of profit. If the estimated sales seem likely to be realized, the administered price is apt to be maintained. If sales should be greater than estimated, the price may be raised. If sales are slow, the seller may lower the price. In the absence of some control over supply, an administered price cannot deviate too far from a free market price. Although administered prices do respond to the influence of demand, they do not fluctuate as frequently or with such amplitude as do purely competitive prices.

In one fashion or another, most product prices are administered prices. Someone has to test the market. The market mechanism does not print out a price, based on demand and supply, for all to see. Someone must try a price to see whether it sticks and how much will be bought at that price. Others may come into the market with the same, a higher, or a lower price. The price may fluctuate until an equilibrium level is found.

WORKABLE COMPETITION

For the past few decades, economists have been discussing a market structure referred to as *workable competition*. According to this model it is not essential for all conditions of pure competition to exist for the best interest of the consumer. It implies that some forms of imperfect competition may be workable under suitable conditions. In order to have workable competition, at least three basic conditions must exist: There must be a reasonably large number of firms in an industry; there must be no formal or tacit agreement among the firms regarding price and output; and new firms should be able to enter the market without serious impediment or disadvantage. Moreover, no firm should be large or powerful enough to dominate or coerce other firms. But even with these criteria it is difficult to define the exact meaning of workable competition. What is meant by a reasonably large number of firms? Is it seven? Twelve? Twenty? Obviously, it will depend on the type of industry. What is meant by "no serious impediment to entry"? Does an exceptionally large capital requirement qualify as a serious bar to entry?

Selecting those industries in which workable competition does exist would in large part depend upon personal judgment. Many economists consider the automobile industry with its relatively few major producers an example of workable competition; others do not. Some put the steel industry into that category, but other economists disagree. Here again we face the problem of applying economic theory in a world of reality. The operation of several oligopolistic industries today might be defined as exemplifying workable competition.

BUYERS' MARKET STRUCTURE

When comparing market models, many analysts think only of sellers. There are, however, varying degrees of competition among buyers, just as there are different types of competition among sellers. In a market in which numerous buyers who are well informed about price and market situations purchase a commodity under identical conditions and in which no individual buyer is large enough to alter total demand or influence the market price, it can be said that pure competition exists among buyers. In a given locality, for example, numerous housewives form a purely competitive buyers' market for the products of the local grocery store. The Avon lady and the encyclopedia salesman also have numerous homemakers as buyers for their products.

Monopsony, is distinguished from monopoly, refers to a market in which there is only one buyer for a product. Although pure monopsony is difficult to find, such a market did exist for many years in the United States when the government was the only purchaser of gold. Monopsonies can be found in rural areas where there may be only one granary to serve the local farmers. Sometimes a near monopsony will exist when a large-scale employer moves into a predominantly rural area where it is the only major employer of labor.

Oligopsony exists when a few buyers dominate the market. In the tobacco market, for example, there are numerous producers but relatively few buyers. It is quite possible for any one of the major tobacco firms to influence the market price by its decision to buy more or less tobacco. Similar market conditions exist in the purchase of commercial aircraft and the buying of original automobile equipment by the big three auto manufacturers. The author of a college textbook faces an oligopsonistic market in seeking a publisher of his manuscript, as does a professional football player in selling his athletic ability.

Monopsonistic competition, a condition in which many buyers offer differentiated conditions to sellers, is prevalent in the American economy. The manufacturer of soap, for example, operates in a monopsonistically competitive market in the distribution of his product. In any large-sized urban community a large number of firms hire labor, offering a variety of working conditions and fringe benefits.

THE MARKET STRUCTURE

The size, variety, and complexity of markets in the United States economy certainly confirm the concept of a mixed economy. Regulated public utilities exist along with unregulated industries, oligopolies stand side by side with highly competitive firms, giant corporations compete with small, single proprietorships, the government regulates some industries and not others, and government operations occasionally compete with private enterprise. Not only is the total economy mixed in this sense, but the market may be mixed for an individual firm. A firm buying its raw materials, labor, and other inputs in purely competitive markets may have a near-monopoly in selling its final product. A multiproduct firm may sell one of its products in a highly competitive market, another in an oligopolistic market, and have a monopoly in the sale of yet another product.

Competitive vs. Monopolistic Pricing

Economic analysis indicates that a high degree of competition is good for the consumer. Under competitive conditions there is a tendency toward lower prices, the use of more resources, and minimal economic profits in the long run. Moreover, to the extent that a high degree of competition exists in an industry, the amount of profit for the average firm tends to decline to the point where price is equal to average total cost. Because of the horizontal nature of the AR and MR lines, the consumer, under ideal conditions, will be able to buy the good at a price equal to the lowest possible average total cost of production for a given scale of operation, as shown in Figure 9-5 (a).

Under long-run equilibrium conditions of pure competition, the

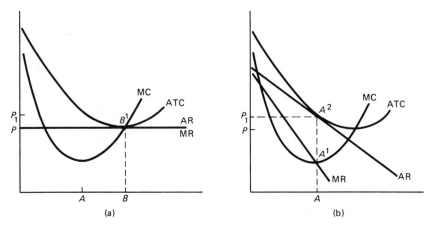

Figure 9-5. Equilibrium Price Under Pure and Imperfect Competition

point at which MR and MC are equal (point B_1) is also the point at which ATC and AR are equal. Thus the price would be at P, and OB units would be produced. Consequently, under pure competition, the price is lower and the output greater than under imperfect competition.

Under conditions of imperfect competition, however, even at the point of no economic profit, where average revenue equals average total cost, as shown in Figure 9-5 (b), the price cannot correspond to the lowest point on the ATC curve. Because of the slope of the AR line, it cannot intersect ATC at the latter's lowest point. Consequently, under identical cost conditions, the long-run equilibrium price will be higher under any form of imperfect competition than it will be under pure competition.

Notice that this analysis assumes that the scale of operation for the firm in pure competition is the same as that for a firm in some form of imperfect competition. Granted that firms in monopolistic competition may be similar to those in pure competition, and therefore their cost curves nearly identical, oligopolies and monopolies generally operate at much larger scales. With a resulting lower ATC curve of the oligopoly or monopoly, it is possible to have an equilibrium price lower than that probable under purely competitive conditions. Even so, the monopolist's or the oligopolist's price will not equal the lowest point on its ATC curve. This can be seen in Figure 9–6, which shows two firms in no-profit equilibrium positions, but one with a lower ATC curve.

Although it may sound paradoxical, it can be said that aggressive competition may lead to monopoly or oligopoly. This is particularly true in heavy industry where the size of the consumer market is small

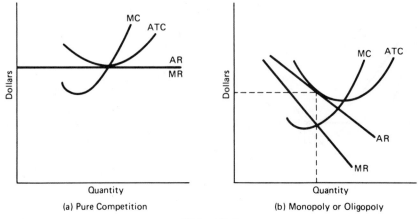

(a) Pure Competition   (b) Monopoly or Oligopoly

Figure 9-6.

compared with the optimum scale of output operations. Envision a long-run situation with various scales of operation as shown in Figure 8-5, and assume an industry with considerable competition among 40 firms. If each firm were operating at scale A and producing 125,000 units, the total market supply would be 5 million units. Assuming the market demand and supply are equal and the firms are in a no-profit equilibrium position, the price would be $20 per unit. If in an endeavor to enhance profit, an innovator and then imitators move to large scale B, and each of the firms then produced 375,000 units, total supply would rise to 15 million units. If they all eventually move to optimum scale C, and each firm produced 625,000 units, total market supply would increase to 25 million units. Sales may very well increase as the market price falls to $16 per unit. But suppose that in the long run, when all the firms were operating at the optimum scale, the total market demand was only 5.625 million units. In that situation, the market would not be large enough to support 40 firms operating at the optimum scale. At scale B, the market demand would support only 14 firms; at optimum scale C, the market would support only 9 firms, each with production levels approximating 625,000 units. Consequently, as competition occurs in both price and scale of operation, some firms, especially marginal and submarginal, will be forced out of business. In essence, if thoroughgoing competition prevails, the character of the industry will move from one approaching pure competition to one of oligopoly.

We have pointed out before that even at equilibrium, all firms in the industry may not have exactly the same cost curves because of temporary or permanent differences in efficiencies. There may be supermarginal, marginal, and submarginal firms all with the same average revenue, about the same size of operation, but with varying average cost curves. So, too, from a practical point of view, not all firms operate at the same scale of operation. At any time there may be firms operating at scales A, B, or C. Even at those sizes, some firms may be slightly smaller or slightly larger. With such a market structure, as the scale of operation increases, production increases and price falls. Firms in the industry may see the handwriting on the wall. Knowing that several of them may be forced out of business, they may overtly or tacitly limit output or fix prices. This is particularly true where there are relatively few firms and an inelastic demand for the product, as in the case cited. Firms at scale B will realize that price competition may hurt them. If a price war occurred, the firms operating at scale C could lower price below the average total cost of firms operating at scale B and still make a profit. Even without any formal agreement, such a market structure could bring about price and output stability.

Concentration Ratios and Resource Allocation

It is difficult to measure the amount or degree of competition, monopoly, oligopoly, or monopolistic competition that exists in the market today. Nevertheless, some indication of the concentration in production can be obtained from an inspection of Table 9-1, compiled by the Senate Subcommittee on Antitrust and Monopoly. The *concentration ratio* as used here is the percentage of total shipments in a given industry made by the four leading firms in that industry. The table shows that imperfect competition in various forms exists in a substantial portion of the United States economy.

According to many economic analysts, pure competition results in allocation of material and labor to the most socially desirable uses. Competition is assumed to promote efficient utilization of these resources. On the other hand, it is claimed by some that imperfect competition does not necessarily allocate resources to their best uses. In some cases, too, firms that have a high degree of monopoly may be less inclined to adopt major innovations and technological changes than they would be if they were subject to rigorous price competition. Numerous examples support this contention. Patent suppressions, or *putting patents to sleep*,[6] and the

---

[6] This term describes the practice of patenting a product or process improvement to prevent competitors from obtaining it, and then withholding it from use because of the cost of making a change. This has happened, for example, in the shoe, paper bag, cash register, cigarette, glass container, and telephone industries. More recently, general use of the more efficient basic oxygen furnace was delayed for years until foreign competition pushed its adoption in the United States.

TABLE 9-1. Concentration in 40 Selected Industries, 1970

		Percentage of Industry Shipments Accounted for by	
		Four Companies	Eight Companies
1	Telephone Apparatus	94	99
2	Motor Vehicles	91	97
3	Cigarettes	84	NA
4	Photographic Equipment	75	86
5	Tires	72	89
6	Soap and Detergents	70	79
7	Aircraft Engines and Parts	68	71
8	Aircraft	65	87
9	Motor Vehicle Parts	58	65
10	Motors and Generators	50	62
11	Radio and TV Sets	48	67
12	Blast Furnaces and Steel Mills	47	65
13	Malt Liquors	46	64
14	Shipbuilding	46	65
15	Nonferrous Wiredrawing	45	62
16	Construction Machinery	42	53
17	Metal Stampings	40	46
18	Toilet Preparations	39	52
19	Petroleum Refining	33	57
20	Weaving Mills, Cotton	33	50
21	Refrigeration Machinery	31	48
22	Bread and Cake Products	29	39
23	Shoes	28	36
24	Paperboard Mills	28	44
25	Periodicals	28	41
26	Paper Mills	26	43
27	Pharmaceutical Preparations	26	43
28	Machine Tools	24	37
29	Meatpacking Plants	23	37
30	Paints and Allied Products	22	34
31	Canned Fruits and Vegetables	21	33
32	Book Publishing	21	35
33	Radio and TV Equipment	19	33
34	Fluid Milk	20	NA
35	Newspapers	16	24
36	Wood Household Furniture	14	23
37	Valves and Pipe Fittings	14	23
38	Soft Drinks	13	20
39	Fabricated Structural Steel	13	18
40	Women's Dresses	10	13

Source: *Statistical Abstract of the United States*, 1974.

continuous use of outmoded equipment, even when new and more efficient equipment is available, are examples. This may result in higher costs and higher prices, than would be the case if the more modern technology and equipment were used. Many analysts think that, over the decades, there has been a noticeable tendency for competition to diminish and to be replaced by monopoly, oligopoly, or monopolistic competition. Unfortunately, we have only limited means by which to judge changes in the extent or degree of competition taking place in the economy. Today's economy has more giant-sized industrial and business firms. The growing size of some firms and the rash of business mergers in the past two decades give the impression that there are relatively few sellers today. However, improved means of communication and transportation facilities have enlarged market areas.

Under conditions of pure competition, price tends to equal production costs. But in many industries, the existence of a sufficient number of firms to meet the conditions necessary for pure competition is neither feasible nor desirable. Moreover, where there are many small firms, prices may be relatively high because few, if any, of the firms are large enough to realize the economies associated with large-scale production. A few large producers may be able to supply a greater variety and quantity of goods at lower market prices than a large number of small firms that, in spite of pure competition, cannot reduce their costs. Would it benefit consumers, for example, to have 100 or more auto manufacturers, of the more than 200 that entered the industry during the past seventy years, still producing automobiles? If the industry had to support that many firms, producers would not be able to operate at the large scale that makes automobile prices as low as they are today. On the other hand, history indicates that when total output in an industry is supplied by too few producers, safeguards may be necessary to protect consumers against exploitative practices by some monopolists and oligopolists. Therefore, as large-scale production becomes more prevalent and desirable — implying in many cases a decrease in the number of producers — there is an evident need to adopt a sound public policy for dealing with business and industry. We will return to this issue in chapter 11.

SUMMARY

Two broad categories of market structure between the extremes of pure competition and pure monopoly are monopolistic competition and oligopoly.

Monopolistic competition is a market condition in which there are many firms, each producing or selling a similar but differentiated product. The differentiation gives the seller some degree of control over price, but the similarity of products limits the degree of price control. Consequently, a firm in monopolistic competition can alter its price up or down somewhat without losing or gaining many customers. If the price change is drastic, however, it will either lose customers or take them away from other firms. Because there are many firms under conditions of monopolistic competition, a firm need not fear the reaction of its competitors to a moderate price change.

Oligopoly is a market structure in which there are relatively few firms. They must be few enough that each has some influence over market price. Moreover, since there are few firms, each one will be concerned about the reaction of its rivals to a change in output or price. Oligopolists may be producing a homogeneous product, such as steel, or a differentiated product, such as automobiles.

The kinked demand line is a characteristic of oligopoly, and it tends to promote price stability. Oligopolistic industry tends to rely on nonprice competition, especially if the industry demand is price inelastic. Such practices as pricing by agreement, price leadership, basing-point pricing, product differentiation, and administered pricing are generally found in oligopolistic industries.

Workable competition is a particular classification of market structure that implies that it may be feasible for firms to compete even under conditions of imperfect competition. On the buying side of the market, perfect competition, monopsonistic competition, oligopsony, or monopsony may exist.

A study of concentration ratios for the United States' economy indicates a market structure in many industries with a high degree of output concentration. In several major industries, as few as four and eight firms produce the bulk of the industry output.

QUESTIONS FOR ANALYSIS AND DISCUSSION

1. Explain how product differentiation permits a firm to exercise a certain degree of control over prices.
2. Why will long-run equilibrium price be higher under conditions or monopolistic competition than it will be under conditions of pure competition?
3. Explain the "kinked demand" line characteristic of oligopoly.
4. Describe the concept of *administered price*.
5. Why must the oligopolist be concerned about the actions or reactions of his rivals?
6. How can a monopoly or oligopoly make a profit and still have a lower price

than a firm engaged in pure competition that is selling its product at a price
that is equal to its cost of production?
7. What is the meaning of workable competition?
8. What are monopsony and oligopsony?
9. What are concentration ratios as applied to United States industries?
10. Do you think that competition is increasing or decreasing in the United
States's economy?

PROBLEMS AND CASES

1. During this century, there has been more than one hundred separate auto-
mobile-producing companies in existence at one time or another. Today
there are relatively few, and the Big Three (General Motors [GM], Chrysler,
and Ford) account for more than 90 percent of domestic production, as
shown in the accompanying exhibit. Within each of the Big Three, however,
different divisions compete with one another. At GM, for example, Pontiac
competes for sales with Oldsmobile and Buick; at Ford, the products of
the Lincoln-Mercury division compete against other Ford cars. In addition,
there are a number of imports from Britain, Germany, France, Japan, and
elsewhere. (See Exhibit 1 on pages 300 to 301).

   (a) How would you classify the United States's automobile industry at the
manufacturers' level?
   (b) Do you think the industry may approach the stage of workable competition, as suggested by some authorities?
   (c) Would you classify the United States's automobile market at the retail
level any differently than classifying it at the manufacturing level? Why
or why not?
   (d) Considering the scale of operations at the manufacturing level, would
you prefer to buy an automobile under the existing oligopolistic market
structure or under conditions of perfect competition in the industry?
Why?

2. The Brass Widget Company is a manufacturer in an industry characterized by
monopolistic competition. It is a marginal firm operating at a no-economic-
profit position. It is, however, recovering all of its costs of operation, both
explicit and implicit, including a nominal profit (entrepreneurial cost). The
state government is considering putting a 5 percent valued-added tax on the
output of this industry of the state. The firm hires you as an economic consultant to show what effect the tax will have on the typical marginal firm in
the industry, assuming that the demand for the product of the industry does
not change. In anticipation of legislative hearings on the tax bill prepare the
following:

   (a) A graphic demonstration, using a marginal-analysis chart, showing the
effect of the tax on output and price.
   (b) An explanation of why price must rise and output decline.
   (c) A response to the possible question by a congressman: Why can the cost
of the tax not be passed on to the customer while maintaining the same
level of output?

EXHIBIT 1.

Auto Production

	Feb. 21-28, 1977		Feb. 21-28, 1977
General Motors		**Ford**	
Chevrolet	13,250	Ford	5,519
Corvette	1,050	Granada	8,935
Chevelle	6,925	Pinto	2,638
Nova	6,250	LTD II	7,284
Camaro	5,025	Maverick	0
Monte Carlo	9,650	Mustang	3,655
Vega	2,025	Thunderbird	7,861
Chevette	2,550	Club Wagon	1,000
Monza	350	Mercury	4,196
Pontiac	4,132	Monarch	3,591
Le Mans	1,965	Cougar	5,178
Firebird	4,209	Comet	0
Grand Prix	4,205	Lincoln	2,557
Astre	810	Mark V	1,378
Sunbird	200	Bobcat	934
Ventura	1,700	**Chrysler**	
Oldsmobile	7,600		
Cutlass	15,700	Plym Gran Fury	1,160
Omega	1,300	Fury	2,370
Starfire	0	Volare	8,580
Toronado	700	Voyager	265
Buick	8,304	Royal Monaco	1,090
Century	7,261	Monaco	1,580
Skyhawk	0	Aspen	6,830
Skylark	2,094	Sportsman	900
Riviera	521	Chrysler	3,400
Cadillac	5,850	**American Motors**	
Eldorado	1,080	Gremlin	950
Seville	990	Matador	1,000
		Hornet	1,600
		Pacer	1,500

Source: *The Wall Street Journal*, March 11, 1977. Reprinted by permission of *The Wall Street Journal*, © Dow Jones & Company, Inc. 1977. All Rights Reserved.

Retail Sales of Leading Imports

	Feb. 1977
Toyota	32,799
Datsun	26,175
Honda	17,669
Volkswagen	16,574
Colt	7,175
Subaru	5,156
Fiat	5,445
Arrow	4,795
British Leyland	4,334
Volvo	3,120
Mercedes-Benz	3,384
Opel	3,998
Audi	2,079
BMW	2,217
Mazda	2,006
Capri	1,948
Porsche	1,265
Saab	1,429
Renault	862
Peugeot	641
Lancia	205
Alfa Romeo	112

Auto Sales Percentage of Total U.S. Market

	1977	1976
General Motors	45.7	45.1
Ford	22.7	22.9
Chrysler	11.9	14.0
American Motors	2.0	3.0
Volkswagen	2.0	2.1
Toyota	4.0	2.9
Datsun	3.2	2.5
Other Imports	8.5	6.5
Total domestic	82.2	86.0
Total Imported	17.8	14.0

(d) An explantion of what might happen to the total production of the industry and the number of firms in the industry.

(e) Advice to the marginal firm of what it must do if it is going to avoid a loss as a result of the tax and consequently continue in business.

3. The Alpha Company is one of five producers in its industry. Each firm is substantial in size and the demand for the product of this industry is price inelastic. Beta Corporation is the dominant producer in the industry, accounting for 38 percent of the total output. The current market price determined by supply and demand in the industry is stabilized at four hundred dollars per unit. The output of each firm is as follows:

	Units (millions)
Alpha Company	2
Beta Corporation	4
Charles, Inc.	3
Delta Co.	1
Ewa Corporation	.5

Under the existing conditions, each of the five firms is making a reasonable profit. The president of Alpha Company, however, is dissatisfied with both the company profit and its market share. He is planning to launch a campaign to improve both. Being part of an oligopoly, he figures that Alpha can increase output by 50 percent and obtain a larger share of the market at the existing price for the product. He asks your advice on the matter and poses the following questions for you to answer.

(a) Will the proposed increased output by Alpha affect the market price in the industry?

(b) Will the total revenue of Alpha change if it increases output and if price declines?

(c) What retailiation, if any, could be expected from the other firms in the industry?

(d) What will happen to the total revenue for the industry as a result of the increased output by Alpha? What will happen to total revenue if all firms increase their production?

(e) If Alpha lowers price in order to increase sales and a price war ensues, what will happen to total revenue and total profit in the industry?

(f) From what little information you have, determine which firms are better equipped to survive a price war. Why?

Did Oil Giants Rig Prices?
The Charges and the Rebuttal

Are Americans paying higher prices than necessary for gasoline because of monopoly practices in the oil industry?

Reprinted from *U.S. News & World Report*, July 30, 1973. Copyright © 1973 U.S. News & World Report, Inc.

Such a claim was made on July 17 by the Federal Trade Commission in a complaint officially filed against the nation's eight largest oil firms.

The firms involved are among the largest corporations of any kind in the U.S., as shown in the table on pages 304 to 305.

Combined, the eight companies account for 55 percent of all gasoline sold in the U.S., 51 percent of crude oil produced, and 58 percent of refining capacity.

The central charge against these industry giants by the Federal Trade Commission was put in these words:

"American consumers have been forced to pay substantially higher prices for petroleum and petroleum products than they would have had to pay in a competitively structured market."

Flat denial. That is flatly denied by the eight firms. Their top officials say that no facts have been provided by the Federal Trade Commission to substantiate the accusation of price rigging.

A spokesman for Standard Oil (Indiana) said the Trade Commission was misleading Americans by "appearing to offer a solution to the energy problem, when nothing could be further from the truth."

The big corporations were given 30 days in which to answer the commission's charges as the first step in what could stretch into years of give and take between Government and industry lawyers. Among other monopoly practices of which the oil firms are accused:

● Eliminating "the most significant source of price competition" by forcing fuel shortages to fall heavily on sections of the U.S. east of the Rockies where independent refiners and marketers are concentrated.

● Obtaining "profits and returns on investment substantially in excess of those that they would have obtained" in a more competitive market.

● Acting to squeeze out smaller, independent refining companies and thus gain unwarranted control over prices of refined products.

FTC complaint. The Federal Trade Commission charges were made in the form of a complaint, rather than in an antitrust suit.

A complaint is issued by the commission when it has "reason to believe" the law has been violated. But this does not imply that the commission has made a judgment of the case.

The Commission's formal complaint did not indicate how it would be followed up. A spokesman indicated the ultimate goal would be to break up the big corporations' refining operations to spur more competition.

Industry answers. The eight companies targeted by the Federal Trade Commission quickly sprang to their own defense.

Mobil Oil placed an advertisement in several big newspapers. It read in part:

"There are 239 refineries in this country, operated by 127 companies. The largest accounts for less than 9 percent of total U.S. refining capacity. No other major manufacturing industry is so little dominated by any one company."

To the charge that the eight firms got together to accommodate the needs of each other, M.A. Wright, chairman of Exxon Company, U.S.A., stated:

"When the facts are fully developed, they will show clearly that the petroleum industry is highly competitive. They will further show that our company is not engaged in any of the alleged illegal acts."

B.R. Dorsey, chairman of Gulf, said that U.S. energy needs were being met at "fair prices," and added:

"This is convincingly demonstrated by the fact that gasoline and other petroleum products have risen at a much slower rate than the general rate of inflation in this country."

Up 16.8 percent. Official figures in the Government's consumer price index show that over the past five years, gasoline prices have gone up by 16.8 percent. This is a little more than half as much as the increase in the cost of living, which has risen 27.1 percent.

In the past year, however, the cost of gasoline has increased by 12.1 percent, compared with a 5.9 percent rise in the cost of living.

Critics refuted. As to charges that this summer's gasoline shortage has been contrived by the industry, Thorton F. Bradshaw, president of Atantic Richfield Company, told "U.S. News & World Report":

"There is an impression that the oil companies have a great deal of gasoline stashed away someplace, and when the price gets high enough, they'll bring it out. The critics never give figures to document this. In fact, the data on inventories are available to everybody and show clearly that there is no surplus gasoline."

Commenting on profits in the oil business, Mr. Bradshaw said:

"Atlantic Richfield's profits last year are a matter of public record — 191 million dollars. Tell that to the average person and he thinks that's a whale of a lot of money, and it is. But it represents a return of slightly more than 6 percent on invested capital. That is less than the cost of borrowed money. Over a period of time, you can go out of business that way. And certainly you cannot attract capital on that basis. The industry should be making 10 or 11 percent. It doesn't come anywhere near that."

Mr. Bradshaw said he faces the fact that people distrust big businesses, but added:

"The oil companies are large, because they have to be. In this day and age we are dealing with vast projects — a 4-million-dollar dry hole in Alaska before we discovered the field at Prudhoe Bay, and a cost of 220 million dollars for a single refinery completed several years ago.

"Looking ahead, it will require 250 million dollars for just one shale-oil plant in Colorado, and about 700 million for a single tar-sands plant in Canada."

The case against the eight oil giants remains to be proved, and that effort is certain to be prolonged. Senator Philip A. Hart (Dem.), of Michigan, who asked the Federal Trade Commission to investigate the oil industry, said:

"We won't get a verdict — and relief — for 8 to 10 years. FTC has to prove not just monopoly power, but anticompetitive behavior."

Most of the oil companies named by the Federal Trade Commission — as well as others — are reporting sharply higher profits thus far in 1973. But officials say these represent a rebound from relatively low levels in 1972.

8 OIL-COMPANY TARGETS — AT A GLANCE*

The eight companies named in a complaint filed by the Federal Trade Commision, on July 17, ranked in order of assets in 1972

1. EXXON The nation's largest manufacturing corporation, with assets exceeding 21.5 billion dollars, sales of more than 20 billion last year.

2. TEXACO Third largest manufacturer in U.S., with assets of more than 12 billion, sales of 8.6 billion.

3. GULF OIL   Assets of more than

9.3 billion, making it sixth largest U.S. manufacturer. Sales exceed 6.2 billion.

4. MOBIL OIL Seventh largest corporation. Assets: 9.2 billion. Sales: 9.1 billion.

5. STANDARD OIL (Calif.) More than 8 billion in assets—ninth largest—and sales of 5.8 billion.

6. STANDARD OIL (Indiana) Assets of 6.1 billion, sales more than 4.5 billion.

7. SHELL OIL Assets: 5.1 billion, sales more than 4 billion.

8. ATLANTIC RICHFIELD Assets of 4.6 billion, sales of 3.3 billion.

*Federal Trade Commission.

(a) How would you classifiy the petroleum industry in terms of market structure?

(b) Do you think that the nature of the industry is conducive to the development of anything approaching conditions of perfect competition at either the refinery level or the retail level?

(c) Do you see any need or justification for joint operations or cooperative activities by the petroleum companies? If so, in what regard?

(d) Is it possible that joint operations at the drilling, producing, and/or refining level could ensure more competition at the retail level?

(e) Would you tend to agree or disagree with the Federal Trade Commission's complaint against the large oil companies? Why or why not?

(f) If you were involved in making a decision in this case, what further evidence or information would you like to have before making a final decision?

In reading the report below of the Hearings of the Joint Economic Committee on the effects of monopoly on inflation, it is well to remember that the Chairman, Senator Paul Douglas, was Professor of Economics at the University of Chicago before he became a Congressman. The other two participants in the discussion are Professor William H. Martin, of Pennsylvania State University, and Howard H. Hines, formerly professor at Iowa State University. (The book referred to is Joan Robinson, *The Economics of Imperfect Competition* [London: Macmillan, 1933].)

The Effects of Monopolistic and Quasi-Monopolistic Practices

Tuesday, September 22, 1959
Congress of the United States
Joint Economic Committee
Washington, D.C.

The Chairman: Gentlemen, we are very appreciative of your coming to Washington to testify on this question of whether we have more or less monopoly and more or less competition as compared with the past.

The Chairman: I would like to ask both of you whether you think Joan Robinson's view on the economics of imperfect competition still holds up. I thought it was a very sound piece of work.

Mr. Martin: I think the best answer I can give the Senator is to refer, probably inaccurately, to Mrs. Robinson's comments on the book at the meeting of international economists devoted to the question of monopoly and competition held three or four years ago. Mrs. Robinson expressed surprise that the book is any longer read, although she evidently was proud of having written it at the time.

The Chairman: It establishes on geometrical and mathematical ground lines of reasoning which seem to be incontestable and conclusions which seem to me important. Check me as I proceed to see whether my memory is accurate.

As I remember it, the differentiation between imperfect and perfect competition is that under perfect competition the fraction of the total part produced by any one firm is so infinitesimal that changes in the output of the firm have no effect upon price, and that therefore the additions to total revenue, which we may call marginal revenue, will be identical with the price per unit, and that therefore there will be equilibrium where marginal cost, or perhaps in the long run average total cost, will be equal to the price. This is the competitive situation.

But under imperfect competition, the output of a given firm performs a sizable fraction of the total output, and therefore expansion in its output will cause the price to fall, and this will cause a still greater decrease in the additions to revenue. Marginal revenue will fall and fall approximately twice as rapidly as price.

Now under these conditions, there will be an equilibrium where output will be determined at the intersection of marginal cost and marginal revenue, which will be a smaller output than you would have under perfect competition.

Is my memory accurate thus far?

Mr. Martin: Indeed it is.

Mr. Hines: I think it is very flattering to have Senator Douglas ask us whether his memory is accurate of the book — for a person of his distinction in the profession.

The Chairman: The more inperfect the competition is and the closer the market approaches complete monopoly, then the greater the difference between the output which you get under monopoly and the output which you would get under perfect competition: with the output always being less under imperfect conditions than under perfect, and being still less the more monopolistic the market is.

Now under those conditions, you do not have maximum employment of labor and capital, and the labor which is not employed in monopolistic industries or in the imperfectly competitive industries is shunted into the competitive industries or less monopolistic industries, with the inevitable result of lowering prices and marginal productivity in those industries.

Now, therefore, can it not be said that on the surface of the case you get an expansion of output by diminishing the degree of imperfect competition and monopoly in the industries which are characterized by these forces?

Mr. Hines: You get a better mix of the products.

The Chairman: And you raise total social productivity, do you not, by transferring labor and capital from areas of low marginal productivity to areas of higher marginal productivity?

Mr. Hines: A better use of resources. That is right.

Mr. Chairman: That is right.

Yes, Mr. Martin?

Mr. Martin: I would point out, however, Mr. Chairman, that the validity of what you say may be confined by the static framework of the analysis. I think it was Professor Schumpter who pointed out that this analysis, all of what you say, is correct only if you have the same cost and demand curves. But it is an open question whether in any real case in the real world you would, in fact, have the same demand-and-cost curves in the monopolistic situation as you would have if the industry were competitive. I think even so, your conclusion is justified: that since entry is blocked into monopolistic industries, resources do not respond to the apparent demand preferences of the community, and in that respect the total social product is reduced. But I would prefer to view it in terms of blocked industry, rather than in terms of the firm's response to specific cost and revenue functions.

The Chairman: As I understood Mr. Hines, while he was emphasizing the importance of conditions of entry into the industry, and probably emphasizing that the possiblility of entry was greater than is sometimes believed, these are mitigating factors to monopoly, but they do not remove the reality of monopoly or of control by a few firms, which we call oligopoly. Is that not true? Those are mitigating factors, but they do not remove the tendency which we deal with?

Mr. Hines: That is right. You quoted me correctly. They mean that the situation is more competitive than is sometimes believed.

The Chairman: That is right.

Mr. Hines: But this does not mean that it is necessarily as competitive as it should be, and also does not mean that these forces operate effectively in every market.

The Chairman: So that the case is strong for trying to get more competition and to diminish the degree of oligopoly and monopoly.

Mr. Hines: I certainly agree, in general. And I think there is practically no chance that we will push it too far in the other direction.

The Chairman: Now, there is another point. And perhaps Mr. Martin will not agree with me on this.

Under monopoly or highly reduced competition you would tend to have a higher unit price than would otherwise be the case, and a higher rate of net profit. To the degree that this continues, because of imperfect entry of competitive firms, then does not this mean that this industry will absorb a larger quantity of net monetary purchasing power, which is sometimes referred to as aggregate money demand, created by the banking system, than would be true in a competitive society for a given volume of output? And does not this withdrawal of monetary purchasing power from other industries create leftward shifts of the demand for these industries, and lower prices than these industries would otherwise have? Therefore, the injury that monopoly has is doubled. On the one hand, it does not absorb its full share of capital and labor. On the other, it absorbs a larger quantity of monetary purchasing power — unless the total money supply expands proportionately. But if the general policies of the Federal Reserve Board, let us say, are carried out, and then the total aggregate demand remains the same, then the more that goes into the hands of monopolies, the less must go into the hands of competitive industries. So that the evil is a dual one.

What would you say to that?

Mr. Martin: I would not be inclined to agree, offhand, at least on the basis of your analysis that unit costs would be higher for monopoly.

Mr. Chairman: I am not saying costs; I was saying prices.

Mr. Martin: Excuse me. I thought in the beginning you had mentioned higher unit costs.

The Chairman: No.

Mr. Martin: Prices may or may not be higher under monopoly. And this, of course, would depend on the behavior of costs.

The Chairman: If less is produced with a given demand curve, the unit price will inevitably be higher, because the demand curve for a product is negatively inclined. And if you have a smaller quantity produced, the unit price will almost by definition be higher.

Mr. Martin: But this is assuming, it seems to me, that in the alternative situation, full competition, the cost curve would be as low for all firms as it is for the single or few firms—

The Chairman: Yes. That is true. But I mean assuming that the cost curves are identical, so far as the demand curves are concerned, the fact that the demand curve is negatively inclined would mean that with less produced than would be true under perfect competition, unit price would be higher.

Mr. Martin: On the basis of that assumption, that is correct; yes, sir.

The Chairman: Then the question turns on whether the large firms can reduce the cost curve by the fact of its size sufficiently so that the ultimate equilibrium will be moved along on the quantity scale.

Mr. Martin: Yes, sir.

(a) According to Chairman Douglas, what happens to output, price, and profit if an industry is characterized by monopoly or oligopoly compared with a more competitive market structure for the industry?

(b) Professor Martin cautions that some of the supposed benefits of perfect competition, compared with imperfect competition, may not be present under existing market conditions. Why might this be so?

(c) According to Chairman Douglas, what effect will the monopolists and oligopolists have on the purchasing power of consumers and the demand for other products? Do you agree with his contention?

(d) How does the subject under discussion in the hearings relate to the material in Chapters 8–9 of this text?

Survival Instinct:
Earnings Crunch Puts Pressure
on Steel Firms To Merge or Retrench

Industry Could Be Reduced To
a Few Big Concerns; The LTV-Lykes Accord

Skyrocketing Prices Ahead?

As the shakeout in the steel industry gathers momentum, some weaker companies can't be certain they'll survive.

Source: David Ignatius, *The Wall Street Journal*, November 8, 1977. Reprinted by permission of *The Wall Street Journal*, © Dow Jones & Company, Inc. 1977. All Rights Reserved.

This is evident to steel buyers like Lloyd Konrad, and a week ago it led him to make an unsentimental decision in behalf of his firm, Walker Manufacturing Co. He would cut off his purchases from two debt-heavy companies he believed were in trouble: LTV Corp.'s Jones & Laughlin Steel Corp., that nation's sixth-largest steelmaker, and Lykes Corp.'s Youngstown Sheet & Tube Co., the eighth-largest.

"If I stay too long with companies that could be belly up, I could get in trouble," Mr. Konrad said in explaining his decision to switch business to larger and more stable producers. As a buyer, he wanted "no surprises" that could disrupt delivery of the 100,000 tons bought annually by Walker, a Tenneco Inc. unit that makes auto-exhaust systems. As for the impact of Mr. Konrad's decision on the two shaky smaller mills, "we can't buy enough to save them," he concluded.

Encouraged by Announcement. But after last Friday's announcement that LTV and Lykes had agreed to merge, Mr. Konrad, who yesterday became the purchasing vice president for Tenneco's entire automotive group, feels more optimistic about the two steelmakers. He says a merger could give them "tremendous freight savings" and other operating efficiencies. If the government allows the merger to go through, he plans to order steel from what would become the nation's third- or fourth-largest steel producer. The merged concern, he believes, will be big enough to survive the shakeout.

The planned combination of LTV and Lykes is dramatic evidence of the pressure for merger or retrenchment facing steelmakers during the industry's current profit crunch. Unless the government moves to blunt these intense market forces, steel could eventually end up like autos, becoming an industry made up of a few giant firms.

Peter F. Marcus, a steel analyst and first vice president at the brokerage firm of Mitchell-Hutchins Inc., views the current situation as a "purge," in which competitive pressures are forcing high-cost plants out of the market. "The profit-system disciplines are brutal," he says, "but they push the survival instinct to the fore, which causes the industry to better utilize its facilities."

Case of Wheeling-Pittsburgh. The current plight of the steel industry is evident in the case of Wheeling-Pittsburgh Steel Corp., the nation's ninth-largest steelmaker, which ranks behind both Jones & Laughlin and Youngstown Sheet & Tube in capacity. Wheeling-Pittsburgh fears that as of Nov. 16, it "may cease to be in compliance" with the net-worth provision of its loan agreement with a consortium of banks. The banks could then call for immediate payment of a substantial portion of the company's debt.

This prospect, the company said in an Oct. 20 filing with the Securities and Exchange Commission, "is largely a result of the operating losses experienced in recent periods." Through the first three quarters of this year, the company lost nearly $21 million.

Right now, Wheeling-Pittsburgh is discussing with its lenders a renegotiation of its loan agreements "so that the corporation may continue to conduct its business in normal fashion." Its president, Dennis J. Carney, expressed confidence in an interview last Friday that the company can solve its problems and "will be producing and selling steel for some time."

Smaller Producers' Woes. Mr. Carney stresses that while the steel industry as a whole is ailing, the smaller producers have special problems. He notes that their "profit, in general, is lower" than that of larger producers, while their "debt is higher." What's more, they depend on steel revenues more than some larger, more diversified firms. When the steel business is booming, the smaller mills prosper—as in the tight market of 1974, when Wheeling-Pittsburgh earned a sweet $20 a share. But at the bottom of the cycle, their difficulties mount.

The smaller companies' debt load is a key worry, since it limits their freedom to act without their lenders' approval. Wheeling-Pittsburgh, for example, had already amended its April 1975 loan agreement seven times before it began its current round of negotiations with the banks. The debt load, combined with low profitability, also hinders Wheeling-Pittsburgh's ability to proceed with a modernization program budgeted at about $600 million in 1975.

Like Wheeling-Pittsbugh, Youngstown Sheet & Tube had indicated in SEC filings that it was near violation of its loan covenants. The Lykes unit had warned that its ability to incur new long-term debt could be "significantly curtailed." In turning for help to a larger steelmaker, Lykes hoped its lenders would bless a merger that promised improved profitability.

Wheeling-Pittsburgh, meanwhile, has developed a novel scheme for raising new equity capital. After abandoning its plan for a conventional offering of preferred stock the company is preparing a preferred offering pitched at its employes and their milltown neighbors in Pennsylvania, Ohio and West Virginia.

The company has advised the SEC that it intends to offer the new preferred issue to these two groups soon, to give them "an opportunity to assist the company in overcoming its current financial difficulties." The earlier plan to offer preferred stock to the general public might have received a chilly reception because operating losses have recently forced Wheeling-Pittsburgh to omit dividends on two already-outstanding preferred issues.

The ultimate dangers facing the smaller steelmakers were highlighted by the demise of Alan Wood Steel Co., a firm about one-sixth as big as Wheeling-Pittsburgh in terms of shipments. Indeed, the start of the industry's current shakeout can perhaps be dated to last June, when this small but venerable producer petitioned for protective court proceedings under Chapter 11 of the Federal Bankruptcy Act.

Looking ahead, the steel shakeout won't necessarily produce the extreme result of more mergers or Chapter 11 proceedings. But the trend toward the closing or sale of unprofitable facilities—evident in the major cutbacks by Bethlehem Steel Corp. and Youngstown Sheet & Tube as well as lesser cutbacks by firms like Kaiser Steel Corp. and Laclede Steel Co.— will probably continue. Even giant U.S. Steel Corp. has said that the future of its Youngstown operations, which employ about 6,000 people, is "quite dismal" unless the industry's profit picture improves.

Economies of Scale. Some observers argue that a merger wave is badly needed to "rationalize" the steel industry and allow smaller steelmakers the benefits of economies of scale. William R. Roesch, former vice chairman and chief executive of Kaiser Steel, believes that the country may be able to support "not more than five integrated producers" in future years, compared to more than a dozen at present. "The more capital-intensive an industry is," he argues, "the fewer companies there should be."

Mr. Roesch also worries that lenders may have too much say in which firms survive and which don't. He fears that bankers' assessments will probably be made more on the quality of a company's balance sheet than on the efficiency of its facilities. It would be "disastrous," he says, "if we wound up with a rationalization from the financial side only."

Whether this rocky "rationalization" goes forward depends largely on decisions taken by the government. The LTV-Lykes merger is likely to prove an interesting test case. In the past, the Justice Department has taken a dim view of big steel combinations. For example, it blocked an effort some years ago by Bethlehem Steel Corp. to acquire Youngstown Sheet & Tube.

But Anthony P. Grassi, a vice president at the First Boston Corp. investment-banking house, who helped put together the LTV-Lykes merger plan, believes that the steel industry's recent troubles may have altered government attitutdes. "In 1974," he says, "you just couldn't have argued that a merger was something necessary to keep Youngstown Sheet & Tube afloat." But in the present crisis atmosphere, he contends, the combination can be defended as "in the nation's interest."

Imports and the Government. The government could probably ease the short-term competitive pressures by sharply restricting steel imports. Many steelmakers have clamored for such relief, which might ease pricing pressure and allow companies to keep open their higher-cost plants. But Mr. Roesch, the former Kaiser Steel chief, contends that "the worst thing that could happen is temporary import relief that allowed marginal producers to prolong their misery."

For those companies that can ride out this year's storm, the future offers considerable hope. By filing dumping cases and pressing for additional government action against imports, the domestic industry has already deterred some steel importers. Buyers report that in recent days, because of the uncertain trade situation, many Japanese and European mills have refused to book orders for delivery after the first quarter.

Perhaps more important, this year's reduction in domestic capacity may hasten the next tight steel market. In a tighter market, steelmakers may be able to raise prices to levels that restore profitability. Mr. Marcus of Mitchell Hutchins predicts, "in the next shortage, prices are going to skyrocket."

Plant closings in 1977 have pared the industry's capacity by about 5.5 million tons, to under 155 million tons, according to Father William T. Hogan, professor of economics at Fordham University, Mr. Roesch predicts that by the middle of next year, the cutbacks in capacity could deepen to as much as 15 million tons.

Leaner and Tougher. As in the classic shakeouts described in the economics texts, the steel firms that survive are likely to emerge leaner and tougher — and with greater pricing power. First Boston's Mr. Grassi notes that one advantage of an LTV-Lykes combination is that the two firms together will have greater "presence in the marketplace" than either had separately. Following the merger, he says, "you've got more clout in a product line or geographical area" and can "hone your product spectrum so that you're not producing stuff you don't make money on."

Ultimately, then, the shakeout is likely to mean higher steel prices and increased profits. But for the moment, most smaller companies are struggling to get through the next several months of continued difficulty.

Wheeling-Pittsburgh, for example, says it is currently offering to sell about 60 million tons of steam-coal reserves, and an unspecified amount of excess high-volatile metallurgical coal. With other hard-pressed steel companies, including Bethlehem Steel, also reportedly attempting to sell coal reserves, it may not be a sellers' market. But Wheeling-Pittsburgh's Mr. Carney says he believes it's time to "sell those assets that don't help you."

Wheeling-Pittsburgh is also taking a tougher stance with its own suppliers, and this has caused some legal battles. A construction firm in Wheeling says it has sued the company in an Ohio court for about $100,000 in a dispute over contract terms. And a Pittsburgh-based engineering firm filed suit last month for $208,000, most of which it claims is due under a "cost-saving" contract provision. Asked about these lawsuits, Mr. Carney responds: "We've been too soft on our suppliers. I'm not going to give a guy $100,000 extra if I don't think he deserves it."

On the bright side, hard times may bolster the industry's case for a respite from environmental pressures. Wheeling-Pittsburgh, for example, has told the SEC that it expects it will be able to settle for "substantially less than $500,000" a fine for over $39.8 million filed last March by Pennsylvania authorities for alleged violation of air-pollution laws.

There are also indications that Wheeling-Pittsburgh is discussing with government officials the possibility of loans and other financial help, which might allow the company to pay for new pollution-control equipment and possibly for new production facilities. Mr. Carney will say only that the company is "working with the state and federal government to solve the pollution and modernization problems" — through a plan that would "save jobs."

(a) Relate the current developments in the steel industry to the long-run, or envelope, curve explained in Chapter 8.

(b) Is the steel industry more concentrated or less concentrated than the auto industry?

(c) Do you see any similarities between what is happening in the steel industry today and what has occurred in the automobile industry in the past?

(d) Why should smaller steel firms suffer more than the larger firms in the industry from such factors as rising cost, environmental requirements, lower sales, and the growth of lower-priced imports.

(e) In 1958 the United States Supreme Court forbade a proposed merger between Bethlehem Steel Corporation, the nation's second largest steel producer, and Youngstown Sheet and Tube Company, the sixth largest producer in the industry, on the ground that such a merger would substantially lessen competition and tend to create a monopoly.

Do you think that the suggested merger of Jones & Laughlin Steel Corporation and Youngstown Sheet and Tube Company should be permitted? Why or why not?

10

Pricing in Practice

Traditional economic theory explains pricing under conditions of perfect competition, perfect monopoly, monopolistic competition, and oligopoly. In the real world of business, however, we do not find perfect textbook models of competition. Rather we find an economy composed of a mixture of market structures and many varieties of competition. Moreover, the decision maker often has incomplete information about costs, revenues, elasticities, markets, competitor reaction, and marginal analysis. In dealing with the problem of production, pricing, and profit the manager must deal with a great many uncertainties.

Frequently a firm is guided by motives other than profit maximization. These include the desire for a reasonable profit, maximization of sales, or increasing market share. The firm or its managers may also be concerned about the good will of customers, community responsibility, antitrust violations, or the desire for personal power or prestige. In addition, the firm may stress long-run profit objectives compared with the short-run profit maximization assumed with marginal analysis. Then, too, a firm may be producing several products, instead of a single-product that is characteristically used as a model of pricing and profit in many of our textbooks. In a situation such as this, the manager must deal with the allocation of cost and pricing of multiple products or services. In the business world of today, pricing decisions and profit objectives are influenced also by a variety of executives, managers, and staff analysts with varied aims and motives.

Traditionally, economic theory provides a good, basic framework and understanding of the market structure of the economy. But the textbook models have to be modified, embellished, patched, or restructured to fit, or explain some of the actual economic decisions that are made. Under such circumstances, the business economist must use his imagination to bridge the gap between theory and practice in order to explain pricing decisions. In terms of economic theory, profit maximization occurs at the point where MR = MC regardless of the type of competitive market structure in which the firm operates. In practice, however, this axiom is not followed to the letter for a number of reasons. First, a firm may not know its marginal revenue or marginal cost. Secondly, the firm may be interested in a reasonable profit as opposed to a maximum profit. What, then, does the firm do in practice? Since traditional economic theory does not always provide the basis for pricing decisions, it may be worthwhile to look at some current practices or methods used for pricing.

MARKET PRICING

If a firm is in an industry that approaches pure competition, such as agriculture or the sale of securities, it must rely on market demand and supply for the determination of price. In the absence of government price supports, the average farmer can obtain for his crops only the price determined by the market. Using this as a given, he can adjust his output somewhat to the market price. Because of price fluctuations, however, the farmer cannot be certain whether he is going to make a profit or suffer a loss. Thus in a year of bumper crops, some farmers may actually suffer losses because of rising costs and lower prices.

Likewise in the securities market an individual, or firm, may seek a price for the sale of a particular security. But it will be tough to get a price other than that established by demand and supply in the securities market.

If a firm desires to enter an existing market, it can assume the average, or near average, price of other suppliers to be the price it will receive. This is often referred to as *going-rate* pricing. The firm can then decide whether or not it can produce and make a profit at the existing average market price or going rate. If the firm decides to produce, it must then decide whether to charge its customers the average price, a premium price, or a discounted price — depending on the product differentiation, advertising, sales promotion, and various other factors.

CUSTOMARY PRICING

Related to market, or going-rate, pricing is the concept of customary pricing. This exists in the sale of some commodities and services that customarily or historically sell for a certain price. For years, if not decades, standard-sized candy bars and chewing gum sold for five cents, coke was a nickel, public-telephone calls a dime, cigarettes fifteen cents, and bus fare was a quarter. A firm wishing to compete in the sale of these commodities or services had to accept the customary price or have a good reason, such as a superior product, to do otherwise. In order to maintain customary prices, producers, at first, tried to offset cost increases with increased productivity, reduction in quantity or quality, and the use of less expensive materials. With the impact of inflation on cost in the past decade, however, producers were forced to raise their customary prices and even shatter their uniformity.

COST-PLUS PRICING

One of the most widely used methods of price determination is cost-plus pricing, sometime referred to as *full-cost pricing*. There are many ways of computing a cost-plus price. A commonly accepted method is to estimate the variable or direct, cost of producing a unit of output, allocating a charge per unit for overhead, or indirect, cost, and finally adding a mark-up, or margin, for profit.

The charge for overhead may be figured in several ways. One way is by estimating the number of units to be produced. The total overhead cost can then be divided by the number of units scheduled for production. Thus, if total overhead were $2.5 million and 500,000 units were to be produced, $5 of indirect cost or overhead would be assigned to each unit of production. The fixed cost can also be assigned by allocating the fixed, or indirect, cost as a percentage of variable, or direct, cost. If the firm's total variable cost for all products is $5 million and its fixed overhead is $2.5 million, it will assign a 50 percent indirect cost to each dollar of variable cost. Thus, if the variable cost assigned to a unit were $10.00, a $5 overhead cost would be added.

While producing 500,000 units, it would allocate $5 million in variable cost and $2.5 million in overhead cost. Each product would show a standard cost of $15 to produce. Added to this cost would be the profit mark-up. Assuming this mark-up to be 33⅓ percent ($15 × 1.33),[1] it would yield a selling price of $20.

The determination of price by the cost-plus method must, of course, be modified to fit the market. If competition is pricing at a figure lower than the twenty-dollar full-cost price or the market will not take 500,000 units at $20 per unit, some adjustment may have to be made in the $20 price.

Cost-plus pricing is a handy method of establishing price, recovering cost, and generating a profit, but the method has its weaknesses. If fewer than 500,000 units are sold, actual cost will be higher than the so-called standard cost. If 400,000 units are sold there will be $500,000 of underabsorbed overhead. If $5 in overhead is assigned

---

[1] This is also expressed as a 25 percent margin on price ($5 ÷ $20 = 25%).

to each of the 400,000 units produced that means that $2 million in overhead was absorbed.[2] In such case the actual overhead burden should be $6.25 per unit of production ($2,500,000 ÷ 400,000 = $6.25) instead of $5 per unit. Total cost will be $16.25 instead of $15; profit would be $3.75 instead of $5; and profit markup would be 23 percent instead of 33⅓ percent.

The problem of overabsorbed and underabsorbed burden (overhead) is not the only weakness of standard-cost pricing. Standard cost is generally based on historical costs, but more important to the manager is cost during the period when production will be taking place. If any changes in costs occur during the course of production, the standard cost will not be a true cost and must be adjusted. (In accounting, this is taken care of through variances.) If higher labor or material costs occur, for example, the standard cost will be too low and will need upward adjustment.

Another difficulty with standard-cost pricing is that it can be misleading. If a manager is pricing a job order for 50,000 additional units, he may very well quote the $20 per unit price based on the standard cost mentioned earlier. Thinking that a $20 price is essential to recover all cost and yield a profit, the manager may reject a counter offer of $17.50 from the potential buyer. As a result, he unnecessarily may lose the job order. In this case, the true cost of producing the additional units may be only $10 per unit instead of $15 per unit, if the order were in addition to the 500,000 units scheduled to be produced. Since the total fixed cost is absorbed with the scheduled 500,000 units of production, it is not necessary to allocate $5 per unit of overhead to the additional 50,000 units. To do so would cause overhead cost to be overabsorbed by $250,000 (50,000 × $5). Consequently, the manager could have met the $17.50 price and made $7.50 profit per unit. Even at a price of $15 the same $5 per unit profit could be made as that on the 500,000 units that were scheduled to be produced and sold at $20 per unit.

INCREMENTAL PRICING

Closely related to marginal-cost pricing is the concept of incremental pricing and profit analysis. It deals with the changes in the relationship between total cost and total revenue resulting from managerial decisions. When a decision is anticipated, its probable effect on total cost and total revenue is the prime object of consideration

---

[2] Also 50 percent of $4 million variable cost (400,000 × $10 = $4,000,000) equals $2 million in fixed cost.

Any decision that will increase net profit is accepted, and those that cause a decrease in net profit are rejected.

In analyzing the effect on total cost and total revenue resulting from the introduction of a new product or service, however, the manager must consider, among other things, the effect of the decision on the cost and revenue of other products or services offered by the firm. In some cases there will be offsetting or adverse changes. In other cases, the decision may have a favorable effect on the costs or revenues of other products or services. The introduction of a new type of camera by itself, for example, may have a minimal effect on net profit. But it might result in substantial sales of a related company product, such as photographic film and increased picture-development service. The production and sale of a student workbook or study guide may produce limited revenue itself, but it may encourage the adoption of the related textbook, increasing net profit. Airline carriers, for example, use incremental analysis in determining whether to add or delete certain flights.

DIFFERENTIAL PRICING
AND PRICE DISCRIMINATION

Differential pricing often exists in the marketing of goods and services. Price discrimination occurs when certain buyers are charged different prices for the same product or service. Price discrimination is possible for a number of reasons. Even an identical price to all buyers may be discriminatory in some instances. Thus, when a product is produced at a central geographic location, such as St. Louis, and priced identically all over the United States, the cost of production plus delivery in and around St. Louis will be less than the cost of production plus the delivery charge to Los Angeles. If customers in each area pay an identical price for the product there is discrimination in favor of buyers in the Los Angeles area. The buyers pay an identical price, but the profit mark-up for the Los Angeles area purchaser is less when transportation cost is factored in. On the other hand, if final sale prices were adjusted for delivery cost differences, price differentials would occur, but they would not be discriminatory. Nevertheless the two terms, *differential pricing* and *price discrimination*, are often used interchangeably. Remember, too, that price discrimination per se is neither morally good nor evil. It is an economic term used to describe a pricing phenomenon. Whether the practice is good or bad must be determined by particular circumstances. The antitrust laws, as we shall see later, prohibit price discrimination where the effect is to lessen competition. Otherwise, price discrimination is not prohibited.

A firm may engage in price discrimination in order to improve or maximize its profit. For price discrimination to be effective, however, certain market conditions must be present. First, the firm must be able to segment the market. It must be able to categorize or isolate different buyers of its product. This is necessary if the firm is going to sell to one category of buyer at a different price from another. Secondly, the price elasticity of demand for each category of buyer must be different. If their elasticities were identical, it would not be worthwhile to segment the market. If all segments had the same price elasticity of demand, profit maximization would require the same price for all.

Price discrimination may be based on different circumstances, such as geographic location, degree of competition, age, sex, need, time, income, and quantity purchased. As pointed out earlier, selling a product at an identical price throughout the country may be a form of discrimination when differences in transportation costs are ignored. In another situation, a sports shop at a plush resort probably can get a higher price for a given product than can a similar shop in a busy shopping center. Beer and hot dogs usually cost more inside the ball park or stadium than they do outside.

Children are often admitted to the theater or on public transportation at a lower price than adults, and senior citizens are frequently given a discount from regular prices. Single women and widows often have greater difficulty in getting credit and pay a higher price for it than male heads of households.

In many cities, people who must rely on buses for going to and from work often pay more than the casual users of public transit who get reduced rates for weekend travel or at daily off-peak hours. Discriminatory pricing for off-peak usage is common in charges for electricity and telephone service. Even the sale of canned goods at 35 cents per can or three cans for $1 is a form of price discrimination against the single-item buyer.

Price discrimination is frequently based on income or wealth. Some merchandisers have higher mark-up prices at their stores in high-income neighborhoods, wealthy homeowners pay higher property taxes for the same municipal services than those in other parts of the city, and doctors generally charge higher-income patients more than lower-income patients for the same medical service.

PRESTIGE PRICING

Frequently a product will be sold at a price higher than the general market price regardless of cost, to maintain or establish its prestige value or "image." Some commodities, such as diamonds, mink coats,

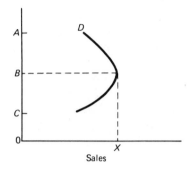

Figure 10-1.

and Rolls Royce cars, are considered prestigious because relatively few people can afford to buy them. If the price of such commodities is reduced, more will be purchased. If the price were reduced to too low a level, however, the product might lose its prestige image, and sales would decline. If the price of mink coats, for example, were reduced, it would stimulate sales, especially if demand is elastic since many additional women would like to own a mink coat. If the price were reduced so low, however, that nearly every women could afford a mink, mink would lose much of its prestige value and sales would no doubt drop. This could produce a backward sloping demand curve, such as that shown in Figure 10-1. As price is reduced, sales increase to a certain level. A critical point can be reached, however, below which lower prices result in declining sales. It can be seen that sales and revenue may increase with lower prices down to Point *B* on the price scale. A price below *B*, however, would bring a reduction in sales.

Certain stores, such as Saks Fifth Avenue and Nieman-Marcus, are well known for selling prestige items. The Cadillac division of General Motors stresses prestige in advertising its cars. One founder and owner of a well-known cosmetic firm established a policy of never charging below a prestige level no matter how little it cost to produce an item.

PRICE LINING

Price lining is a practice often found in retail merchandising, particularly in department and specialty stores. Price lining is found in the sale of dresses, suits, hosiery, furniture, and a host of other items. Some claim that the practice simplifies pricing decisions. Once established, prices are held fairly stable, with adjustments in quality made to maintain mark-up or price lines. Several different price levels may be established via the price-lining method. For effectiveness, a minimum of three levels representing "good," "better," "best" merchandise is usually established. A department store, for example, may establish a line of summer dresses at $16.95, $19.95, $24.95, and $29.95. Although the department-store's buyer may pay varying prices for dresses, each spring he or she must decide into which price category each dress should be placed. Predetermined pricing simplifies the pricing process when the merchandise arrives and permits the buyer to devote more time to other functions, such as sales promotion, inventory handling, merchandise display, personnel motivation, and related activities. The buyer must, however, decide what to buy from the manufacturer — quality "B" dresses for $12, or quality "A" dresses for $13, or some combination of the two — to fit into the $16.95 retail price level. One must estimate the probable sales volume of quality "A" dresses versus quality "B" dresses at the $16.95 price, and project total profit on each line of dresses. If the department store manager desires to maximize profit, he or she needs to equate marginal revenue to marginal cost.

MULTIPLE-MODEL PRICING

A practice somewhat similar to price lining is using different models of a basic product in order to maximize revenue and profit. This form of pricing is often found in the sale of automobiles, tires, encyclopaedias, airline tickets, pleasure boats, and appliances, such as refrigerators and sewing machines. It is a means of extracting consumer surplus. On a given demand line, according to economic theory, once the market price is established by the interaction of demand and supply, all consumers pay that price. Some buyers, however, would be willing to pay a higher price for the product. Some other customers who would like to buy the product are deterred from doing so because the market price is too high for them. Even if the demand is price elastic and total revenue would be increased by lowering the price, the gain in total revenue may be substantially less than it would be if those willing to pay a higher price did so. If at the same time, price could be lowered for those not willing to buy at the higher price, total sales and revenue would be further increased.

One way of taking advantage of this situation is by offering two or three models of the product or service, such as a "deluxe" model at the basic market price, a "supreme" model at a higher price, and a "standard" model at a lower price. In this way, similar to that shown on the demand line on page 115, the seller can take advantage of some customers' willingness to pay a price higher than the basic market price and others' readiness to buy only at a price less than the basic market price. A given product or service can be used for the basic model to be sold at the average market price; the same basic model with extras can serve as the higher-priced model, and a stripped-down version of the basic model can be used for the lower-priced model. This is a common marketing practice in the auto industry. In 1975, for example, the Ford Motor Company in one line offered an LTD 500, an LTD Brougham, and an LTD Landau, as its lower-, middle-, and higher-priced models, respectively, of one car. Although basically the same car, each model had different features, accessories, and trim.

This is simply a method of taking full advantage of demand as explained through the use of the demand line on page 115. At the retail level, many sellers advertise the price of the stripped-down model to lure customers into a store. Once the customer appears, however, the seller may try to induce him to buy a "better" or higher-priced model. This is a common practice of a good, aggressive salesperson. Unfortunately, undue pressue may be applied to get the customer to buy the higher-priced model. In some cases, only a very limited number of the lower-priced model may be available. This practice is called *bait and switch* and is frowned upon by the Federal Trade Commission.

PUBLIC-UTILITY PRICING

Public utilities provide a special case for pricing. Franchises are granted by municipalities or other governing bodies to one firm[3], giving it a monopoly to provide a service, such as gas, electricity, or transportation in a particular geographic area. In exchange for the franchise, the public-utility firm must accept regulation by the appropriate public-service commission.

It is the practice of the regulatory body to permit the utility to make a fair return on a fair investment. The utility can set its prices or rates for service accordingly. It must, however, obtain permission from the public-service commission to establish, or change, its prices and it must provide services designated by the commission.

Public-utility pricing is strongly influenced by two major issues: What is a fair return? What is a fair investment? Answers to these questions vary according to public service commissions and courts throughout the United States. Numerous public-utility-commission

---

[3] Sometimes where markets are large, franchises are given to two or more firms.

hearings have been recorded, orders issued, and court decisions rendered on the question of a fair return. Should the decision be made by comparing the return of one utility with that of different utilities or to nonutilities in the same geographic area? Should a fair return be based on what similar utilities are making in other geographic areas? Decisions vary from 6 percent to 9 percent to 14 percent, depending on the type of utility, its location, and the nature of its investment.

A more difficult decision is determining the value of the investment, which forms the base on which the fair return is to be allowed. The concept of a fair investment is easier to state than to determine. The rate base, or fair investment, may be calculated by using the original, or historical, cost of the investment. It may be determined, also, by using the replacement cost of the investment. Many public-service commissions favor the use of original cost. It is easier to calculate and provides a more definite measure of the investment the company has made in the business. Most utilities prefer to use replacement cost, especially during periods of generally rising prices or inflation. They feel that it more adequately reflects the current and true value of the investment. Moreover, replacement cost measures the cost involved in replacing depreciated assets and the cost of purchasing additional assets that may be needed for the expansion of service.

With a given rate of return, such as 8 percent, it can make a substantial difference in public utility rates for customers and in total profit for the company if original or replacement cost is used for determining the investment. If original cost were $100 million, for example, the utility would be able to price in order to yield an $8 million total profit ($100,000,000 × .08). If replacement cost were $150 million because of the rising price of assets, and $150 million became the rate base, the firm could set rates to yield a $12 million total profit ($150,000,000 × .08). This could mean a substantial difference in the rates charged consumers.

There are nearly as many formulas for determining the rate base as there are public-service commissions. Many of them use some combination of original and replacement cost in determining fair investment. One public service commission, for example, used replacement cost new, less depreciation (RCNLD). This provides an estimate of how much it would cost currently to replace the investment. But the commission then adjusts this figure downward to take into account the age of the existing facilities.

Public-service commissions also monitor actual investment and current expenditures of regulated firms to make sure that they are not overinvesting or padding their costs with unnecessary expenses.

In addition, they monitor service to make certain that all customers are cared for. The firm that provides electricity or bus service, for example, may have to serve an unprofitable area of the city. But it must do so, since the cost will be offset by its general rate charges. It is evident, then, that public-utility pricing is similar to full-cost pricing, insofar as the firm will recover all costs, both fixed and variable, and be permitted a mark-up for profit.

SKIMMING VS. PENETRATION PRICING

The pricing practices at opposite ends of the spectrum are *skimming* and *penetration*. Skimming is used to take advantage of a boom market that may fade away. It can be said also that it is pricing according to a possible life cycle for the product. Penetration is used to break into or develop a market for the product. Both techniques are generally used in connection with a new good or service.

In the case of price skimming, the firm may anticipate a strong demand, perhaps enhanced by heavy promotion, for a new product. The product will then be priced high to take advantage of those buyers willing to pay a high price. This can be abetted by holding output in short supply. As the supply of the good eventually becomes more plentiful, especially with the entry of competitors, the price will fall and profit will decrease. Thus the strategy is to initiate and maintain a high price until the supply expands. This, in effect, will skim the cream (profit) off the market before prices are forced downward. A form of price skimming occurred in the initial years of television sales and the sale of such items as ballpoint pens, hula hoops, and hand calculators. Price skimming is often used in the sale of items that are one-time purchases, or infrequently purchased. Items with relatively inelastic demands are conducive to price skimming.

Market-penetration pricing, on the other hand, is a practice of pricing low in the hope of inducing many consumers to buy and thus gain widespread acceptance of the product. This type of pricing is used when a competitor wants to penetrate an existing market. It is used also when the seller of a new product wants to establish a market for his product. It is frequently employed in selling retail items, such as soap or toothpaste, which are bought repeatedly. Low initial prices will, it is hoped, attract buyers and get consumer acceptance for the product. Once the market has been developed or penetrated, the price can be raised to yield a better profit. This form of pricing is often applied in the cents-off coupon and buy-one, get-one-free sale. Once consumers have accepted the product and the market has been penetrated, the price can be raised. This can be done easily by phasing out the cents-off coupon or eliminating the two-for-one sale. Products with short-run price elasticities, those whose production is subject to economies of scale, and those exposed to rigorous competition are likely candidates for the use of penetration pricing.

MARGINAL-COST PRICING

Marginal-cost pricing, which equates price to marginal cost, is rarely practiced. From a theoretical viewpoint it could be used under ideal conditions of perfect or pure competition, since the marginal revenue (MR) is equal to the average revenue (AR), or price. Under such conditions profit will be maximized at the point where MR = MC. Since AR = MR, this is also the point where price is equal to marginal cost. Moreover, economic theory assumes that all products of the firm are sold at an identical price. In such case, if the firm produced up to the point where MR = MC, or AR (price) = MC, all buyers would receive the product at a price equal to marginal cost as shown in Figure 10-2. It can be seen on the graph that the firm would produce and sell Quantity X at a market price equal to marginal cost. It would not produce and sell more than Quantity X, however, because the marginal cost of producing additional units would be greater than the market price, and the firm's profit would be reduced. Yet it is often stated that a major social advantage of pure competition is that the firms will produce and sell up to the point at which the consumer is willing to pay an amount equal to the marginal cost of production. Little pure competition exists, however, in the United States' or in any other economy.

Moreover, under conditions of perfect competition the market price is established by aggregate demand and supply. The firm must

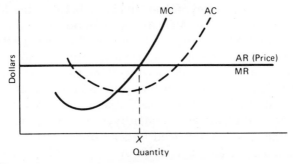

Figure 10-2.

accept this market price and adjust its output to the point where MR = MC. Insofar as the aggregate of the marginal-cost lines of the various firms in the industry becomes the aggregate supply line for the industry, it can be said that some semblance of marginal-cost pricing exists.

If true marginal-cost pricing occurred, however, the price charged to all buyers would be equal to the marginal cost of the last unit produced. In such a situation, as a firm increased its output, and its marginal cost rose, its price would increase for all buyers. Profit would increase as marginal cost and price rose above average cost. If buyers were not willing to pay the higher price, however, the firm could not use marginal-cost pricing. On the other hand, if marginal cost were below average cost, the firm would suffer a loss by using marginal-cost pricing. Under conditions of perfect competition, the only level of output at which marginal-cost pricing occurs is at the equilibrium output where MR = MC. At that point AR (price) also equals MC. At any other level of output, price will be either greater or less than marginal cost. To have true marginal-cost pricing, the price would have to change as the marginal cost changed.

Under conditions of imperfect competition, such as monopoly, oligopoly, and monopolistic competition, the use of marginal-cost pricing is less practical. Even from the theoretical viewpoint, the firm will not produce up to the point at which price equals marginal cost because of the nature of the demand or average revenue line. Under conditions of imperfect competition, the AR line slopes downward, instead of being horizontal as in the case of pure competition. As we observed in Chapter 8, this means that the MR line also will slope downward, but at a faster rate than the AR line. In any case the firm will maximize profit at the point where MR = MC. But since the MR line deviates from the AR line (price), the point where MR = MC is not the same point where AR = MC. In Figure 10-3, it can be seen that the firm will produce and sell up to Quantity X where MR = MC. At that point, however, AR is greater than MC. Nevertheless, the firm will not produce beyond Quantity X because the MR of each additional unit is less than MC. Any production beyond Quantity X will reduce the firm's profit, even though the price (AR) is greater than, or equal to, marginal cost. Hence, some economists say that such a firm is not maximizing social welfare, since it will not produce up to the level of Quantity Y, where price is equal to MC.

Marginal-cost pricing can be used in situations in which prices to consumers are not identical. Frequently, a firm using full-cost pricing will realize that it does not need to get a price greater than, or equal to standard cost on all items sold. As explained in Chapter 7, for example, a firm may fill an order for a price less than its standard

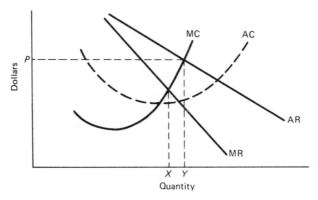

Figure 10-3.

cost, so long as the price is equal to, or greater than, its variable or marginal cost. Any revenue over the marginal cost makes a contribution to overhead (profit), even though it does not cover standard cost. This is especially true when production is exceeding standard operating capacity. It is profitable to engage in such marginal-cost pricing only because other buyers, those paying full cost, are covering the overhead or fixed costs. To use marginal-cost price successfully, it is necessary to have some form of price differentiation. If everyone sold the product at an identical price equal to the marginal cost, the firm would suffer a loss, unless the marginal cost were above the average cost.

A form of marginal-cost pricing has been used by the airline industry when carriers decided to add or discontinue certain flights on the basis of marginal revenue and marginal cost. Marginal-cost pricing is occasionally used by manufacturers and jobbers when bidding on various job orders. Marginal cost is the basis for off-peak pricing in the transportation industry and for off-season pricing in the resort and vacation industries. Utilities use a form of marginal-cost pricing in setting rates for different users, such as residential, commercial, and industrial.

In that respect public utilities present a special case for marginal-cost pricing. Utilities — gas, electricity, water, public transit, and telephone service — are usually decreasing-cost industries. Most public-service commissions allow the utilities to use some form of full-cost pricing. But a number of economists and others suggest that public utilities should use marginal-cost pricing. They argue that marginal-cost pricing relates the value consumers put on a service, as measured by the price they are willing to pay, compared to the added or marginal-cost incurred to produce that service. Since the public utility is granted a monopoly to provide the services, advocates of marginal-cost pricing contend that the utility should be required to sell some of its services at a price equal to marginal cost. Difference in cost is in fact the basis for off-peak pricing, discounts to large users, and delivery of services to different geographic areas.

If all users received the service at a price equal to marginal cost, it could mean that the company would suffer a loss. In such case, however, some proponents of marginal-cost pricing recommend paying a subsidy to the public utility so it can cover all its cost. Others suggest public ownership of utilities on the ground that not all cost would have to be covered from operating revenues. This often happens when a municipality takes over a public utility. A few years ago, when the city of Cincinnati took over the public-transit company, for example, passenger fares were reduced. But the city earnings tax was increased to help make up the deficit of the newly owned city-transit company.

Figure 10-4 can be used to demonstrate different pricing possibilities for a public utility with decreasing cost. It can be seen on the graph that if the industry were unregulated and a monopoly existed, the firm would maximize its profits by producing Quantity X, where MR = MC, and charge price A, which is above both AC and MC. If the monopoly were regulated and permitted to recover all its cost, it would produce Quantity Y and price at B, where price would equal AC but still be above MC. If the firm were required to price at marginal cost, it would produce Quantity Z and charge price C, which is equal to marginal cost. In this last case, however, unlike the first

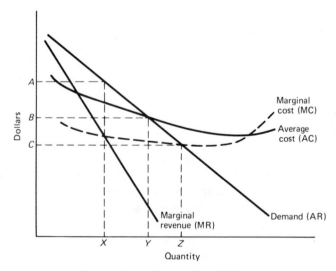

Figure 10-4. Pricing Possibilities

two situations, the price would be below the average cost and the firm would suffer a loss. This loss would have to be made up through some other means, such as a subsidy.

OTHER PRICING TECHNIQUES

There are many other variations of pricing, among them, *experimental pricing* — which is akin to test marketing — to determine price elasticity. A firm may price in different markets to ascertain its best price. The use of trade and quantity discounts is also a form of establishing prices. At one time, fair-trade pricing, or resale price maintenance, which permitted the manufacturer to establish the price at which its commodity was to sell at retail, was a prevalent form of pricing.

Many firms also must engage in pricing for intracorporate sales. This occurs when one division of a company sells commodities or services to another. Determining the right transfer price becomes more difficult when there is no external market for the commodity or service. Charging a higher or lower transfer price may not affect the total profit of the corporation, but it can affect the profit of different divisions. This pricing becomes more complicated when divisions of the company are located in different states with varying corporate profit tax structures.

PRICING GOALS

Individual firms have various pricing objectives. Overall, a firm may price to maximize its profit, or it may be content with a reasonable profit. This is sometimes referred to as *target* pricing; the firm prices to achieve a specifically defined target. A firm may set its price objective to attain a certain profit rate of return on stockholders' equity before taxes, such as 13 percent or 20 percent. Another firm may target for a 5 percent profit per dollar of sales. Once a firm sets its price(s), however, it still must contend with market forces, such as custom and competition. Conditions in the market will usually determine whether target prices can be implemented.

Studies indicate that General Motors, for example, once aimed for prices that would yield a 20 percent after-tax return on investment, whereas a company like ALCOA used a 20 percent before-tax target. In the steel industry, U.S. Steel Corporation sought an 8 percent after-tax target.

Some firms may have a pricing policy designed to obtain a targeted share of the market. This objective may or may not be compatible with target pricing for profit, particularly when low prices are needed for market penetration and there exists an inelastic demand for the product. Gaining an additional share of the market might just put a dent in profits. Target pricing to achieve market share may be applied in the opposite direction as well. A firm may desire to reduce its market share in a given line for antitrust or for other economic reasons, such as desire to devote its resources to more profitable uses. In this case, the pricing strategy may be to raise prices to reduce its share of the market. Pricing for market share, in either direction, may be abetted by product quality, product service, advertising, and other market considerations.

Some firms merely target to meet the market price or to meet the price of a certain competitor. Frequently this is the pricing objective followed by small firms competing against a limited number of larger firms. It is a pricing policy also used often by firms that are not certain of their costs. In this respect, a firm may be forced to lower its price because of competition or other market forces. On the other hand, it may raise its price, even though its cost has not risen, simply because its competitors have done so. In certain oligopolistic industries, such as autos, oil, steel, aluminum, and in commercial banks (interest rates), prices of competitors in the market tend to rise and fall almost simultaneously.

Another common objective is the achievement of stable prices and stable output. This objective is based on the philosophy that orderly market conditions are easier to deal with than highly volatile prices and output. With stable prices and output, planning is easier, profit return more certain, marketing less hectic, and consumers less confused. This is true provided that a given market price yields a comfortable rate of return on investment. Firms in many cases prefer stable prices, as opposed to those that might fall during slack or recession periods, then rise significantly during periods of prosperity. Stable prices, of course, would yield a smoother flow of profits over the business cycle. In many cases, it may be necessary to adjust output to attain some price stability. An outstanding case of the objective of price stability is that of agriculture with government-support prices and acreage allotments used to limit supply to achieve price stability.

SUMMARY

Although economic analysis, stressing profit maximization, provides a basic understanding of pricing theory under assumed market conditions, pricing in practice tends to vary considerably. Firms in industries approximating conditions of pure competition must rely on demand and supply to determine the market price they must accept. In other markets, prices are established by custom and firms follow the customary price.

Most firms, however, have established some type of cost-plus, or full-cost, pricing technique. This usually allows for the recovery of all cost plus a mark-up for profit. Often standard cost is used as a basis for the profit mark-up. In other situations incremental pricing is utilized. This considers the impact on total revenue and total cost of managerial decisions. Decisions that contribute more to revenue than to cost usually are given the go-ahead signal since they will enhance profit.

In some cases, differential pricing and even discriminatory pricing exist. Market conditions, especially price elasticities of demand, serve as a basis of price differentials and price discrimination. Another price objective is prestige pricing. Associated with this is the backward-sloping demand curve, sometimes referred to as an *inferior demand*.

Price lining is often used by retailers. This policy establishes predetermined price categories for certain items, such as women's dresses or men's suits. Items of various qualities are then fitted into each of the price categories. Akin to price lining is the practice of marketing different models of a given basic product to appeal to consumers willing to pay different prices for a commodity.

Depending on the nature of the product, the competition in the market, and the price elasticity of demand a firm may engage in price skimming by initiating a high price and gradually reducing it. On the other hand, a firm may desire to enter the market with a low price as a means of penetrating the market.

Public-utility pricing is in a category by itself. Usually a public-service commission allows a public-utility firm to price in a manner that permits it to earn a fair return on a fair investment. But opinions differ, however, on what constitutes a fair return. The determination of a fair investment also is controversial, since the investment may be valued at original or replacement cost. Most public-utility commissions have a formula they follow in determining pricing.

Business firms seldom use marginal-cost pricing. In some instances, public utilities have experimented with it, as have the airlines. Some firms do use a form of marginal-cost pricing in accepting certain job orders at prices lower than those based on standard cost.

QUESTIONS FOR ANALYSIS AND DISCUSSION

1. Traditional economic theory explains pricing under what type of market conditions? What useful application does this pricing theory have?
2. What does it mean to say that a firm is meeting the market price? Are there

any markets in which the price is determined primarily by demand and supply?

3. What is cost-plus, or full-cost, pricing?

4. What is standard cost? How does it relate to average cost? What effect does underabsorbed or overabsorbed burden have on pricing decisions?

5. How does incremental pricing differ from marginal-cost pricing?

6. Does differential pricing imply price discrimination? Under what conditions would differential pricing be or not be discrimination?

7. Explain the so-called inferior demand curve associated with prestige pricing. What do you think of prestige pricing?

8. Describe price lining and explain how product quality can affect profit for a given price line.

9. Explain the relationship between multiple-model pricing and price elasticity of demand.

10. Explain the rate basis of public utility pricing. Do you prefer original cost or replacement cost as a basis for determining public utility investment?

11. Under what circumstances would a company prefer price skimming to penetration pricing? Give some examples of price skimming.

12. Explain marginal-cost pricing. Under what circumstances could it lead to a no-profit, or a loss, situation for its user?

13. Why would an oligopolist not continue to produce up to the point at which price equaled marginal cost?

14. Evaluate the various pricing objectives for a firm.

PROBLEMS AND CASES

1. In 1977, American farms produced a bumper crop of corn, in excess of 6 billion bushels. That fall, many farmers throughout the nation were withholding large supplies of corn from the market by storing it in their own bins. They maintained that the market price of corn, about two dollars per bushel, was too low compared with the cost of production. At the same time, the United States Department of Agriculture was considering the feasibility of reducing acreage allotments for the production of corn by 10 percent for the 1978 growing season. It was also reported that the Soviet Union would probably purchase 15–20 million metric tons of United States grain, including more than 1 million tons of corn, within the next few months. The People's Republic of China, too, stated its intention to purchase large supplies of grain from the United States. Earlier in the 1977 season, corn had been selling for $2.78 per bushel. A similar situation existed in the production of wheat.

As a student of managerial economics, explain the following:

(a) What type of pricing was involved in the grain market?

(b) How will the action of the farmers affect the price of corn?

(c) If the government reduces the acreage allotments for 1978, this should affect the price of corn in what way?

(d) Is there anything inconsistent in the action of the farmers' storing the grain and the proposed reduction in acreage allotments by the Department of Agriculture?

(e) Could the potential Russian grain deal influence the action of the farmers to store grain and the action of the government to reduce acreage allotments? If so, how?

2. A world-renowned copper-market analyst speaking before an international group meeting in Geneva in the fall of 1977 stated that the world copper price would rise from its current fifty-four cents per pound to seventy cents within a year and to one dollar per pound by the mid-1980s. His prediction was based on a forecasted copper shortage to occur about five years hence.

   The speaker indicated that the price of copper was depressed because of the action of major copper-producing nations. Many producers were pumping ever-increasing amounts of copper into world markets as a means of offsetting lower income resulting from falling prices. Anticipating that these nations would not cut copper production, he suggested that if output were held at current levels and if 25 percent of world output were held (stockpiled) by independent parties, such as international banks, the pressure on prices would be alleviated. He stated that the mere announcement that copper was going to be stockpiled would give prices a boost. If such a plan were followed, the producing countries would benefit from the short-term increase in the price of copper; the stockpiler, from the long-term increase in price.

   The expert predicted a copper shortage because the current low price for copper does not offer much incentive to invest in the new copper mines that some day would be needed. He pointed out that in the past several years, copper consumption had been increasing at the rate of 5.5 percent annually, while production had been increasing at an annual rate of 4.2 percent. Moreover, because of the lack of incentive, copper production would increase at less than 4 percent annually in the next several years.

   In the United States, for example, the price of copper in 1973 was seventy-seven cents per pound and stockpiles rose from 338,000 short tons to more than 519,000 tons in 1975.

   (a) In terms of demand and supply, explain what probably was going on in the world copper markets.
   (b) What type of pricing was involved in the world copper markets?
   (c) Do you think that the speaker's plan to raise the price of copper is a good one?
   (d) What risk would the stockpiler be taking in the speaker's suggested plan of action?
   (e) How is his plan related to the action of the farmers in the previous problem?

3. The Fast-Tick Corporation produces small clocks that it sells under its own brand name for $20. It produces 250,000 clocks annually. It normally operates at 80 percent capacity, and its employees are on a 40-hour, 4-day-week work schedule. No overtime payment is necessary under these conditions. Fast-Tick has been using the following standard cost in pricing its product:

Labor cost	$ 6.00
Material cost	4.00
Overhead	4.00
Total	$14.00

The corporation is approached by Swing-Time Jewelers to supply an otherwise identical clock with the Swing-Time label. Swing-Time is willing to pay $12.50 for the clocks and will order 50,000 clocks annually. Fast-Tick, in considering the proposal, knows it can do the work on Fridays, but will have to pay its employees time and one-half under the Fair Labor Standards Act. The additional (only) materials, however, can be purchased at a 10 percent discount.

(a) What is the total overhead burden of Fast-Tick?

(b) What will be the marginal cost of producing the additional 50,000 clocks?

(c) If 300,000 units (250,000 + 50,000) are produced, will the standard cost of $14 shown above contain overabsorbed or underabsorbed burden and to what extent?

(d) Will Fast-Tick, with the $12.50 price, be able to cover the marginal cost of producing the additional clocks?

(e) Should Fast-Tick accept the Swing-Time order? Why or why not?

4. A moderate-sized shop specializing in women's wear established price lines of $14.95, $17.95, and $19.95 for its inexpensive categories of summer dresses. In ordering for the $17.95 price line, the buyer has the opportunity to purchase one quality dress for $12 or a better-quality dress for $13.50. It is anticipated that at the price of $17.95, sales of the $12 quality dress will be approximately 250; sale of the $13.50 quality dress at a price of $17.95 will be 350. If the $12.00 dress is sold at $14.95, sales would be 450. There is no thought of selling the $13.50 dress in the $14.95 price line. Another option for the buyer is purchasing some $12 and some $13.50 dresses for sale in the $17.95 price line.

(a) Should the buyer select the $12 or the $13.50 quality dress for the $17.95 price line? Why?

(b) What would the gross profit be on the sale of each quality of dress?

(c) If the $13.50 rather than the $12 dress is selected, what is the marginal cost of each of the extra 100 dresses that will be bought? Will the marginal cost be above or below the marginal revenue?

(d) The buyer chooses to split the order and buy 125 dresses at the $12 price and 175 at $13.50. Will gross profit be more or less than it would be under the other two options?

5. The brewer of a regionally distributed beer is interested in expanding its sales territory. Its first targets are two moderate-sized cities located on the periphery of its current sales territory. The beer is considered of good quality and taste, and the price is in line with other nonpremium beers sold in its territory.

The brewmaster of the company maintains that the quality of the beer is such that the beer will sell itself with the help of a little introductory advertising. The sales manager, on the other hand, recommends heavy advertising, distributor discounts, and promotional schemes to accompany the introduction of the beer into the two cities. The president asks whether such ballyhoo may tarnish the current good image of the beer.

You are asked, as a newly hired business economist, to comment on the proposals. What would you say?

6. Jim English and Jock MacDade, two of your former classmates, plan to write and publish a local sports magazine for a metropolitan city that has a population of one million. They estimate that within a year, circulation will reach and stabilize at 35,000 copies. Checking with the printer, they learn that they can have 35,000 copies printed for $8,750 or 50,000 for $10,000. At a selling price of 60 cents per copy, and sales of 35,000, they can cover all costs and make a reasonable profit.

(a) What is the average cost of printing 35,000 copies versus printed 50,000 copies?

(b) What is the marginal cost per copy of printing the additional 15,000 copies?

(c) If they approached you about their sales and pricing plans, what would you advise them?

7. To better understand some existing pricing policies, complete the following exercises:

(a) List several products that have been subject to price skimming. Is there any characteristic common to these products?

(b) Make a list of several products or services for which multiple-model pricing takes place. Do these products or services have any common characteristics?

(c) Make a list of several products that appear to be objects of prestige pricing. Do these products have any common characteristic(s)?

8. A small electric-utility company over the years invested $100 million in plant, equipment, and other assets. The public-utility commission permits the firm to price in a manner to yield 8 percent return on this investment. Sixty percent of the investment was made in 1955, 20 percent in 1960, and the remainder in 1965. All assets are subject to a 40-year straight-line depreciation. In 1975, the company petitioned the public-utility commission to permit the use of replacement cost in determining the value of investment. In 1975, the Consumer Price Index was 161, compared with 95 in 1965, 89 in 1960, and 80 in 1955.

The electric-utility company asks you to assist in preparing its case and to serve as an expert witness during the hearings on the matter. In preparing the data for the case, be sure to have answers for the following questions:

(a) What, in your judgment, is the value of the company's investment based on replacement cost?

(b) If an 8 percent rate of return is allowed on the replacement value of investment, what total profit would the utility be permitted to make?

(c) What percentage of change in customer rates would have to be imposed in order to make an 8 percent rate of return on replacement cost of investment?

Competition in Automobile Prices*

A. **The Manufacturer's Suggested Price.** In accordance with law, each new car offered for sale has the Manufacturer's Suggested Price (MSP) attached. It is this price from which the dealer and the customer negotiate the transaction price. It applies only to the specific car and its equipment. In addition to the list price, only a part of which the manufacturer receives, the MSP includes the suggested dealer delivery and handling charge and a provision for the Federal excise tax, which tax, of course, goes to the government.

The MSP represents a complex balancing of many and sometimes opposing factors. These include the competitive advantages the manufacturer believes his new product line offers in relation to his and other prior models, his estimate of the customer appeal of new competitive products, the prices of his competitors, his estimates of change in the cost of production and his appraisal of the market potential.

In his approach to new product pricing, the manufacturer is constrained within narrow limits by the competitive realities of the market on the one hand and the facts of cost change on the other. As is evident from the foregoing discussion of product competition, a new car offering specified qualities and features can be sold only if its price is at least roughly comparable with that of other similar cars. Since all manufacturers recognize this fact, competitive makes, models and body styles are offered for sale at closely similar prices, after adjustment for differences in features.

The evidence of intense price competition is impressive. For example, General Motors' 1969 model prices, announced in the form of list prices, were lower than the list prices announced earlier by Chrysler. Shortly thereafter Chrysler adjusted its prices to remove or reduce disparities on competitive models and body styles. Similar price rollbacks to adjust to competitors have occurred in other recent years. Exhibit 1 indicates that competitive actions and responses in list prices which occurred with the announcement of the 1969 cars. As is evident from the range of price changes, the adjustment of prices with respect to models and body styles is in response to competitive pressures in the industry. Moreover, a comparison of the average price change indicates the nature and the amount of the adjustments which took place. For example, following Chrysler's initial average increase of $84, and after the announcements by General Motors and Ford of lesser increases, Chrysler rolled back to a $52 average increase, a reduction of $32.

The same competitive pressures which forced these price reductions by Chrysler forced General Motors to change previously announced plans to include head restraints as standard equipment on all its 1969 cars. This was discussed in a General Motors press release of September 23, 1968, as follows:

> Head restraints, which help protect against possible whiplash injuries, will be required in every car after January 1, 1969. We had announced our plan to make these head restraints standard equipment

*This case is taken from a statement by the General Motors Corporation. It was prepared for the United States Senate Subcommittee on Retailing, Distribution and Marketing Practices and the Subcommittee on Monopoly of the Select Committee on Small Business.

EXHIBIT 1. Summary of 1969 Model List Price Changes
(1969 vs. 1968 models)

Date	Range of Dollar Change $	Average Dollar Change $	Average Percent Change %
Sept. 16, 1968 Chrysler (Original Prices)	−66 to +164	+84	2.9
Sept. 23, 1968 General Motors	−1 to +144	+49	1.6
Sept. 25, 1968 Ford	−89 to +149	+47	1.6
Sept. 26, 1968 Chrysler (Revised Prices)	−69 to +188	+52	1.8
Sept. 27, 1968 AMC	−74 to +437	+37	1.5

Source: Published Company Data.

on all 1969 models. However, the pressures of competition force us to continue them as optional equipment until January 1. Until then, we will offer them as an option at new and substantially reduced list prices of $15, $16 or $17, depending on the model. On January 1 they will be standard equipment and basic list prices will be increased by these amounts.

In assessing the competitive position of his products, the manufacturer has an up-to-date body of market data on which to draw. New car transactions, averaging some 30,000 per selling day in recent years, provide a guide to the customer's judgment of each product in relation to other competitive new and used cars. There is no appeal from this verdict. Each manufacturer's new models and the corresponding suggested prices must reflect these market-determined judgments.

Year-to-year changes in new vehicle announced prices must take into account the competitive challenge which each product line, model and body style is expected to meet. This is a highly particularized product and price analysis which leaves no opportunity for inflexible pricing procedures or for sweeping generalizations. Again, the 1969 model price announcement is illustrative. While labor and material increases applied to production of all 1969 models, price adjustments were determined by market forces and varied from model to model. As shown in Exhibit 2, 1969 model list price changes in relation to 1968 prices for 4-door General Motors cars ranged from a $1 reduction to a $144 increase. In terms of percent, the price changes ranged from a small decrease to an increase of 2.7 percent for the models shown.

The average price increase for General Motors 1969 cars was $49 per car, or 1.6 percent. This was less than already-known cost increases would have justified if cost were the only consideration. Payroll costs, for example, will increase by nearly 6 percent, and the costs of certain materials, principally steel, copper and nickel had already increased. In addition, important safety features were incorporated. On the other hand, estimated cost savings, resulting from the change in our warranty policy, were also taken into account. General Motors, however, anticipated — but could *only* anticipate — further efficiencies in production of cars still to be built, and the customer's acceptance of cars still to be displayed.

Although car prices are announced at the beginning of each model year,

EXHIBIT 2. Change in General Motors List Prices for Selected 4-Door Models
(1969 vs. 1968)

Make	1968 Models $	1969 Models $	1969 Model Change from 1968 $	%
Chevy II Nova 4	2,104	2,103	-1	—
Chevy II Nova 6	2,163	2,177	+14	+0.6
Tempest Custom 6	2,429	2,459	+30	+1.2
Chevelle Malibu 8	2,459	2,469	+10	+0.4
Impala 6	2,656	2,701	+45	+1.7
Catalina 8	2,797	2,862	+65	+2.3
Cutlass Supreme 8 Hardtop	2,860	2,895	+35	+1.2
Skylark Custom 8 Hardtop	2,908	2,933	+25	+0.9
Electra 225 8	3,884	3,964	+80	+2.1
Cadillac DeVille 8*	5,405	5,549	+144	+2.7

*Includes Front Disc Brakes
Source: Published General Motors Data.

how much profit — if any — may be earned will not be known until the end of each year, and will depend upon how well the company performs against competition — in the factory and in the showroom.

Each manufacturer attempts to recover known changes in labor and material costs through efficiency improvement, price adjustments or both. However, there is no formula he can apply to this, and there can be no assurance when the model year opens that he will be able to accomplish it.

The discipline of price competition is clearly evident in the new model price announcements made by manufacturers each year. For example, in the announcement of its 1969 model prices, General Motors reviewed the interaction of volume, cost, market and competitive factors as follows:

> The Index of Wholesale Auto Prices compiled by the United States Bureau of Labor Statistics, shows that, since 1959, auto prices have declined about 2.5% throughout the industry. And General Motors' prices for the average car are currently lower than those of our competitors. In contrast, the consumer price index has risen about 20% and the wholesale price index of all industrial commodities has increased about 8%.
>
> Reduction in the Index was achieved during a period in which GM's hourly employment costs rose 63%; and the costs of steel (prior to the August increase) rose 9%, lead 14%, nickel 27%, zinc 35% and copper 58%.
>
> In these ten years, General Motors countered its rising costs with imaginative efforts to increase efficiency and to develop and sell 'more car per car' — more optional equipment and a higher proportion of top-of-the-line models. For the first several years, our results were further favorably influenced by a rapidly expanding market as car sales doubled from 1958 to 1965.

Exhibits 3 and 4 contain the new car wholesale and retail price indexes prepared by the Bureau of Labor Statistics, both of which take into ac-

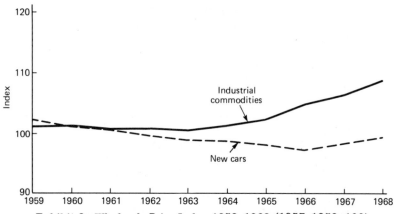

Exhibit 3. Wholesale Price Index 1959–1968 (1957–1959=100)

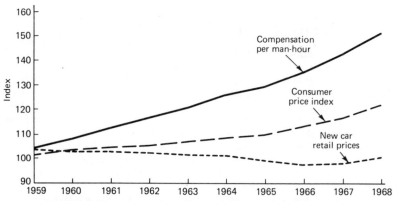

Exhibit 4. Wages, Cost of Living and Car Prices 1959–1968 (1957–1959=
100)

count improvement in car quality. These are compared with relevant comprehensive indexes of price change in the economy and with the index of compensation per man-hour. As shown in Exhibit 3, while the index of industrial commodity prices is now about 9 percent above the 1957–59 base level, the index of new car wholesale prices is at about the base period level.

As the Consumer Price Index shows (Exhibit 4), the past decade has been one of general price inflation with the Index now some 22 percent above the 1957–59 base period. While compensation per man-hour increased 51 percent, the indexes of new car wholesale and retail prices have been remarkably stable. They currently are approximately the same as the base period level. Particularly in this period of general inflation and rising cost pressures, the new car price tends are remarkable — a clear indication of the strength of the competitive forces that govern the production and sale of new cars.

B. **The Price the Customer Pays.** The Manufacturer's Suggested Price brings into focus all the competitive and cost factors affecting each new model. With the increase in new car models and body styles and the availability of a great variety of optional equipment for each car, the MSP has become an important adjunct of new car retailing. The "price sticker" not only identifies the specific car make and model but all items of optional equipment on the car. This assists the customer in his evaluation of the product choices available at various prices with the result that competition with respect to the car itself, optional equipment and price has become increasingly keen.

The MSP, which provides a basis for negotiations between the dealer and the customer, normally does not change during the model year. It is a price at which the dealer is usually willing to sell. However, since each new car transaction is a result of individual bargaining between the dealer and his customer, the actual transaction price can and does vary substantially from one transaction to the next during the model year.

The extent of this variation is suggested by a study of trading practices in the Chicago area reported in *The Journal of Business* in October, 1959.[1] Bargaining transactions were conducted with 28 Chicago Chevrolet dealers in February and August, 1959. In both months the range of individual bargaining was over $150 per car.

Thus, while the MSP is a specific price of a specific model as equipped, the individuality of each transaction further reflects the negotiation between the dealer and his customer. As a result, the transaction price varies and is usually below the MSP or sticker price. The extent of this difference depends on many considerations, such as the demand for a particular model and the ability of the manufacturer and dealer to satisfy the demand promptly. In addition, special sales incentive programs and product promotion allowances, which are an integral part of each manufacturer's marketing effort, can be sources of price variation at the retail level.

Conditions of supply and demand in local marketing areas also influence retail prices. Moreover, since marketing areas tend to overlap, changes in one area tend to be transmitted to contiguous areas.

Competitive pressures also affect each dealer's approach to his marketing opportunity. Each dealer, of course, strives to retain as large a part of the difference between the wholesale price and the MSP as competitive conditions in his area, combined with a desire for sales, permit. Subjective factors such as the dealer's reputation for service as well as the reputation of the product and its manufacturer importantly affect the dealer's ability to build his business on a profitable basis. Selling practices of other dealers as well as the size of new car stocks are also factors. Finally, the bargaining skill of both buyer and seller is important.

These factors, which are of critical importance to the individual dealer trying to sell a car, are just as important to the manufacturer. Ultimately, therefore, these various aspects of the dealer–buyer transaction determine prices, marketing programs, and sales volumes at the manufacturing level. Every auto manufacturer analyzes these trends as carefully as possible to determine what product, price, and marketing adjustments should be made to meet the needs of competition.

---

[1] Allen F. Jung, "Price Variations Among Automobile Dealers in Metropolitan Chicago," *The Journal of Business* (October 1959): 31–42.

EXHIBIT 5. New Lower-Price Makes Offered by U.S. Manufacturers
(by model years)

	1960	1961	1962	1963	1964	1965	1966	1967	1968
Corvair (GM)	●	●	●	●	●	●	●	●	●
Falcon (Ford)	●	●	●	●	●	●	●	●	●
Valiant (Chrysler)	●	●	●	●	●	●	●	●	●
Comet (Ford)	●	●	●	●	●	●	●	●	●
Tempest (GM)		●	●	●	●	●	●	●	●
F-85 (GM)		●	●	●	●	●	●	●	●
Special (GM)		●	●	●	●	●	●	●	●
Lancer (Chrysler)		●	●						
Chevy II (GM)			●	●	●	●	●	●	●
Fairlane (Ford)			●	●	●	●	●	●	●
Meteor (Ford)			●	●					
Dart (Chrysler)				●	●	●	●	●	●
Chevelle (GM)					●	●	●	●	●
Mustang (Ford)					●	●	●	●	●
Coronet (Chrysler)						●	●	●	●
Belvedere (Chrysler)						●	●	●	●
Barracuda (Chrysler)						●	●	●	●
Charger (Chrysler)							●	●	●
Camaro (GM)							●	●	●
Montego (Ford)							●	●	●
Firebird (GM)							●	●	●
Cougar (Ford)								●	●
Javelin (AMC)									●
AMX (AMC)									●

Source: Ward's Automotive Reports.

C. Pricing Considerations in Product Development. The measurement of trends in new car wholesale and retail prices (Exhibits 3 and 4) is based on a comparison of the prices of comparable high volume models offered each year. As a result, the indexes do not take into account shifts in customer product and price preferences.

The price implications are equally significant. Starting with the 1960 model year, a wide selection of small and intermediate-size cars was introduced at prices below the high-volume Chevrolet Impala V-8 and competitive makes. Exhibit 5 shows the model years in which these cars were introduced and continued in production.

As a result, the lower priced models shown in Exhibit 5, which accounted for only 16 percent of registrations in 1960 increased to 41 percent by mid-1968 (Exhibit 6). Thus, in terms of product change there was, over this period, a significant expansion, both absolutely and relatively, in the variety of new domestic lower price makes.

In terms of new car price analysis, the implications of these trends are fully as significant as the index of price changes for "comparable models". They reflect the long-term efforts of each manufacturer to anticipate trends in customer preference, to strengthen areas of weakness in his product line and to counter competitive challenges.

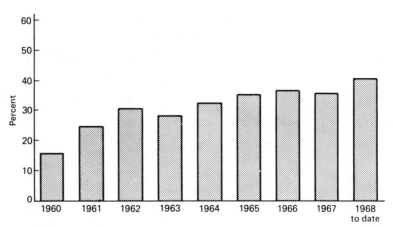

Exhibit 6. Percentage of Industry Registrations Accounted for by New Domestic Lower Price Makes (1960-1968 to Date)

Each manufacturer must work back from competitive trends in the market which establish basic vehicle specifications and price requirements. The key test is whether a product of the type specified can be produced at a cost which will enable the manufacturer to sell at a profit in the defined areas of the price structure. Most manufacturers have had the experience of building prototype cars which could not meet this test and were not put on the market. In addition, many models were introduced which showed promise of meeting the test but subsequently failed. There are many classic examples — the "pregnant" Buick, the Air Flow Chrysler and the Edsel, to name only a few.

In deciding about a new product, the manufacturer must estimate, as best he can, the rate of return on investment expected in order to determine whether it will be worthwhile to make the investment required to undertake production. However, the existence of estimated or budget profit does not in any way mean that the manufacturer has any ability or power to secure it. Frequently, a new product decision depends on a comparison of the estimated earnings loss which would result for the business as a whole if the new product is not introduced, as against the estimated overall earnings of the business with a new proposed competitive model. In addition, the competitive performance of the new car may be greater or less than anticipated. It may affect the sales volume of other cars in the manufacturer's line to a greater or lesser degree than estimated. The most that can be said is that the manufacturer hopes the new product will make a profit contribution to the business.

The manufacturer cannot engage in a mechanistic calculation of price changes based on cost changes. Cost estimates merely suggest which products may be marketed on a profitable basis. While cost changes do exert pressure on prices, cost is only one element in the complex of factors to be considered. The other elements include the competitive efforts of other manufacturers, volume expectations and, most importantly, the customer who must be satisfied by the product values offered.

Management's ability to maintain the business on a profitable basis is measured by its success in anticipating customer demand two or more years in advance; its willingness to risk large expenditures on product research and development, to invest in plant and equipment in advance of the market and its determined efforts to control costs at all levels of the business.

(a) Describe the pricing procedure in the automobile industry.

(b) To what extent is pricing in the automobile industry pricing to meet the market?

(c) There is no mention of supply and demand in the formulation of the manufacturer's suggested price. Does this mean that demand and supply are ignored in the pricing process?

(d) If products are really differentiated in the industry, why did Chrysler reduce its initial price increase in 1969?

(e) It is stated that for the 1969-model year General Motors increased the price of its car an average of forty-nine dollars or 1.6 percent. On the other hand, it is stated that payroll cost alone would increase by 6 percent. Does this mean that profit would be reduced? Why or why not?

(f) What is the function of the Manufacturer's Suggested Price (MSP)?

(g) What are some of the many factors that can cause the transaction price of a new car to deviate from the sticker price (MSP)?

(h) How do you relate the increased sale of new lower-priced models during the 1960s to the movement of the Wholesale Price Index of New Cars?

(i) To what extent do automobile manufacturers use a cost-plus pricing policy as opposed to pricing to meet the market?

(j) Would you describe the pricing in the auto industry as purely competitive, monopolistic, or oligopolistic? Why?

A New Product Comes to Market*

How Did it all Get Started?   No one thought up *Pampers*, the disposable diaper, overnight. The process began when a grandfather was baby-sitting for his first grandchild, a job which, of course, included changing diapers. He decided that there had to be something better than cloth diapers, and that the disposable diapers then on the market weren't the answer. The cloth diaper met a need, but not very well. The disposable diaper also met a need, but not very well. It was not as absorbent as cloth, and it wasn't really "disposable."

The grandfather, a consumer, was also a Procter & Gamble engineer. He knew his company was in business to solve consumer problems like this. And so, he brought his problem to his associates. He was persuasive enough to make the company want to verify his instincts. At this point, the company had to decide whether or not to try to develop a better way of dia-

*This case is adapted from a manual, *Consumer Choice*, published by Educational Services, The Procter & Gamble Company. © The Procter & Gamble Company, 1977. Reproduced with permission.

pering babies. Since Procter & Gamble, like every business and every individual, has limited resources and unlimited ways of using them, the company had to decide if diapering babies was a consumer need it could satisfy, better than others.

Before embarking on a project that would cost millions of dollars, the manager making decisions for Procter & Gamble had to be able to answer three basic questions:

1. Was there a real consumer need for an alternative method of diapering?
2. Did Procter & Gamble have the scientific and technological ability to develop the product?
3. Is the potential "market" for such a product large enough to offer some promise of making a profit?

To confirm that other consumers shared the engineer's need for an alternative diapering method, Procter & Gamble used market research. Such research can take many forms — interviews with consumers in their homes, telephone interviews, questionnaires, discussion groups. The objectives, however, are always the same: find out what consumers want by finding out how they use existing products, what they think of these products, and what their daily habits are. Procter & Gamble, for example, looks for clues in the interviews it conducts with more than a million consumers annually. These clues can help the company recognize a need that consumers have not been able to verbalize.

In the case of Pampers, thousands of mothers were asked how they diapered their babies and how they felt about their current diapering methods and products. The research showed that mothers found that cloth diapers were uncomfortable for their babies. The cloth diapers bunched up, did not keep the babies dry enough, and required plastic pants which could irritate a baby's tender skin. Obviously, there was a real need for a better way since this consumer problem was larger than just the messy task of storing and laundering soiled diapers.

The company had the expertise to develop the product since it had a good deal of experience inventing and manufacturing absorbent paper products like paper towels and facial and toilet tissue.

Now, P&G specialists in product research, engineering, marketing, and advertising all began to examine the basic idea of a single-use, disposable diaper. Could it be made? How? Would it satisfy the consumer need? Could it be sold at a profit?

All these questions were critical ones, but the final question — profit — was the most critical of all. If a company cannot make a profit on it, there is no incentive to develop a new product.

Market opportunity — the potential size of a new market — is crucial in determining profit. A company has to have some promise of return on the millions of dollars required to develop a product from the idea stage to mass production. Procter & Gamble learned that there were over fifteen billion diaper changes a year in the United States. This was certainly an impressive market, if an effective and efficient alternative diapering system could be invented.

Such a market would lend itself to a mass-produced product, one that could be produced in high volume but at a relatively low cost per unit. This was important because the company knew the new product would have to have a price that could compete with cloth diapers, but at the same time provide some return (profit) on its investment.

Although each diaper sold would return only a tiny amount of the investment required, the return possible from millions of sales could make the effort worthwhile. Spreading huge research and investment costs over millions or billions of units of a product is an example of what economists call economy of scale.

Along with finding a real consumer desire or problem, and having the technical capacity to fill that wish or solve the problem, the company decided there was a large enough potential market for such a product to justify the investment required to get the product from idea to mass-producing reality. In deciding that Pampers was a promising investment for its time and money — compared with possible development of other product ideas or improvement of existing products — Procter & Gamble made its economic choice to go ahead.

Starting Product Development. The chain of action and reaction that began with the consumer was developing rapidly. The idea of a disposable diaper had reached the *product development* phase. Chemists and engineers were now given the task of inventing a product that would solve the problems consumers had with their current diapering method.

The objective was to develop a product that would be comfortable for the baby to wear (better fit, keep the baby drier than cloth), easy to store, disposable, and competitively priced with cloth diapers. The raw materials would have to be safe for babies and the environment in which these diapers would be disposed. After nine months of research, the product development team came up with a diaper pad for insertion in plastic pants. The pad used a special pleat for better fit, was absorbent, and flushable.

The new disposable diaper was now ready for a *pilot test*, another form of market research. So a small supply of these unnamed diaper pads and plastic pants was made by hand, and given free to mothers in Dallas, Texas. Results? Dallas parents turned thumbs down on the product by an overwhelming majority!

What went wrong? The diaper was okay as far as comfort and absorbency were concerned, but the specialists forgot one thing. It gets very hot in Dallas, and while 80% to 90% of the babies up North wore elasticized plastic pants, Dallas parents weren't about to subject *their* babies to a Turkish bath.

So it was back to the drawing boards again.

Dallas consumers having spoken, it took another six months to develop a radically new diaper design. Scientists looked for new raw materials, and they had to be checked thoroughly for human and environmental safety. Finally, six months later, a new diaper — changed to correct the Dallas problem — emerged. The company kept the things Dallas parents liked about the diaper pad product — the special pleat for comfort and absorbent materials for dryness. The new product also retained the disposability feature. This time, however, plastic pants were replaced with a newly invented, thin plastic backsheet that kept the moisture in but allowed some circulation to help alleviate the "hot house effect" of plastic pants. Another invention — a porous topsheet between the baby and the absorbent material — allowed fluid to get to the absorbent material, but kept most of it from coming back through. This kept, baby drier and more comfortable.

When the new product was thought ready for another try-out, 37,000 diapers were made by hand. This time, consumer reaction was overwhelmingly favorable. Parents liked the new single-use diaper and said they would keep on buying it.

Test Marketing a New Product. A product had been designed which appeared to meet consumers' needs for an alternative to cloth diapers. Next step was to introduce the product into the market to see if consumers really agreed that the product solved their problem effectively and efficiently. Despite the checks and rechecks that had already been conducted with consumers, the only way to determine if the product really solved the problem was to put it on sale under actual market conditions.

Remember—Pampers was a totally new product. All manufacturing up to this point had either been done by hand, or on a small scale manufacturing line, and raw materials had been purchased only in the small quantities needed. A decision to make the product available to consumers across the country would require the construction of manufacturing facilities, purchase of equipment, hiring of additional people, and contracting for the huge quantities of raw materials. This would mean expenditures of millions of dollars.

If, despite the research and testing, not enough consumers bought the product, the company would lose money on the product, and its capital investment in machinery would be down the drain.

To avoid gambling on such an investment, many companies first introduce a new product in a limited area called a *test market*. In a test market, a product that has already been proven safe and effective is put on sale in one or more selected cities with populations that correspond to the composition of the country as a whole. The product is sold exactly as though it were on sale nationally, with advertising, cents-off coupons, store displays, the whole array of modern mass marketing. The idea is to see if what looked good to the company, and to those consumers who tried the product for free in the preliminary research, still looks good to consumers under actual buying conditions. After a period of time in test market, sales can be analyzed and projections made about the number of consumers who would buy the product if it were available nationally.

P&G's completely redesigned diaper seemed to solve all the problems consumers had with cloth diapers. But before the company could move ahead with test marketing, a lot of work had to be done.

Engineers had to translate their thinking and drawing into machines that could mass produce this new product in quantities sufficient to supply the test market, but with the same consistent quality as the handmade versions. To do this, they had to invent a totally new manufacturing process. It took a year, but P&G engineers managed to design and build a small scale production line. The machinery, a complex array of metal, wires, and pulleys that was the first of its kind anywhere, had to be adjusted and readjusted, but finally the line was running smoothly enough to produce enough for the test market. Once the machinery was running with at least some consistency, 100 cases of the product were given to consumers to try in their homes, to make sure that the machine-made ones were as satisfactory to consumers as the hand-made ones had been.

Marketing the New Product. While engineering specialists were developing a way to make the product in quantity, with quality, and at high speed, the company's marketing groups were moving into motion behind the new product.

Market researchers went back to consumers for help in giving the new product a name. They tried all kinds of names — Tenders, Dri-Wees, Winks, Tads, Solos, Zephyrs — and, of course, the winner, Pampers.

Those parents interviewed felt that *Pampers* best conveyed the feeling of tender, loving care that they gave their babies. The company agreed and thought it was a name that could be easily recognized and remembered.

P&G's newly named product also needed a package — so packaging experts worked toward a solution that would be the right size, protect the contents, and catch the eye. Today's consumer products compete not only in meeting consumer needs, but in visibility.

Other marketing specialists coordinated by an "advertising brand group" — a team set up to manage the total marketing of each product — began reviewing what consumers had said they wanted, and comparing it with what the new product had to offer. Their job was to create advertising messages that communicated these benefits effectively to the potential consumers. At the same time, distribution experts were determining how to ship the product from point of manufacture to point of sale.

Still other technical experts and buying experts were searching for the best sources of supply, at the lowest possible price, for the raw materials that they hoped would be needed in vast quantities.

The Pricing Problem.   Accountants kept track of the costs being calculated by all the other groups: the cost of the raw materials, the cost of manufacturing the product and distributing it. Each group had to figure not only the actual cost of getting Pampers ready for the test market but also the cost if Pampers was mass produced to sell nationally. The accountants and the advertising brand group developed a price based on estimates of how many Pampers they could sell in terms of the total potential market (fifteen billion diaper changes every year) and how many people would use this new diapering method.

For its first test market (Peoria, Illinois, in 1961), Pampers was offered for sale at a cost of about 10¢ per diaper. This figure was determined by taking the costs involved to produce about 400 million diapers annually, which is the number of Pampers the company estimated could be sold nationally at a price mass production would permit. However, a company always loses money in a test market because the product costs much more to produce in the small quantity needed than it would when finally in mass production.

The Peoria test was a major disappointment.

Instead of the projected national sales level of 400 million diapers, the Peoria test indicated that the most P&G could hope to sell was less than half of this amount.

The company could not afford to invest any more in equipment and machinery needed to mass produce Pampers if this was the best they could expect. But that's what test markets are for — rechecking what the consumer wants, alerting the company to changes that need to be made in packaging, marketing, or even the product. The company could have moved ahead without the test market, but it would have involved possible loss of the total investment made for national production and introduction of the product. As it was, P&G already had spent millions of dollars on a product which now looked like a failure.

Market research soon found the trouble: *price*. Collectively, consumers liked the disposable diaper idea, but they decided that 10¢ a diaper was too much to pay. The trade-off of 10¢ of their resources for one disposable diaper wasn't worth it to them.

Why hadn't P&G discovered this before? One reason is that what consumers say they will do, and what they actually do, can be two different things. Also, consumer habits, needs, wants, and priorities may change from day to day. At this point, test market research confirmed that parents who tried Pampers liked them, but not at the price asked.

(a) What type of pricing technique was involved with Pampers?
(b) Was there any suggestion of price skimming or penetration pricing evident in P&G's pricing approach?
(c) Is there any way P&G might have avoided going as far as it did before finding out that its proposed price was too high?
(d) What would you recommend that P&G do next regarding its new product?

Marginal Cost Pricing — An Example

A recent proposal for pricing telephone service in Dallas, Texas, illustrates some of the problems involved when average total costs spread over several types of service, rather than marginal costs of specific services, are used for regulated prices. A public official recently called for a study of the "tremendous advantages" that seemingly could result from a system of toll-free calls throughout the Dallas-Fort Worth metropolitan area. Southwestern Bell's immediate response was that the system would be "extremely expensive."

At present, average cost pricing is applied to the residential class of customers within the Dallas phone system. Each residential customer pays the same price per month for all local calls irrespective of the customer's contribution to the capacity cost of the system through varied frequency and time of use. Toll-free calls can be placed between a number of cities in the Dallas phone system, but calls to Fort Worth and other cities in the metropolitan area incur long-distance charges. If the current price system has been properly designed, further differentiation of individual users' costs of service would add more to metering and billing costs than it would contribute to efficient use of the system.

A customer who contributes to system costs by making a long-distance call can be identified and billed at relatively little expense. With this billing procedure, the customer wishing to make a long-distance call has to decide whether the benefit of the call will exceed the additional cost of receiving the service. Faced with the marginal benefits and costs, he takes voluntary action in deciding to place or not place the call. The telephone company has a measure of the desirability of committing more resources to the long-distance exchange capacity, and this measure is based on individual valua-

Source: *Review*, Federal Reserve Bank of Dallas, November 1977.

tions of using the resources in alternative ways. Additional capacity is provided when marginal benefits exceed marginal costs.

Consider the alternative system that has been suggested — average cost pricing throughout the Dallas-Fort Worth metropolitan area. The cost of the new product (toll-free calling over the wider area) is averaged over residents in the area. For families that find little or no immediate benefit in the additional service provided the additional charge per customer may be small relative to the cost of protesting plus any potential benefits. Persons who are heavy users of long-distance services will be relieved by paying their true contributions to costs and will provide active support. Customers who actually use the long-distance service will be subsidized in their consumption by those who place few or no calls. Also, some households may no longer purchase the services of a residential telephone at its higher marginal cost to the household.

The long-term effects are quite predictable. Once a toll-free plan is adopted and the higher cost added to each customer's bill, the marginal cost of placing calls that were previously long-distance calls becomes zero for each customer. As the number of such calls increases and congestion arises in the telephone system, additional capacity will be "needed." Resources will be poured into the project without a test of their potential marginal contributions to satisfaction of consumer wants in alternative uses, now or later.

(a) From a customer's point of view, should Southwestern Bell implement a system of toll-free calls between Dallas and Fort Worth? (The distance between Dallas and downtown Fort Worth is approximately 30 miles).

(b) From the company's point of view, should Southwestern Bell adopt such a toll-free system?

SELECTED READINGS

Burck, G. "The Realities of Corporate Pricing," *Fortune*, April 1972.

Eckstein, Otto, and Gary Fromm. "The Price Equation." *The American Economic Review*, December 1968.

Electric Utility Rate Reform. Washington, D.C.: American Enterprise Institute for Public Policy Research, September 1977.

"Flexible Pricing" (Industry's new strategy to hold market share changes the rules for economic decision-making), *Business Week*, December 12, 1977.

Haynes, Warren. *Pricing Decision in Small Firms.* Lexington, Ky.: University of Kentucky Press, 1962.

Kahn, Alfred E. *The Economics of Regulation*, Vol. I. New York: John Wiley & Sons, Inc., 1971.

Kaplan, A.D.H., J. Dirlam, and R.F. Lanzillotti. *Pricing in Big Business.* Washington, D.C.: The Brooking Institution, 1958.

Leftwich, Richard H. *The Price System and Resource Allocation.* Hinsdale, Ill., Dryden Press, 1973.

Mulvihill, Donald F., and Stephen Paranka. *Price Policies and Practices.* New York: John Wiley & Sons, Inc., 1967.

Oxenfeldt, Alfred R., and William T. Baxter. "Approaches to Pricing: Economist vs. Accountant." *Business Horizons*, Winter, 1961.

Sherry, Edward. "Cutting the Marginalists' Gordian Knot," *Public Utilities Fortnightly*, February 17, 1977.

Sizer, John. "The Accounts Contribution to the Pricing Decision," *The Journal of Management Studies*, May 1966.

Tybout, Richard A. "Marginal Cost versus Rolled-in Pricing for Natural Gas," *Public Utilities Fortnightly*, March 3, 1977.

Watson, Donald S. *Price Theory in Action.* Boston: Houghton Mifflin Company, 1973.

Antitrust Regulation

Americans have always believed that a high degree of competition is beneficial for the U.S. economy and, particularly, for the American consumer. Since early times there have been laws to protect, preserve, and promote competition. Before the Civil War, much of this law was contained in our common law inherited from Britain. With the rise of corporations, the development of large-scale businesses, and the formation of trusts in the United States after the Civil War, however, many common law restrictions were incorporated into statutory law. This began on a broad scale with the passage of the Sherman Antitrust Act in 1890.

SHERMAN ANTITRUST ACT (1890)

Using its authority to regulate commerce, Congress formally declared monopolies, trusts, conspiracies, and other restraints of trade to be illegal. The heart of the act is contained in three sections. Section 1 states that "every contract, combination in the form of trust or otherwise, or conspiracy in restraint of trade or commerce among the several states or with foreign nations is hereby declared to be illegal." Section 2 states that "every person who shall monopolize, or attempt to monopolize or combine or conspire with any other person or persons to monopolize any part of the trade or commerce among the several states . . . shall be deemed guilty of a misdemeanor. . . ."

Both sections of the act go on to say, ". . . and on conviction thereof, shall be punished by a fine not to exceed five thousand dollars, or by imprisonment not exceeding one year, or by both said punishments, in the discretion of the court. . . ." The maximum fine is currently one hundred thousand dollars on individuals and one million dollars on companies; the maximum imprisonment, three years. In addition to such punishment, Section 7 provides for triple damages by making it possible for an injured party to "recover threefold the damages by him sustained and the cost of the suit . . ." from a defendant who has been convicted of violating the law.

As with the enforcement of other laws, the courts are "invested with the jurisdiction to prevent and restrain violations of this act; and . . . to institute proceedings in equity to prevent and restrain such violations." Actually, three charges may be preferred under the law. Criminal conspiracy charges brought by federal attorneys, proceedings in equity instituted by the antitrust division to enjoin and restrain violations of the law, and triple damage suits by private parties injured "by reason of anything forbidden or declared to be unlawful by this act."

Enforcement

If charged with violating the act, a defendant may plead guilty, not guilty, or *nolo contendere* ("no contest"). In pleading nolo contendere, the defendant does not admit guilt, but may agree to accept a consent decree issued by the court. Such a decree will state specific alleged violations of the law. In accepting the consent decree, the defendant agrees to correct the alleged violations. By doing so, the defendant avoids a costly court defense and adverse publicity. Frequently, before prosecuting a case, the court will offer the defendant a consent decree. In other cases, especially when violations are serious, such as they were in the electrical price-fixing conspiracy of the late 1950s, the judge will order the defendant(s) to plead guilty or not guilty and stand trial.

Another advantage of accepting a consent decree is the probability of avoiding suits by injured parties. Many times injured parties may not want to risk the time, effort, and money to bring suit against an alleged violator. But if the government brings suit against a defendant for criminal or equity violations of the law and the defendant is found guilty, it paves the way for third parties injured by the violation to bring suit for triple damages against the defendant. Such suits may go to trial or be settled out of court. Such was the case in the electrical price-fixing case in which the defendants, who were found guilty, subsequently had to pay millions of dollars to damaged parties.

In early years, enforcement of the Sherman Act was limited, in part because of inadequate staff and minimal budget provided for enforcement. The antitrust division of the attorney general's office, for example, was unsuccessful in its attempt to break up the sugar trust, which controlled more than 95 percent of the domestic sugar refining industry. The government lost its case on the grounds that the manufacturing process "only incidentally and indirectly affects commerce," and therefore was subject to state rather than federal regulation.[1] Similar rulings were applied in two cases against livestock dealers in Kansas City a few years later.

The antitrust division met with more success in prosecuting a group of Western railroads for fixing rates,[2] and in breaking up a territorial,

[1] *United States* v. *E.C. Knight Co.*, 1895.
[2] *United States* v. *Trans-Missouri Freight Association*, 1897.

or market, pool comprising six manufacturers of steel pipe who assigned each member a certain territory in which to sell its products free of competition from the others.[3] In 1904, the Supreme Court found defendants guilty of attempting to monopolize certain segments of the railroad industry[4] and dissolved their holding company. Later, the duPont explosives combination was dissolved by the court.[5] In 1908, a labor union was found guilty of violating the law, through a boycott, and triple damages of two hundred twenty-two thousand dollars were assessed against the union.[6]

Rule of Reason

Two landmark cases in antitrust history were heard in 1911—the Standard Oil case[7] and the American Tobacco Company case.[8] Although the Sherman Antitrust Act states that *every* contract, combination, trust, conspiracy, or monopoly in restraint of trade is a misdemeanor, in the oil and the tobacco cases the court held otherwise. In both cases, the defendants were found guilty of violating the law on several counts, and the cases led to the subsequent dissolution of the oil and tobacco trusts. In its decision, the Court declared, however, that the antitrust law was not intended to condemn all restraints of trade, but only *unreasonable* restraints of trade. Thus a firm, because of its size, or because it is a monopoly, may have certain cost advantages that make it difficult for other firms to compete or stay in business. This could be construed as reasonable restraint of trade, particularly if the large firm took no overt action to restrain trade.

As a result of this interpretation of the law, a shoe-machine manufacturer was found not guilty of violating the law, even though it required lessees of its bottoming machines used to attach soles to uppers not to use them in series with machines manufactured by others. Such "tying clauses" enabled the company to force a complete line upon any shoe manufacturer who found one of its machines indispensable. The court held that since the defendant had a patent on its bottoming machine and leased the machines to shoe manufacturers, rather than selling them outright, the defendant could designate the conditions under which its machines might be

---

[3] *United States* v. *Addyston Pipe and Steel Co.*, 1897.

[4] *Northern Securities Co.* v. *United States*, 1904.

[5] *United States* v. *duPont de Nemours & Co.*, 1911.

[6] *Loewe* v. *Lawlor*, 1908.

[7] *United States* v. *Standard Oil Company of New Jersey*, 1911.

[8] *United States* v. *American Tobacco Company*, 1911.

used.[9] In another case involving United States Steel Corporation, which at that time produced approximately 50 percent of the nation's steel, the court held the company not to be in violation of the law.[10] It stated that "the law does not make mere size or the existence of unexerted power an offense." Since the company had not recently committed serious overt acts to restrain trade, it was not in violation of the law. This principle of "mere size not being an offense" was reinforced in the International Harvester case.[11] There, International Harvester, which was formed by combining the three leading agriculture-implement (farm machinery and equipment) producers in the nation, controlled 65 percent of farm equipment output. Although other firms were forced out of business because they could not compete with the low prices of International Harvester Company, the Court held that such lessening of competition was a normal occurrence. In both the United States Steel and the International Harvester cases, the courts held that the companies made no attempt to use compulsory regulation of pricing or other unfair means to prevent competition. In fact, in both situations the market shares of each firm had declined in the previous decade. United States Steel's share dropped from 60 percent to 50 percent and that of International Harvester fell from 85 percent to 65 percent.

The principle of "mere size not being an offense" against the antitrust laws, as held in the United States Steel and the International Harvester cases, was overturned a few decades later in the ALCOA case (1945) and the second United States Shoe Machinery case (1953).

ALCOA was charged with monopolizing the manufacture of virgin aluminum and the sale of various aluminum products. The monopoly was made possible by control of patent rights and raw materials. ALCOA manufactured 90 percent of the virgin-aluminum ingots used in the United States. The rest were imported. Although the Court considered the point that "mere size is not an offense," it concluded otherwise. The Court in this case held that the distinction between unexerted and exerted monopoly power was purely formal. The distinction "would be valid only so long as the monopoly did not operate; for when it did . . . it must sell at some price and the only price at which it could sell is a price which it itself fixed."[12] Price fixing, according to the court, was inherent in monopoly.

[9] *United States v. United Shoe Machinery Company*, 1918.
[10] *United States v. United States Steel Corporation*, 1920.
[11] *United States v. International Harvester Co.*, 1927.
[12] *United States v. Aluminum Co. of America*, 1945.

Although ALCOA had attained its dominant position in the industry by reinvesting earnings and expanding output as the market grew, rather than through acquisition, the court held that it could have avoided the development, or continuation, of monopoly power by not growing as fast as the market, thus leaving room for competitors. On another score, the company maintained that it had engaged in no predatory practices and had not abused its monopoly power. The Court responded that "the law did not condone good trusts and condemn bad ones; it forebade them all." Although the government sought to have ALCOA broken into two companies, the Court denied the government's request. But it did require the company to license its patents to other domestic producers.

The precedent established in the ALCOA case was followed the next year in a case against three tobacco companies. Here the Court held that the companies could be convicted of monopolization under Section 2 of the Sherman Antitrust Act without proof that they had abused their power.[13] The mere existence of power, according to the Court, was all that was needed to be in violation. A similar decision was made in the Paramount Pictures case in 1948, which involved five major producers of motion pictures who also operated chains of first-run theaters in major cities and chains of smaller theaters throughout the nation. The Court held that ". . . monopoly power, whether lawfully or unlawfully acquired, may itself constitute an evil and stand condemned under Section 2 even though it remains unexercised."[14] The Court thereupon ordered a separation of the production and exhibition of motion pictures. The companies were subsequently divided into ten: five movie producers and five chains operating movie theaters.

On the basis of the precedent set in the ALCOA case, United States Shoe Machinery Company, which forty years after its first trial was still the dominant producer in its industry, was again charged with monopolization in violation of Section 2 of the Sherman Antitrust Act.[15] Unlike the first case, in which the Court had held the company not to be in violation because of patent rights, the Court found the company guilty in 1953. The Court held that a charge of *attempt to monopolize* requires proof of intent. But the *violation of monopolizing* does not. Even though the means to obtain a monopoly are lawful, the Court held that monopolization itself is not lawful. These three cases, and others, reversed earlier decisions declaring "mere size not an offense."

[13] *American Tobacco Co.* v. *United States*, 1946.

[14] *United States* v. *Paramount Pictures*, 1948.

[15] *United States* v. *United Shoe Machinery Corp.*, 1953.

CLAYTON ACT (1914)

Because of the ineffectiveness of the Sherman Antitrust Act, Congress moved to bolster and clarify the antitrust law with the passage of the Clayton Act in 1914. Section 2 of the act declared specific actions to be unlawful. Among other things, the Clayton Act prohibits the following: (1) price discrimination among buyers; (2) certain tying contracts, which force a seller, retailer, or supplier to handle exclusively the products of a particular manufacturer; (3) certain intercorporate stock acquisition; and (4) interlocking corporate directors. Moreover, Section 6 of the act holds labor to be neither a commodity nor an article of commerce. Consequently, it declares the usual activities of labor unions to be outside the jurisdiction of the antitrust laws.

There are qualifications to each of the prohibitions just cited. The law is violated when the effects of such action "may be to substantially lessen competition or tend to create a monopoly in any line of commerce." Regarding price discrimination, for example, nothing in the law prevents price discrimination among purchasers of commodities on account of differences in grade, quality, or quantity of the commodity sold, or makes due allowance for differences in the cost of selling or transportation, or discrimination in the same or different commodities made in good faith to meet competition. One salient practice that Congress was attempting to outlaw by this section was temporary price cutting by a firm with large resources as a means of eliminating a financially weaker competitor. In the matter of interlocking directors and intercorporate stock acquisition, the action must be among competitors and it must substantially lessen competition to be a violation of the law. Moreover, the ban on interlocking directors applies only to corporations with net worth in excess of $1 million. Penalties for violating the Clayton Act are similar to those of the Sherman Antitrust Act.

FEDERAL TRADE COMMISSION ACT (1914)

In the same year that Congress passed the Clayton Act, it established the Federal Trade Commission (FTC). It is the function of the Commission to prevent persons, partnerships, and corporations that are subject to the Federal Trade Commission Act from using unfair methods of competition in commerce. The FTC has investigative powers and the authority to issue orders to "cease and desist" from unfair practices. If necessary, it can apply to federal circuit courts for enforcement of its orders. The Federal Trade Commission seeks primarily to prevent violations of the antitrust laws. Again, punishment similar to that provided in the Sherman and Clayton Acts can be imposed for noncompliance with FTC investigations or orders.

The FTC was also given the authority to make recommendations to Congress for additional legislation to prevent restraint of trade and to outlaw unfair competitive practices. In 1938 Congress passed the Wheeler-Lea Act, which gave the Commission power to initiate action to restrain business practices detrimental to the public interest, including false advertising and the adulteration of manufactured products.

Initially, unfair methods under common law included diversion of customers from competitors by deceitful means, misappropriation of competitors' confidential information, and interference with business relations of competitors. In declaring unfair methods of competition to be unlawful, through the Federal Trade Commission Act, however, Congress intended to permit the words *unfair competition* to expand in meaning to meet changing circumstances.

ROBINSON-PATMAN ACT (1936)

Two decades and numerous court decisions left some uncertainties about the meaning of Section 2 of the Clayton Act, regarding price discrimination. In order to clarify the issue of when the effect of such discrimination may be to lessen competition substantially or tend to create a monopoly in any line of commerce, Congress enacted the Robinson-Patman Act in 1936 as an amendment to the Clayton Act.

The Robinson-Patman Act modifies the clause "in any line of commerce" in Section 2 to indicate that a violation may occur without lessening a *whole* line of competition in commerce. A violation can occur when competition between only certain persons or individual firms may be injured, destroyed, or prevented. In addition, the Robinson-Patman Act does not condemn all price discrimination, but only *undue discrimination*. In effect, one can say that the act prohibits price discrimination except to the extent of any cost savings involved. Or one may say that the Robinson-Patman Act permits price discrimination to the extent of any cost savings involved. Due allowances in the selling price can be made for differences in the cost of manufacture, sale, or delivery resulting from the different methods or quantities in which such commodities are sold or delivered. Section 2 of the Clayton Act was amended to read:

> That it shall be unlawful for any person engaged in commerce, in the course of such commerce, either directly or indirectly to discriminate in price between different purchasers of commodities of like grade and quality, . . . where the effect of such discrimination may be substantially to lessen competition or tend to create a monopoly in any line of commerce, or to injure, destroy or prevent competition with any person who either grants or knowingly receives the benefit of such discrimination, or with customers of either of them.

It is obvious from the preceding excerpt that the law applies to both the seller and the buyer. Other parts of the law specifically prohibit granting any commission, brokerage fee, compensation, discount, or promotional allowances in connection with the sale or delivery of commodities, except for services rendered in connection with the sale or delivery of the commodities involved. Another part of the act specifically declares illegal regional discrimination for the purpose of "destroying competition or eliminating a competitor."

Moreover, the law states that any payment or consideration offered by the seller must be available on proportionately equal terms to all other customers competing in the distribution of such products or commodities.

The Robinson-Patman Act is sometimes called the "anti-chain-store" act, since it was in part the intent of Congress to prevent large buyers, such as chain stores, department and grocery stores, and mail-order houses from exerting undue pressure, through their large demand, on manufacturers for price concessions that were larger than any savings in cost involved in the manufacture, sale, or delivery of the commodities. Before the passage of the Robinson-Patman Act, for example, the FTC had filed a complaint against the Goodyear Tire and Rubber Company. In 1926, Goodyear entered into an agreement with Sears, Roebuck and Company to supply Sears with all its tire needs on the basis of cost plus 6 percent. Except for the label and tread design, the tires were identical to those that Goodyear distributed under its own brand name to approximately 25,000 retailers throughout the country. The FTC found the net average price discrimination over a number of years to be between 12 and 22 percent in favor of Sears. This enabled Sears to undersell independent retailers by 20–25 percent. The FTC held that this was a difference in excess of the savings in cost involved. Goodyear appealed to the circuit court, which reversed the FTC's order. Subsequently, as a result of the enactment of the Robinson-Patman Act, Goodyear discontinued the contract.[16]

Numerous cases involving price discrimination have been heard. In the Morton Salt Company case, in 1948, for example, the Supreme Court upheld the FTC approach to eliminate discriminatory quantity discounts.[17] The Court reasoned that Morton's quantity discounts were not justified on the basis of savings in cost, and stated that of four quantity discounts, prices ranging from $1.60 to $1.35 per case, only five large grocery chain stores qualified for the $1.35 price. The Court held that, although the discounts were in theory equally available to all, actually they were not. Moreover, it held that the discounts could affect the final retail price and therefore could injure competition.

In another case, in 1952, the FTC charged Standard Oil of Indiana[18] of violating the law by selling its Red Crown gasoline at two different wholesale prices. It delivered the gas to jobbers, who might sell at wholesale or at retail, at a lower price than it delivered to service station customers. Consequently, some jobbers reduced their retail gasoline prices below prevailing prices in the area. The FTC maintained that this action resulted in injuring, preventing, and destroying competition. Standard Oil maintained that the reduction in price was not based on cost differentials, but given in good faith to retain the jobber as a customer, and in order to meet an equally low price offered by one or more of Standard's competitors. On the basis of good faith and the need to meet competition, the Court set aside the FTC order against the company.

Several other cases regarding price discrimination have been before the courts. In some, the FTC's orders were upheld; in others, they were not. The Robinson-Patman Act contains both criminal and civil sections. The criminal section makes three offenses, or violations, punishable by fine and/or imprisonment: charging different prices for identical products, selling at a lower price in one geographic area than in another, and selling at an unreasonably low price for the purpose of destroying competition or eliminating a competitor.

FAIR-TRADE PRICING

Another controversy regarding price competition centered on the fair-trade laws, which permitted resale price maintenance. Under

---

[16] *Goodyear Tire and Rubber Company v. Federal Trade Commission*, 1937.

[17] *Federal Trade Commission v. Morton Salt Company*, 1948.

[18] *Federal Trade Commission v. Standard Oil Company of Indiana*, 1958.

resale-price maintenance, the manufacturer can designate the price at which his product is to be sold at retail. In 1931, California passed the first Fair Trade Act, which gave manufacturers legal authority to enter into agreements with retailers to set the price at which the manufacturers' products would sell at retail. Only those retailers who signed agreements, however, were bound by the so-called fair-trade price. The act was subsequently amended to permit the manufacturer to compel nonsigners of the agreement to sell at the suggested retail price. In short, as long as the manufacturer could get one or a few retailers to accept the suggested retail price, all retailers could be forced to sell at that price, whether they agreed to or not.

Other states adopted fair-trade laws, and much controversy arose over the constitutionality of these laws. Were they or were they not in conformity with the antitrust laws? Did they protect or did they prevent competition? The basic question was settled in 1936 when the Supreme Court upheld the constitutionality of the California and Illinois fair trade laws.

Miller-Tydings Act (1937)

In 1937, Congress passed the Miller-Tydings Act, which, in effect, amended the Sherman Antitrust Act to permit fair trade–pricing. The Miller-Tydings Act declared that fair-trade pricing was legal in any state that had a fair-trade law. The effect of the act was to encourage states to enact fair-trade legislation, and, subsequently, 45 of the 48 states did. The exceptions were Missouri, Texas, and Vermont, plus the District of Columbia. Fair-trade pricing was widespread after World War II. In its heyday, however, a blow was struck against fair pricing. In 1951, the Supreme Court in the Schwegmann cases declared that the nonsigner clause in the Louisiana fair-trade law was unconstitutional.[19] In these cases, Calvert and Seagram had made contracts with some retailers setting the price of their whiskeys at $4.24 a fifth. Schwegmann refused to sign and sold the whiskey at $3.35. Calvert and Seagram sued Schwegmann, and Schwegmann appealed. The Court held that only voluntary agreements to maintain resale prices were permissible under the Miller-Tydings Act. This court decision cut at the foundation of fair-trade pricing. Within a few weeks, retailers in New Orleans, New York, Detroit, and other but not all major cities were cutting fair-trade prices by 20–30 percent. After a price war of several weeks, however, prices began returning to their previous levels. Whether the retailers were happy

---

[19] *Schwegmann Bros.* v. *Calvert Corporation*, 1951; *Schwegmann Bros.* v. *Seagram Distillers Corp.*, 1951.

to get rid of fair-trade pricing or whether they were using the court order as an excuse to get rid of excess inventories is still debatable. Nevertheless, the following year Congress enacted the Maguire Act (1952), which established the legality of the nonsigner clause.

The End of Fair Trade

Even though the constitutionality of the Maguire Act was upheld, several states subsequently abandoned their fair-trade laws. By 1963, the number of fair-trade states had been reduced to forty. Of these, only twenty-three had nonsigner clauses, and fair-trade pricing was in disarray. As late as 1970, a bill called the Quality Stabilization Act was introduced into Congress. This was nothing more than an attempt to obtain a national fair-trade law. With the spread of discount stores and the emergence and development of *consumerism* among the American people, the application of fair-trade pricing, or resale trade pricing, weakened. In 1975 alone, 15 states repealed their fair-trade laws. The final blow to fair trade came in December 1975, when Congress enacted legislation that nullified fair-trade pricing in the remaining 21 states that still had their fair-trade laws.

THE ANTIMERGER ACT (1950)

The Clayton Act forbids incorporate stock acquisitions between competing corporations; nevertheless, some firms, with the sanction of the courts, have in a number of cases found ways of getting around the law. One such technique was to acquire the assets of a corporation, rather than its stock. This was done in the meat industry by Swift & Co.[20] and in the shoe industry when International Shoe Co., the largest producer, acquired the assets of the fourth largest producer.[21] In both cases the courts found no violation of Section 7 of the Clayton Act. Another technique was to acquire the stock of competing corporations, but distribute it to shareholders. The shareholders could then vote to merge the two corporations. This was done and declared by the court not to be illegal in the Arrow-Hart & Hegman Electric Co. case.[22] Prior to 1950, fewer than 30 cases were brought before the courts by the government under Section 7 of the Clayton Act, which prohibited intercorporate stock acquisitions among competing corporations that lessened competition.

---

[20] *Swift & Co.* v. *FTC*, 1926.

[21] *International Shoe Co.* v. *FTC*, 1930.

[22] *Arrow-Hart & Hegeman Electric Co.* v. *FTC*, 1934.

Several of the loopholes in Section 7 were closed in 1950, however, with the enactment of the Celler-Kefauver Antimerger Act. This act amended the Clayton Act to prohibit the acquisition of assets as well as of stock. The act has been used also as a means to abort proposed mergers. It states:

> "No corporation shall acquire, directly or indirectly, the whole or any part of the stock or other share capital and no corporation subject to the jurisdiction of the Federal Trade Commission shall acquire the whole or any part of the assets of one or more corporations engaged in commerce, where in any line of commerce in any section of the country, the effect of such acquisition, of such stocks or assets, or the use of stock by the voting or granting of proxies or otherwise, may be substantially to lessen competition, or tend to create a monopoly...."

Armed with this new antitrust weapon, the government became more active and aggressive in breaking up and preventing mergers that would lessen competition. Within five years, more than 150 cases involving horizontal, vertical, and conglomerate mergers were brought to court by the antitrust division of the Justice Department and by the Federal Trade Commission under the Celler-Kefauver Act.

The government did realize an important victory, however, in 1957, under the original clause of Section 7 of the Clayton Act. In the duPont case, the Supreme Court, reversing a lower court, declared that duPont's acquisition of General Motors stock gave duPont sufficient control to influence General Motors' use of duPont products, such as automobile finishes and fabrics, in making GM cars.[23] The Court, therefore, ordered duPont to dispose of its General Motors stock by distributing it among duPont shareholders.

The initial major case to be tried under the Celler-Kefauver Act concerned the proposed merger of two steel companies, Bethlehem Steel Corporation and Youngstown Sheet and Tube Company.[24] Bethlehem, the industry's second largest producer, notified the Justice Department that it planned to acquire Youngstown, the nation's sixth largest steel producer, as a means of improving its competitive position vis-à-vis the industry's dominant producer, United States Steel Corporation. The acquisition would raise Bethlehem's share of the market from 15 to 20 percent compared with the approximately 30 percent held by United States Steel.

Bethlehem contended that it had no production facilities in the Chicago area, the nation's fastest growing steel market, and that the acquisition and expansion of Youngstown's Chicago plants would provide those necessary facilities. The steel companies also

[23] *United States v. duPont*, 1957.

[24] *United States v. Bethlehem Steel Corporation*, 1958.

contended that Youngstown was not in a financial position to expand its Chicago facilities.

Although the companies did produce some similar types of steel, they defended the merger because Bethlehem produced structural steel, which was in strong demand and short supply in the Chicago market, whereas Youngstown did not. Conversely, Youngstown produced certain types of steel not produced by Bethlehem. In addition to the benefit to stockholders of both companies of greater product diversification, the companies contended that the merger would provide wider geographic diversification. The Youngstown plants, primarily in Youngstown, Ohio, and Chicago, would provide Bethlehem with its desired facilities in Chicago and the Mid-continent area. On the other hand, the Bethlehem plants in the eastern part of the United States would provide Youngstown with an entry into those markets. Moreover, both companies maintained that they would provide more vigorous competition to United States Steel, the only fully integrated, geographically diversified steel producer in America.

In spite of the fine arguments presented by both companies, the Court held otherwise. It stressed that the law does not distinguish between good mergers and bad ones. Furthermore, it pointed out that Bethlehem had other ways to obtain facilities in the Chicago or Mid-continent area. The Court indicated that the proposed merger, if permitted, could set off a chain reaction of mergers in the steel industry. Smaller firms seeking to compete more efficiently with the Big Two might want to merge. This would lead eventually to a triploy in the steel industry. The Court also found that competition in the common products of the two firms probably would be lessened by the merger. It concluded, therefore, that there was a reasonable probability that the merger would lessen competition and tend to create a monopoly in violation of the law. Consequently, in a 4 to 3 decision, with two members abstaining, the Court forbade the proposed merger. The companies did not appeal and dropped their plans to merge. Subsequently, both companies expanded their production facilities in the Chicago market area, including a large new plant erected by Bethlehem Steel Corporation at Burns Harbor, Indiana.

In a second major case, the Supreme Court, in a unanimous decision, declared a merger involving a much smaller market share to be unlawful. The Brown Shoe Company, which produced 4 percent of the nation's shoes, acquired the Kinney Shoe Company, which produced 0.5 percent of the nation's shoe supply. Brown was also the third largest shoe retailer, with more than twelve hundred outlets, Kinney was the eighth largest retailer, with 350 stores. The Court expressed concern about growing concentration in the shoe industry and the possibility that Brown could prevent its competition from distributing shoes through Kinney retail stores. The court declared the merger to be anticompetitive and ordered it dissolved.[25]

For like reasons, the Court ordered divestiture in a case involving ALCOA. The producer of nearly 30 percent of the nation's aluminum conductors, ALCOA had acquired Rome Cable Company, which produced 1.3 percent of the market output. Nevertheless, the Court held that Rome Cable Company, although a small producer, was an aggressive competitor, a pioneer in the field with special aptitudes and skills, and that its competitive potential should be preserved.

In these and several other cases that the government has won since the enactment of the Celler-Kefauver Act, the courts have not, by design, established any set criterion for deciding quantitatively what market share constitutes a monopoly or even a restraint of trade. In the Paramount case, Justice Learned Hand suggested that a 90 percent share constituted a monopoly, that a 33 percent share did not, and that 64 percent may or may not. But this suggestion has not been followed. In fact, in many cases the courts have refused to quantify specific percentages.

Even if the market share question were decided, a second question remains. What constitutes a market? Is structural steel a market by itself, or is it part of all steel output combined? Do aluminum conductors or aluminum and copper conductors make up the market? Is it only cellophane or all packaging material that makes up a market? Is it rugs or all types of floor covering? Is the sport-shoe market different from the dress-shoe market?

Questions about market share, composition of the market, and the like are frequently decided on an individual basis, with each case judged by the court on its own merits. Consequently, it is not easy for the average business executive, or even the economist, to ascertain what is and what is not going to be a violation of the law. If a major company, with all its expert legal talent, frequently runs afoul of the law, it is easy to realize that decision-making in the entire area of antitrust can be perplexing to the middle- or small-sized firm.

WEBB-POMERENE ACT (1918)

The antitrust laws, particularly the Sherman Act, the Clayton Act, and the FTC Act, applied to foreign commerce as well as to domestic interstate commerce. This, of course, made international operations

---

[25] *Brown Shoe Co.* v. *United States*, 1962.

more difficult for many United States firms competing with foreign cartels. In many foreign nations, cartelization — which uses price fixing, marketing quotas, and pooling arrangements — is legal. Any United States firm entering into such an organization or using similar tactics would be in violation of the antitrust laws.

In order to help United States firms compete more effectively and readily in foreign markets Congress in 1918 passed the Webb-Pomerene Act. According to the act, nothing in the antitrust laws is to be construed as declaring illegal "an association entered into for the sole purpose of engaging in export trade and actually engaged solely in such export trade, or an agreement made or act done in the course of export trade by such association, provided such association, agreement, or act is not in restraint of trade within the United States and is not in restraint of the export trade of any domestic competitor of such association." The act is clear on this latter point, stating further that the act does not permit firms to "enter into any agreement, understanding, or conspiracy or do any act which artificially or intentionally enhances or depresses prices within the United States . . . or substantially lessens competition within the United States or otherwise restrains trade therein."

According to the preamble of the Webb-Pomerene Act, its purpose is to promote export trade. The act legalizes the formation of combinations for engaging in foreign sales. It permits the use of cartel tactics, such as price fixing, pooling, and market quotas to promote sales. The FTC and the courts have vacillated on whether the act permits United States firms to join foreign cartels. Only a limited number of combinations, perhaps not many more than fifty, have been formed under the act. There have been some findings and court orders against some whose actions affected the United States domestic market. Although the Webb-Pomerene Act was intended to help American businesses, especially small firms, engage in export trade and compete successfully with foreign cartels, it has been large companies, rather than small companies, that have used its provisions. In some cases, United States firms merely became participants in European cartels.

OVERT AND INADVERTENT VIOLATIONS

In some cases it appears obvious that there was an attempt to evade or defy the law. Such was the evidence in the Electrical Price Conspiracy case of the late 1950s and early 1960s. In that case, the court found guilty and fined 29 manufacturers of electrical equipment $1,787,000. In addition, several executives were fined. About 30 of them were sentenced to prison for their parts in the conspiracy, but most of the sentences were suspended because of age, health, or other mitigating circumstances.

The companies and the executives' fixing the prices of electrical equipment included predetermined rigging of sealed bids on the sale of equipment to the government. Ample evidence was uncovered, in the form of letters, phone calls, code numbers, and secret meetings, that proved that the executives were or should have been aware that what they were doing was in violation of the law. The industry leaders, including General Electric, Westinghouse, Allis-Chalmers, Federal Pacific, and I-T-E Circuit Breaker Company, were heavily fined.

In addition to criminal-conspiracy convictions, the companies were also charged in civil suits. Most of these were settled out of court with consent decrees. This put the government in a position to obtain immediate injunctions against any of the companies that might subsequently fail to comply with the cease and desist orders. As a result of the government suits, nearly 2,000 private suits for triple damages were filed by various companies, particularly utilities, that had purchased equipment from the guilty companies. The companies paid dearly to settle these suits. General Electric Company, for example, paid out $225 million; Westinghouse, $110 million; and Allis-Chalmers, $45 million.

In many recent cases, too, evidence of overt violations of the antitrust laws have been found. These include price fixing, bid-rigging, and contract allocation in the sale of reinforcing bars in the Texas market by major firms in the steel industry; the setting of prices and discount rates for plastic fittings for drainage pipe by five leading producers; and price fixing of women's apparel over a five-year period by prestigious New York stores. More recently (1976), four steel executives were fined for conspiring to fix prices of steel in the Florida market.

On the other hand, in many cases, the companies or individuals involved do not know, or do not believe, that their actions are in violation of the law. In the case of motorcycle distributors in the Los Angeles area, for example, their association even published and distributed minutes of the motions and votes of members to keep prices high and crack down on reluctant distributors. In another case, a leading meat wholesaler publicly stated at a trade association meeting what price he expected to get for hamburger. This provided evidence that resulted in fines against him and the other company executives who followed his price. Yet the Court found no evidence of collusion, for example, in the government's case against the Big Three auto producers charged with attempting to fix prices in establishing the sale prices for fleets of autos. Papercraft is disputing the FTC charge that Papercraft's acquisition of another company, giving Papercraft a 22 percent share of the gift wrapping and ribbon industry, was a violation of the Clayton Act. Fruehauf (a truck-trailer manufacturer) is vigorously challenging an FTC charge that Fruehauf's merger with Kelsy-Hayes (a truck- and auto-parts manufacturer), one of its suppliers, is a violation of the Clayton Act. The court refused to force General Dynamics to divest itself of United Electric Coal Co., as ordered by the Antitrust Division of the Department of Justice. General Motors is contending that its present distribution of crash parts (fenders, grills, etc.) is not restraining trade, as charged by the government.

In 1976, the appeals court ruled that Dunkin' Donuts, Inc., did not violate federal antitrust laws by encouraging its franchise holders to buy equipment, signs, real estate, and supplies that it sold. But Sears, Roebuck and Company gave up its fight and was seeking to settle an FTC charge that Sears used "bait and switch" tactics to sell sewing machines and other household appliances.

In addition to the current charges against General Motors for its part distribution and Fruehauf regarding its merger actions, at present numerous suits, charges, and appeals are pending against alleged violators of the antitrust laws. The Justice Department, for example, is charging in two separate suits that the nation's two largest tire producers, Firestone and Goodyear, are independently attempting to monopolize the replacement-tire market. The Federal Trade Commission is charging Hertz, Avis, and National of controlling 96 percent of the airport car rental service and forcing customers to pay artificially high rates. The FTC has charged the companies with fixing prices, conspiring against and harassing competitors and making deals with the Big Three auto producers for advertising payoffs. In another case, the Justice Department has charged six major manufacturers of gypsum board with price fixing. A federal grand jury in 1976 indicated 23 manufacturers of cardboard cartons for conspiring during 14 years to fix prices. A&P, the large grocery chain, is currently appealing a $32.7 million triple-damage verdict awarded to six cattlemen. The four leading breakfast-cereal producers, who account for 90 percent of market share, are being charged by the FTC with a number of unfair methods of competition. Xerox, which controlled 85 percent of the plain-paper-copier market, in 1975 accepted a consent decree, requiring it, among other things, to license its competitors to use more than twelve hundred of Xerox's current patents plus some future patents, and further limited Xerox's rights to obtain patents from its competitors.

In 1977, the H.J. Heinz Company filed a $105 million damage suit against the Campbell Soup Company for alleged violations of the antitrust laws in the manufacture and domestic sale of soups. Heinz claimed that Campbell used predatory pricing practices that foreclosed or lessened competition. Five oil companies and a trade association were convicted of conspiring to fix retail gasoline prices between 1967 and 1974 in six mid-Atlantic states. In addition, four resin manufacturers were charged with price fixing between 1971 and 1974. Four major firms pleaded no contest to fixing cane sugar prices in 1972 and 1973.

Besides these and other pending actions, Congress, the Justice Department, and the Federal Trade Commission are currently preparing large-scale actions against the Big Three automobile manufacturers, AT&T, and the major oil companies. In regard to the automobile industry, it is proposed, among other measures, that General Motors Corporation divest itself of its Chevrolet Division, the largest and perhaps most profitable segment of the company, as a means of improving competition in the industry. To improve competition in the telephone industry, it is proposed that AT&T divest itself of Western Electric Company, AT&T's manufacturing unit, and divest itself also of all or part of its Long-Lines Division, which handles long-distance calls.

With respect to the major oil companies, a Senate Antitrust Subcommittee has recommended a bill that would break up the giants of the industry. The functions of the petroleum industry would be divided into three categories: crude oil production, refining and selling, and pipeline transportation of oil. Many of the major companies, who now perform all three functions, would be required to divest themselves of one or two of their present functions. A company that chose to retain its crude oil production, for example, might not be permitted to retain its pipeline facilities. This proposal would require a huge divesture program to be supervised by the FTC. All eighteen major companies would be required to get rid of one or more of their current components.

Recently penalities have been increased, and the FTC and antitrust division of the Department of Justice have accelerated enforcement of the laws. In December 1974, a new antitrust law raised price fixing from a misdemeanor to a felony, increased the maximum fine against individuals from $50,000 to $100,000 and the maximum fine against corporations from $50,000 to $1,000,000. In addition, the maximum jail sentence for violating the law was raised from one to three years. In the past few years, the government has doubled the number of suits brought against businesses. For example, it now files about 20 price-fixing suits against individuals and companies annually, compared with about 10 suits annually a half-dozen years ago.

In a recent two-year period, the government filed more than 100 antitrust suits. The number of suits filed by injured parties is also rising. In the same two-year period, nearly 2,500 private suits were filed by individuals against alleged violators. This compares with less than 300 per year in the early 1960s.

Since price-fixing restrictions are easily violated, both purposely and inadvertently, top executives, middle managers, field managers, and salesmen should be properly warned that the following actions may constitute a violation of the law and result in stiff penalties:

1. Agreeing with competitors to maintain or raise prices.
2. Coordinating discounts or other conditions of sale.
3. Agreeing with competitors to rotate low bids on contracts to the government or other firms.
4. Discussing prices or other matters related to prices at trade-association meetings or other business or social gatherings.
5. Agreeing with competitors on production limitations or cutbacks to stabilize prices.
6. Arranging with competitors to issue new price lists on a common date.
7. Agreeing with competitors to establish maximum prices in the purchase of supplies.
8. Joining with competitors to purchase distressed supplies to prevent prices from declining.
9. Joining with others to force suppliers to boycott price-cutting competitors.
10. Lowering prices or conspiring with some competitors to lower prices for the purpose of destroying other competitors.

THE ROLE OF THE ECONOMIST IN ANTITRUST

Even though antitrust suits involve much technical knowledge about the economics of competition, supply and demand, price determination, elasticity, and the nature of oligopoly and monopoly, economists were not used in antitrust cases until 1945, when a modification in the rules of judicial procedure permitted judges to use economists as expert witnesses to analyze and interpret economic facts.

The antitrust division of the Department of Justice now has a staff of thirty economists, in addition to its three hundred lawyers, and the FTC has its own Bureau of Economics. Economists, too, are often called upon to testify at congressional hearings by many committees, such as the Senate Committee on Antitrust and Monopoly.

Today companies frequently use business economists in helping to prepare the defense for antitrust suits brought by the government and by others against the company. In many cases, company executives would do well to consult professional economists on pending actions with antitrust implications. Just as the government prefers preventive to remedial action in antitrust matters, so too, in the absence of an overt attempt to violate the antitrust laws, many inadvertent violations could be avoided by checking with well-informed persons before acting.

In this respect, it is well to remember that today a manager, executive, or company must be careful. It is possible to violate the antitrust laws in many ways, such as the following:

1. By entering into a contract, combination, or conspiracy in restraint of trade.
2. By monopolizing, attempting to monopolize, or combining or conspiring to monopolize trade.
3. By acquiring stock or assets of a competing corporation.
4. By entering into exclusive or tying contracts.
5. By discriminating in the matter of price among buyers, except to the extent of any cost savings involved.
6. By discriminating among buyers by giving special allowances, brokerage fees, quantity discounts, and otherwise, except where cost savings are involved.
7. As a buyer by inducing or knowingly receiving a discriminatory price advantage.
8. By serving as a director of competing corporations.
9. By using unfair methods of competition.
10. By employing unfair or deceptive advertising practices.
11. By engaging in collusive price bidding.
12. By agreeing with others to limit output or set prices.
13. By allocating territories.
14. By agreeing to pool profits.
15. By any other means that tend to lessen competition.

In the absence of specific legal advice, the business economist should be able to keep managers and executives fairly well informed about actions that might violate the antitrust laws. If the manager has no economist or legal adviser to turn to, he should be aware that engaging in any of the actions listed could constitute a violation of the law and that such actions can be costly to the manager or the firm.

PENDING ANTITRUST LEGISLATION

Antitrust law and its application are constantly changing. Besides variations in Justice Department and FTC enforcement procedures and changing court interpretation of current legislation, there is much discussion in Congress regarding amendments to antitrust law.

The mood of Congress seems to be for more enforcement of present law.

One bill, for example, would double the amounts available for antitrust enforcement over a three-year period. Another would overhaul antitrust laws and make the plea of no contest admissible as prima facie evidence of a violation in a triple-damage suit. In addition, this bill would allow any state attorney general to bring a civil antitrust damage suit against a company on behalf of citizens of his state. That is known as the *parens patriae* (parent of the state) concept, which was used in British common law to describe the king's power as guardian of the state and its people. The principle would be invoked primarily in price-fixing cases.

Still another Senate bill, the Hart Industrial Reorganization Bill (S.1959), would make it unlawful to possess monopoly power. It would also create an industrial-reorganization commission to prosecute violators before a special industrial reorganization court. The bill would presume the existence of monopoly power in instances in which there was no sign of price competition among two or more corporations in any line of commerce for a period of three consecutive years. or in which four or fewer firms accounted for 50 percent or more of the sales in any line of commerce in any year. The commission would be empowered to issue orders for the reorganization of corporations found to possess monopoly power in order to restore effective competition.

SUMMARY

On the premise that a high degree of competition is healthy for an economy, Congress in 1890 passed the Sherman Antitrust Act, which declared monopolies, trusts, conspiracies, and other restraints of trade to be illegal. The law provided that anyone monopolizing or attempting to monopolize or otherwise restrain trade, was guilty of a misdemeanor and subject to a fine of $5,000 and/or imprisonment not exceeding a length of one year. Today, the fine may be as high as $100,000 for individuals, $1 million for corporations, and imprisonment for up to three years. Charges of criminal conspiracy, charges in equity, and triple-damage suits may be filed against violators of the antitrust laws.

The provisions of the Sherman Act were subsequently clarified and expanded. The Clayton Act (1914), for example, prohibits specific violations, such as price discrimination, tying contracts, intercorporate stock acquisitions, and interlocking directors. The Federal Trade Commission Act (1914) spells out various forms of unfair methods of competition. The Robinson-Patman Act (1936) clarified the price-discrimination concept by declaring it illegal except to the extent of any savings in cost involved. The Miller-Tydings Act (1937) approved of resale price maintenance in states that had fair-trade laws. In effect, the act gave rise to the growth of state fair-trade laws. When the nonsigner clause of fair-trade laws was declared unconstitutional by the United States Supreme Court, Congress passed the Maguire Act (1952) to establish the legality of the nonsigner clause. It did not stem, however, the tide of the movement to repeal the fair-trade laws. The Antimerger Act (1952) expanded the prohibition of intercorporate stock acquisitions to cover intercorporate acquisition of assets. The Webb-Pomerene Act (1918), of course, gave United States firms engaged in foreign operations some relief from the antitrust laws.

The law is one thing. Interpretation of the law may be another. Consequently, there has been much litigation regarding the meaning and interpretation of the antitrust laws. The Standard Oil and the United States Tobacco cases in 1911, for example, gave us the "rule of reason." The United States Steel case (1911) and the International Harvester case (1927) stated that "mere size is not an offense" against the law. This principle was overturned, however, in the ALCOA case (1946) and the Paramount Pictures case (1948). The Supreme Court opinion in 1958 prohibiting the proposal merger of Bethlehem Steel and Youngstown Sheet and Tube reinforced the provisions of the Antimerger Act.

Many charges of restraint of trade, pratically price fixing, have been brought against United States business firms. Since enforcement is becoming more vigorous, fines more severe, and damage-suit awards higher in cost, managers need to exercise more caution regarding possible violations of the antitrust laws. Moreover, a number of bills introduced in Congress would provide for wider coverage and tougher enforcement of the antitrust laws.

QUESTIONS FOR ANALYSIS AND DISCUSSION

1. State the basic provisions of Sections 1 and 2 of the Sherman Antitrust Act (1890).
2. Explain what type of charges may be brought against alleged violators of the antitrust laws and what penalties may be levied against those convicted.
3. What is the rule of reason? Is it reasonable?
4. Is bigness per se a violation of the antitrust laws? Do you think that it should be?
5. State the major provisions of the Clayton Act (1914).
6. What is the function of the Federal Trade Commission?

7. How does the Robinson-Patman Act (1936) treat price discrimination? Why is it sometime referred to as the "anti-chainstore" act?

8. Is fair-trade pricing legal today? Explain its checkered history.

9. How did the Antimerger Act (Kefauver-Celler Act) of 1950 amend the Clayton Act?

10. Indicate some of the actions that may constitute price fixing.

11. What is the current status of the Hart Industrial Reorganization Bill (S.1959)? Do you think that it should be enacted?

12. Do you think that a conflict of national antitrust policy is involved in the Webb-Pomerene Act compared with other antitrust laws? Explain.

PROBLEMS AND CASES

1. Refer to the case of the Lightfoot Shoe Company, in the "Problems and Cases" section of Chapter 6. In light of the Robinson-Patman Act prohibition against price discrimination, how could the company possibly sell shoes to the discount store for $14 per pair, even if it were profitable to do so, when it was selling to its regular customers at a price of $18 per pair?

2. Assume that Congress is planning a review, evaluation, and possible revision of the Webb-Pomerene Trade Export Act. Since three divisions in your company engage in export trade, your company president and chief executive officer (CEO) is asked if he will appear as a witness at the congressional hearings on a proposed revision of the Webb-Pomerene Act. Two of the three divisions engaged in export sales are members of an export trade association. The CEO asks you, as an economist, to prepare a brief for him indicating the primary purpose of the Webb-Pomerene Act, its major provision(s), some of the pros and cons of the act, and if, for the good of the free-enterprise system, the act should be maintained, repealed, or amended. He informs you not to worry about the effect the provisions of the act may have on company profits. He is going to have the company treasurer prepare that statement.

3. The Robot Manufacturing Co. is engaged in difficult and lengthy bargaining sessions with the union. They are almost at a deadlock on the matter of a wage increase. During a late-afternoon coffee break, Joe Bellino, the chief union negotiator, takes Jim Smith, the head company negotiator, aside. In an off-the-record remark, he suggests that the company accede to the union's wage demand, and then use the wage increase as a reason for increasing prices. Bellino suggests that if the company were to do so, the union would throw its full support behind the need for a price increase. Smith agrees that it may be a good way to solve the bargaining deadlock, but expresses concern that discussing and planning a price increase under such circumstances could be construed as a violation of the Sherman Antitrust Act. Bellino assures him that the union is exempt from the antitrust laws under Section 6 of the Clayton Act. Without making any commitment, Smith says that he will consider the matter and respond to it the next day.

After the bargaining sessions are over for the day, Smith calls you, the company's economist, at home to discuss the proposal. Since he is not sure that he will be able to call you the next morning, he asks if you will leave a memo on the matter with his secretary by 10:00 A.M. He can then read your memo during the morning coffee break in the bargaining session. What would you advise Smith?

4. A group of hospital-administration students are discussing the high cost of medical service. One of them remarks that some doctors are making more than $100,000 per year administering to Medicare patients alone. Another states that many doctors charge what the traffic will bear, and that patients with higher incomes pay more for the same service than those with lower incomes. Another states that it is the other way around; the doctor reduces the fee for those who cannot afford the regular cost. Another student claims that such pricing is merely a way for doctors to justify service to many low-income families. In his opinion, it is a method of subsidizing low-income patients. A quotation from one leading physician is read stating his "fee structure bears a close resemblance to the government's progressive income tax."

Since you are an economics major, the students ask your viewpoint on the matter. Whatever else such a pricing structure may be, they ask, is it not a form of price discrimination? As such, is it not tantamount to a violation of the Robinson-Patman Act? Explain this aspect to the students.

5. As a junior economist in the economic-analysis department of a large retail chain, you are asked by Dr. Ian MacTavish, vice president and economist of the company, to attend the monthly sales meeting while he is out of town. At one of the sessions you learn that the company is going to engage in a large-scale promotion campaign to introduce a new vacuum sweeper in the fall. At the meeting, the sales manager informs the managers and salespersons of the appliance departments that there will be two models: a deluxe and a deluxe supreme. The deluxe model will sell for $69.95; the deluxe-supreme model for $99.50. He indicates further that in order to attract buyers only the deluxe sweeper will be advertised on radio, television, and in newspapers, at the price of $69.95. He emphasizes, however, that salespersons should not sell the deluxe model, but should push the deluxe-supreme model at $99.50. In fact, he states that deliveries to each store will be only 5 percent deluxe models, and that these are to be used primarily for display and and demonstration. He advises the salespersons that it is necessary to have a few deluxe models available to authenticate the sale price of $69.95 to be used in the advertising campaign. He explains that since there is a 50 percent mark-up on each model, more profit will be made by selling the deluxe supreme compared with selling the deluxe model, and that the sales target is 500,000 units combined.

Toward the end of the meeting, the sales manager politely asks you what you think about the marketing strategy involved. What would you comment?

(a) In doing so, calculate the gross profit that would be made if 475,000 deluxe-supreme units and 25,000 deluxe units were sold and the gross profit if 250,000 of each model were produced and sold.

(b) Is there any danger of economic loss in following the sales manager's marketing strategy?

A & S Auto Supply

A & S Auto Supply Distributors sold its products in a large Midwestern city and the surrounding area. Its customers were jobbers, garages, auto supply stores, and gas stations. One of its best-selling products was a line of gaskets called Everseal, manufactured by the Xemex Corporation. The brand name, Everseal, was in auto supplies as well known as Coke and Kleenex in their respective industries. Everseals were widely used in the auto-supply business, and few buyers would accept substitute gaskets. Xemex, which had a patent on Everseal, had early in 1963 given A & S an exclusive franchise to handle its products in its territory. With just cause either party could cancel the contract upon ninety days notice.

Everseal gaskets became one of the best-selling product lines for A & S. Forty-five percent of A & S customers bought Everseal gaskets. Some bought only gaskets, but most customers purchased other items as well. The total sales of Everseal gaskets and other supplies to these customers in 1973 accounted for about 40 percent of A & S's total sales, $2 million annually. Average markup on these products was 30 percent. Everseal gaskets accounted for 5 percent of A & S's total sales. Sixty percent of A & S's total sales were made to customers who bought no gaskets.

In the early 1970s, Xemex introduced a new line of auto supplies. One of the products in this new line was Plug-it, a radiator sealer, designed to eliminate leaks. Most of the other new products were designed for the teenage auto market. Plug-it was to be sold in direct competition with Stop-Leak, a well-known and established radiator sealer. As part of its exclusive franchise, A & S was required to carry the new Xemex product line. A & S, however, experienced difficulty selling the new line of products. They attributed this in large part to the minimal advertising allowance for the new line and to the larger discount that Xemex's competitors gave their customers for carrying their products.

In mid-1973, Xemex canceled its franchise arrangement with A & S Auto Supply Distributors because of the poor sales performance on the new line of products. Although A & S had sufficient inventory of Everseal gaskets to last through the remainder of 1973, it finally had to stop selling Everseal gaskets in 1974 because of stock depletion. It had, however, before the end of 1973 received a large order on another line of gaskets. Sale of these new gaskets in 1974 was disappointing, and total sales of A & S merchandise dropped by 20 percent in 1974 compared with those of 1973. A & S concluded that it was losing sales because it no longer had Everseal gaskets to sell. Not only was there a loss of sales to those who bought only gaskets from A & S, but there was a loss of sales of other items by those who bought both gaskets and other items. A & S concluded that many customers who purchased Everseal gaskets and other items from A & S had ceased buying from A & S because Everseal gaskets were no longer available. In fact, A & S was able to produce a list of such customers that showed that sales of non-gasket items to its former gasket customers fell to $324,000 in 1974.

In 1974, gaskets made up only 1 percent of A & S total sales. In addition, A & S observed that sales to those customers not ordering gaskets increased by 5 percent during the year.

Early in 1975, A & S placed an order with Xemex for Everseal gaskets.

Xemex refused delivery on the ground that it had given the exclusive franchise to another firm. When sales continued at low levels during 1975, A & S decided to bring a triple-damage suit against Xemex for restraint of trade.

The lawyer for A & S, who is a friend of yours, asked your aid in determining the total damages (loss of profit) resulting from the cancellation of the contract. He asked you to draw up a report on the damages and to serve as an expert witness regarding the damages in the event that the suit went to trial. What will your report and testimony consist of?

Consent Decree

In 1975, the Justice Department filed a proposed consent decree to settle a civil antitrust suit for price fixing brought against eight major manufacturers of paper labels. The consent decree would prohibit the eight companies from fixing prices or other conditions of sale of paper labels, allocating markets, and sharing price and related information with one another. In addition, all the companies would be required for ten years to send annual reports to the court and to the Justice Department describing steps taken to comply with the decree. Some of the companies would be required to send an official to the court to provide sworn testimony about their compliance.

Earlier, some of these companies, along with company officers, were charged with criminal conspiracy for price fixing. In a no-contest plea, the companies and their officers were fined a total of $282,500. In addition, several company officials were sentenced to deliver speeches before civic and business organizations once a month telling of their experience and what they had learned from the price-fixing case. The speechmaking was a condition of probation for the company officers, who received suspended sentences.

(a) What do you think of the speechmaking idea as a penalty for violating the antitrust laws?

(b) As an economist for one of the companies involved, you are asked by one of those sentenced, your vice president, to help him prepare the speech he must make in order to comply with his sentence. He suggests that if you give him two or three double-spaced typewritten pages on the evils of price fixing and what he should have learned from his experience, he will use that as the core of his speech and embellish it with related data. Write the paper for him.

FTC Charges General Motors with Parts Monopoly

In March 1976, the Federal Trade Commission charged the General Motors Corporation with monopoly control of crash replacement parts for its automobiles. It alleged that the GM practice was costly to the public and to independent repair shops. Crash parts include items such as fenders, doors, bumpers, and grills. The director of the FTC Bureau of Competition stated that General Motors "has intentionally maintained a monopoly and monopoly power over the distribution of crash parts." He indicated that GM sold crash parts exclusively through its twelve thousand franchise dealers. Many of these dealers sold the parts at wholesale as well as installed the parts. Moreover, the approximately thirty thousand independent body-repair shops were forced to purchase parts from franchised dealers, often at prices marked up from what the dealer paid for them.

The proposed FTC order required GM to make parts directly available to all dealers, body shops, and independent wholesalers at the same price, terms, and conditions of sale — subject to reasonable, cost-justified quantity discounts and stocking allowances.

The FTC order was based on three separate studies on auto parts over the past ten years. It also came shortly after a Senate commerce subcommittee hearing on the matter. Testimony at the hearings indicated that the prices of crash parts had risen at a substantially faster rate than the Consumer Price Index. An insurance executive, for example, testified that the price of crash parts increased 64 percent from January 1, 1974, to the spring of 1976. Some witnesses suggested that the cost of parts had been raised to help offset the decline in new car sales associated with the recession of 1974–75. At the hearing, the Big Three auto representatives denied such allegations and insisted that the increases were due to higher costs of raw materials, production, packaging, and transportation.

At the hearings it was further brought out by the director of the FTC Bureau of Economics that approximately 70 percent of crash-part expenses were covered through automobile insurance.

In its charge, the FTC stated that "General Motors has a primary responsibility to the people who buy its cars to have crash parts available when needed." In response to that statement, Thomas R. Murphy, Chairman of the Board of General Motors Corporation, claimed that "the present system of distribution does that faster, at lower cost to the consumer and more efficiently than any other system we know. We are convinced that the current distribution system does not violate any law and we intend to defend it vigorously." He further stated that "the action which the FTC has instituted to force modification of General Motors' current distribution system is ill-advised because it would neither improve the availability of 'crash parts' nor lower their cost to consumers. In fact, it would probably have the reverse effect."

(a) From the information cited, determine which antitrust laws seem to have been violated.

(b) Since both the Ford Motor Company and Chrysler Corporation have similar parts-distribution systems, how would an adverse decision on General Motors affect them?

(c) If you were an economist for General Motors, how would you attempt to defend the existing parts-distribution system?

(d) If GM appealed the order and lost the court decision, how would you propose that GM comply with the order?

Toward Economic Freedom — A Plan for
Coping with Bigness*

Industrial power. Now let us turn to the concentration of industrial power. One of the factors that prevents needed action is the public misconceptions about the advantages of colossal size in industry. Actually, there is some basis for union and public opinion that colossal industrial power justifies colossal union power. I believe our antitrust laws, which were enacted in the early stages of our industrial development, need to be modernized and strengthened to cope with new problems created by excess industrial power.

This need is illustrated by federal subsidization to create and maintain adequate competition. During and after World War II, the government finally broke the monopolistic position of the Aluminum Company of America by using indirect government subsidization to establish four additional aluminum companies. In the case of the automobile industry, the President of the United States, about three years ago, directed the use of Defense Department procurement powers to indirectly subsidize the continuation of one of the five remaining passenger car companies.

Now, the competitive principle enables consumers to reward companies that successfully meet their preferences and to reject companies that fail to do so. Elimination, or economic death, *is* and *should be* the penalty of economic failure in a competitive society. It keeps our economy healthy and responsive to consumers' desires and needs. However, in most of our basic industries, the competitive discipline of the market place has now reduced the number of companies to a mere handful. In the case of the automobile industry, in my opinion, the five passenger-car companies left barely constitute the minimum number necessary for adequate consumer choice and discipline.

How can we continue to have the benefit of at least five competing passenger-car companies? I think there are only these alternatives:

1. The ability of each of the remaining companies to permanently escape economic failure. In light of earlier competitive history, this would appear impossible.

2. The restraint of competitive effort to permit the survival of weaker competitors. To the extent that this practice exists, it deprives our nation and individual consumers of the benefits of genuine competitive effort, and may lose for us the struggle for international leadership. We cannot afford competitive slowdowns.

3. Government action to subsidize weak competitors. As far as I am

*From an address given by George Romney at the 13th Annual School of Business Alumni Conference, Indiana University, on March 20, 1959, and adapted for printing in *Business Horizons*, Vol. 2, No. 2 (Summer, 1959), pp. 21–28, Graduate School of Business, Indiana University. (Mr. Romney was formerly Chairman and President of the American Motors Corporation, and is a former Secretary of Housing and Urban Development.) Copyright, 1959, by the Foundation for the School of Business at Indiana University. Reprinted with permission.

concerned, this approach is unthinkable as a matter of national policy. It leads to statism.

4. Some form of government regulation. This approach would either involve arbitrary government action to preserve marginal or sub-standard producers or would lead to industrial concentration and monopoly. It, too, is statism.

5. Provision for economic birth as well as economic death. I believe preservation of the competitive principle in America depends on provision for economic birth as well as economic death in our major basic industries.

Before the Kefauver committee last year, I made these specific recom-mendations for economic birth based on the degree of market domination in such industries: When an individual company engaged in only one basic industry is doing more than 35 percent of the business, or, when a com-pany engaged in more than one basic industry is doing more than 25 per-cent of the business, this company should be required to submit to a specified public agency its own program for reducing its percentage of the particular business involved. An obvious way to do this would be through the creation of more than one company from the old company — in other words, by the process of division, or economic birth. Adherence to such percentage figures guarantees only the future existence of four or five companies in each basic industry. It does not require the breaking up of General Motors, or any other company, into more than two companies.

This proposal would reward, not penalize, a company like General Motors for being successful. It would give us the advantage of two com-panies with the potential competence of General Motors, instead of one. It is the only way such an enterprise can grow without restraint or limit in a free competitive economy.

When a company acquires a large share of control over a basic industry, it begins to fear the shadow of adverse government action. It must neces-sarily begin to restrain itself, to hobble its skill. We need all of the com-petitive skill we can get. We must seek to increase it, not restrain it.

My proposal is not made for the purpose of reducing General Motors' competitive strength. I do not make it because it would reduce competi-tion for American Motors. Actually, it would *increase* competition. My proposal is made with the national need in mind, not American Motors' needs. It would not deprive customers of the benefits of mass production efficiency in the automobile or other industries. Experience shows that the optimum efficiency volume is well below 25 or 35 percent of the industry.

A point of grave national concern is that the championship level of General Motors' profits has become the focal point of the UAW's collec-tive bargaining demands against the entire industry. The auto union has used General Motors' greater ability to pay to convince the public that the union's demands can be met by General Motors without serious financial difficulty. General Motors' settlements are then used as an industry pat-tern. A key question raised by the UAW collective bargaining strategy is "Are General Motors' profits too high?" This question must be answered to the satisfaction of the American public.

I think that, to find the true answer, people need to know this fact: Un-less we are willing to substitute some other means of disciplining our econ-omy for the principle of competition — and the only other means I know of involves absolute authority of either a public or private character—then the question of whether a particular company is making too much money depends on whether that company has adequate competition. If the company is earning the money in the face of an adequate number of competent competitors, then its profit becomes a measure of its efficiency and ability and a reward for its contribution.

Now what is the situation in this respect in the automobile industry? Mr. Yntema* spelled out with great clarity before the Kefauver committee a year ago the fact that no automobile company other than General Motors has sufficient financial strength to be reasonably certain of continuity.

Citizens and consumers must be satisfied that profits being earned by a company are achieved in competition with an adequate number of competent competitors. Unless they are satisfied, those now attacking our economy may well be able to persuade the people that the government should intervene in some manner that will seriously impair the functioning of our competitive system. In this dangerous age, America cannot afford to have highly efficient companies restraining their competitive efforts to avoid government action. Nor can the nation permit giant unions to continue to use the profits of General Motors or the steel industry as a target for uneconomic wage demands, which result in costly concessions that become the basis for pattern bargaining demands across American industry.

My proposal for economic birth has as its objective the further development of competition in this country. If we are to fulfill our economic goals, realize our Space-Age potentials, and meet the challenge of communism, we need to encourage the power of creative individuals and organizations—not smother that power by forcing them to conform to the dictates of unions and business concentrations that exercise an excessive degree of control. It is important to emphasize that the problem is not one of *size* or *bigness*. Bigness per se is not necessarily bad. Indeed, bigness is essential in a modern industrial economy. Under my proposal, a company would be as large as the nature of the industry required for efficient, competitive operation, and no arbitrary fixed limit is suggested. The problem is the degree of control over a major economic, social, and political segment.

Adoption of a birth policy would, I believe, again unleash the principal factors of industrial growth without enactment of new laws but simply modernization of the old. Paving the way for the elimination of the conflict in our national economic policy—for conflict between the competitive policy of the antitrust laws and the monopolistic policy of the labor laws—would result in the organization of employer and union responsibilities on common economic principles of mutual interest and would end the economic conflict based on class warfare throughout American industry.

Finally, it would reduce the threat of government regulation and, by a more adequate division and dispersion of private power, decrease the justification for excessive concentration of federal power.

(a) Evaluate Mr. Romney's concept of "economic birth."
(b) Relate the concept of economic birth to the Supreme Court decision in the United Fruit Case of 1958, in which the company agreed to set up a competitive firm to take over about 35 percent of its banana-import business.

*A vice president of the Ford Motor Company.

(c) Do you see any similarities between Mr. Romney's concept of economic birth and the Hart Industrial Reorganization Bill?

(d) What similar major problems do you see in both the Romney and the Hart proposals?

SELECTED READINGS

Adams, Walter. *The Structure of American Industry*. New York: Macmillan Publishing Co., Inc., 1971.

American Enterprise Institute for Public Policy Research. *Antitrust — Paren Patriae Bill. Legislative Analysis* No. 7, 1975.

Blair, John M. *Economic Concentration: Structure, Behavior, and Public Policy*. New York: Harcourt Brace Jovanovich, Inc., 1972.

Demsetz, Harold. *The Market Concentration Doctrine*. American Enterprise Institute for Public Policy. *Policy Study* 7, August 1973.

Fusilier, H. Lee, and Jerome C. Darnell. *Competition and Public Policy: Cases in Antitrust*. Englewood Cliffs, N.J.: Prentice-Hall, Inc., 1971.

Galbraith, J. Kenneth. *The New Industrial State*. Boston: Houghton Mifflin Company, 1967.

———. *Economics and the Public Purpose*. Boston: Houghton Mifflin Company, 1973.

"Is John Sherman's Antitrust Obsolete?" *Business Week*, March 23, 1974.

Jacoby, Neil H. *Corporate Power and Social Responsibility*. New York: Macmillan Publishing Co., Inc., 1973.

"Price Fixing Crackdown under Way." *Business Week*, June 2, 1975.

Scherer, F.M. *Industrial Market Structure and Economic Performance*. Chicago: Rand McNally & Company, 1970.

Weiss, Leonard W. *Case Studies in American Industry*. New York: John Wiley & Sons, Inc., 1971.

12

Capital Expenditure Analysis

Perhaps the biggest single step a business firm must take is the decision to buy or not to buy additional plant and equipment. Very few decisions tend to fix so irrevocably the course of a firm's future. Capital budgeting procedures typically result in long-term commitment of large amounts of funds. Moreover, the level and effectiveness of capital expenditures strongly affect the direction, rate of growth, and profitability of a business enterprise. Hence, obviously capital expenditure decisions are among the most important tasks performed by the firm's managers.

CAPITAL EXPENDITURE DEFINED

What are capital expenditures? They might include such items as acquisitions of capital assets, major repairs and improvements, replacements of existing equipment, as well as important outlays that are ordinarily listed as expenses by accountants (such as costs of training programs, advertising campaigns, and research programs). How does a capital expenditure differ from an operating expenditure? One important distinction between them is the length of time required to realize returns from the expenditures. With most operating expenditures, such as labor and material costs, it is hoped that cash benefits will be forthcoming within a few months, or at least during a normal accounting period. The returns to be realized from capital expenditures, however, are expected to be received over a period of years. Because of this highly important factor of time, it follows that making decisions about capital expenditure involves much more uncertainty and forecasting judgment than making decisions about current or operating expenditures. As a result, budgeting for capital investments and net cash flows involves basically different general principles and procedures than those used in budgeting for operating expenditures and income.

This chapter will discuss decision making about capital expenditure and related problems. We will turn our attention to the ways in which firms rank potential capital expenditures and the methods used to arrive at accept-reject decisions for these investments. Chapter 13 concentrates on financing capital expenditures and calculating the cost of capital.

THE CAPITAL BUDGETING PROCESS

A business manager is assumed to have available at a given time a number of alternative investment possibilities or projects. The act of investment, in turn, opens up the possibility of a flow of cash benefits, in the form of decreased cost or increased income, resulting from the use of the assets.

The capital budgeting process is an analytical approach that has as its purpose an indication of the value each investment proposal might contribute to the net present worth of the firm. The analytical problem is how to find a logical framework for comparing a number of investment proposals — all likely to differ in dollar amount and in timing — in order to select the more desirable ones from the financial point of view.

As our discussion of the capital budgeting process develops, we shall see that the basic quantities we are trying to measure and compare are two flows of cash. If new equipment is needed to replace outdated machinery, for example, there must be estimates of the costs involved to buy and to put the equipment into production, as well as estimates of the incremental cash inflows resulting from the manufacture and sale of the units of output. Thus, the first step in the capital budgeting process is the projection of the dollar amounts of the cash outflows and inflows related to a proposed project, together with the time dimension of each flow. The outflow of cash we will term *net cash investment*; the inflow will be called *net cash benefits*.

First, each of these flows will be discussed. Then, since cash outflows are apt to occur at different points in time than cash inflows, we will consider another important matter — the time value of money. This is the underlying concept involved in the capital budgeting process, since it enables us to relate cash outflows and inflows that occur at different times to a common point of reference. Once we have developed an understanding of the foregoing elements of a typical cash-flow analysis, we shall have accumulated the relevant factors necessary to permit us to move into an examination of the various methods of evaluating proposed capital expenditures.

Net Cash Investment

The problem of deciding which factors should be considered in calculating net cash investment is not always easy to solve. The firm should, however, use a net cash investment that is based to a substantial degree on its own unique situation, rather than on broad generalizations. Nevertheless, the following list, although not intended to be all-inclusive, illustrates some basic factors to consider in the calculation of net cash investment.

1. For purposes of capital budgeting decisional analysis, accounting costs are usually a starting point when computing net cash investment. The costs of acquiring assets, such as invoice price, freight charges, and installation costs, are examples of normal accounting outlays. A true economic evaluation of a proposed capital expenditure, however, demands that we add to or subtract from this accounting cost various ingredients, such as those that follow.

2. Permanent increases in working capital, resulting from implementation of the proposal, should be added to accounting costs.

3. Nonacquisitive outlays, directly related to the capital expenditure, should be included as investment cost. Research, development, advertising, and trial-run expenses are examples of items included in this category.

4. Capital expenditures or repair costs for old machinery, which can be avoided by the purchase of replacements, should be deducted from the outlay for the new machinery.

5. In proposals for replacements, the salvage value of the old machinery should be considered. The salvage value of the old machinery minus the costs of removal and disposal, should be deducted from the new investment. Moreover, the salvage value should be adjusted for the tax effect. In many situations, the costs of removal and disposal could exceed the revenue obtained from the sale of the machinery. This negative figure, of course, would be added to the investment cost of the new machinery. If the replaced machinery is used in another capacity within the firm and this eliminates the need to purchase similar assets, its value as a substitute should be used to reduce the investment cost of the new machinery.

Should the accounting *book value* of an asset to be replaced by new equipment be considered when determining net cash investment or net cash benefits? That is, should this unrecovered *sunk cost* of the replaced machinery be added to the cost of the new machinery? The answer is clear. Money previously expended for existing fixed assets is not altered by current or proposed decisions regarding the disposition of existing assets. Past history is just that. Consequently, the net cash investment for a proposed capital expenditure is in no way affected by a prior investment and its current book value. For the reasons just stated, there is no practical justification for considering the unrecovered cost an incremental outflow on existing assets when determining net cash inflows on new assets. The consequences of erroneously considering sunk cost of the replaced asset when calculating net cash investment of the new asset can be costly. Gains from profitable new assets might be lost, for example, simply because the assets to be replaced have a large accounting-book value.

Thus, the incorrect approach could lead to the accumulation of obsolete, inefficient fixed assets.

The simplest net cash investment to illustrate is that of a proposal to buy new equipment. Assume that a new machine may be purchased at an invoice price of $17,500. Freight charges are $800 and it will cost $1,700 to install the machine. It is estimated that $2,500 additional cash must be invested in inventory and accounts receivables each year if the new machine is used. Training employees to operate the new machine will require an additional outlay of $700. Since the training costs are expensed, they are tax deductible. If the tax rate is 48 percent, the net cash investment is calculated as follows:

Example 1

Invoice price		$17,500
Freight charges		800
Installation cost		1,700
Basis for depreciation		$20,000
Cash invested in inventory and accounts receivable		2,500
Training expense	$700	
Less: taxes (48%)	336	
After tax training expense		364
Net cash investment		$22,864

Now, assume that in addition to the facts set forth in Example 1, the new machine is to be acquired to replace an obsolete machine, and that purchase of the new machine necessitates the sale of the old machine. Assume, further, that the old machine has an accounting-book value of $7,000, but can be sold to a used equipment dealer for $5,000. This means that the firm would suffer a $2,000 loss on the sale of the old machine. Because of current tax laws, however, the $2,000 loss provides a tax benefit for the company. For simplicity we shall assume that the savings in taxes will be 30 percent of the capital loss, or $600 ($2,000 × .30 = $600). Thus, the net cash investment is adjusted as follows:

Example 2

Net cash investment (first example)		$22,864
Proceeds from sale of old machine	$5,000	
Tax benefit on $2000 loss	600	
Proceeds plus tax benefit		5,600
Net cash investment		$17,264

Again let us keep the same initial facts as in our first example, but change the assumptions added in the second example. Assume now that, instead of selling the old machine for a loss, we can dispose of it to a dealer for $10,000. Since the book value of the old machine was $7,000, we are faced with a gain of $3,000 and, thus, a tax disadvantage. If we find that the tax rate on the sale is 30 percent, our tax disadvantage will be $900 ($3,000 × .30 = $900). Our net cash investment under these conditions would be $13,764.

Example 3		
Net cash investment (first example)		$22,864
Proceeds from sale of old machine	$10,000	
Tax disadvantage on $3000 gain	900	
After tax proceeds		9,100
Net cash investment		$13,764

Net Cash Benefits

The second flow of cash involved in making decisions on capital expenditure is the net of incremental inflows minus incremental outflows. If we buy new equipment, we can expect a change in the operating cash flows — both inflows and outflows — which are in addition to outflow for net cash investment. Our concern is the net change in these operating flows, and our objective is to estimate a net cash benefit for each time period beyond the time of the initial outlay for the investment.

Perhaps revenues will be increased by additional sales resulting from the expansion of output when one uses a new machine. Various costs, on the other hand, might be increased or decreased if the new machine is put into operation. We might estimate that material and direct labor costs will decline significantly, but advertising and selling expenses might increase outlays. Incremental increases and decreases in these and other inflows and outflows of cash will, of course, vary from firm to firm. In any case, an economist's concern is with the differential cash flows, over time, that should result from the purchase and use of the new equipment. Inasmuch as we are calculating a *cash flow*, however, depreciation or any other item that does not involve a current payment of cash is not subtracted from revenue in determining our totals.

Assume that the Hayes Corporation, for example, plans to purchase a new machine to replace an obsolete one. After careful study, the firm estimates that upon installation of the new machine it can increase first-year revenue from sales by $10,000. Moreover, various costs, such as direct labor, indirect labor, and overhead, can be reduced by $5,000 during the initial year of operation. Hence, incremental benefits for the first year add up to $15,000. The invoice price of the new machine is $13,000, freight charges total $500, and $1,500 must be expended for installation of the new machine. Thus, the net cash investment and the basis for depreciation is $15,000. If the firm uses straight-line depreciation and the estimated economic life of the machine is three years, annual depreciation is $5,000 ($15,000 ÷ 3 years). The firm's records show that the old machine has a book value of $6,000 and is depreciated on a straight-line basis of $2,000 for the next three years. Incremental benefits for years two and three are assumed to be $11,000 and $7,000.

The following approach may be used to compute net cash benefits after taxes:

	Year 1	Year 2	Year 3
Incremental benefits (changes in revenues less net changes in operating costs)	$15,000	$11,000	$7,000
Depreciation New machine $5,000 Old machine 2,000	3,000	3,000	3,000
Earnings before taxes	$12,000	$ 8,000	$4,000
Income taxes (50%)	6,000	4,000	2,000
Earnings after taxes	$ 6,000	$ 4,000	$2,000
Net cash benefits after taxes	$ 9,000	$ 7,000	$5,000

As indicated in the accompanying table, the net cash benefits after taxes to be derived from the use of the new machine are $9,000, $7,000, and $5,000 for the three-year economic life of the equipment. Notice that both income taxes and depreciation must be considered when calculating annual net cash benefits. Even if we do not purchase a new machine, the old machine may be depreciated for three more years, or $2,000 per year. The new machine is to be depreciated on a straight-line basis of $5,000 annually for three consecutive years. Since we must consider increments, our concern with depreciation is the net difference between the old and new depreciation, or $3,000 per year. Once we have determined the net annual depreciation of $3,000, the first-year incremental benefit of $15,000 is reduced to taxable income of $12,000. For simplicity we assume a 50 percent tax rate to determine earnings after taxes of $6,000. The first year's annual net cash benefit after taxes ($9,000) is merely earnings before depreciation and taxes ($15,000) adjusted for the tax effect of $6,000. Net cash benefit after taxes may also be calculated by adding the net increase in depreciation ($3,000) and the earnings after taxes ($6,000). The foregoing approach is, of course used to compute the net cash benefits after taxes of $7,000 and $5,000 for the last two years of the machine's economic life.

In passing, we should note that if our example had included an assumed scrap value of the new machinery of, say, $2,000, this total would be subtracted from the $15,000 outlay for the new machinery, thus changing to $13,000 the accounting basis for computing each year's depreciation. Moreover, the $2,000 scrap value would be added to the last year's net cash benefit after taxes. Thus, in our example, the third year net cash benefit would total $7,000 instead of $5,000. Likewise, if our project tied up $1,000 in additional working capital during the life of the project, we would not only increase net cash investment by $1,000, but would return the released working capital at the end of the project's economic life of three years. Thus, the third-year benefit after taxes would be increased $1,000, owing to the return of the working capital. No tax effect would be involved in either of these two examples of increases in last-year benefits, since we are dealing with nontaxable items. Often a firm incurs a disposal cost to remove and haul away a machine at the end of its useful life. If we assume that the disposal of our new machine will require an outlay of $500, the last year's taxable income should be reduced by that amount before after-tax earnings (and thus net cash benefit after taxes) are computed.

Time Value of Money

Funds for capital expenditures are committed only in expectation of enchancing the value of the owners' equity in the firm; that is, it is hoped that future inflows resulting from an investment will exceed outflows. A key question is: How do we measure the value of these inflows and outflows of funds? Should the absolute total-dollar amount of $5,000 received as five consecutive yearly inflows of $1,000, for example, be compared with a net cash outflow of $2,000? The answer should be obvious. A prudent person places a higher value on a dollar received today than on a dollar received one year from today because the dollar received today can earn a return and thus be worth more than the dollar received one year hence. If, for example, an investment opportunity offered an annual return of 12 percent, a dollar invested today would be worth $1.12 at the end of one year. This can be put into a simple formula: If P is the principal or beginning amount, i is the interest rate, P_i, of course is the principal times the interest rate, and S_1 is the sum received at the end of one year, then

$$S_1 = P + P_i = P(1 + i)$$
(12-1)
$$= \$1.00 + \$1.00\,(.12) = \$1.00\,(\$1.12) = \$1.12$$

Similarly, if today's dollar is worth $1.12 a year from now, it must be worth even more two years hence. Thus if $1.12 is reinvested for a second year at the same rate of interest, compounded annually, the balance at the end of two years will be $1.25. The same result may of course be obtained as

$$S_2 = S_1 + iS_1$$

where S_2 is the value at the end of two years, iS_1 is the interest earned on S_1 during the second year. Substituting from Eq. (12-1) for S_1 we have

$$S_2 = P(1 + i) + iP(1 + i)$$

Factoring $P(1 + i)$ gives

$$S_2 = P(1 + i)\,(1 + i) = P(1 + i)^2$$
$$= \$1.00\,(\$1.12)\,(\$1.12) = \$1.25$$

If we continue the compounding process by reinvesting all the funds for n years at i rate of return, then

(12-2)
$$S_n = P(1 + i)^n$$

This, of course, is the compound interest formula.

Obviously, if we can invest $1 at a compound annual interest rate of 12 percent, the process can be turned around. Instead of calculating the ending value, an unknown beginning value of a known future value can be found by simply reversing the process and solving the compound interest formula for P. The amount of P is called the *present value* of a future amount of money. The rate that equates the beginning amount and the future or ending amount is the *dis-*

count rate. Using our previous example, we see that the $1.12 received at the end of one year has a present value of $1. This is obtained by solving the compound interest formula for P and letting P represent the present value of money. Thus,

$$P = \frac{S_1}{1 + i} = \frac{\$1.12}{1 + .12} = \$1.00$$

If $1.25 received two years hence is discounted back to the present at a rate of 12 percent, the beginning amount of $1 (rounded off) is calculated as

$$P = \frac{S_2}{(1 + i)^2} = \frac{\$1.25}{(1.12)\,(1.12)} = \$1.00$$

Similarly, the present value of an amount, S_n, received at the end of n years is found by

(12-3)
$$P = \frac{S_n}{(1 + i)^n}$$

where i is the discount rate and S_n is the amount to be received at the end of n years.

Assume that a series of identical cash benefits are received by a firm, e.g., $1 at the end of each year for three consecutive years. If this stream of inflows is discounted back to the present at a 12 percent rate, the present value of the flow is $2.40.

The present value of the first year's benefit of $1 is

$$P = \frac{S_1}{1 + i} = \frac{\$1.00}{1.12} = .893$$

and the values of each $1 received at the end of each of the remaining two years are

$$P = \frac{S_2}{(1 + i)^2} = .797$$

$$= \frac{S_3}{(1 + i)^3} = .712$$

The sum (V) of all these present values is simply

$$V = \frac{S_1}{1 + i} + \frac{S_2}{(1 + i)^2} + \frac{S_3}{(1 + i)^3}$$

$$= .893 + .797 + .712 = 2.402$$

Fortunately, standard tables are available to reduce our work load. Table 12-1 gives us the present value of $1 received at the end of n year at various discount rates. Table 12-2, on the other hand, shows the present value of $1 received at the end of each year for n years for a wide range of discount rates. Other detailed tables are readily available, ones that assume that cash flows are available throughout the year. Although Tables 12-1 and 12-2 assume that benefits are received at the end of each year, they could be used to evaluate monthly, or even quarterly or semiannual flows, by simply considering each time period as months, quarters, or half-years. Obviously, under those assumptions, internal rates of return derived from the use of such tables would be monthly, quarterly, or semiannual, but could easily be converted to annual rates.[1]

The use of Tables 12-1 and 12-2 is illustrated in the following problems:

Problem 1: Find the dollar amount which must be invested today at 8 percent compounded annually in order to receive $8,500 at the end of seven years.

Solution 1: Under the "years" column of Table 12-1, we locate year 7. We then move across the table to the 8 percent column and find that the present value of $1 received at the end of seven years is $.583. However, we are dealing with $8,500 instead of $1. Thus, $8,500 × .583 gives us $4,955.50, the present value of $8,500 received at the end of the seven years. In other words, if we can invest $4,955.50 for seven years at 8 percent compounded annually, we could receive the one-time payment of $8,500 at the end of the seven years.

Problem 2: Find the present value of $4,000 received at the end of each year for five consecutive years, if the flow is discounted at 10 percent.

Solution 2: Table 12-2 may be used to find the present value of

---

[1] The calculation of the internal rate of return from a capital expenditure will be explained later in this chapter.

TABLE 12-1. Present Value of $1 Received at the End of Period

Years Hence	1%	2%	4%	6%	8%	10%	12%	14%	15%	16%	18%	20%	22%	24%	25%	26%	28%	30%	35%	40%	45%	50%
1	0.990	0.980	0.962	0.943	0.926	0.909	0.893	0.877	0.870	0.862	0.847	0.833	0.820	0.806	0.800	0.794	0.781	0.769	0.741	0.714	0.690	0.667
2	0.980	0.961	0.925	0.890	0.857	0.826	0.797	0.769	0.756	0.743	0.718	0.694	0.672	0.650	0.640	0.630	0.610	0.592	0.549	0.510	0.476	0.444
3	0.971	0.942	0.889	0.840	0.794	0.751	0.712	0.675	0.658	0.641	0.609	0.579	0.551	0.524	0.512	0.500	0.477	0.455	0.406	0.364	0.328	0.296
4	0.961	0.924	0.855	0.792	0.735	0.683	0.636	0.592	0.572	0.552	0.516	0.482	0.451	0.423	0.410	0.397	0.373	0.350	0.301	0.260	0.226	0.198
5	0.951	0.906	0.822	0.747	0.681	0.621	0.567	0.519	0.497	0.476	0.437	0.402	0.370	0.341	0.328	0.315	0.291	0.269	0.223	0.186	0.156	0.132
6	0.942	0.888	0.790	0.705	0.630	0.564	0.507	0.456	0.432	0.410	0.370	0.335	0.303	0.275	0.262	0.250	0.227	0.207	0.165	0.133	0.108	0.088
7	0.933	0.871	0.760	0.665	0.583	0.513	0.452	0.400	0.376	0.354	0.314	0.279	0.249	0.222	0.210	0.198	0.178	0.159	0.122	0.095	0.074	0.059
8	0.923	0.853	0.731	0.627	0.540	0.467	0.404	0.351	0.327	0.305	0.266	0.233	0.204	0.179	0.168	0.157	0.139	0.123	0.091	0.068	0.051	0.039
9	0.914	0.837	0.703	0.592	0.500	0.424	0.361	0.308	0.284	0.263	0.225	0.194	0.167	0.144	0.134	0.125	0.108	0.094	0.067	0.048	0.035	0.026
10	0.905	0.820	0.676	0.558	0.463	0.386	0.322	0.270	0.247	0.227	0.191	0.162	0.137	0.116	0.107	0.099	0.085	0.073	0.050	0.035	0.024	0.017
11	0.896	0.804	0.650	0.527	0.429	0.350	0.287	0.237	0.215	0.195	0.162	0.135	0.112	0.094	0.086	0.079	0.066	0.056	0.037	0.025	0.017	0.012
12	0.887	0.788	0.625	0.497	0.397	0.319	0.257	0.208	0.187	0.168	0.137	0.112	0.092	0.076	0.069	0.062	0.052	0.043	0.027	0.018	0.012	0.008
13	0.879	0.773	0.601	0.469	0.368	0.290	0.229	0.182	0.163	0.145	0.116	0.093	0.075	0.061	0.055	0.050	0.040	0.033	0.020	0.013	0.008	0.005
14	0.870	0.758	0.577	0.442	0.340	0.263	0.205	0.160	0.141	0.125	0.099	0.078	0.062	0.049	0.044	0.039	0.032	0.025	0.015	0.009	0.006	0.003
15	0.861	0.743	0.555	0.417	0.315	0.239	0.183	0.140	0.123	0.108	0.084	0.065	0.051	0.040	0.035	0.031	0.025	0.020	0.011	0.006	0.004	0.002
16	0.853	0.728	0.534	0.394	0.292	0.218	0.163	0.123	0.107	0.093	0.071	0.054	0.042	0.032	0.028	0.025	0.019	0.015	0.008	0.005	0.003	0.002
17	0.844	0.714	0.513	0.371	0.270	0.198	0.146	0.108	0.093	0.080	0.060	0.045	0.034	0.026	0.023	0.020	0.015	0.012	0.006	0.003	0.002	0.001
18	0.836	0.700	0.494	0.350	0.250	0.180	0.130	0.095	0.081	0.069	0.051	0.038	0.028	0.021	0.018	0.016	0.012	0.009	0.005	0.002	0.001	0.001
19	0.828	0.686	0.475	0.331	0.232	0.164	0.116	0.083	0.070	0.060	0.043	0.031	0.023	0.017	0.014	0.012	0.009	0.007	0.003	0.002	0.001	
20	0.820	0.673	0.456	0.312	0.215	0.149	0.104	0.073	0.061	0.051	0.037	0.026	0.019	0.014	0.012	0.010	0.007	0.005	0.002	0.001	0.001	
21	0.811	0.660	0.439	0.294	0.199	0.135	0.093	0.064	0.053	0.044	0.031	0.022	0.015	0.011	0.009	0.008	0.006	0.004	0.002	0.001		
22	0.803	0.647	0.422	0.278	0.184	0.123	0.083	0.056	0.046	0.038	0.026	0.018	0.013	0.009	0.007	0.006	0.004	0.003	0.001	0.001		
23	0.795	0.634	0.406	0.262	0.170	0.112	0.074	0.049	0.040	0.033	0.022	0.015	0.010	0.007	0.006	0.005	0.003	0.002	0.001			
24	0.788	0.622	0.390	0.247	0.158	0.102	0.066	0.043	0.035	0.028	0.019	0.013	0.008	0.006	0.005	0.004	0.003	0.002	0.001			
25	0.780	0.610	0.375	0.233	0.146	0.092	0.059	0.038	0.030	0.024	0.016	0.010	0.007	0.005	0.004	0.003	0.002	0.001	0.001			
26	0.772	0.598	0.361	0.220	0.135	0.084	0.053	0.033	0.026	0.021	0.014	0.009	0.006	0.004	0.003	0.002	0.002	0.001				
27	0.764	0.586	0.347	0.207	0.125	0.076	0.047	0.029	0.023	0.018	0.011	0.007	0.005	0.003	0.002	0.002	0.001	0.001				
28	0.757	0.574	0.333	0.196	0.116	0.069	0.042	0.026	0.020	0.016	0.010	0.006	0.004	0.002	0.002	0.002	0.001	0.001				
29	0.749	0.563	0.321	0.185	0.107	0.063	0.037	0.022	0.017	0.014	0.008	0.005	0.003	0.002	0.002	0.001	0.001	0.001				
30	0.742	0.552	0.308	0.174	0.099	0.057	0.033	0.020	0.015	0.012	0.007	0.004	0.003	0.002	0.001	0.001	0.001	0.001				
40	0.672	0.453	0.208	0.097	0.046	0.022	0.011	0.005	0.004	0.003	0.001	0.001										
50	0.608	0.372	0.141	0.054	0.021	0.009	0.003	0.001	0.001	0.001												

Source: R.N. Anthony, *Management Accounting: Text and Cases* (Homewood, Ill.: Richard D. Irwin, Inc., 1969).

A.

TABLE 12-2. Present Value of $1 Received Annually at the End of Each Period for N Periods

Years (N)	1%	2%	4%	6%	8%	10%	12%	14%	15%	16%	18%	20%	22%	24%	25%	26%	28%	30%	35%	40%	45%	50%
1	0.990	0.980	0.962	0.943	0.926	0.909	0.893	0.877	0.870	0.862	0.847	0.833	0.820	0.806	0.800	0.794	0.781	0.769	0.741	0.714	0.690	0.667
2	1.970	1.942	1.886	1.833	1.783	1.736	1.690	1.647	1.626	1.605	1.566	1.528	1.492	1.457	1.440	1.424	1.392	1.361	1.289	1.224	1.165	1.111
3	2.941	2.884	2.775	2.673	2.577	2.487	2.402	2.322	2.283	2.246	2.174	2.106	2.042	1.981	1.952	1.923	1.868	1.816	1.696	1.589	1.493	1.407
4	3.902	3.808	3.630	3.465	3.312	3.170	3.037	2.914	2.855	2.798	2.690	2.589	2.494	2.404	2.362	2.320	2.241	2.166	1.997	1.849	1.720	1.605
5	4.853	4.713	4.452	4.212	3.993	3.791	3.605	3.433	3.352	3.274	3.127	2.991	2.864	2.745	2.689	2.635	2.532	2.436	2.220	2.035	1.876	1.737
6	5.795	5.601	5.242	4.917	4.623	4.355	4.111	3.889	3.784	3.685	3.498	3.326	3.167	3.020	2.951	2.885	2.759	2.643	2.385	2.168	1.983	1.824
7	6.728	6.472	6.002	5.582	5.206	4.868	4.564	4.288	4.160	4.039	3.812	3.605	3.416	3.242	3.161	3.083	2.937	2.802	2.508	2.263	2.057	1.883
8	7.652	7.325	6.733	6.210	5.747	5.335	4.968	4.639	4.487	4.344	4.078	3.837	3.619	3.421	3.329	3.241	3.076	2.925	2.598	2.331	2.108	1.922
9	8.566	8.162	7.435	6.802	6.247	5.759	5.328	4.946	4.772	4.607	4.303	4.031	3.786	3.566	3.463	3.366	3.184	3.019	2.665	2.379	2.144	1.948
10	9.471	8.983	8.111	7.360	6.710	6.145	5.650	5.216	5.019	4.833	4.494	4.192	3.923	3.682	3.571	3.465	3.269	3.092	2.715	2.414	2.168	1.965
11	10.368	9.787	8.760	7.887	7.139	6.495	5.988	5.453	5.234	5.029	4.656	4.327	4.035	3.776	3.656	3.544	3.335	3.147	2.752	2.438	2.185	1.977
12	11.255	10.575	9.385	8.384	7.536	6.814	6.194	5.660	5.421	5.197	4.793	4.439	4.127	3.851	3.725	3.606	3.387	3.190	2.779	2.456	2.196	1.985
13	12.134	11.343	9.986	8.853	7.904	7.103	6.424	5.842	5.583	5.342	4.910	4.533	4.203	3.912	3.780	3.656	3.427	3.223	2.799	2.468	2.204	1.990
14	13.004	12.106	10.563	9.295	8.244	7.367	6.628	6.002	5.724	5.468	5.008	4.611	4.265	3.962	3.824	3.695	3.459	3.249	2.814	2.477	2.210	1.993
15	13.865	12.849	11.118	9.712	8.559	7.606	6.811	6.142	5.847	5.575	5.092	4.675	4.315	4.001	3.859	3.726	3.483	3.268	2.825	2.484	2.214	1.995
16	14.718	13.578	11.652	10.106	8.851	7.824	6.974	6.265	5.954	5.669	5.162	4.730	4.357	4.003	3.887	3.751	3.503	3.283	2.834	2.489	2.216	1.997
17	15.562	14.292	12.166	10.477	9.122	8.022	7.120	6.373	6.047	5.749	5.222	4.775	4.391	4.059	3.910	3.771	3.518	3.295	2.840	2.492	2.218	1.998
18	16.398	14.992	12.659	10.828	9.372	8.201	7.250	6.467	6.128	5.818	5.273	4.812	4.419	4.080	3.928	3.786	3.529	3.304	2.844	2.494	2.219	1.999
19	17.226	15.678	13.134	11.158	9.604	8.365	7.366	6.550	6.198	5.877	5.316	4.844	4.442	4.097	3.942	3.799	3.539	3.311	2.848	2.496	2.220	1.999
20	18.046	16.351	13.590	11.470	9.818	8.514	7.469	6.623	6.259	5.929	5.353	4.870	4.460	4.110	3.954	3.808	3.546	3.316	2.850	2.497	2.221	1.999
21	18.857	17.011	14.029	11.764	10.017	8.649	7.562	6.687	6.312	5.973	5.384	4.891	4.476	4.121	3.963	3.816	3.551	3.320	2.852	2.498	2.221	2.000
22	19.660	17.658	14.451	12.042	10.201	8.772	7.645	6.743	6.359	6.011	5.410	4.909	4.488	4.130	3.970	3.822	3.556	3.323	2.853	2.498	2.222	2.000
23	20.456	18.292	14.857	12.303	10.371	8.883	7.718	6.792	6.399	6.044	5.432	4.925	4.499	4.137	3.976	3.827	3.559	3.325	2.854	2.499	2.222	2.000
24	21.243	18.914	15.247	12.550	10.529	8.985	7.784	6.835	6.434	6.073	5.451	4.937	4.507	4.143	3.981	3.831	3.562	3.327	2.855	2.499	2.222	2.000
25	22.023	19.523	15.622	12.783	10.675	9.077	7.843	6.873	6.464	6.097	5.467	4.948	4.514	4.147	3.985	3.834	3.564	3.329	2.856	2.499	2.222	2.000
26	22.795	20.121	15.983	13.003	10.810	9.161	7.896	6.906	6.491	6.118	5.480	4.956	4.520	4.151	3.988	3.837	3.566	3.330	2.856	2.500	2.222	2.000
27	23.560	20.707	16.330	13.211	10.935	9.237	7.943	6.935	6.514	6.136	5.492	4.964	4.524	4.154	3.990	3.839	3.567	3.331	2.856	2.500	2.222	2.000
28	24.316	21.281	16.663	13.406	11.051	9.307	7.984	6.961	6.534	6.152	5.502	4.970	4.528	4.157	3.992	3.840	3.568	3.331	2.857	2.500	2.222	2.000
29	25.066	21.844	16.984	13.591	11.158	9.370	8.022	6.983	6.551	6.166	5.510	4.975	4.531	4.159	3.994	3.841	3.569	3.332	2.857	2.500	2.222	2.000
30	25.808	22.396	17.292	13.765	11.258	9.427	8.055	7.003	6.566	6.177	5.517	4.979	4.534	4.160	3.995	3.842	3.569	3.332	2.857	2.500	2.222	2.000
40	32.835	27.355	19.793	15.046	11.925	9.779	8.244	7.105	6.642	6.234	5.548	4.997	4.544	4.166	3.999	3.846	3.571	3.333	2.857	2.500	2.222	2.000
50	39.196	31.424	21.482	15.762	12.234	9.915	8.304	7.133	6.661	6.246	5.554	4.999	4.545	4.167	4.000	3.846	3.571	3.333	2.857	2.500	2.222	2.000

Source: R.N. Anthony, *Management Accounting Text and Cases* (Homewood, Ill.: Richard D. Irwin, Inc., 1969).

the level sequence of inflows. We move down to the fifth year and across the table to the 10 percent column to find the factor of 3.791. Thus, the present value of $1 received at the end of each of five straight years is $3.791 (factor for five years at 10 percent times $1). Again, however, we are working with some multiple of $1. Thus, the present value of our cash flow is $4,000 times the factor of 3.791, or $15,164.

Problem 3: Using a discount rate of 12 percent, calculate the present value of $2,000 received for three consecutive years, followed by $5,000 received at the end of years 4 or 5.

Solution 3-A:

PV of $2,000 for 5 years = 3.605 × $2,000	
(Table 12-2) =	$ 7,210.00
PV of $3,000 for years 4 and 5 only	
(from Table 12-1)	
.636 × $3,000	1,908.00
.567 × $3,000	1,701.00
Total PV of cash flow	$10,819.00

Solution 3-B: Use Table 12-2 to find the difference between the fifth year factor and the third year factor (3.605 less 2.402 = 1.203). Then:

PV of $2,000 for 3 years = 2.402 × $2,000 =	$ 4,804.00
PV of $5,000 for years 4 and 5 =	
1.203 × $5,000 =	6,015.00
Total PV of cash flow	$10,819.00

These solutions are just two of several approaches used to calculate the present value of the uneven series of payments.

The Hurdle Rate

Once the concept of the present value of money is clearly in mind, we are ready to turn to the question posed in any capital budgeting process: Is A or B the preferable investment project? We shall illustrate several commonly used methods designed to help provide an answer to this critical question. Before proceeding, however, it behooves us to consider the discount rate, or *hurdle rate*, which should be used in our calculations.

The concept of the cost of capital (which will be discussed in detail in the next chapter) is the standard for choosing among new investment opportunities. This standard is universally accepted among business economists and financial theorists. The reasoning is both clear and persuasive. An investment proposal should be judged as to whether it provides a return equal to or greater than that required by the firm's investors. Clearly the basic purpose of an investment is to add to the value of the owners' equity. That value can be increased only if the net incremental profit from a new investment exceeds the cost of capital required to obtain the extra net income. Thus, the cost of capital may be referred to as a hurdle rate or cutoff rate to be used when evaluating proposed capital expenditures by the rate of return method. If an investment opportunity offers a rate of return greater than the cost of capital, then from a monetary viewpoint, it is favorable. On the other hand, the owners of the firm would be worse off if the cost of capital for a given project exceeded its rates of return. For similar reasons, the cost of capital is the discount rate for the present value method of evaluating proposed investment projects. By using the cost of capital as a discount rate, we compare the present value of the net cash benefits with the cost of the proposal. It follows that if the present value of the net cash benefits exceeds the present value of the net cash investment, the return is greater than the cost, net monetary benefits are gained, and owners' equity is enhanced.

In order to simplify our discussion of the various methods used to evaluate proposed capital expenditures, in this chapter we merely assume a cost of capital (discount or hurdle rate). In the following chapter the cost of capital will be the subject of a detailed discussion.

MUTUALLY EXCLUSIVE, INDEPENDENT, AND DEPENDENT INVESTMENTS

When projects in a group of investment proposals are compared, it is necessary to determine whether the projects are substitutes for one another (mutually exclusive), or are independent of each other. Mutually exclusive proposals imply that the selection of one project rules out the others. For example, assume that a firm is investigating the possibility of placing its bookkeeping and other clerical operations on computers and has a choice between two types of equipment. The choice of one computer excludes the use of the other equipment. In other words, two mutually exclusive projects cannot both be accepted.

Assume that, in addition to the computer installation, the company plans to replace obsolete machines with more efficient equipment. The expected yield or rate of return derived from the use of the new machines is not affected by one's accepting or rejecting other proposals. Thus, the new machine is said to be *independent* of all other investment proposals. A *dependent* proposal, on the other hand, is one whose selection depends upon the acceptance of one or more other proposals. The acquisition of a large data-processing installation that requires the construction of additional office space would be an example of a dependent investment proposal.

METHODS OF EVALUATING PROPOSED CAPITAL EXPENDITURES

Four methods of evaluating proposed capital expenditures are frequently utilized. They are:

1. The net present-value method.
2. The internal rate of return method.
3. The accounting rate of return method.
4. The payback method.

These will be explained and illustrated and the strengths and weaknesses of each discussed.

Net Present-value Method

A popular approach to evaluating proposed capital expenditures is the present-value method. This approach involves the calculation of the present value of all future cash inflows computed at the cost of capital or at an arbitrary rate of interest.

Assume that an investment proposal is being evaluated and promises a net cash benefit at the end of the first year of $9,000, $7,000 the second year, and $5,000 the third year. If the net cash investment is $15,000 and the cost of capital is 10 percent, the present value of this project would be computed as follows:

$$PV = \$9000 \left(\frac{1}{1 + 0.10}\right) + \$7000 \left(\frac{1}{1 + 0.10}\right)^2$$
$$+ \$5000 \left(\frac{1}{1 + 0.10}\right)3$$

Present Value of *Net Cash Benefits*	*Net Cash Benefits —end of year*		
	1	2	3
	$9,000	$7,000	$5,000

$ 8,181.
  5,782.
  <u>3,755.</u>

$17,718.   Total — Present Value of Net Cash Benefits

If one uses the Present Value of $1 Table (Table 12–1), the present value of the net cash benefits are computed by handling the problem of unequal receipts as a series of one-year inflows received at successively later time periods. Since the net cash benefit for each year is different, the computations must be made separately for each year. Hence, the present value of $1 at 10 percent is multiplied by the net cash benefit for each year to obtain the present value of each net cash benefit. The present values for each year are totaled to obtain the present value of the investment. For example, the present value of $1 received at the end of the first year is $.909, at a discount rate of 10 percent. However, since we are dealing with $9,000, the present value of the first year benefit is $9,000 × .909 = $8,181. The factor for the second year at 10 percent is .826. Thus, the present value of $7,000 received at the end of two years is $5,782 ($7,000 × .826 = $5,782). Finally, the benefit of $5,000 times the third year factor of .751 gives a present value of $3,755. The sum of the present values for each year ($17,718) is the total present value of the net cash benefits.

Once the present value of the benefits is computed, it may be used several ways. One obvious and simple acceptance criterion is to compare the present value of the net cash benefits with the net cash investment. If the present value of the benefits exceeds the net investment, then from a financial viewpoint, the project should be accepted. In our illustration, the decision using this criterion would be to accept the project since:

$17,718 (PV of cash benefits) > $15,000 (net cash investment)

Another way of expressing the preceding criterion is to calculate net present value; that is, present value of net cash benefits minus the net cash investment. Thus, an investment proposal would be accepted if the net present value exceeds zero. In the example just given, net present value is $2,718 ($17,718 present value of cash benefits less $15,000 net cash investment).

Profitability Index. The profitability index provides a convenient method of ranking investment proposals that require identical net cash investments. This index is obtained by dividing the present value of net cash benefits by the present value of net cash investment.

$$\text{Profitability index} = \frac{\text{PV of net cash benefits}}{\text{PV of net cash investment}}$$

According to the example previously presented to illustrate the present value method, the profitability index is 1.18.

$$\text{Profitability index} = \frac{\$17,718}{\$15,000} = 1.18$$

If the index is greater than 1.0, the investment proposal is acceptable. Obviously, for a given project, the present-value method and the profitability index give the same results. Although the profitability index may be suitable for selecting mutually exclusive proposals, a great deal of care is called for when there are substantial differences in the net cash investments required for various investment opportunities. The following illustrates this point:

	PV of Net Cash Investment	Profitability Index	Net Present Value
Project A	$ 10,000	1.24	$ 2,400
Project B	70,000	1.20	14,000
Project C	160,000	1.16	25,600
Project D	80,000	1.05	4,000

If we are concerned only with the amount returned per dollar invested, then the ranking by profitability index numbers is correct. But if we assume that the firm can raise enough capital, project C (or even B and D) provides a much greater overall benefit to the company, although its profitability index is less than project A. Thus, it can be argued that the net present value is a better measure than the profitability index, since it states in absolute terms the estimated economic contribution of each project to the firm. The profitability index, on the other hand, merely expresses the relative profitability of each project.

Internal Rate of Return

The other discounted cash-inflow method to consider is the internal rate of return. Like the present-value method, the internal rate of return takes account of both the timing and the magnitude of cash benefits in each year of a project's expected life.

The internal rate of return is the discount rate that equates the present value of net cash benefits with the present value of the net cash investment. Thus, the internal rate of return is the special case when the net present value of an investment is zero. It is represented as follows, if the net cash investment is at time 0 (the present):

$$A0 = \frac{A1}{(1+r)^1} + \frac{A2}{(1+r)^2} + \ldots + \frac{An}{(1+r)^n}$$

where $A0$ represents the net cash investment at time 0; A_1, A_2, A_n represent the stream of net cash benefits; r is the internal rate of return or the discount rate, which is used to obtain a present value of net cash benefits equal to net cash investment.

When the cash benefits are an uneven series, solving for the internal rate of return involves a trial-and-error procedure. The rate is determined by trying several discount factors to find the one that equates discounted net cash benefits with net cash investments. To illustrate the method, we use our previous investment project. To determine the internal rate of return, we must find the rate that discounts the stream of future net cash benefits of $9,000, $7,000, and $5,000 to equal the net cash investment of $15,000. By trial and error we are able to determine the appropriate rate of discount. Assume that we try discount rates of 20 percent and 22 percent.

Years	Net Cash Benefits	20% Discount Factor	22% Discount Factor	20% Present Value	22% Present Value
1	$9000	.833	.820	$ 7497	$ 7380
2	$7000	.694	.672	$ 4858	$ 4704
3	$5000	.579	.551	$ 2895	$ 2755
				$15250	$14839

Since the net cash investment is $15,000, we see that the internal rate of return lies somewhere between 20 percent and 22 percent. We can approximate the actual rate by interpolation.

Discount rate   Present values

20% $\begin{cases} \$15250 \\ \$15000 \\ \$14839 \end{cases}$ $411

$250

Internal Rate of Return $15000 $411

22% $14839

$$\frac{\$250}{\$411} \times 2\% = 1.2\% \qquad\qquad 20.0\% + 1.2\% = 21.2\%$$

Thus, the internal rate of return is approximately 21.2 percent. Since the relationship between the two discount rates (20 percent and 22 percent) is not linear relative to present value, the internal rate of return is necessarily an approximation. For most situations, however, the approximate internal rate of return is more than adequate.

When the cash benefits stream is a sequence of identical payments for each of the three years, trial and error is not necessary to determine the internal rate of return. If the net cash investment today is $12,000, and net cash benefits at the end of each year for three consecutive years are $5,000, we merely divide $12,000 by $5,000 to obtain a factor of 2.4. Our next step is to find an annual rate of interest that, when applied to an annuity of $1 for three years, provides a factor of 2.4. Using Table 12-2, we move down to year three and across the table, until we find the factors nearest 2.4. At 12 percent and at three years, the factor is 2.402. Since the factor at 14 percent is 2.322, we know that the actual rate lies between 12 percent and 14 percent. Again, interpolation may be used to obtain the approximate internal rate of return.

The accept–reject criterion employed with the internal-rate-of-return method is to compare the internal rate of return with a hurdle rate (often the firm's cost of capital). If the internal rate of return is greater than the hurdle rate, the investment should be accepted. In the example just given, if the hurdle rate were 10 percent, the project would be accepted, whereas a hurdle rate of 18 percent would result in a rejection.

Internal Rate of Return and Present Value Methods Compared. Usually the internal-rate-of-return method and the present-value method give the same investment decisions. Figure 12-1 illustrates the two methods graphically. Net present value (present value of net cash benefits less net cash investment) is shown on the Y axis; the discount rate, on the X axis. Notice that at very low interest rates, the present values of net cash benefits exceed net cash investment by

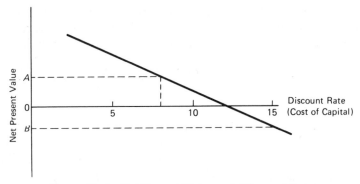

Figure 12-1. Net Present Value and Discount Rate

substantial amounts. As discounts rates increase, the present values of net cash benefits decrease relative to net cash investment. Eventually, at discount rates in excess of 12 percent, the present values of net cash benefits are less than net cash investment, and net present values are negative. At the intercept of the present-value curve and the X axis, the present-value of net cash benefits is equal to present value of the net cash investment (the net present value is zero). It follows that the discount rate of 12 percent at this point of interception is the internal rate of return.

As indicated in Figure 12-1, if the hurdle or cutoff rate were 8 percent, a favorable net present value of the investment would be A. In addition, the internal rate of return of 12 percent exceeds the required rate of 8 percent, an "accept" result for the rate-of-return method. Therefore, under the assumptions illustrated, we would accept the investment project, regardless of the method of evaluation used. The graph also reveals that we would reject the investment proposal under either method, if the hurdle or cutoff rate exceeded the internal rate of return. If the hurdle rate were 15 percent, for example, then the internal rate of return of only 12 percent would not justify an expenditure for the investment. Likewise, the proposal would be rejected under the present-value method of evaluation, since a discount rate of 15 percent would give a negative net present value of B.

Net Present Value vs. Internal Rate of Return. Although Figure 12-1 indicates that both the internal rate-of-return and the net present-value method give the same accept-reject decision when we evaluate a single investment project and use the same cutoff (discount) rate in both cases, significant problems may occur when we are required to rank mutually exclusive proposals. Two or more proposals are mutually exclusive if the acceptance of any one would eliminate from consideration all others in the mutually exclusive group. The following table illustrates the nature of the problem.

Years	Net Cash Benefits	
	A	B
1	$9000	0
2	$7000	$ 6000
3	$5000	$18,000
Internal Rate of Return	21%	18%
Net Present Value (with 10% discount rate and net cash investment of $15,000)	$2718	$ 3474

Obviously we have a conflict. With an assumed investment of $15,000, project *A* has an internal rate of return in excess of project *B*. Using a discount rate of 10 percent, however, the net present values reveal that project *B* is preferred over project *A*.

The different rankings of projects occur because of the different assumptions we make relative to the reinvestment of net cash benefits from each project. The present-value method is based on the assumption that funds are reinvested at a rate equivalent to the required or cutoff rate (discount rate); the internal rate-of-return method implies reinvestment at the internal rate of return.

Figure 12-2 reveals that at low discount rates, the net present value of project *B* exceeds the net present value of project *A*. At higher discount rates, however, the net present value of project *A* is greater than the net present value of *B*. Projects such as *A*, whose net cash benefits are largest in earlier years, in general will have higher net present values at higher discount rates; projects whose net cash benefits are larger in later years, e.g., *B*, will have lower net present values at higher discount rates. This results because the projects with greater net cash benefits in later years are penalized by the lower values of the discount factors in later years. For example, Table 12-1 indicates that at a 10 percent discount rate, the present value of $1 at the end of the first year is .909, compared with .621 at the end of the fifth year. The net present value of project *B* remains higher than the net present value of *A* until a discount rate of about 15 percent. Beyond the interception of *A* and *B*, the net present value of project *A* exceeds the net present value of project *B* by increasing amounts.

The *internal rate of return* is the rate that equates the present value of net cash benefits with the net cash investment (zero net present value). This is indicated on the graph at the points where the net present-value lines for A and B intercept the horizontal axis (zero

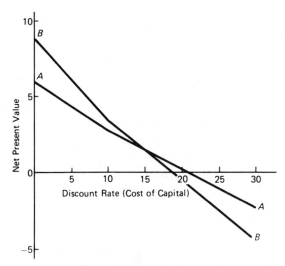

Figure 12-2. Net Present Value, Discount Rate, and Internal Rate of Return

net present-value line). Therefore, the internal rate of return of project B is about 18.4 percent; for project A, it is about 20.6 percent.

At the point of intersection of A and B at approximately 15 percent, the projects have identical net present values. If we assume that cash inflows could be reinvested at about 15 percent, then project A and B would be equally ranked. On the other hand, implied reinvestment rates other than 15 percent would require that we prefer one proposal to the other. Thus at reinvestment rates of less than 15 percent, project B ranks higher than project A; at rates in excess of 15 percent, project A would be preferred.

Selecting the Best Method. Although Figure 12-2 shows that the internal rate of return of project A is greater than that of project B, for various reasons we cannot say unambiguously that project A is preferred over B. The graph indicates that at a discount rate of 5 percent, for example, project B ranks higher than project A. In contrast, at discount rates in excess of 15 percent the net present values of project A exceeds those of project B.

The answers to the question of which method of evaluation provides the best solutions depends on the appropriate reinvestment rate for cash inflows. As previously indicated, the net present value method implicitly assumes that the cash inflows generated during the economic life of a project can be reinvested at the hurdle or cutoff (discount rate), whereas the implied reinvestment rate under the internal rate-of-return method is the calculated internal rate of return. The implied reinvestment rate for the present-value method is

405

the same for both proposals *A* and *B*. Moreover, the discount rate used for the present-value method is often the firm's cost of capital, or the market price the firm must pay for capital. On the other hand, the internal rate of return is merely a number obtained by equating the present value of net cash benefits with the net cash investment. One can argue that it is much more realistic to assume that a firm can reinvest its net cash benefits at rates currently available in the capital market, rather than at a rate that it happens to compute by equating the present value of net benefits with the net cash investment. Therefore, when and if a choice must be made, the present-value method generally is considered superior and thus provides an unambiguous answer.

Payback Method

The payback method involves calculating the period of time required to return the original investment:

$$\text{Payback period} = \frac{\text{Net cash investment}}{\text{Net cash benefits}}$$

Referring again to our previous example, if the net cash benefits received at the end of each year are $9,000, $7,000, and $5,000, our net cash investment of $15,000 is recovered in less than two years. Firms using the method usually establish a minimum acceptable payback period. If three years is our accept–reject criterion, the project would, of course, be acceptable. Since this method measures the number of years needed to recover the proposed investment, it differs from the other three methods of evaluation, in that it indicates liquidity, not profitability.

The weaknesses of the payback method occur because it ignores portions of the information about the investment. It does this in two ways.

1. It does not consider the time value of money. The time pattern of net cash benefits, whether before or after the investment is recovered, is ignored. Assume that projects *A* and *B* each require a net cash investment of $30,000. The sums of the net cash benefits for *A* and *B* are $30,000 each, received over a three-year period as follows:

Years	Project A	Project B
1	$15,000	$ 5,000
2	10,000	10,000
3	5,000	15,000

If we consider *only* the payback period, each investment is recovered in three years. Clearly, however, the projects are not equally attractive, since a much greater dollar amount is recouped during the first two years of the economic life of A than is the case for B, as shown in the preceding table.

2. The payback method measures only liquidity, since net cash benefits beyond the payback period are not considered. The following table indicates that net cash investments of $15,000 each for projects A and B are recovered in two years in each case.

Years	Project A	Project B
1	$7500	$7500
2	7500	7500
3		7500

But profit is a function of the net cash benefits received after the investment is recouped, rather than the length of time required to make the recovery. Thus, project *B* is the preferred investment. These are indeed serious criticisms. Yet the payback method is widely used by business firms. It is therefore important to consider why.

The major advantages of this much-maligned method are that it is very simple to compute, and offers significant information about liquidity. Obviously, a measure of liquidity is highly important for firms that encounter unstable revenues and cash flow problems. In situations with a high degree of uncertainty about cash benefits to be received for a number of years, an economist may find it desirable to simply ignore the more distant inflows. In addition, if an economist or business manager is comparing alternative investments from among a group of investment possibilities having about the same economic life and profile of benefits, then the major criticisms of this approach tend to be less significant.

Finally, given certain conditions, the reciprocal of the pay-back period may be used to provide a relatively good estimate of the internal rate of return of an investment project. The reciprocal of the payback period is

$$\frac{1}{\text{Payback period}}$$

Assume that we find that the payback period for a proposal is three years. The reciprocal of 3 is 1/3. Thus the estimated internal rate of return is 33 percent, if the following conditions prevail.

1. The estimated life of the project is double the payback period.

2. Each year's net cash benefits after taxes are identical.
3. The estimated salvage value of the new project is zero, or an insignificant amount.

If an investment of $100,000 has no salvage value at the end of its economic life, but provides net cash benefits of $30,000 for each of ten consecutive years, the payback period is 3 1/3 years. The reciprocal of the payback is 3/10. Thus, a fair estimate of the internal rate of return is 30 percent. The calculated internal rate of return is 27.4 percent. As the estimated economic life of an investment increases relative to the payback period, the reciprocal of the payback becomes an increasingly more accurate estimate of the internal rate of return, although this estimate will always exceed the actual internal rate of return.

Accounting Rate of Return

The accounting-rate-of-return method of evaluating proposed capital expenditures is based upon accounting income rather than cash flow. It is calculated by dividing the average annual net income after taxes by the average investment in the project. By using average investment, we are accounting for shrinking investment. That is, the average amount of the declining book value of the project over its estimated life is used as the investment base.

Assume that a machine costing $20,000 is expected to produce average annual net income after taxes of $4,000 for five years. If the equipment is not expected to have a salvage value at the end of its economic life and we assume straight-line depreciation, the average investment will be $10,000 ($20,000 ÷ 2). In other words, the book value of the machine will shrink each year by $4,000, from $20,000 to $16,000 to $12,000 to $8,000 to $4,000 and finally to zero.

The ratio of the average annual net income after taxes to the average investment gives us the accounting rate of return for the project:

$$\frac{\$4000}{\$10,000} = 40\% \text{ accounting rate of return}$$

This provides a suitable measure of the profitability of a proposed project and thus lends itself to comparison with the profitability of other similarly measured proposals or with some minumum level of acceptability. For this reason, many business firms often use it.

The accounting rate of return provides a fairly good estimate of the internal rate of return, and a better estimate than the reciprocal of the payback period, under the following conditions:

1. The estimated life of the project is less than double the payback period.
2. Each year's earnings after taxes are the same.
3. The estimated salvage value of the new project is zero, or insignificant.

Assume that a net cash investment of $100,000 has an economic life of five years. The firm receives an annual savings before depreciation and taxes of $40,000. If straight-line depreciation is used and the tax rate is assumed to be 50 percent, the payback period and accounting rate of return are calculated as follows:

	Books of Account	Net Cash Benefits
Savings each year	$40,000	$40,000
Depreciation (100,000 ÷ 5 yrs.)	20,000	
Added taxable income	20,000	
Taxes (50%)	10,000	10,000
Added earnings after taxes per year	$10,000	
		$30,000

The accounting rate of return is

$$\frac{\text{Average earnings after taxes}}{\text{Average net cash investment}} = \frac{\$10,000}{\$50,000} = 20\%$$

The payback period is 3 1/3 years, since $100,000 ÷ 30,000 = 3 1/3. The reciprocal of the payback period is 3/10, or 30 percent. Thus, since the life of the project is less than twice the payback period, the accounting rate of return is the better estimate of the actual internal rate of return of 15.2 percent.

This method also has serious deficiencies. First, the time value of money is ignored. Moreover, no allowances are made for variations in annual earnings or in their distribution through time. In our example, the accounting rate of return would be stated at 40 percent, whether or not most of the total net income after taxes is earned during the first two years or in the last year of the project.

SUMMARY

Capital budgeting procedures usually result in long-term commitment of large amounts of funds. The level and effectiveness of capital expenditures greatly affect the direction, growth rate, and profitability of a firm. Thus, capital expenditure decisions are among the most important tasks to be performed by the managers of a firm.

Capital expenditures include acquisitions of capital assets, major repairs and improvements, replacements of existing equipment, and important outlays often expensed by accountants, such as training programs, advertising costs, and research programs. These expenditures contribute to earning power over an extended period of time.

The capital budgeting process is an analytical approach designed to indicate the value each investment proposal might contribute to the net present worth of the firm. The first step in the process is the projection of the dollar amounts of cash outflows and inflows related to a proposed project. The outflow of cash we term *net cash investment*; the inflow we call *net cash benefits*.

Once net cash investment and net cash benefits are determined, various methods may be used for ranking investment proposals. The four methods described are widely used. The net present value method and the internal rate-of-return method are preferred over other methods, since each approach considers the time value of money. Annuity tables designed to lessen the work load may be used to bring back to the present the expected net cash benefits of a proposed capital investment. Thus, cash inflows from competing projects may be compared on a current dollar value basis. Under the present-value method, if the present value of future net cash benefits exceeds the net cash investment, the project is acceptable. If the internal rate of return is greater than a predetermined hurdle rate, the project is also acceptable.

The payback method involves calculating the period of time required to return the net cash investment. The accounting rate of return is the average annual net income after taxes divided by the average investment in the project. Each of the latter methods ignores the time value of money and suffers from other serious deficiencies.

QUESTIONS FOR ANALYSIS AND DISCUSSION

1. The annual net cash benefits from a proposed investment project has a present value of $22,000, if discounted at a rate of 14 percent. If the net cash investment required for the capital expenditure is $23,500, will the internal rate of return be greater or less than 14 percent? Explain.
2. Discuss the differences between the accounting book value of a capital ex-

penditure and the net cash investment used for capital expenditure analysis. Give examples of each.

3. Distinguish between an operating expenditure and a capital expenditure and give at least three examples of each.

4. Explain the economic importance of the concept "time value of money" in terms of capital expenditure analysis.

5. Assume that a firm is studying the possibility of replacing an old machine with a new machine. Which of the following should a manager ignore, add to, or deduct from, the accounting cost of the new machine when calculating net cash investment? Ignore tax effects in each case.

   (a) The expense of dismantling and removing the old machine.
   (b) The old machine may be sold for a price of $3,000 above its accounting book value.
   (c) If the new machine is purchased, $2,000 will not have to be expended to repair the old machine.
   (d) The use of the new machine will require an increase of $2,600 annually in outlays for inventory and accounts receivable.

6. "If the profitability index of a proposed capital expenditure is 1.0, it follows that the internal rate of return for the project must be equal to weighted cost of capital." Do you agree or disagree? Why or why not?

7. Use examples to explain the major differences between the internal rate of return and the accounting rate of return of a proposed capital expenditure.

8. What assumptions are made about the reinvestment rate for net cash benefits generated during the economic life of an investment project when we use (a) the present-value method and (b) the internal rate-of-return method of evaluating proposed capital expenditures?

9. Discuss the types of outflows and inflows to be considered when calculating the net cash benefits resulting from a proposed capital expenditure.

10. Under what conditions might it be wise to employ a method of evaluating proposed capital expenditures that ignores the time value of money?

PROBLEMS AND CASES

1. Compute the present value of the following cash inflows. Use a discount rate of 10 percent in all cases.

   (a) $6,500 received at the end of four years.
   (b) $4,000 received at the end of each year for five consecutive years.
   (c) $6,000 received at the end of years two and three, with no cash inflow for the first year.
   (d) $4,000 received at the end of each year for three consecutive years, followed by $2,500 received at the end of years four and five.

2. The Walls Manufacturing Corporation plans to purchase a new machine to replace an obsolete one. The old machine has an accounting-book value of $4,000, but may be sold for $8,000. The invoice price of the new machine is $14,000. Freight charges total $800 and installation costs for the new machine are $1,200. The firm estimates that if it retains the use of the old machine, an outlay of $3,000 for repairs will have to be made within a few weeks. The company is in the 48 percent tax bracket. Calculate the net cash investment for the new machine and explain your computation.

3. The Nichols Company is currently using a machine whose original basis for depreciation was $32,000. The machine is being depreciated over an eight-year period on a straight-line basis and will have no salvage value at the end of its economic life. It is now four years old and the firm has determined that the machine may be sold to a used-equipment dealer for $8,000. Mr. Nichols is considering the purchase of a new machine that will cost $64,000 and have an estimated salvage value of $8,000. Straight-line depreciation is used over an eight-year economic life of the machine and the cost of capital is 16 percent. The company is in the 40 percent tax bracket and it is estimated that savings before depreciation and taxes is $27,000 annually. Calculate the net present value of the investment project.

4. The Penny Pipe Corporation has been presented with two investment opportunities, each of which requires a net cash investment of $84,000. The firm's economic advisor estimated that its weighted cost of capital is 12 percent. In addition, he reported that the net cash benefits after taxes for each of the proposed capital expenditures are as follows:

Year	Expenditure A	Expenditure B
1	$38,000	$12,000
2	38,000	22,000
3	20,000	22,000
4	10,000	22,000
5	10,000	22,000
6		22,000
7		40,000
8		40,000

(a) Calculate the following for *each* proposed capital expenditure, A and B.
   1. Net present value.
   2. Internal rate of return.
   3. Payback period.
(b) Use a graph to obtain the internal rate of return with net present value shown on the vertical axis and cost of capital on the horizontal axis.
(c) Discuss any apparent conflicts in ranking the two projects when using the three methods of evaluation listed in part A.

5. The Sizemore Company is considering the purchase of new machinery. The firm is trying to decide which of three alternative projects it should accept. The following data are available for each project.

	Project A	Project B	Project C
Invoice price of machinery	$8,000	$14,000	$9,000
Installation cost	800	0	200
Employee training cost	0	500	400
Additional working capital	2,200	500	800
Salvage value	1,000	2,000	0
Method of depreciation	Straight-line	Straight-line	Straight-line
Estimated life of machinery	4 years	6 years	6 years

Estimated annual cash benefits before depreciation and taxes are as follows:

Year	Project A	Project B	Project C
1	$5,000	$10,000	$12,000
2	5,000	10,000	12,000
3	5,000	10,000	12,000
4	5,000	8,000	3,000
5		8,000	3,000
6		8,000	3,000

If we assume a cost of capital of 14 percent and a tax rate of 50 percent, calculate the following for each project:

(a) net present value.

(b) internal rate of return.

(c) accounting rate of return.

(d) payback period.

6. (a) Calculate the discounted cash benefits at 0 percent, 6 percent, and 12 percent for the following proposed capital expenditure:

Year	Net Cash Benefits
0*	($2500)
1	1400
2	500
3	500
4	500
5	500

*Year 0 is the here and now. The negative $2,500 is the net cash investment.

(b) Explain how you obtained your figures for the 0 percent rate.

(c) Calculate the internal rate of return for the proposed capital expenditure.

7. The Harsh Manufacturing Company is in the process of determining its capital expenditure program for the near future. It currently has available the following investment opportunities.

Investment Opportunity	Net Cash Investment	Annual Net Cash Benefits			
		1	2	3	4
A	$12,000	$ 5,000	$ 5,000	$ 5,000	$ -0-
B	40,000	20,000	18,000	15,000	10,000
C	52,000	40,000	20,000	10,000	10,000
D	25,000	8,000	8,000	8,000	8,000

(a) Compute the internal rate of return for each investment opportunity.

(b) Use the graph method of computing the internal rate of return.

(c) If the weighted cost of capital is 14 percent (and this is the hurdle rate accepted by the firm), which investment opportunities should be undertaken?

(d) Explain why the weighted cost of capital may be used as a hurdle rate.

SELECTED READINGS

Bauman, W. Scott. "Evaluation of Prospective Investment Performance." *Journal of Finance*, 23 (May 1968): 276-95.

Bierman, Harold, Jr., and Seymour Smidt. *The Capital Budgeting Decision.* New York: The Macmillan Co., 1971.

Bones, A. James. *Capital Budgeting.* New York: Praeger Publishers, 1972.

Dean, Joel. *Capital Budgeting.* New York: Columbia University Press, 1951.

Johnson, Robert W. *Capital Budgeting.* Belmont, Calif.: Wadsworth Publishing Company, Inc., 1970.

Kiammer, Thomas. "Empirical Evidence of the Adoption of Sophisticated Capital Budgeting Techniques." *Journal of Business* (July 1972), 387-97.

Lerner, Eugene M. "The Integration of Capital Budgeting and Stock Valuation." *American Economic Review*, 54 (September 1964): 682-702.

Mao, James C.T. "Survey of Capital Budgeting: Theory and Practice." *Journal of Finance*, 25 (May 1970): 349-60.

Solomon, Ezra. "The Arithmetic of Capital Budgeting Decisions." *Journal of Business*, 29 (April 1956).

——. *The Theory of Financial Management.* New York: Columbia University Press, 1963.

Van Horne, James. *Financial Management and Policy.* Englewood Cliffs, N.J.: Prentice-Hall, Inc., 1971.

13

Cost of Capital

One reason the cost of capital concept is important is that within the capital budgeting framework discussed in Chapter 12, it is one of the two determinants, along with internal rate of return, of the dollar volume of funds that business firms seek and allocate for new investment opportunities. The cost of capital may be compared with the internal rate of return in order to judge whether or not to proceed with a proposed project. In terms of accept–reject criteria a business economist would recommend an investment if the internal rate of return exceeds the cost of capital. Moreover, a proposed project should be accepted if the net present value of the cash flow is positive when discounted at the cost of capital. In theory, if these two accept–reject rules are followed over the long run, the value of a firm's stock should be maximized.

The basic purpose of capital investment is to add to the value of each owner's share of the firm. This share can be increased only if incremental profit earned from the new investment exceeds the cost of capital required to realize the additional net income. Consequently, the cost of capital sets the hurdle rate which capital investment projects must clear before a firm's funds are committed. Thus *cost of capital* is the rate of return on a project that will leave unchanged the market price of a company's stock.

The discussion that follows will show that we are not in an area of hard and fast rules. The cost of capital is a controversial and difficult issue. Although most authorities would agree that cost of capital is an appropriate hurdle rate for a firm, widespread differences of opinion occur on the issue of how this cost should be determined. A large portion of this chapter is devoted to methods of measuring the after-tax costs of funds. Although our figures will look precise, we shall see that, for various reasons, our calculations may be open to question. As we proceed, however, we shall underscore some of the analytical problems involved in computing cost of capital. After considering various approaches used to measure the costs of individual sources of financing, we shall combine these into an overall weighted cost of capital. To accomplish this, we will weigh the cost of each component of debt and equity in a firm's capital structure by its relative weight in the total of funds sought.

CAPITAL STRUCTURE

A firm's capital structure may include bonds, common stock, preferred stock, retained earnings, and depreciation flows. Bonds are a debt to the firm, since they involve an obligation to repay funds. The others are considered as part of the owner's equity, since the owners of the business contribute these funds. Rarely is there any obligation to repay these funds. Each of these is a source of funds. Which source(s) will or should be used for additional funds will depend on their costs.

BONDS

The cost of long-term debt capital is more easily determined than the cost of equity, since holders of debt receive a fixed amount over a contract period. Thus there is much agreement about the method of computing the cost of this source of funds.

The cost of bonds is the investor's yield to maturity, adjusted for the tax effect. In this regard, cost to maturity, not just initial or current costs, is considered. When calculating yield to maturity, the interest cost to a definite date of maturity (which is known and stated) is related to the net proceeds to the firm from the sale of the bond. Net proceeds are determined by subtracting from the price paid to the seller by the investor (buyer), the underwriting and other costs of the bond issue. Finally, we must remember that a bond may sell at a discount or premium.

Approximate Yield to Maturity Method

Yield to maturity is determined either by approximation or by the accurate or exact method provided by the use of bond tables. To determine the yield to maturity by approximation, one need only divide the average annual cost of funds by the average annual funds available to the firm.

Assume that a $1,000 par value 7 percent, 20-year bond is sold via underwriters for $1,005. If underwriting and related costs amount to $65, the net proceeds to the firm for each bond sold are $940. What is the approximate yield to maturity?

The 7 percent coupon rate requires that the borrower pay an annual interest of $70. But the yearly cost does not end here. Although the net proceeds for the sale are only $940, the firm has agreed to repay at maturity a principal amount of $1,000. We can assume that the difference of $60 can be spread equally over twenty years at the rate of $3 per year. Thus, our total average annual cost is now $73 ($70 + $3 = $73).

Since the actual annual outlay is only $70, the company, in a sense, holds back $3 annually from bondholders over the twenty-year life of the bonds. Therefore, the firm has use of both the proceeds and the amounts held back. Hence, the annual amount of funds available to the firm is the average of the $940 net proceeds and the par value of $1,000 due at the maturity of the bonds. This amounts to $970.

$$\frac{\$940 + \$1,000}{2} = \$970$$

The approximate cost of the bond then is determined by dividing the average annual cost to the firm by the average annual funds available, as follows:

$$\frac{\$\ 73}{\$970} = .07526 \quad \text{or} \quad 7.53\%$$

Because the cost of capital is to be used as a discount rate to compute the present value of after-tax cash flows, or to compare with an internal rate of return based on after-tax cash flows, we must express these costs on an after-tax basis. If the federal income tax rate (t) for a firm were 48 percent, then the after-tax cost of bonds in our example would be

$$7.53\% \times (1 - t) = 7.53 \times .52 = 3.92\%$$

The same result may be derived by means of the following formula:

$$\text{Yield to maturity} = \frac{C + \dfrac{M - P}{N}}{(M + P)/2}$$

C = annual dollar amount of coupon interest
M = maturity or par value of the bond
P = net proceeds to the firm
N = number of years to maturity.

By substitution we can calculate the yield to maturity.

$$\frac{\$70 + \dfrac{\$1,000 - \$940}{20}}{(\$1,000 + \$940)/2} = \frac{\$70 + \$3}{\$970} = 7.53\%$$

If a bond is sold at a premium price which provides net proceeds in excess of the par value of the bond, our approach when computing the approximate cost of the bond differs only slightly. Assume that the firm receives net proceeds of $1040, instead of $940, for the afore-mentioned 7 percent $1000 par value bond which matures in twenty years. Using the formula, we calculate the approximate yield as follows:

$$\frac{\$70 + \dfrac{\$1,000 - \$1,040}{20}}{(\$1,000 + \$1,040)/2} = \frac{\$70 - \$2}{\$1,020} = 6.67\%$$

If the tax rate is 48 per cent, the after-tax cost of the bond sold at a premium is

$$6.67\% \times (1 - t) = 6.67 \times .52 = 3.47\%$$

Accurate Method

The accurate method simply reduces the yield to maturity to a discount rate that equates the net proceeds of the bond issue with the present value of all interest and principal payments. Using our last example to calculate the accurate yield to maturity, we would have to find a discount rate that would give us a sum of present values of all $70 interest payments plus the present value of $1,000 received at the end of twenty years, which would be equal to the proceeds of $1,040. Precise bond tables are available that provide yields at various maturities and coupon rates, thus making an otherwise involved computation very simple. Without the table, we would have to solve for i in the following formula:

$$P = \frac{C}{(1 + i)} + \frac{C}{(1 + i)^2} + \frac{C}{(1 + i)^n} + \frac{M}{(1 + i)^n}$$

P = dollar amount of net proceeds,
C = annual dollar amount of coupon interest paid,
M = maturity or par value of the bond, and
n = number of years to maturity.

COMMON STOCK

Of the various sources of funds available to a business firm, the cost of equity capital, particularly common stock, is by far the most difficult to measure. There are several reasons for this. For example, the investor in a share of equity capital has far more complex and uncertain expectations than does the investor in preferred stock or debt instruments. Common stock has neither a floor nor a ceiling in terms of returns to the investor. Earnings on equity capital may go up or down. Since dividends are residual returns to owners and there is no promise or guarantee of anything, dividend payments may or may not reflect earnings retention, so that capital gains are uncertain.

The problem is particularly complex because the stockholder can derive returns in two basic ways — through dividend payments or through price appreciation. It can be argued that the expected returns are actually the earnings available to stockholders after taxes, whether paid out in dividends or retained by the firm. On this premise, one could contend that the only significant benefit received by the owner of stock is dividends. Because of current progressive tax structures, however, one could argue that the dividend payment is not indicative of the kind of benefit stockholders expect in the long run. Therefore, the ratio of expected dividends to the market price of a stock is not a realistic measure of the cost of common stock. Dividends alone do not meet the requirement of earning a reasonable return for investors.

Because of the problems involved with using dividend pay-out as a measure of cost of common stock, one might argue that the earnings yield is the appropriate measure. This approach would relate the expected future earnings per share to the net price obtained for a share of stock. The net proceeds received by the firm for a new issue of stock is relatively simple to calculate, but earnings per share expected by owners are much harder to measure. True, under normal market conditions, price-earnings ratios on similar securities might be used to determine stockholder expectations. During wide swings in market values, however, these ratios clearly are not very realistic indicators of investor anticipation. Hence, considered separately, both dividend pay-out and anticipated earnings per share leave much to be desired as measures of the cost of common stock. A better approach is based upon the assumption that a firm's owner, both existing and future, has in mind some minimum rate of return — from both dividends and capital gains — when investing in shares of the company. When his expected rate of return meets or exceeds his personal threshold of investment, he will invest; otherwise, he will disinvest. In other terms, the cost of equity capital is the minimum rate of return that a firm must earn on the equity-financed portion of an investment in order to leave unchanged the market price of the common stock.

The problem of measuring the cost of equity in this manner is closely linked to the problem of measuring the market value of the common stock. The value of a stock to an investor (the market price he agrees to pay) is determined by the present value of the expected future stream of dividends plus some terminal value (the market price of the stock when he chooses to sell it).

The following examples illustrate this contention:

Example 1: Assume that an investor plans to buy a share of common stock, receive an annual dividend, and then sell it at the end of one year. The value of the stock to him is the dividend plus the terminal value, each discounted back to the present at his expected minimum rate of return. This can be expressed:

$$(13\text{-}1) \qquad P_o = \frac{D_1}{1+k} + \frac{P_1}{1+k}$$

where P_o is the current price of the stock, D_1 is the first-year dividend, P_1 is the price of the stock at the end of one year, and k is the discount rate (expected rate of return).

Example 2: Now Assume that the investor expects to receive dividends for two years and then sell the stock at the end of that period. To obtain the value of the stock to him, Equation 13–1 is adjusted as follows:

$$(13\text{-}2) \qquad P_o = \frac{D_1}{(1+k)^1} + \frac{D_2}{(1+k)^2} + \frac{P_2}{(1+k)^2}$$

Example 3: Thus we see that the terminal value or selling price of the stock in Example 2 is merely the present value of the discounted stream of dividends plus the discounted terminal price, regardless of the time period involved. In turn, the terminal value is only the price paid by a second investor, and this price is determined by this discounted value of the second investor's expected stream of dividends plus the discounted terminal value, and so on. Hence, the value of a share of common stock *in general* is expressed as

$$(13\text{-}3) \qquad P_O = \frac{D_1}{(1+k)^1} + \frac{D_2}{(1+k)^2} + \frac{D_3}{(1+k)^3} + \cdots + \frac{D_n}{(1+k)^n}$$
$$+ \frac{P_n}{(1+k)^n}$$

Example 4: The foregoing equations indicate that the intrinsic value of a stock depends upon its future dividends. Thus

$$(13\text{-}4) \qquad P_0 = \frac{D_1}{1+k} + \frac{D_2}{(1+k)^2} + \frac{D_3}{(1+k)^3} + \cdots$$

If dividends are assumed to remain constant, it follows that the value of the stock is merely

$$(13\text{-}5) \qquad P_0 = \frac{D}{k}$$

Example 5: On the other hand, if we assume that a firm's common dividends will grow at a constant rate, g, and if D_0 is the current dividend, then the dividend for any future year, D_n, is expressed as $D_n = D_0(1+g)^n$. Equation (13-4) becomes

$$(13\text{-}6) \qquad P_0 = \frac{D_0(1+g)}{1+k} + \frac{D_0(1+g)^2}{(1+k)^2} + \cdots + \frac{D_0(1+g)^n}{(1+k)^n}$$

Or, if k is greater than g, Equation (13-6) reduces to

$$(13\text{-}7) \qquad P_0 = \frac{D_0}{k-g}$$

Solving for k, the discount rate (and, as previously indicated, the cost of common capital), we have

$$(13\text{-}8) \qquad k = \frac{D_0}{P_0} + g$$

Thus, if a share of a firm's stock is selling for $40, the current dividend is $4, and dividends have been growing at the rate of 4 percent annually, then the after-tax cost of common capital is

$$k = \frac{\$4}{\$40} + 4\% = 14\%$$

Example 6: The basic valuation formula may be used to derive the value of the shares of a firm which is expected to go through various stages of its life cycle. For example, if we estimate that a company's dividends will grow at a rapid rate of 12 percent for six years and then taper off to 4 percent thereafter, the value of its shares may be determined as

$$(13\text{-}9) \qquad P_0 = \sum_{t=1}^{6} \frac{D_0\,(1+gr)^n}{(1+k)^n} + \sum_{t=n+1}^{\infty} \frac{D_n\,(1+gc)^n}{(1+k)^n}$$

where gr is the rapid growth rate and gc is the constant growth rate. The rapid growth period is represented by the first summation, the second one is the present value of the constant rate of growth. Hence, we can see that as long as we know the timing and magnitude of changes in the growth pattern of the firm, the basic formula Equation (13-6) may be used to obtain a stock's intrinsic value (or the cost of common capital) by solving for k.

Clearly the preceding examples are based on the assumption that the price of a stock is determined by its stream of dividends in perpetuity. But can we make this statement about the market value of a firm that has never paid a dividend? How can we explain investors' being willing to pay a high price for a share of such stock? Obviously, such investors expect a high terminal value when the stock is sold sometime in the future. Rather than paying dividends currently, the company is retaining earnings, building its future earning power and thus its future potential to pay substantial dividends. Therefore, we can see that the intrinsic value of the stock of a "no current dividend" firm is also determined by a future stream of dividends.

RETAINED EARNINGS

Because retained earnings provide funds without any corresponding increase in obligations or equity securities outstanding, it is easy to erroneously regard them as a cost-free source of capital. Yet clearly they are not a free source of funds. Rather, there is a definite opportunity cost borne by the owners of the firm. Since retained earnings legally belong to the owners, it is generally assumed that a company withholds earnings from them only if it can expect returns on these earnings to be at least equal to, or greater than, the benefits the owners themselves could earn from alternative investments of similar risk. The opportunity cost is, of course, the dividend payments foregone by the shareholders. Before taxes, this is the cost of equity capital; that is, the cost determined by the return that owners expect to receive. The cost of this internal source of equity capital in this instance is based upon the current market price of the common stock, not the net proceeds from the sale of a new issue.

One approach to calculating the cost of retained earnings holds that this opportunity cost is less than the cost of new common stock for two reasons. First, when dividends are paid out, they are taxable income for the stockholders. Second, if we assume that the owner reinvests dividends received, he is likely to incur brokerage expense. The following example illustrates these points.

Assume that a corporation has determined that the cost of equity capital (the minimum rate of return expected by investors in the ownership of the firm) is 10 percent. The company earns $500,000 and pays out the entire amount in dividends. If all stockholders are in the 35 percent marginal tax bracket and if brokerage cost on re-invested dividends is 3 percent, the cost of retained earnings would be computed as follows:

1. Dividend payment $500,000
   Less: taxes $175,000
          brokerage cost   9,750   184,750
          (3% of $325,000)
   Net dividends reinvested $315,250

2. If the stockholders reinvest dividends at 10 percent (the cost of external equity capital to the firm) their earnings on the new investment is $31,525 ($315,250 × .10 = $31,525).

3. Since stockholders have a lesser net amount available for investment in other alternatives ($315,250) than would the firm if earnings were retained, it follows that the company would have to earn much less on the retained earnings of $500,000 than on external sources of equity capital, in order to provide the owners the benefits they could receive elsewhere. In our example, the internal rate of return of the firm required to provide $31,525 in benefits to stockholders is only 6.305 percent ($500,000 × 6.305 = $31,525). Therefore, shareholders are equally well off whether the company earns only 6.3 percent on internally financed investment opportunities or pays out dividends which are reinvested by recipients at a yield of 10 percent. Thus 6.3 percent is the cost of retained earnings.

The example just given illustrates that the cost of retained earnings may be computed by the following formula:

$$kr = ke \ (1 - t) \ (1 - b)$$

   kr = cost of capital for retained earnings,
   ke = cost of capital for external equity capital,
   t = income tax rate, and
   b = percentage brokerage cost for reinvested dividends.

$$kr = 0.10 \ (1 - 0.35) \ (1 - 0.03) = 6.305\%$$

The method just described for measuring the cost of retained earnings from the point of view of stockholder alternatives seems reasonable at first glance, but it suffers from a very significant weakness: the cost depends upon the tax bracket of the stockholder. Inasmuch as the marginal tax rates for a typical body of stockholders could range from 0 to 70 percent, this approach prohibits us from arriving at the "one correct answer." Some authorities suggest that we should not let this problem deter us. An "educated estimate" of the marginal tax rate of the firm's stockholders is urged as a means of overcoming the apparent obstacle. Others prefer to use average marginal tax rates for individual stockholders in general. Still others recommend that we base calculations on the minimum federal income tax rate of 14 percent. Nevertheless, since marginal tax rates vary widely and the other proposals appear rather arbitrary, the use of any of the suggested rates seems somewhat unrealistic.

What, then, is the proper measure of the cost of retained earnings? A reasonable position would hold that the cost of retained earnings is the same as the cost for external equity funds (common stock). It seems logical to assume that the cost is what these funds can earn in comparable income-risk packages outside the firm. This type of external opportunities rate gives us an earnings yield that satisfies the market for the common stock itself and thus is the better measurement of opportunity cost for retained earnings. Both funds received from stockholders and retained earnings are in effect funds to be invested in the same type of venture at similar rates.

DEPRECIATION

Depreciation is an internally generated source of funds. As a matter of fact, business firms consistently report in such publications as the *Economic Report of the President* that depreciation is one of their most important sources of capital funds. Thus, management tends to be fully aware that a part of available cash does indeed result from the recovery of the cash spent on fixed assets at some prior date. The question that arises is, for capital budgeting, should depreciation be measured as a source of funds when computing weighted cost of capital? Even though traditional financial and economic thinking views depreciation as a source of funds, is it similar to common stock, preferred stock, or debt obligations? Should a cost be assessed against depreciation? If so, how should this charge be determined?

We submit that reinvestment of these funds should be tested as carefully as the reinvestment of capital derived from any other source and that the cost of this internal capital is equal to the cost of common stock and retained earnings. The reasoning behind this approach parallels that used in measuring the cost of retained earnings. As in the case of undistributed profits, management, through the write-off of depreciation, has the use of these internally generated funds and in effect avoids outside equity funds by using them. Theoretically, the firm could distribute the funds to its owners who, in turn, could reinvest them in the stock of similar corporations or other alternative projects of similar risk and earn a benefit equal to their required rate of return. Logically, if the firm cannot earn at least this required rate equal to the owners' opportunity cost, and thus maintain the market value of the outstanding stock, then the funds should be paid out to the stockholders.

PREFERRED STOCK

The calculation of the cost of preferred stock is less complex than for debt obligations, since preferreds have no maturity date or repayment obligation. Hence, we avoid the complicating factors of a payment at maturity and the amortization of a discount or premium over the life of the security. Moreover, the preferred stockholder does not relate future earnings to the price he is willing to pay for the stock, because the dividend return is fixed. Therefore, the cost of preferred stock is the amount of the dividend divided by the net proceeds realized by a firm from the sale of the stock after deductions for underwriters' cost or spread and other costs of the issue.

Assume that a 6 percent $100 par value preferred stock nets a firm $95 after underwriting and other costs. The cost of this source of funds to the firm would be

$$\frac{\text{Annual dividends}}{\text{Net proceeds}} = \frac{\$6}{\$95} = 6.32\%$$

Since dividends are not tax-deductible, we are dealing with after-tax dollars, and 6.32 percent is the after-tax cost.

WEIGHTED COST OF CAPITAL

In order to determine a hurdle rate (minimum return on investment) which a firm must earn to justify the use of funds, the cost of each individual source of capital is of very limited use. The reasons are quite apparent. If a 1977 investment project's internal rate of return of 12 percent, for example, is matched against the after-tax cost of a bank loan of 7 percent, then very likely the investment should be made. If in 1978, however, our individual source of funds is 14 percent equity capital, then new projects earning less than 14 percent would not be considered. Thus this approach would result in widely fluctuating and unreasonable cutoff rates each year.

There are further reasons against using an individual source of funds as a hurdle rate. Assume that a firm's cost of equity capital is estimated as 14 percent and the after-tax cost of debt obligations is 6 percent. Obviously, we cannot contend that if just the debt obligations are used to finance a new investment, then the cost of capital of the new project is only 6 percent. Unless the debt obligations had an adequate equity base, they could not be sold. Bond interest, for example, must be covered by earnings, mainly derived from the equity base, if bonds are to be marketed successfully. In other words, we can readily see that decisions on the minimum level of return required for any project should not be determined by reference to the cost of a specific source of funds that, on occasion, may be used. To do so would be erroneous because the source of funds selected for a specific investment will eventually affect the cost and the firm's overall flexibility in choosing other sources for future investments. Changes in the proportions of debt, for instance, tend to change the riskiness of the equity and thus the cost of the latter component. In other words, a firm cannot assume any debt level it chooses and simply ignore the effect on the market value of its stock. Further, to avoid a capital structure that is top heavy in debt, the firm currently using debt as a source of funds could be forced to switch to equity in subsequent years. Considerable evidence indicates that the average cost of equity increases as additional *sums* of such funds are obtained. Similarly, it would be somewhat unreasonable to assume that debt cost will remain the same in subsequent years as more and more funds are required.

Often the lowest-cost sources are not used as a means of financing a particular project, since the decision frequently requires balance between risk and cost. Thus, even though the costs of common stock and retained earnings are usually higher than other sources, they often tend to be selected because of the relatively low risk to the firm. Therefore, the after-tax cost of individual sources of funds have little practical meaning. Again we see that hurdle rates should be based on the average cost of capital, rather than the cost of a specific source of funds.

Clearly, the average cost of capital becomes even more significant when the weights of each source of capital are taken into consideration. That is, average cost of capital is adjusted by weighting the cost of each component of the capital structure by the relative proportion of that source to the total. The computation of the weighted cost may be illustrated in Tables 13-1 and 13-2.

The preceding book value approach indicates that a firm had after tax costs of capital of 4 percent for bonds, 6 percent for preferred stock, and 10 percent for equity capital (common stock, retained earnings, and depreciation). The balance sheet of the company shows that the book value of the capital structure is $20 million, with 35 percent of the structure in bonds, 5 percent in preferred stock, and 60 percent in equity. The weighted cost of each source of funds is obtained by multiplying the proportion of the capital structure (column 2) by the after-tax cost (column 3). The sum of the weighted costs of the three sources of funds is the weighted average cost of capital, or 7.7 percent.

Now assume that the current market value of the common stock plus the retained earnings and depreciation totals $32.8 million and the market values of both bonds and preferred stock are $100,000 greater than the book values of each. As illustrated in the market value approach, different percentage capital structures are obtained, and consequently a different overall weighted cost of capital of 8.9 percent is computed.

This example leads us to this question: Should the proportions of capital structure be expressed in terms of book values or market values? The answer is quite important, since book and market values often differ substantially. Because of these differences, it follows that weighted cost of capital based on book value is apt to differ significantly from one measured in terms of market values.

Our previous discussion indicates that we measure cost of capital of various sources of funds in reference to the market. The valuation of various securities issued by the firm is a focal point under this approach. The determination of the cost of common stock, for

TABLE 13-1.

		Book Value Approach					
Source of Funds	(1) Book Value	(2) Proportion of Structure		(3) After-tax Cost		(4) Weighted Cost	
Bonds	$ 7,000,000	35.0%	X	4.0%	=	1.4%	
Preferred	1,000,000	5.0	X	6.0%	=	0.3	
Equity	12,000,000	60.0	X	10.0%	=	6.0	
	$20,000,000	100.0%				7.7%	

TABLE 13-2.

	(1)	(2)		(3)		(4)
Source of Funds	Market Value	Proportion of Structure		After-tax Cost		Weighted Cost
Bonds	$ 7,100,000	17.3%	X	4.0%	=	0.7%
Preferred	1,100,000	2.7	X	6.0%	=	0.2
Equity	32,800,000	80.0	X	10.0%	=	8.0
	$41,000,000	100.0%				8.9%

Market Value Approach

example, required that we consider the market value of the stock. That is, the cost of equity capital is the discount rate which gives us a present value of expected dividends equal to the current market value of the stock. Therefore, to be consistent with the basic investor orientation of the cost-of-capital concept, we use market value when weighting various proportions of each source of funds.

The weighting procedure set forth is based upon various assumptions: First, we assume that acceptance of an investment project does not alter the business-risk complexion of the company; that is, the effect of business risk upon the valuation of the firm, and thus its cost of capital, is held constant. Then, we assume that the firm will maintain a constant dividend payout. Finally, we hold constant the capital structure of the firm; that is, a company will continue to finance its needs over a period of time in about the same proportions as currently reflected in the market values of each source of funds. This is not to say that each time a firm needs funds it will issue securities made up of proportionate shares of bonds, preferred stock, common stock, and so forth. Rather, we assume that common stock may be issued at one period, bonds at another, and later another source of funds may be utilized. However, we assume that, over time, the proportions of the capital structure are maintained.

SUMMARY

The basic purpose of capital investment is to add to the value of each owner's share of the firm. This share is increased, however, only if incremental profit earned from a new investment exceeds the cost of capital required to realize the additional income. Hence, the cost of capital sets the hurdle rate that a project must clear before a firm's funds are committed. Cost of capital, therefore, is the rate of return on a project that will leave unchanged the market price of a firm's stock.

The cost of capital is an opportunity cost established by the market. Although most authorities agree that the cost of capital is an appropriate hurdle rate for a firm, wide differences of opinion occur when we consider how this cost should be calculated. One approach holds that the cost of capital is determined by first measuring the costs of individual sources of financing, then, combining these costs into an overall weighted cost of capital. To accomplish this, we weigh the cost of each component of debt and equity in a company's capital structure by its relative weight in the total of funds sought. A firm's capital structure may include bonds, common stock, preferred stock, retained earnings, and depreciation flows.

The cost of bonds is yield to maturity, net after taxes. The costs of common stock and preferred stock, like the cost of bonds, are based on market values of these securities. The cost of common stock is that rate which equates the stream of future dividends to its market price; the cost of preferred stock is the amount of annual dividends divided by its market price. Like common stock, the cost of retained earnings is difficult to measure. However, a reasonable position would hold that the cost of these funds is the same as the cost of common stock. Depreciation is an internally generated source of funds which should be tested as carefully as the reinvestment of capital derived from any other source. This cost is equal to the cost of common stock and retained earnings.

The overall, or weighted, cost of capital is determined by calculating a weighted average of the costs of the separate components of the capital structure. That is, average cost of capital is adjusted by weighting the cost of each component of the capital structure by the relative proportion of that source of the total.

QUESTIONS FOR
ANALYSIS AND DISCUSSION

1. Why is the cost-of-capital concept of great importance to the economist or manager of a firm when calculating various methods of evaluating proposed capital expenditures? Explain fully.
2. "Retained earnings are a costless source of funds to a business firm." Do you agree or disagree? Why or why not?
3. Defend the position that the weighted cost of capital is an appropriate hurdle or cutoff rate for a firm when making capital expenditure decisions.
4. What are the reasons for using market values instead of accounting book values of individual sources of funds for computing the weighted cost of capital?
5. Discuss both the practical and theoretical problems involved when an attempt is made to calculate the cost of common stock.

6. Distinguish between the approximate and accurate methods of computing the cost of bonds to a firm.

7. Assume that you hold a position as economic advisor to the President of the United States. If it were felt that the economy would benefit by additional capital investment, what fiscal and monetary policies would you recommend to affect cost of capital and to stimulate capital expenditures by business firms?

8. Under what conditions might an arbitrary discount rate, rather than the cost of capital, be used as a hurdle rate when computing the net present value of an investment project?

9. What are the arguments for using the cost of depreciation when calculating the weighted cost of capital of a firm?

10. How are opportunity costs used when determining the weighted cost of capital?

PROBLEMS AND CASES

1. The L.C. Walter Corporation presently has the following capital structure:

    A. $12 million par value 7 percent bonds due in twelve years. The current market price of a $1000 par value bond is $960.

    B. $8 million 6 percent $100 par value preferred stock. The current market price of the stock is $112 per share, with 80,000 shares outstanding.

    C. 4 million shares of common stock are outstanding. Each share is currently earning $3 and paying a $2 dividend. The firm's earnings, dividends, and common stock price have all been growing at a rate of 3 percent a year, and management expects this growth pattern to continue for a number of years. The current market price of the stock is $36 per share. The corporation is in the 48 percent tax bracket.

    Calculate the weighted cost of capital.

2. McClain Computer Services, Inc., has provided you with the following information regarding its various sources of funds:

Bonds	(6%)	$2,000,000 (Book Value)
Preferred stock	(6%)	$2,000,000 (Book Value)
Common stock		$8,000,000 (Market Value)

The 20-year bonds are selling for $980 and have a par value of $1000. Preferred stock is $100 par value and has a current market value of $92 per share. Common stock has a market value of $40 and is earning $2 per share. Dividends are $1 per share. Earnings have been growing 6 percent annually, and this growth rate is expected to continue. The tax rate is 48 percent.

   (a) The company has asked you to compute its weighted cost of capital. Based on the information given, what is this cost?

   (b) If you had access to the firm's financial records, what additional data would you seek, if any? Why?

3. The common stock of the Taylor Products Corportation is currently selling for $94 per share. After careful study, management estimates that the

earnings, dividends, and market price of the stock should continue to grow at an annual rate of 2.75 percent. Current earnings per share are $9 and the annual dividend is $7.65. The stockholders' required rate of return is estimated to be 10 percent. Assume all stockholders are in 35 percent marginal tax bracket, and brokerage fee for reinvestment of stockholders' dividends is 3 percent.

(a) Review the two methods of calculating the cost of retained earnings given in the text and use each method to compute the cost of this source of funds.

(b) Discuss the arguments used to support each of the two methods of calculating the cost of retained earnings.

4. The Bryant Corporation has been producing bicycles and related accessories, games, and a limited line of toys for forty-eight years. Except for three years (1935–38) the firm has been very profitable. After the death of its founder seven years ago, however, the company has experienced a slight decline in sales, although profits have been increasing at a rate of about 2 per cent annually during the past seven years. Nevertheless, management has done nothing to modernize plant and machinery. Joseph Martin was recently appointed financial manager and assigned the task of formulating a capital expenditure program designed to update the firm's machinery. Since the company has never used the present-value method or the internal rate-of-return method of evaluating proposed capital expenditures, its management had not attempted to compute a weighted cost of capital. One of Martin's first assignments was to analyze the following data and to calculate a weighted cost of capital.

1. The liability and net worth section of the balance sheet indicated the following:

Bonds 6%	$500,000
Preferred stock 6%	$400,000
Common stock (par $1.00)	$600,000
Retained earnings	$200,000

2. The corporation's tax rate is 40 percent.

3. Bonds are 15-year term, par value $1000, with a current market value of $1030.

4. Preferred stock is $100 par value and currently selling on the market at $96 per share.

5. Earnings on common stock are $1.20 per share. Dividends are $.80 per share. Despite the firm's overall decline, earnings have been growing at a rate of 2 per cent annually for the past several years. The current market price of common stock is $30 per share.

6. The firm's fixed assets are old and somewhat obsolete and are fully depreciated.

(a) Calculate the weighted cost of capital.

(b) Defend the method used to compute the after-tax cost of each source of funds.

5. Your instructor will assign you the task of computing the weighted cost of

capital of a large, well-known corporation. The following suggestions are intended to ease the burden of your research and computations.

(a) Determine the coupon rate, the maturity date, and the current market price of outstanding bonds. Then calculate the approximate yield to maturity to obtain the cost of bonds. Since the complexities of sinking funds are beyond the scope of this text, ignore any sinking funds and simply assume a common maturity date for all bonds.

(b) Find the dividend rate and current market price of preferred stock. Again, compute the cost of this source of capital, but ignore sinking funds, if any.

(c) Examine the market for the common stock to find the current market price and the recent dividend paid. Study past growth trends, current conditions, and possible future earnings expectations; then estimate the future growth rate of earnings. Then compute the cost of common stock.

SELECTED READINGS

Bierman, Harold, Jr., and Seymour Smidt. *The Capital Budgeting Decision.* New York. The Macmillan Co., Inc., 1971.

Brigham, Eugene F., and Myron J. Gordon. "Leverage, Dividend Policy, and the Cost of Capital." *Journal of Finance* (March 1968): 85-103.

Gordon, M.J. *The Investment, Financing and Valuation of the Corporation.* Homewood, Ill.: Richard Irwin, Inc., 1962.

———. "Security and Investment: Theory and Evidence." *Journal of Finance* (December 1964): 607-618.

Mao, James C.T. "The Valuation of Growth Stocks; The Investment Opportunities Approach." *Journal of Finance* March 1966): 91-102.

Modigliani, F., and M.H. Miller. "The Cost of Capital, Corporation Finance, and the Theory of Investment." *American Economic Review* (June 1958).

Soldofsky, R.M. "The Cost of Capital Function of a Firm." *Controller* (June 1958): 263-68.

———. "A Note on the History of Bond Tables and Stock Valuation Models." *Journal of Finance* (March 1966): 103-111.

Solomon, Ezra. "Leverage and the Cost of Capital." *Journal of Finance* (May 1963): 273-79.

Vandell, Robert F., and Robert M. Pennell. "Tight-money Financing." *Harvard Business Review* (September-October, 1971): 82-97.

Weston, J. Fred, and Eugene F. Brigham. *Managerial Finance,* 3rd ed. New York: Holt, Rinehart and Winston, 1969.

Wippern, Ronald F. "Financial Structure and the Value of the Firm." *Journal of Finance* (December 1966): 615-33.

14

Employment
of Human Resources

Labor cost is the largest single cost faced by most business firms. Although a firm's labor costs may range from 10-90 percent of total cost, wage and salary payments constitute 75 percent of our national income. Not only are labor costs large, they are in most cases recurring; costs that must usually be paid weekly or biweekly. They cannot easily be delayed or deferred. Nor can they, like material cost, be paid on a 2 percent, net 30, basis. The responsibility and stringency of making wage and salary payments is often manifest in the question "Has he ever met a payroll?" put to test the capabilities of a potential new manager or to question the theories of a professor of economics.

Changes in labor costs, whether in wages or fringe benefits, can have a pronounced effect on total cost, on profit, and on the final price of a product or service. The cost of labor, also has a definite influence on its use as a resource. This cost helps determine where labor is used, and whether or not it should be used at all or perhaps be replaced by capital.

HISTORICAL WAGE THEORIES

One of the first attempts to explain wages was in terms of the *subsistence theory*. According to this theory, prevalent during much of the nineteenth century, wages were determined by the amount of necessities required to keep a worker and his family alive. Economic factors, it was held, would cause an adjustment in market wages if they were above or below the subsistence level. This theory was followed by the *wages-fund* theory, which held that wages were dependent upon a special fund (the wages fund) set aside by employers out of previous profits. Wages were determined by the size of the fund relative to the population. The greater the population, the less the wage rate, and vice versa. The *residual theory of wages* also was typical of nineteenth- and early twentieth-century economic thinking. It held that wages were determined by the amount of the total product left after all other factors of production, including rent, interest, and profit, had been compensated.

CURRENT WAGE THEORIES

Bargaining Theory

There is a widespread belief today that wages are determined by bargaining. The *bargaining theory*, as it is known, suggests that wages are set somewhere between a maximum that the employer will pay and a minimum that the employees, or their union, will accept. Although the union demands more than it expects to get, it generally has a minimum below which it will not go, at least without a strike. On the other side of the bargaining table, management generally will offer less than it can pay, but there is a definite level above which it will not go. Through bargaining, the wage rate is established somewhere between the minimum acceptable to the union and the maximum tolerable to the employer. A number of factors, such as the state of the economy, the financial condition of the company, the strength of the union, and wage rates offered elsewhere all affect the actual wage rate.

Nevertheless, the bargaining theory is more a description of how actual wages are set than it is a true theory of wages. It does not explain what determines the minimum and maximum levels established by the employer and the union. What, for example, determines the minimum the union will accept? Is it the subsistence level, or "natural wage," or is it based on some notion of an American standard of living? Certainly the minimum acceptable wage will be determined by a multitude of factors, such as the cost of living, wages elsewhere, the aggressiveness of the union, the militancy of the workers, and the union's evaluation of the workers' productivity. The maximum wage level above which the company will not pay, on the other hand, will be influenced by the firm's profitability, its measure of workers' productivity, the wage rate of its competitors, its policy toward the union, its financial ability to risk a strike, and many other factors. To find these answers to the question of delineating the minimum and maximum perimeters of the wage determination, one must look elsewhere, to the subsistence theory, supply and demand, and the marginal productivity theory of wages.

At the present time, the bargaining theory of wages, moreover, cannot be a general theory of wages since it does not apply to wage determination in all cases. In many situations in the economy today wages are determined in the absence of bargaining, collectively or otherwise.

The theory of wages most widely recognized today is the marginal-productivity theory. It endeavors to explain how wages are determined by using a large number of assumptions. The marginal-productivity theory holds that wages will be determined by the value of the goods produced by the marginal worker, and that the employer will not hire another worker if the value of the added goods produced by the worker is less than the wage that must be paid. In a practical situation, if you could hire workers at $30 per day to make goods that sold for more than $30, you could make a profit by hiring them. On the other hand, if the products they made brought you only $25 per day, you would not hire them. In the latter case, you could not pay them more than $25 per day without losing money.

But far be it from economic analysis to put forth a simple theory. Many complications enter the picture: The product of each worker differs, and when adding people to a work force, the contribution of each additional member may differ, depending on the machinery, equipment, and number of people already in the work force. Remember that when adding workers to a work force, we must always contend with the law of diminishing returns. Complications also exist in selling the product of the workers. Perhaps additional products can be sold at a uniform price, but if imperfect competition prevails, the price obtainable will decrease as output increases.

1. Assumptions of the Marginal-productivity Theory. In essence the marginal productivity theory assumes the following conditions (which resemble pure competition): (1) free competition exists between employees for jobs; (2) free competition exists between employers for workers; (3) both labor and capital are mobile between industries and localities; (4) labor is fully employed, except for those who seek a wage above the value of their productivity; (5) both employers and workers have a means of knowing the value of the worker's marginal product; (6) there is a given contribution by the other necessary factors of production; (7) workers in the same grade are interchangeable; (8) every worker in the same grade is paid the same wage; (9) the employer desires to maximize profits.

2. Marginal-productivity Theory under Pure Competition. Under conditions of pure competition, both the price of the product and the price of labor will be determined by the force of supply and demand. Thus, assume a hypothetical situation in which the employer can hire all the labor he wants for a wage of $30 per day.

Assume further that the price at which he can sell his product is $6 per unit, and that his production effort is subject to the law of non-proportional output.

In Table 14-1, Column 1 shows the number of workers hired. Column 2 indicates the total output (units) resulting from the use of a specific number of workers. The marginal product, the increase in total product per additional unit (labor) used, is shown in Column 3. Observe that the point of diminishing marginal productivity, 52 units, is reached with the employment of the fourth worker. Column 4 represents the total fixed cost, with which you are already familiar. Column 5 shows the wage rate, $30, as determined by the market forces of supply and demand or other forces. This wage or amount is also known as the *average outlay* (AO) because it is the average amount of money that the employer must pay for each worker hired. (In this case it is the average variable cost, since we are assuming that no other variable cost exists. Notice that this differs from the term *average total cost*, used in earlier chapters, which refers to the average of both fixed and variable cost.) Column 6 is the total cost, made up of both the total variable and the total fixed cost. Column 7 represents the *marginal outlay* (MO), which may be defined as the increase in total cost per additional unit of input (worker) hired. Notice that it differs from the term *marginal cost*, defined, in Chapter 7, as the increase in total cost per additional unit of output. Keep in mind, too, that it is a constant amount because, under conditions of pure competition, an individual employer can hire any number of workers at the given market price determined by supply and demand.

On the revenue side, Column 8 represents the market price for the final product. This price is also known as the *average revenue*. Remember that, under conditions of pure competition, an individual firm can sell an infinite number of units at a given market price. The total revenue, Column 9, is obtained by multiplying the average revenue (price) by the total output. The *marginal revenue product* (MRP), shown in Column 10, is defined as the increase in total revenue resulting from the use of an additional unit of input (labor). Notice that it differs from marginal revenue, which is the increase in total revenue resulting from the sale of an additional unit of output. Any time an additional unit of labor increases the total product by more than one unit, the marginal revenue product will be some multiple of the average revenue and be greater in value than the marginal revenue. It can be observed further that the marginal revenue product, after a certain point, declines as output increases. This is due to the operation of the law of diminishing marginal productivity.

TABLE 14-1.

(1) Units of Labor	(2) Total Units of Output	(3) Marginal Product	(4) Total Fixed Cost	(5) Average Outlay (wage)	(6) Total Cost	(7) Marginal Outlay	(8) Average Revenue (price)	(9) Total Revenue	(10) Marginal Revenue Product	(11) Total Profit
1	10	—	$200	$30	$230	—	$6	$ 60	—	-$170
2	22	12	200	30	260	$30	6	132	$72	-128
3	36	14	200	30	290	30	6	216	84	-74
4	52	16	200	30	320	30	6	312	96	52
5	67	15	200	30	350	30	6	402	90	52
6	80	13	200	30	380	30	6	480	78	100
7	90	10	200	30	410	30	6	540	60	130
8	98	8	200	30	440	30	6	588	48	148
9	104	6	200	30	470	30	6	624	36	154
10	108	4	200	30	500	30	6	648	24	148
11	110	2	200	30	530	30	6	660	12	130
12	110	0	200	30	560	30	6	660	0	100

If the firm wants to maximize profit, it will continue to add workers so long as total profit increases. Since marginal revenue product is the increase in total revenue per additional unit of labor utilized, and the marginal outlay is the increase in total cost per additional unit of labor used, whenever the marginal revenue product exceeds the marginal outlay, total profit will increase or total loss will diminish. If the marginal revenue product is less than marginal outlay, however, the total profit will decrease. Since the marginal revenue product (MRP) eventually declines as workers are added and marginal outlay (MO) remains constant, an equilibrium point is reached at which the MRP equals the MO. At this point the firm will have maximum profit. Accordingly, a firm will hire workers so long as the MRP is greater than the MO.

In analyzing the data in Table 14-1, notice that the firm will hire the first nine workers because in each case the MRP of each worker hired is greater than the MO required to hire the worker. One can see, too, that with each worker total loss is decreased or the profit increased by the amount of the difference between MRP and the MO. The firm will not hire the tenth worker or any more, however, because the MRP of the tenth, and subsequent workers, is less than the MO. To hire more than nine workers would cause total profit to decline. Maximum profit, $154, is made with the ninth worker. This assumes that the firm hires only full-time and no part-time employees. Otherwise, according to the graph, it would maximize profit with 9 1/2 workers. If the firm is using fewer than nine workers, it can increase its profit by increasing the number of employees. On the other hand, if it is using more than the equilibrium number of workers, it can raise its profits by reducing the number of workers.

The marginal productivity theory of wages assumes that all workers of the same grade are interchangeable. Therefore, if the first or the fifth worker were hired in the place of the ninth worker, his marginal-revenue product would be no greater than that of the ninth worker. Thus, it is concluded that the wage paid to any worker should be no more than the value of the marginal revenue product (MRP) of the last worker hired.

The marginal productivity theory is not only a theory of wages, it is also a theory of employment. There is a definite relationship between productivity, wages, and employment. This can be demonstrated in the figures that follow. Figure 14-1 assumes conditions shown in Table 14-1 with a wage of $30. Since the wage for all workers is the same, the AO and (MO) are depicted by a horizontal line. Observe that, for all workers up to and including the ninth, the MRP of each worker is greater than the MO. For the tenth and each subsequent worker, the MRP is less than the MO. Hence, the equilib-

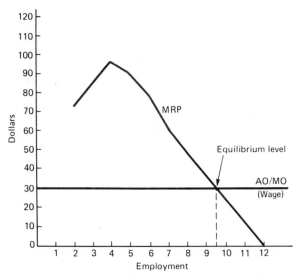

Figure 14-1.

rium level of employment is at nine workers, where the maximum profit is made. Less profit will be made if the employer hires fewer or more than this number of workers.

A change in the wage, of course, can change employment. Suppose the wage were increased from $30 to $40. In this case it would no longer be profitable for the firm to hire the ninth worker, since the MRP, $36, of the ninth worker shown in Table 14-1 is less than the new wage. On the other hand, if wages were reduced to $20, it would become profitable to hire the tenth worker, whose MRP is $24. This would increase profit by $4, and every dollar counts. Thus the theory holds that an increase in wages will decrease employment and a decrease in wages will increase employment. This conclusion is shown in Figure 14-2, where a wage increase to $40 reduces employment to eight workers and a decrease in wages to $20 causes an expansion of employment to ten workers.

It is also possible that workers' productivity will change. Suppose that because of better production techniques, the productivity of all workers rose and that of the tenth worker in particular increased from $24 to $36. In such a case his MRP would become greater than the MO, and it would be profitable to hire him. This is shown in Figure 14-3. On the other hand, if productivity were decreased for some reason or other, such as inefficiency or union limitation, to such an extent that the MRP of the ninth worker fell from $36 to $24, his MRP would be less than the MO, and it would no longer be

442

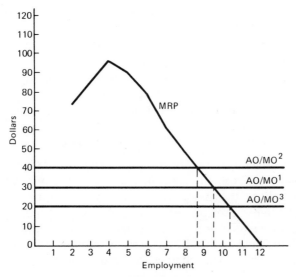

Figure 14-2.

profitable to hire him at $30 per day. Since the MRP is affected not only by the number of units produced but also by the price received for each unit produced, the MRP can be influenced by price changes. If prices rise, the MRP will increase and employment will increase, and vice versa. Thus, the theory holds that if the MRP increases for

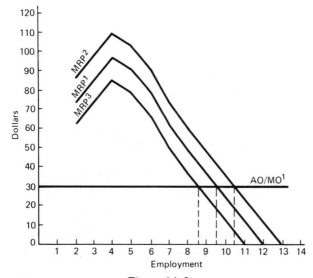

Figure 14-3.

any reason, the level of employment will rise and if the MRP decreases, the level of employment will fall.

If wages increase, it is not necessary that employment decrease, however, provided that offsetting changes take place. Likewise, if wages decrease, employment will not necessarily increase if offset by a decreasing marginal revenue product. One of the possible offsetting changes is shown in Figure 14-4 where the wage increase is more than offset by an increase in productivity. In such a situation, employment actually increases rather than decreases.

3. Marginal Productivity Theory under Imperfect Competition. As one moves away from the assumptions of pure competition into the world of reality, the marginal productivity theory becomes more complex. Under conditions of monopoly or oligopoly, for example, the selling price received from the sale of each additional unit produced will decline as output increases, as explained in Chapter 8. This condition, naturally, will change the shape and the slope of the marginal revenue product line.

Moreover, in the labor market, if monopsony, oligopsony, or monoposonistic competition exists, an individual employer will not be able to hire an infinite supply of labor at a given market price. Because of the nature of imperfect competition, higher wages will be required to hire additional units of labor. As a result, the wage, or average outlay, will no longer be identical to the marginal outlay, as it was under conditions of pure competition. If it is assumed that

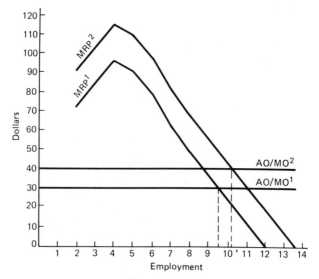

Figure 14-4.

the wages of all workers will be the same, it means that when an additional worker is hired at a higher rate, the total cost will increase substantially. Marginal outlay will rise not only by the wage of the additional worker but also because the wage of all other workers will be increased to the new higher wage of the last worker hired.

Graphically, both the wage (AO) and the MO will be represented by lines sloping upward to the right. But the MO will increase at a faster rate than the AO, or wage rate. At the point of maximum profits, the marginal revenue product will equal the marginal outlay (MRP = MO); but the AO (wage), will be less than the MRP of the last worker hired. Under conditions of imperfect competition, the MO and the AO (wage) diverge. Therefore, the wage will not tend to equal the marginal revenue product of the worker. This can be seen in Figure 14-5, where the MRP intersects the MO at $48, but the AO (wages) is only $34 at the equilibrium level of employment, 8 workers.

4. Further Reservations. Only a limited amount of pure competition exists in our economy. It must also be remembered, too, that the marginal productivity is based on a number of unrealistic assumptions. Some employers, for example, are not interested in maximizing profits but in making reasonable profits. Workers may not be as mobile as the theory assumes. Monopsonists do not necessarily pay the lowest possible wage. In most cases, neither the worker nor the employer knows the value of the marginal revenue product of the

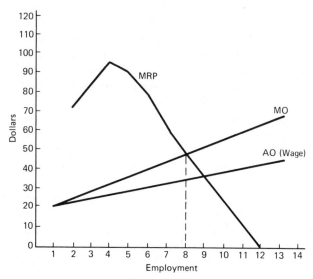

Figure 14-5.

worker. Moreover, modern industrial firms cannot easily hold all factors constant except labor, and then by hiring additional workers measure the marginal revenue products of such workers. These and other complications have led businessmen and most union leaders to question the value of the marginal productivity theory of wages.

Nevertheless an employer generally will admit that the firm will not hire additional workers unless it results in higher profit. Thus it appears that, in a practical sense, the business is following the guiding principle established by the marginal productivity theory.

5. Validity of the Marginal-productivity Theory. Even under conditions of pure competition where the wage equals the marginal revenue product of the last worker hired, is the wage really determined by the marginal productivity of the worker? Or does the wage plus a given marginal productivity determine the number of workers that will be hired? In an actual labor market, the latter seems to be true. Usually the wage is determined by some other force, such as supply and demand, collective bargaining, or legislation. Given a certain wage, as determined by supply and demand, for example, the employer will hire workers as long as the marginal productivity of the worker is greater than the wage that must be paid. Thus one may more appropriately say that the wage will tend to equal the marginal productivity of the worker (and it does so simply because the employer is interested in maximizing profits) than to say that the wage will be determined by the marginal productivity of the worker. On the other hand, it is also true that the wage paid workers, regardless of how it is determined, cannot be more than the marginal revenue product of the worker, or the employer will lose money. The theory does, however, relate wages to productivity and does indicate that the worker, through his productivity, can influence his wage and, for that matter, his employment or unemployment.

Moreover, the marginal productivity approach is a useful tool of analysis in attempting to determine the effects of a rise in the legal minimum wage on total employment. It can also be used by a business firm to ascertain the probable effects of a rise in wage rates or fringe benefits. Changes in prices, productivity, and other factors affecting the productivity of the worker can be analyzed via the marginal productivity approach.

No one theory completely and adequately explains wage determination. Nor are the theories mutually exclusive; they overlap in some degree. Since no one theory, or even combination of theories clearly and satisfactorily explains how wages are determined, one might ask: why bother to study those theories? The answer is twofold: (1) A study of the theories gives us some idea of the complexity and difficulty of wage-rate determination. (2) Although no one theory adequately explains wage determination, each adds something to our understanding of the problem. Furthermore, since some progress has been made in developing wage theory during the past few hundred years, knowledge of older theories lays a foundation for their improvement. Certainly familiarity with existing wage theories, whatever their weaknesses and limitations, makes the analyst's task much easier as he searches for an improved theory or seeks to make current theory more practical.

But how are wages actually determined by the business firm, or the worker, or the government? Here you may have almost as many different answers as you have employers. Some firms maintain that they pay a cost-of-living wage and even gear their wages to the Consumer Price Index. Others claim to be paying comparative wage rates, that is, they pay the same rate as workers receive in comparative firms in the industry. But here again one might ask, what determines the wage rate in comparative firms? Still other firms say that they are paying community rates; that is, rates in line with those general in the community. These wages are not so high that they disturb the general wage structure of the community and incur the wrath of fellow employers, nor so low that the employer is looked upon with disdain by workers and the community as a whole. Many firms pay the competitive rate determined, in large part, by the supply of, and demand for, workers. Others claim that they are paying the union rate, whatever that may be.

Also to be explained in actual wage determination are wage differentials. Besides the usual differences, wage differentials often exist between workers of the same grade. There are also inter- and intra-industry differentials. Wages differ between regions, between urban and rural workers, and between organized and unorganized workers. In still other cases, in spite of recent legislation, differences in wage rates exist between male and female workers and between workers of different races.

Complications in wage determination are intensified when hourly rates are compared with piece rates, and with the utilization of complex incentive, bonus, and profit-sharing systems. Then there are the numerous fringe benefits, including holiday pay, vacation pay, insurance, medical benefits, supplementary unemployment benefits, pensions, and the like that must be considered, especially since, on the average, they are equal to about 30 percent of the standard wage rate.

FACTORS AFFECTING LABOR COSTS

Labor costs, therefore prices and profits, are affected by a multitude of factors that the business firm must consider. These factors include the method of wage payment, the minimum wage, hours of work, social security payments, pension funds, profit sharing, and the activities of labor unions, just to mention a few.

Methods of Wage Payment

The total cost, the wage rate, the cost per unit of output and profit can be affected by the method of wage payment. A *piece-rate* system may be used that ties a worker's wage directly to his productivity. Usually a worker is paid so much per unit of output, or the worker may receive a percentage pay bonus when output exceeds a stipulated level. There are numerous variations of piece rate payment. It may be paid on an individual or group basis; it may be a straight or variable rate; it may or may not contain a bonus system. Many firms think that a piece rate schedule serves as an incentive to workers and enhances worker productivity. Employers also contend that it gives them better control over labor cost.

Piece-rate systems, however, are sometimes difficult to implement and administer. Job requirements change, periodic time studies are required, and production standards must occasionally be altered. In many cases, workers and unions resist or resent piece rate systems. In addition, a piece rate formula cannot be applied to all jobs.

The hourly rate method of wage payment is much more common. It is easier to apply, it eliminates pay differences on identical or similar jobs, time studies are required less frequently, and hourly rates are more readily accepted by workers and labor officials. With the use of hourly rates, it is important to establish job requirements and production standards in order to get an optimum amount of production from each job or person holding that job. It is harder, also, to relate wage payments to specific job productivity. Hourly rates limit worker incentive, since there is no specific or direct reward on the job for being more productive.

Regardless of the type of wage payment, the frequency of the pay period can have a noticeable effect on total labor cost. If a company has a sizable payroll and is accustomed to paying its employees biweekly or semimonthly and then changes over to a weekly pay period it will add considerably to the company expenses. First, it will need more clerical and computer time to get checks out every week. Secondly, there can be a substantial loss of interest income from the more frequent payout. Paying on a biweekly basis compared to a weekly basis, for example, permits the company to hold on to funds a week longer. These funds can be invested in short-term cash reserve portfolios to earn an interest income.

Minimum-wage Laws

Federal and state minimum wage laws have a pronounced effect on the cost and profit of a business firm. If a firm is using marginal labor and paying the minimum wage, it certainly will have its cost increased noticeably whenever the minimum wage rises. When the federal minimum wage was increased from $2.30 per hour to $2.65 per hour in January 1978, a number of marginal firms were forced out of business because of the increase in labor cost. A number of empirical studies have been made that show the adverse effect of a rising minimum wage on employment. Scheduled minimum-wage increases to $2.90 in January 1979, $3.10 in 1980 and $3.35 in 1981 will no doubt take their toll on employment in marginal firms.

A minimum wage increase not only affects those at the minimum wage level, but others in the company as well. This is so because in many firms wage differentials between jobs are firmly established. If the wage on the lowest-paying job is raised, others expect their wages to rise to maintain the differentials. Consequently, other wage rates go up simultaneously, or subsequently; this adds to the company payroll cost. This latter phenomenon occurs even in companies that have no workers near the minimum wage level. Frequently, a firm may be paying competitive rates or community rates. If wages rise generally because of an increase in the minimum wage rate, the firm may find it necessary to increase its wage rates.

There is also a tendency for rising wage rates to accelerate the substitution of capital, automation, and other labor-saving devices for labor power. Elevator operators, grocery store bag boys and checkout cashiers, bowling alley pin setters, clam diggers and certain agricultural workers, to name a few, have been put out of jobs because of rising minimum wage rates.

From an aggregate point of view, a rise in the minimum wage rate can cause a decrease in employment, as graphically depicted by the marginal productivity theory of wages, unless offset by increases in productivity or by higher prices. A rise in the minimum wage makes it more difficult for marginal workers, especially teenagers, minority workers, or others who lack skills and training, to find jobs. Since their productivity, or the productivity of jobs for which they may be hired, is marginal, an employer may not find it worthwhile to retain such positions.

Production and labor costs are affected also by hours of work. Most workers today put in a 40-hour workweek. Some, however, particularly those on a weekly or monthly wage, such as office clerks, typists, sales clerks, work less than 40 hours per week. When salaried personnel work less then 40 hours per week, or course, their total production may be reduced accordingly. This has an upward bias on cost of production. Whether lunch is eaten on the employee's own time or on company time affects costs and production. The number and length of relief periods or coffee breaks can adversely affect production and costs. The loss of time involved may be offset, however, if the breaks refresh the worker and stimulate him to greater production before or after such breaks. In many cases, a fifteen-minute morning and afternoon work break plus lunch on company time results in a 7-hour work day though the employee may be receiving pay for 8 hours. This results in higher labor cost per unit of output.

An important change affecting production and cost is the move toward a shorter work week. The proposal takes a variety of forms, such as 7 hours, 5 days; 6 hours, 6 days; and 8 hours, 4 days. A new variation of the workweek adopted by many firms in the past few years is the 4-day, 40-hour week. Workers work 10 hours per day for 4 days and enjoy a three-day weekend. But in whatever form, a shorter workweek with the same pay usually results in higher cost of production. Often the short workweek necessitates hiring more workers. This is particularly true where there is need for 24-hour operations, such as fire and police protection, steel mill operation, and plant protection.

Regarding hours, a business firm must also take into consideration the likelihood of overtime. Legally, according to the Fair Labor Standards Act, overtime over 40 hours per week or 8 hours per day must be paid for at the rate of time and one-half of the standard pay rate. Some union contracts define the workweek as something less than 40 hours, such as 35 hours, and the employer pays overtime rates for anything beyond 35 hours at the rate of time and a half or more. In fact, on a number of occasions, unions have negotiated to reduce the so-called standard workweek not so much with the idea of reducing the number of hours worked per week as for the sake of receiving more overtime pay. In other cases, unions have requested a reduction in the workweek without any reduction in weekly take-home pay. Any such changes have a substantial effect on the cost and profit of a company.

Labor Turnover and Layoffs

Another important cost factor is *labor turnover*, which the Bureau of Labor Statistic (BLS) defines as the movement of all wage and salary workers from one employment status to another. It is composed of accessions, new hires, quits, and layoffs. Paramount to us here is the *accession rate* which is defined as the average number of persons added to a payroll in a given period per 100 employees. The *separation rate* is the average number of workers dropped from a payroll per 100 employees. *Quit rate* is the number who voluntarily terminate their employment.

One gets some idea of the cost impact of labor turnover from looking at BLS manufacturing turnover rates for the past few years.[1] The quit rate in manufacturing in 1974, for example, averaged 2.3 per month. This means that 2.3 percent of the employees quit each month. Extending that on a yearly basis means that the quit rate in manufacturing was 27 percent last year. This does not necessarily mean that more than one-fourth of the workers quit their jobs. It is possible that a very high quit rate on a few jobs forces the average upward. A firm may have 100 employees and 100 jobs. If, in one month, four different employees were hired and subsequently quit the same job, the quit rate would be 4 for the month. But 99 of the original 100 workers retained their jobs.

Both quits and acquisitions must be considered in keeping cost down. A quit usually results in the loss of an experienced worker. Such loss can have an adverse effect on production schedules. Moreover, the cost of acquiring and training a replacement is more than meets the eye, especially when one considers the low level of productivity of new hires during their training period.

On a related matter, when a need for increased production exists, the firm must consider the alternative costs between working existing employees overtime versus hiring additional new employees. If acquisition and training cost are high, a manager may find it more economical to have overtime work; this would be the case particularly if the need for higher production were know to be temporary or management was uncertain about its continuation.

Holiday and Vacation Pay

The number of holidays and the length of paid vacations affect costs and profits. Today it is customary for most workers to get at

---

[1] Labor turnover rates are published monthly in the *Monthly Labor Review*

least six paid holidays. Many workers receive 8 to 10 paid holidays. A company may desire to be generous in this matter, but it must remember that it is paying out money for which it gets no corresponding increase in production. Each additional holiday given is equivalent to giving a .4 percent pay raise. Management must keep in mind, also, that if it desires to have workers come in on a holiday, they usually receive overtime pay at the rate of time and a half, double time, or according to some union-management contracts, triple time.

Paid vacations have a similar effect on costs and profits. Paid vacations of one to four weeks, or more, can have a serious impact on the cost of operation of a business firm.

Social Security Taxes

It must be remembered, too, when hiring additional workers, that social security taxes have to be factored into labor cost. At present, in most states, the employer pays the unemployment tax at a basic rate of 3 per cent of payroll. Most states use an experience-rating formula which reduces the tax rate for employers with lower rates of unemployment. This, of course, can encourage employers to minimize layoffs. Unemployment compensation taxes should be especially considered when deciding to hire additional workers on a temporary basis versus working existing employees overtime.

Federal Old Age, Survivors, Disability, and Health Insurance tax must be paid also. One-half, 6.05 percent, is paid by the employer; the other half by the employee. Currently the tax rate is 12.10 percent on individual earnings up to $17,700 per year. Both the rate and the earnings base are scheduled to increase in the near future, as shown in Table 14-2.

Pension and Profit-sharing Plans

Many companies have private pension plans (other than social security) and/or profit-sharing plans. These, too, must be considered a part of labor cost. When such plans do exist, it is important that they qualify for tax exemption under the Internal Revenue Code, otherwise they will be more costly to the employer. If they qualify under the tax code, payments into pension and profit-sharing funds can be considered as legitimate cost of doing business for tax purposes. If they do not qualify, the company must pay income taxes even on that portion of its earnings that is paid into the employee pension and profit-sharing plans. Assume a company, for example, earned $5 million in profit and was in a 50 percent corporate income

TABLE 14-2. Social Security (FOASDHI)[1] Tax Rates
Rate According to 1977 Amendments

Year	Wage Base[2]	Employer Tax Rate[3]
1977	$16,500	5.85
1978	17,700	6.05
1979	22,900	6.13
1980	25,900	6.13
1981	29,700	6.65
1982	32,100	6.70
1983	34,800	6.70
1984[2]	—	6.70
1985	—	7.05
1986	—	7.15
1990	—	7.65

[1] Federal Old Age, Survivors, Disability, and Health Insurance
[2] Wage Base changes have not been scheduled beyond 1983.
[3] Employee pays the same amount.
Source: Economic Report of the President, 1978.

tax bracket. If the company contributed $1 million into an employee pension or profit-sharing fund, that did not qualify under the tax code, it would have to pay $2.5 million in income taxes ($5,000,000 X .50). The company's profit after taxes would be $2.5 million. If $1 million were paid into a qualified pension or profit-sharing fund, however, the company would be exempt from paying taxes on that million and required to pay taxes on only the $4 million. Consequently, its tax would be $2 million instead of $2.5 million, and its profit after taxes would be $2 million. In this way, the cost of the pension or profit-sharing plan would be only half of what it would be without the tax incentive.

Total Fringe Benefits

Other fringe benefits add to the cost of production. These include payments like those for medical benefits, such as Blue Cross and Blue Shield, for dental service, life insurance, auto insurance, and educational benefits for employees. It is estimated today that total fringe benefits cost over $3984 per employee or somewhere between 30 to 35 percent of total payroll. Obviously these costs add substantially to the labor cost of operating a business.

Moreover, fringe benefits are increasing faster than basic pay rates. A recent U.S. Chamber of Commerce study shows that fringe benefits in a ten-year period, 1965–75, rose 165 percent compared

	1965	1975		
Fringe benefits	$1,502	$3,984	Increase in "fringes"	Up 165%
Pay for time worked	$5,460	$9,709	Pay increase Up 78%	
Total employment costs	$6,962	$13,693	Total increase Up 97%	

Figure 14-6.

with a 78 percent increase for basic work pay. Figure 14-6 also, shows that a worker with a work income of $9,709 per year received $3984 worth of fringe benefits. A breakdown of these fringe benefits is given in Table 14-3. Additional information shows that the following fringe benefit costs were paid in various manufacturing industries, chemicals, 42.2 percent; primary metals, 40.6 percent; rubber, 40.4 percent; transportation, 39.9 percent. In nonmanufacturing businesses, the leaders were public utilities, 37.5 percent; banking, 37.3 percent; insurance, 35.2 percent, and department stores, 28.4 percent. These and other data are shown in Table 14-4.

Sometimes, however, it costs less to grant a fringe benefit than to give an increase in basic wages. A 10 percent increase in the standard hourly rate of pay will cost just that. It will automatically increase the pay rate for overtime, holidays, vacation pay, unemployment taxes, and probably FOASDHI taxes. The equivalent of a 10 percent increase in the standard hourly rate in the form of a fringe benefit may cost less because there will be no increase in overtime, holiday, and vacation pay rates. Nor will unemployment taxes or other social security payments be raised.

Frequently, in negotiating certain fringe benefits with manage-

TABLE 14-3.
Where Benefits Go
Of the $3,984 in fringe benefits per employee in 1975

Social Security (employer's share)	$636
Pension plans	$620
Insurance	$582
Paid vacations	$580
Paid rest, lunch periods	$408
Paid holidays	$376
Workmen's compensation	$141
Paid sick leave	$134
Profit sharing	$123
Unemployment compensation	$114
Other benefits	$270

TABLE 14-4.
How Industries Rank in Pay Supplements
Percentage of payroll costs going into "fringes" in 1975

Manufacturing Industries			
Chemicals	42.2%	Pulp, paper, lumber, furniture	32.7%
Primary metals	40.6%	Printing, publishing	32.2%
Rubber, leather, plastic	40.4%	Textile products, apparel	27.8%
Transportation	39.9%		
Petroleum	39.2%	*Nonmanufacturing Industries*	
Food, beverages, tobacco	36.2%	Public utilities	37.5%
Nonelectrical machinery	36.1%	Banking	37.3%
Stone, clay, glass	35.1%	Insurance	35.2%
Fabricated metal products	35.1%	Department stores	28.4%
Electrical machinery	35.0%	Trade	28.2%
Instruments	34.8%	Hospitals	24.0%

Source: Reprinted from *U.S. News and World Report*, Oct. 25, 1976. Copyright 1976 U.S. News and World Report, Inc.

ment, unions will stress their tax-exempt status in order to emphasize that such benefits will cost the company only about half the actual payout because of the savings in taxes.

MONEY WAGES VS. REAL WAGES

Workers are interested not only in money wages and fringe benefit, but in real wages, or what their money will buy. *Real wages* are the purchasing power of money wages. Real wages are usually determined by comparing the purchasing power of a current money wage with the purchasing power of the money wage in a previous year. This is done by using a price index, usually the consumer price index (CPI), to adjust money wages for the effects of price changes. Using a 1967 base year when the CPI equaled 100, the weekly money wage of $114.90 would buy $114.90 worth of goods and services in terms of 1967 prices. Since the real wage is determined by dividing the money wage by the CPI, the money wage and the real wage were equal.

We can obtain some notion of the total increase in real wages or purchasing power for the average worker from Table 14-5. In this table the money wage (column 2) shows average weekly earnings in all manufacturing industries. Column 5 is the real wage, or the purchasing power of the money wage, in constant 1967 dollars. Column 6 shows the percentage of real wage in a given year compared to the base year 1967. The *real wage* in column 5 is determined by dividing

TABLE 14-5. Money Wage vs. Real Wage, 1960-1977: Average Weekly
Earnings in Manufacturing Industries (selected years)

(1) Year	(2) Weekly Money Wage	(3) Money Wage as Percentage of Base Period	(4) CPI (1967 = 100)	(5) Real Wage 1967 Prices	(6) Real Wage as Percentage Increase of Base Period 1967
1960	89.72	78	88.7	101.15	88.8
1967	114.90	100	100.0	114.90	100.0
1968	122.51	107	104.2	117.57	102.3
1969	129.51	113	109.8	117.95	102.6
1970	133.73	116	116.3	114.99	100.1
1971	142.04	127	121.3	117.10	101.9
1972	154.69	135	125.3	123.46	107.4
1973	165.24	144	133.1	124.15	108.1
1974	176.00	153	147.7	119.16	103.7
1975	189.51	164	161.2	117.56	102.3
1976	207.60	181	170.5	121.76	106.0
1977	226.89	197	181.5	125.01	108.8

Source: *Economic Indicators* (June 1978).

the money wage in column 2 by the consumer price index (1967 =
100) in column 4. For example, the real wage for 1970 was $114.99
($133.73 ÷ 116.3 × 100 = $114.99). The money wage for 1977,
$226.89 was divided by the price index for that year, 181.5, which
deflated the money wage to a real wage of $125.01 in terms of
1967 dollars.

Some interesting observations can be made from Table 14-5.
Notice that the money wage increased by 97 percent between 1967
and 1977, but because of price increases the real wage increased by
only 8.8 percent. In effect price increases obliterated most of the
advantages of higher wages during the period. Moreover, since the
average worker was placed in a higher income bracket because of his
higher money wage, his real wage further adjusted for higher income
taxes was probably close to what it was in 1967. In addition, the
table reveals that in some years, such as 1970, 1974, and 1975, the
worker experienced a decrease in purchasing power in spite of his
higher money wage. Situations of this nature often accentuate the
demand for higher wages by workers and unions.

Indexation

One way to prevent the erosion of purchasing power or real wages,
is by using a wage escalator clause which ties money wages to changes
in the cost of living. Before World War II, very few wage contracts

had such a clause, but in 1948 it was negotiated into the auto workers' union-management contract. It provided that workers' pay was to be adjusted every three months for changes in the Consumer Price Index (CPI). At that time they were to receive a one-cent hourly increase for every 1.14 percentage point rise in the CPI. There was no upward limit to the rise, but there was a downward limit of 5 cents per hour.

Since 1948, the use of escalator clauses has spread. It is estimated that approximately 5 million workers now have their wages tied to the CPI. In addition, the pensions of retired federal employees and military personnel are somewhat tied to the CPI, and in 1975, Social Security payments of 29 million persons were indexed to the CPI. Furthermore, economists, labor leaders, and legislators have seriously proposed widespread indexation of most forms of income. The arguments for and against indexation are abundant. Nevertheless, since workers' incomes and firms' labor costs can be affected directly or indirectly by change in the CPI, further insight into the nature and limitations of the CPI can help us to see its effects.

Consumer Price Index

A *price index* compares the average price of a group of commodities and services in one period of time with the average of the same group in another period. Prices for a group of goods or services are determined for a base period and prices in all subsequent or previous years are measured in relation to the base-period prices. The Bureau of Labor Statistics (BLS), which calculates the Consumer Price Index, used the "Laspeyres' formula."[2]

The CPI maintained by BLS compares the price of a group of 400 basic commodities and services out of the more than 1400 required by an average family of four in moderate-sized industrial communities. The items in the "market basket" are weighted according to the percentage of total spending applied to each of several categories, such as food, rent, apparel, transportation, recreation, and medical care. A separate index is calculated for each category as well as a composite for all commodities. Indexes are published for each of 37

---

[2] In its simplest form, the formula reads:

$$R_i = \frac{\Sigma q o p_1}{\Sigma q o p_0}$$

where qo is the average quantities of each item used by families in the wage-earner group in the base period, P_0 is the price for these items in the base period, and P_1 is the price in the current period.

TABLE 14-6. Hypothetical Price Index

(1)	(2)	(3)	(4) Price Index (1958 base year)	(5) Price Index (1967 base year)
Year	Commodities	Cost		
1952	a b c d e	333	92	80
1958	a b c d e	363	100	87
1960	a b c d e	375	103	89
1965	a b c d e	396	109	95
1967	a b c d e	417	115	100
1970	a b c d e	483	133	116
1975	a b c d e	672	185	161
1976	a b c d e	713	196	171
1977	a b c d e	759	209	182

metropolitan areas and for 14 nonmetropolitan urban areas as well as for the United States as a whole.[3]

Hypothetical Index. In order to obtain an accurate price index it is essential to hold the items, whose prices are to be measured, constant both in quantity and quality. Table 14-6 includes a hypothetical set of figures that show briefly the general principle by which an index is calculated.

Assume that it costs $363 per month to buy the market basket of commodities (goods and services) represented by a, b, c, d, and e in 1958. The price index in column 4 represents the percentage cost of the commodities in each year compared with their cost in the base year of 1958. The index for 1958 must be 100, since the cost of the commodities in 1958 was 100 percent of their cost in that year. By 1965, however, these same commodities cost $396. In general, then, the price of these commodities had increased 9 percent. Therefore, the index for 1965 was 109; that is, the prices were 109 percent of what they were in 1958 ($396 ÷ 363 = 1.09 = 9 percent). By 1970 the various commodities cost $483, and prices were 133 percent of what they were in 1958. In 1977 the price level reached 209, which meant that prices increased 109 percent in the period 1958–1977.

The index for any given year can be obtained by dividing the cost of the market basket in that year by its cost in the base year. Any specific year can be compared with another by noting the change in the index between the years. The index thus gives us a method of comparing the prices in any given year with the level that existed in the base period or any other year.

[3] Information on the CPI and real wages can be found in the *Monthly Labor Review.*

Changing the Base Period. For a number of reasons, the base year must be changed periodically. Spending habits change over the years; new goods and services enter the market; and the spending proportions (weights) assigned to various categories of goods and services change. In addition comparison of current prices with prices in some earlier period means less to many people, especially younger persons, as the years pass. The CPI was once based on the 1910-14 period. In the late 1920s the base was changed to 1926. Later, the base year became 1935-39. Early in the 1950s it shifted to a 1947-49 base. Later the BLS turned to a 1957-59 base period. It now uses 1967 as base year.

Remember that a change in the base period does not change actual, or existing prices. It merely changes the year to which actual or current prices are compared. If the base year for the hypothetical index in Table 14-6 were changed to 1967, for example the actual cost of buying the commodities in 1977 would still be the same. The index, however, would read 182 ($759 ÷ 417) instead of 209 as it does when the index is based on 1958 prices.

A new base year can be established by dividing the series of data whose base is to be changed by the value of the data for the new base period. For example, the figures in the Hypothetical Price Index, 1967 base, shown in Table 14-6, were calculated by dividing the 1967 figure of $417 into each of the other figures in column 3. This approximates the values of other years compared to a 1967 base-year figure.[4] Such a method, however, should not be used as a permanent substitute. A periodic revision of current index numbers, and the construction of a new index is not that simple. Because of changes in the basic commodities and services in the market basket and changes in the weights assigned to various items, the absolute cost of buying the current "market basket" may be more or less than the absolute cost of buying the former basket of goods and services.

Structure of CPI. The CPI market basket, as indicated earlier, is made up of various components. Included are such categories as all items, all commodities, durable goods, nondurable goods, food, apparel, all services, rent, transportation, new cars, medical-care services, and household services. Some of these in turn have sub-indexes. Since prices of some goods and services change faster than others, it is important to use appropriate geographic areas and item categories when utilizing the index for specific purposes. Figure 14-7, for example, indicates that the prices of services have been rising faster

[4] A conversion to a new base year can be made also by dividing the CPI for the newly selected base year into the CPI for every other year.

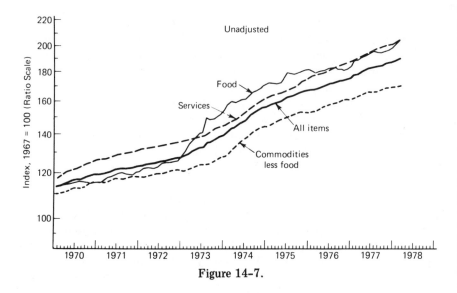

Figure 14-7.

than the prices of commodities. It also shows the surge in food prices particularly in the 1973-75 period.

Reservations about the CPI. The Consumer Price Index reflects the relative change in the cost of living. It does not measure the actual dollar cost of living. A higher CPI in one city does not necessarily indicate that prices are higher there than elsewhere. It simply means that the cost of living since the base period has increased more rapidly in that city than it has in others. Assume that in 1967, for example, the actual cost of the CPI market basket for a family in City A was $500 per month, and the cost in City B was $600 per month.[5] Both of these costs would be represented by a CPI of 100 for the respective cities in the base period, 1967. If the actual cost of living in both cities increased by the same amount, say $300 per month, by some subsequent period, such as 1977, the actual cost in City A would be $800 per month and that in City B would be $900 per month. The consumer price index for City A would be 160, however, while that for City B would read 150. A city whose current cost of living is lower may have a higher CPI number than a city with higher living costs. The actual cost of living for a family in Dallas in 1976 was $14,699; in Milwaukee, it was $17,307. The 1976 CPI for Dallas, however, was 170.3; that for Milwaukee was 162.7 (1967 base year). A measure of the actual cost of living can be obtained by

---

[5] Costs may vary because the prices of items in the market basket may differ in each of the cities during the same base period.

Figure 14-7. (Continued)

(1967 = 100)

Period	All Items	Food	Commodities Less Food	Services	All Commodities	Food		Commodities Less Food	
						Food at Home	Food Away from Home	Durable	Non-durable
					Unadjusted				
1970	116.3	114.9	112.5	121.6	113.5	113.7	119.9	111.8	113.1
1971	121.3	118.4	116.8	128.4	117.4	116.4	126.1	116.5	117.0
1972	125.3	123.5	119.4	133.3	120.9	121.6	131.1	118.9	119.8
1973	133.1	141.4	123.5	139.1	129.9	141.4	141.4	121.9	124.8
1974	147.7	161.7	136.6	152.1	145.5	162.4	159.4	130.6	140.9
1975	161.2	175.4	149.1	166.6	158.4	175.8	174.3	145.5	151.7
1976	170.5	180.8	156.6	180.4	165.2	179.5	186.1	154.3	158.3
1977	181.5	192.2	165.1	194.3	174.7	190.2	200.3	163.2	166.5
					Seasonally Adjusted				
1978: Jan	187.2	199.2	168.6	202.0	179.9	197.0	208.4	167.6	170.6
Feb	188.4	202.0	168.8	203.5	180.8	199.5	210.5	168.7	170.1
Mar	189.8	204.2	170.0	204.9	182.3	202.5	212.5	169.5	171.2

Note. — Beginning January 1978 data relate to all urban consumers. Earlier data relate to urban wage earners and clerical workers.
Source: Department of Labor, Bureau of Labor Statistics.

461

referring to the BLS City Worker's Family Budget which is maintained for several major cities.

Another reservation in using the CPI is required because it is not a completely pure price index. BLS statisticians readily admit that certain elements of quality change may be reflected in the index. In measuring price changes each month over a period of time there may well be quality alterations in some of the standard items in the market basket. It is difficult to determine how much a change in the price of a particular commodity, for example, is due to a general change in the price and how much is due to quality change. BLS does not have the time or resources to ferret out all such changes in quality. Consequently, the CPI does reflect some value for change in quality of goods and services contained in the market basket. Various studies indicate that the size of the bias in the index resulting from quality change and other sources of imperfection in collecting, measuring, and processing CPI data approximates one to two percentage points annually.

Other Price Indexes. Remember that the CPI tries to measure changes only in the prices of consumer goods and services. Since these account for only about two-thirds of the total spending in the economy, the CPI does not give a full account of what is happening to prices. It does not take into consideration changes in the prices of machinery, equipment, buildings, raw materials, or even houses. The broadest price measure is the "GNP implicit price deflators," which endeavors to measure changes in the prices of all goods and services produced by our nation's economy.

Other BLS indexes are available for use in economic analysis, including the Wholesale Price Index (WPI) with its various components, Spot Market Price Index, Import and Export Price Indexes, Weekly Food Price Index, various Retail Price Indexes, and the Construction Materials Index. These indexes are often used by business economists and managers to do forward pricing. Many job orders, especially on heavy machinery, equipment and buildings, cannot be completed for several months or sometimes years. By projecting a trend of prices, the jobber can better estimate his future cost and prices of finished products.

VALUE OF MONEY

Price indexes are also useful for calculating the value of money or the purchasing power of the dollar. The value of money is determined by the volume of goods and services that a given amount of money will buy. If prices rise, a given amount of money will buy less; the value of money decreases. If prices fall, the value of money increases since a given amount of money will buy more. To state it another way, a rise in prices decreases the purchasing power of the dollar and vice versa.

The value of the dollar's purchasing power can be determined at any time by dividing the dollar by the current price index and multiplying by 100. Thus, the value of the dollar in 1939, using the then current price index, was $1.00 ($1.00 ÷ 100 × 100 = $1.00). In 1977 it was valued at .23 cents ($1.00 ÷ 436 × 100 = .23). This means that, because of higher prices, a 1977 dollar would buy what 23 cents would have bought in the pre-World War II period. Remember, however, that the value or purchasing power of the dollar is only a relative concept. There is nothing inviolable about this value. One can easily show that in 1977 the dollar was worth about 55 cents, instead of 23 cents, simply by using the current 1977 CPI value of 181.5, which is computed on the 1967 base period. ($1.00 ÷ 181.5 × 100 = .55). In fact, you can always make the dollar equal to a dollar by using the current year as a base period equal to 100. As stated earlier, an important issue is how many dollars one has in relation to its value.

The CPI Wage-escalator Ratio

Early in 1978, BLS made a change in the CPI. Whatever changes are made, whether in the base year or in the composition of the market basket, they affect wage agreements tied to the CPI. Until 1978 the market basket had been designed to take into account the needs and spending of urban wage earners and clerical workers. Since the percentage of the labor force in this category, however, had been declining, BLS decided to broaden the scope of measurements to "all urban families." Some groups, such as labor unions, opposed this change because the CPI historically has been calculated on a wage-earner basis. Consequently, BLS now publishes two CPI's, one for "wage earners and clerical workers" (CPI-W); the other for "all urban families" (CPI-U). These will be continued for at least three years while BLS studies them and decides whether to continue both or maintain only one or the other index.[6]

We mentioned previously that early escalator clauses granted workers a 1 cent per hour wage increase for every 1.14 percentage point rise in the CPI. There was no upward ceiling, but there was a

[6] Julius Shiskin [Commissioner of Labor Statistics], "Updating the Consumer Price Index," *Monthly Labor Review*, July 1974.

five-cent per hour limit on the down side. BLS was then using a 1935–39 base period. When the base year changed, however, the cost of the market basket in the new base year was generally higher than it was in the previous base year. Consequently, it required a larger dollar increase in the actual cost of living, to equal a 1.14 percentage change in the new higher-cost market basket. This meant that a worker received a lesser adjustment from a given dollar price increase. In our hypothetical index shown in Table 14–6 for example, a 1.14 percentage point increase in the 1958 cost of the market basket equals $4.14 ($363 × .0114). But a 1.14 percentage point increase using a 1970 market basket cost equals $5.51 ($483 × .0114). This means that it would take a one-third larger than dollar rise in the CPI for the worker to get a 1 cent hourly increase in pay with the new base year. Consequently, each time the base year is changed, the wage-escalator ratio must be changed to prevent workers' real income from deteriorating. In the auto workers' 1975 contract, for example, the workers receive a 1 cent hourly increase in wages for each .3 percentage point increase in the CPI.*

Indexing an individual wage to the CPI has many advantages and disadvantages. From a labor cost point of view, one should remember that the cost of living segment of wages is not usually part of the standard wage rate for purposes of computing overtime, holiday pay, vacation pay, and other fringe benefits. Consequently, if a worker were receiving $5.00 per hour plus a 50 cents cost-of-living allowance, his two-week holiday pay allowance would be $400 ($5.00 × 80 hours) rather than $440 ($5.50 × 80 hours). Hence, periodically, a union will negotiate to have all or a part of the cost-of-living-allowance (COLA) incorporated into the standard rate of pay, especially when the cost of living allowance becomes sizable.

City Worker's Family Budget

The city worker's family budget (CWFB) was designed to measure how much it costs a four-person urban family to purchase the goods and services required to maintain a "modest but adequate" level of living in various areas. The list of items included in the budget was developed for a family composed of an employed 38-year-old hus-

---

*In the fall of 1978 an estimated 960,000 auto industry workers received an 18 cent per hour cost of living increase, the largest COLA payment in the industry since the escalator formula was adopted 30 years ago in 1948.

Ford Motor Co., for example, reported that its COLA cost since it adopted the plan in 1950 has gone up $3.17 per hour. Eighty-four cents of this was under the current 3-year contract signed in 1975.

General Motors indicated that the latest 18 cent COLA boost would lift average earnings for its hourly-rated workers to $8.29 per hour.

band, a wife not employed outside the home, and two children, an 8-year-old girl and a 13-year-old boy.

The annual cost of an "intermediate" level of living for a four-person family in 1977 ranged from a high of $20,609 in the Boston area to a low of $14,776 in Austin, Texas, according to BLS estimates of the city worker's family budget in 38 metropolitan areas in the contiguous United States. Outside the continental United States, Honolulu was higher still, with a $20,883 budget; Anchorage, Alaska, was the highest with a $24,019 budget. The average budget for the urban United States was $17,106. The BLS calculated a *lower* budget for the urban United States, at a less adequate level of living, at $10,481, and a *higher* budget at $25,202.

The budgets do not purport to show how an "average family" actually spends, or is supposed to spend, its money. The budgets merely give the total cost of a representative list of goods and services considered essential by urban families to provide health, efficiency, the nurture of children, and some participation in social and community affairs. The budgets calculated by the BLS for 1977 are shown in Table 14–7 (pp. 466–67). Of the $17,106 intermediate budget about 76 percent is allocated to items of family consumption. The remainder covers the cost of personal taxes, Social Security and disability deductions, and occupational expenses. Notice that 24 percent of family income was spent for food and 18 percent went for housing. The budgets shown in Table 14–7 may be updated by adjusting them for the increase in prices since 1977. The urban U.S. intermediate budget for 1978, for example, would be over $18,000 when adjusted upward because of rising prices.

SUMMARY

Since the early days of economics, economists have been concerned with theories of wages. Among those they developed were the subsistence, the wages-fund and the residual theories of wages. The modern bargaining theory of wages is a description of how wages are arrived at, rather than a theory of wages.

The most sophisticated theory of wages is the marginal productivity theory. It states that wages tend to equal the marginal productivity of the last worker hired, and equilibrium in employment exists where MRP = MO. The theory, however, rests on a number of assumptions that may or may not be applicable. The theory does show a relationship between wages, marginal productivity, and employment. An increase in the wage rate, other things being equal, for example, will cause a decrease in employment, and vice versa. On the

TABLE 14–7. Annual Costs of an Intermediate Budget for a 4-Person Family, Autumn 1977

Area	Total Budget	Total Consumption	Food	Housing	Transportation	Clothing	Medical Care	Social Security & Disability Payments	Personal Income Taxes
					Family Consumption				
Urban United States	$17106	$13039	$4098	$4016	$1472	$1182	$ 985	$ 961	$2342
Metropolitan Areas	17498	13299	4160	4130	1480	1187	1017	975	2452
Nonmetropolitan Areas	15353	11880	3823	3510	1434	1160	842	896	1853
Northeast:									
Boston, Mass.	20609	15302	4426	5585	1817	1211	902	965	3499
Buffalo, N.Y.	18298	13683	4229	4239	1583	1484	831	981	2848
Hartford, Conn.	17796	14041	4413	4438	1625	1198	886	965	1992
Lancaster, Pa.	16322	12473	4222	3655	1466	1186	736	954	2151
New York–Northeastern N.J.	19972	14702	4653	5071	1376	1121	1075	992	3456
Philadelphia, Pa.–N.J.	17792	13268	4572	3914	1420	1063	1002	974	2779
Pittsburgh, Pa.	16516	12553	4266	3563	1450	1091	867	965	2252
Portland, Maine	17578	13648	4448	4155	1509	1359	920	965	2180
Nonmetropolitan Areas	17052	12974	4147	4168	1512	1164	892	990	2327
North Central:									
Cedar Rapids, Iowa	16681	12572	3664	3880	1489	1339	884	965	2397
Champaign–Urbana, Ill.	17223	13296	3944	4166	1500	1399	977	965	2190
Chicago, Ill.–Northwestern Ind.	17330	13378	4176	4150	1537	1105	1060	965	2212
Cincinnati, Ohio–Ky.–Ind.	16547	12717	4125	3740	1469	1243	893	965	2113
Cleveland, Ohio	17411	13485	4085	4222	1486	1268	999	965	2182
Dayton, Ohio	15695	12223	3970	3465	1402	1202	895	918	1819
Detroit, Mich.	17427	13212	4038	4094	1454	1181	1105	965	2481
Green Bay, Wis.	16768	12301	3658	3906	1418	1190	818	965	2764

466

Indianapolis, Ind.	16695	12936	3989	3850	1592	1243	949	965	2034
Kansas City, Mo.-Kans.	16486	12702	4041	3577	1523	1301	914	962	2070
Milwaukee, Wis.	18230	13262	3819	4363	1448	1360	935	965	3232
Minneapolis-St. Paul, Minn.	17813	12754	4018	3868	1439	1189	877	965	3341
St. Louis, Mo.-Ill.	16377	12637	4213	3582	1531	1162	866	959	2032
Wichita, Kans.	15994	12455	3845	3572	1513	1255	945	936	1860
Nonmetropolitan Areas	15658	11977	3773	3616	1424	1225	797	914	2041
South:									
Atlanta, Ga.	15483	12066	3980	3256	1388	1226	917	907	1781
Austin, Tex.	14776	11848	3659	3234	1490	1234	922	866	1340
Baltimore, Md.	17204	12705	4008	3764	1409	1214	1008	965	2783
Baton Rouge, La.	15283	12074	4119	3130	1424	1209	849	895	1584
Dallas, Tex.	15313	12241	3777	3420	1517	1104	1114	895	1442
Durham, N.C.	16369	12319	3819	3673	1372	1134	1026	959	2353
Houston, Tex.	15488	12356	3953	3364	1482	1189	1098	907	1486
Nashville, Tenn.	15290	12218	3798	3553	1465	1331	836	895	1442
Orlando, Fla.	14910	11953	3721	3386	1414	1159	998	872	1360
Washington, D.C.-Md.-Va.	18026	13409	4193	4314	1486	1042	1006	965	2876
Nonmetropolitan Areas	14471	11395	3738	3192	1417	1123	826	850	1520
West:									
Bakersfield, Calif.	15686	12123	3790	3406	1569	1000	1146	1032	1800
Denver, Colo.	16711	12729	3937	3666	1457	1470	918	965	2264
Los Angeles-Long Beach, Calif.	17126	13103	3915	4024	1520	1162	1236	1079	2178
San Diego, Calif.	16721	12816	3809	3936	1514	1149	1172	1079	2070
San Francisco-Oakland, Calif.	18519	14071	4101	4657	1548	1256	1143	1079	2570
Seattle-Everett, Wash.	17211	13603	4229	4125	1492	1342	1055	965	1860
Honolulu	20883	15103	4932	4939	1541	1185	1077	1022	3922
Nonmetropolitan Areas	15334	11715	3703	3445	1386	1176	878	989	2004
Anchorage, Alaska	24019	17764	4849	6561	1871	1431	1568	1035	4291

other hand, an increase in marginal revenue product will cause employment to increase and vice versa. Offsetting or augmenting changes may occur in wages and productivity that will have an impact on employment.

Applying the marginal productivity theory is different under conditions of imperfect competition. With a monopsonistic or oligopsonistic employer, for example, the wage will not equal the marginal productivity of the worker. Equilibrium employment will occur where MRP = MO, but that is not the point where MRP = AO (wage). Nevertheless, the marginal productivity theory serves as a good tool for wage and employment analysis.

In existing labor markets labor costs are affected by many different factors. These include the method of wage payment, minimum wage laws, hours of work, labor turn-over and layoffs, holiday and vacation pay, social security taxes, pension and profit-sharing plans, and a host of other fringe benefits.

Although workers and their employers are affected by money wages paid, the real wage, or the purchasing power of the money wage, is more important to the worker. The money wage can be converted into a real wage by dividing the money wage by the Consumer Price Index (CPI). A substantial number of workers have their wages indexed to the CPI. Since indexation of wages and other forms of income is becoming more commonplace in the United States economy, an understanding of index numbers and of reservations in using the CPI takes on added importance. A knowledge of the City Worker Family Budget is also significant for the analysis of wages and income.

QUESTIONS FOR ANALYSIS AND DISCUSSION

1. What do you see as the major weakness of the wages-fund theory?
2. In the marginal productivity theory of wages, why will the wage tend to equal the marginal revenue product of labor?
3. Use marginal productivity analysis to explain how an increase in wages can cause a decrease in employment.
4. Can the bargaining theory be used to explain the determination of wages in a nonorganized industry?
5. Do you think conventional wage theories are appropriate to explain how wages are determined in today's economy? Why? Why not?
6. Do you prefer the concept of piece work or hourly rated pay? Give your reasons.
7. Explain how labor turnover can increase the cost of production.
8. How can an employer pay less than the full cost of a pension plan for his employees?

9. What is the average cost of fringe benefits to an employer?
10. Do you think that wages should be tied to the Consumer Price Index? Why? Why not?

PROBLEMS AND CASES

1. You are among a small group of students involved with a group of young business executives in a series of discussions about economic and business issues. In a discussion on wages the students maintain that wages are determined according to the marginal productivity theory. Jim Profitt, one of the business executives, disputes that. He states that marginal productivity sounds good in theory, but that it does not apply in practice. One of the students, Joe Ledger, questions whether Profitt, and businessmen generally, really understand the theory. The meeting ends in a heated debate. You are asked by the group to prepare, for the next discussion, a graphic explanation of the marginal productivity theory of wages.

   In doing so, show the following:

   (a) How to determine the equilibrium level of employment with a given wage level and marginal revenue product curve.
   (b) What happens to employment when wages are increased or decreased.
   (c) What happens to employment when productivity per worker or product prices are increased.
   (d) How it is possible to have rising wages without a decline in employment.
   (e) In what manner does marginal productivity determine wages.
   (f) Conditions under which the wage at equilibrium employment does not equal the marginal revenue product.

2. The Jones Manufacturing Company has 300 employees. Their wages range between $4.85 and $7.20 per hour, with an average pay of $5.77 per hour. All employees work 40 hours per week, except for two-week vacations and 8 paid holidays.

   In the fall of 1978, the union negotiated a 10 percent across-the-board wage increase to take effect January 1, 1978. In addition, the company granted 2 extra paid holidays and agreed to put 10 cents per hour per worker into an employee insurance plan. Moreover, an increase in social security taxes is scheduled to go into effect in January 1979 (See table 14-2, page 453). The company is in a 50 percent income tax bracket. Assuming there is no increase in productivity, how much will the wage package and increased social security tax cost the company in 1979?

3. Ford Motor Company has 440,000 employees world wide, of which 220,000 are employed in U.S. operations. Excluding fringe benefits, average per hour earnings for U.S. hourly employees were $8.03 in 1976.

   How much will the increase in the social security tax rate cost the company in 1979?

4. The Brass Rivet Company is negotiating a new wage contract. Members of the union negotiating team demand a 30-cent per hour pay raise. Management representatives offer a 15-cent hourly increase. After some lengthy bargaining sessions, management is about ready to agree to a 23-cent wage increase. As a member of the company negotiating committee, you suggest

that the company stick to its original offer of 15 cents on wages, but add 8 cents per hour per worker to the employees' existing pension plan. Certain company representatives ask you to explain your reasons for the suggestion.

5. The Daylight Transit Company pays its drivers and other $5.75 per hour plus a cost-of-living allowance (COLA). The cost-of-living allowance is based on the CPI, using a 1967 base year. The wage escalator clause negotiated in 1973 provides for a 1-cent increase or decrease in pay for each subsequent 0.3 percentage point change in the CPI. In 1973, as was customary when the wage contract was renewed, all of the cost-of-living wage allowance, with the exception of 5 cents, was incorporated into the base wage rate of $5.75 per hour. Using the CPI data shown in Figure 14-7, calculate the following:

    (a) What was the total size of the cost-of-living wage allowance in 1977? If all but 5 cents of this allowance were incorporated into base pay, what would be the new base pay?

    (b) To what extent will other labor cost be affected by the change in (a)?

    (c) If the CPI were changed in 1978 to a 1975 base year, approximately what change should be made in the CPI wage-escalator ratio in order that workers do not suffer a loss of purchasing power?

    (d) If workers were given a straight 10 percent increase in base pay before conversion to the new CPI base year mentioned in (c), how much would it cost the company? What would the same 10 percent cost if given after conversion to a 1975 base year?

6. The Joy Manufacturing Company operates one shift five days per week. Employees start at 7:30 A.M. and work until 4:00 P.M., with one half hour, 12:00 noon to 12:30 P.M., for lunch. Employees eat lunch on their own time. Workers usually average three hours overtime per week. Occasionally, about once per month, they work four hours on Saturday morning. Their straighttime hourly pay rate is $5.00. There has been an official request by employees, through their union, to change the workweek to four days, ten hours per day. As the wage & salary administrator for the company, you are asked to draw up for management consideration, the advantages and disadvantages to both the employees and company of the four day, 40 hour workweek, and recommend whether the company should adopt the proposal or offer a counter proposal.

As UAW Begins Pre-Bargaining Parley, Job Security Tops List of Issues This Year*

DETROIT—Three years ago, as the United Auto Workers union began sifting possible demands to be made in the approaching 1973 contract talks with the "Big Three" auto makers, one issue kept floating to the top of the pile: the right of a weary auto worker to refuse to work unlimited overtime.

It was a powerful issue. For more than two years the industry had been booming. Ten-hour days and six-day weeks were common, and although rank-and-filers' paychecks had never been larger, many workers were sick of overtime. Finally, after striking Chrysler Corp., the union won at least limited rights for its members to turn down extra work.

Now the union is again sifting demands for its triennial talks this summer. And again one issue has floated to the top: assuring there is enough work to go around, or failing that, protecting worker incomes when there isn't.

For a lot has changed in three years. The auto industry has been through its worst slump in decades. At one point more than a third of the UAW's 700,000 or so Big Three members were on the street. Now employment is slowly rising, but tens of thousands still are jobless. And those back in the plants have fresh memories of hard times.

Search for Security. So when some 1,000 UAW delegates troop into this town today for the first of three pre-bargaining Auto Worker conventions, most will have one thing high on their lists of demands: "It's the age-old search and quest of the working man for security for himself and his family," a UAW vice president, Douglas A. Fraser, says. Judging from feelings already expressed on both sides, that quest could lead to some of the toughest auto bargaining in years.

A specific UAW battle plan for more job security won't emerge until hard bargaining begins closer to the Sept. 14 expiration date of Big Three contracts. But it is already clear that of the numerous plans being advanced, all are likely to be viewed as costly and restrictive by auto makers.

No one at this time, of course, sees a strike coming from all this. Top UAW officials, including President Leonard Woodcock, insist a walkout can be avoided. But they also contend that even though auto workers may be in shaky personal financial condition after two lean years, they wouldn't shrink from a fight.

"Obviously, we'd be concerned about the effect of a long strike," Mr. Woodcock says. "But that doesn't mean we shouldn't do some of the things we need to do." By mid-September, the union is expected to have accumulated a record $150 million strike fund.

GM's Tough Stand. Predictably, the posturing by auto companies at this early stage is just as tough. General Motors Corp., which strongly influences the stance of its smaller rivals, recently issued an unusually early and strong blast at the still-unformed job-security demands; it termed them detrimental to productivity. "The solution to joblessness lies not in short-sighted make-work or share-the-work programs. In the long run they'll mean fewer jobs, not more," GM Chairman Thomas A. Murphy argues.

Whether a confrontation can be avoided depends on the shape taken by the UAW demands. One general strategy will be a bid to reduce the number of hours worked by each employee during a year, on the theory that in the aggregate other workers will then be needed. "You can't measure it precisely, but obviously if they're going to produce the same number of units, they'll have to have more people on the job or fewer layoffs," UAW Vice President Irving Bluestone says.

One form this demand almost certainly won't take is a simple four-day, 36-hour week at 40 hours' pay —even though a powerful alliance of local leaders is expected to push for that approach. Top auto executives have already tagged that idea as inflationary and, more importantly, have complained it would interfere with maximum use of their costly facilities.

"It would jeopardize our world-wide position if we lost the use of 20% of our capacity," Ford Motor Co. Executive Vice President William O. Bourke says.

Top UAW officials don't quarrel with the notion that auto makers need to run their plants as much as they can to pay for the huge capital investment. But that, in their view, doesn't rule out many plans to reduce the work time of individual employes while scattering the impact so that regular five-day, eight-hour work turns, or even overtime output, could go on as usual.

Pact at Farm-Gear Firms. Mr. Woodcock, for example, cites what he calls "embryonic plans" won three years ago at farm-implement companies, where a worker earns a half-hour off for each full week worked. "This has two advantages," Mr. Woodcock says. "It doesn't idle capital equipment, and a worker who has accumulated time off takes it periodically and for a short time that eliminates the possibility of holding a second job." One drawback to a simple four-day week, Mr. Woodcock explains, is that it might not lift employment nationally because "the more vigorous workers" might take a second job.

Variations on this theme are blossoming. For example, J.P. Hale, a delegate to this week's convention here from Ford's Chicago stamping plant (where 600 of 4,200 workers are still laid off), says he will urge two hours time off for each full week worked. And UAW Vice President Ken Bannon theorizes about one full day off every other week — in effect a 36-hour week when averaged, but perhaps with less impact on plant operating schedules.

The simplest method of reducing individual work time, however, is the added holiday, personal business day off, the longer vacation or even a few more minutes of relief time. And the UAW is expected to push for some or all of these. That could be the method most palatable to the auto makers, too, because in effect they have been moving in that direction for years.

By most estimates, auto workers now spend only about 33 to 34 hours of each 40-hour week directly on their jobs after vacations, holidays and other time off is factored in. "Another holiday costs an auto maker four cents an hour," union Vice President Fraser says. "What's the difference whether they give us a holiday or four more pennies for the paycheck?"

Improvements in other existing contract provisions could also have the related effect of changing at least the make-up of the work force, if not its size. For example, some UAW members are pushing for sweetened terms — and perhaps mandatory application — of the previously won "30-and-out" plan that lets workers retire after 30 years on the job even though they aren't 65 years old. "The younger people know if the older ones retire, there'll be new openings all along the line," says John Schlepphorst, a 44-year-old truck driver at GM's Buick engine plant in Flint, Mich. But he and others note that many workers with more than 30 years of employment still work because the UAW's cost-of-living allowance doesn't apply to pensions and they fear inflation would erode retirement income.

Difficult Sales Job. Selling some of these ideas to both the companies and the workers could be difficult. For example, three years ago the union locked itself into a six-year pension agreement, and the auto makers are certain to resist any move to reopen the pact. And rank-and-file union members clearly want some fairly visible job-security provisions. Mr. Bannon, the UAW vice president, worries, "We can have the best contract in the world, but if people don't feel we've given them job security, they won't ratify it."

In fact, Mr. Bannon sees some especially knotty issues at Ford—the auto company whose workers he specifically represents. Ford has been importing parts for some of its U.S.-made small cars and recently disclosed plans to import a German-built mini-car to compete with GM's new Chevette, rather than build one domestically.

"When we start talking about this at the bargaining table, it's going to be different than talking about money. But it's a job-security issue," he says. Because of Ford workers' strong feelings, he calls it "one of the most important issues at Ford in 1976." He predicts, "If we have a strike, it'll be over that."

Closely tied to efforts to keep more workers on the job in times of slow auto sales is a drive to take better care of those laid off if furloughs can't be avoided. For 20 years, auto workers have been covered by some kind of company-paid supplemental unemployment benefit (SUB) funds. Currently SUB, when added to public unemployment benefits, is supposed to provide eligible workers with up to 95% of their usual take-home pay for up to a year.

But the dramatic layoffs of the past two years put such a strain on these plans that at both GM and Chrysler they ran dry, leaving thousands of workers without checks they counted on. When the GM plan went broke the first time last spring, for example, it was paying out benefits at the rate of $10 million a week and taking in only $1.4 million under the formula for company contributions. At that point it had disbursed more than $400 million in benefits in less than 18 months.

"SUB is a major matter and we don't know quite how to tackle it," Mr. Woodcock, the UAW president, concedes. "The plan is fundamentally sound; I just don't know how you can devise a scheme" that would protect workers against wholesale layoffs like those of the past two years. (Originally SUB was intended to tide workers over relatively short annual new-model changeover layoffs.)

But it's clear the UAW will seek both a restructured and beefed-up SUB plan, possibly through larger company contributions and a two-tier payout system that earmarks at least part of available funds for senior workers.

One of the big difficulties in the recent slump was that low-seniority workers were laid off first, when the funds were in relatively good shape. Later, when senior workers were idled, they faced fast-dwindling SUB funds. As further protection for these long-term workers, the union may also seek a layoff plan based on reverse seniority—allowing older workers to volunteer for any layoffs that are slated. In the past, auto makers have opposed that idea, however, in part because it could leave them with a low-experience work force.

Traditional Pay Demands. While such job and pay security issues—most of which would be costly to auto companies—would be tough to win anytime, this fall's bargaining will be further complicated by the fact that traditional wage and benefit demands are as important as ever. According to one source, a simple extension of current pacts would push auto labor costs up more than 7.5% a year because of usual base-pay boosts, cost-of-living adjustments and rising costs of current benefits.

"Some people are saying wage increases aren't a big thing this time because they assume there'll be some," Mr. Woodcock says. "But that's an elusive thing." Big wage settlements in other industries this spring and summer "may fuel these desires" among auto workers, he says.

And for many workers, "benefits are by far not forgotten," says James Babb, vice president of Local 36 at Ford's Wixom, Mich., assembly plants. "In an inflationary economy, the only way to keep more money in your pocket is not to have to reach in there so much." And that could go down hard with auto makers. For example, as of Feb. 1 in Michigan, Chrysler will be paying $133 a month, equal to 77 cents an hour, for Blue Cross and Blue Shield insurance for workers with families. That's up 34% from the current rate without any change in benefits.

(a) Make a list of the probable UAW demands for 1976.
(b) Evaluate the proposal for a 36-hour week at 40 hours pay.
  (i) What percentage wage increase would be necessary to satisfy that demand?
  (ii) Considering that Ford Motor Company has approximately 70,000 production employees, what would be the total wage cost of implementing the proposal?
  (iii) Approximately how many more workers would have to be recalled from layoff or hired if the 36-hour week were implemented?
  (iv) What other costs would be involved in the 36-hour workweek plan?
  (v) What cost impact would the 36-hour week have if Ford Motor Company returned to full production at 40 hours per week plus some overtime?

SELECTED READINGS

"Annual Cost of City Workers Family Budget." *Monthly Labor Review*, May 1978.

Essays on Inflation and Indexation. Washington, D.C.: The American Enterprise Institute for Public Policy, 1974.

Ferger, Edgar L., and Douglas D. Pearce. "Wage-Price Control Experiment — Did It Work?" *Challenge*, July/August 1973.

Humphrey, Thomas M. "The Concept of Indexation in the History of Economic Thought," Federal Reserve Bank of Richmond, *Economic Review.* November/December 1974.

Hushey, R.P. "Work Incentives and the Cost — Effectiveness of Income Maintenance Programs." *Quarterly Review of Economics and Business*, Spring 1973.

Manpower Report of the President. Washington, D.C.: U.S. Department of Labor, 1975, 1976, and 1977.

Myers, A. Howard, and David P. Twomey. *Labor Law and Legislation.* Cincinnati, Ohio: South-Western Publishing Co., 1975.

Rosenthal, Neal, and Hall Dillon. "Occupational Outlook for the Mid-1970's." *Occupational Outlook Quarterly*, Winter 1974.

Schrank, Robert. "Work in America: What Do Workers Really Want?" *Industrial Relations.* May 1974.

Skiskin, Julius. "The Consumer Price Index: How Will the 1977 Revision Affect It?" *Business Economics,* March 1976.

Social Security Bulletin. Washington, D.C.: U.S. Department of Health, Education and Welfare, June 1975.

"The U.S. Labor Force: Projections to 1990." *Monthly Labor Review,* July 1973.

"U.S. Manpower in the 1970's." Washington, D.C.: U.S. Department of Labor, 1970.

Yang, Jai-Hoon. "The Case for and against Indexation. An Attempted Perspective." *Review,* Federal Reserve Bank of St. Louis, October 1974.

15

The Changing
Economic Environment

476

During the past few decades the operation of the typical business firm has been affected by a number of economic, social, and political changes. These changes include the imposition of environmental controls, the implementation of new worker-safety regulations, the enforcement of equal employment opportunities, and the adoption of consumer product safety legislation. These impose both a challenge and a cost to the business firm.

ENVIRONMENTAL CONTROLS

Air and water were once considered resources abundantly available to industry. Since no price was paid for them, they were regarded economically as "free goods." They could be used and then returned to the atmosphere, or earth, either clean or polluted. Free use of air and water led to their abuse; eventually, much of the air and water became polluted. Clean air and pure water became scarce and in many respects are now considered as economic goods that must be paid for. Somebody must pay for antipollution measures and devices or for depollution mechanisms. The cost may be borne by the firm, the consumer, or the government. Although the costs ultimately reach the consumer in one fashion or another, the business firm suffers a direct increase in cost as a result of numerous antipollution regulations and controls imposed on a voluntary or compulsory basis.

So, too, is it with noise and solid-waste pollution. It costs money to preserve the natural environment, to provide clean water, pure air, noise abatement, and to prevent solid-waste pollution. These costs cannot be ignored. The decision-making process of most business firms must take these costs into account.

Environmental factors have been instrumental in closing down certain industrial plants, in determining the location of new chemical plants, oil refineries, and airports, in sealing off mines, closing fishing grounds, delaying the Alaskan pipeline, retarding the growth of nuclear energy, and cutting off public funds for developing an American supersonic transport (SST). In many ways concern about pollution of various types has had considerable effect on the livelihood of millions of people.

Air Pollution

Although air is never completely pure, certain pollutants, visible and invisible, affect the atmosphere. Carbon monoxide, sulphur oxides, hydrocarbons, nitrogen oxides, and particulate matter, befoul the air and create health hazards. Much of the pollution emitted comes from cars, trucks, industrial processes, fuel combustion, and even solid-waste disposal. These pollutants can cause or aggravate such illnesses as lung cancer, emphysema, bronchial asthma, and chronic bronchitis. They can cause property damage, injure crops, and endanger auto, truck, train, and plane passengers. The cost of air pollution damage to health, vegetation, materials, and property values has been estimated at almost $20 billion a year.

Pollution costs for the business firm can result from the need to depollute air before using it in a productive process. A direct cost is involved also if the firm must use antipollution devices in productive processes such as smelting, to prevent emissions from polluting the air. The cost to the firm can be affected also by pollution standards that must be met in the use of the firm's final product, such as autos, airplanes, speedboats, and incinerators. Spending for depollution and antipollution devices increases cost without necessarily increasing productivity. Changes and improvements in the manufacture or fabrication of certain products to meet antipollution standards, frequently raise the cost of production. Whether a firm can, in whole or in part, pass such costs forward to consumers, or backward to suppliers, depends on the respective elasticity of demand and supply.

Environmental Regulations

Both the federal government and state and local governments impose air pollution standards. Federal regulation began in 1955 with the passage of the Air Pollution Act. This was followed by the Clean Air Act of 1963, the Air Quality Control Act of 1967, and the Clean Air Act of 1970. Each law tightened the standards and broadened the application of the standards. The 1970 law established a national uniform air quality standard based on geographic regions. The Environmental Protection Agency (EPA) has authority to enforce two sets of standards: Primary air quality standards establish the minimum levels of air quality essential to prevent illness. Secondary standards are designed to promote the public welfare and prevent damage to animals, plant life, and property in general. State governments determine how the national air pollution objectives are to be attained within various geographic regions.

In many parts of the nation, state and local government regulation of the air preceded federal regulation. In some states today the state regulation may be stricter than the federal standard. California's auto emission standards, for example, preceded and helped to set the stage for federal regulation of auto emissions.

Auto emission standards have received considerable attention since 1970. The 1970 act declared that 1975 automobiles should emit 90 percent less carbon monixide than 1970 automobiles, and that 1976 autos were to discharge 90 percent less carbon monixide than the 1971 autos. In effect we were to have nearly pollution-free autos by 1976. Although meeting these standards was postponed until 1978 because of high costs and the energy shortage, substantial advances have been made toward developing an automobile which is minimally polluting.

This has not been without a cost, however. The average car is several hundred dollars dearer because of the necessary antipollution equipment. Moreover, it costs more to run in terms of fewer miles per gallon, the cost of servicing equipment, and higher prices for lead-free gasoline.

EPA enforces air emission standards for factories, power plants, incinerators, chemical plants, and dozens of other sources of pollution. Meeting these standards imposes a cost on business, and raises the average cost and the marginal cost of operating. Although these additional costs are usually passed on to the consumer, there is ample evidence that hundreds of firms have been forced out of business since 1970 because they could not meet the cost of abiding by EPA air pollution standards.

The Union Carbide plant in West Virginia was once known as the smokiest factory in the world. It was on the verge of closing as a result of EPA requirements. In 1971, however, it began taking steps to correct environmental conditions. It was able to meet EPA standards by reducing emissions by 97 percent. But it had to spend $33 million for antipollution devices, and it added $3 million annually to its operating cost for maintenance of antipollution systems.

Reserve Mining Company, which processes taconite, was ordered by the court to shut down its operation in Silver Bay, Wisconsin, because of the pollution it caused to Lake Superior. The order affected thousands of families and the company's existence, as well as the operations of companies to whom it supplied iron ore. The order was subsequently modified to give Reserve Mining time to correct the environmental pollution.

More recently, an EPA official publicly called United States Steel Company the worst offender against environmental regulations and said that its bad record was giving all industry a black eye. A company spokesman, however, branded the charges false and stated that the company was proud of its efforts in the environmental area; he pointed out that the company had already spent $1 billion on pollution control facilities.

Dozens of cases have been cited and orders issued against the automobile industry and the chemical industry. Municipal sewage treatment plants are frequent offenders. Hundreds of orders have been issued against smaller plants and processors. In some cases plants have been closed; in others much time, effort, and money, have been spent in correcting the environmental situation.

Besides complying with air quality standards, a firm must be careful of water pollution. Although a federal Water Pollution Control Act was passed in 1956, stricter standards and enforcement came with the Federal Water Pollution Control Act amendments of 1972. Commonly referred to as the *Clean Water Act*, this legislation is designed to end the pollution of America's waterways by 1985. The act authorized nearly $25 billion to be spent during the first three-year period. Most of this, about $18 billion, went to sewage treatment facilities. In this regard a firm must be concerned with the content of its effluents and also with their temperature. Again the process of cleaning and/or cooling water before returning it to its source can be a costly matter, which needs to be considered when pricing a product or service.

The 1972 law established a new system of permits for discharges into the nation's waterways. No discharge of any pollutant from any point is permitted without a permit. Not only industrial dischargers but publicly owned sewage treatment plants and municipally controlled discharge points must obtain permits. Permits are issued by the states, which have programs that meet EPA guidelines. EPA has emergency powers to seek an immediate court injunction to stop water pollution that poses "an imminent and substantial endangerment" to public health, or to someone's livelihood.

Polluters must keep proper records, install and use monitoring equipment, and sample their discharges. Penalties for violating federal water pollution control standards range from a minimum of $2000 to a maximum of $25,000 per day and a maximum of a year in jail for the first offense. Subsequent violations carry a penalty up to $50,000 per day and two years in prison. Even unintentional violations entail civil penalties, fines up to $10,000 per day.

In 1972 Congress also passed a strong noise control bill which permits EPA to set decibel standards for various sources of noise, such as factories, aircraft, pile drivers, and many other noise makers.

Not only does compliance with various environmental standards increase the cost of doing business and the price of products and services, but failure to comply with the regulations can result in criminal indictments. These can involve fines and other penalties. Consequently, environmental regulations must be taken into account when establishing a business, producing and marketing a new product, or continuing current operations.

OCCUPATIONAL SAFETY AND HEALTH

As industry grew, it was forced into greater concern for the safety and health of workers. Measures were taken, laws were passed, and insurance was paid to prevent industrial accidents, to protect worker's health, and to compensate for occupational disabilities. This, of course, added to the total cost of production for the business firm or employer.

OSHA

In 1970 Congress passed a new, comprehensive law, the Occupational Safety and Health Act. The federal agency responsible for implementing the act is the Occupational Safety and Health Administration (OSHA), an agency of the Department of Labor. Congress declared that the purpose of the act and hence OSHA's mission was "to assure so far as possible every working man and woman in the Nation safe and healthful working conditions and to preserve our human resources."

Responsibilities and Rights. The Act requires each employer to provide a workplace that is free from safety and health hazards and to comply with OSHA standards. Employers are required to keep records of work-related injuries or illnesses, to report to OSHA each injury or health hazard that results in a fatality or the hospitalization of five or more employees, to post information about employee rights under the law, to cooperate with OSHA compliance officers during site inspections, and to post citations of violations of the law.

Employers, on the other hand, have certain rights under the law, such as the right to request proper identification of OSHA personnel before inspection visits, to be informed of any reason for an inspection, notified of the inspection date, accompany the OSHA compliance officer on the inspection walkaround, file a protest against any OSHA citation or penalty, and even to apply for temporary variance from OSHA standards if material, equipment, or personnel needed to comply are unavailable within the required time. Employees, too, have responsibilities and rights under the law. They have responsibilities to comply with the OSHA standards, to follow the safety and health rules of the employer, such as wearing prescribed protective equipment, and reporting hazardous work conditions to the supervisor. Employee rights include freedom to obtain OSHA information, to request information from the employer regarding safety and health hazards in the work area, to have a worker representative accompany the compliance officer on the inspection walkaround, to observe the monitoring or measuring of hazardous materials, to request that NIOSH[1] determine whether any substance in the work place has a toxic effect, to request OSHA to inspect the work place, to have his name withheld from his employer when filing a complaint, and to be told what OSHA has done about the complaint. In addition, the employee may file another complaint with OSHA if he feels that he is being discriminated against in any fashion by his employer for exercising his rights under the law.

The Standards.   For purposes of the act a *standard* is defined as a legally enforceable regulation governing conditions, practices, or operations to assure safe and healthful workplaces. The standards are published in the Federal Register. These standards are divided into three major categories: general industry, maritime, and construction. An updated version of the standards is available through the OSHA Subscription Service, a looseleaf periodical in large type. Besides standards for the three listed categories there is a volume on interpretations and a compliance operation manual, which can be helpful to any firm desiring to avoid violations of the law.

OSHA has been carrying out inspections based on a "worst-first" program. It has inspected industries with injury frequency rates more than double the national average. These include longshoring, meat and meat products, roofing and sheet metal, lumber and wood products, and miscellaneous transportation equipment, such as the manufacture of mobile homes, campers, and snowmobiles. The second area of investigation is focused on the five most commonly used and hazardous toxic substances: asbestos, carbon monoxide, cotton dust, lead, and silica. In addition inspections are made in response to complaints. Eventually, OSHA will carry out periodic inspections of other workplaces.

During an inspection, the compliance officer, along with the employer and employee representative, walk through the establishment, and each work station is inspected for compliance with OSHA standards. After the walkaround the compliance officer discusses possible violations with the employer and the time needed to correct violations. The compliance officer then writes his report and discusses it with his area director. The area director or his superiors determine what citations will be issued and what penalties will be levied. These are then sent to the employer by certified mail. The employer can comply with or contest the orders by appealing to

[1] The act established this new agency, the National Institute for Occupational Safety and Health, in HEW, to carry out the research and educational functions assigned to HEW under the act.

the OSHA Review Commission. Of course if no violations are found, no citations are issued or penalties imposed.

Penalties. In the event of violations, citations may be issued and penalties imposed on offenders. There are several types of violation: (1) *De minimis*: a condition that needs correction but has no direct or immediate relationship to job safety or health. An example of this would be the lack of proper restroom facilities or supplies. (2) *Nonserious violation*: a violation that is directly related to job safety and health but not likely to cause death or serious physical harm. This could be a tripping hazard, inadequate height space, slick floors, or the like. A proposed penalty up to $1000 may be imposed for such violations. (3) *Serious violation*: a condition where there is a definite probability that death or physical harm could result. To be classified as a serious violation, however, the employer must know, or should have known, about the hazard. Examples of this would be unguarded punch presses and saws and inadequate protection from falling materials. In case of serious violation a proposed penalty up to $1000 is mandatory. This penalty may be adjusted downward, depending on a number of conditions, such as the size of the business, the history of previous violations, and the good faith of the employer in correcting the violation. Any employer who willfully, or repeatedly, violates the act may be assessed penalties up to $10,000 for each such violation. Criminal penalties are also provided for under the act. Any willful violation resulting in death of an employee, upon conviction, is punishable by a fine of not more than $10,000 or by imprisonment for not more than six months or both. Subsequent conviction doubles these maximum penalties.

Citations can be issued also for violations of other OSHA regulations, such as giving false information, failure to maintain proper records, failure to report fatalities or catastrophes, failure to post notices, and failure to post citations. Upon receiving a citation the employer may comply with or contest the citation. If the employer disagrees with the citation or the proposed penalty he can request a meeting with the area director to discuss the matter. He also can appeal the case to the OSHA Review Commission, which is separate from, and not related to, the Department of Labor.

Since compliance may impose a hardship on some firms, the act makes it possible for small businesses to obtain long-term loans through the federal Small Business Administration to help them get into compliance with the standards.

Congress, through the act, also directed OSHA to encourage states to develop and operate their own job safety and health programs. The federal government provides money for planning and developing such state programs and can provide 50 percent of the operating cost once a state program is approved and instituted. To receive OSHA approval and funding, state programs must be "at least as effective as" federal standards.

Costs. Clearly, compliance with OSHA standards involves a cost to most business firms. Especially affected are firms that have been operating with minimal safety and health conditions. Although it is a policy of OSHA to implement the standards fully and firmly, it wishes to do so without harassing employers and employees. Fortunately, much of the cost in meeting standards involves a fixed cost. Such items as machine guards, ventilators, fire prevention equipment, environmental controls, personal safety equipment, decibel controls, safety screening, sanitary facilities, and safety signs are one-time costs that can be spread over a wide range of production. Other costs, such as the need to keep records, to hire qualified crane operators; to use safer, but more expensive, raw materials, and stacking requirements — all can add to the variable cost of operation. Firms must also take into account the possibility of penalties for violations.

EQUAL EMPLOYMENT OPPORTUNITY

Another area of government regulation, which has considerable cost effects on the operation of a firm, is that of equal employment opportunity. Title VII of the Civil Rights Act of 1964 places an affirmative obligation upon employers, labor unions, and employment agencies not to discriminate because of race, color, religion, sex, or national origin. The nondiscrimination provision applies not only to hiring, but also to promotion, transfer, and other matters of employment. An Equal Employment Opportunity Commission was established to enforce these provisions of the act. The commission subsequently published guidelines on employee selection procedures, including testing procedures for training, promotion, and transfer.

Equal Employment Opportunity Act (1972)

In 1972 the concept of employee nondiscrimination was expanded and strengthened with the enactment of the Equal Employment Opportunity Act. The provisions of the act apply to all employers engaged in an industry affecting commerce who have 15 or more employees. According to the act it is "an unlawful employment practice" for an employer:

1. to fail or refuse to hire or to discharge any individual, or otherwise to discriminate against any individual with respect to his compensation, terms, conditions, or privileges of employment because of such individual's race, color, religion, sex, or national origin
2. to limit, segregate, or classify employees or *applicants for employment* in any way which would deprive or tend to deprive any individual of employment opportunities or otherwise adversely affect his status as an employee, because of such individual's race, color, religion, sex, or national origin.

Similar clauses apply to labor unions and employment agencies. There are a few exceptions to the act, such as those involving Communists, the employment of persons for jobs of national security, and certain preferential treatment for veterans and American Indians. Although the act prohibits discrimination, it does not, on the other hand, require preferential treatment for any particular category of workers. Section 703(j) states specifically:

Nothing contained in this title shall be interpreted to require any employer, . . . to grant preferential treatment to any individual or to any group because of race, color, religion, sex, or national origin of such individual or group on account of an imbalance which may exist with respect to the total number or percentage of persons of any race, color, religion, sex, or national origin employed by any employer . . . in comparison with the total number of persons of such race, color, religion, sex, or national origin in any community, state, section, or other area, or in the available work force in any community, state, section, or other area.

Moreover the act does not prohibit the application of different standards of compensation, or different terms, conditions, or privileges of employment based on bona fide seniority or merit system, or a system which measures earnings by quantity or quality of production, or to employees who work in different locations, provided that such differences are not the result of any intention to discriminate because of race, color, religion, sex, or national origin.

Even in advertising job openings, an employer must be very careful not to violate the law. Ads for general employment that state "men wanted" or "salesladies" are usually held to be in violation of the law. In no way may the employer indicate a preference, for example, for a man or woman, for a Catholic or Protestant, for a Black or White, unless such difference is a bona fide occupational qualification for the job. The employer must also be careful in using tests to determine hiring, promotion, and transfer. Tests that are more difficult for the culturally disadvantaged may be held to be unlawful.

Under the law, employers are required to make and keep records relevant to determinations of whether unlawful practices have been or are being committed, and to make them available at the request of the commission. If a company has an apprenticeship or training program, for example, it must keep a list of applicants who wish to participate, including the chronological order in which they apply. It must also on request give the commission a detailed description of the manner in which persons are selected for the apprenticeship or training program. A firm may in no way discriminate against married women. Pregnancy, for example, must be treated as any disability and a reasonable leave given at the proper time. It may not be used as a reason for firing a worker or forcing an early or extended leave on her. In fact, the list of restrictive activities that an employer must avoid to stay in compliance with the law grows continually.

Affirmative Action

All firms covered by the act are required to take affirmative action to prevent discrimination from occurring and to assure fair and equal treatment to all persons in employment matters, such as hiring, promotion, and transfer. It is difficult to define *affirmative action* precisely, however, and different approaches and measure have been taken in the name of affirmative action. Although the law states that it is not necessary to give preferential treatment to any individual or group on account of an imbalance which may exist with repsect to the percentage of that group in an employer's work force compared to the percentage of that group to the total population or to the available work force, the Equal Employment Opportunity Commission and the courts have often publicly demanded to know what actions some firms have taken to hire more minority people. In regard to firms with public contracts an affirmative action program is considered to be a set of specific and result-oriented procedures to which a contractor commits himself. An acceptable affirmative action program must include an analysis of areas within which the contractor-employer is deficient in the utilization of minority groups and women, and further a statement of goals and timetables to which the employer's good faith effort must be directed to correct the deficiencies. Minorities include Blacks, Spanish-surnamed Americans, American Indians, and Orientals. Numbers and percentages are often utilized by the commission as evidence of discrimination. At times the commission has enforced numerical goals and timetables on employers in order to reduce imbalances. This is so particularly where the composition of the work force gives indication of discrimination over past years.

In 1971, for example, it was required that academic institutions develop written affirmative action programs. To be acceptable, these affirmative action programs had to include an analysis of deficiencies in the utilization of minority groups and women and the establishment of goals and timetables for increasing their employment in order to correct the deficiencies.

The EEOC is not the only government agency that enforces antidiscrimination policies, the Department of Labor and HEW also have a role. In fact, at times two or more government agencies have issued conflicting directives, to the dismay of the employer.

As stated in the *Affirmative Action and Equal Employment Guidebook for Employers*:

> The message conveyed by these legal rulings is clear: If a statistical survey shows that minorities and females are not participating in your work force at all levels in reasonable relation to their presence in the population and the labor force, the burden of proof is on you to show that this is not the result of discrimination, however inadvertent. There is a strong probability that some part of your system is discriminating, and that unless you make changes you may be subject to legal action.

Courts have in many cases required fundamental changes in hiring, promotion, and transfer practices; they have specified numbers and percentages of minorities and females to be hired, trained, or promoted until certain goals are reached. Women, for example, in most firms have not been found in significant numbers at the management level. Thus in many cases the Equal Employment Opportunity Commission has directed firms to take affirmative action to include women in management training programs.

When, because of discrimination, overt or inadvertent, a firm is directed by the commission to take affirmative action, the order may require very specific and extensive analysis and record keeping. This can include a detailed description of each job, an analysis of each category of employee with respect to race, color, religion, sex, etc., an analysis of the qualifications of each employee in regard to jobs available, a list of the sources of applicants for work, a review of tests utilized, and a myriad of other items, including an analysis of neighborhood conditions surrounding the place of employment to determine whether they are conducive to attracting applicants from groups that may suffer discrimination.

A job applicant, an employee, a union, or the commission may file a complaint of discrimination against an employer. After investigation and hearing any employer found guilty of discrimination in violation of the act may be enjoined from engaging in such unlawful employment practices. Moreover, the employer may be ordered to take appropriate action, including, but not limited to, reinstatement of employees or hiring of applicants with or without back pay. An employer may have canceled or be deprived of obtaining federal contracts or funds because of noncompliance with the Equal Employment Opportunity Act.

To cite some of the more noteworthy penalties, Anaconda Aluminum Company was ordered to pay $190,000 in back wages, along with court cost to 276 women employees because of discrimination on so-called heavy jobs. Virginia Electric Power Company was ordered to pay a quarter of a million dollars to compensate Black workers for wages they would have earned had discrimination not denied them promotion. The company also had to stop requiring a high school diploma and using aptitude tests as hiring and promotion criteria for blue-collar jobs. Household Finance Corporation paid over $125,000 to white-collar female workers who were denied promotion because of sex. Under the agreement the company also consented to hire more females and minority workers for their offices.

Sardis Luggage Company was ordered to pay $120,000 in back wages to Black plaintiffs, and ordered to hire Black workers in the ratio of 2 to 1 for four years until their work force reached a proper racial balance. Corning Glass Works had to pay $1 million in back pay for discriminating against women employees and against employees of both sexes regarding pay differential between day and night shift workers. Detroit Edison, a utility, is appealing a federal court order that it increase hiring and promotion of black workers and pay more then $4 million to Blacks who were judged to be victims of racial discrimination.

After two years of litigation, American Telephone and Telegraph Company agreed to pay $15 million in one-time payments to thousands of its employees who, it was claimed, suffered from discriminatory employment practices. AT&T also had to start making an estimated $50 million in yearly payments for promotion and wage adjustments to minority and female employees. In addition the company had to set specific hiring and promotion goals in order to increase significantly the utilization of women and minorities in every job classification. It was required, also, to set goals for employing males in previously all-female jobs. Lastly, all women college graduates hired in the previous eight years had to be assessed to determine their interest and potential for higher-level jobs, and a specific development program was to be established to prepare these women for promotion.

Costs

Obviously compliance with EEOA standards has a price. Keeping detailed records is costly and inconvenient. The employer's expenses rise when it is necessary to search out and interview applicants in order to avoid discrimination. Establishing and implementing an affirmative action program is time consuming and can distract the people involved from other functions and duties. More time and expense may be needed to train workers to qualify for higher-level jobs, promotions, and transfers. One of the largest costs, moreover, can be loss of production because it is not necessarily the best-qualified and most productive workers who get the jobs or promotions. This is true particularly when quota goals are established for hiring minority workers and women.

Unfortunately, a number of employers have taken exaggerated measures for affirmative action, either voluntarily or as a result of action from the commission, and engaged in reverse discrimination. In some instances a minority or female worker can get a job, promotion, or transfer more easily than a white male can. Recently the federal district court, for example, ruled that the city of Detroit discriminated against thirty-six white firemen when it by passed them to promote Black fire fighters with less seniority under a so-called affirmative action program. The court held that the action of the city was an absolutely clear, unequivocal violation of the rights of the individual plaintiffs under the 14th Amendment.

CONSUMER PRODUCT SAFETY

For decades manufacturers have been careful about the uses and safety of the products they produce and sell. Although a high degree of competition can keep prices low and improve the quality of product, this is not always true. Business firms have been known to produce and sell shoddy and unsafe products. Consequently a number of laws, such as the Flammable Fabrics and Refrigerator Safety Acts, were passed to prevent such abuses.

Not until 1972, however, was a rather comprehensive act passed to prevent the production, distribution, and sale of unsafe products. The Consumer Product Safety Act of that year was designed to protect the public against unreasonable risks of injury associated with consumer products, to develop uniform safety standards for consumer products, and to promote research and investigation into the causes and prevention of product-related deaths, illnesses, and injuries.

The act established a new independent federal regulatory agency, the Consumer Product Safety Commission (CPSC). The primary goal of the commission is a substantial reduction of injuries associated with consumer products. The commission has broad authority to issue and enforce safety standards governing the design, construction, performance, packaging, and labeling of more than 10,000 consumer products from architectural glass, stairs, and power tools to stoves, ladders, and lawnmowers. The commission can ban hazardous products. Any product that presents an imminent hazard of death, serious illness, or severe injury is liable to immediate seizure under a court order. The act provides for civil and criminal penalties against offenders. Known violations of the act can result in civil penalties up to a maximum of $500,000. Criminal penalties for knowing and willful violation after notice of noncompliance carry a maximum fine of $50,000 and imprisonment of one year.

Standards. A major task of the commission is establishing mandatory safety standards for consumer products which pose unreasonable risks to consumers. The act permits anyone to submit an existing voluntary standard for adoption as a proposed mandatory standard. The commission may accept any of several offers or develop its own standard. Manufacturers, importers, private labelers, distributors, and retailers of consumer products have specific responsibilities under the act. Most important is the requirement to notify the commission immediately if a product has a defect that could pose substantial risk of injury. The commission may then require notification about the defect to the general public and to those in the distribution chain; and it may order repair or replacement of the product or refund of the purchase price.

During its first year of operation the commission heard from about 130 companies. The defects involved over 14 million product units. Most of the companies voluntarily agreed to notify consumers of these defects and agreed to repair or replace the product or refund the consumers' money.

490

In addition to the Consumer Product Safety Act, the commission is responsible for implementing several previously existing laws, including the Flammable Fabrics Act, the Federal Hazardous Substances Act, the Poison Prevention Packaging Act, and the Refrigerator Safety Act. Any of these can have an effect on the operations of a firm.

Costs. Again it is easy to see that it may be costly to comply with the various safety standards of the CPSC. As a result of voluntary or mandatory product standards, a firm may have to use costlier and safer raw materials. It may have to redesign its product and retool its machinery for production; it may have to develop better product containers; and it may have to be more specific in labeling its products. Such labeling might make consumers less ready to buy the product.

If a hazardous product has been distributed there is a cost involved in notifying and tracking down its purchasers, a cost to repair or replace the merchandise, and the cost of possible suits for personal injury that may have been caused. Violations, too, can result in stiff financial penalties. In addition, any notification or suit may tarnish the image of the product in the minds of consumers and result in the loss of sales.

CPSC orders to ban products can be even more damaging. A few years ago a ban on cranberry sauce led to irreparable damage to some firms in the industry. Later a mushroom producer in the Middle West went out of business when its products were banned. The mercury poison scare hurt the sales of fish. Some dyes have been declared unsafe, and certain lipsticks have been taken off the market. Annually hundreds of thousands of automobiles are recalled to repair defects. Since implementation of the Consumer Product Safety Act the sale of some 1800 children's toys have been banned, and the safety of aerosol cans is now being investigated.

OTHER RELATED REGULATIONS

In addition to regulations previously discussed, producers must be aware of still other regulations affecting production. The Federal Food, Drug and Cosmetic Act, as amended in January 1975, established standards and penalizes violators in those industries. Firms in the transportation industry are regulated. The railroad and trucking industries are subject to Interstate Commerce Commission jurisdiction; the airlines must observe FAA regulations. Public utilities are regulated by public service commissions in the various states; even farmers must deal with acreage allotments and support prices.

Any firm already in business, or about to go into a certain business, needs to know and understand the standards, regulations, and restrictions that will be placed upon it. The costs those regulations generate can be substantial and sometimes prohibitive. Consequently, a producer should analyze the financial impact of such standards and regulations upon its cost and on the bottom line of statements of income and expense. Between 1972 and 1975, for example, Americans paid $2.4 billion more for the automobiles they bought to cover the cost of mandatory safety equipment. It is estimated that the average automobile may soon cost $1000 more to cover the cost of anti-pollution equipment, safety devices, and other government-mandated changes in company operations.

Cost-benefit Analysis

Cost-benefit analysis is a technique of measuring the total social benefit versus the total social cost of a given proposal.[2] It has been used for the past several decades by economists to determine the feasibility of government projects, such as flood control (dams), highways, bridges, recreation facilities, and weapons systems. In using the technique all costs and benefits, both explicit and implicit, are measured. No distinction is made between private and social cost and/or benefits. If a social benefit comes at the expense of the private sector of the economy, that would not deter recommendation of a proposal, so long as the total benefit exceeded the total cost.

The measurements of aggregate cost and aggregate benefit for a given proposal or project are not easy. Yet, the cost may be easier to calculate than the benefit. One can readily compute the capital cost associated with constructing a project, such as a dam, and the cost of maintaining it after it is in operation. But even here there may be costs that are not so readily measured. Estimates must be made for the loss of land inundated by the water, the loss of income to businesses forced to move because of construction of the project, and the possible loss of jobs and income in the area.

On the benefit side a judgment has to be made regarding the enhancement of land values to those owning property that abuts the new lake shoreline, the income and spending effects of new businesses that may locate in the area, and the increased value of land and its crop output resulting from less frequent floods in the area. It is also necessary to place a value on such intangibles as the benefit from any water and park recreational facilities developed as a part of

---

[2] Often called *benefit-cost* analysis

the project, and even the value of enjoyment drawn from improved landscaping and scenery.

Sometimes where several proposals are recommended, a benefit-cost ratio is calculated for each project. Consequently, Project A may have a benefit-cost ratio of 2 to 1, which would indicate that the total social benefit is double the social cost of the project. Another project may have a 1.7 to 1 ratio, another a 1.5 to 1 ratio, and a fourth project a .8 to 1 ratio. Projects with ratios equal to, or greater than, 1 to 1 are considered economically feasible. Those with a ratio of less than 1 are not economically feasible. The ratios can then be considered, along with many other inputs, such as size of the financial outlay in assigning priorities to the projects.

Cost-benefit analysis has often been applied to public projects. Environmental projects have recently been included in such proposals, and there, too, benefit judgments must be made about the value (benefit) of cleaner air and purer water for people's health, the value of improved land values, and the value of lower costs for maintaining residential properties.

Similar difficulties arise in applying cost-benefit analysis to occupational health and safety regulations, equal employment opportunity requirements, and consumer products safety regulations. These proposals are often evaluated in terms of cost-benefit analysis in reference to total society. Since a firm does not consider social costs (external cost) in its profit and loss statement, however, the answer, or ratio, one gets from a conventional cost-benefit analysis may be much different than a cost-benefit analysis, or marginal analysis, based strictly on the conventional revenue-expenditure analysis of the firm. Presently, some firms because they do not cover all cost, including the social or external cost, are being subsidized by society. The firm is making more profit or consumers are getting the product for less than would be the case if the firm had to cover both internal and social cost. If a project such as a pollution control project, is constructed that internalizes these costs, the firm may need to pay more of the social cost of doing business. On the other hand, some firms or their customers may actually be subsidizing society if the social benefit from the firm's operation exceeds the social cost of operation, or if a firm is assessed a cost for a project that exceeds its own external cost.

SUMMARY

The economic environment in which businesses operate is changing continually, Recently business firms have had to contend, among other things, with various environmental measures, worker safety rules, equal employment opportunity regulations, and consumer product safety standards. These are issues that did not loom large on the economic horizon before the middle 1960s. Each of them, along with other regulations, rules, and standards, has an economic impact on the profit and loss statement of many firms.

Today, for example, a firm must be concerned about the noise it creates and its discharge of pollutants into the air or water. Meeting new EPA regulations on noise, air, and water pollution standards involves a cost to a company and/or its customers.

The Occupational Safety and Health Administration imposes certain standards regarding the safety and health of workers. Although a standard can be beneficial to workers, it can add to the cost of doing business.

The Equal Employment Opportunity Commission also imposes certain requirements regarding the hiring and promotion of workers. In addition, many firms today are required to implement affirmative action programs for hiring and promotion of minorities and women. These programs often mean additional cost to the employer, without increasing revenue. The Consumer Products Safety Commission has established and enforces safety standards governing the design, construction, performance, and packaging of many products.

From a public point of view cost-benefit analysis, based on social cost and social benefit, may be used to determine the economic feasibility of an EPA standard or a consumer product safety regulation. The implementation of such a standard or regulation having positive economic feasibility, however, can be costly to a business firm.

Stiff financial penalties can be levied upon violators of these and other standards. Consequently, a firm must be aware of its responsibilities under the ever-growing standards and regulations being imposed by various federal, state, and local agencies, and, it must exercise care in conforming with the standards, requirements, and regulations affecting various aspects of its operations.

QUESTIONS FOR DISCUSSION

1. Do you think that the government, private enterprise, or consumers should bear the cost of cleaning up the environment? Explain.
2. It has been suggested that we should strive toward ZEG (zero economic growth) as a means of preventing further deterioration of the environment. Do you agree or disagree? Why?
3. Why did it take so long for our nation to recognize pollution for the hazard that it is?
4. When there is a conflict between pollution standards and energy conserva-

tion regulations, as there has been in the auto industry, for example, which do you believe should prevail? Why?

5. It is stated that the closer we move toward completely clean air and pure water the greater the marginal cost. Why should this be so?

6. Do the financial penalties for violating EPA standards seem minimal, optimal, or excessive to you? Why?

7. Do you think that employers should be forewarned of OSHA visits? Why or why not?

8. Explain the four different categories of violation under the Occupational Health and Safety Act.

9. How can a small marginal business afford safety equipment required to meet OSHA standards?

10. What categories of persons is the EEOA trying to protect against discrimination?

11. Is there any incongruity between the Equal Employment Opportunity Act and Equal Employment Opportunity Commission orders and court orders regarding numbers or quotas?

12. What is affirmative action? Why and how is it used?

13. What kind of penalties can be imposed for violations of the Equal Employment Opportunity Act?

14. What obligation does a firm have if it produces and distributes a defective product?

15. What kind of penalties can be imposed for violation of the Consumer Product Safety Act?

PROBLEMS AND CASES

1. Your firm, the Valley Foundry Company, has been ordered by EPA to install antipollution equipment, which is estimated to cost $2 million. Furthermore, it is indicated that a new maintenance man must be hired at a wage of about $15,000 a year to take care of the antipollution equipment. Company sales amount to $5 million annually; its net profit is about $250,000 per year. It is calculated that the cost of the equipment can be written off (depreciated) over a twenty-year period. Preliminary discussion with a local bank reveals that the $2 million needed for the equipment can be borrowed and repaid over a ten-year period at an interest rate of 10 per cent annually. As a member of the company's financial analysis division you are asked to calculate what effect the purchase and use of the antipollution equipment will have on profit and to suggest how much of an increase in prices is necessary to maintain the current profit level.

2. H.E. Sachs was recently hired as the personnel manager for a small manufacturing company employing 150 workers. After working about six weeks he is informed that the company for economic reasons is moving its operations to another state more than one thousand miles away. He is informed, further, by the vice president that, as personnel manager, he (Sachs) will be completely responsible for the transfer and/or hiring of new employees to fill the jobs at the new location. As a management trainee for the company,

you are designated to assist Sachs in carrying out his assignment. What policies and measures would you recommend to him?

3. The Jaywalk Shoe Company has a plant in a rundown slum area adjacent to the central business district in a large town. The area has a large number of bars and the reputation of a tough and unsafe neighborhood. There is a high crime rate in the neighborhood. The company has decided to add a night shift at the plant because of increased sales. The company has limited parking facilities. Most workers who drive must park on the street or in private parking lots a block or two from the plant. Those who use the bus must walk a block and a half to the bus stop. In addition to a 10 percent night shift premium, the vice president tells you, the employment manager, that because of the neighborhood conditions the company will pay an extra 5 per cent to attract workers for the night shift. The going rate of pay for the day shift is $4.00 per hour. The vice president gives you a list of 100 jobs to be filled and indicates that you can transfer workers from the day shift and/ or hire new workers. Because he is concerned about the safety of women workers as they come and go in the neighborhood, he states specifically that you are to hire only males for the night shift. What problems do you foresee in regard to the Equal Employment Opportunity Act?

4. As a recently appointed product manager for a toy manufacturer you have just completed a successful marketing program for a line of toy trucks and cars. Two million units at a cost of $2.00 per unit have been distributed to wholesalers and retailers at a price to them of $3.50 per unit. The suggested retail price is $5.00. While enjoying your apparent success and preparing an advertising program for Christmas sales, you are informed by a young chemist in the company that the paint used on the toy trucks and cars contains a substance that can be harmful to children if they eat it. He states that it can cause a mild case of lead poisoning lasting for two or three days. He assures you, however, that it cannot be fatal to children or adults.

You discuss the paint with the product manager. He says that he used a cheaper paint because you asked him to keep the cost down. He assures you that it is good paint that has been used by the company before on other types of toys, and that they have never had a complaint about its causing any harm to children. You calculate that it would cost 75 cents per unit to recall and repaint the toys, if you can get them all returned. This would cut down your profit margin. Moreover, it would take two to three weeks to get them back into the wholesalers' and retailers' hands. This would make them late for the Christmas season. In discussing these various points with the production manager he suggests that you forget about the whole thing. What would you do?

5. Workers in your plant complain, through their union, about unsafe working conditions in the plant. The union, after talking to the production manager and receiving no satisfaction, files a complaint with OSHA. OSHA notifies the company of the complaint and establishes an inspection date. Although the production manager has the plant in good housekeeping order on the date of the inspection, the compliance officer points out 15 violations of OSHA standards during the walkaround. These violations include unprotected cutting machines, sparks flying from grinding wheels, and unguarded punch presses. Although the general manager disagrees with the compliance officer about the seriousness of the hazards, he reluctantly agrees to correct them. Subsequently, OSHA issues an order confirming the general manager's agreement to correct or eliminate the hazards. When the order

arrives, two days later, the general manager, who is scheduled to leave the next day for a four-week European vacation, hands the letter to you with instructions to talk to the production manager about the situation. In your capacity as assistant to the general manager, you mention the orders to the production manager. He tells you to forget about them, that the violations were not serious, that correcting them costs too much, and that OSHA doesn't know what it is talking about. Furthermore, he indicates that the punch presses would have to be shut down for two days to install safety equipment and that the company cannot afford the loss of production. What argument would you put forth to convince the production manager that the hazards need to be removed or eliminated?

6. The Turner Division of Cleanweld Products, Inc., a small manufacturer of fuel cylinders in Illinois, was ordered by OSHA to install engineering controls to reduce the noise to a 90-decibel level in parts of its plant. The Turner Company, formerly owned by Olin Corporation when the order was issued, protested stating that it met the 90-decibel noise standard by requiring workers to wear earplugs. The cost of the engineering controls was estimated to be $30,000. The Department of Labor contended that engineering controls are "feasible" when a company can afford them. The company filed suit in federal court protesting OSHA's order. Company representatives claimed that the outcome of the case could mean $8-billion to industry in general.

(a) Do you think that the company has a case? Are earplugs a reliable means of protection?

(b) What type of cost-benefit analysis can be made in this case?

(c) What was the decision of the U.S. Court of Appeals (Chicago)?

(d) What differences or similarities do you see between the outcome of this case and the outcome of the Mahoning Valley steel case? (Following)

Mahoning River Valley

In March 1976 the federal Environmental Protection Agency, in a striking departure from its clean water policies, exempted eight steel plants from new regulations governing the iron and steel industry. All eight plants were located in a 24-mile stretch of the Mahoning River Valley situated near Youngstown, Ohio, and the Pennsylvania border. The eight plants are owned and operated by three major steel companies: United States Steel Corporation; Republic Steel Corporation; and Youngstown Sheet and Tube Company.

The new EPA guidelines require the iron and steel industry to reduce uncontrollable discharges of oil and grease by 99.8 percent and suspended solids by 99.5 percent before 1983. This would make the waters clean enough to permit fishing and water recreation, according to EPA.

All eight plants are older facilities, some dating to the early 1900s, and use open-hearth furnaces that are less efficient and more pollution prone than newer types of furnaces, such as the basic oxygen furnace.

The EPA decision was based on an analysis indicating that the companies, since they had facilities elsewhere, might choose to close the plants rather than make the required large outlays for pollution control devices. Closing the plants would jeopardize 20,000 to 25,000 jobs, or 14 per cent of the total employment, in the Mahoning Valley area. In its exemption statement EPA said, "This provision of relief on the basis of regional economic impact is a unique situation, due to a combination of the large number of jobs involved and the large portion of the labor force affected."

The EPA exemption excused the steel companies from meeting the interim standards in 1977. But they would still have to meet the final standards by 1983, unless they applied for another exemption. It is estimated by EPA that the exemption for 1977 saved the companies between $30–$60 million. A representative for the steel companies said that they welcomed the exemption because the eight plants were not profitable enough to justify spending about $140 million for pollution controls by 1983.

The decision of EPA was immediately severely criticized by environmental groups. Some charged the EPA was creating a pocket of pollution not envisioned by the Clean Water Act. The Natural Resources Defense Council, based in Washington, stated that, "The EPA has opened a loophole, and who knows how many other steel plants or even other industries will try to take advantage of it." The Sierra Club and the state of Pennsylvania challenged the exemption. The state was concerned about western Pennsylvania communities that use the Mahoning River as a water supply after it crosses into Pennsylvania below the steel plants. A suit was filed in federal court challenging the EPA exemption order.

(a) What would be the approximate annual loss in wages to the community if the plants were to close down?

(b) How does this estimated loss compare to the cost of implementing the antipollution devices?

(c) Do you see any solution to the problem?

(d) If you were asked to serve as an expert witness in the court case, what type of economic arguments would you make for the company? For the environmentalists?

(e) How did the court decide the case? Do you think that it was a good decision?

SELECTED READINGS

A Compilation of Laws Administered by the Consumer Products Safety Commission. Washington, D.C.: U.S. Consumer Products Safety Commission, 1973.

Affirmative Action and Equal Employment (A guidebook for Employers). Washington, D.C.: U.S. Equal Employment Opportunity Commission, 1974.

Ellwood, P.M., Jr. and M.E. Herbert. "Health Care: Should Industry Buy It Or Sell It?" *Harvard Business Review*, July 1973.

Enthoven, Alain C., and A. Myrick Freeman III. *Pollution, Resources and the Environment.* New York: W.W. Norton & Company, Inc., 1973.

"Into A New Era — How Your Life Will Change." *U.S. News and World Report*, March 3, 1975.

Laws and Rules You Should Know. Washington, D.C.: U.S. Equal Employment Opportunity Commission, 1975.

"Reverse Discrimination — Has It Gone Too Far?" *U.S. News and World Report,* March 29, 1976.

Savage, Donald, et al. *Economics of Environmental Improvement.* Boston: Houghton Mifflin Company, 1974.

Schachter, Ester Roditti. *Enforcing Air Pollution Controls.* New York: Praeger Publishers, 1974.

Smith, Robert S. *The Occupational Safety and Health Act: Its Goals and Achievements.* Washington, D.C.: American Enterprise Institute for Public Policy, 1976.

Sowell, Thomas. *Affirmative Action Reconsidered.* Washington, D.C.: American Enterprise Institute for Public Policy, December, 1975.

The Clean Air Act. Washington, D.C.: U.S. Environmental Protection Agency, 1974.

The Occupational Safety and Health Act of 1970. Washington, D.C.: U.S. Government Printing Office, 1973.

Toward Cleaner Water. Washington, D.C.: U.S. Environmental Protection Agency, 1974.

Weiss, Leonard W. *Economics and Society.* New York: John Wiley & Sons, Inc., 1975.

Index

A

Accession rate, 451
Accounting profit, and economic profit, 29-32
Actual vs. potential GNP, 145, 146
Affirmative action, 486-87
  penalties, 488-89
Affirmative Action and Equal Employment Guidebook for Employers, 487
Air pollution, 477-78
Air Pollution Act (1955), 478
Air Quality Control Act of 1967, 478
American Economic Association (AEA), 8
American Economic Review, 8
Analysis, processes of, 12-13
Annual forecast, 170-71
"Anti-chainstore" act, 359
Antitrust laws, 4
  violation, 371
Antitrust legislation, pending, 371-72
Antitrust violations, overt and inadvertent, 366-70
AO. (*See* Average outlay)
AR. (*See* Average revenue)
Arc elasticity, 97

Arithmetic straight line fitted by least squares to Gross National Product, 182
A & S Auto Supply case, 376-77
ATC. (*See* Average total cost)
Auto industry registrations, due to lower price makes, 342
Automobile prices:
  competition in, 336-43
  lower, 341
Auto production, 300
Auto sales:
  percentage of total U. S. market, 301
  retail sales of leading imports, 301
AVC. (*See* Average variable costs)
Average fixed cost, 221
Average outlay (AO), 439
Average product, 217-18
  defined, 217
  input, output, marginal product and, 216
  relationship of marginal product to, 217
Average revenue (AR), 226, 247
Average total cost (ATC), 221, 247, 248